AF663463

The Essence of Jaina Scriptures

Pravachanasara of Kundakunda

By the Same Author

Fundamentals of Jainism

Salvation through Self-Discipline: *Niyamsara* of Kundakunda

The Art and Science of Self-Realization: *Prushartha-Siddhyupaya* of Amrtachandra Suri

The Enlightened Vision of the Self: *Svarupa Sambodhana* of Akalanka Deva (Editor)

Spiritual Englightenment: *Paramatma Prakash* of Yoginu Deva (Editor)

Spiritual Insights: *Ishtopadesh* and *Samadhi Shatak* of Pujyapada (Editor)

The Essence of Jaina Scriptures

Pravachanasara of Kundakunda

with *Tattvadipika* Commentary
by Amrtachandra Suri

Edited with an Introduction by
Jagdish Prasad Jain

2014
Kaveri Books
New Delhi - 110002

First Published in 2014

ISBN: 978-81-7479-163-4

Published by
Kaveri Books
4832/24, Ansari Road
New Delhi-110002 (India)
Tel: 011-23288140, 23245799
E-mail : kaveribooks@vsnl.com
kaveribooks@gmail.com
Website: www.kaveribooks.com

Typeset in AGarment Font at
Delta Book World, New Delhi - 110 002.

PRINTED IN INDIA

Dedicated to
Shrimati Shakuntala Devi Jain
and
Late Shri Madan Lal Jain
Jain Familiy Trust

Contents

List of Abbreviations

AC	*Amrtachandra*
AM	*Apta Mimansa* of Samantabhadra
BA	*Baras Anuvekkha* of Kundakunda
DS	*Dravya Sangraha* of Nemichandra
JS	*Jayasena*
KK	*Kundakunda*
MMP	*Moksha Marg Prakashak* of Pandit Todarmal
NN	*Nishchaya Naya*
NS	*Niyamsara* of Kundakunda
Outl.	*Outlines of Jainism* by Jagmander Lal Jaini (J.L.Jaini)
Pk.	*Prakrit*
PKS	*Panchastikayasara* of Kundakunda
PP	*Pramatma Prakash* of Yogindu Deva
PS Kalash	*Pravachanasara Kalash* of Amrtachandra
PSU	*Purusharthasiddhyupaya* of Amrtachandra
RKS	*Ratna Karanda Shravakachara* of Samantabhadra
SAS	*Savarthasiddhi* Commentary on *Tattvartha Sutra* (TS) of Pujyapada
Sk.	*Sanskrit*
SS	*Samayasara* of Kundakunda
TRV	*Tattvarta Rajvarttika* Commentary on *Tattvartha Sutra* (TS) of Akalanka
TS	*Tattvarta Sutra* of Umasvami or Umasvati
TSV	*Tattvarta Sholka Varttika* of Vidyananda
VN	*Vyavahara Naya*

Preface

Acharya Kundakunda, the author of *Pravachanasara,* is one of the greatest philosophers and foremost spiritual thinkers of the world. Being a multifaceted personality, he was an outstanding thinker, reformer, organizer, philosopher, teacher, poet, saint as well as a living legend. His importance within both Jainism and the Jaina philosophical tradition is incomparable. In fact, in the Digambara sect of Jains, he is revered next only to Lord Mahavira and his apostle Gautam Ganadhara. As the leader of *Mula Sangha* (basic ascetics), he was indeed the most prominent. The origin of almost all the lineages of the Digambara monks is therefore traced to Kundakunda.

Though Kundakunda occupies a very prominent place in Jainism and commands the highest respect, the literature on his life continues to be both scant and controversial. The existing literature contains numerous legends and is replete with incredible miracles, exaggerations, contradictions and inconsistencies. For instance, the *Epigraphic Carnatica* states that due to his excellent religious conduct, Kundakunda possessed miraculous power to move in the air four fingers above the ground. There is also a controversy about Kundakunda's air travel to Videh where he is said to have directly heard the divine discourses of the omniscient Lord (*Tirthankara*) Simandhara Swami. Different views are also prevalent regarding the dates of his life, which range from 108 BC to 5th-6th century A.D. A. N. Upadhye however maintains that Kundakunda flourished in the beginning of the Christian era.

The real name of Kundakunda is said to be Padmanandi. According to Shrutasagar's commentary on *Bodh Prabhrat,* Kundakunda was also known as Vakragreeve, Elacharya and Graddhapichha. Kundakunda is said to have had a number of preceptors (*gurus*). These include *shruta kevali* Bhadrabahu (see *Bodh Prabhrat*, verses 61-62), Kumarnandi Siddhantadeva (see Jayasena's observation in *Panchastikayasara*), or Jinbhadra (see Nandisangha's *Pattavali*).

All these descriptions, beliefs or opinions about the life of Kundakunda are based on *pattavalis*, rock inscriptions or eulogies in books written in the 10th century or thereafter. These books are not historical biographies in the modern sense of the term. In fact, till today we do not have absolutely reliable materials from which it is possible to reconstruct the life or writings of Kundakunda with any degree of certainty. Five of his works, viz. *Panchastikayasara* (PKS), *Samayasara* (SS), *Pravachanasara* (PS), *Niyamasara* (NS), and *Baras Anuvekkha* (BA) (Twelve Reflections or Affirmations) may be safely ascribed to him. Of these five treatises, the first three have been commented upon in Sanskrit by Amrtachandra in the tenth century and by Jayasena in the thirteenth century, which contains a number of interpolations (in Jayasena's recension). However, Kundakunda's authorship of *Ashta Pahuda*, *Rayanasara*, *Kural*, etc. is disputed. All of Kundakunda's works have been written in Shaurseni Prakrit.

The treatise *Pravachanasara* (*Pavayanasara* in Prakrit the name of treatise mentioned in PS 275) has been written by Acharya Kundakunda.

The word "*pravachan*" consists of *pra+vachan* in which "*pra*" means "*prakrisht*", i.e. the best, the excellent and immaculate, while "*vachan*" means description, exposition or instruction. And *sara* means the essence. In reality, such *pravachan* can only be delivered by those who are pure and perfect, and by those who have conquered all their shortcomings, limitations and impurities of deluded view, attachment, aversion, etc. They can be delivered only by those who know the reality of things since they are imbued with a desire to foster the well-being of all living beings.

The *Tirthankaras* are the promulgators of *dharma-tirtha* (the path of *dharma*), i.e. the rules and guidelines for the well-being and the moral and spiritual upliftment of living beings through their discourses (*pravachana* or sermons) which are the source of scriptures (*Jinvani* or Jain *Agama*). These scriptures provided invaluable insights into the reality of things and provide guidance to all living beings even when *Tirthankaras* or *Jinas* are not available.

Pravachanasara, thus, contains the "Essence of Divine Discourses", i.e. the essence of the sermons or the teachings of Lord Mahavira — the last of the 24 *Tirthankaras.* These teachings are said to have been organized subject-wise, in a systematic manner by his apostle Gautam and have been preserved for generations through being memorized by the learned people of both the Digambara and Shvetambara sects of Jains. These teachings were later enshrined/encoded in the canons/ scriptures of the two sects. Kundakunda inherited these teachings and his work *Pravachanasara,* therefore, contains the Essence of Divine Discourses, i.e. sermons or the Essence of the Jain Scriptures.

The treatise is based on the solid foundation of the scriptures or Jain texts and the principles contained therein. Kundakunda was not only well-versed in Jain scriptures, but was imbued with a mission to communicate the spiritual knowledge of the *Tirthankaras* to his readers. He was also well versed in other systems of philosophy as well as psychology, ethics, spiritualism and social aspects that facilitate a better understanding of human life in all its ramifications. All of Kundakunda's works have been written in Prakrit. They are full of enlightening wisdom and contain deep insights of the inner recesses of human nature. Being an excellent poet, he had the creative ability (*pratibha*) or the intellectual capacity of expressing new ideas and interpreting things in his own inimitable style.

One may encounter certain difficulties in understanding Kundakunda's works, especially if the reader proceeds from a purely analytical, descriptive and objective perspective. Things that were quite clear to him may not seem so to the lay reader. The reader must therefore have the intellectual ability to understand the inner meaning to see the hidden insights and to experience the enlightening wisdom himself. Kundakunda never wanted to impose his views, ideas or concepts on readers on the authority of the Revealed Word (the scriptures) of the Lord. He also did not ask people to accept his description of the reality because it is based on his own experience. He wanted people to read, listen, think, critically examine, and never to suspend their own judgment because one should accept them only after verification by one's own experience (SS 5). This is similar to what Buddha said: "Don't take my word for it; find out for yourself."

Pravachanasara discusses important concepts such as the definition of *dharma* (PS 6), the nature of the self (PS 7 and 192), equanimity (PS 7 and 24), *jnayaka bhava* (something that is essentially of knowing nature) (PS 200 and 35), the pure and good or auspicious conscious attentiveness, and the bad effects of evil or inauspicious psychic disposition (PS 11-14, 45, 69-79, 85, 92, 208-221, 236-240, 245-270). It also discusses the concepts of omniscience (PS 15-20), *svayambhu* (self-evolved enlightenment) (PS 16), knowledge (PS 21-58), the exposition of joy (PS 53-68), including sensorial pleasure, and of the knowable substance, including *jiva,* both in general (PS 93-126) and particular aspects (127-144), the mechanism of bondage (PS 169-189), and the path of liberation (PS 232-244), good conscious attentiveness (PS 245-270), the concepts of *ahimsa* (non-violence), *aparigraha* (non-possessiveness) and the conduct of *samana* (noble, self-restrained person), etc.

My appraisal of the significant concepts contained in *Pravachanasara* is given in the extensive Introduction, in which I have sought to present these concepts in their proper perspective in order to dispel misperceptions that readers may have. The detailed Introduction is extremely useful in dispelling various misrepresentations/distortions of Kundakunda's ideas by scholars of other religions, who lack a proper understanding of Jain principles and Jain scholars. These include some biased Shvetambara and Kanjipanthi scholars of the Digambara sect, who tend to take a one-sided, distorted view of Kundakunda's basic concepts. Among these, we may include many other well-meaning scholars of the Digambara sect, who have translated and commented in different languages and have given different interpretations. It also includes several foreign scholars like W.J. Johnson, who has created considerable confusion about Kundakunda's works, especially *Samayasara* and *Pravachanasara.*

The subject matter of *Pravachanasara* is serious, subtle, and profound requiring thoughtful investigation. In order to properly comprehend it, it is necessary for one to be a dedicated reader and one need not necessarily be an ascetic as is sometimes mistakenly believed. Repetitions are inevitable in a work of this nature especially as one seeks to clarify the issues and remove the misperceptions pertaining to the essential concepts dealt with in this superb treatise. In fact, repetitions are said to be characteristics of all Indian spiritual and philosophical treatises. The critical reader may not appreciate them, but the assiduous *sadhaka* (spiritual seeker) will value them immensely.

Pravachanasara is composed in Prakrit, which was once the common language of the people However, it is almost a dead language now. This poses serious problems. Even the first commentary thereon by Amrtachandra in Sanskrit (which again is understood by few people and is not understood by lay men) was written after nine centuries when Prakrit was neither spoken nor written. One cannot say with any certainty how proficient Amrtachandra was in Prakrit. It is very likely that he wrote his commentary on the basis of the Sanskrit rendering of Prakrit *gathas* (verses).

It is therefore not surprising that the word "*mayacharo*" (PS 44), which in Prakrit means "conduct" that is natural to *maya*, i.e. *mata* or mother, has been mistakenly equated with the Sanskrit word "*maya*" (deceitfulness), even by Amrtachandra, which is considered a characteristic natural to women. Accordingly, the sitting, standing, teaching of moral rules, etc. activities of *arihant* (Enlightened Lord, worthy of worship) are compared not to the natural conduct of the mother (Samantabhadra has compared the Enlightened Lord to mother), but with the aptitude of deceitfulness considered natural to women (PS 44 AC and JS). This not only denigrates the image of the Worthy Lord, but tarnishes the image of women as well.

That Prakrit and Sanskrit words have several meanings often pose another serious problem. This has given rise to gross misperceptions regarding the nature of the self. For instance, the word "*suddham*" (in Prakrit or "*shuddha*" in Sanskrit) in both languages means not only pure in the sense of impurity/purity, faultless, sinless, blameless, but also unique, unmixed, pure and simple in the sense of nothing else, only (*kevala*). This has created a very serious problem in a proper understanding of the inherent nature of the self in Kundakunda's works, especially *Pravachanasara* and *Samayasara.*

In his commentary on *Pravachanasara* 192, Amrtachandra has interpreted the nature of the self as pure (*atmanah shuddhatvam*) in the sense that it is distinguishable, different, and discriminated from other substance(s) (*para-dravya vibhagena*) and indistinguishable or not to be discriminated from its own properties or traits (*sva-dharma avibhagena*) with which it maintains an indivisible unity (*ekatvam cha*). In his commentary on *Samayasara* verse 6 also, Amrtachandra states that the self is said to be "*shuddha*" (pure), in the sense that the *jiva* (soul or conscious entity) can never become non-soul, or non-living (*ajiva*) material entity, and *ajiva* can never become *jiva*. These two substances, viz. life and non-life or the spirit and matter, are not liable to lose or interchange their inherent nature. *Jiva* can never assume or have the characteristic attributes of touch, taste, smell, etc. of non-living material entity or its modes/states of evolution (*evashesha dravyantara bhinnatvena upasyanman shuddha iti abhilipyate*) (SS 6 AC).

Jayasena, on the other hand, has deliberately translated and interpreted the word "*suddham*" as being devoid of all distortions or impurities of attachment, etc. (*ragadi samasta vibhava rahitam*) (PS 192 JS). In his *Samayasara* verse 6 commentary, he interprets it as "pure soul" or "pure consciousness" (*shuddhatma*) even though he had access to Amrtachandra's commentary. Jayasena's interpretation in this regard is inappropriate since it does not differentiate the nature of the self from the Advaita Vedanta and the Sankhya system of philosophy. It also fails to distinguish the embodied souls in the empirical existence from the liberated souls, who alone are devoid of all impurities and all kinds of *karmas*.

None of the Hindi and English translations of the Prakrit verses of Kundakunda in either *Samayasara* or even *Pravachanasara*, or the Sanskrit commentaries of Amrtachandra and Jayasena including those in Hindi can be said to be immaculate. This creates a serious problem for those not knowing Prakrit and Sanskrit. The problem of translating and interpreting Kundakunda's concepts of the complex subject of spirituality in English, a foreign language, is all the more difficult.

Prakrit and Sanskrit are not understood by the common folk as well as most scholars. Jainism is considered to be a universal religion. The propagation of such a religion far and wide (*dharma prabhavana*) is held to be one of the necessry prerequisites of an enlightened person. Since English is the *lingua franca* of the world, it is imperative that Jain scriptures are increasingly translated in the English language as well as other languages. A proper translation is as necesssary as a proper interpretation of the ideas contained in the Jain scriptures. As Jaina concepts are often very subtle and rich in meaning, it is usually difficult to explain them in English. In fact, an English translation poses a large number of problems compared to those of Hindi translation.

The terminology constitutes one of the most important and difficult part of any translation from one language into another one. The Hindi translators could use the same Jaina technical terms as in the original. However, this facility is not available in English. A number of early scholars like J.L. Jaini, A. Chakravarti, and A.N. Upadhye have translated many scriptures, including those authored by Kundakunda. I have been benefited by these translations as well as by the translations of terminology such as J.L. Jaini's *Jaina Gem Dictionary*, N.L. Jain's *Glossary of Jain Terms*, and Ramesh Chand Jain's *Sudha Sagar: Hindi-English Jaina Dictionary*. However, quite often these translations including those of *Pravachanasara*, whether in English or Hindi, have been found wanting in one respect or other in properly explaining the true purport or meaning of the subtle concepts. I have, therefore, tried to elaborate the technical terms as far as possible so that the reader may grasp the actual meaning of the term. I have also retained many original terms like *jiva*, *karma*, etc. as these are quite common nowadays. Other problems encountered in the English translation of the scriptures pertain to the paucity of scholars proficient in the English language and the subject matter or the lack of financial and/or literary encouragement.

Moreover, the task of a proper understanding of Kundakunda's concepts and ideas is further complicated by the preferences of some biased Shvetambara scholars and the one-sided interpretations of Kundakunda's concepts by the Kanjipanthi writers. Even some Digambara scholars and writers seek to give a certain twist to Kundakunda's ideas in favour of asceticism and external austerities, etc. The proper understanding of this scripture *(The Essence of Jaina Scriptures)* and the reality of things, Amrtachandra states, requires the right mental perspective and the purified enlightenment, which is free from any bias, preference or prejudice, which is obtained by the practice of conduct and the power of knowledge of the doctrine of *syadavada* (PS 275 AC and PS *Kalash*, 20-22).

In my detailed introduction, I have tried to highlight the significant points covered in *Pravachanasara* giving my own translation wherever necessary in order to present a correct and balanced view of the various issues to the best of my ability without any bias or preference. To that end, I have made full use of existing translations and commentaries in Sanskrit, Hindi and English. I have also drawn heavily on Kundakunda's other works, especially *Samayasara* (The Essence of Spirituality, Consciousness and the Transcental Self) together with various translations and commentaries thereon in different languages. I have benefitted greatly from dozens of other books and articles on the subject, written by numerous Indian and foreign scholars.

The present translation of the treatise *Pravachanasara* is based on the English translation by Professor Barend Faddegon, a Dutch Indologist, of the Prakrit *gathas* (verses) of *Pravachanasara* of Kundakunda together with the Sanskrit commentary, *Tattva-dipika*, by Amrtachandra. To that end, Faddegaon has indeed rendered a great service to the Jains since it is probably the only significant Digambara text authored by Kundakunda, which has been translated by a European scholar. Faddegon deserves credit for undertaking the painstaking task of translating the complicated Sanskrit sentences of Amrtachandra, which, as F.W. Thomas observes, "renders the work of interpretation and translation extremely difficult". He undertook this laborious task at the "behest" of Prof. Thomas, even when he was not feeling well due to a constitutional nervous disease for "the joy of a deeper and better understanding" of the Jain religion.

Faddegon has translated not only the text of *Pravachanasra* but also the *Tattvadipika* commentary of Amrtachandra thereon honestly and sincerely with an open and critical mind, which is reflected in his notes. At some places, the notes give a comparative perspective of various systems of philosophy including Jainism, Buddhism and Vaisheshika on certain issues. It is indeed a matter of deep concern and regret that no Jaina or non-Jaina scholar, Indian or foreign, has so far deemed it necessary to translate the other two commentaries by Amrtachandra of Kundakunda's two other outstanding works, viz. *Panchastikayasara* and *Samayasara*. A.N. Upadhye has translated only Kundakunda's verses of *Pravachanasara* text, but not Amrtachandra's commentary thereon. Faddegon's translation of both Kundakunda's text and Amrtachandra's commentary thereon, A.N. Upadhye says, reached his hands very late, when all the forms of his translation and Introduction had already been printed.

Faddegon's mastery of Sanskrit is evident from the fact that he taught the *Mimansa* and *Nyaya* systems of philosophy and *Vyakaran* (Sanskrit Grammar) to Ludo Rocher and wrote on Panini and the Vaisheshika system. Even Upadhye, who has called his own translation of *Pravachanasara* text of "tentative character", states that he is "benefitted by some of the ideas of the late B. Faddegon who has so carefully translated into English the *Pravachanasara* along with the Sanskrit commentary of Amrtachandra".

Since Faddegon was not exclusively devoted to Jaina philosophy and religion, he was not very well conversant with the intricacies of all the Jaina concepts and technical terms, such as "*sarvagata*," "*samyak*," "*para-samaya*," "*dravyatva*", etc. Therefore, his translation of Kundakunda's verses and even Amrtachandra's commentary thereon in a number of places does not seem to be proper. For instance, following the Vedanta tradition, Faddegon has translated the word "*sarvavyapi ekchid-rupa*" (PS Kalash 1) as "pure intelligence pervading everything," which I have corrected as *atman* being "one principle or reality of consciousness-as-such that permeates all its attributes and modes".

The literal translation of "*achal*" as "immobile" (in PS 192) and of "*rupa*" in "*yathajata rupam*" as "colour" (in PS 204 and 207) are also not correct. I have therefore translated "*achal*" as "stable" and "*rupa*" as "form" or "character," which in my opinion are more appropriate translations in conveying the sense and purport of the author. Since Faddegon was not very familiar with Indian conditions, he could not understand that *sahakara* fruit (in PS 104 AC) means mango fruit, which evolves by itself from the green state into the yellowish state, not a "white" state as he has translated the term "*pandu*". The word "*pandu*," like many other terms, has more than one meaning. When it is used in the context of silver, it means "white" but when it is used with respect to mango fruit "yellowish" is more appropriate.

The translation of "*samyak*" as "absolute" in Amrtachandra's commentary on *Pravachanasara* 241, and of "*samyak-darshan*" as "perfect faith" in Amrtachandra's commentary on *Pravachanasara* 242 is not proper. Similarly, translation of *vyavahara* and *nishchaya nayas* as "view of common acceptance" and "view of strict verity" respectively (see PS 191) or "theoretical point of view" and "practical point of view" respectively in Amrtachandra commentary (see PS 242) do not seem to be appropriate. In my view, a better translation of the word "*samyak*" is "enlightened", of *nishchaya naya* as "internal, self-referential point of view" and of *vyavahara naya* as "external, other-referential point of view". Since most Indian scholars have also not translated these terms properly, Faddegon alone should not to be blamed.

I have sought to revise, correct and modify Faddegon's translation of Kundakunda's Prakrit verses wherever considered ncecessary. I have also used Upadhye's translation of *Pravachanasara* in this regard. Faddegon's translation of Amrtachandra's commentary has also been modified and revised at a number of places. I have also removed a few question marks noticed in his translation.

In his translation of Amrtachandra's commentary on *Pravachanasara* in verse 207 concerning *pratikraman/pratyakhyana*, Faddegon has left out one long sentence pertaining to the fourth *avashyaka* (essential daily duties), which has been translated and inserted in the proper place by the present editor of this volume. As a result, Faddegon only mentioned five of the six essential daily duties. This possibly occured because the copy of *Pravachanasara* available to him did not contain that sentence in Sanskrit. This sentence in Amrtachandra's Sanskrit commentary is missing even in the *Pravachanasara* book, edited and published by A.N. Upadhye.

Moreover, while Faddegon had a good command over Sanskrit, he apparently did not have much knowledge of Prakrit. Like most other translations, his translation of the Prakrit text of Kundakunda is based on the Sanskrit rendering (Sanskrit *chhaya*) of Prakrit verses. As a result, when he translates the two Prakrit verses quoted by Amrtachandra which do not have a Sanskrit rendering in his Appendix on 47 points of view, his translation has been found to be incorrect and even perverse. The Sanskrit rendering and English translation of these two Prakrit verses by J. L. Jaini available in *Gommatsara Karmakanda* Part II (Verses 894-895) published in 1937 was also not available to Faddegon at the time of his translation of this treatise (1934). I have translated these two Prakrit verses and also reproduced Faddegon's translation thereof.

Barend Faddegon's translation, edited with an introduction by F.W. Thomas, was first published in 1935. Its publication was made possible by the "liberality and Testamentary Provision" of Rai Bahadur Jagmanderlal Jaini (J. L. Jaini), to whose memory the publication was dedicated.

The footnotes coming at the bottom of the page in Faddegon's translation have been shifted towards the end of the book. Moreover, the numbering of the verses in Book II and III have also been made consecutive so as to tally with the Prakrit text, given at the end of the book and numerous publications on *Pravachanasara.* Since a number of books on *Pravachanasara* in Hindi as well as A.N. Upadhye's English translation thereof, follow the pattern of book-wise numbering, e.g. II.5 (for PS 97) and III.8 (for PS 208), I have also retained that pattern for Book II and Book III along with consecutive numbering for the whole book for the convenience of the readers.

Like Amrtachandra's commentary of *Samayasara*, Amrtachandra's commentary of *Pravachanasara*, though written in prose, also contains poetic compositions or verses, called *Kalash* (246 in *Samayasara*, and 22 in *Pravachanasara*). I have revised translations of these *Kalash* verses. I have also numbered them and kept them separate from the commentary in prose. The English translation of Faddegon of the 36 additional verses given only in *Tatparyavrtti* commentary of Jayasena has been given after Amrtachandra's commentary. The glossary in the book has been reproduced from *Pravachanasara*, translated and edited by A.N. Upadhye. However, references to verses (*gathas*) have been changed to the consecutive numbering for the whole book, instead of book-wise numbering.

I express my sincere gratitude to Shri Ashok Jain of Jain Family Trust for sponsoring the publication of this book. I express my sincere thanks to my sons, Rajendra Kumar Jain and Pradeep Kumar Jain, and my daughter-in-law, Sunita Jain, for their encouragement, support and help of various kinds. I thank my grand-daughter Ruchika and grandson Anekant, who have helped in various ways including proofreading. I also thank Vaishali Gupta for typing the bulk of the manuscript and carrying out corrections.

12 March 2014 — JAGDISH PRASAD JAIN

1

Introduction

Jagdish Prasad Jain

Kundakunda and His Works

Acharya Kundakunda is held in very high esteem among the Jains, particularly the Digambara sect. In fact, he is revered next only to Lord Mahavira and his apostle Gautam Gandhara. Many Jain monks deem it a proud privilege to trace their spiritual lineage from Kundakunda, who is considered to have flourished in the beginning of the Christian era. R.G. Bhandarkar describes Kundakunda as "one of the earliest Digambara authors whose works are referred to by subsequent writers".[1] Peterson characterizes him "a teacher of great antiquity and renown".[2] Kundakunda's works, all of which are in Prakrit (Pk.) dialect[3], are read with respect by all sects and sections of Jains. The hallmark of all his works is their focus on spirituality, i.e. attention to our inner dimension.

There are five significant works of Kundakunda (KK), viz. *Panchastikayasara* (PKS), *Samayasara* (SS), *Pravachanasara* (PS), *Niyamasara* (NS) and *Baras Anuvekkha* (BA) (*Twelve Reflections or Affirmations*), Of these, the first three have been commented upon in Sanskrit (Sk.) by Amrtachandra (AC) (in the 10th century) and Jayasena (JS) (in the 13th century). Thus, we have two recessions of these three works.

Panchastikayasara (PKS) deals mainly with the six substances. *Samayasara* (SS) – which is widely recognized to be the most important of Kundakunda's works – deals essentially with the supreme reality of the transcendental nature of the self. The self is said to have unity or oneness *(ekatva)* with the embodied soul and material *karman* and the resultant influx of *karmas*, etc. modes or categories *(padartha)* in the transmigratory existence yet maintains its distinctness *(vibhaktpana)* from them. In *Pravachanasara* (PS), there is a systematic, philosophical, logical and scientific examination of the following issues – knowledge, the knowables, karmic bondage, auspicious *(shubha),* inauspicious (*ashubha*), pure (*shuddha*), psychic-attention, violence and non-violence, and description of equanimity and conduct, etc.

Two Recensions of *Pravachanasara* (PS)

Kundakunda did not divide *Paravachanasara* into books, chapters or sections. Amrtachandra has, however, divided it into three Books dealing with the principles of knowledge (*jnana*), the knowable (*jneya*) and conduct. Apart from the benedictory (PS 1-5) and preliminary verses relating to the nature of the self and its states-of-evolution (PS 7-12), Book 1 contains four chapters: Pure Psychic-attention (*shuddhopayoga*) (PS 13-20), Exposition of Knowledge (PS 21-52), Exposition of Joy (PS 53-68), and Good (*shubha*) Psychic-attention (PS 69-92). Book II has three chapters: Knowable (Substance) in General (*dravya samanya*) (PS 93-126), Substance in Particular (*dravya vishesh*) (PS 127-144), and Distinctive Characteristics of soul substance (*jiva dravya*) (PS 145-200). Book III has four sections, viz. Conduct including negligence (PS 201-231), Path of Liberation (PS 232-244), Good Psychic-attention (*shubha upayoga*) (PS 245-270), and the five jewels (PS 271-275) pertaining to principles of transmigration (*sansara*) (PS 271), liberation (PS 272), means of liberation (PS 273-274), and the benefits of understanding the treatise (PS 275).

Of the two recensions, Amrtachandra's recession of *Pravachanasara* contains 275 *gathas* (verses) divided into three *Shrutaskandhas* (Books) each dealing with the exposition of *Jnana-tattva* (knowledge principle), *Jneya-tattva* (knowable principle) and *Charana-tattva* (conduct principle) and containing 92, 108 and 75 *gathas* (verses) respectively. Jayasena's recension, however, adopts the three divisions and terms them *adhikaras* (Chapters), which deal with *jnana* (knowledge), *darshan* (intuition, view) and *charitra* (conduct). The number of *gathas* (verses) in Jayasena's recension are 311 with each *adhikara* having 101, 113 and 97 *gathas* (verses) respectively. Thus, the recension of Jayasena contains 36 additional verses (9 in Book I, 5 in Book II, and 22 in Book III).

The verses have been numbered according to the Prakrit text given at the end of this book. Thus, if Jayasena's verses are coming before Amrtachandra, it is numbered as 19/1 and 93/1, while Amrtachandra's verses are numbered as 19/2 and 93/2. Similarly, if Jayasena's verses are coming after those of Amrtachandra, they are numbered as 52/2, 135/2, 217/2, 217/3, etc., while Amrtachandra's verses are renumbered as 52/1, 135/1, 217/1, etc. (this has been the case in the rest of the verses). The additional verses given only in Jayasena's commentary of *Tattparya-vrtti* have been given at the end of the book. The subject matter and contents of Book II indicate that Jayasena's designation thereof as *darshan* does not seem to be quite correct. At times, he also gives alternative readings and two interpretations of the same verses (e.g. see for instance II.46-47 (PS 138-139).

Additional Verses in Jayasena's Recension

After examining the contents and the general nature of the additional verses in the longer recension of Jayasena and the position they occupy in the text, Upadhye comes to the conclusion that of the 36 additional verses, 8 verses (viz. 52/2, 68/3, 79/3, 82/2, 92/2 and 92/3 of Book I and 93/1, 200/2 of Book II) contain "salutation and benediction". The second group of 12 verses (viz. 19/1, 68/2, 79/2 of Book I and 135/2, 146/2 of Book II; and 217/2-3, 229/2-4, 239/2, and 268/2 of Book III) contain some "explanation and amplification". These twenty verses, Upadhye observes, "even if they are dropped their absence would not be felt, and even if they are present they do not materially add to the contents of *Pravachanasara* as a whole."[4]

These twenty verses include an additional verse (viz. verse no. 19/1 of second group). In this context, Upadhye observes: "It is something like a gloss on the previous *gathas* and does not disturb the context very much."[5] On careful examination of this verse and previous verses, the present author feels that this additional verses does disturb the context as is implied from Upadhye's qualifying phrase "very much". This verse has no relation whatsoever with either the previous or the subsequent one. However, it does contain two novel assertions or innovative ideas. To the best of my knowledge, it is not mentioned in any other Jain texts and, therefore, seem to be creations of Jayasena's own fertile mind.

Two remarks about this additional verse are required. Firstly, verse 19/1 mentions a new definition of *samyak-darshan* (enlightened view) when its introductory remark states: "Those who believe in [the] omniscient are *samyak-drashti* (one having *samyak-darshan* i.e. enlightened view)." The followers of all religions consider their Gods to possess absolute or complete knowledge, i.e. omniscience. They believe in them and therefore can be said to be upholders of enlightened view. In this regard, verse 80 of *Pravachanasara* states that he who knows the true nature of the self, through the medium of *Arhat* (*kevali* or omniscient) in relation to substance, quality and modification, his infatuation (*moha*) perishes, i.e. such a person is called *samyak-drashti* (one having enlightened view about the self), and not simply someone who merely believes in the omniscient Lord.

Secondly, the additional verse 19/1 states that those who believe in the best of all objects, i.e. omniscient soul(s), honoured by the gods of heaven, etc., have their miseries brought to nought. The very next verse (19/2 or rather verse 19 of Amrtachandra's recension and also acceptable to Jayasena), on the other hand, affirms: "He whose destructive *karman* has perished... he himself evolves into knowledge and bliss," i.e. has his miseries brought to nought. In other words, the elimination of miseries or attainment of salvation takes place not simply by belief (i.e. enlightened view), but by the trinity of enlightened view, knowledge and conduct.

Jayasena's additional verse 19/1 is being misinterpreted by H.C. Bharill, a follower and spokesperson of Kanjipanthi, in support of his one-sided assertion: "If from the beginningless time the soul is miserable, its only cause (*ek matra karana*) is absence of *samyak-shraddhan*, or *samyak-darshan* (i.e. false belief or deluded view); freedom from it is the real freedom, i.e. liberation."[6] *Samyak-shraddhan* is imperative for liberation but as Kundakunda has clearly stated that one having *samyak-shraddhan* but lacking self-restraint (*sanjad* in Pk. or *sanyat* in Sk.) does not attain liberation (PS 237). In this context, Amrtachandra remarks:

> And for one without self-restraint what can belief, which consists in apprehension (*pratiti*) of the truth of the self as described, or knowledge, which consists in experiencing (*anubhuti*) of the truth of the self as described have any effect? Therefore, from belief or knowledge, devoid of self-restraint, there is no attainment of liberation; hence [the idea] that

> non-simultaneity of Scripture knowledge, belief in the principles or the categories, and self-restraint could be the path of liberation is refuted. (PS 237 AC)

In so far as the third group of remaining 16 verses (viz. 187/2 of Book II and 220/2-4, 224/2-12, 227/2 of Book III) are concerned, A.N. Upadhya observes, one wonders whether the additional information contained in them is consistent with the contents of Kundakunda's other works. If there is any inconsistency, one has to question their authenticity. However, if similar contents are found in other works of Kundakunda, they can be considered acceptable.[7]

After undertaking a strict scrutiny of these 16 verses, Upadhye remarks:

> The position of II.95*4 [187/2], especially in that particular context, is doubtful. The remonstration against the use of clothes, in 220/2-4, is only an amplification of one of the 28 primary virtues (PS 204, 208-209), and this subject is discussed in detail in *Charittapahuda* (20 ff.), *Suttapahuda* (17 ff.), *Bodhapahuda* (51 ff.)... That women cannot attain liberation, as set forth in 224/2-12, is a topic which represents the Digambara view against that held by the Shvetambaras. It is not only here, but also in *Suttapahuda* (22 ff.) that Kundakunda states his views almost in the same tone.... The contents of 227/2 have nothing special, though the *gatha* disturbs the context.[8]

Of the 16 additional verses of the third group, the only consistency with the contents of the five major works of Kundakunda is about his objection to the use of clothes (verse 220/2-4), which Upadhye considers to be only an "amplification" of one of the 28 primary qualities (*mulgunas*) of a *shraman* in *Pravachanasara* verses 204 and 208-9. If this has already been discussed in three verses of *Pravachanasara,* it was not necessary to further elaborate it by the introduction of three more verses by Jayasena. Upadhye concurs that two of these additional verses (187/2 and 227/2) disturb the context. For the remaining eleven additional verses in this third group of 16 verses, the only comparable references that Upadhye could cite, are related to *Ashta Pahuda,* in which case Kundakunda's authorship is said to be somewhat doubtful.[9]

These 11 verses of the third group maintain that women cannot attain liberation in the same birth. The Digambaras endorse this view whereas the Shvetambaras disagree. Unlike additional verses 220/2-4,

Upadhye does not give any comparable reference to the subject in these additional 11 verses to any of the verses in the *Pravachanasara* of Amrtachandra recession or in any of the other significant works of Kundakunda mentioned above, and also these 11 verses could not be said to be an "amplification" or elucidation of other verses.

Another controversy between Shvetambaras and Digambaras relates to eating of food by the *kevali* (*arihanta*, the enlightened soul, who has gotten rid of the four *ghatia* (destructive) *karmas*, i.e. those *karmas* which obscure the four excellent attributes of the enlightened soul). This point has been raised and discussed in detail by Jayasena in his commentary on *Pravachanasara* verse 20. In fact, there does not seem to have been any particular need to introduce this topic at this point since the verse merely states that the *kevali* does not experience bodily pleasure or pain since he has transcended the realm of the senses. In his commentary, Amrtachandra reiterated this by arguing that just as fire, which has no contact with an iron ball, is not subjected to the heavy blows by a hammer, the pure soul, having transcended the senses does not experience either bodily pleasure or pain.

On the other hand, Jayasena discusses the sectarian issue of *kevali* at length in almost three pages. It seems that he dwells on this controversial topic in order to score a point against the rival sect by using Kundakunda's "literary reputation" and seeks to display his own intellectual skills (*panditya pradarshan*). To that end, Jayasena tends to tarnish the image of a great thinker like Kundakunda whose works are the common heritage of all mankind. In fact, at a number of other places, Jayasena's commentary seems to be unnecessarily lengthy. For instance, while Amrtachandra's commentary of *Pravachanasara* verses 261 and 262 as well as verses 264 to 267 is provided in only one sentence, Jayasena's commentary runs to as many as 8 to 20 sentences.

Thus, the additional verses of Jayasena in *Pravachanasara*, especially the 11 verses of the third group, "appear to be a subsequent interpolation".[10] (Besides *Pravachanasara*, additional verses also appear in Jaysena's recension of the text of two other works of Kundakunda, viz. *Samayasara* and *Panchastikayasara*). Jayasena has not given any explanation for the additional verses and the circumstances point to him being the author of the verses.[11]

The additional interpolatory verses in all three works of

Kundakunda seem to be "the work of someone who had mastered the language in the manner of the original, from which they are considered to be indistinguishable".[12] This "someone", it seems, is no other person than Jayasena himself as all his three Sanskrit commentaries start with translation meanings or explanations in Sanskrit of each Prakrit word or phrase coming in Kundakunda's verse. This is indicative of his proficiency and mastery of the Prakrit language. However, Amrtachandra does not adhere to this practice.

In his introduction in English to the 1959 edition of *Samayasara*, published in Hindi by Rajkrishna Jain of Ahimsa Mandir, Delhi, i.e. almost two decades after Upadhye edited *Pravachanasara*, A.N. Upadhye seems to have revised his opinion about Jayasena. He observes:

> To the modern mind there is something heinous in any one tampering with old texts like this. In India, however, many old works have received such treatment even from authors of great merit and originality, who have preferred to remain anonymous, not with the idea of committing a fraud, but from a sense of modesty and selflessness. It is possible that Jayesena put in the additional verses in a similar frame of mind, but the controversial verses in *Pravachanasara* do not support this charitable interpretation. Many Jaina writers begin their work by inviting the reader himself to rectify mistake of omission and commission on their part.[13]

Amrtachandra was not only older to Jayasena but far more learned of the two Sanskrit commentators. In his commentary, he has incorporated a number of independent Sanskrit poems (known as SS *Kalash* or PS *Kalash*). As a renowned scholar, he has himself written a number of excellent works.[14] Amrtachandra's commentaries of the three works of Kundakunda, viz. *Samayasara*, *Pravachanasara* and *Panchastikayasara*, are generally recognized as outstanding. He has sought to elaborate certain points, which would have otherwise been very difficult to understand. However, his commentaries incorporate his own ideas and preferences at certain places. In my own evaluation of the significant concepts and ideas presented in *Pravachanasara*, I have sought to present as honestly as possible what Kundakunda himself would have wanted to say. To that end, I have even given my own translation at a number of places and have also used the commentaries of Amrtachandra and Jayasena, as well as highlighted views and translations of other scholars wherever necessary.

Motivations behind Jayasena's Commentaries

We must seek to examine the issue as to what motivated Jayasena to write his commentaries of the three works of Kundakunda. It seems that Jayasena's motives in mastering the Prakrit language and undertaking the laborious task of writing the extensive Sanskrit commentaries of three outstanding works of Kundakunda was to insert additional Prakrit verses. He also apparently sought to orient these works towards asceticism, emphasize omniscience and pure conscious attentiveness (*shuddha upayoga*). Moreover, he sought to highlight that these works, especially *Samayasara,* dealt with the pure self or pure consciousness and, therefore, they needed to be read only by either saints or ascetics.

Unlike Amrtachandra, Jayasena in his commentaries has deliberately interpreted "*shuddha*", even in describing the inherent nature of the self as "free from attachment etc. passions", i.e. pure self. He thus equated the Jaina view regarding the nature of the self with those of Advaita Vedanta and Sankhya. Moreover, Jayasena has endeavoured to interpret the words "*shraman*", "*muni*", etc. from the perspective of ascetics.

Jayasena apparently sought to enhance his reputation by exhibiting his intellectual skills by incorporating the stages of moral and spiritual advancement (*gunasthan*), and seeking to explain issues through some innovative ideas of his own (see the discussion on his additional verse 19/1). In the process, he made various divisions and subdivisions of different points of view which has only created confusion in the minds of scholars and people alike.

Instead of an independent work, Jayasena preferred to present his ideas through his commentaries of the works of Kundakunda. Unfortunately, people are generally reluctant to criticize any commentator, even though it may be eating into the very essentials of Jainism, lest it diminishes the common man's faith in the scriptures. This probably explains why Upadhye felt that "excepting" a few verses, which he felt were "dubious in that context" he did not find "that there is any strong case against Kundakunda's authorship, as a composer or compiler, of these additional *gathas.*"[15] He wonders why Amrtachandra did not include these *gathas* in his commentary. He answers the question himself: "My tentative conjecture is that Amrtachandra was too spiritualistic to enter into sectarian polemics;

and possibly he wanted to make his commentary along with it the sublime utterances of Kundakunda, acceptable to all the sects by eliminating the glaring and acute sectarian attacks."[16]

The use of the words "strong case", "tentative conjecture," and "exceptions in regard to few verses" indicates that Upadhye was not averse to acknowledging that a case could be made for considering the additional *gathas* (verses) of Jayasena of "dubious authencity".[17] However, subsequently, as stated earlier, A.N. Upadhye revised his views in his Introduction to *Samayasara.*

Thus, the translation of a religious text, its interpretation or writing its commentary should be undertaken with a sense of responsibility and not for name, fame or personal reputation, lest it distorts the meaning and creates confusion in the minds of people.

Even though Jayasena's commentaries are not as good as those of Amrtachandra, his commentaries at some places do contain some good points or explanations.

Problems in Translation of Old Scriptures

There are several problems in the translation of old scriptures. Firstly, apart from the problem of tampering with the old texts, particularly Kundakunda's works, in the form of additional verses, a far more serious problem is tampering with the concepts and ideas of Kundakunda and distortion of their sense and meanings through commentaries, translations, interpretations, and explanations. This has prevented correct presentation and proper understanding of the great psychological insights and philosophical concepts contained in Kundakunda's works.

Secondly, another problem is that *Pravachanasara* is composed in Prakrit, which at one time was the common language of the people, but is now virtually a dead language. Amrtchandra's first commentary on the scripture was in Sanskrit (which is also not understood by common people) and was written after nine centuries when Prakrit was neither spoken nor written. Thus, one cannot say with certainty as to Amrtchandra's proficiency in Prakrit. It is very likely that he wrote his commentary on the basis of the Sanskrit rendering of Prakrit *gathas* (verses). At times, this tends to create confusion. For instance, the word "*mayacharo*" (in PS 44), which in Prakrit means "conduct", which is natural of *maya,* i.e. *mata* or mother, has been erronously equated with Sanskrit word "*maya*" (deceitfulness), which is considered an aptitude natural to women, by both Amrtchandra and Jayasena in their Sanskrit commentaries.

Accordingly, the sitting, standing, teaching of moral rules, etc. activities of *arihant* (Enlightened Lord, worthy of worship) are compared not to the natural conduct of the mother, but with the aptitude of deceitfulness considered natural to women (PS 44 AC and JS), which not only denigrates the image of the Worthy Lord but also is damaging to women-folk. In *Svayambhu Stotra* (35), Samantabhadra eulogizes enlightened Lord Suparshva for giving spiritual instruction and rendering advice for the well-being of living beings in a manner akin to that of a mother to her children.

Thirdly, people hesitate to criticize the interpretation of the two Sanskrit commentators even when it is not proper at some places in conveying the true sense of the original author (Kundakunda). But for the proper understanding of the significant concepts of the author, it is necessary to point out the shortcomings in the commentaries and not hesitate to criticize them. Without the rectification of defects, the faultless presentation of the sense or purport of the author becomes impossible.

Hence, we should no longer allow any tampering or distortions to tarnish the image of Kundakunda – an outstanding philosopher, an original thinker and a great scientist of the inner recesses of human nature. The absence of proper presentation of the Jaina concepts has prevented Jainism from occupying its rightful place of becoming a world religion.

Significant Concepts in *Pravachanasara:* An Appraisal

Pravachanasara is an outstanding work containing a systematic exposition of Jaina ontology, epistemology, psychology and ethics. In the first four verses, Kundakunda pays homage to *Tirthankar* Lord Mahavira (*Vardhman*), who has annihilated the four destructive *karmas* (*ghatia karman*, i.e. those distorting the nature of the self). As a result, he has become worthy of worship. He is the promulgator of *dharma-tirtha* (the path of *dharma*, righteousness and piety), i.e. the rules and guidelines for the well-being and moral and spiritual upliftment of living beings. His discourses (*pravachana*) are the source of the scriptures. All the other promulgators of *dharma-tirtha* are also liberated souls (*siddhas*), who have purified (*vishuddha*) their souls.

The Concept of Equanimity (*Samya*)

After paying homage to all the most revered souls, Kundakunda states that having approached their holy station, and devoted primarily to purifying (*vishuddha*) one's world-view and knowledge, "I rely upon the conduct of equanimity, (*sammam* in Pk. or *samya* in Sk.), which leads to the attainment of *nirvana* (liberation)" (PS 5).[18]

Conduct based primarily upon an enlightened world-view and knowledge leads to the attainment of the prosperity and happiness in this world and heaven hereafter as well as enduring happiness of liberation (*nirvana*) (PS 6). Thus, Kundakunda speaks of both *abhyudaya*, i.e. attainment of prosperity and high status in this world as also *nihshreyas* (*moksha*, i.e. liberation). Of the two, *moksha* is considered superior and indeed the highest goal of human endeavour according to both Jaina scriptures as well as Indian tradition. Kundakunda is no exception to this. It is precisely for this reason that Amrtachandra asserts that liberation is preferable to the transitory happiness of either this world or of heaven (PS 6 AC).

Describing the nature and significance of conduct based on equanimity (*samo* in Pk., *samya* in Sk.), Kundakunda states: "Conduct is *dharma. Dharma* is defined as equanimity (*sama);* and equanimity is said to be a state-of-evolution (*parinama)* of the soul, in which it is free from infatuation (*moha)* and disturbance *(kshobha*)" (PS 7).

In his commentary on this verse, Amrtachandra explains that conduct is behaving according to one's innate nature because *dharma* is defined as the nature of things *(vastu svabhavat dharma),* which is the manifestation of one's pure consciousness. This constitutes equanimity since it encompasses the inherent qualities of the self. Equanimity, he adds, is a state-of-evolution *(parinama)* of the soul. This is exempt from the flaw of infatuation (*moha*), which is the result of the rise *(udaya)* of view-deluding *karman* and mental agitation or perturbation *(kshobha)* caused by the arising of conduct-deluding *karman,* i.e. attachment *(raga)* and aversion *(dvesh)* (PS 7 AC). *Moha, raga* and *dvesh* are the greatest enemies of the soul in the path of the liberation – the highest goal of human endeavour.

Conduct, according to Jayasena, is regarded as *dharma.* This, in turn, is said to be *samo* (meaning *shama* or *shaman,* i.e. quietitude, calming, subsidence or restraint), which signifies the state-of-evolution of soul devoid of infatuation *(moha)* and *kshobha,* i.e. attachment and aversion. In other words, it means behaving in accordance with one's pure nature of the consciousness, which is free from the blemish of delusion, attachment and aversion, which are the cause of the transmigratory existence (PS 7 JS).

Behaving according to equanimity constitutes the essence of spiritual enlightenment since it seeks to essentially purify one's world-view and knowledge and leads to liberation (PS 5). However, before discussing this further, it is necessary to understand the word *sama, samo, samabhava, samaya, samaiyam* (*samayika* in Sanskrit), used in the sense of equanimity. It is also desirable to understand one's own nature (*svabhava*), *dharma*, pure thoughts, *charitra* (conduct), freedom from attachment and hatred (*veetragata*), *shama* or *shaman* (subsidence of passions, i.e. *vikara-shaman*) and *shrama* and *shraman* (*saman* in Prakrit), which is suggestive of hard work or labour (*shrama*, effort), which are considered equivalent words. (see *Samansuttam*, a compilation of Prakrit verses of both Digambara and Shvetambara traditions, verses 78, 100, 230, 232-233, 275, 327-328, 336, 341, 343, 346-347, and 422-423).

The emphasis in *Pravachanasara* verse 7 signifies that enlightened view and knowledge are not able to achieve the objective of happiness unless they are accompanied by enlightened conduct based on equanimity and freedom from infatuation or deluded view (*moha*) and mental agitation (*kshobha*), caused by attachment and aversion, anger, etc. passions (PS 7). In other words, the self has the potential to become purified (*vishuddha*). This means that one has to make efforts to become pure by practicing conduct (*charitra*) of *sama* (equanimity) and *shama* or *shaman* (subsidence of passions, i.e. *vikara-shamana*) and undertake *shrama* (hard work, i.e. be *samana* in the true sense of the word).

Accordingly, that *samana*, who practices five self-regulations (*samiti*), the three self-restraints (*gupti*) of mind, speech and body, controls his five senses, has conquered his passions (*kashaya*) like anger and is fully endowed with intuition and knowledge, is called self-restrained (PS 240). Further, it is stated that *samana,* the practitioner of *sama*, is he, who considers groups of enemies and friends as the same, pleasure and pain as the same, praise and blame as the same, clay and gold as the same and moreover, maintains equanimous attitude in regard to life and death. (PS 241)

In the daily recital of Acharya Amitgati's song on equanimity (*samayika),* a person is asked to remain equanimous not only among groups of pleasant and unpleasant and enemies and friends, but also even in association or conjunction with love and tragic separation therefrom, and while living in palace or in forest; as also not to have any attachment whatsoever with any one of them. The Buddhists speak of four sets of contrasting conditions or traits (*dhammas*), viz. praise and blame, gain and loss, pleasure and pain, and fame and disrepute. One is asked to maintain a balanced and equanimous attitude towards them because they are impermanent. The *Gita* also talks of remaining equanimous in pleasure and pain, victory or defeat, friend and foe, fame and disrepute (*Gita* 2.38 and 12.18).

Self-restraint and Equanimity

In his commentary on *Pravachanasara* verse 241, Amrtachandra observes:

> Self-restraint is conduct accompanied by enlightened [*samyak*] intuition or world-view and knowledge. Conduct is *dharma; dharma* is equanimity; equanimity is a state-of-evolution devoid of infatuation (*moha*) and perturbation or mental agitation (*kshobha*). Therefore, equanimity is the characteristic of the self-restrained. (PS 241 AC)

Self-restraint is the necessary condition of equanimity, which enables a person to remain calm, retain an equanimous attitude in favourable and unfavourable circumstances, and to transcend the five dichotomies, groups or pairs of contradictory traits (*dvandas)* of enemies and friends, pleasure and pain, etc. (PS 241) as well as five other dichotomies – preferences, biases, fixations, complexes or knots (*granthi*). These are mentioned by Amrtachandra as follows:

> This is mine *(mum)* or this one belongs to me and this is other (*para*); this is a joy or pleasant to me and this is a torment or unpleasant; this is an elevation to me and this is humiliation; this man or object is useless to me and this one is helpful or of benefit; this is worth holding or maintaining of myself and that is a complete destruction.

All these dichotomies or dualities (*dvaita*), Amratachandra states, are the result of infatuation. They are based on attachment and aversion. However, in the absence of these traits one continually experiences the self as having for nature pure spiritual vision and knowledge (PS 241 AC).

Such an enlightened person, Amrtachandra adds, recognizes the groups of enemies and friends, pleasure and pain, etc. as indistinguishable, i.e. the same, merely as knowables (PS 241 AC). By nature, they are transitory states or conditions, like waves on the surface of water. On the other hand, the knowing subject, which is the substratum of all these states, remains unperturbed like the bottom of the ocean since it truly possesses equanimity in all respects. Therefore, he is neither dejected/perturbed in miseries/failures nor is he elated/hankering amidst pleasures or successes, but maintains his calm in all circumstances.

Amtrachandra concludes his commentary by stating that equanimity can be said to be a characteristic of someone who exercises self-restraint, who brings perfection in terms of simultaneity of self-knowledge and knowledge of the scriptures, conviction in principles and categories and self-restraint (PS 241 AC). In other words, if a person is not ignorant of the real nature of the self and the reality of things, considers pleasure and pain etc. to be "merely knowables", is not infatuated with reference to objects, and does not feel attachment or aversion, then inevitably he destroys various *karmas* resulting in liberation. (see PS 243-244 and PS 243-244 AC)

Bhagavdagita also emphasizes that equanimity is the characteristic of those who exercise self-restraint when it states that *samatva,* i.e. equanimity is said to be *yoga* (*Gita* 2.48) because *yoga* is defined as restraint of mental processes (*chittavrtti nirodha*) (Patanjali, *Yogasutra* 1.2). Our mind generally tends to always sway in extremes of likes and dislikes. Either we are intensely attached to someone or start hating him madly. Therefore, the balance of mind or intelligence is described as the essence of *yoga.*

In *Atmabodha* (knowledge of self) (50), Adi Shankracharya repeats what Kundakunda has said (in PS 7), when he states: "Having crossed the ocean of delusion (*moha*) and gotten rid of attachment and aversion, or likes and dislikes, which are the cause of mental agitations, the self restrained (*yogi*), united with peace, revels in his own *Atman.*"

Samayika

The daily practice of *samayika* (equanimous state of mind for a fixed period, usually 48 minutes twice or thrice in a day) in Jainism is aimed at keeping oneself aloof from all sinful and injurious activities by controlling one's mind, body and speech. *Samayika* also cultivates an equanimous state of mind by renouncing attachment and aversion to the objects of the world.

The purpose of *samayika* is the cultivation of: (1) equal goodwill (sympathy) (*samabhava*) towards all religions, towards all races and castes, and towards men and women; (2) equality and evenness (*samata*) regarding all living beings equal with one's own self and to maintain equanimity of mind both favourable and adverse occasions; and (3) maintaining tranquillity (*sama*) or balance of mind through restraint or subsidence (*shama* or *shaman*) of passions. Thus, by the constant practice of *samayika* one seeks to attain gradually "inward balance" or mental equipoise and tranquility of mind. It is, in fact, an exercise in *samaya*, etymologized as the state-of-evolution of self (*aya*) in equanimity (*sama*).[19]

Transcendental Nature of the Soul

In *Samayasara*, the supreme reality (*paramartha*) is said to be verily *samaya* (*paramartha khalu samao* in Pk. or *paramartha khalu samayah*, SS 151), i.e. soul's equanimous state-of-evolution or transcendental quietitude (tranquility or balance), or transcendental nature of soul (*samayasara*). This transcends all relative modes and viewpoints (SS 142-144), including contrary traits of bound with *karmas* or not bound with *karmas* (SS 142), passionate or not passionate (SS 6), as also dichotomies or dualities of pleasure and pain, praise and blame, etc.

Transcending contrary traits or pairs of dichotomies does not necessarily imply negation or annihilation of contradictions or contrary traits. Transcendence signifies that one should not be attached or affected by them. One should remain neutral and maintain one's peace and equipoise. Mental harmony and equipoise is indeed a great spiritual attainment.

The self who is devoted to its real nature (*samaya pratibaddha*) does not favour or take sides with either of them by being attached to one and despising or deprecating the other side or viewpoint (SS 143) but maintains its equipoise, balance or neutral state (*madhyastha*, PSU 8). As a result, it has no attachment or aversion in regard to any viewpoint. The dual reactions of likes and dislikes or attraction towards the pleasant and repulsion towards the unpleasant arise out of attachment or desire and aversion or hatred. To be happy or miserable is the result of the coming into operation or rise (*udaya*) of *karmas* (SS 254). Therefore, the enlightened soul, who maintains the insight or vision of equanimity (*sammaditthi*), does not have any attachment for the sensuous pleasures (SS 370). The *Gita* also speaks of equal vision (*sama-darshan*) (Gita 5.18, 6.29).

In *Niyamsara*, it is clearly stated that continuous practice of discriminative insight (*bhed-abhyasa*) enables the self to distinguish its transcendental nature of consciousness-as-such from human, sub-human, etc. conditions or modes (NS 77), soul-quests, soul-classes and spiritual stages, classified on the basis of senses, psycho-physical differences or moral and spiritual progress of souls (NS 78), attachment, aversion and infatuation (NS 80) and anger, pride, greed, etc. passions (NS 81) and thus becomes established in its own nature (*majjhattha*) (NS 82) or *madhyastha*, thereby attaining equanimious conduct (NS 82). Accordingly, he endeavours to maintain his equipoise (*sammam*) towards all living beings, has enmity or ill-feeling towards none, renounces all desires and expectations, and observes supreme equanimity (*samadhi*) (NS 104).

Characteristics of Equanimity

In a separate chapter devoted exclusively to equanimity in *Niyamsara*, Kundakunda states that a person, who meditates on his real nature free from attachment and observes self-restraint is said to possess supreme equanimity (*param samadhi*) (NS 122-123). For a person devoid of equanimity (*samadarahiyassa* in Pk. or *samata rahitasya* in Sk.), residing in a forest, mortification of the body, observance of various fasts, study of the scriptures, and keeping silence, etc. are of no use (NS 124).

Again, the characteristics which qualify a person to be considered possessing steadfast equanimity (*samayika*) are the following: freedom from all demeritorious and unwholesome (sinful) actions; observance of three-fold restraint (of body, mind and speech) and control of one's senses (NS 125); an equanimous attitude towards all living beings (NS 126); proximity to his real self during the practice of self-restraints, observances of rules (*niyam*) and austerities (NS 127); freedom from psychic dispositions of attachment and aversion (NS 128); abstention from mournful and cruel concentrations (NS 129); consistent renunciation of meritorious and demeritorious or sinful psychic dispositions (NS 130); renunciation of scornful laughter, indulgence, sorrow and hatred (NS 131); renunciation of disgust, fear, sexual-inclinations of all kinds (NS 132); and practice of righteous and pure concentrations (NS 133).

Samya or *samata* (equanimity) is rated very highly in *Pravachanasara* and other works of Kundakunda. Equanimity is described as the characteristic of *saman*, a person who is equanimous and self-restrained, who is said to be one who considers the dichotomous pairs or groups, such as enemies and friends, pleasure and pain, praise and blame, clay and gold and life and death as the same (*samo* or *samah* in Sk.). In other words, he is devoid of dichotomies of attachment and aversion, etc. In the absence of equanimity, there is only attachment, aversion, passions, violence, discontent, lack of contentment, cruelty, etc.

During the transmigratory existence (*sansara*), things are neither the same nor maintain their natural state or condition of equilibrium (*sahava samavatthido* in PK, and *svabhava, samaavasthit* in Sk.) (PS 120). As a result, the soul (*jiva*), although permanent in regard to substantiality (*dravyatva*), is non-permanent with respect to modifications, since such is the inherent nature of *sansara* (PS 120 AC).

In other words, all our interactions in life between our senses and the objects are bound to produce mutually contradictory feelings of pleasant and unpleasant, likes and dislikes, owing to our attachment and aversion, which are the main causes of bondage. In the circumstances, an enlightened person, who seeks to maintain equipoise of mind or equanimity devoid of attachment and aversion that are the cause of deluded view (*moha*) and mental agitation (*kshobha*), has indeed acquired real spiritual attainment and a characteristic of a liberated soul. Thus, it is stated: "If the soul whose infatuation (deluded view) has gone and who has properly grasped the reality of the equanimous, nature of self forsakes attachment and aversion, then it realises the pure self" (PS 81).

In *Paramatma-Prakash* (100), Yogendu Deva clearly states that he who gets rid of attachment and aversion and is established in equanimity, attains liberation in a short time.

The *Bhagavada Gita* also speaks quite highly of *sama* (*Gita* 2.38,

2.48, 4.22, 6.8, 6.9, 6.32, 12.4, 12.18, 13.9, 13.27, 13.28) *samya* (*Gita* 5.19 and 6.33), *sama-darshinah* (*Gita* 5.18 and 6.29) and *samatva* (*Gita* 2.48). In *Vivekchudamani* (440), Shankara specially states that he who maintains his psychic state of equanimity, when praised or worshipped by the noble people and also when teased, taunted and abused by the wicked people, is indeed a *jivanmukta* (liberated soul even in the embodied existence).

Definition of *Dharma*

Kundakunda has defined *dharma* in broad and non-sectarian terms in several ways:

1. *Dharma* signifies moral self-restraint and spiritual self-discipline or conduct (PS 7) based on or accompanied by an enlightened world-view and knowledge (PS 6). Thus, the trinity of enlightened view, knowledge and conduct is declared to be *dharma*.

2. *Dharma* is the inherent or essential nature of a thing or object (*vastu svabhavat dharma*) (PS 7 AC), which exists in all three times (*traikalika svabhava*). The essential nature of the self (*jiva*) is sentiency or consciousness (*chaitanya*) and its function or manifestation (*upayoga*) (PS 127; see also PKS 16 and 27).

3. *Dharma* is also defined as equanimity (*samya*) (PS 7) which means the possession of the qualities or the characteristics of the self (*atmaguna*) as they are (*yathavasthita*) (PS 7 AC).

4. Equanimity, which is said to be the synonym of *dharma*, is described as a state of evolution (*parinama*) of the soul. It is a state which is completely exempt or free from infatuation (*moha*) and mental disturbance (*kshoba*) (PS 7), caused by conduct-deluding *karma,* i.e. attachment, aversion and anger, etc. passions.

5. *Dharma* of the soul is also said to be the nature which it holds, takes, assumes, and possesses (*dharanant dharmah*) or through which it evolves during the time of evolution (PS 8), since it consists of that and is absorbed or engrossed in that (*tanmaya*). Thus, the soul accepts or assumes the character of its state-of-evolution. When it evolves through the good, or the evil, or the pure, it becomes good, evil, or pure (PS 9).

6. Lastly, *dharma* is said to be the state-of-evolution of the soul conjoined with pure (*shuddha*) conscious attentiveness (*upayoga*), which is the direct cause of the happiness as also the state-of-evolution of

the soul endowed with good, righteous or auspicious (*shubha*) conscious attentiveness, which is the cause of heavenly happiness (PS 11) and gradually leads to the attainment of the highest happiness of liberation (PS 254 AC). Hence, those possessing *shuddopayoga* or *shubhopayoga* are both considered *saman* (*shraman* in Sk.) (PS 245), i.e. those treading the path of liberation (*moksha marg*). *Shuddha upayoga* is defined in *Pravachanasara* verse 14, *shubha upayoga* is described in *Pravachanasara*, 69-70, 157 and 246-249 while *ashuba upayoga* is described in verse 158.

Nature of *Dharma*

Sometimes, *dharma* is equated with self-restraint (*samyamah khalu Dharma*) or enlightened world-view (*darshan mulo dhammo*) or compassion and kindness (*daya dharma ka mool hai*). A comprehensive definition is provided in *Karttikeyanupreksha* (verse 478). It states: "*Dhammo vastu sahavo, khamadi-bhavo ya das-viho dhammo; rayanttayam cha dhammo, jivanam-rakkhanam dhammo.*" In other words, the intrinsic nature (*svabhava*) of an object or living being is known as its *dharma*; forgiveness, etc. ten moral virtues is *dharma*; three jewels comprising of enlightened world-view, enlightened knowledge, and enlightened conduct – the three combined is also *dharma*; and non-violence or protection of living beings from any injury or harm is *dharma*.

Dharma in Jainism consists of a set of principles, values, and virtues; it is the science of well-being. Jainism is not, as is generally assumed and believed or as is very often preached and asserted, merely a set of doctrines and dogmas, a bundle of practices, forms, rites, rituals, a code of dietetics, a mode of social life, or a routine of daily conduct. These are not the essentials of Jainism. Jainism is, in fact, a way of life that ensures peace, happiness, and social well-being. It is a prescription for leading a good, peaceful, virtuous and happy life, which can only be realized by conquering our inner enemies, attachment and aversion, anger, greed, etc. passions.

Dharma, according to Jainism, does not merely consist in worship, fasts, contemplation, penance or asceticism. They are all means and should not be confused with the ends. The discipline of asceticism is a method and a means, it is not an end. It serves as a means to liberate consciousness from its attachment to instinctive impulses, subconscious motivations and instincts and egoism in order to attain equanimity.

Nature of the Self or Soul

The self or soul (*jiva*) is a substance (*dravya*), an existent reality, whose essential nature or distinguishing characteristic is (*chedana uvaogamao* in Pk. and *chetana upayogamaya* in Sk.) (PS 127, PKS 16), i.e. sentiency or consciousness (*chetana*) and manifestation, function of consciousness or psychic attention (*upayoga*). (In *Tattvartha Sutra* (TS 2.8), *upayoga* alone is described as the defining distinguishing characteristic of *jiva*). Although both *chetana* and *upayoga* are said to be the nature of the self, they are not identical. *Upayoga* is the application, manifestation, mode, or rather the active, functional and the attentive aspect of consciousness, but not consciousness-as-such (*chetana*) which is the essence of *jiva* or the soul substance. *Upayoga* is the manifestation, modification or the state-of-evolution (*parinama*) of *jiva*, which has the form of functioning of the soul substance (PS 127 AC). Thus, the nature of the self in Jainism is eternal (*nitya*) as well as evolvent (*parinami*), or *parinami nitya*, i.e. evolvent and yet eternal, not "unchanging eternal" of Advaita Vedanta and the Sankhya system of philosophy.

Panchastikayasara 27 states that *jiva* is conscious entity (*cheda*), whose particular characteristic is *upayoga* (*jivo tti havadi cheda uvaoga visesido* in Pk., and *jiva iti havati chetayita upayoga visheshitah* in Sk.) (PKS 27). Amrtachandra explains it by stating that from the internal, self-referential standpoint (*nishchaya naya*), *jiva*, in its mundane empirical existence, state or condition (*samsara avastha*) is consciousness-as-such, because it is endowed with the essence, the internal life source, inalienable psychic or conscious vital force (*bhavaprana dharnat*). From the external, other-referential point of view (*vyavahara naya*), the *jiva* is endowed with or possesses physical, objective, external manifestations of *jiva*, i.e. *dravya pranas* (the physical insignia of life), viz. the bio-energies or physical, corporeal characteristics [of five senses, the three energies of mind, body and speech, life duration and respiration] (PKS 27 AC).

Chetana (consciousness) remains the eternal, constant factor (*dhrauvya*) of *jiva* or soul substance, which is the substratum of all its attributes and modes and exists in all its states or conditions and at all stages of the evolution of the self, including *upayoga*, in all three times. On the other hand, *upayoga* can transform itself in either direction: enlightened or deluded, towards purity or impurity, good or evil.

Since there is no object without a state-of-evolution (*parinama*), the self is said to be evolvent in nature, i.e. subject to change or modification. It possesses the nature of that through which it evolves during the time of the evolution (PS 8). In other words, it accepts the character of its state-of-evolution (PS 9).

Conjunction of the self with other substance, i.e. *karman*, results in a particular type of *upayoga*, i.e. manifestation of *chetana*, which has two modes of psychic-attention or awareness, viz. *jnana* and *darshan* (PS 155). When the awareness of an object has some form (*sakara*), it is said to be *jnana* (cognition or knowledge). If it is without form (*nirakara*), it is considered *darshan* (intuition) (PS 155 and PS 155 AC). These two modes of awareness are intimately related to *karmic* changes and the relation may be said to be in inverse ratio. The intensity and quality of these two *upayogas* decreases as the *karmic* veil becomes thicker and stronger, but they have the chance of fuller manifestation when the *karmas* either decay or disappear.

Shubha (good or auspicious) *upayoga* and *ashubha* (bad or inauspicious) *upayoga* are also related to interaction with *karma*. In *shubha*, anger, etc. passions become feeble or mild due to their subsidence, with the result that the *karmas* also get reduced. *Shubha*, therefore, has the effect of purifying (*vishuddhi*) of the self. In *ashubha*, on the other hand, which witnesses an intensity of passions, the bondage of *karma* is increased, and the self is imbued with affliction, distress or morbidity (*sanklesh*) (PS 155 AC).

If the manifestation of consciousness is auspicious, the soul accumulates merit (*punya*); if inauspicious, demerit or sin (*papa*). In the absence of both, there is no accumulation (PS 156) of either, with the result that only "pure" [in the sense of being unconditioned, unencumbered (*nirupadhi*), natural (*svabhavika*) (PKS 58 AC), unmixed, only, *kevala* (exclusively one's own),[20] alone, of the nature of only consciousness-as-such] remains (*avatishthate*). This is not the cause of conjunction with other substance (*sa punah akaranam eva para dravya sanyogasya*) (PS 156 AC). In other words, it has no relation with *karman* whatsoever and is devoid of any conjunction with any other substance; it is consciousness (*chetana*) itself. It is said to be "pure" because it is consciousness-as-such alone (*chinmatra*, SS 73 AC) or possessing only conscious force (*chit shakti matra*, SS 36 AC) and because it is not conditioned by *karman*. In other words, it is non-relational to *karman* (*karma-nirpeksha*) *parinamika bhava*, which is the natural, intrinsic or the inherent nature of *jiva* or soul, independent of any bias or prejudice of any relative aspect with other (object) (*anya nirpeksha*) (NS 28) and unconditioned by *karman*.

Pariamika Bhava

Because of *karmic* adjunct, association, entanglement (*upadhi*) or *jiva*'s interaction with the *karmas*, Kundakunda speaks of five fundamental qualities (*panchagga guna*) (PKS 53, *jiva gunas*, PKS 56), or *jiva bhavas* (thought characteristics, psychic dispositions or emotional, affective states of consciousness). One of these states of consciousness is the *parinamika bhava* (consciousness-as-such), which is without beginning and end, the intrinsic, natural state of the self (*svabhavika*) and is of *nirupadhi* character (PKS 58 AC), i.e. independent and unconditioned by *karman*, i.e. *karma-nirpeksha* (PKS 56 JS). Amrtachandra calls it the essential nature of *jiva* (*parinamika bhava*), the essential natural state of consciousness-as-such (*sahaj chaitanya lakshan parinamika bhava*) (PKS 53 AC).

In *Yogasara-Prabhrata* (1.52) of Amitgati, the self (*atman*) is said to be devoid of *karma* and *no-karma* (gross, physical body), non-corporeal (*amurta*), beyond old age and death, free from particularities (*nir-vishesha*) and completely non-relational (*asambandha*).

The *parinamika bhava* is said to have neither beginning nor end (PKS 53). In other words, as spiritual existence it is eternal; neither is it created nor can it be destroyed. It is called *parinamika* because of its evolvement nature (*parinamena yukta parinamika* PKS 56 AC), i.e. subject to change, modification or evolution (*parinama*), though it is considered to be neutral in the sense that in itself it is neither pure nor impure; it is the basis and the substratum of the other four states of consciousness (*jiva bhavas*), which are the modes or modifications (*paryaya*) of consciousness-as-such, and signify the purifying and not sc, i.e. impure psychic states.

These four psychic dispositions or conditions of consciousness are the states of coming into operation or the rising of *karmas* (*audayika*), subsidence (*aupshamika*), the mixed process or state of partly destruction and partly subsidence (*kshayopashamika*), and destruction (*kshayika*) of *karmas.* All of them are causally connected with or related to physical (*dravya*) *karma* or *karma-upadhi* (PKS 56 AC). Since these psychic states cannot happen in the consciousness of a *jiva* without corresponding changes in material or physical *karman,* they are said to be the effects of physical *karma* (*karma krta*) (PKS 58 and PKS 58 AC).

Of these four psychic states, the *audayika,* accompanied as it is with the coming into operation or rise of deluding *karma,* is the supportive factor (*nimitta*) or the auxiliary cause of *karmic* bondage (PKS 56 JS) and *samsara* (transmigratory existence of the cycle of births and deaths) and hence represents the impure condition.

The other three states of consciousness have a purifying effect (*vishuddhi*) and are the cause of liberation or emancipation (*moksha*) (PKS 56 JS). Of these three, the *aupashamika* and *kshayopashamika* gradually lead to liberation. *Moksha* (liberation), signifying as it does liberating the self from the *karmic* entanglement, as a result of inhibition of fresh *karmas* and the annihilation of previously bound *karmas,* is also *karma*-referential.

The *parinamika bhava* (consciousness-as-such) is not causally connected with either (*karmic*) bondage or liberation (PKS 56 JS). Jayasena here cites an old verse which says: "The *parinamika bhava* is inactive (*nishkriya*); the *audayika bhava,* i.e. coming into operation or rise of *karmas* is the cause of bondage, while the other three *bhavas* are the cause of liberation" (PKS 56 JS). Even when *parinamika bhava* is considered to be inactive, the manifestation of consciousness or psychic-attention (*upayoga*) makes the soul active (*sakriya*).

Being *karma-nirpeksha* and *nirupadhi* in character, i.e. independent of and being unconditioned by *karman,* the *parinamika bhava* is not causally connected with either *samsara* (the mundane worldly existence of births and deaths) or *moksha* (liberation). It is said to be neither bound nor unbound (SS 142), neither passionate (*pramatta*) nor dispassionate (*apramatta*) (SS 6), neither pure nor impure. Moreover, the *parinamika bhava* is an existent reality in all living beings. Since it is already available to them and is "not a thing or condition to be attained as such," one sometimes contends that "theoretically its articulation should make no difference to the behaviour" of living beings, particularly the moral and spiritual practitioners or seekers (*shraman*).

Such thinking or belief in reality is not correct. The knowledge and the firm conviction (*shraddhan*) in regard to the real nature of the self is imperative to distinguish between *jiva* and *pudgal* (matter), soul and body. Without this discriminative insight (*bhed-vigyan*), one cannot have an enlightened view (*samyak-darshan*) of the fundamental principles of life or the reality of things as they are. Moreover, since this enlightened view is the first necessary precondition in the path of liberation, one cannot attain liberation in its absence. Of course, one has to make efforts by adopting moral and spiritual discipline (conduct) to attain the objective of libration.

Pravachanasara verse 159 speaks of the self (consciousness) having the nature or the character of knowing (PS 159) and of establishing itself unswervingly in its own conscious attentiveness (*upayoga*) (PS 159 AC). In the subsequent verses, the self is distinguished from body, mind and speech, which are declared to consist of material (*pudgal*, unconscious) substance, while the self (the subjective awareness of "I") is distinguished from them since that awareness of 'I' is not composed of matter (PS 160-162).

Jiva Nikaya

In *Pravachanasara* verse 182, the soul substance (*jiva dravya*) is distinguished from the six classes of earth-bodied, etc. immobile and mobile souls or group of *jivas* (*jiva nikaya*),[21] which are said to be other (*anya*) than *jiva* (PS 182). *Jiva* [*jivatva*, *jiva tattva* or *atma dravya*, i.e. consciousness-as-such], is one unitary self, its own substance (*sva dravya*) (PS 182 AC). This is considered to be other (*anya*) from these several classes of souls (PS 182), because these [conjoint psycho-physical conscious entities] have elements of material or physical bio-energies (*dravya pranas*) (the body, mind, senses, etc.), made up of unconscious material substance (*achetanatvat*) (PS 182 AC) or that the *jiva nikaya* are the product of the coming into operation or rise of *nama karman* (PS 182 JS). The six classes of *jiva nikaya* are not "pure" consciousness-as-such, but are mixed with some elements of unconscious material substance, just as an ornament is not pure gold but is gold mixed with various elements like silver and copper. The perverse-minded people, however, errneously feel that the composite or combination of *jiva* and *karma* or soul and body comprises the self (SS 42).

These *jiva nikaya* are, in fact, the extrinsic manifestation of consciousness, i.e. the heterogeneous (*asamanjatiya*) modes (*paryaya*) of *jiva dravya* (PS 93 AC), having earth-bodied, etc. immobile class of *jiva* or animal, human, etc. mobile modes of *jiva*. The *jiva* (soul), i.e. the self (*appanam* in Pk. and *atmanam* in Sk.) is to be distinguished from other (*para*, i.e. non-self) according to their own characteristic nature (*svabhavam asadya*) (PS 183). *Jiva* or soul is a sentient, non-corporeal, conscious entity, possessing subjective attributes of cognition, feeling and volition. Matter or body, however, is non-sentient, corporeal, inanimate entity possessing characteristic sense qualities of touch, taste, smell and colour.

Just as in *Pravachanasara*, *jiva nikaya* are distinguished from *jiva*, i.e. consciousness as such, so also in *Samayasara* (SS 65-66) the different classes of living organisms (*jiva sthana*) (SS 66) are distinguished from *jiva*. The different classes of *jiva*, comprising of 1, 2, 3, 4 and 5 sensed living beings, whether they are subtle or gross and fully developed or partly developed are no doubt the classes of living beings (*jivas*). However, since all these are (different) sub-species of body-building *nama karma*, i.e. the result of the fruition of that *karma*, how can they be called *jiva* (consciousness-as-such)? (SS 65-66). Since all these types of *jiva*, basically refer to the varieties of the bodies and are conventionally applied to *jiva*, they are said to belong to the soul only from *vyavahara naya* (SS 67).

Whosoever does not through their respective characteristic natures (*svabhava*, as consciousness and unconsciousness), know or see the distinction of the self or *sva* (own) and non-self or other (*para*), *jiva* and *pudgala* that *jiva* (soul) has through infatuation the perverse conviction (*adhyavasana*) of other substance being considered self or identified as self, i.e. *aham* "I am this" [the body, etc.] or this [wealth, etc.] or "this is mine" (*mamedam*) (PS 183 and PS 183 AC), and does not abandon such notions in regard to body and wealth, etc., takes the wrong path (PS 190). This signifies that it is necessary to discover and distinguish between the real "I" or "true self" (*jiva* as such or *jiva-tattva*) from the various classes of souls (*jiva-niyaka*), comprising of mind, body, senses, etc. The former is the substratum while the latter (also an existent reality during the period of their existence) are its manifest forms or modes.

It is this *jiva tattva*, the essential nature of *jiva*, i.e. *chetana*, sentiency or consciousness-as-such (*parinamika bhava*), which is existent in all states, stages in the three times (past, present and future) of *jiva*, whether in its transmigratory and embodied condition or its liberated state, and is said to be other (*anya*) than the six classes of transmigratory and embodied *jivas* (*jiva nikaya*) (PS 182). *Jiva tattva* is not separate from them (*jiva nikaya*), though distinguished from them in the sense that it is their underlying substratum. (For a detailed discussion about the distinction between separateness (*prathakatva*) and otherness (*anyatva*), see *Pravachanasara* 106).

Bhava and *Dravya-pranas*

Consciousness is considered to be the essence of *jiva* or its essential nature or property because it is the animating principle, which enlivens a particular living organism and infuses life into the body, the senses and all other bio-energies. In its absence, all the bio-energies remain inactive and lifeless. In other words, the *parinamika bhava* or *bhava prana* (the inner, subjective, underlying spiritual reality of *jiva*, or the internal life source, the inalienable psychic or conscious vital force) is other than the *dravya pranas* (the physical, objective, external manifestations, the bio-energies, i.e. the ten *pranas* comprising of five senses, the bio-energies of mind, speech and body, life duration and respiration).

In its embodied from of existence, *jiva* is a conjoint psycho-physical, conscious entity, consisting of both *dravya-prana* and *bhava-prana.* As such, *dravya-prana* cannot exist in isolation without *bhava-prana*, which cannot exist without *dravya-prana* in *jiva*'s transmigratory, embodied existence. However, *dravya-pranas*, which are the product of the arising of *nama-karman* (PS 182 JS), do not exist in the liberated state. While *dravya-prana* is said to be unconscious material substance, the conjoint psycho-physical conscious entity of *jiva nikaya* cannot be said to be unconscious (*achetan*).

Bhava-prana, i.e. consciousness-as-such or *jiva-tattva*, is the underlying substratum of all classes of *jiva-nikaya*, which are modes or forms of *jiva-tattva.* Like *dravya* (substance) and *paryaya* (mode of substance), they (*jiva-tattva* and *jiva nikaya*) cannot be separated though they can be distinguished as manifester and manifested. One class of *jiva*, like one mode, can cease to exist and some other class of *jiva* or mode may arise. But *jiva* as such (i.e. *jiva tattva*), being the existent reality in all three times and all states, conditions, stages, forms, or modes, is neither produced nor destroyed.

Amrtachandra states that the six classes of mobile and immobile *jiva-nikaya* (group of *jivas*) are, indeed, other (*anya*) than *jiva* (consciousness-as-such) because they have unconscious, inanimate physical vitalities or bio-energies (*achetanatva*) in them and *jiva* is also other (*anya*) than those due to its essential principle or property of consciousness (*chetanatva*) (PS 182 AC).

In the second sentence of his commentary (of PS 182), Amrtachandra states that although the six *jiva nikaya* are or have the underlying substratum *atman* (consciousness) (Faddegon has usually translated *jiva* as soul and *atma* as self), they are *para-dravya*, i.e. other substance [in the sense that when conscious *jiva* is united or bound with other inanimate substance (material *karman*)] it takes the form of heterogeneous modes of soul substance, the conjoint psycho-physical altered entities [as is the case of six classes if *jiva nikaya*] and that the self (*atma*) alone (*eva*) is its own substance (*sva-dravya*) (PS 182 AC).

Although the vitalities of body senses, etc., which are composed of unconscious material substance, are commingled or mixed up in view of occupying the same space with *jiva tattva* in the six *jiva-nikaya*, *jiva tattva* and the inanimate vatalities (*dravya pranas*) always maintain their own intrinsic nature (PKS 7) without losing their respective qualities.

In his commentary of *Pravachanasara* 182, Jayasena has also sought to distinguish the immobile and mobile *jiva-nikaya* from the innate nature of *jiva* (*jiva svabhava*). He states that they are other (*anya*) than or different (*bhinna*) from *chaitanya svabhava* (conscious nature) of *jiva* because they are the product of fruition, coming into operation or arising of mobile and immobile *nama-karman*, which are *achetan* (unconscious, inanimate) (PS 182 JS). Although *nama-karman* is unconscious material substance and the six classes of *jiva*s are undoubtedly not devoid of *karman*, but, as conjoint psycho-physical conscious entities, they are not devoid of consciousness in their embodied existence. However, one desirous of liberation (*mokshartbi*) abstains from [attachment] to other (*para*) substance [including body] and becomes inclined to concentrate on its own substance (*sva-dravya*) (PS 182 JS).

Jiva is said to be different from *jiva niyaka* (in PS 182). It is the soul substance (*jiva bhava*, PKS 16-17) or *jiva-guna*. As such, the (essential nature or) qualities of soul, viz. consciousness (*chetana*) and its attentiveness or function (*upayoga*) (PKS 16) is never destroyed (PKS 17). It is distinct both from its modes (*paryaya*) of six classes of mobile and immobile living beings and from the states, conditions or modes of human, animal, denizens of hell and heaven (PKS 16-17), which have transitory or temporal existence. Both *jiva nikaya* and human, etc. embodied souls are psycho-somatic states or heterogeneous modes (*asamanjatiya paryaya*, PS 93-94 AC) of the soul substance consisting of the (combination of) two distinct substances, soul and matter or soul and body. They possesses their own respective distinctive characteristics. *Jiva* or soul possesses its subjective attributes of cognition, feeling and volition, in all three times and in all stages of life journey, whether transmigratory existence or liberated state. The material body, on the other hand, is an inanimate entity which possesses its own characteristic sense qualities of touch, taste, smell and colour. For instance, though gold and silver are combined or united in making of ornaments, they do not lose their inherent qualities of yellowness and whiteness, i.e. the two can never become one in nature really (SS 27 AC).

Similarly, though the soul and body are found together or united in an embodied individual, they retain their own distinctive characteristics. It is only from an external, other-referential viewpoint (*vyavahara naya*), they are said to be one, i.e. having unity (*ekatva*) or oneness, but from the internal, self-referential viewpoint (*nishchaya naya*) the two can never become one singular substance (SS 27).

The human, etc. modes are impure or distorted states or modes (*ashuddha* or *vibhava paryaya)* of the soul substance because they are produced or caused by connection or relationship with other substance (PKS 16 AC). In other words, the soul substance in itself, i.e. its natural state or mode (*svabhava paryaya*) or that its essential nature is pure because it does not have regard to or is independent of any relation with other object (*anya nirpeksha*, NS 28). Kundakunda declares: "My soul is ever one, eternal, characterised by knowledge and intuition; all other are external substances (*bhava*), since they all have the characteristic of being accidental to me." (NS 102)

Pure Nature of the Soul

The self ("I") is one "exclusively one's own (*kevala*), alone, uncompounded, not connected with anything else" (i.e. *anya nirpeksha*, NS 28). It is therefore truly pure (*aham ekko khalu suddho*, SS 38, 73) so much so that not even the subtlest atom of other thing (substance) whatsoever (living or non-living) is mine or related to me as mine (SS 38), and that no other or none else is mine (*nirmam*) (SS 73, BA 20).

Amrtachandra explains the nature of the self as pure as follows:

> The self is one, alone, only, of the nature of consciousness (*chinmatra*) and as such it is pure because of being extremely distinct from the nine categories or principles (*nava tattva*), characterised from the external, other referential view-point (*vyavahara naya*) as human, animal etc. particular forms, states or modes of soul substance (*jiva vishesh*), non-living, unconscious matter (*ajiva*), virtue, sin, influx of karmas, inhibition of karmas, shedding off or destruction of karmas, bondage and liberation (SS 38 AC).

Unlike both Kundakunda and Amrtachandra, Jayasena maintains that the self ("I") is pure because it is different from, i.e. devoid of the impurities of attachment, etc. psychic states or dispositions (*ragadibhavebhyoh bhinna aham iti shuddhah*) (SS 38 JS). As a result, it is free from the *karmas* as in the state of liberation. A similar discrepancy is found in the views of Kundakunda and Amrtachandra and those of Jayasena regarding *Pravachanasara* verse 192 (see infra).

In this context, one must mention that the word "*suddha*" (in Pk. or *shuddha* in Sk.) in Prakrit and Sanskrit is used in both senses of not having any relation with other (*anya nirpeksha*, NS 28) and free from attachment, etc. impurities by both Kundakunda in his works as well as by Amrtachandra in his commentaries thereon in different contexts. However, Jayasena's interpretation of *shuddha* as free from impurities regarding the nature of the self fosters considerable misperception and confusion. In order to dispel such confusion, Amrtachandra distinguishes the nature of the self from bondage and liberation (see *supra*). To describe nature of the self as pure in the sense of being devoid of or free from all distortions of attachment, etc. impurities (*raagadi samasta vibhava rahitam*) (PS 192 JS and SS

38 JS) implies the denial of soul's transmigratory nature and signify the inability to adopt means (*sadhan*) to purify impurities (like attachment, etc.) of the self in order to attain liberation.

The word "*suddha*" in Pk. or "*shuddha*" in Sk. means cleansed, clean, pure (*pavitra*), faultless, blameless (*nirdosh*), without impurity (*nirmal*) sinless, as also "pure, i.e. simple, *kevala* (only), genuine, true, unmixed (i.e. not mixed with any other substance or contaminated), unmodified, unqualified, veritable, unequalled." The word "*kevala*" is translated as "exclusively one's own, alone, only, mere, sole, one, excluding others, not connected with anything else, isolated, absolute, simple, pure, uncompounded, unmingled, entire, whole." Pure and simple means nothing else, only natural, while 'mere' means only (*kevala*).[22]

Clarifying the sense in which the nature of the self is said to be pure, Kundakunda states:

> I (*aham*) deem the self (*appagam* in Pk., *atmakam* in Sk.) as pure (*suddha*) because it is knowledge and intuition, a supra-sensual supreme reality (*mahartha*) eternal or permanent (*dhruva*), stable (*achal*), without prop or support (PS 192).

In his commentary on the above verse, Amrtachandra explains that the self is in fact pure, and only the pure self is *dhruva* (permanent, eternal) because it is an existent reality (*sat*) ([it exists in all three times, past, present and future, in all living beings]), without a cause (*ahetuka*), without beginning or end (*anadyantah*) and it is self-established [or self-proved], nothing else is so. And the self is pure (*shuddha*) because it is distinguishable or can be discriminated from another substance. It is also indistinguishable or non-discriminated from its own properties with which it has unity (*ekatva*). This (unity) consists of knowledge and intuition because it transcends the senses and knows the sense qualities of touch, taste, etc. It also remains unperturbed, unaffected and stable (*achal*) by the various discernible modifications corresponding to impressions of objects, and being without any prop or support of any kind from "other" substance. Thus, the self is pure because it is *chin-matra* (consciousness-as-such alone) (PS 192 AC).

While the self, which comprises psychic attention (*upayoga*), is eternal (*dhruva*), neither the body nor possessions, neither pleasure nor pain, neither enemies nor friends, are eternal, (*dhruva*) for the soul (PS 193), i.e. they are impermanent (*asat*) (PS 193 AC). In other words, body, possessions, etc. have a transitory existence. The use of the term "*asat*" here cannot be said to be "non-existent" or "unreal" as is misconstrued by W. J. Johnson. He, who having thus discerned the pure self contemplates on the supreme reality of the soul (*param appagam* in Pk., *paramatman* in Sk.), be it a householder or an ascetic, destroys the evil bondage of infatuation (*moha*) (PS 194).

The nature of the self, which is considered pure in the sense of being constant or eternal (*dhruva*), stable, without any support (PS 192), being alone (*aham ekko khalu suddho*, SS 38, 73, BA 20), having no relation with any other (*nirpeksha*), is not the same as pure which is devoid of *karmas* (*karma-rahita*). In this case, it is said to be pure only when the soul gives up infatuation (*moha*), etc. (PS 79), when it is free from attachment and aversion (PS 81) or has unity or oneness (*aiyatta*) with the pure (*suddha*) self. As such, it is worth acquiring (*upadaya*) (BA 20), viz. the objective to be achieved, and that the self which becomes purified (*visuddha*) by giving up attachment, etc., thereby getting rid of karmic bondage (SS 290).

Jayasena's Faulty Explanation of Pure

Unlike the statements of Kundakunda and Amrtachandra in *Pravachanasara* (192 above), Jayasena explains that the word "pure" (*suddham* in Pk., *shuddham* in Sk.) is devoid of all distortions of attachment, etc. impurities (*raagadi samasta vibhava rahitam*) (PS 192 JS). In the commentary on *Pravachanasara* 7, while Amrtachandra argues that the nature of a thing is its *dharma* (*vastu svabhavat dharma*), Jayasena feels that the adoption of pure consciousness devoid of distortions and impurities by the self is its *dharma* (*nirvikara shuddha chaitanya dhartiti dharmah*). Again, according to Amrtachandra, conduct (*charitra*) is "behaving according to one's own nature" (*svarupe charanam*). For Jayasena, conduct is activity in accordance with its nature of pure consciousness (*shuddha chit svarupe charanam*) (PS 7 AC and PS 7 JS).

Similarly, in their commentaries on *Panchastikayasara* verses on the nature of the self, while Amrtachandra speaks of *parinamika bhava* (PKS 53 AC), and *parinamikah* (PKS 56 AC), Jayasena uses "*shuddha parinamika bhava*" (PKS 53, 56, 58 JS). In his commentary of

Samayasara 6 as well, Amrtachandra explains the nature of the soul, i.e. consciousness (*jnayak bhava*) as "*shuddha*" in the sense that it is quite different from all other substances, their states, conditions, modes and attributes and that the self is said to be "*shuddha*" (pure), in the sense that *jiva* (soul or conscious entity) can never become a non-soul and non-living (*ajiva*) material entity can never become *jiva.* The two substances, viz. life and non-life or the spirit and matter, are not liable to lose or interchange their nature and that *jiva* can never assume or have the characteristic attributes of touch, taste, smell, etc. of non-living material entity or its modes or states of evolution (*evashesha dravyantara bhavebhyoh bhinnatvena upasyanman shuddha iti abhilipyate*) (SS 6 AC).

Jayasena seems to be responsible for the prevalence of the mistaken belief among a large number of Jain scholars, especially the Kanjipanthi (a sect belonging to Kanji Svami), that the nature of the self is "pure" in the sense of being free from impurities. This view is similar to that upheld in both Advaita Vedanta and the Samkhya system of philosophy. Lest there be any doubt regarding the nature of the self as being neither pure nor impure is dispelled by Kundakunda himself through his emphatic assertion in *Pravachanasara* 8 cited above as well as *Pravachanasara* 9 which states: "The soul accepts the character of its state-of-evolution. When the soul evolves through the good or the evil, it becomes good or evil. When it is pure, it becomes pure" (PS 9).

Lastly, when the word "pure" is used in the sense of purity, i.e. faultless, blameless sense, it signifies the potential to become pure (*shuddha*). In other words, one has to make efforts to make it pure. If the innate nature of the soul or self is considered to be "pure", i.e. "pure consciousness", it indeed becomes problematic to account for the impurity of the self as to how the "pure self" becomes impure. Moreover, if the self is already "pure", there is no need to either make any efforts or adopt any means such as moral self-restraint, spiritual self-discipline, austerities, etc. to purify the impurities of attachment, aversion, deluded view and anger, pride, greed, etc. passions. Without such efforts, it is not possible to remove the impurities in the self. Without the removal of impurities, the soul cannot attain the highest objective of human endeavour, i.e. the supreme state of Godhood (*Paramatma*) or liberation.

Meaning of the Pure Nature of the Soul

Thus, the word "*shuddha*" (pure) regarding the innate nature of the self or the true identity of the soul (consciousness) signifies the unmixed, *chin-matra* (consciousness-as-such alone), unconditioned state, or non-relational to *karmas* (*karma-nirpeksha*) condition of the self. while the word "*vishuddha*", "*vishuddhi*" (purifying) (in PS 2, 5, 15, 78, 194, 220, etc. and PS 155, 180 AC) is generally used by Kundakunda in the sense of purifying the self, which is the result of the subsidence (*aupshamik*), partly subsidential and partly destruction (*ksayopashamika*) or destruction (*kshaya*) of passions that leads to liberation from the bondage of *karman.*

The material *karman* (the neuro-physiological processes) cannot be obliterated by physical surgery alone. The conditioning effect and fresh bondage of the self as a result of material *karman* can only be nullified by the eradication of attachment, aversion, passions and the consequent freedom from *karmas* (*karma-rahita*). Kundakunda, therefore, lays greater emphasis on internal aspects or the mental attitude in regard to bondage as well as liberation. Renunciation (*tyaga*) of worldly concerns devoid of all consideration, regard, relation or expectation of any sort (*nirvekkho* in Pk., *nirpeksha* in Sk.) does not occur without purity (*vishuddhi*) of intention. When the mind (*chitta*) is not-pure (*avishuddha*), how can there be annihilation of *karman*? (PS 220).

In *Pravachanasara* 192 and *Samayasara* 38 and 73, *jiva* and its nature is said to be "pure" in the sense that it does not transform itself into another, unconscious inanimate substance (*dravyantara*) (SS 6 AC) and in *karma-nirpeksha parinamika bhava* sense. *Jiva* is also said to be of a knowing nature (*jnayak bhava* or *jnayak svabhava*). In other words, consciousness of something of knowing nature, which can be either pure or impure, does not necessarily mean that it is enlightened. However, it has the potential to become a pure, enlightened and supreme soul (*paramatma*). Potential means one has to make efforts to realize that potential.

Thus, the nature of the soul (*sabhava* in Pk. or *svabhava* in Sk.) is declared to be *janago* (*jnayak* in Sk.), i.e. something knowing or essentially something-that-knows (PS 200). Since the soul is *jnayak* alone (*eva*) through its nature, the only relation it has with other objects is only that of knower and knowable (*jneya jnayak*). It has no other connection like that of possession and possessor. One should, therefore, renounce the notion of "mine" in regard to other objects, including body, wealth, etc. (PS 183, 190, 200 and PS 183, 190, 200 AC and SS 19-23).

The unique characteristic of the conscious self is consciousness. The *jnayak bhava* (the nature of conscious awareness) is not to be confused with cognition or knowledge, which is only one of the attributes or aspects of consciousness. In *Pravachanasara* 35, Kundakunda observes: "He who knows is knowledge (*jo janadi so nanam*); but the self does not by the help of knowledge becomes something-that-is-knowing (*jnayak*); knowledge evolves by itself, and all the objects reside in knowledge." Clarifying the last point in this verse, Amrtachandra observes: "All the objects which are the causes of all the knowable appearances which are (really) the effects of the self-evolving knowledge, in a certain way reside in knowledge" (PS 35 AC). Knowledge is evolution (*parinama*) of the soul knowing, though the evolution cannot be separated from the evolvent self. Therefore, the forced supposition (*klesha kalpana*) of a separation of knower and knowledge is superfluous. The concept of *jnayak bhava* is discussed in detail in *Samayasara* 6, 7 and 356, etc.

The *parinamika bhava* is described in *Samayasara* as: (1) *bhutarth* (SS 11), i.e. the existent reality which exists in all living beings, in all conditions or states, including liberated state, and in all three times (past, present, and future), is without beginning and end (*anadinidhan*, PKS 53); (2) *paramarth*, i.e. the highest or the deeper inner reality of self; (3) *pakshatikranta* (SS 142), i.e. the transcendental state, which is independent of *karmas* (*nirupadhi*), neither bound by *karmas* nor unbound by *karmas* (SS 142) and as such neither pure nor impure, and beyond all biases and prejudices of different perspectives or viewpoints (*naya paksha*), bound, unbound, etc.; and (4) *Samayasara* (SS 142), the essential nature or the essence (*sara*) of self (*jiva*).

In *Pravachanasara*, the word "*shuddha*" (pure) as in pure conscious attentiveness (*shuddha upayoga*), is used in the sense of blameless, faultless, pure consciousness, devoid of *karma* (*karma rahita*) as also in the sense of being unaffected, unmixed, only, *kevala*, or unconditioned by *karman*, i.e. *karma-nirpeksha* (non-relational to *karmas*) *parinamika bhava*, consciousness-as-such or the nature of self. The nature of the self is considered to be pure because it is consciousness-as-such (*chin-matra*) and also because it is unique and unmixed and being *karma-nirpeksha*, having no relation whatsoever with *karmas*. It is not causally connected with either *samsara* or *moksha*, either bondage or liberation. Though the soul is associated with *karmas* since beginningless time and as such impure but that is not considered the inherent nature of the self.

Upayoga

The word "*uvaoga*" (*upayoga* in Sk.), a "rarity in Shvetambara books", but referred frequently in Kundakunda's works is translated in several different ways. (See Introduction by F. W. Thomas). This word has been generally translated in *Pravachanasara* as "psychic attention" by Faddegon and as "manifestation of consciousness" by A.N. Upadhye. [In his footnote to PS 69, Upadhye states: "The term *upayoga* is very difficult to be rendered into English; the shade of its sense often depends on the context; similar is the case with *dharma* and other words."][23]

W.J. Johnson translates *upayoga* as "application". Jacobi translates it as "realization of its [soul's] developments" whereas Deleu translates it as "spiritual function". Frauwallner translates it as *Betaetigung*, i.e. "work" or "activity", but Johnson prefers to translate it as "perhaps 'activation' 'actuation'." P.S. Jaini translates *upayoga* as "awareness" and Nathmal Tatia terms it as "active consciousness" (see Nathmal Tatia, *Studies in Jaina Philosophy*, p. 55; on page 70, however, Tatia translates *upayoga* as "consciousness," which is said to be the defining characteristic of soul) (TS 2.8) which would be better."[24]

In *Tattvartha Sutra* (TS 2.8), *upayoga* is said to be the differentia, the definition or the distinguishing characteristic (*lakshan*) of *jiva* (soul). The word "*upayoga*" in *Tattvartha Sutra* is translated as "attention, consciousness, attentiveness" by J.L. Jaini; "consciousness" and "active or attentive consciousness" by S.A. Jain; and "sentience," which in turn, is explained as "awareness or consciousness" by Nathmal Tatia.[25]

Unlike *Tattvartha Sutra* (2.8) wherein *upayoga* (conscious attentiveness) is described as the (only) distinguishing characteristic of the soul (*jiva*), in Kundakunda's works (PKS 16, 27 and PS 127), the nature of soul is said to consist of *chetana* (consciousness) and *upayoga*, which constitute the main quality of soul (*jiva guna*, PKS 16). In *Panchastikayasara* (PKS 16, 27), Chakravarti translates *chetana* as "consciousness" and *upayoga* as "manifestation of consciousness" in two ways or two modes of consciousness, *darshan* (perception) and *jnana* (knowledge), which "are mainly cognitive or thought elements". Consciousness also includes emotion and will. The affective and volitional or conative element is also recognized in Jaina system.[26]

In *Pravachanasara* (PS 127), Faddegon translates *upayoga* as "psychic attention of thought (*chetana*)" "manifestation (*parinama*) of thinking (*chetana*), august, in the form of consciousness (*samvrtti*)" (PS 127 AC), while A. N. Upadhye states that *jiva* is constituted of "sentiency" (*chetana*) and "manifestation of consciousness (*upayoga*)". In *Pravachanasara*, Kundakunda mainly describes three kinds of *upayoga* – pure (*shuddha*), auspicious (*shubha*) and inauspicious (*ashubha*), which are defined in verses 14, 69 (also 157) and 158 respectively.

Three Aspects of Consciousness

Kundakunda also refers to the three aspects of consciousness (PS 123-125, see also PKS 38-39), viz. *jnana chetana*, *karma chetana* and *karmaphala chetana*. In other words, the evolution of consciousness (*chetana*) is considered with reference to knowledge (*jnana chetana)*, which comprehends objects, the self and other, deed or action (*karma chetana*), which is undertaken by the soul, and fruit of action (both past and present action) (*karmaphala chetana*), which is either pleasure or pain (PS 123-124). And every soul, according to its own status in the course of evolution is capable of being in its own way the knower (*jnata*), the actor (*karta*) and enjoyer (*bhokta*).

Various other Translations of Upayoga

In the various translations of *Samayasara*,[27] the term "*upayoga*" is translated as "conscious attentiveness" (SS 88, 90), "attentive soul" (SS 89), "conscious attention" and "attention" (SS 100) by J. L. Jaini. A. Chakravarti has translated *upayoga* as "being of the nature of self" (SS 88), "the Self of the nature of *upayoga* (pure thought and perception)" (SS 89, 90), and "mental activity" (SS 100). The affective, cognitive and volitional or conative modes or functions of consciousness are also known as the three kinds of *upayoga*, referred to in *Samayasara* (SS 88-90, 94-95), viz. *darshan* (this *darshan* is different from perception and is translated variously as feeling, intuitive awareness, view, world-view, belief, faith), *jnana* (knowledge or cognitive awareness) and *charitra* (conduct, volition) [these could be enlightened but when deluded they are known as deluded view (*mithyatva* or *mithya-darshan*), deluded or wrong knowledge (*mithya jnana*) and wrong conduct (lack of moral and spiritual self-restraints (*avirati* or *mithya-charitra*)].

Jethalal S. Zaveri, a Shvetambara scholar, translates *upayoga* as "consciousness" (pages 90, 100, 135, 138, 151, 163) and "activity of the soul" (page 146). The characteristic quality of the soul is said to be "consciousness (*upayoga*)," a complex of two cognitive faculties – knowledge and intuition. Of this twofold *upayoga*, knowledge is described as "apprehension of an object with its contents" and intuition as "apprehension of a thing without its contents" (page 91). Knowledge, he adds, "includes intellect, competence and technique" (page 91). And Vijay K. Jain translates *upayoga* as "consciousness" (SS 88-90).

Chetana and *Upayoga* are not the same

Thus, it is evident that those who follow the line of thinking of *Tattvartha Sutra* often make no distinction between *chetana* and *upayoga*. I. C. Shastri insists that *upayoga* alone is the essential definition or characteristic of the soul (*jiva*) on the basis of Shvetambara scriptures (*Bhagavati* (II, 10) and *Uttaradhyayana Sutras* (28, 10)) and *Tattvartha Sutra* (TS 2.8). He does not refer to Kundakunda's statement that the essential definition or the distinguishing characteristic of the soul substance (*jiva dravya*) is consciousness (*chetana*) and manifestation, attention or function of consciousness (*upayoga*) (PS 127, PKS 16, 27), which are not the same. *Upayoga* is the application, manifestation, mode, or rather the active, functional and the attentive aspect of consciousness, but not consciousness-as-such (*chetana*) which is the essence of *jiva* or the soul substance and is the underlying substratum of all its attributes, modes, conditions and even forms of *upayoga*.

Upayoga is the manifestation, modification or the state-of-'evolution' (*parinama*) of *jiva*, which has the form of function or mode of soul substance (PS 127 AC). Shastri, however, persists in following the line of thinking of *Tattvarta Sutra* (2.8), in spite of the fact that he himself quotes Digambara philosopher Vidyananda to the effect that "*upayoga* means attention or application of consciousness (*chaitanya*) which is the essence (*svatattva*) of *jiva*. Vidyananda points out the difference between essence and definition (*lakshana*) by stating that "the essence is a definition as well as the definee. It occupies both the positions; while mere definition is not necessarily given that position." (TSV, p.318).

The self or the soul is declared to be *cheda* (conscious entity) (PKS 27) and as such is identified with consciousness (*chetana*). Since *upayoga* (conscious attentiveness) is only a particular mode of consciousness, it cannot be identified with self. In this context, Shastri states that *upayoga* is an essential definition of the self. We cannot separate it from the latter. There is no soul without *upayoga* and there is no *upayoga* without soul. Yet, we cannot say that they are absolutely one and the same thing. *Upayoga* is only a part of the psychical function. Other functions are feeling, willing, etc. which, according to Jainism, are not included into *upayoga* which is the activity of cognition only, a particular expression of consciousness (*chaitanya*) which covers the entire range of psychical life. This is also one of the reasons for regarding it as the essence and *upayoga* as the definition of soul.[28]

In his introduction to *Gommatsara Jivakanda*, Jaini observes:

> Consciousness... is the mighty real characteristics of life. It is the most essential differentia between the living and non-living... you must be alive to read these words. You must be attentive to feel that something is there. You must conate [in the sense of intuition, *darshan*] these words. Then again you must be attentive to perceive, then alone you begin to know them, i.e. have perception, conception, judgement, retention, memory, recognition, induction, or deduction from them.

Consciousness is an active, responsible agent; it is the Doer of all actions; and it is the Enjoyer of the fruits of these actions, good or bad. It is necessary to remember these, lest we should fall into the error of exempting the soul, *ego* or individual consciousness from all responsibility for his actions, good or bad, and thus at one stroke uproot all ethical distinctions and fullstop to discriminate actions.[29]

In Kundakunda's works, *jiva* or *appa* (*atma*), i.e. soul or the self, is said to be of the nature of *chetana* (consciousness) and *upayoga* (conscious attentiveness, the application, or function of consciousness) (PS 127) [in PKS 16, *chetana* and *upayoga* are said to be the qualities or attributes of *jiva* (*jivaguna*)], while in PKS 27, *jiva* is said to have life, consciousness, i.e. conscious entity (*cheda* in Pk. and *chetayita* in Sk.) with *upayoga* as its distinguishing property, special or particular characteristic (*upayoga visheshitah*). *Chetana* and *upayoga* are not the same.

Three Kinds of *Upayoga*

Pravachanasara 155, states: "The self (*appa* in Pk. *atma* in Sk.) is of the nature of or has for self psychic-attention (*upayogatma*) and *upayoga* is stated as knowledge and intuition [vision]." And this psychic-attention of the self is also auspicious (*shubha*) or inauspicious (*ashubha* [good or evil] (PS 155), depending on the character of its state-of evolution. When it evolves through the pure (*shuddha*), it becomes pure (PS 9). In other words, it possesses the nature of that through which it evolves during the time of the evolution (PS 8).

In his commentary, Amrtachandra draws our attention to some significant aspects in regard to *upayoga*. The particular *upayoga* characteristic of the self (i.e. consciousness) accounts for the absolute distinctness (*atyanta vibhakta*) of the self [from inert inanimate matter, etc. other substances] and is [also] the cause of the self's conjunction (*sanyoga*) with other substance (Introductory remark to PS 155 and PS 155 AC). Moreover, *upayoga*, indeed, is the nature of the self, since it evolves in obedience to its (the self's) character of consciousness (*chaitanya anuvidhayi parinama*) (PS 155 AC, also SAS commentary of Pujyapada and Akalanka's TRV commentary on TS 2.8), i.e. it (*upayoga*) has sameness (*anvyayi*) of nature or character as consciousness.

Continuing his commentary on *Pravachanasara* 155, Amrtachandra states: "And that (*upayoga*) is knowledge and intuition, since consciousness, according as it is definite or indefinite, has both forms. Now this psychic–attention is specialized in two ways, according to purity and impurity. Of these the pure is without attachment; the impure is with attachment, which again is two-fold good or auspicious (*shubha*) and evil or inauspicious (*ashubha*), because of the two-fold character of the attachment, as being in the form of sanity (purifying, *vishuddhi*) or affliction, distress and morbidity (*sanklesha*)" (PS 155 AC).

The impure psychic-attention (*upayoga*) is evident or visible in the form of *vishuddhi* or *sanklesh*. It thus has a dual aspect of *shubha* and *ashubha* or double aspect of *punya* (righteousness or piety) and *papa* (evil or vicious). This is the cause of the soul's conjunction with other substance (*para dravyasya sanyoga karana*). In the absence of *punya* and *papa*, only pure psychic-attention remains and that is not the cause of conjunction with another substance (PS 156 AC). In other words, consciousness-as-such (*chetana*) is not the cause of conjunction with other substances. It is only the imure psychic-attention (*upayoga*) in the form of *shubha* or *ashubha*, which is the cause of conjunction with other substance. In other words, it acts as the supportive factor or the auxiliary cause (*nimitta karana*) of bondage with other substance (material *karman*). Good thoughts (*shubha parinama*) is the cause of *dharma* (righteousness or piety, i.e. *punya*) *karma*, and bad or evil thoughts (*ashubha parinama*) is cause of *adharma* (sin or *papa*); giving up both leads to pure, as a result of which no bondage of *karma* takes place (PP 2.71).

Akalanka's Definition of Upayoga

Upayoga is defined by Akalanka as *bahya-abhyantara hetu dvaya sannidhane yathasambhavam uplabdhyu chaitanya anuvidhayi parinam upayogah*, (Akalanka, *Tattvarthavartika: Rajavartika*, TRV commentary on TS 2.8), i.e. conscious attentiveness is the state-of-evolution in obedience to its (the self's) character of consciousness, of the nature or character of psychic state, mode or attention resulting from "available" two types of external and two kinds of internal conditions or auxiliary causes being placed together as far as possible in the vicinity or close proximity of one another. The two types of external conditions or auxiliary causes are: (1) *atma-bhuta*, (intrinsic), i.e. eye, ear, etc. senses, which are formed or developed in the body and associated with consciousness; and (2) *anatma-bhuta* (extrinsic), i.e. lamp, sunlight, electricity, etc. The two kinds of internal conditions or auxiliary causes of *upayoga* are: (1) *anatma-bhuta* (extrinsic), i.e. vibrations in the soul resulting from the material clusters (*vargana*) suitable for constituting body (gross and subtle), speech, and mind (i.e. structural aspects of physical mind, such as nervous system and brain); and (2) *atma-bhuta* (intrinsic), i.e. cognition, etc. mental or psychic states dependent on external or internal factors, personal experiences, and the inner capacity and vigour of soul.

The word "available" in this definition indicates conditioned state of consciousness, implying thereby that consciousness-as-such is the state of only or purely consciousness, which is the very nature of the soul and the substratum of all its attributes, modes or forms of conscious activity, pure and impure. In other words, even the specific transformations, evolutions or mutations of psychic states, including distorted, perverted, impure states, of soul (consciousness) is known as functional or applied forms or modes of consciousness (*upayoga*), just as the transformed states or distorted (*vikar*) modes or forms of gold such as bracelet, ring, ear-rings and armlet, etc. being in obedience to the character of goldness, are known as gold, which remains their substratum.

The Samkhya argue that pleasure, pain and infatuation that are states-of-evolution which adhere to the self's character as consciousness should be characterised as manifestation of consciousness (*upayoga*). In this context, however, the various transformations of *upayoga* are said to be the distorted states-of-evolution of knowledge and intuition. Though the two views seem to be contrary or inconsistent to one another, there is no flaw here, since consciousness remains the substratum as much of knowledge, etc. as of pleasure, pain, delusion, etc.

Consciousness is the extraordinary general characteristic of the soul or nature (*dharma*) of the self (*atma*). *Jiva* does not lose its nature or property of consciousness, even in close proximity of other substances, which is found in the forms of knowledge, intuition, etc. as also in the forms of pleasure, etc. Though different substances commingle or are mixed up and mutually interpenetrating, they are distinguished by their own distinctive intrinsic natures or characteristics. Just as gold though united with silver is distinguished by its extraordinary property or characteristics of yellow colour, density or weight, etc., so also the self, though united (*ekatva*) with material substance (say body) from the perspective of bondage, is distinguished by its own intrinsic defining characteristic of knowledge, etc. conscious attentiveness (*upayoga*).

The defining characteristic of *upayoga* is of two kinds: *atma-bhuta* (intrinsic, inalienable or inseparable) and *anatma-bhuta* (extrinsic, alienable or separable). Heat is the inseparable characteristic of fire whereas the stick of Devadatta is the separable characteristic. *Upayoga* is the inseparable characteristic of self (*atma*). (Akalanka's TRV commentary on TS 2.8). Similarly, *jivatva* (consciousness-as-such) is an inseparable characteristic of the soul but the human or animal condition (*gati*) of existence, is a separable state or mode of *jiva* (soul).

Moreover, unlike *jivatva*, the six classes of immobile and mobile souls (*jiva nikaya*, PS 182), the 14 soul classes (*jiva samasa*), classified primarily on the basis of differences of body, senses and mind, the soul quests (*margana sthana*) (SS 53) based on psycho-physical living organisms, including sex, passion, etc., and various kinds of living beings (*jiva sthana* SS 55 and 65-67), having one to five senses and both completely developed and incompletely developed, subtle and gross, are other than consciousness-as-such and separable modes of *jiva* (soul or consciousness). All of them or all these modes pertaining to the body are given the appellation of *jiva* or are said to be *jiva* in the scriptures from the external, other-referential point of view (*vyavahara naya*) (SS 56 and 67).

Rarity of the Concept of Upayoga *in Shvetambara Texts*

Commenting on F.W. Thomas, remark that the conception or the doctrine of *upayoga*, is a "rarity in Shvetambara books [texts]," – which is "at the heart of Kundakunda's soteriology in the *Pravachanasara*", Johnson states:

> Among the earliest surviving texts there appears to be no direct reference to *upayoga* in the *Ayaramga*, the *Suyagadamga*, or the *Dasaveyaliya Sutras*. The term does appear, however, at *Uttarajjhayana* XXVIII. 10, where it is said that the characteristic of the *jiva* is manifestation (or application) through (or with) 'knowledge, perception, (*darshan*), happiness and suffering' (*jivo uvaogalakkhano nanenam damsanenam ca suhena ya duhena ya Utt.* XXVIII.10). Jacobi translates this as 'The characteristic... of the soul [is] the realization (*upayoga*) of knowledge, faith, happiness and misery' – 1895, p. 153. It is not clear whether *upayoga*, which can have the meanings 'application', 'manifestation' or 'employment,' should be taken here in its full technical sense of 'application' or 'manifestation of consciousness.' The passage could mean that *nana* (*jnana*, knowledge), *damsana*, (*darshan*), etc., are particular types of *upayoga*, or that *upayoga* is one of a number of characteristics of the *jiva*; but in either case it need not mean 'consciousness' as such, although the assumption among commentators and translators is that it does.[30]

Kundakunda distinguishes between *chetana* and *upayoga*. He identifies the soul (*jiva*) with *chetana* or consciousness-as-such or considers *chetana* to be the essence of *jiva*, having the nature of *upayoga* (*upayogamaya*) (PS 127) or the particular characteristic of (*upayoga visheshita*) (PKS 27). In *Panchastikayasara* 16, he states that *chetana* and *upayoga* are the attributes of *jiva* (*jiva guna*) (PKS 16). However, Amrtachandra, in his commentary thereon argues that *chetana* can be of the nature of experiencing pure consciousness of knowledge of the self or impure consciousness of the fruits of one's *karma. Upayoga*, on the other hand, evolves in obedience to the soul's character of consciousness pure or impure depending on whether it is with or without thought constructions (*vikalpa*) (PKS 16 AC).

The following verse of (*Uttarajjhayana* XXVIII. 11), Johnson remarks, has a different system of classification, [which makes it] clear that *uvaoga* (*upayoga*) is one among a number of characteristics of the *jiva*, and not yet the defining characteristic. The characteristics of the soul (*jiva*) are knowledge, faith, conduct, austerities, energy (*viriyam*) and *uvaoga* (application). Jacobi (ibid.) translates *uvaoga* here as realization (of its developments).

According to Johnson, these two verses of chapter XXVIII of *Uttaradhyayana Sutra* (*Uttarajjhayana Sutta* in Pk.), which he acknowledges was "a relatively late addition to the body of the *Uttarajjhayana*" [this "late addition" could be posterior or subsequent to Kundakunda, and as such the Shvetambara text seems to have borrowed or inherited the concept of Kundakunda's *upayoga*, though Johnson feels it otherwise since in his mistaken view Kundakunda flourished in the early 5th century AD or later].

Johnson maintains that the "formal division" of *upayoga* into *jnana* and *darshan* has not yet been made. He ignores Kundakunda's works, *Tattvartha Sutra* (TS 2.9) and even the Shvetambara text *Vihayapannatti* (*Bhagavati*) (II. 10a (147b), which states that *guna* (essential property or attributes) of the *atthikaya* (fundamental entity) *jiva* makes possible *uvaoga* (the spiritual function) (Deleu's translation). And at (*Bhagavati* II.10c (149a) it is asserted that the "characteristic (*lakkhana*) of soul is the spiritual function (*uvaoga*)". The soul by its own nature (*aya-bhavenam*) possesses will (*viriya*) "which enables it to apply this spiritual function in the infinite number of possibilities or modes (*pajjava* or *paryaya*) of knowledge (*jnana*) and intuition (*darshan*)" – thus the "true nature of soul" (*jiva bhava*) is revealed through *upayoga* (*Vihayapannatti* II. 10c).[31]

Five Psychic Dispositions of Jiva

In *Tattvartha Sutra* (TS 2.1), Umasvami or Umasvati has described *jiva* in terms of *bhavas* (psychic dispositions or states of the soul) of five kinds arising from the four types (subsidential, destructive, partly subsidential and partly destructive, and coming into operation or rise of *karmas,* i.e. the fruition of karmas), or conditions of *karmas* plus the *jiva's* natural or inherent *bhava* (*parinamika bhava*), independent of *karmas.* These five *bhavas* are said to be the soul's own psychic states (*svatattva*).

In other words, *parinamika bhava* is the natural state of the *jiva,* which is the substratum of, or has the potential to undergo modification(s) [in the form of subsidential, etc. four *bhavas* (modes)] under the influence of *karman* and for that very reason, it is in itself non-relational to *karman,* i.e. *karma nirpeksha,* independent or different from the subsidential, etc. four types of modifications, not free from or devoid of *karman* (*karma rahita*).

Evolvement Nature of the Soul

At *Viyahapannatti* XVIII. 10e (760a), Somila, a Brahmin, asks Lord Mahavira whether he is "one or two imperishable (*akkhaya*) eternal (*avvayaya*) and stable or constant (*avatthiya*) or has he different forms in past, present and future (*anega-bhuya-bhava-bhaviya*)?", In his reply, Lord Mahavira states:

> He is all of these, since from the point of view of [the] essence [of his soul, *Abhayadeva's vrtti* on *Viyahapannatti*] (*davv atthayae*) he is one, from the point of view of knowledge and vision (*nana-damsan atthayae*) he is two; as to *paesas* or *pradesh* [space points] he is imperishable (*akkhaya* or *akshaya* in Sk.), immutable (*avvayaya*) [its correct translation should be eternal] and stationary (*avatthiya*) [its correct translation should be stable or constant]... [but as to *uvaoga* he] has different forms [(or modes, *paryaya*)] in past, present and future. Here it is interesting to note that the form of *uvaoga,* as 'spiritual function is something that changes'; [it signifies that it is evolvent (*parinami* or *parinamansheel*) and yet eternal and stable or constant]; moreover, it is essentially something that the soul changes itself (Note also that *jnana* and *darshan* share the same context as *upayoga* here).[32]

This translation of the Shvetambara scripture by Johnson makes it amply clear that the translations of both Deleu and Johnson of the word "*avvava*" (*avvayaya* in Sk.) as immutable, i.e. unchanging and of *avatthiya* (*avasthita* in Sk.) as stationary in Somil's question and in Lord Mahavira's reply thereto are not correct (see *Paea sadda mahannavo Prakrit-Hindi Dictionary,* ed. K.R. Chandra (Ahmedabad: Prakrit Jain Vidhya Vikas Fund, 1987).

Moreover, *Viyahapannatti* also uses the terms "*anagarovautta*" and "*sagarovautta*" to designate two types of *uvaoga*. Following Schubring's translation of *sagara*-and *anagara-uvaoga*, (see Schubring 1962, para 82), Deleu renders these as "faculty of abstract or indistinct imagination" and "faculty of concrete or distinct imagination" respectively (see, for instance, *Viy.* VI.3.5 (257b), and XIX.8 (770b)). *Uvautta* is the *Prakrit* from the Sanskrit *upayukta*, meaning 'employed' or 'applicable to'; similarly, *upayoga*,... have the meaning of 'application,' 'manifestation', or 'employment' (of consciousness).[33]

Deleu's use of "imagination" (see above) to translate the term "seems eccentric". But at *Viyahapannati* V. 4 (221b), he renders *uvautta* as "attentive". At XVIII.8.3 (755a) he defines "*sagara*" as "formally distinct" and *anagara* as "formally indistinct". The Prakrit term "*agara*" corresponds to the Sanskrit *akara* "form" or "figure". Thus, Deleu considers *uvautta* as "attentive," *sagarovautta* as "attentive to something with form," and *anagarovautta* as "attentive to something without form" (i.e. determinate or indeterminate cognition/manifestation of consciousness), corresponding to the two kinds of *upayoga*, *jnana* and *darshan* ('knowing' and 'perceiving').[34]

The concept of *upayoga* (conscious attentiveness) which occupies a prominent place in Kundakunda's works, plays a significant role in life. It is stated that "a substance (including the soul substance) possesses the nature of that through which it evolves during the time of the evolution" (PS 8) and that "the soul accepts the character of its state-of-evolution. When the soul evolves through the good or the evil, it becomes good or evil. When it is pure, it becomes pure." (PS 9) In other words, it is up to the individual soul how he wants to evolve in the only time he has before him, i.e. the present. Being the lord or the architect (*prabhu*) of his own destiny (PKS 27), the self is free to evolve through the impure or distorted mental states of anger, etc. passions and attachment, aversion and deluded view, which are the cause of bondage, or desist from them.

If the activity of the soul is performed with conscious awareness/conscious attentiveness, the use of intellect (*buddhi-purvak*) and sense of responsibility, the self will not prefer to choose a course of action which is detrimental to its interests. However, if an action is undertaken without conscious attentiveness and use of intellect, i.e. *abuddhi-purvak* and as such under subconscious compulsions, instinctive urges and impulsive drives, under the influence of the neuro-physiological processes/brain states, i.e. physical *karma*, and as such "unconsciously planned and executed," it will be full of "telling errors of perception, memory and judgement" according to neuroscientist Gazzaniga.[35] These are obviously lacking in coherence, a balanced and detached view, discriminative insight and unity of conscious experience, which are the prerogatives of conscious entity and the domain of conscious attentiveness (*upayoga*).

Importance of *Upayoga* compared with Mindfulness in Buddhism

The concept of *upayoga* occupies a significant place in Jainism. This may be compared to the importance attached to "mindfulness" in Buddhism. *Upayoga* enables us to focus one's attention (conscious attention) to the task at hand by concentrating all the energy of both mind and body on one specific target or goal at a time. If one wants to fulfill one's potential, one must focus one's attention on the present, here and now. At that one moment in time, what has happened in the past does not really matter because it has already been, while what may happen in the future is yet to come.

Success in life is not possible without the attentiveness of consciousness (*upayoga*) or mindfulness. Conscious attention, mindfulness is so powerful because it gives us the ability to take charge of our thoughts and feelings. If we do not fully attend to these – if we live our lives in a state of constant distraction – we are condemned to keep experiencing whatever thoughts, interpretations and emotions habitually recur.[36]

It is only by the power of attentiveness or mindfulness, i.e. concentrating or focusing all our energy on the present, that one will be able to direct one's cognitive, emotional and conative or volitional faculties or aspects/modes of consciousness in the fulfillment or accomplishment of the objective. In *Power of Now*, as Eckhart Tolle points out that it is only by becoming deeply conscious of the present moment that one can hope to transform one's mode of consciousness. Otherwise, one will only be a slave to one's instinctive impulses, biases or habits and emotional responses that silently or unconsciously shape the most important attitudes and decisions in one's life.

In order to propagate the powerful and wide-ranging benefits of mindfulness practice, extensive research is being conducted by the

Centre for Mindfulness in Medicine, established at the University of Massachusetts in 1995 by Jon Kabat-Zinn, under the inspiration of Dalai Lama, the Buddhist leader.

The Issue of *Shudha, Shubha* and *Ashubha Upayoga*

The self of the nature of *upayoga* is described to be of two kinds, viz. *darshan* (intuitive awareness) and *jnana* (cognition or knowledge) (TS 2.9 and PS 155). In *Samayasara, upayoga* is said to be three-fold, *darshan, jnana* and *charitra* (volition or conduct (SS 89-90, 94-95). In a ethico-spiritual context, Kundakunda has also deemed it necessary to discuss *upayoga* in the sense of pure (*shuddha*) (PS 14), good or auspicious (*suho* in Pk. or *shubha* in Sk.) conscious attentiveness (PS 11, 69-70 and 157) and evil or inauspicious (*asuho* in Pk. or *ashubha* in Sk.), psychic disposition or attention (PS 12 and 158).

Most people agree that *ashubha* (inauspicious, unwholesome thoughts or sinful activities) are to be completely abandoned (*atyanta heya*, PS 12 AC), and *shuddha* (pure or the absence of passions, attachment, aversion, and deluded view), which is the direct cause of liberation (*nirvana*), should be sought in every way. There are several misperceptions and a great deal of controversy in regard to *shubha.* There are acute differences about its role in liberation of the soul and whether it can be considered desirable and to be followed and practiced (*upadeya*) or is it undesirable and worth renouncing and abandoning altogether (*heya*)?

A group of people known as Kanjipanthi (the followers of Kanji Svami, a Shvetambara monk, who along with thousands of his followers joined the Digambara tradition), firmly affirm that the activity and psychic disposition or conscious attentiveness of *shubha* or *punya* (auspicious, wholesome thoughts, righteousness, piety or moral conduct of self-restraint) is as much undesirable and worth abandoning (*heya*) as *ashubha* or sinful (*papa*) activity. In the process, they blur the distinction between *shubha* and *ashubha upayoga* by emphasizing that both of them are impure (*ashuddha*) *upayoga.* This is a gross misrepresentation of Kundakunda's views in this regard as presented in his works, including *Pravachanasara,* as well as other Jaina texts.

The evolution of the self accompanied by attachment, aversion and a deluded view is the cause of bondage of the physical *karman.* Of these, deluding view (*moha*) and aversion (*dvesha*) are evil or inauspicious (*ashubha*). Attachment is of two kinds: *shubha* and *ashubha.* Good (*shubha*) attachment (*prashasta raga*) has a purifying (*vishuddhi*) effect whereas *ashubha* attachment (*aprashasta raga*) has the effect of affliction, distress and morbidity (*sanklesh*) (PS 155 AC and PS 180 AC). Thus, it is asserted that those, who are devoid of evil psychic-attention (*ashubha upayoga*) by annihilating a deluded view, aversion and disapproved attachment (*aprashasta raga*) and are sometimes possessed of pure psychic-attention (*shuddha upayoga*), by putting an end to the arousal of passions (*kashaya*), and sometimes possessed of good psychic-attention (*shubha upayoga*) through ripening of excellent attachment (*prashasta raga*), are, through being themselves abodes of liberation, saviours of men; and others who manifest excellent feelings of devotion to them become partakers of merits (*punya*) (PS 260 AC).

Thus, *ashubha* attachment (*aprashasta raga*) is considered undesirable and worth abandoning (*heya*), whereas *shubha* attachment (*prashasta raga,* i.e. excellent attachment) is not deemed to be undesirable. In fact, *shubha raga* is considered commendable, praiseworthy, desirable and worthy of acquisition (*upadeya*). A clear distinction is also made between *ashubha upayoga* (evil psychic-attention) and *shubha upayoga* (good psychic-attention), which is not condemned as undesirable or worth abandoning.

Mistaken View of Kanjipanthi in Equating *Shubha* and *Ashubha*

In support of their mistaken view that "there is no difference" whatsoever between *punya* (righteousness, piety or merit) and *papa* (evil or sin) and that both are equally undesirable and worth abandoning, the Kanjipanthi state that both *shubha* or *punya* and *ashubha* or *papa* are the cause of karmic bondage just as both gold and iron fetters bind a person (PS 77 AC; also SS 146). *Shubha* also undeniably binds a person but that does not imply that there is "no difference" between *shubha* or *punya* and *ashubha* or *papa.*

Let us now examine the above contention of Kanjipanthi by carefully scrutinizing *Pravachanasara* verse 77 and Amrtachandra's commentary thereon in the light of Kundakunda's statement in this regard at several places in this very work as well as some of his other works and Amrtachandra's commentaries thereon. In *Pravachanasara* verse 77 Kundakunda states:

He who does not believe that there is nothing particular or special (*nasti vishesha* in Sk., *natthi viseso* in Pk.) between *punya* and *papa* [i.e. the two are similar] in the way or sense stated above (*evam*) [this refers to previous verses] moves about, covered with infatuation or muffled in delusion (*moha sanchhanna*) in the cycle of transmigratory existence.

This verse does not suggest that "there is no difference", whatsoever, as most scholars, including Faddegon, translate it in both English and Hindi. Moerover, the qualifying phrase "*moha sanchhana*" is very significant in that it signifies that it is primarily because of infatuation (*moha*) that the self (*jiva*) wanders aimlessly in the cycle of transmigratory existence. In *Pravachanasara* 43, it is clearly stated that in the condition of coming into operation or the rise (*uday*) of *karman*, only one, who is filled with a deluded view, attachment and aversion necessarily incurs bondage. In other words, the self alone is responsible for bondage by being deluded, attached, etc.

This verse (PS 77), as Kundakunda and Amrtachandra point out, has to be understood in the context of previous verses. The immediately preceding verse explains that the sensorial pleasure, of which *shubba upayoga* is the means (*sadhan*), is misery alone (*eva*) (PS 76). Kundakunda states: "Happiness acquired by means of the senses, is dependent, accompanied by obstacles or distractions, interrupted or terminable, cause of bondage and unequal, and hence it is indeed misery only (*eva*)" (PS 76), or that it is misery in disguise.

Commenting on it, Amrtachandra observes:

> Sensorial pleasure, although originating from merit, is actually misery, for it is dependent, accompanied by obstacles or distractions, interrupted, cause of bondage, unequal; It is depenent, for it rests on something else, since it has in something else its condition. It is accompanied by obstacles or distractions, for it is utterly confused, since it is attended by different longings, such as hunger, thirst, etc. It is interrupted, for oppositions are noticed in it, since we realize it as proceeding by the rise of good emotional-*karman* (*sad-vedya=sata-vedaniya*) disturbed by the rise of bad emotional-*karman*. It is a cause of bondage, for in its outcome it is hard to bear, since it is covered with a thick mass of dust of *karman*, collecting in the train of the army of the vices, passion, etc., trailing along the road of sensual enjoyments. It is unequal, for it is utterly unsteady, since it evolves through increase and decrease. And it is, indeed misery only. Thus, even merit turns out to be, like sin, the means of misery (PS 76 AC).

It the earlier two verses (PS 74-75), it is stated: "If manifold merits, resulting from (good psychic states of) evolution make the souls, including those of the gods, to necessarily thirst or crave for sense-objects (*vishaya trashna*) [they are the cause of misery] (PS 74 and PS 74 AC; and that these (souls), then, due to their thirst roused and made unhappy by such thirstings, or cravings, wish for obtaining till death the pleasures of sense-objects, thereby being burnt by misery" (PS 75), since expectation of obtaining joy or pleasures from sense objects is incorrect understanding of the reality of things, i.e. deluded view; it is like a deer's desire of finding water from mirage (*mrgatrashna*) (PS 75 AC)].

In his expectation of obtaining pleasure in sense objects, and feeling unhappy in having unpleasant sense objects, the soul develops likes and dislikes, i.e. attachment and aversion towards them. Attachment, aversion and a deluded view are the direct causes of the influx as well as consequent bondage of *karmas* since indulgence in sense objects and anger, etc. passions or attachment and aversion, are the characteristics of evil (*ashubha*) or sinful (*papa*) psychic attention (PS 180 JS). Given the persistence of the above conditions and circumstances, *punya*, thus, turns out to be similar to *papa.*

In his commentary on *Pravachanasara* 77 also, Amrtachandra explains how there is "nothing particular or special" between *punya* and *papa* alongwith the purport of this verse. He states that the circumstances in which the two (*punya* and *papa*) seem to be similar or that the dichotomy or duality of merit (*punya*) and sin (*papa*), like a duality of good and evil psychic-attention or of pleasure and pain, is hardly maintainable or sustainable in several circumstances:

(1) when things are viewed from transcendental nature of the self (*paramarthatah*) [*karma-nirpeksha parinamika bhava*, i.e. consciousness-as-such having no relation to *karmas*, which is beyond dualities and relative opposites of good and evil]. As a result, both *punya* and *papa* cannot be considered to be an attribute of the soul and as such they are said to be similar, i.e. "there is nothing particular or special" between *punya* and *papa* (*anatma-dharmatva avisheshatvat*);

(2) when prosperity and higher status, etc. is acquired through or as result of *punya karma*, which is also the condition thereof, one takes pride, in his superior status, position or condition. This leads to an egotistical (*ahankarik*) difference between *punya* and *papa*, like a gold and iron fetter, [thereby giving rise to *adhyavasana bhavas* (the psychic

dispositions of pride, greed, etc. passions)];

(3) if such a person chooses the path of righteousness, good or virtuous activities (*dharma* or *punya*) [for the purpose, desire or the expectation of obtaining position of lord of heaven (*Indra*), etc. prosperity, wealth, etc. and sense pleasures in the future (i.e. *nidan*) [*dhammam bhoga nimittam*, and not for demolishing the *karma* (SS 273-275)];

(4) as a consequence thereof, one's psychic attention or cognitive, volitional and emotional activities, functions and processes of the mind (*chitta bhitti*) becomes darkened, obscured or coloured (*uparakta*) [with the *adhyavasana bhavas* of pride, greed, etc. passions, delusion (*mithyatva*), lack of self-restraints (*avirati*), attachment, aversion, etc.]; and

(5) as a result, one comes to scorn or disdain one's property, energy, vigour or capacity (*shakti*) for purification (*vishuddhi*)] or pure psychic-attention (*shuddha upayoga*). In this way, he experiences or suffers bodily misery [and mental distress] as long as the transmigratory existence of the cycle of births and deaths (*samsara*) lasts (PS 77 AC).

Conscious of the above-mentioned sombre aspects of *punya*, one should keep oneself away from being attached to pleasant objects of senses or nurturing a feeling of aversion towards unpleasant objects, and orient oneself in the direction of purification of one's psychic-attention (PS 78 and PS 78 AC) through self-restraint (*samyam*) and austerities (*tapa*), etc. (PS 14).

By behaving in the manner described above, i.e. indulgence in and attachment to sense objects (*vishaya*) and pride, greed, etc. passions (*kashaya*), which are the characteristics of evil (*ashubha*) attachment (PS 180 JS), those endowed with auspicious or good psychic-attention (*shubha upayoga*) and great deal of merits (*punya*) will be acting like those imbued with evil or sin (*papa*).

The pleasures of sense objects, acquired by the virtuous activities (*punya*), eventually lead to misery (PS 76 and PP 2.59). The worldly prosperity and name, fame (*vaibhava*), etc. obtained by virtuous deeds leads to pride (*mada* or *ahankara*), and pride generates deluded intellect (*mudha mati*), which, in turn, leads to sinful, vicious acts (*papa*); such *punya* is not desired (PP 2.60).

Both Kundakunda and Amrtachandra were well aware that their description between *punya* and *papa* was selective when they stated that under these circumstances, there is nothing "particular or special (*vishesha*)" between *punya* and *papa* (PS 77) and that the dichotomy or the duality (*dvaita*) between them is not sustainable (PS 77 AC). Similar sentiments were expressed when they argued that "how can (*shubha* or *punya*) be considered to be good, virtuous or desirable (*sushil*) when it leads (*jiva*) into the transmigratory existence of the cycles of births and deaths (*samsara*)" (SS 145), binds the soul, as *ashubha* does, in the same manner as fetters made of gold or iron bind a person (SS 146) and is destructive of independence of the self (SS 147).

Kundakunda and Amrtachandra were aware that there is considerable difference between *punya* and *papa*, or *shubha* and *ashubha* [see PS 11-12, SS 145 AC]. Amrtachandra points out that *shubha* differs from *ashubha* on four grounds, i.e. in its nature (*svabhava*), cause (*karana*), effect (experience or *anubhava* of fruition of *karmas*) and in substratum (*ashraya*) being supportive of the path of liberation. *Shubha* (*punya*) is the path of liberation (*moksha marg*), while *ashubha* (*papa*) is the way to only *karmic* bondage (*bandha marg*), (*shubhashubhau moksha bandha margau*) (SS 145 AC, see also SS 145 JS]. While evil (*ashubha*) or *papa* is to be absolutely abandoned (*atyanta heya*) (PS 12 AC), *shubha*, endowed with commendable or excellent (*prashasta*) attachment, has purifying (*vishuddhi*) effect (PS 155 AC and PS 180 AC), which gradually (*kramatah*) brings about the highest happiness of *nirvana* (liberation) (PS 254 and PS 254 AC), and, thus, not only ieads to liberation of oneself (PS 259 and PS 259 AC) but also help others to attain liberation (PS 260 and PS 260 AC).

If Kundakunda omited mention of the worthy attributes and the commendable role of *punya* and *shubha* and preferred to emphasise the more sombre aspects of *shubha* or *punya* (in PS 77, and in SS 145-147), then he had a reason for doing so. He leaves it to the reader to discover why he chooses to do so [Amrtachandra has endeavoured to help the reader in this respect through his commentaries of PS 77 and SS 145]. Th situation is somewhat similar to Andrew Hacker's comment about Machiavelli. Hacker states:

> Only a few have the intelligence and insight to cut through the ideological prisms which distort the perceptions and wrap the mind . . . Machiavelli says: "It may be said of men in general, that they are ungrateful, voluble, dissemblers, anxious to avoid danger, and covetous of gain." . . . [this] is

not the whole truth . . . Machiavelli is no fool, and he knows full well that his description is selective and one-sided. He is aware that men are often trustworthy and loyal, helpful and friendly. If he omits mention of these worthy attributes and chooses to emphasize the more sombre ones, then he has a reason for doing so. It is the reader's responsibility to discover why Machiavelli selects this particular emphasis . . . The theorist's main tools, in short, are the depth of his intelligence and the range of his imagination. . . .

Men are both brave and cowardly, trustworthy and deceitful, good and evil. The trouble with taking account of all the facts is that it admits all the ambiguities . . . Generalizations are always risky, but to be meaningful they must come down on one side or the other. A political [spiritual] theorist has to be committed to a point of view, and this often entails uttering a half-truth or selecting a single tendency for disproportionate emphasis. He must, in sum, have the courage to speculate on the important questions and to put the facts aside when they get in his way . . . Albert Einstein has this to say: "In the field of politics and social science there has grown up a justified distrust of generalizations pushed too far. When thought is too greatly dominated by such generalizations misinterpretations of specific sequences of cause and effect readily occur doing injustice to the actual multiplicity of events. Abandonment of generalization, on the other hand, means to relinquish understanding altogether. For that reason I believe one may and must risk generalization so long as one remains aware of its uncertainty." *Out of My Later Years* (New York: Philosophical Library, 1950), p. 252. . . . The goal of theory is to enhance the understanding. And great knowledge rises out of those insights which only the engaged mind and the quickened insight are able to create.[37]

After stating what he does (in PS 77), Kundakunda states: he who understands the reality of things thus and no more entertains attachment or aversion towards objects, thereby purifying his psychic attention (*upayoga*), puts an end to pain originating from the body (PS 78). In the very next verse, he states: "If any one, after giving up sinful undertakings and even getting ready to undertake efforts in good conduct, does not get rid of infatuation, etc., then he does not attain the pure self." (PS 79) Here Kundakunda emphasises giving up sinful undertakings, but does not speak of giving up good *(shubha)* conduct.

Even *punya* (merit), it is argued, turns out to be like sin, the means of misery (PS 76 AC), *if* the result is experiencing of misery, born from the body (PS 72), and leads only to thirst, craving or longing for sense objects (PS 74 and PS 74 AC).

Shubha is preferable to *Ashubha*

When Kundakunda says that there is "nothing particular or special (*vishesha*)" about *punya* (righteousness, virtuous), as compared to *papa* (sin), he implies that when viewed in general or as generalization, *punya* and *papa* appear similar, he is well aware that, when viewed in their particular aspects, there is an obvious difference between them and that *punya* or *shubha* is definitely preferable to *papa* or *ashubha*.

This is evident from the following:

(1) The difference between good and evil is reflected in the definition of good (*shubha* or *punya*) (PS 69, 157) and sin or evil (*ashubha* or *papa*) (PS 12, 158), which represent dissimilar characteristics and consequences of the two;

(2) if *punya* or *dharma* (righteousness and piety) was not preferable to evil, Kundakunda would not have spoken of refraining from sin (*papa*) and of striving for virtuous activities, thereby joining the path of righteousness (PS 259);

(3) If there was no difference between *punya* and *papa*, Kundakunda would not have spoken of being devoid of evil or inauspicious psychic attentiveness or conscious manifestation, having pure or good psychic attention, and of being devoted to what is excellent (*prashasta*) (PS 260);

(4) a *samana* can be either of pure (*shuddha*) or good (*shubha*) psychic attention (PS 245, 260), but Kundakunda nowhere states that a person having evil or inauspicious (*ashubha*) psychic attention can be a *samana*; and

(5) of the *shubha* and *ashubha* psychic states or modes, infatuation (*moha*) and aversion (*dvesh*) are evil or inauspicious, while attachment (*raga*) is inherently both auspicious (*shubha*) and inauspicious (*ashubha*) (PS 180).

Clarifying this, Amrtachandra observes that attachment, which is said to be both good and evil, has a dual role or character. Whereas auspicious, excellent or commendable attachment has a purifying (*vishuddhi*) effect, *ashubha* leads to affliction, distress or misery (*sanklesh*) (PS 155 AC and PS 180 AC). In other words, just as from similar germs [seeds] there is variance of produce due to variance of soil, so from similar psychic-attention characterised as excellent attachment, there is variance of fruit, due to variance of receptacle or beneficiary (*patra*), since different occasions lead to different effects (PS 255 and PS 255 AC).

Kundakunda goes on to give two additional explanations:

(6) The activities imbued with good or auspicious attachment are not censurable (PS 247, 253), implying thereby that evil or inauspicious activities are censurable.

(7) Whereas *ashubha* is imbued with affliction, distress or morbidity (*sanklesha*) (PS 155 AC and PS 180 AC), *shubha* (auspicious, wholesome thoughts or meritorious activities), i.e. *punya* or righteous conduct should not be completely abandoned (*sarvatha* or *atyanta heya*) even though it is imbued with commendable attachment (*prashasta raga*) and as such leads to karmic bondage since it leads one towards sanity and has a purifying effect (*vishuddhi*) (PS 155 AC and PS 180 AC). Moreover, it enables one to gradually (*kramatah*) attain the highest happiness of *nirvana* (libration) (PS 254 and PS 254 AC). Thus, it not only leads to liberation (PS 259 and PS 259 AC) but also helps others to attain liberation (PS 260 and PS 260 AC). Those who are imbued with sin or evil and indulge in sense objects and passions (*vishaya kashaya*), [do not attain liberation and] cannot become saviours [of other] (PS 258). Excellent attachment (*prashasta raga*), thus, has a dual role.

Kundakunda's description in the above-mentioned verses in *Pravachanasara* or in *Samayasara* 146 that just as a shackle whether made of gold or iron, binds a person, so also activity good (*shubha* or *punya*) or bad (*ashubha* or *papa*), equally binds the *jiva*, is deliberate. He seeks to draw our attention to the fact that the good or evil nature of an activity depends on the good or evil intention of a person and that the attachment that exists in *shubha* is commendable or excellent (*prashasta*) or contrary to that, i.e. *aprashasta*.

If the prosperity, good birth, health, etc. obtained through virtuous *karmas* (deeds) is wasted or exhausted in sensual pleasures, such pleasures of sense objects, acquired by the virtuous activities (*punya*), is indeed misery (PS 76 and PP 2.59).

In this context, one should note that when *shubha* or *punya* is considered merely a "means of sensorial pleasure" (PS 69 AC), it facilitates sensual enjoyments, which enable one to get attached to or indulge in sense objects. However, they do not compel us to be either attached or indulge in them or debase us. *Shubha* or *punya* is not inherently bad. It basically depends on one's intentions and how one chooses to make use of the facilities at his disposal. One may either squander one's wealth in gambling, drinking, etc. or prefer to make judicious use thereof. Human life offers numerous opportunities to swerve from the path of righteousness and piety (*dharma*).

Merits (*punya*) are of different kinds (see below) and play different roles. It is *only when* (*jadi* in Pk., *yadi* in Sk.) it gives rise to the craving for sense enjoyments (*visaya tanha* in Pk., and *vishaya-trashna* in Sk., PS 74), then only such people wish to obtain sense pleasures, which leads to unhappiness and misery and eventually death (PS 75). Mundane souls are usually seen to have a tendency towards indulging in such craving for sense objects (PS 74 AC). They covet them in the hope of enjoying them. As a result, they are afflicted by them until the end (PS 75 AC), since craving for sensorial pleasure is the cause of bondage (PS 76), even if it originates from merit (*punya*) (PS 76 AC). "Detached from the senses, you are free. Attached, you are bound." (*Ashtavakra Gita* 15.1-2) Kundakunda deemed it necessary to warn people beforehand so that they could be cautious, alert and on guard in regard to this general tendency.

It is in this context that Kundakunda states (*Pravachanasara* 77) that there is "nothing particular or special" between *punya* and *papa.* Similar to the duality of good and evil (*shubha* and *ashubha*) *upayoga* or of pleasure and pain, he adds, the duality of *punya* and *papa* does not exist or is not maintainable from the transcendental perspective (*paramartha*) as they are not of the nature of the self (PS 77 AC). In other than a transcendental perspective, the difference between the above pairs of duality does exist. In fact, the two can never be equated. It would be a gross misperception and a totally wrong view to assert that there is no difference whatsoever between the two.

Shubha (auspicious, wholesome) righteous moral conduct is undoubtedly preferable to *ashubha* (inauspicious, unwholesome thoughts or sinful activities), which is worth abandoning (*heya)* on all counts. If conscious attentiveness is good or auspicious (*shubha*), the soul accumulates merit (*punya*); if evil or inauspicious (*ashubha*), sin (*papa*). In the absence of both, there is no accumulation of *karmas* (PS 156). The *ashubha upayoga* "must be completely abandoned" (*atyanta heya*) (PS 12 AC) because its growth or accretion leads the self to become a rogue, an animal or inhabitant of hell. It is also continuously beset by thousands of pains, as a result of which it strays incessantly (PS 12).

Moreover, a person whose psychic attention is evil or inauspicious (*ashubha*) is steeped in sensual pleasures and passions, addicted to wicked words, bad thoughts or evil intentions and bad companionship. He also tends to be violent or cruel and inclined to perverse ways (PS, 158). However, a person characterized by "cessation from sin, who possesses equanimity towards all righteous (*dharmika*) persons and strives for the totality of meritorious or virtuous qualities has entitlement for following the right path" (PS 259). As a result, such a person is the abode (*aayatan*) of liberation (*moksha*) and merit (*punya*) (for oneself as also others (*svayam parasya*) (PS 259 AC).

Such persons, who are free from *ashubha upayoga* by annihilating all deluded views and aversion, are sometimes possessed of pure (*shuddha*) conscious attentiveness as they have put an end to all passions from arising. They are also sometimes possessed of good or auspicious (*shubha*) conscious attentiveness through the arising of commendable or excellent attachment (*prashasta raga*). They are themselves (*svayam*) the abode of liberation and are saviours of [other] men and those who manifest feelings of devotion to them become partakers of merits (*punya*) (PS 260 and 260 AC).

In *Pravachanasara* 180, Kundakunda clarifies that infatuation and aversion is *ashubha*, attachment (*raga*) is either *shubha* (good) or *ashubha* (evil). Attachment, Amrtachandra observes, has a dual role or character: it is *shubha* [or *prashasta*] when it is purifying or oriented towards sanity and purity (*vishuddhi*), and it is *ashubha* when it is imbued with affliction, distress or morbidity (*sanklesha*) (PS 155 AC and PS 180 AC). Thus, *shubha* has purifying (*vishudhi*), beneficial effect whereas *ashubha*, which is imbued with affliction and distress (*sanklesh*), and invariably leads to bondage, is harmful to the self.

A person who refrains from sin (*papa*) and strives for meritorious (*punya*) qualities is an adherent of the path of liberation (PS 259 and PS 259 AC). Those, who are free from *ashubha* and are endowed with pure or auspicious (*shubha*) psychic-attention, are not only themselves able to cross the (mundane existence of transmigratory cycle of births and deaths), and attain liberation but also help others to attain liberation (PS 260 and PS 260 AC). A person with auspicious (*shubha*) psychic-attention, having commendable or excellent (*prashasta*) conduct, has the ability to gradually (*kramtah*) attain the highest happiness of *nirvana* (liberation) (PS 254 and PS 254 AC). Therefore, *ashubha* and *shubha* cannot be equated with one another.

The status or the position of the *arahantas* (those who have annihilated the destructive *karmas* and are therefore worthy of worship) is the fruit of *punya*, i.e. virtuous or meritorious *karmas* and their activities is the result of the arising of the *karmas* (*audayika karman*). They are considered to have annihilated the cycle of *karman* (*kshayika*, i.e. pure) since they are free from infatuation, etc. (PS 45). As such, they do not cause any damage or distortion to consciousness (*chaitanya vikar*), or karmic bondage (*bandha*), but are in effect the cause of liberation (*moksha*) (PS 45 AC).

Leaving aside the exceptional case of *arahantas*, the coming into operation or the rise (*audaiyika*) of *karmas* is generally considered the cause of karmic bondage. The annihilation (*kshaya*) of passions or *karmas* represents the purity or the pure (*shuddha*) state of consciousness, which was earlier impure.

The other two conscious states of subsidence of passions (*aupshamik*) and subsidence-cum-destruction (*kshayopshahmik*) have the effect of purifying (*vishuddhi*) the impurities of *karman* or passions existing in the soul or consciousness. All these four conscious states (*bhavas*) are *karma*-referential and are said to be the modes or modifications (*parinama* or *paryaya*) of consciousness-as-such. The fifth conscious state of *parinamika bhava*, which is the innate nature of the self, is non-relational to *karmas* as it is independent of *karmas* (*karma nirpeksha*). It is the substratum of the first four *bhavas*, i.e. states of consciousness. It is eternal, constant or stable (*dhruva*), i.e. existent in all three times (past, present and future). It is considered neither pure nor impure, even though it has the potential to become pure. This signifies that that the self has to make efforts to make it pure.

Thus, *vishuddhi* presupposes the existence of the *karma*-infected self and includes subsidence or partial abatment of passions. In the state or condition of subsidence of passions, the self is in a position to undertake the good, auspicious or meritorious (*shubha*) activities of self-restraint, which have a purifying effect, and are a necessary means to complete freedom from passions or eradication of *karmas*, i.e. liberation.

It has already been clarified by Amrtachandra in *Pravachanasara* 180 that commendable attachment [i.e. *prashtha raga* or good psychic attention (*shubha upayoga*)] has a purifying effect (*vishuddhi*), while *ashubha* (inauspicious or evil) attachment is of the nature of affliction, distress and morbidity (*sanklesha*) (PS 180 AC). Moreover, good evolution leads to merit (*punya*) while *ashubha* is the cause of sin (*papa*) (PS 181). Explaining *shubha* and *ashubha*, Jayasena states that devotion of the five revered souls (*panch parameshthi*), etc. is *shubha* (auspicious) attachment [i.e. commendable or excellent (*prashasta*) attachment], while attachment to sense objects (*vishaya*) and anger, etc. passions (*kashaya*) is *ashubha* [i.e. worth abandoning or not praiseworthy (*aprashasta*)] attachment (PS 180 JS).

When a person's mind is in the grip of intense emotional agitation caused by passions or sinful, evil, and unwholesome thoughts (*ashubha*), his impulsive actions and reactions are conditioned by *karmas*, i.e. instinctive impulses, so much so that one behaves like a puppet in the hands of *karmas* and is wholly dependent on them. It is only in the state of *upashama* (subsidence of passions), when the deluding *karma* is held up, even if temporarily, that the soul can have a glimpse of the truth of the reality. It is only then that the self can have peace of mind in which one can assess the situation calmly and dispassionately and develop a definitive self-conscious predilection which illumines the spiritual journey leading to the ultimate goal.

In other words, the calmness of mind resulting from the subsidence of passions alone enables a person to think properly regarding the choices, evaluate the consequences of one's actions and to arrive at appropriate decisions. It also enables one to make efforts (*purushartha*) and use one's conscious attentiveness (*upayoga*), independently of *karma-upadhi*, i.e. the instinctive impulses and subconscious motivations, in the direction of moral and spiritual advancement.

The process of *upashama* (subsidence or abatement of passions), thus, occupies an important place in the spiritual thought and moral conduct of the Jains. Thus, the Jaina concept of self-restraint, control and conquest of senses and subsidence of passions is quite different from value-free Freudian psychology of repression. The subsidence or abatement of passions (like feebleness of anger, pride, greed, etc.)

is an auspicious (*shubha*) thought activity whereas the severity and intensity of passions (*kashaya*) is an inauspicious (*ashubha*) thought activity.

One does not become a purified soul (*visudha appa* in Pk., *vishuddha atma* in Sk.) at one go or in one step. The purification of the *jiva*, infected with *karmas* since beginningless time, takes place by degrees (PS 5 AC). In this way, a person who is endowed with *shubha upayoga* or subsidence of passions gradually (*kramtah*) attains the highest happiness of *nirvana* (liberation) (PS 254 AC). The attainment of the state of pure self or pure consciousness free from *karmas* is always gradual, i.e. from *ashubha* to *shubha* and then to *shuddha* (pure). In *Pravachanasara* it is specifically stated that *shubha* is purificatory (*vishudhi*) (PS 180 AC) unlike *ashubha*, which is of the nature of morbidity, affliction and misery (*sanklesha*) (PS 180 AC), and gradually leads to liberation (PS, 254 AC). Acharya Vidayasagar has stated: "*bin shubha upayoga ke hot na shuddha upayoga*", i.e. there cannot be pure conscious attentiveness without first having wholesome thought activities or good or auspicious conscious attentiveness (*shubha upayoga*).

Strangely, the Kanjipanthi want to enjoy the fruit of *moksha* (*nirvana*) without practicing self-restraint of moral rules of non-violence, etc., i.e. the good and meritorious activities of *shubha upayoga* (good or auspicious attentiveness) which have a purifying effect (*vishuddhi*) for the self and are the means (*sadhan*) of liberation. In his lectures, H.C. Bharill doggedly persists in his one-sided mistaken view and continues to insist that *shubha* (good or auspicious) is not different from *ashubha* (evil or inauspicious) psychic disposition and is the cause of only bondage.

Misperceptions persist not only about good or virtuous activities but also regarding the effects or consequences thereof. This is the reason that Samantabhadra referred to instances where many hermits, ascetics, etc. are seen performing sacrificial acts with the expectation or desire of begetting children, wealth and a berth in heaven or the best of the other world (*Svayambhu Stotra* 49).

Thus, it is quite apparent that Kundakunda, Samantabhadra, etc. *acharyas* (preceptors) were fully aware of the tendency of people to indulge in several good activities (such as worship, devotion, charity, fasting, etc.), external austerities and refrain from physical injury or violence, even when their psychic dispositions are not purified of the impurities of passions like attachment, aversion, anger, pride, etc. Kundakunda, therefore, had to observe that he who practices austerities, moral rules (non-violence, etc. *vrata* or vows), observances (*niyam*) and virtuous activities, but is devoid of *paramartha*, i.e. do not understand the real transcendental nature of the self and are not devoted to the purification of the soul by giving up impurities of attachment, passions, etc. do not attain liberation (*nirvana*) (SS 152-153).

In *Pravachanasara*, it is clearly stated that in the absence of the proper understanding, or an enlightened view of things [which sets the goal (*lakshaya*), the direction and the orientation of one's activities (whether towards inner peace and happiness or towards worldly attractions and sense pleasures)], the practice of vows like non-violence, observances (*niyam*), study, comtemplation (*dhyana*) and charity (*dana*) does not lead to the attainment of liberation from rebirth. It results in one obtaining a state characterised by pleasure (PS 256). In *Samayasara*, it is also stated that good deeds (i.e. *dharma* or *punya*, i.e. righteousness and piety comprising of vows, carefulness, i.e. *samiti*, restraints of mind, speech and body (*gupti*), rules of conduct and austerities) should be performed not for the purpose of future enjoyment (*bhoga-nimittam*) but for the destruction of *karmas* (*karma-kshaya-nimittam*) (SS 273-275).

The mention of the word "*evam*," i.e. "in the way described" in verse 77 of *Pravachanasara* refers to preceding verses (PS 63-68 and 69-76), which deal with sense enjoyments with good or auspicious (*shubha*) psychic attention (*upayoga*) being the means (*sadhan*) thereto. If the soul thirsts merely for sense objects as a result of good or virtuous (*punya*) activtities (PS 74) and as happiness acquired by means of senses is, indeed, misery (PS 76), how is there any (distinction between) good or evil psychic attention? (PS 72).

Pravachanasara verse 77 is to be viewed in the above context. This verse makes it amply clear why Kundakunda omits mention of the worthy attributes of good or auspicious psychic attention, selects the particular description (of PS 77) as such, thereby choosing to emphasize the more sombre aspects. One should always be vigilant, lest one slides back into sense enjoyments or be deluded by attractions of worldly prosperity, name, fame and success, etc.

Moreover, since it is necessary that after giving up evil (*papa*) activities, one has to adopt good or auspicious psychic attention in order to attain pure psychic attention, Kundakunda stresses that one should not be content with all that one can achieve by good psychic attention. One should, he argues, should strive to make use of all the facilities or the means of good health, noble birth, etc. afforded by *punya,* to advance further in moral and spiritual development in order to attain durable and lasting peace and happiness. One should not forget that "if anyone, although giving up sinful undertakings and even getting ready to undertake efforts in good conduct, does not get rid of infatuation, etc., then he does not attain the pure self" (PS 79), but moves about, covered with infatuation or deluded view (*moha*), in the terrible transmigratory existence of the cycle of births and deaths (PS 77).

In *Pravachanasara* 180, Amrtachandra clarifies that commendable attachment (*prashasta raga*), i.e. good psychic attention (*shubha upayoga*), has a purifying effect and is part of purification (*vishuddhi*). *Ashubha* (evil), on the other hand, is of the nature of affliction (*sanklesha*). Good state-of-evolution of psychic disposition, he adds, leads to merit (*punya*), while *ashubha* is the cause of sin (*papa*) (PS 18).

Shuddha and *Shubha Upayoga*

Pravachanasara 11 states that when the state-of-evolution of the soul or consciousness through *dharma* (conduct, duty, equanimity, righteousness, moral precepts or piety) is accompanied, conjoined or endowed with pure (*shuddha*) conscious attentiveness, in the sense of practising self-restraints (*sanyam*) and austerities (*tapa*) (PS 14), it leads to the happiness of *nirvana* (liberation). When it is endowed with good or auspicious (*shubha*) attentiveness, it leads to the happiness of heaven. Both are adherents of *dharma* and also followers of the path of liberation.

While *shuddha* (pure) *upayoga* is capable of being the direct cause of liberation, *shubha upayoga,* being conjoined with attachment and therefore somewhat lacking the efficacy of directly accomplishing its objective of liberation is in some respect (*kathanchit*) productive of contradictory effect (*viruddh karya*) of bringing about the bondage of heavenly happiness. For instance, whereas massage of hot butter (*ghee*) is helpful in reducing pain, but it also causes some pain in the process. Hence, *shuddha upayoga* is preferable to *shubha upayoga* (PS 11 AC). A person, who is endowed with *shubha upayoga* and has excellent conduct, experiences the pure consciousness with a certain degree of attachment, gradually (*kramtah*, or *kramashah*) attains the highest happiness of *nirvana* (liberation) (PS 254 AC).

Interestingly, Kundakunda has used conscious attentiveness (*upayoga*) in regard to *shuddha* (pure) and *shubha* (auspicious) in *Pravachanasara* 11, because *upayoga* is in obedience to conscious awareness (*chaitanya anuvidhayi*). This is not the case with *ashubha* for which the word coming into operation or "arising" (*uday*) of *karma* has been used (PS 12) since it is based on instinctive impulses and sub-conscious motivations, even though the *ashubha* mode is also a pscychic disposition. What is the reason for this? The point that Kundakunda seems to emphasize here is that in the state of *shuddha* and *shubha*, consciousness plays an active role and the functionality of consciousness is accepted. In the state of *ashubha*, the self apparently ignores the attentiveness or alertness of the conscious entity and follows the diktat or the proddings of instinctive impulses and subconscious motivations, in which the neurophysiological processes or brain states (*dravya karma*) acts as an extrinsic, auxiliary cause (*nimitta karana*).

Moreover, while a person who is endowed with *shuddha* or *shubha upayoga* is considered to be an adherent of *dharma* (*dharmatma*) (PS 11), a person endowed with *ashubha* psychic disposition is not a follower of *dharma.* The latter is a sinner, hypocritical person, and a rogue, an animal or inhabitant of hell and always beset by thousands of pains, and strays incessantly (PS 12). Such a person "must be completely abandoned" (PS 12 AC) since he strays very far from the path of liberation as his vicious activities lack self-restraint.

In his commentary of *Pravachanasara* verse 245, Amrtachandra points out that *shubha upayoga* (wholesome psychic attentiveness) is identical to or in harmony with *dharma*, i.e. righteousness or piety (*dharmena sah ekarth samvaya*). Because of its favourable disposition towards *dharma* (*dharma sadbhavat*), even those having *shubha upayoga* are also called *shraman.* But they are not at the same level as those who possess pure conscious attentiveness, who have renounced all passions and as a result are without karmic inflow. A person, who is capable of attaining pure psychic attention, can adopt a course of action which is desirable. However, a person, who is not able to adopt such a course of action, should adopt the *vyavahara* path of righteousness of *shubha* (good, auspicious). This is useful, desirable and worth adopting (*prayojanavana*) in order to restrain delusion, gratification of sense objects, and passions like anger, etc. and concentration on evil (SS 12 JS).

In *Pravachanasara*, it is stated that "Even though there should result a small stain (some karmic bondage) yet a layman or a saint who is a follower of *Jina* should through compassion render disinterested aid (*nirvekkham* in Pk. *nirpeksha* in Sk.) [i.e. without any consideration or expectation of any kind] to all" (PS 251). In this context, Jayasena observes that catering to the well-being of the other with compassion produces some bondage. Such good or auspicious (*shubha*) psychic attention or activity is righteousness (*dharma*) and should be undertaken. Such *shubha* activities should be *nirpeksha*, i.e. devoid of any desire or expectation of name, fame and gain (*khyati puja laabha*), which is destructive of pure intentions (PS 251 JS).

When good or auspicious psychic attention, Jayasena adds, is imbued with an enlightened view, it leads to the bondage of good or virtuous *karmas* and conventionally (*paramparya*) leads to liberation. However, if it is not imbued with an enlightened view, it leads only to the bondage of good or virtuous *karmas* (PS 255 JS).

Such a clear and detailed description of *ashubha, shubha* and *shuddha* as given in Kundakunda's works, particularly *Pravanchanasara*, is not found in such detail or clarity in any literature of the world or even in other Jain texts.

Shuddha, Shubha and *Ashubha* in other Works of Kundakunda

In Ashta Pahuda

In *Bhava Pahuda* (76), Kundakunda states that while unwholesome or bad (*ashubha*) thought activities (*bhava*) are painful (*arta*) and wicked or wrathful (*raudra*), *shubha* (wholesome, good) *bhavas* are *dhammam* (*dharmam* in Sk.), i.e. virtuous, righteous and valuable. In *Bhava Pahuda*, he clarifies that mere practice or observance of external rules of conduct, including austerities and scriptural study, will not lead to purity or the accomplishment of the objective of liberation, if there exists a slight taint of psychic impurities of pride, expectation, deluded view, etc. If a person continues to be imbued with internal infatuation or attachment to things, even renunciation of external attachment to objects and possessions is of no use (*Bhava Pahuda* 44-53).

On the other hand, a householder, who is endowed with an enlightened view and is well set in the path of liberation and is free from internal infatuation and deluded view, is declared to be superior to an ascetic who is imbued with a deluded view (Samantabhadra, *Ratna Karanda Shravakachara* (RKS 33).

A person should also have compassion for all living beings (PS 157), knowledge and virtue (*Sheel Pahuda* 2), observe the five great vows (NS 56-60, *Charitra Pahuda* 30) and possess virtues like contentment (*Sheel Pahuda* 19), forgiveness (*Bhava Pahuda* 107), modesty (*Bhava Pahuda* 104), moral emotions like fearlessness (SS 228), and universal love [*maîtri* or friendliness] (*Charitra Pahuda* 7) and propagation of values (*Charitra Pahuda* 7) – all these are intrinsically desirable. Experience of these intrinsic values is good in itself. Kundakunda states that good experience [or psychic dispositions or mental states] (*shubha bhava*), is intrinsically valuable (*Bhava Pahuda* 76). He speaks of *shubha bhava* as representing all that is intrinsically valuable (PS 9 and 46).[38]

In *Sheel Pahuda* (verse 28), it is pointed out that although the sea is full of gems, it is called sea because of the water, in the same way as *jiva* possesses many gems like austerity, reverence, virtue (*sheel*) and charity. However, it is because of virtue (*sheel*) that a person attains the excellent state of liberation (*nirvana*). The five rules of moral conduct including non-violence come under *sheel*.

Commenting on *Ashta Pahuda* (verse 121), Pandit Jaichand Chhabra observes that auspicious attachment (*shubha raga*) is the condition or the supportive factor (*nimitta*) of the bondage of good karmas (*punya bandha*). However, since it has a purifying effect, it is also the cause of shedding of bad or evil *karmas* (*papa karmas*).

All religions place a premium on good conduct and virtue. The observance of *sheel* (virtue) is the *sine qua non* of a spiritual life. Lord Buddha laid great emphasis on *sheel* (virtue) and regarded it as the pre-condition for making any progress in a spiritual journey. *Sheel* (virtue), *samadhi* (concentration) and *prajna* (discriminating insight), according to him, are the three important milestones on the road to *nirvana*. Without observing *sheel*, one will not be able to practise concentration of mind and develop discriminative insight. *Sheel* is also considered important for developing a higher spiritual life as well as for practicing meditation and attain *prajna*.

Buddhists are mostly satisfied with only mental action (viz. the intention). However, Kundakunda does not rely solely on intention alone even though he too lays greater emphasis on internal aspects of psychic disposition or intentions of the person. He stresses that the role and importance of external conduct (actions) cannot be completely lost sight of or ignored. In fact, it is our actions which reflect our intention and character. They are also the reliable yardstick of the purity or otherwise of one's intentions. For Kundakunda, conduct is *dharma*. He defines *dharma* as equanimity (*samya*), which, in turn, is said to be a state-of-evolution of the soul devoid of infatuation or deluded view and mental disturbance (*kshobha*), i.e. conduct-deluding *karma* of attachment and aversion (PS 7). In this way, Kundakunda sought to harmonise internal and external aspects.

One cannot realise *nishchaya charitra*, Pandit Sadasukh argues, unless one gives up five sins (*papa*) of violence, etc. and adopts *vyavahar* (conduct) of the character of the magnificence of internal and external activities (commentary on RKS 49). In other words, one can attain *nishchaya charitra* only by renouncing sinful tendencies and adopting the excellence of *vyavahara* conduct of goodness (*punya*) in both internal and external aspects.

In Baras Anuvekkha (BA)

Kundakunda categorically states that the good, auspicious or wholesome activity of mind, speech and body (*shubha yoga*) purifies (*pavitti*) and is instrumental in the inhibition (*samvar*) of the influx of evil, inauspicious, unwholesome activities (*ashubha yoga*). Restraint (*nirodh*) of the auspicious thought activity is possible by means of pure thought activity (BA 63). And since that which is the cause of inhibition of *karma* is also the cause of the shedding of *karmas* (*nirjara*) (BA 66), *shubha* is also the cause of shedding or elimination of *ashubha karma*. It is quite obvious that so long as one does not attain direct pure conscious attentiveness (*shuddha upayoga*), one has to depend on the *vyavahara* of the nature of auspicious (*shubha*) activity.

In Niyamsara (NS)

Although karmic bondage is caused by both *punya* and *papa*, there is a great deal of difference between the two in many respects. In *Niyamsara*, self-restraint of the mind (*manogupti*) is described as avoiding impurities of attachment, aversion, etc. inauspicious (*ashubha*) dispositions (NS 66).. *Vyavahara* (external, other-referential) conduct is said to consist of five vows (*vrata*), including non-voilence, five carefulness or self-regulations (*samiti*), and the three self-restraints (of mind, speech and body) (*gupti*) (NS 56-70). They constitute practice of austerities from the *vyavahara* point of view (NS 55) and part of enlightened conduct. This signifies that good or virtuous psychic dispositions and activities are helpful and supportive factors in the purification of the self (*atma shuddhi*).

Shubha activity of the nature of virtuous (*punyamaya*) *vyavahara dharma* (righteousness) is a factor in the influx and consequent bondage of *karma*, However, at the same time, the abstaining or refraining from inauspicious activity of the nature of evil (*papamaya*) that takes place is to that extent leads to inhibition or restraint (*samvara*) and destruction or dissociation (*nirjara*) of *karmas*. Thus, *shubha* or *punya* has a dual role.

According to *Niyamsara*, one should abstain from unwholesome activities (*ashubha bhavna parihar*) (NS 66), which are said to be sinful or defiled, deluded, instinctive or impulsive behaviour, imbued with feelings of attachment and aversion, etc. (NS 66); engage in wholesome (*shubha*) thoughts and practice moral rules of self-restraint, thereby observing *vyavahara* conduct of righteousness (NS 55); and endeavour to purify one's thought activities through self-disciplinary methods of repentance, etc. (*nishchaya* conduct) so as to completely eradicate passions (NS 77-158).

The three maxims mentioned above can be summed up in one sentence: "Avoid doing of all evil, practice moral conduct of righteousness and accomplish purity of one's own psychic dispositions."

In Samayasara

In order to realize the supreme state of pure consciousness free from *karmas*, one has to transcend not only *ashubha* but also *shubha*, because attachment to *shubha* also causes bondage of *karmas*, which leads to mundane wanderings and is destructive of independence of the soul (SS 145, 147 and 154). *Punya* is also a hindrance in the attainment of liberation (*Nishithachurni*, 3329).

It was in that context that Kundakunda asserted that both a gold as well as an iron fetter binds a person just as both *shubha* (wholesome) and *ashubha* (unwholesome) bind the *jiva* (self) (SS 146). *Rishibhashitani* (45/5) also states that bondage, whether of a golden or of an iron fetter, is bondage, which is the cause of misery or suffering. The pain caused by a golden stick is also pain. Therefore, one should not be attached to them (SS 147) for an attached person binds *karmas* (PS 179, SS 167).

In *shubha upayoga*, the self is able to find and tread the proper path (of liberation), but in *ashubha upayoga* there is no possibility thereof. In his commentary on *Samaysara* verse 145, Amrtachandra points out that *shubha* differs from *ashubha* on four grounds, i.e. in its nature (*svabhava*), cause (*karana*), effect (experience or *anubhava* of fruition of *karma*) and in substratum (*ashraya*), i.e. being supportive of the path of liberation. He has also specifically stated that while *shubha* (*punya*) is the path of liberation (*moksha marg*), *ashubha* (*papa*) is the way to karmic bondage (*bandha marg*) (*shubhashubhau moksha bandha margau*) (SS 145 AC). So long as one does not attain pure conscious attentiveness (*shuddha upayoga*), one has to depend on *vyavahara* conduct of the nature of auspicious (*shubha*) activity.

A proper understanding of *Pravachanasara* 151, 191 and 194 and *Samayasara* 188, 189 and 206, advises one to practice meditation (*dhyana*) in order to destroy deluded view and attain the best or the highest happiness in life. However, this does not necessarily negate auspicious (*shubha*) or commendable attachment (*prashasta raga*), which leads to righteous or virtuous meditation (*dharma dhyana*, also called *prashasta dhyana*), as compared to inauspicious (*ashubha*) thoughts which lead to mournful (*arta*) and cruel (*raudra*) inauspicious meditation (*aprashasta dhyana*).

Similar to inauspicious (*ashubha*) or detestable, unwholesome (*aprashasta*) meditations and auspicious (*shubha*) or righteousness, commendable (*prashasta*) meditations are (*aprashasta*) and (*prashasta*) thought paints or emotional tints (*leshya*). The (*aprashasta*) or sinful (*papa rupa*), i.e. *adharma leshyas* are: (1) black *leshya*, which is characterized by wrathful, hostile or pugnacious temperaments, wicked, i.e. devoid of piety and compassion, engrossed in sense objects, pride, etc; (2) blue *leshya*, which signifies envious and deceitful, passionate behaviour, having intense desire for worldly riches, etc; and (3) grey (*kapot*) *leshya*, characterized by angry thoughts, a deluded view, sorrow, fear and envy and is not straightforward.

The *prashasta* (*shubha*) or righteous (*dharma*) *leshyas* are: (1) yellow (*tejo*) *leshya*, characterized by an understanding or discerning knowledge as to what is fit or unfit to do, humility, straightforwardness, and practice of compassion and charity, etc., righteousness or virtuous activities, (2) pink (*padma*) *leshya* comprising of detachment, forebearance, dispassionate conduct, etc.; and (3) white (*shukla*) *leshya*, characterized by self-restraint (*gupti*) of mind, speech and body, equanimity, etc. According to *Uttaradhayana* (34/32), a person endowed with *shukla leshya* can be both with attachment [excellent attachment] or without attachment (*veetraga*).

Shubha and *Ashubha* in *Panchastikayasara* (PKS)

The psychic states or psychological conditions determining auspicious (*shubha*) or righteousness (virtue, *punya*) and inauspicious (*ashubha*) or vice (evil, sin, *papa*) are described in *Panchastikayasara* (PKS) verses 131, 132 and 135-140. These verses clearly state that whenever a *jiva* is endowed with the mental states of a deluded view (*moha*), which clouds one's faculty of perception and conviction, attachment (*raga*) and aversion (*dvesh*), which distorts the conative, conscious will or volitional (conduct) faculty of consciousness, then they manifest in a mental state characterized by inauspicious, sinful, undesirable, bad thought activities (*ashubha parinama*). However, the restraint and subsidence of psychic dispositions like attachment, etc. results in peace and happiness of the psyche (*chitta prasad*). This, in turn, manifests in a desirable, good, virtuous and auspicious mental state (*shubha parinama*) (PKS 131).

Describing the subjective states of good (*shubha* or *punya*) and evil (sinful, i.e. *ashubha* or *papa*), *Panchastikayasara* (verse 132) states that good or auspicious (*shubha*) thought activity, state or condition (*parinama*) is righteousness (*punya*), while evil or inauspicious (*ashubha*) thought activity is sin (*papa*).

In *Panchastikayasara* (verses 135-140), Kundakunda makes a clear-cut distinction between *shubha* and *ashubha* while describing the components of *punya* or *shubha parinama* (wholesome psychic dispositions, inclined or oriented towards righteousness) and *papa* (evil thoughts and sinful activities). The constituent elements of *punya*, he states, are (a) *prashasta raga* (commendable or excellent attachment, noble thoughts and aspirations) (PKS 135), such as reverence of perfect souls, devotion to *dharma* (piety or righteousness), self-restraint and observance of rules of moral conduct in life [PKS 136 and PKS 136 AC]; (b) *anukampa* (compassion), i.e. feeling of goodwill and sympathy at the sight of needy and the sufferers and the offering of charity or active relief to the thirsty, the hungry and the miserable; and (c) *akalushata*, i.e. freedom from evil impulses and passions (anger, pride, deceit and greed or covetousness) (PKS 135), which constitute the impurity of the soul (PKS 135-138). The subsidence or abatement of anger, etc. passions, signifies purification (*vishuddhi*) (PS 180 AC).

The three auspicious or good (*shubha*) psychic dispositions or mental states (*bhava*) are commendable attachment (*prashasta raga*), feeling of compassion (*anukampa*) and in whose mind there are no evil impulses or passions (*akalushata*) (PKS 135 AC). *Kalushata* (impurity) is said to be coming into operation or appearance in mind of *jiva* (self) of the intense (*teevra udaya* or rise) of anger, pride, deceit and covetousness or greed, etc. passions, which create a severe mental disturbance (*chittasya kshobha*) affecting the calmness/peace and balance of mind. The abatement (less intensity or *manda udaya*) of those passions is one of the necessary conditions of *shubha* (righteousness or good). One can have auspicious *shubha* or righteous dispositions only when there is calmness of mind (*prasham bhava*) due to subsidence (*upasham*) of passions resulting in calmness of mind, which is also purity or *akalushta* (PKS 138 AC).

The necessary prerequisites of *samyak darshan* (enlightened view) are *prashasta raga* (which is equivalent of *samvega*, i.e. psychic energy geared or disposed towards righteousness), *anukampa*, and *akalushata* (i.e. subjective purity arising out of subsidence of passions, which is equivalent or synonymous of *prasham*). *Samyak darshan* is considered to be the foundation of *dharma* (*dansan mulo dhammo*) and the necessary first step in the direction of salvation. Without it neither knowledge nor conduct can be *samyak* (enlightened). Kundakunda could not possibly condemn these constituent elements of *punya* (*shubha*) and prerequisites of *samyak darshan* by equating them with *papa* (evil) or *ashubha* (unwholesome thoughts). While *ashubha* results in sinful thoughts and activities, *shubha* is helpful in righteousness.

Panchastikayasara describes the springs of evil (*papasrava*) as *pramadcharya* (negligent acts, thoughtless behaviour, including unnecessary, useless, time-wasting gossiping); negative and impure emotions (*kalushata*) like anger; hankering for and indulging in sensual pleasures, causing anguish or harm to fellow beings; slandering people openly or covertly; the animal instincts or instinctive impulses and sub-conscious motivations; the soul-soiling emotional tints (*leshya*), yielding to the temptations of the senses; mournful (*arta*) and cruel (*raudra*) *dhyana* (concentration or meditation), which are said to be *ashubha* or *aprashasta* (inauspicious, distorted and perverted) *dhyana*; evil thoughts and delusion which corrupts the faculties of intuition and will. On the other hand, *shubha* (auspicious) or *prashasta* (commendable or excellent) psychic dispositions or thoughts lead to righteous or virtuous meditation (*dharma dhyana*), which is the necessary concomitant (*avinabhavi*) of enlightened view (PKS 139-140 and 139-140 AC).

Commenting on the *Panchastikayasara* Verse 171, Jayasena observes that one who considers pure self to be worth acquiring and for that matter undertakes vows like non-violence and austerities, etc. and has a psychic disposition free from the desire for future sense pleasures, is the person endowed with an enlightened view. Such a person binds good or meritorious *karma* (*punya bandha*) in the present transmigratory existence due to one's inability to continue to stay in the state of pure self. However, in the next transmigratory existences that person necessarily attains liberation by remaining stable in the contemplation of the supreme reality of self (PKS 171 JS).

In his comment on the next verse, Jayasena states that those who believe in *vyavahara mokhsa-marg* (path of liberation) as a means to the *mokhsa-marg* leading to pure self and are persons of enlightened view due to having enlightenment with attachment and the practice of observing charity, etc. also customarily (*parampara se*) attain liberation (PKS 172 JS).

Shubha and *Ashubha* in other Jain Texts

In Jai Dhavala

Acharya Virasena, in his *Jai Dhavala* (Book 1, p. 5) commentary on *Kashaya-Prabhrata* (*Kashaya-Pahuda*), one of the most authentic Jain texts of Digambaras, has acknowledged the possibility of both *samvara* (inhibitation of influx of *karma*) and *nirjara* (eradicating of *karmas*) by stating that "if eradication of *karmas* is not considered possible by *shubha* and *shuddha* (pure) psychic disposition (*parinama*), then eradication of *karmas* will not be possible at all". In other words, while complete absence or freedom from passions may be said to be pure (*shuddha*), *shubha* is partial purity (*shuddhata*) or purification (*vishuddhi*) (PS 180 AC) of thoughts, i.e. the means (*sadhan*) of purity or the path of liberation (PS 254 AC). The bondage of *punya karma* is not the only consequence of *shubha. Shubha* also leads to the inhibition (*samvara*) and dissociation (*nirjara*) of sinful (*papa*) *karma.* It also results in a gradual yet continuously higher purification of the self (*atma-vishuddhi*). Without first having *shubha* (auspicious) psychic dispocition, one cannot have pure thoughts, which are the most important means of *samvara, nirjara* and *moksha,* i.e. the imhibition, dissociation and complete annihilation of karma. This is the conclusion reached in *Jai Dhavala.*

In Adipurana

In *Adipurana,* Acharya Jinasena writes that as a result of *punya,* one gets or obtains the status of *Tirthankara* and salvation. Without the particular method or way of first having *shubha* psychic disposition (*parinama*), it is not possible to attain pure *parinama* in one go (*Jai Dhavala,* Book 14, p. 155). This description is not meant for ordinary people, but for those great noble souls, who are likely to attain salvation in the same birth by destroying the conduct-deluding *karmas,* thereby advancing fast in spiritual development through the destructive ladder (*kshapak shreni*).

In Jai Dhavala

In his commentary on *Jai Dhavala,* Acharya Yativrashabha remarks: "The *parinama* is purified in the case of *jiva* who is starting to destroy conduct-deluding karmas. In this way, this aphorism signifies that more and more *shubha* and *shuddha* (pure) *parinama* is possible only by the destruction of *ashubha parinama.* This has happened through the infinite times purification (*vishuddhi*) from the lower thought activity (*adhah pravrtakarana*)," or the lowest vile stage (*jaghanya parinama*) (SS 171).

Explaining this further, Kanaknandi remarks:

Since *shubha parinama* is the cause of *shuddha* (pure) *parinama*, there cannot be *shuddha parinama* without *shubha parinama*, because without the cause the accomplishment of the task is not possible in the three times in the three worlds. In the preliminary stages, therefore, *shubha parinama* is considered desirable (*upadeya*), not worth-abandoing (*heya*) for the practitioner or the aspirant (*sadhak*) of the path of liberation. . . . *Shubha parinama* is not only the cause of *shuddha parinama*, but it is also the cause of inhibition (*samvara*) and dissociation or falling off (*nirjara*) of *karmas*. Moreover, the destruction of *karmas* cannot take place without *shubha* and *shuddha parinama*.[39]

The purport (*abhipraya*) that is sought to be conveyed by the words "*suha-suddha parinamehi*" is that abstaining or refraining from evil and inauspicious (*ashubha*) activities involved or implied in good, virtuous (*punya*) or auspicious (*shubha*) activities leads to or results in the inhibition (*samvara* or *nirodha*) and destruction or dissociation (*nirjara*) of *karmas*, i.e. purification of the self. Moreover, in the empirical existence, the destruction of the intensity or fruition (*anubhaga*) of commendable (*prashasta*) *karmas* does not take place. On the contrary, the destruction of the intensity or fruition of only *aprashasta karmas*, i.e. those karmas which are not commendable or excellent, takes place and considered useful (*Jai Dhavala*, Book 14, p. 153).

In Tattvartha Sutra (TS)

In *Tattvarthasara* (verses 103-104 of Chapter IV), Amrtachandra states that *punya* (righteousness or meritorious act) and *papa* (sinful act or demerit) are different from one another in both cause (*hetu*) as well as effect (*karya*), even though both are the source of transmigration. The cause of *punya* is auspicious thought activity (*shubha bhava*). Its effect is calmness and peace of mind, happiness or joy, while the cause of *papa* is unwholesome or inauspicious thought activity (*ashubha bhava*) and its effect is misery.

In *Tattvartha Sutra* (TS 6.3), *asrava* is said to be of two kinds: (1) *shubha* (good or auspicious) is the cause of *punya* (righteousness, piety or virtue), while (2) *ashubha* (evil or inauspicious) is the cause of *papa* (sin). In this context, (TS 6.3), Acharya Pujyapada remarks:

> Violence, stealing incontinence, etc. are negative, evil activities of the body. Falsehood, harsh and uncivil language, etc. are the evil activities of speech.

> Thoughts of violence, envy, calumny, etc. are evil activities of the mind. The good activities are counter to these . . . . the good or evil nature of an activity depends on the good or evil intention of the person. Although good or virtuous activities are the cause of *punya*, i.e. beneficial *karma*, they are also admitted to be cause of bondage of knowledge-obscuring etc. *karmas*. That which purifies the soul or by which the soul is purified is *punya*. [In this way, *punya* is considered a supportive factor in spiritual awakening and development (*sadhana*)]. The general effect of good activity is happiness and that of evil activity is pain.[40]

In his *Sarvarthasiddhi* commentary on *Tattvartha Sutra* (TS 7.1 and TS 6.12), Pujyapada stresses that self-restraint (*samyam*), i.e. to restrain oneself from evil, undesirable, inauspicious (*ashubha*) activities of injury, etc. and observance of vows like non-violence, truthfulness, etc. is considered as morality, virtuous activities (*punya*), or righteousness and piety (*dharma*). Five of the ten moral virtues (*dharma*) (TS 9.6) are only positive aspects of five moral rules (vows) of conduct like non-violence, etc. and are described to be one of the ways of inhibiting (*samvara*) of karmic inflow (TS 9.2, 9.3). According to *Pravachanasara* this is the necessary concomitant of partial purification (*vishuddhi*) (PS 155 AC and 180 AC), partly because it signifies desisting or abstaining from evil, vicious (*papa*) activities. The five moral rules are said to have a paradoxical dual nature and are instrumental in inhibiting the influx of *karma* when practiced with detachment and without any vestige of passion. They also generate karmic influx of beneficial (pleasure producing) *karma* when practiced with attachment (*sarag samyam*) as being compassionate towards living beings in general in the worldly sense.

Punya and *papa* are considered significant concepts and separate categories in *Samayasara*. In fact, no verse in the *asrava* chapter of *Samayasara* makes any reference to *punya* or *papa* as being part of *asrava* (influx of *karmas*) since *punya* is not merely the cause of influx and consequent bondage of *karmas*. *Punya* has a dual role in fostering karmic bondage as well as having a purifying effect (*visuddhi*) (PS 180 AC) and gradually leading to liberation (PS 254 AC).

In Tattvartha Rajvarttika (TRV)

Presenting the logical exposition of *punya* and *papa*, Akalanka Deva further explains it as follows:

It is said that just as fetters of both gold and iron have the effect of binding a person, thereby making him dependent, so also both *punya* and *papa* are the condition (*hetu*) or the auxiliary (*nimitta*) cause (*karana*) in making the self dependent. Thus, there appears nothing special between the two, yet there is difference between them due to one (*punya*) being the *nimitta* of desirable or favourable (*ishta*) effect (*phala*) and the other (*papa*) of undesirable or harmful effect (*anishta phala*). That which is the condition (*hetu*) of desirable or favourable condition of existence (*gati*), genus, caste or class of being (*jati*), body (*sharira*), the objects of senses (*indriya vishaya*) is *punya*. And that which is the *hetu* of undesirable *gati, jati,* body and the objects of senses is *papa*. Thus, there is difference between *punya* and *papa*.[41]

As a result of *punya*, one is endowed with thirteen qualities including prosperity, health, family and friends, devotion to triple jewels of enlightened view, knowledge and conduct, control of senses, etc.[42] Thus, *punya* is desirable not only for the success in the worldly life but also for the attainment of liberation. In this context, Vidyananda remarks: "The attainment of liberation also (*api*) is possible by the supremely excellent *punya* and the effort (*purushartha*) for distinctive conduct pertaining to enlightened view, knowledge and conduct." (Akalanka's *Ashta-shati* commentary on Samantabhadra, *Apta-Mimansa*, p. 257.)

Shubha (*punya*) has a double or two-fold role: it has binding effect and for that reason considered undesirable from the perspective of *shuddha* (pure), which is the direct cause of liberation, and to be given up. At the same time, it plays a significant role in getting rid of the impurity of evil (*ashubha* or *papa*) and has purifying (*vishuddhi*) effect (PS 155, 180 AC), and as such regarded a helpful factor in the liberation of soul, in the same way as soap is helpful in cleaning the dirt of the cloth. And just as, for the whiteness of the cloth the presence of soap is unnecessary and is also to be removed or separated, so also in the pure state, *punya* is unnecessary and is also to be given up. But as the soap cleans the dirt and, after cleaning the dirt, gets itself separated, in the same way *punya* also is helpful in getting rid of the dirt of the impurity of evil (*papa*) and after *papa* is gotten rid of and purity is realized, *punya* itself is also given up.

Explaining the role and contribution of *shubha*, Akalanka Deva further points out:

It is not our conception or idea that *shubha* is the cause of only *punya*, but *punya* is [definitely] caused by *shubha* alone (*eva*). Hence, it is not denied that *shubha* can be the condition (*hetu*) of *papa* (sin) [or *ashubha*], since good or auspicious activities are also admitted to be cause of bondage of knowledge-obscuring etc. *karmas*. . . . Intensity of bondage is primary (*pradhan bhuta*); it is the auxiliary (*nimitta*) cause of pleasure and pain. The superior purifying (*vishuddha*) disposition (*parinama*) is the *nimitta* of all the excellent or superior (*utkrashta*) intensity of bondage of the nature or class (*prakrti*) of *shubha*. Likewise, the most severe disposition imbued with affliction, distress or morbidity (*sankless*) is the *nimitta* (auxiliary cause) of the most intense bondage of all the *ashubha* class of *karmas*. Although excellent *shubha parinama* is also the condition of the low or the minimal (*jaghanya*) intensity of bondage of the *ashubha* class of *karma*, yet *shubha* is considered to be the cause or the condition (*hetu*) of *punya* (beneficial karma). This is because even if one might incur the minimal, slight or little bit of harm, affront, disservice, or misconduct (*apakara*), it produces or results in a great deal or vast amount of beneficence or beneficial effect (*upakara*) and, therefore, it is considered to be beneficial (TRV commentary on TS 6.3).

Similarly one should understand the aphorism: "Evil, inauspicious or unwholesome (*ashubha*) actions cause harmful or sinful (*papa*) karma" [TS 6.3]. It is said: "By purification (*vishuddhi*), the excellent intensity of the *shubha* class of bondage takes place, while by distressful or afflicting (*sanklesh*) dispositions *ashubha* class of bondage takes place. The sequence (*krama*) of low or minimal (*jaghanya*) intensity of bondage is reverse of that, i.e. by *vishuddhi* the *jaghanya* bondage of *ashubha karma* and by *sanklesh* the *jaghanya* bondage of *shubha karma* (*Panchsangraha* 4/445, cited by Akalanka in his TRV commentary on TS 6.3).[43]

Shubha yoga (the joining of *jiva* with auspicious vibratory activities, which is the condition of righteousness), according to Vidyananda, is the outcome of *shubha* dispositions (*parinamas*) such as the disposition of non-violence, speaking of truth, respect of scriptures and contemplation of consciousness (*atma chintan*), etc.[44] It is of the nature of vibration in the space-points of consciousness (*atma*), engrossed in or devoted to, as also well disposed towards an enlightened view, sex fidelity, speaking beneficial words, inclination or liking for austerities (*taporuchi*), etc., because it is part of purification (*vishuddhi*). In other words, *shubha yoga* is the cause of purification. It is the deed or action (*karya*) of *vishuddhi*, being the outcome of previous *vishuddhi*. It is in itself of the nature of purification of soul (*atma vishuddhi*). The case of *ashubha yoga* is the antithesis of all that since it is engrossed in a deluded view, etc. and is the cause, the outcome, and is in itself of the nature of affliction, misery, distress and morbidity (*sanklesh*).[45]

In Apta Mimamsa (AM)

The spiritual content and the influx of *karmas* and the consequent bondage of *punya* and *papa* is not determined by the hedonic aspects of pleasure and pain caused to others (AM 92) or the self (AM 93). All this depends on whether pleasure and pain are part of purification (*vishuddhi*) or affliction or morbidity (*sanklesh*) (AM 95). This state of affairs, as Akalanka's commentary clarifies, is known or understood by the existence or the absence of concentrations or meditations (*dhyana*) of affliction, sorrow or mournful (*arta*) and cruel or wrathful (*raudra*) characterized by inclination or tendency towards violence, falsehood, stealing, and safeguarding possessions or objects of sensual gratification.

Thus, if it is maintained that sin is necessarily accumulated as a result of causing pain to others while virtue is the result of causing pleasure to others, then even an inanimate entity or a person who is free from passions like anger, pride, greed, etc. should possibly suffer bondage inasmuch as both can somehow be a supportive or an auxiliary factor (*nimitta*) in causing pain and pleasure to others (AM 92). Inanimate objects like milk and butter are the cause of happiness to others, whereas poison and weapons result in causing pain or harm (even killing) to others. Similarly, dispassionate enlightened souls become a supportive factor in causing unhappiness to the relatives of the person who is being initiated in asceticism. At the same time, they impart happiness to disciples through their lectures.

If it is maintained that virtue is necessarily accumulated as a result of causing pain to oneself while sin is the result of causing pleasure to oneself, then even a conscious entity (e.g. a sage or a noble person who is free from attachment) can possibly acquire a stock of sins/virtues inasmuch as even such a person can be a supportive factor in causing some kind of unhappiness/happiness to himself in certain situations (AM 93). A detached person who practices austerities often causes pain to his body and experiences happiness from the contentment and equanimity derived from his understanding of the reality of things. If these are considered to cause bondage to a person, then one would not be able to attain liberation.

It may, therefore, be stated that the influx (*asrava*) of meritorious or virtuous and demeritorious/sinful genre of *karmas* through pleasures or pain caused to others or to oneself, is contingent upon if such acts performed are part of purification (*vishuddhi*) or affliction/morbidity (*sanklesha*). In the absence of purification or afflication, those acts will remain ineffective insofar as the influx of *punya* or *papa* is concerned (AM 95).

Ashtashati commentary of Akalanka (on AM 95) clarifies the nature of *sanklesha* and what is *vishuddhi* as follows:

> The psychic states, modes or forms of concentration of anguish, affliction, pain, sorrow (*arta dhyana*) or of cruel, wrathful concentration (*raudra dhyana*) are *sanklesha*, while *vishuddhi* is the absence thereof signifying auspicious (*shubha*) or meritorious or virtuous (*punya*) psychic states leading to purification and spiritual development, which takes place by the virtuous or righteousness concentration (*dharma dhyana*) and pure concentration (*shukla dhyana*).

Thus, it is quite evident that the virtuous or sinful character of an act does not depend on how it externally affects the persons involved (qua 'agent' or 'qua' 'other') in this act but on whether it has been performed with bad, evil or good, righteous intentions.[46] Moreover, *vishuddhi* is described as the stage of being situated in one's own consciousness (*svatman avasthanam*). In other words, when *punya* achieves *vishuddhi*, it fosters spiritual progress whereas sinful or *papa* leading to *sanklesh* is conducive to the downfall of the soul. Therefore, righteousness (*punya*) is said to be excellent/commendable (*prashasta*) and sin (*papa*) is not considered to be excellent/commendabie.[47] *Shubha,* Vidyananda opines, is the condition (*hetu*) of the objective (*sadhya*) of purity of the self, with which it has necessarily concomitant (*avinabhava*).[48]

In his commentary on *Apta Mimansa* (AM 95), Akalanka has defined (*sanklesh*) as the result, effect or the state (*parinama*) of mournful, distressful (*arta*), and cruel or wrathful (*raudra*) concentration (*dhyana*), and *vishuddhi* as the absence thereof. Waiting in the shade is preferable to standing in the heat of the sun (*Mokshapahuda* 25 and Pujyaypada, *Ishtopadesh,* 3).

Thus, *shubha* is definitely better than *ashubha.* Unlike *shubha* and *ashubha, shuddha* and *shubha* are not dichotomous. While *shubha* is the opposite of *ashubha, shubha* is said to be dovetailed into and transcended in *shuddha*. However, there seems to be an apparent contradiction between *shubha* and *shuddha*, which is succinctly summed up by Voltaire as: "The best is the enemy of good."[49] This is a perfectionist attitude. The reality, however, is that the good (*shubha*), which has a purifying effect (*vishuddhi*) (PS 180 AC) and is partial purity (*shuddhata*), is continuously purified (*vishuddha*) until it becomes pure (*shuddha*).

In Mulachara

In *Mulachara* (234) it is stated that *punya* (merit) is the state of evolution of the self through an enlightened view (*sammatta* in Pk. and *samyaktva* in Sk.), knowledge of the scriptures and restraint/ subsidence (*nigraha*) of passions. Its opposite is evil (*papa*). Compassion (*anukampa*) and pure conscious attentiveness (*shuddha upayoga*) are said to depend upon or considered to be the result of meritorious *karmas* whereas evil *karmas* have the opposite effect (*Mulachara* 235).

Under no circumstances does Kundakunda equate *ashubha* (unwholesome) thought activities with *shubha* (wholesome) *bhavas* like compassion, amity, goodwill, etc. which are the outcome of subsidence of passions. In Kundkunda's schema, *shubha* is hierarchically integrated with *shuddha* (pure *bhavas*). The higher *shuddha* does not spurn and repudiate "the lower" *shubha*. To talk of *shuddha* repudiating *shubha* is false dichotomizing. *Shuddha*, in fact, is not only built upon and rests upon *shubha*, but encompasses *shubha*.

In Dravya Sangraha (DS)

In *Dravya Sangraha* (verse 45), good or auspicious (*shubha*) activity is described as restraint from evil, harmful/inauspicious (*ashubha*) tendencies. *Vyavahara charitra* (conduct) is said to consist of vows, carefulness or self-regulations and self-restraints of mind, speech and body.

Punya (merit) is helpful in liberation, while *papa* (sin) is an obstacle in liberation. Hence, conduct (*charitra*) is described as refraining from what is harmful (*ashubha*) and engagement in what is beneficial (*shubha*) (DS 45).

That which binds the self (*atma*) or leads to its downfall is evil or sin (*papa*) (*Uttaradhyayana churni* 2). Like poison, evil or sin (*papa*) is not beneficial to *jiva* (the self) (*Maransamadhi* 613). According to Hemchandra, *punya* is indicative of feebleness of inauspicious (*ashubha*) *karmas* and the onset of a commendable/excellent (*prashasta*) state, which is the result of the coming into operation/ rise (*udaya*) of *shubha karmas.*

Dual Role of *Shubha*

Shubha performs a dual role. Since as a result of good/auspicious psychic dispositions (*shubha bhava*), delusion, passions, etc. become feeble/mild, the bondage of *karmas* is also somewhat reduced. As a result, one is able to practice moral rules of self-restraint. *Shubha* has a purifying effect (*vishuddhi*), which acts as the means (*sadhan*) of liberation. Since a certain degree of attachment persists, even if it is commendable (*prashasta raga*), it also results in the bondage of good or meritorious *karmas.*

Subsidence/feebleness or abatement of intense passions is the necessary precondition of undertaking *shubha* (auspicious) vows and moral self-restraints, righteous/virtuous (*punya*) activities, and spiritual self-discipline. It is only when passions like deluded view, attachment, aversion, anger, etc. subside and one is inclined to moral rules/valules like non-violence, that one develops a clearer perspective of the nature of things, especially the nature of the self and the non-self as well as the relation between the soul and *karma,* their nexus and interaction. It is only then that one comprehends the difference between *papa* and *punya,* including the dual role of *punya* in causing karmic bondage as well as inhibition and dissociation of *karmas.* This, in turn, has a purifying (*vishuddhi*) effect (PS 155 and 180 AC) which eventually leads to liberation (PS 259 and 260 AC). It also enables one to develop a clear understanding of *asrava* (influx of *karmas*), etc. and other categories/principles of one's journey in life.

The subsidence of delusion, passions, etc. enables the self to be aware of the eventual goal and the direction/capacity/potential of the soul to realize the objective of liberation. In this regard, it is significant to remember that while everyone is striving in their own way for the realization of the ultimate state of emancipation, the quest becomes a self-conscious effort only when a measure of purity has been achieved by the soul. The processes of the deluded *karman* [both view-deluding and conduct-deluding] play an important role in the making up of the worldly existence. It is only subsidence (*upashaman*) of this *karman* that gives the soul a glimpse of the reality of the nature of things. This process leads to spiritual awakening or an enlightened world-view (*samyak darshan*). It is also a definitive self-conscious predilection which illumines the spiritual journey leading to the ultimate goal. The process of 'subsidence,' thus, occupies a very important place in the spiritual thinking of the Jainas.[50]

In the case of *ashubha bhavas* (inauspicous thought activities), on the other hand, the delusion, passions, etc. become intense and therefore the bondage of *karmas* is also enhanced. Observance of moral rules of self-restraint (vows, etc.) is more desirable than indulging in "unrestrained conduct". By the arousal of *ashubha karmas*, the self becomes a rogue, an animal or inhabitant of hell and is always beset with thousands of pains (PS 12, see also PS 158), while the result of good and meritorious *karmas* is good human birth or heavenly happiness (PS 11).

Mokshamarg Prakashak (MMP)

Pandit Todarmal, a keen observer of spiritualism and quite conversant with Kundakunda's works, has categorically stated that unlike *ashubha* (inauspicious) *upayoga*, *shubha upayoga* (conscious attentiveness) is not altogether/absolutely or on all counts, in all respects (*sarvatha*) worth abandoning or not to be adhered to (*heya*), thereby refuting the contention of those who seek to equate *shubha* and *ashubha*. He has adduced several reasons in that regard under the heading (*Shubhopayoga sarvatha heya nahin hai*). This heading has been omitted in Kanjipanthi (who hold Pandit Todarmal in high esteem and quote him quite often in support of their one-sided assertions) publications so as not to highlight its utility and significance.[51]

Todarmal observes that those persons who hold a deluded view because of misconceptions about *nishchaya naya* (internal self-referential viewpoint, i.e. *nishchayabhasi mithyadrasthi* (a characteristic that is applicable to Kanjipanthi], regard acts like worshipping, to be the cause of the influx of auspicious *karmas*. These *karmas*, he adds, should not be adhered to if in renouncing them one keeps onself engrossed in (*shuddha*) *upayoga*, i.e. pure conscious attentiveness. It is only in that condition/situation/circumstance, is it desirable/

beneficial to abandon them. However, if one indulges in inauspicious (*ashubha*) acts like sensual pleasures or passions, then one would only harm oneself.[52]

Aversion, Pandit Todarmal adds, results in the bondage of sins whereas non-violence, etc. excellent attachment (*prashasta raga*) leads to the bondage of merit or virtue (*punya*). Since both are the cause of bondage, both of them ought to be given up. The passionless state wherein one is free from attachment and aversion is a state where one remains a mere observer and knower (*drashta jnata*). This state is without any bondage and hence worth attaining (*upadeya*), However, until such a (passionless pure) state is achieved, one must engage in or continue to observe and follow the conduct of excellent attachment (*prashasta raga*), i.e. *shubha upayoga.*[53]

By *shubha upaygoa*, i.e. good or auspicious *upaygoa*, one may get a berth in heaven. One may even get an enlightened view of the reality of things by good intentions or it may be good auxiliary cause (*nimitta*) for the reduction of the duration and fruition of *karmas.* However, bad or inauspicious (*ashubha*) *upayoga* result in one getting a berth in hell or *nigoda*, etc. Bad intentions or being bad may be an auxiliary cause which increase the duration and fruition of *karmas.* As a result, the attainment of an enlightened view, etc. becomes extremely difficult.

Shubha upayoga enfeebles passions or makes them mild whereas *ashubha upayoga* makes passions more intense. Therefore,

> indulging in the acts of intense passions by giving up acts of mild passions is comparable to not eating bitter things but eating poison instead. This is utter ignorance or foolishness.[54]

In this regard, he (the *nishchayabhashi*) [Kanjipanthi] (adherent of a deluded view) mistakenly argues that *shubha* and *ashubha* are said to be alike in the scriptures (*shastras*). (This alludes to SS 146 and PS 77 and PS 77 AC in which they are described as golden and iron chains binding a person, i.e. being the cause of *karmic* bondage.) It is not, therefore, advisable to delve deeper into their special/particular characteristics. In his reply to this argument, Pandit Todarmal points out that for people, who consider *shubha upayoga* to be the cause of liberation (*moksha*) and consider it worthy of adoption (*upadeya*) and are not therefore able to recognize [the significance of] *shuddha* (pure) *upayoga, shubha* and *ashubha* are said to be similar from the point of view of impurity of karmic bondage. However, when a comparison is made between the two (*shubha* and *ashubha*) as between themselves (*paraspara*) then it becomes apparent that in case of good/auspicious (*shubha*) thoughts/mental states, passions tend to become feeble. This leads to a reduction of the bondage of *karmas*. In case of bad or inauspicious (*ashubha*) thoughts, passions become intense and thereby lead to an increase in the bondage of *karmas*. Thus, viewed from this perspective, the good or auspicious (*shubha*) is considered to be better than the bad or the inauspicious (*ashubha*) in Jaina scriptures and philosophy. For instance, the disease is only bad irrespective of whether it is less or more serious. However, in comparison to a more severe disease, a less severe disease is better.[55]

Therefore, so long as *shuddha upayoga* (state of pure conscious attentiveness) or passionless conduct is not attained, it is desirable to keep oneself engaged in *shubha* (auspicious thought activities or virtuous conduct) by getting rid of *ashubha* (inauspicious thought activities or vicious conduct). But it is not desirable to indulge onself in the *ashubha* (vicious conduct) by forsaking *shubha* (virtuous conduct).[56]

Again, he (the *nishchayabashi* adherent of a deluded view) argues that "The inauspicious tendency of satisfying the desire of lust or hunger, etc. cannot be avoided and one has to engage in inauspicious proclivity willfully; and he who holds enlightened view wants to avoid desires, therefore, making effort of *shubha* (pious conduct) is not desirable."[57]

In response, Pandit Todarmal stresses that engagement in good and auspicious (*shubha*) *upayoga* increases the sense of detachment. As a result, the intensity of sexual urge, etc. as well as the pain and restlessness caused by hunger, etc. is reduced. Hence, it is desirable to practice *shubha upayoga.*[58] In spite of making such effort, if lust and hunger, etc. still cause distress, then in order to satisfy those urges, one should be careful in committing less sin. However, indulgence in unrestrained behaviour in sinful acts by forsaking good and auspicious (*shubha*) *upayoga* is not at all desirable.[59]

Further, as for the (*nishchayabhasi*) argument that a person who has an enlightened view does not seek any desire while the practice of *shubha upayoga* requires willful effort, it may be said that

> though a person does not want to give even a little amount of his money yet wherever he feels that great amount of money is likely to be lost, he

> makes effort willfully to give some quantity of money. Similarly, one who holds enlightened view, does not want to engage himself even in an act involving slightest amount of passion but wherever he feels that inauspicious acts will results in intense passion, he willfully makes effort to engage himself in auspicious acts involving less passions.[60]

Thus, it is evident that wherever it is possible to attain to pure (*shuddha*) *upayoga* of a passionless state, the engagement/involvement in auspicious acts is not desirable. However, where there is a likelihood of inauspicious *upayoga*, one should make efforts to willfully engage oneself in auspicious *upayoga*. In this way, indulgence in unrestrained behaviour by forsaking all kinds of external, other-referential moral and other religious practices (*vyavahara dharma*) is declared to be undesirable and forbidden.[61]

While one should not exclusively lay emphasis on external practices or means (*bahya sadhanadi hi*) of *dharma*, it must be clearly understood that in comparison to indulgence in sinful acts, external moral and religious practices (*vyavahara dharma*), such as adoration (*bhakti*), donation (*dana*), fasting, etc. penance (*tapa*), vows/moral rules of conduct like non-violence, acts of worship and promotion of *dharma*, etc. and study of scriptures are not prohibited even though they cause bondage of *punya* (merit, virtue) or auspicious karmic bondage. One should not, however, remain satisfied by the mere observance of such *vyavahara* practices but continue to make efforts for the attainment of liberation.[62]

In brief, Pandit Todarmal comes to the conclusion that

> knowing attachment, etc. passions as bad and harmful, one must make efforts to uproot them. There *anukrmavishai* (step-by-step) [this is exactly the same as Amrtachandra's *kramtah*], i.e. gradually or step-by-step (PS, 254 AC)], first of all, one should give up inauspicious acts by forsaking intense passions, etc. and should engage oneself in auspicious acts. Thereafter, even by forsaking feeble passions, one should give up auspicious acts also and evolve to the dispassionate or passionless state of purity (*shuddhopayoga*).[63]

Good or auspicious thought activities or moral rules of self-restraint, which are accompanied by subsidence of passions, have a purifying effect (*vishuddhi*). They are a means of spiritual development and liberation. However, when good or auspicious (*shubha*) activities or righteousness (*dharma*) are practiced only for the sake of sensual pleasures (*bhoga nimittam*) (SS 275 and *Bhavapahuda* 182) or indulged in with passions like attachment or pride, etc., they result in bondage and misery. They do not lead to the destruction of *karmas*, i.e. liberation. Good deeds (*shubha karma*) are not to be performed for extraneous considerations, selfish ends or personal gain of name and fame in this world or to seek a berth in heaven, but as a means of purification of the self, keeping in view the final goal of liberation.

Kundakunda makes it abundantly clear that those who ignorantly or slavishly observe vows, restraints, etc. moral conduct or practice austerities (*tapas*) and yearn for *punya* (merit) in order to get a berth in heaven, attain miraculous powers or even *moksha* (salvation) in the next world do not know the transcendental (*paramartha*) nature of the real self (*parinamika bhava*). They act in violation of the true interests of the self, i.e. peace and excellent happiness (*uttam sukha*) (*paramartha bahira*). They neither know the rationale or cause of salvation (*moksha-hetu*) in the true sense nor are they able to attain *nirvana* (liberation) (SS 153-154).

In order to destroy the cause of conjunction of the soul with other substances (Amrtachandra's introductory remark to PS 159), viz. material or physical *karman* (*pudgala karman*), which act as an auxiliary cause of passions like attachment, aversion, and anger, etc. perverted, harmful, psychic dispositions, resulting in karmic bondage, what is required of the self is to get rid of evil psychic attention. It should not remain stuck in good conscious attentiveness but become established in the real nature of the self (*majjatth* in Pk., *madhyastha* in Sk.), meaning neutral or indifferent and meditate upon the self which is of the nature of something knowing (PS 159) and strive for the liberation of the soul.

Morality and Spirituality

In view of what has been stated in the preceding pages, a futile attempt is made by some people to pit morality against spirituality by obstinately equating *punya* and *papa* by relying solely on their bondage aspect, and denying the dual role of *punya*, including its significant role in purifying (*vishuddhi*) and liberation. Moral rules of conduct, which provide guidelines to man in leading his life in relation to others in the empirical world, cannot be divorced from the world of his inner thoughts and feelings.

True spirituality is only inner. However, it usually involves some outward expression and manifests itself in moral conduct. The spiritual goal of self-realization or inner purity cannot be achieved by immoral means of *himsa* (violence), untruth, etc. Thus, the internal and external aspects of spirituality and morality are inter-related, inter-connected and inter-dependent. Morality without spirituality is meaningnless, and spirituality without morality is spirituality only in name. Morality and spirituality or *vyavahara* and *nishchaya charitra* is not an either/or situation. They are intimately related to one another and can neither be considered as mutually exclusive nor compartmentalized into watertight compartments.

A spiritual culture is inconceivable without an ethical culture. Morality goes hand-in-hand and coexists with spirituality. In fact, the two are inseparable. They are also interdependent in the sense that spirituality helps morality. In turn, morality facilitates/fosters the attainment of the spiritual goal of self-conquest or the eradication of evil tendencies and impurities of the self. Thus, in Jainism, spirituality is the essence of morality and morality is intertwined with spirituality.

Spirituality and morality are not identical but they are not separate as they are the internal and external aspects or the obverse and reverse sides of the same conscious entity or the self. Spiritual goals can only be realized by the pursuit of a life of morality, which is the pursuit of righteousness and piety. Spirituality is concerned with internal purity and individual perfection, which is unthinkable without morality. Moral self-restraints are necessary for attaining freedom from instinctive impulses and subconscious motivations.

Thus, morality and spirituality are closely related and complementary to one another. Spirituality is the foundation and the basis of morality and morality is its natural offspring and manifestation. In the absence of spirituality, morality would be deprived if its moorings. Without morality, spirituality will degenerate into "mere experiential" mysticism or an intellectual exercise devoid of either content or result.

Overall Appraisal of *Shubha*

Shubha (good) psychic-attention (*upayoga*) is regarded as auspicious (*mangala*) causing well-being and fostering merit, virtue, or righteousness (*punya*). It plays an important role in our life. It is therefore regarded as desirable thing worth-acquiring (*upadeya*) in all religions of the world. On the other hand, evil or vicious (*ashubha*) *upayoga* is considered inauspicious, undesirable and worth abandoning (*heya*). When good (*shubha* or *punya*) karma becomes operational, one gets worldly prosperity, good health, manifold sensual pleasures, including those of heaven, etc. (PS 70, PS 11). If *shubha* or the excellent attachment (*prashasta raga*) is oriented towards sanity and purification (*vishuddhi*) (PS 155, 180 AC), it gradually (*kramtah*) leads to liberation (PS 254, 259-260). However, with the rise (*udaya*) of the evil (*ashubha*) *karma*, the self becomes a rogue, an animal or inhabitant of hell. It is always plagued by thousands of pains, and strays incessantly (PS 12).

After transcending the stage of *ashubha* (evil) *upayoga*, the self ascends the stage of *shubha upayoga*, and thereby embraces the love of righteousness (*dharma anuraga*), which manifests in respect for the worthy Lord and the enlightened souls like teachers (*guru*) and saints as well as virtues like charity, moral precepts/moral conduct of self-restraints of non-violence, etc. (PS 69 and PS 69 AC) and compassion towards living beings (PS 157), etc. *Ashubha upayoga*, on the other hand, consists of infatuation, both view-deluding (i.e. infatuation) and conduct-deluding (i.e. attachment and aversion). It is inclined towards perverse ways. It is engrossed in sense-gratification (*vishaya*), and passions (*kashaya*), practicing passionate bad thoughts, bad hearing, bad intention, bad companionship and violence (PS 158 and PS 158 AC).

Explaining *shubha* and *ashubha* attachment in *Pravachanasara*, Jayasena states: "Devotion of the five revered souls (*panch parameshthi*), etc. is *shubha* attachment [i.e. commendable or excellent attachment, *prashasta raga*], while attachment to sense objects (*vishaya*) and anger, etc. passions (*kashaya*) is *ashubha* attachment" (PS 180 JS), [i.e. worth abandoning or not praiseworthy and not excellent attachment, i.e. *aprashasta raga*.

In *Samayasara,* it is also stated that for people, who are at a lower stage of spiritual development, the *vyavahara* path of *shubha* (good, auspicious) is useful, desirable and worth adopting (*prayojanavana*) in order to inhibit or restrain passions like delusion, gratification of sense objects, anger, etc. and evil concentration (SS 12 JS).

Kundakunda says that if the psychic-attention (*upayoga*) is good (*shubha*), it leads to accumulation, generation or increase of *punya* (virtue, merit, righteousness, piousness). If the psychic-attention is evil or inauspicious (*ashubha*), it leads to accumulation or increase of sin or sinfulness (*papa*). In the absence of both, there is no accession, accumulation or increase of either (PS 156), i.e. bondage of *punya* and *papa karma* (PS 156 JS).

When psychic-attention (*upayoga*) is influenced by attachment in the form of sanity or purifying effect (*vishuddhi*) or affliction, distress and morbidity (*sanklesha*), it is of a dual aspect, viz. good and evil. It is active as a cause of conjunction with other substances, which receive a double aspect of either merit and sin. However, when non-existence of this impure in both forms is effected, then only pure psychic-attention remains. This is no cause of conjunction with any other substance (PS 156 AC).

The evolution of the self into infatuation (*moha*) and aversion (*dvesh*) is *ashubha*, while its evolution into attachment is both good (*shubha*) and evil (*ashubha*) since attachment has a dual role whereby it is imbued with either sanity having a purifying (*vishuddhi*) effect or is imbued with affliction, distress and morbidity (*sanklesh*) (PS 180 and 180 AC).

In *Tattvartha Sutra,* virtuous activities (*punya*) are also said to have a paradoxical dual nature/role of generating karmic influx and bondage as well as of inhibiting (*samvara*) of karmic influx (SAS commentary on TS 6.3, and 9.2.3).

In *Purusharthasiddhyupaya* (PSU 221) and in his commentary on *Pravachanasara* (PS 11), Amrtachandra has described the contradictory effects of good (*shubha*) psychic-attention by citing the example of hot clarified butter (*ghee*), which makes things delicious, but if *ghee* is heated by fire it also causes pain of burning. One should not, therefore, reach the wrong conclusion that contradictory effects occur simultaneously.

Dual Role of *Shubha*

Shubha has a dual role in generating *karmic* influx and bondage as well as inhibiting (*samvara*) *karmic* influx, which in turn influences the purification of the self. This signifies that it is not to be blindly or indiscriminately adhered to. As a means to sensorial pleasures (PS 69 AC), it leads to misery (PS 76), *if* people having plenty of *punya,* resulting from *shubha upayoga* indistinguishably experience, like those with evil (*ashubha*) *upayoga*, simply misery, conditioned by the body, i.e. by the five sense-organs. Since both miss innate happiness of a transcendental nature (*parmartha*), a relation of separateness (*prthakatva*) between good and evil psychic-attention does not hold (PS 72 and PS 72 AC), especially *if* they (such people) are necessarily perceived as craving for only (*eva*) sense objects (*vishaya trashna*) (PS 74 and PS 74 AC). In order to denigrate *punya*, the Kanjipanthi try to ignore qualifying word "if".[64]

Thus, a person who is immersed in this way in infatuation (*moha*), continuously moves about in the terrible cycle of transmigratory existence. As a result, according to deeper truth of the transcendental nature of the self (*paramartha*), a duality of merit and sin, like a duality of good and evil psychic-attention or of pleasure and pain, does not exist. The primary reason for this is that on both sides equally there is no property (*dharma*) which really belongs to the soul (PS 77 AC). The last sentence of this paragraph has been distorted by Bharill to signify that for the devotees of *dharma* of the self (*atma dharma*), both *punya* and *papa* are equally *adharma* (unrighteous, evil, sin) only.[65]

In this regard, Amrtachandra describes the way in which one must act to avoid circumstances when *punya* is similar to *papa*:

(1) If one feels egoistical (*ahankarika*) pride in practicing *punya* (acts of righteousness such as charity, compassion, etc.) (PS 77 AC) [because the worldly prosperity and name, fame (*vaibhava*), etc. obtained by virtuous deeds leads to pride (*mada* or *ahankara*), pride generates deluded intellect (*mudha mati*), which, in turn, leads to sinful, vicious acts (*papa*); such *punya* is not desired (PP 2.60)];

(2) when one has expectation of enjoyments of sense objects in future (*nidan*) as a result of *punya* because pleasure of the senses indeed spells misery (PS 76 and PP 2.59);

(3) if his state of consciousness (*chitta bhumi*) becomes coloured (*uparakta*) [with intense attachment, aversion, etc.] due to *punya*; and

(4) if due to *punya*, he censures, disdains or disrespects, i.e. goes against the purity of the self (*suddhatmano vipreet*) and does not consider *punya* as a means (*sadhan*) of or supportive factor of] pure (*shuddha*) *upayoga* (PS 77 AC).

However, it is incorrect to equate *shubha* and *asubha*, or *punya* and *papa*. *Shubha*, Amrtachandra clarifies, differs from *ashubha* on four grounds, i.e. in its nature (*svabhava*), cause (*karana*), effect (experience or *anubhava* of fruition of *karmas*) and in substratum (*ashraya*) and fosters the path of liberation because *shubha* (*punya*) is the path of liberation (*moksha marg*) whereas *ashubha* (*papa*) is the way to *karmic* bondage (*bandha marg*), (*shubhashubhau moksha bandha margau*) (SS 145 AC). *Punya* is therefore desirable (*upadeya*) or worth practicing.

From an external, other-referential point of view (*vyavahara naya*), Jayasena elaborates, there is a difference between *punya* and *papa* in regard to the condition (*hetu*) of *karmic* bondage, nature (*svabhava*), effect (fruition or experience) and substrata (*ashraya*). If virtuous activities (*punya*), such as self-restraint of moral rules of non-violence, etc. vows (*vrata*), charity (*dana*) etc., are accompanied by or associated with an enlightened view of things (*samyaktva*), they become the traditional (*paramparaya*) cause of liberation (SS 145 JS).

Due to attachment, the self [even with good, excellent or commendable attachment (*prashasta raga*) (PS 254-255) also] binds *karman* (PS 179). However, when oriented towards sanity and purification (*vishuddhi*), (PS 155 and 180 AC), thereby experiencing the [transcendental nature of] the pure self, gradually (*kramatah*) brings about the highest happiness of *nirvana* (liberation) (PS 254 and PS 254 AC). Thus, it not only leads to liberation of oneself (PS 259 and PS 259 AC) but also helps others to attain liberation (PS 260 and PS 260 AC).

Shubha occupies a middle position between *ashubha* and *shuddha.* It can degenerate into *ashubha,* if the prosperity and high position, etc. obtained by good or virtuous deeds, leads one to indulge in sense pleasures and pride, greed, etc. passions. Alternately, it can rise to become the pure self as it also has a purifying (*vishuddhi*) effect if it is oriented towards sanity, righteousness, self-restraint and piety. It all depends on the use one makes of it. If Kundakunda has pointed out the sombre aspects of *shubha* or *punya,* i.e. the possibility of its misuse, that does not imply that one should discard *punya* or *shubha* altogether considering it as worth abandoning (*heya*) like evil (*ashubha*) or sinful (*papa*).

Misperceptions and Distortions of *Kanjipanthi* regarding *Shubha* or *Punya*

In spite of what has been stated above, Kanjipanthi still harbour numerous misperceptions in regard to good (*shubha* or *punya*) by selectively using out of context certain portions of the text and deliberately twist/distort meanings and wrongly interpret various statements. These misperceptions are:

1. *That both good (shubha) and evil (ashubha) are both impure (ashuddha) psychic-attention (upayoga).* Therefore, they are equally worth abandoning[66] and emphasis should be laid on getting rid of both of them.[67] In response, one may argue that Kundakunda describes *upayoga* to be of three kinds (viz. *ashubha*, *shubha* and *shuddha*), and not of two kinds (viz. pure and impure) as Kanjipanthi seem to suggest. In *Pravachanasara* verse 9, Kundakunda specifically states: "The soul accepts the character of its state-of-evolution. When the soul evolves through the good or the evil, it becomes good or evil. When it evolves through the pure, then it becomes pure." (PS 9) In his commentary on this verse, Amrtchandra observes that the states-of-evolution (*parinama*) of consciousness or psychic-attention (*upayoga*) of soul (*jiva*) is good, evil and pure (PS 9 AC), i.e. three kinds.

In *Pravachanasara* 155, *upayoga* characterized by knowledge and intuition is said to be good or evil. However, in his commentary, Amrtachandra states that *upayoga* is sub-divided in two ways according to purity and impurity. The impurity which is characterized by attachment, is again two-fold, viz. good and evil [yet these two are not the same].The good is characterized by sanity having purifying (*vishuddhi*) effect, while evil is characterized by affliction, distress or morbidity (*sanklesha*) (PS 155 AC). Jayasena considers this *shubha* of the nature of attachment or affection for *dharma* (righteousness or piety) and *ashubha* of the nature of attachment to sense objects, aversion and deluded view (*vishaya anuraga rupa*, *dvesh moha rupa*) (PS 155 JS). The nature of good (*shubha*) and evil (*ashubha*) *upayoga* is described in *Pravachanasara* verses 157 and 158, which amply brings about the difference between the two.

Thus, the states-of-evolution of consciousness are said to be of three kinds: (a) of the nature of *sanklesh*, which is characterized by overwhelming, non-abstinent, most intense or severe passions (*teevra kashaya*); (b) *vishuddhi* characterized by mild or moderate passions (*manda kashaya*); and (c) pure, which is devoid of passions of anger, pride, greed, etc. It is only when passions subside, that the soul has a mental state (*bhava*) which is oriented towards veneration of the worthy Lord and moral conduct of self-restraint [such as non-violence, etc. vows, self-regulation (*samiti*) and restraints of mind, speech and body (*gupti*)]. Therefore, these activities are considered to have a purifying (*vishuddhi*) effect, which in turn acts as the cause of attaining pure psychic-attention and the pure self.

Pandit Todarmal categorically states that less intensity or mild passion is better that greater intensity of passion, just as less severity of disease is better than more severity of disease.[68] Only the soul with mild passion is likely to evolve into even more milder state(s) of passion and ultimately become devoid or free of passions, i.e. pure (*shuddha*). It is for this reason that Acharya Vidyasagara has stated: "One cannot have pure psychic-attention without good psychic-attention (*bin shubha upayoga ke hot na shuddha upayoga*)."

2. *There is no difference whatsoever, according to Bharill, between punya (good, virtuous, righteousness) and papa, (evil, sin).* A person who thinks that there is a difference between them, he asserts, is a deluded person (*mithyadrashti*).[69] [This is nowhere written in any Jain scripture.] This is a serious mistake, which leads to the inevitable result of *nigod* (rebirth in the lowest state of development of soul). The avoidance of that mistake leads to an enlightened view of things (*samyak darshan*) resulting in *moksha* (liberation). Even if any difference between *punya* and *papa* is accepted or acknowledged even from an external, other-referential aspect (*vyavahara naya*), Bharill adds, one should consider that difference to be secondary (*gauna*) and negate or deny that difference (*gauna karake nishedha karna hai*).[70] Thus, this kind of thinking on the part of Kanjipathi is not only patently wrong and misplaced but also dangerous.

Impurity (*kalushata* or *ashuddhi*) primarily consists in the intensity of anger, etc. passions, and evil impulses. The natural result of good (*shubha*) psychic-attention (*upayoga*) or the operationalization of virtuous (*punya*) deeds leads to the subsidence of passions reflecting calmness of mind (*prasham bhava*), commendable attachment (*prashasta raga*), which is oriented towards sanity and purification (*vishuddhi* or *akalushata*), compassion (*anukampa*) and psychic energy geared or disposed towards righteousness (*samvega*). They are said to be necessary prerequisites of an enlightened world-view (*samyakdarshan*). Therefore, to equate them with evil (*papa*) or consider them to be the cause of delusion (*mithyatva*) is a gross distortion of facts and what is written in Jain scriptures, including the works of Acharya

Kundakunda.

3. *That punya and papa are only the cause of influx (asrava) of karmas (TS 6.3) and consequent bondage alone.*[71] From this, the Kanjipanthi seek to prove that they both are to be considered as part of influx and bondage of *karmas*. This is said to be the view expressed in *Tattvartha Sutra*, which speaks of only seven principles of life (*tattvas*) (TS 1.4). In his works particularly *Samayasara*, Kundakunda, specially mentions nine *tattvas* or categories (*padarthas*) (SS 13 and PKS 108) including *punya* (righteousness and piety) and *papa* (sin, vice). As in the case of *asrava, bandha*, etc. *padarthas*, a separate chapter is devoted in the case of *punya* and *papa*, which are considered significant concepts and separate categories; in fact, it is significant to note that no verse in the *asrava* chapter of *Samayasara*, makes any reference to *punya* or *papa* as being part of *asrava* (influx of *karmas*), since *punya* is not merely or simply the cause of influx and consequent bondage of *karmas. Punya* has a dual role of *karmic* bondage as also having a purifying effect (*visuddhi*) (PS 180 AC) and gradually leading to liberation (PS 254 AC).

4. *That Jain texts do not mention that good (shubha) activities and virtuous (punya) deeds, such as veneration of the worthy Lord, etc. lead to inhibition of karmic influx.*[72] In response, it may be stated that the *Sarvarthasiddhi* commentary on *Tattvartha Sutra* (TS 6.3 and 9. 23) specifically points out that the virtuous activities (*punya*) have a paradoxical dual role in generating *karmic* influx and bondage as well as inhibiting (*samvara*) *karmic* influx.

5. Kanji Svami's assertion that "*the objective (dhyeya) of good psychic dispositions (shubha parinamas) is sensorial pleasure*"[73] *is also quite incorrect and misleading.* In his commentary, Amrtachandra has described good psychic attention as the means (*sadhan*) of sensorial pleasure (PS 70 AC). However, neither Kundakunda nor Amrtachandra have considered sensorial pleasure to be the objective of *shubha parinama*, because in their view, the pleasure, acquired by means of the senses, is indeed misery (PS 76).

6. Bharill's assertion that *one gets only external material (of sense enjoyments) as a result of shubha or punya and not peace of self,*[74] *or less intensity of passions (kashaya mandata)*[75] *is not correct.* Apart from prosperity, one also gets calmness of mind due to subsidence of passions (*prasham bhava*). This is possible only in the conditions of a

good mental state (*shubha bhava*) and not in the circumstances when a person's mind is in the grip of intense emotional agitation caused by intensity of passions or sinful evil thoughts (*ashubha*).

7. *That good psychic-attention is the cause of karmic bondage.*[76] This assertion is not correct since good psychic-attention, as stated earlier, has a dual role: it is the cause of both bondage and inhibition of *karmas* and purification (*vishuddhi*) (PS 180 AC) and leads to liberation (PS 254 and 259 AC).

8. *That good (shubha) psychic-attention is not dharma or that it cannot be considered to be dharma.* The real *dharma* is pure psychic-attention or pure state-of-evolution of the self alone, which is the cause of freedom from *karmic* bondage.[77] In this context, *Pravachanasara* states that the innate nature of the soul is to evolve through *dharma*. This evolution can be pure (*shuddha*) psychic-attention or good (*shubha*) psychic-attention (PS 11 and PS 11 AC). When the self is not partaking at all of the evolution of *dharma*, it gives itself up to the evolution of evil (*ashubha*) psychic-attention, which lacks even a grain of (lawful or righteous) conduct (PS 12 AC). As a result, it experiences the bondage of a thousand pains and misery, and wanders about as rogue, animal or inhabitant of hell and must be completely abandoned (PS 12 AC).

Moreover, good or virtuous mental states and acivities, which are characterised by subsidence of passions and oriented towards self-restraints, sanity and purification (*vishuddhi*), also act as the cause of pure psychic-attention as also of pure self. The commendable attachment (*prashasta raga*) in good psychic-attention gradually (*kramatah*) brings about the highest happiness of *nirvana* (liberation) (PS 254 and PS 254 AC). Thus, it not only leads to liberation of oneself (PS 259 and PS 259 AC) but also helps others to attain liberation (PS 260 and PS 260 AC) as has already been stated.

Moreover, Acharya Virasena, in his *Jai Dhavala* (Book 1, p. 5) commentary on *Kashaya-Prabhrata* (*Kashaya-Pahuda*), one of the most authentic Jain texts of Digambaras, has acknowledged the possibility of both *samvara* (inhibitation of influx of *karma*) and *nirjara* (eradicating of *karmas*). He states: "If eradication of *karmas* is not considered possible by *shubha* and *shuddha* (pure) psychic disposition (*parinama*), then eradication of *karmas* will not be possible at all."

9. Kanji's contention that *the psychic disposition of punya is not the*

means (sadhan) of dharma, but is the cause of affliction (*klesha*)[78] is not correct because *Pravachanasara* clearly states that good or virtuous (*shubha* or *punya*) is oriented towards sanity, righteousness, or piety (*dharma*) and purification (*vishuddhi*). Evil (*ashubha*) and sinful mental state, on the other hand, is of the nature of affliction, distress and morbidity (*klesha* or *sanklesh*) (PS 155 and 180 AC).

10. *To say that there is no other dharma except the discourse, sermon or instruction (deshana) of the worthy Lord,*[79] *is only partially true.* Similarly, to argue that the attainment of inclination to understand and grasp the reality of things such discourses (*deshana labdhi*) is the only auxiliary cause of the nature of supportive factor of an enlightened world-view (*samyakdarshan*) is again a partial truth because there are several other factors, such as subsidence of passions, commendable attachment (*prashasta raga*), compassion (*anukampa*), etc.

11. Kanji's statement that the self's good or virtuous (*punya*) psychic dispositions of compassion or kindness (*daya*), charity (*dana*), etc. take place by forgetting the nature of the self, comprising of perception, cognition and being blissful,[80] implying thereby that such activities are against the nature of the self and that *punya* only gives rise to longing (*trashna*) for and the tendency of enjoying sense-objects[81] is patently wrong. In *Dhavala*, one of the most authentic texts of Jainism, compassion is declared to be the innate nature (*svabhava*) of *jiva* (self) (*Dhavala*, Book 13, p. 362).[82]

In reply to Kanji's assertion that *punya* only gives rise to longing and tendency for sense-enjoyments, it may be stated that *punya* does not say or compel a person to have longing for or indulge in sense-enjoyments. Ultimately, it is upto the person, who is the architect and master of his destiny (PKS 27), how one makes use of the facilities and opportunities of prosperity, good health, human birth, etc., obtained as a result of virtuous deeds (*punya karma*). One may put them to good use or waste and squander his energies and facilities in sense-enjoyments.

The Kanjipanthi persist in their mistaken view that there is no difference between good (*shubha*) or righteousness (*punya*) and evil (*ashubha*) or sinful (*papa*) activities whatsoever, that both are the cause of bondage of *karma*. In so doing, they are: (1) blurring the difference between the two; (2) ignoring the dual role of *shubha* or *punya* pointed by Amrtachandra that it is not only cause of bondage but also of purification (*vishuddhi*), which gradually leads to liberation (see PS 155-156, 180 and 254 AC); (3) pitting *shubha* against *shuddha* (pure), even though (*shubha*) is the supportive factor and cause of *shuddha*; and (4) denying the significant role of self-restraints (*samyam*) and austerities (*tapa*) in attaining liberation.

The reason why the Kanjipanthi want to deliberately distort the nature of *shubha* or *punya* by insisting that there is no difference whatsoever between *punya* and *papa* and that both of them are worth abandoning (*heya*) seems to be to present an easy path of liberation to people so that they do not have to either adopt means (*sadhan*) of moral conduct and spiritual self-discipline or undertake efforts of self-restraints (*samyam*) and austerities to attain pure psychic-attention, pure self and liberation.

Knowledge of the self (*atmajnana*), or obtaining an enlightened view of the self through overcoming of delusion (*mithyatva*) and meditation of the self (*atma dhyana*), which is [mistakenly defined by Bharill as] continuing to know the self, is considered sufficient for getting rid of *karmas* and attaining liberation. In so doing, they seek to revise Kundakunda's teaching and scriptural prescription that an enlightened world-view of the reality of things as they are, including the self, the non-self and the resulting categories of influx of *karmas*, etc. due to their interaction, knowledge thereof and enlightened conduct devoid of attachment and aversion–the trinity constitute the path of liberation.

With a view to circumvent this age-old path of liberation, the Kanjipanthi do not hesitate to propagate that delusion (*mithyatva*) is an "internal" fault[83] and the most terrible, the most serious, dangerous and great heinous sin or crime (*maha bhayankara papa*).[84] It alone is said to be responsible for the transmigratory existence of the soul, and to belittle, or undermine the significance of conduct-deluding attachment and aversion by stating that they are "external or superficial only".[85]

Bharill has the audacity to make such patentently wrong and absurd assertions even when it is specifically declared that "attachment, aversion and deluded view are soul's own inalienable states-of-evolution or modes (*ananya parinama*)" (SS 371) and that after delusion (*mithyatva* or *moha*) [deluded-view] has gone or is given up, "*if*, [i.e. only when] the self gets rid of attachment and aversion, then [and then only] it obtains the pure self (*shuddha atma*) (PS 81), i.e. attains liberation, not otherwise.

This is because a deluded-view, attachment and aversion are considered *asrava-bhava* (psychic states responsible for the influx and consequent bondage of *karmas*) (SS 176-177). In their absence, the soul is not liable to bondage (SS 167, 178). Without these *asrava-bhava*, even the four factors (*pratyaya*) of delusion (*mithyatva*), lack of moral self-restraints of non-violence, etc. vows (*avirati*), anger, etc. passions and vibratory activities of mind, speech and body (*yoga*), that affect, influence, and condition psychic states (SS 109), which are usually considered to be the causal factors of bondage (SS 109), are not able to bind the soul (SS 176, 178).

The Characteristics of Infatuation (*Moha*) and the Issue of Compassion (PS 85)

There is considerable controversy regarding *karuna* (mercy, kindness or compassion) mentioned in *Pravachanasara* verse 85. It states: "The [three] characteristics of *moha* (infatuation) are: (1) the tendency to view things differently or other than what they really are, i.e. wrong perceptions or perverse ascertainment of things or deluded view (*mithya darshan*); (2) *karunabhavo* towards animals and men; and (3) indulgence in sense objects." Due to its inclination towards sense objects, the self is inclined to develop attachment (*raga*) towards affectionate, pleasant or agreeable objects and aversion (*dvesh*) in regard to objects considered unaffectionate, unpleasant or disagreeable things (PS 85 AC).

Evidently, where only *moha* is used, it usually (unless context indicates otherwise) implies the above-mentioned three characteristics, viz. deluded view, attachment and aversion. Where *moha* is used along with *raga* and *dvesh*, it signifies only *mithya darshan*, which consists of *mithyatva* (delusion) plus the most intense or tenacious anger, etc. passions (*anantanubhandhi kashaya*). *Mithya darshan* is called view-deluding (*darshan mohaniya karma*), while *raga* and *dvesh* are considered conduct-deluding (*charitra mohaniya*) *karma*, i.e. the faults of conduct in Jaina terminology.

Different Works and Scholars on Compassion

The controversy regarding *karunabhavo* relates to deciding whether "*karunabhavo*" (or *karunabhava* in Sanskrit) signifies feeling of compassion (*karuna+bhava*), i.e. *samas* (conjoint word) in grammar or absence of feeling of compassion (*karuna+abhava*), i.e. *sandhi* (joining of two words) in grammar. Barend Faddegon, following Amrtachandra, has translated *karunabhavo* as "feeling of compassion (*karuna*)", while A.N. Upadhye has translated it as "absence of kindness (*karuna*)" (PS 85).

There is, thus, a serious difference of opinion as regards what Kundakunda meant by *karunabhavo.* Amrtachandra interprets it as feeling of compassion (*karuna+bhava,* i.e. *samasa* between two words). A number of scholars, on the other hand, maintain that it means absence of kindness (*karuna+abhava,* a joining, or combination, i.e. *sandhi* of two words). This, they argue, is evident from what has been stated by Kundakunda in his works, including *Panchastikayasara* and *Pravachanasara,* and other Jain texts. It is argued how the feeling of compassion which is a wholesome, good (*shubha*) thought-activity and which is a constituent of an enlightened world-view, can be said to be the characteristic of *moha,* that needs to be destroyed? If compassion is not *dharma,* can the absence of compassion, i.e. cruelty to animals and fellow beings be called *dharma*?

Ashta Pahuda (AP)

In *Bodh Pahuda* (25), Kundakunda states that *dharma* (righteousness, piety) is that which is purified by compassion (*daya visudhho dhammo*). In *Bhava Pahuda* (133), *muni* (saints) are instructed to have compassion towards all six classes of living beings and such compassionate people are said to destroy all sins (Verse 159). Whosoever is compassionate to living beings is considered to have good psychic attention (*shubhopayoga*) (PS 157). In *Sheel Pahuda* (19), kindness to living beings, control of senses, truthfulness, non-stealing, chastity, contentment, enlightened view, knowledge and austerity are said to (constitute) the family of virtue.

Niyamsara

In *Niyamsara,* Kundakunda speaks of *sparahidam* (*sva-para hita* in Sk.), i.e. the well-being of self as well as others (NS 62). In *Panchastikayasara,* compassion (*anukampa*), a feeling of goodwill, sympathy and kindness (*karuna*) at the sight of needy and the sufferers and the offering of charity or active relief to the thirsty, the hungry and the miserable (PKS 137), is considered (see above) as one of the necessary prerequisites of *samyak-darshan* (enlightened world-view), which is quite opposite of infatuation or deluded view (*moha*).

Compassion is, thus, said to be one of the constituents or prerequisites of *shubhopayoga* as also of enlightened world-view (*samyak-darshan*). The additional verse *Pravachanasara* 268/2 of Jayasena recension defines compassion as: "He who, seeing one thirsty, hungry or miserable, is pained in mind and through pity assists him is compassion." (PS 268/2)

Dhavala

In *Dhavala*, compassion (*anukampa*) or kindness (*karuna*) is described as one of the four characteristics (together with *samvega*, i.e. inclination towards righteousness, avoidance of evil deeds, i.e. *prasham* or subsidence of passions, and *astikya*, i.e. firm conviction about the reality of things or the fundamental principles of life) of *samyaktva* (enlightened view) (*Dhavala*, Book 10, p. 1151). If compassion is the characteristic of *samyaktva* (enlightened view, which is opposite of *moha* or *mithya darshan*), how could it be said to be the characteristic of a deluded view (*moha*). Compassion is also declared in *Dhavala* to be the innate nature (*svabhava*) of *jiva* (self) (*Dhavala*, Book 13, p. 362), just the same way as the lamp removes the darkness of itself as also of others.

Pujyapada

There is a natural tendency or inclination in living beings to feel concerned at the sight of the miserable condition of other beings. Defining compassion, Pujyapada states: "Compassion is the feeling of sympathy of one whose mind is moistened by kindness or distress for the suffering of others as if it were one's own" (*Sarvarthasiddhi* commentary on TS 6.12). To be sensitive (*samvedan-sheel*) in regard to the suffering of others is quite natural. Compassion is not only essential for our own peace and mental stability but also essential for human survival as it is the very basis of society. It is because of compassion and kindness (*karuna bhava*) that the enlightened Lords deliver sermons or discourses for the well-being of living beings. Likewise, the saints give spiritual instruction (*upadesha*) for the good of the people.

Shakespeare

Shakespeare talks of mercy, as a virtue which is "twice blest; it blesses him that gives and him that takes" (*Merchant of Venice* – IV, I). Indeed, purely from one's own point of view and for one's own benefit, it would be necessary to cultivate this virtue of mercy, as also another virtue which invariably goes with it – compassion. Both of these are the two sides of the same coin. One cannot exist or be embellished without the other.

Dalai Lama

In this regard a question may be asked that while one spends his time, energy and money, only others benefit? In other words "how is mercy or compassion" to be considered "twice blest" as is claimed? According to the Dalai Lama, "The first beneficiary of compassion is always oneself" as it "reduces our fear, boosts our confidence and brings inner strength." It is spirituality of the highest order for it leads to positivity and contentment. It is negation of the feeling of hatred, revenge and criticism of fellow sentients. Compassion, as the Dalai Lama says, is that unique sense of caring which binds people into a single human family.

Patanjali

Patanjali, while including compassion (*karana*) as one of the necessary virtues for obtaining peace and felicity (*chittaprasadnam*), based his exhortation on practical wisdom. This is because when a person is involved in act of mercy or compassion, he emerges, though for a short while, out of his own cloistered world within, to that real and vast world, where suffering poverty, inequity and despair abound.[86] Commenting on it, K. Vijayaraghavan observes:

> In this comprehensive view of things, one's own problems, concerns and anxieties would appear less daunting. He would also comprehend that the world outside also includes those immumerable persons and also animals and birds who, though deprived, have much strength, toughness and resilience within.
>
> Such exposers have an inspiring impact whereby the resultant broadness in outlook serves to erase the accumulated prejudices, grudges, resentments, conflicts and self-pity from the mind. The 'space' now created within permits entry of noble thoughts and healthy vibrations. Improved focus, which comes about naturally, ensures accomplishments in all ways. The person concerned is, thus, more than compensated for his efforts. Importantly, he is also at peace, in the feeling that he has done his bit.[87]

The Bible

[These virtues] bring with them that fulfillment within, which only practical experience can vouch for. . . The Bible aptly pionts out "He that has pity upon the poor lendeth into the Lord" (Proverbs: 19, 17). . . [Since such] virtues benefit oneself too, it would also be necessary to inspire and motivate oneself continually.[88]

Example of Abraham Lincoln

It is said that when Abraham Lincoln was a young lawer (later the future sixteenth President of the United States) was travelling, he saw a piglet hopelessly stuck in the mud. The poor creature was struggling very hard to extricate itself from the marshy land but the more the animal struggled to get free, the more it stuck itself in the mud and was sure to die of thirst or starvation ultimately. Lincoln was wearing a new suit he hadn't owned for very long and most thoughts of compassion or rescue were not really in his priority list right then. Lincoln felt distressed or grieved by its pitiable condition, so much so that when he reached office he could not get the pig out of his head and concentrate on his work. His mind could not be at ease until he got that pig extricated from the mud. He, therefore, went to that place, got down from his carriage to help it out. When he was praised for his goodness, he remarked that what he did was merely to remove a thorn from his own mind which would have pricked him throughtout his life, if he had not done this simple affordable act. "By showering mercy, compassion, generosity and altruism," Vijayaraghavan remarks, the person concerned does a service to himself too. [Hence mercy is] "twice blest".[89] Thus, it signifies that one renders aid to others primarily for relieving the anguish, grief or regret (*kheda*) from one's own mind, thereby ensuring his own peace of mind. In this sense, compassion is also justified from the internal, self-referential point of view (*nishchaya naya*).

Panchastikayasara (PKS)

Kundakunda himself has stated that since one's mind [naturally] gets afflicted by grief or distressed (*duhkhit mana*) at the sight of the thirsty, the hungry and the miserable, he offers relief to them, out of pity (*kripa*); then such behaviour of that person is compassion (*anukampa*) (PKS 137), which is the second condition (after noble or commendable attachment, (*prashasta raga*) generating *punya* (merit or virtue). The act of compassion implies the feeling of sympathy at the sight of the needy and the sufferers as well as active relief to them.

This kind of compassion is common to the ordinary mortals and it manifests in only temporary relief. But in the case of the wise ones (*jnani*) *anukampa,* i.e. feeling of grief or regret (*kheda*) manifests in a higher form at the sight of the struggling souls in the ocean of *Samsara* (PKS 137 AC) and they manifest a generous sympathy and help them towards emancipation. Thus, *anukampa* is of two kinds, lower and higher according as its result is temporary and superficial or radical and permanent.

Tattvartha Sutra (TS)

Like compassion or mercy, giving charity (*dana*) is also for mutual benefit as it benefits both the giver and the recipient. The giver gives for his own benefit with a sense of gratitude to the recipient. Charity, thus, practiced with a pure heart helps weaken *karmic* bondage (TS 7.38). As a result of charity, one also accumulates merit (*punya*), thereby benefitting oneself as it is one of the causes of the influx of pleasure-producing (*sata-vedaniya*) *karma* (TS 6.12). Charity also benefits others by relieving their suffering. Those who practice these virtues will not harbout any national, racial, religious or class hatred.

Thus, the external behaviour of rendering help or assistance to others, resulting from compassionate feeling, naturally leads to the discontinuance or removal of pain of the self and other (*sva-para dhukha nivrtti*). As a result, it is the cause of peace, happiness and well-being of oneself as well as others (*sva-para hita* or *sva-para anugraha heto*). The well-being of oneself is primary and precedes the well being of others. In being kind to oneself (*sva-daya*), one is being kind to others as well (*para-daya*). *Sva* (self) and *para* (other) or internal and external are inter-related.

The accomplishment of any task or deed requires or depends on coordination of both internal and external causes (the intrinsic cause is regarded as primary or the substantive cause, while the extrinsic cause is considered as secondary, supportive or auxiliary cause) is said to be in the very nature things (*dravyagatah svabhavah*) (Samantabhadra, *Svyambhu-stotra*, Verse 60).

Since *karuna* is not *audayika bhava,* i.e. the mental state resulting from the coming into operation or the rise of *karman,* it cannot be the cause of *karmic* bondage (*Dhavala*, Book 13, pp. 381-382). Compassion (*karuna*) (as described in PKS 137) can be said to be the natural inclination or tendency to be sensitive (*samvedansheel*) to the suffering of others, signifying willingness to be helpful towards them. In *Jai Dhavala* (Book 1, p. 96 commentary), compassion results in the influx of *punya* (merit, righteousness) and of pure conscious attentiveness (*shuddha upayoga*), while the opposite thereof, i.e. absence of compassion, leads to influx of sinful *karmas*. Thus, the two most authentic Digambara texts speak highly of compassion.

Karuna in Sanskrit means active sympathy, gentle affection and willingness to bear the pain of others. It is a wish for all beings to be free from suffering. The Pali word is "*metta*", which means loving kindness, friendliness, benevolence, fellowship, amity, concord, inoffensiveness and non-violence. It is a strong wish for the welfare and happiness of others (*parahita-parasukha-kamana*) without any self-interest. *Metta* is universal, unselfish and all-embracing love. It is a wish for the happiness of all. It is an antidote to selfishness, anger and fear.

Compassion and Infatuation are Different

Compassion or kindness (*karuna*) and infatuation (*moha*) are quite different. As already stated, compassion is said to be the nature (*svabhava*) of *jiva* (self), the characteristic of an enlightened world-view (*samyaktva*) as also the cause of *punya* or *shubha* (good, auspicious), *dharma* (righteousness, piety) having a conscious role (*bhumika*) of attentiveness. Infatuation is said to have three roles (*bhumika*), viz. of false perception of things, including nature of self (i.e. *moha* or delusion), attachment (*raga*) and aversion (*dvesha*) (PS 83 AC). It is the perversion of the conscious states, quite opposite of an enlightened view of things and conduct. It leads to sinful (*papa*) activities, which are considered to be *adharma* (absence of righteousness, piety, *dharma*). The absence of compassion signifies mercilessness, cruelty or wrathful meditation (*raudra dhyana*), which can in no way be described as wholesome, righteous or virtuous meditation (*dharma dhyana*), and as such can only be considered *adharma* (*Dhyanshatak* 27).

Infatuation prevents a person from being able to grasp the real nature of the self. One is therefore engrossed in sense pleasures, attached to external objects, and utterly selfish, "having a sense of me and mineness in other substances" (PS 183 and SS 19-23). This makes one forget one's duties. One even tries to exploit others for the satisfaction of one's desires. A kind-hearted person, on the other hand, endeavours to help the needy and the poor by sacrificing his money and comfort for their benefit.

The activities – mental, vocal or physical – of the mundane self, for the well-being of others are called *punya.* Such activities of the nature of *punya* are of two kinds: (1) those that are done for the selfish reasons in the world; and (2) those that are done as a matter of duty and without any expectation. Of the two, the second one is the real *punya* activity. A unique example of this is 80 years old "birds hospital' in the precincts of Jain Red Temple just opposite Red Fort in Delhi. Such activities include reverence or worship of the Lord who is non-attached, study of and reflection on scriptures, being imbued with non-attachment and rendering service to disinterested and detached preceptors and practice of rules of moral and spiritual self-discipline that awakens the power of self-reliance.

Kindness to living beings (*jiva daya*) is of three kinds: the virtuous (*punya*) activity, which is the cause of the influx and consequent bondage of auspicious (*shubha*) *karma.* It involves getting rid of unkindness of the nature of evil or inauspiciousness and represents less intensity or mildness of passions like anger, pride, greed, etc. It is a factor in inhibition (*samvara*) and dissociation (*nirjara*) of karmas. It also implies kindness to living beings of the nature of virtuous activities that is also imbued with the "pure" or purifying intrinsic nature and *nishchaya dharma* (self-referential righteousness). Moreover, it is of the nature of other-referential righteousness and piety (*vyavahara dharma*), which is the supportive factor or auxiliary cause of the *jiva daya* of the nature of *nishchaya dharma.* All these three kinds of *jiva daya* have their own existence and significance.

Compassion and Non-violence

Compassion or kindness (*daya*) is considered the positive psychic aspect of non-violence, which is said to be the basis of all other rules of moral conduct (PSU 42). Since non-violence is said to be the root or the foundation (*mula*) of *dharma* (righteousness and piety) (*Uttaradhyayana vritti* 1-11), *daya,* being the positive psychic aspect of non-violence, is also said to be *mula* (foundation, basis or root) of *dharma* (*Dharmaratna Prakarana*) because all other practices or observances (*anushthana*) follow from that.

From the description of kindness (*daya*) in *Bhagavati Sutra*, it is quite evident that it is considered synonymous to non-violence. There are various forms of compassion (*anukampa*) which are not a condition or cause of any harm, sorrow, weeping, etc. or fear, to all living beings (*Bhagavati Sutra* 6-7). The definition and nature of non-violence is also similar. Moreover, kindness (*daya*), self-restraint (*samyam*), sense of decency or modesty (*lajja*), absence of disgust or censure (*jugupsa*), lack of insincerity or deceit (*kapatheenata*), endurance or forbearance (*titiksha*), non-violence and modesty (*hri*) – all these are said to be synonymous (*Uttaradhyayana Niryukti* Chapter 3).

In Jainism, non-violence has two aspects: not to cause harm, injury or violence and that of friendliness or amity (*maitri*), compassion or kindness (*karuna*) and service (*seva*). The first one is primarily that of abstinence (*nirvrtti*) whereas the second is primarily disposed towards active life (*pravrtti*). Both aspects are interdependent and, therefore, non-violence is contained in both of them.

While infatuation (*moha*) is worth renouncing (*heya*), compassion, kindness, mercy (*daya*), charity (*dana*), service (*vaiyyavrttya*) are all noble qualities, which represent good and auspicious psychic dispositions (*shubha bhava*). They are an excellent or commendable attachment (*prashasta raga*) and a meritorious activity (*punya*) that needs to be cultivated. One is asked to contemplate, meditate and practice friendliness towards all living beings, appreciation of other's good qualities, compassion or kindness for the afflicted and equanimity towards those who are ill-behaved. (TS 7.11)

In a frenzy of anger, etc. passions, one is almost possessed by instinctive impulses and sub-conscious motivations, as a result of which one is no longer one's own master. By the practice of compassion, one starts rising above the muddy world of desires, greed and anger, etc. passions, and is able to transform his energies in the direction of sanity, righteousness and piety.

Moreover, Samantabhadra states that Lord Mahavira's teaching lays emphasis on compassion, self-restraint, renunciation and meditation (*daya-dama-tyaga-samadhi*) (Samantabhadra, *Yuktyanushashan*, Verse 6), which are the four components of *karma-yoga*. In his commentary thereon, the commentator Vidyananda points out that compassion or non-violence is the auxiliary cause of self-restraint; self-restraint is the cause of renunciation (limitation or giving up of attachment to worldly possessions), and renunciation leads to meditation (*dhyan aur samadhi*).[90]

Compassion (*daya*) is rightly said to be the basis of both *dharma* (righteousness or piety) and *ahimsa*, which is the negative aspect of compassion. Non-violence is described not only as *param dharma* (supreme duty), but also *param Brahma*[91] – the supreme divine principle or the supreme law for living beings. In *Svayambhu Stotra*, Shri Shanti Jina is described as the embodiment of compassion and kindness – *dayamurti*. (Samantabhadra, *Svayambhu Stotra*, verse 76) The non-attached (*veetragi*) form (*mudra*) of Shri Ara Jina reflects *vidya-dama-daya-param*, i.e. being totally engrossed in the pursuit of knowledge, control of senses, and being full of compassion or kindness reflecting *dosha-vinigraham*, (*Svayambhu Stotra*, verse 94), i.e. absence of all evils like attachment, lust.

In *Pravachanasara* itself (PS 251), the householders (laymen) as well as saints who are followers of *Jina* (conquerors of internal enemies) are enjoined to render detached or disinterested (*nirvekkha* in Pk., *nirpeksha* in Sk.) aid or help (*uvayaar* in Pk. *upakara* in Sk.) through compassion to others without any consideration or expectation of any kind, even though that might lead to a small stain.

In worshipping the Worthy Lord, the devotee might incur, out of attachment, indulgence or omission, slight impiety or sin (*savadya-lesho*). However, that is of not of much significance in comparison to the vast amount of *punya* (virtue) (*bahu punya rashau*) that one earns thereby, since a small quantity of poison does not affect or pollute an ocean full of cool and exhilarating water. (Samantabhadra, *Svayambhu Stotra*, Verse 58). Similarly, compassion or kindness might lead to a small stain, but that is quite insignificant in comparison to great benefits which accrue particularly to the self in the form of self-restraint or peace of mind, renunciation and contemplation, meditation, etc.

The word "*nirpeksha*" is crucial. It signifies that help to others should be rendered without any interest, desire, expectation or any extraneous consideration of name, fame, etc. (*khyati*, *puja*, *labha vanchha rahitam*, as Jayasena states in PS 251 commentary). Not only householders but also *sadhus* and *shramanas* of good psychic disposition are enjoined to render service and help (PS 249-254) with humility and respect (PS 250) to those suffering from disease, hunger, thirst or exhaustion with all their power (PS 252). The only condition is that in rendering service and help one should not hurt living beings (PS 249-250).

Commenting on it, Amrtachandra observes that the minds of the followers of *Jina* are purified by unalloyed kindness. Owing to *anekant*, their activity is directed towards pure knowledge and intuition of the self. Such people are not forbidden to undertake such an activity characterized by rendering of aid to others (*paropakara*). If, as a result of compassion, such persons acquire a small stain, it does not matter because the objective is the attainment of the pure self (PS 251 AC). Such activity, Jayasena remarks, is the cause of a small stain but results in a great deal of *punya* (*savadyalesho bahu punyarashi*) (PS 251 JS).

Rendering help to a person suffering from disease, hunger, thirst or exhaustion occupies a prominent place among the duties of a saint who is enjoined to render such assistance and service with all his power or to the best of his capability (PS 252). This assistance should be *nirpekhsa* (PS 251), i.e. without any interest, desire (*ichchha*), expectation, mental clinging (*murchcha*), sense of mineness (*mamatva*) and superiority or pride (*ahamkara*). Even with such activity or conduct of excellent attachment (*prashasta raga*), the *shramans* (saints) and householders attain the highest or the supreme (*param*) happiness (*sokkham* in Pk., *saukhyam* in Sk.) of [liberation, *moksha*] (PS 254).

Moha (infatuation) has three roles (*bhumika*) of false perception in regard to things, including the nature of the self (*darshan moha* type of delusion) and attachment (*raga*) and aversion (*dvesha*), which are conduct-deluding or *charitra-moha.* The means to destroy them are discussed in *Pravachanasara* 83-89. The subjects of compassion or kindness (*anukampa* or *karuna*), *vaiyavrttya* or *upakaar* (rendering service and help to others), service (*vaiyyavrttya*) are described in *Pravachanasara* 249-254. Cruelty or violence (the absence of kindness) towards animals or human beings cannot be justified under any circumstances. They cannot also be considered *dharma* in the sense of the inherent nature of the self (*vastu svabhavo dharma*)and the ten moral virtues (*das dharma*) of righteousness or piety (*dharma*) of forgiveness, etc.

Amrtachandra's Comment on Compassion

In view of what has been stated above, it is paradoxical that an eminent scholar like Amrtachandra maintains that the feeling of kindness or compassion towards animals and human beings is the second characteristic of infatuation (*moha*) (PS 85 AC). A number of scholars in Hindi have followed Amrtachandra in their translation of *Pravachanasara* 85. A few others, especially Acharya Jnanasagar, have stated that the word "*karunabhavo*" in *Pravachanasara* 85 should be understood in the sense of an attitude of cruelty (*nirdayata*) or absence of kindness towards animals and human beings as the characteristic of infatuation (*moha*), [not in the sense that compassion is the characteristic of *moha*], along with two other characteristics of *moha*, viz. deluded view and indulgence in sense objects, resulting in attachment and aversion.

To say that a feeling of kindness or pity (*daya*) is the characteristic of *moha*, Acharya Jnanasagar adds, signifies that such a compassionate or kind person is a deluded person (*mohi*, *mithyadrashti*), i.e. having false perception regarding things, including the real nature of the self, terrible sinner and *bahiratma*, i.e. exterior self engrossed in sensual pleasures, slave of his desires and attached to external objects and relations. The interpretation or meaning that compassion is the characteristic of *moha*, he points out, goes against all Jain scriptures. Compassion and goodness is respected in all religions. This error on the part of Amrtachandra, he feels, could be the result of negligence (*pramad*) or it could be the mistake of some other person.

To accuse an eminent *acharya* of the stature of Amrtachandra of negligence (*pramad*) does not seem to be proper. It is also inappropriate to conclude that it could be the mistake of some other person because the version of Amrtachandra's commentary of the verse (PS 85) that the sense or thought of kindness or mercy (*karunya buddhya*) towards sub-human and human beings is (one of the) characteristics of infatuation (*moha*) is found in several copies of *Pravachanasara*. Then what could be the reason of Amrtachandra statement?

Circumstances in which Compassion could be Deluding

Evidently, a moral principle or rule of conduct, including kindness or pity, cannot be universally or absolutely followed blindly by all people in all circumstances and in all times and places, towards all people. In *Pravachanasara* 257 Kundakunda himself categorically states: "Service, assistance or gift [charity, kindness], etc. activities, bestowed on persons who do not know the transcendental (*paramartha*) nature of reality and in whom indulgence in sense objects and passions (*kashaya*) predominate, result (in a rebirth) among low level of gods (*devas*) or men"(PS 257).

In his work, *Purusharthasiddhyupaya*, Amrtachandra has pointed to a number of instances in which the thought of kindness may be quite tempting but could indeed be deluding and counterproductive since it may really be misplaced and lead to the perpetration of violence or killing which is not justified and can in fact be avoided.

For instance, one can argue that killing of one (say tiger, lion, etc.), who kills a number of animals, is justified since it would lead to the protection of many others (PSU 83), that it would be an act of mercy or kindness towards other animals (Amrtachandra, a great votary of non-violence, does not favour that killing). This plausible argument is often raised by sportsmen. They defend hunting on the ground that by doing so they protect humanity from the ravages of ferocious animals. But in reality, apart from the excitement of sport, the feelings that actuate them in killing a lion may be the expectation of reward, praise or being called bold men.

Again, Amrtachandra states: "These kill many lives, and accumulate grave sin." On this basis, it is sometimes said that killing such beings would be an act of mercy towards them. This kind of argument is also misleading. Even those who injure others should not be killed for that reason (PSU 84), since it is also a fallacious argument.

Then again, "Those in great suffering will on being killed soon obtain relief from their agony". (PSU 85) This is called mercy-killing (not only of animals, dog, horse, etc. but also human beings) or euthanasia or doctor-assisted death (in which life support is withdrawn from the patient permanently disabled or suffering from incurable disease). This is legalized in one of the states (Ohio) of USA and one of the countries (Netherlands) in the world. In Egypt, some people considered it a pious religious duty to stab their old parents to death, in the belief that by doing so, they relieved them of miseries and infirmities of old age. It is a misconception and indeed a delusion to call such practices an act of mercy.

In a number of cases of such mercy-killing of the distressed one, which Amrtachandra does not approve (PSU 85), people, including relatives, may be guided more by ulterior motives of saving money for their own use rather than spending it in the hospitalization and treatment of the patient and avoiding the botheration of visiting the patient in the hospital or taking care of the person at home.

The practice of so-called mercy-killing is quite different from the Jaina concept of *sallekhana*, *santhara* or *samadhi-marana*. The latter is a bold and noble attempt to face death willingly or voluntarily in a peaceful, natural, noble way. This is done by the person concerned, who undertakes or engages in it, of his own free will through emaciation of one's passions (anger, pride, greed, etc.). Such a person puts aside all enmity, attachment, acquisitiveness, thereby attaining peace of mind and equanimity. He either undertakes a fast or subsists only on liquid food like milk, buttermilk, fruit juice or only warm water. In some cases, this could even result in curing the disease and averting imminent death. In such cases, one should not forcibly and unnecessarily invite death. (For detailed discussion in this matter see Jagdish Prasad Jain, *Fundamentals of Jainism*, New Delhi: Radiant Publishers, 2005, pp. 215-219).

Amrtachandra has also drawn our attention to several other instances where kindness or mercy could be misplaced or deluding. Thus, the belief that "The happy shall, if killed in state of happiness, will continue to be happy [in their next life]" (PSU 86). "A disciple desirous of piety . . . cutting off the head of his own preceptor when he, by means of constant practice, has attained such perfection of concentration, as leads to a good condition of life" (PSU 87); or "a person killing himself by zealously giving one's own flesh as food to another starving person, seen approaching in front" (PSU 89). (Self-sacrifice, literally speaking, was at one time considered an act of religious piety, but it is undoubtedly *himsa* and attempt at suicide is a criminal offence.)

After citing the above examples, Amrtachandra observes: "Which person is there who, having an enlightened and pure intellect, having served teachers, well-versed in the various points of view, and having realized the essence of Jaina philosophy, would yield to [any kind of] delusions and misconceptions under the guise of *ahimsa*" (PSU 90).

Thus, in practicing compassion or kindness (*karuna*), one must consider whether one is yielding to (any kind of) delusion and misperception, or is one's kindness accompanied with an enlightened view or is that kindness anchored on the transcendental nature of the self, i.e. the innate nature of soul devoid of delusion and attachment.

This is similar to the observance of vows like non-violence and the practice of austerities, etc., which are considered childish in the absence of an enlightened view of things, or when they are devoid of transcendental nature of the self (*paramartha bahira* in Pk. and *paramartha bahya* in Sk.) (SS 152-153). Similarly, it has to be considered whether all the good, virtuous (*punya*) or auspicious (*shubha*) activities, such as kindness, non-violence, etc. we are performing or engaged in, are the cause of transmigratory existence (SS 153) or leading us gradually to liberation (PS 254 AC).

Viewed from the above perspective, it may be said that since Kundakunda was not only a philosopher but also a teacher, he used many key terms that are polysemous and thus capable of more than one meaning (this built-in ambiguity need not necessarily be a defect, but rather an asset). He may have employed the term "*karunabhavo*" in *Pravachanasara* 85 to mean that, depending on the context or the circumstances of the case, kindness (*karuna*) can be considered in both the senses (of *samasa* and *sandhi*). In other words, in certain circumstances, the feeling of kindness may be misplaced and considered as a characteristic of infatuation (*moha*). In other circumstances, the absence of kindness towards sub-human and human beings can be said to be the characteristic of infatuation (*moha*).

Another significant consideration in this regard is whether the person involved or concerned in the act of kindness/absence of kindness (i.e. use of violence or non-violence) is an ordinary layman (say householder) or an ascetic or a spiritual person of a higher stage of moral and spiritual development. When Gandhiji once asked Shrimad Rajchandra, whether we were justified in killing a lion attacking a cow or us?, he replied how can he agree to what leads one to go to hell and result in transmigratory existence? To Gandhi's further remark that the feeling of protecting oneself is a *shubha bhava* (good psychic disposition), Shrimad Rajchandra stated that any cruel or violent thought and act of killing, even for the sake of protection, is not possible without the thought of affliction (*sanklesh*), which results in the bondage of sin.

A person of the stature of Shrimad Rajchandra, who was much advanced in spiritual discipline, or an ascetic, who had renounced all things, is enjoined, to observe perfect and unqualified conduct (*sakal charitra*) (RKS 50), may not entertain any violent thought even in self-defence. On the other hand, a householder, who is still entangled in the world is enjoined to abstain from the deliberate or intentional violence (e.g. such as hunting, offering animal sacrifices, killing for food, amusement or decoration, etc.), which can be avoided by every thinking person without any difficulty and harm to himself. However, he cannot avoid some sort of violence or injury to living beings, that are inevitable in the performance of necessary household activities, such as preparation of food, construction of house, etc. and protection of himself, family members and property against robbers, assailants, etc.

Gandhi, a great votary and proponent of non-violence, was fully committed to the principle that violence should be avoided no matter what, since he was quite confident "about the capacity of human nature for degradation or exaltation" (*Collected Works of Mahatma Gandhi*) (CWMG) (87: 180). In his Nobel 'Peace' Prize acceptance speech, US President Barack Hussein Obama declared to the world that although he has not seen anything weak, passive and naive in the creed and live (life) of Gandhi, he expressed the view that a non-violent movement could not have halted Hitler's armies and that sometimes, the use of force might be necessary and morally justified. In this regard, the following observation is quite relevant.

Although Gandhi insisted that German Jews could have followed a non-violent resistance with a high price to invoke the consciousness of 'ordinary Germans', he thinks even a violent struggle is justifiable in this special case. He states:

> The German persecution of the Jews seems to have no parallel in history. The tyrants of old never went so mad as Hitler seems to have gone. And he is doing it with religious zeal. For he is propounding a new religion of exclusive and militant nationalism in the name of which any inhumanity becomes an act of humanity to be rewarded here and hereafter. The crime of an obviously mad but intrepid youth is being visited upon his whole race with unbelievable ferocity. If there ever could be a justifiable war in the name of and for humanity, a war against Germany, to prevent the wanton persecution of a whole race, would be completely justified. But I do not believe in any war. A discussion of the pros and cons of such a war is therefore outside my horizon or province. But if there can be no war against Germany, even for such a crime as is being committed against the Jews, surely there can be no alliance with Germany. How can there be alliance between a nation which claims to stand for justice and democracy

and one which is the declared enemy of both? *Complete Works of Mahatma Gandhi,* 74: 239-40).

Jayasena's Commentary on Compassion

Jayasena was apparently uneasy or concerned about Amrtachandra's commentary (of PS 85), which did not seem quite right to him. The feeling of kindness, he felt, was being contradictory to the self-restraint of supreme indifference (*param-upeksha samyamvipreet*), which is the characteristic of achievement of pure soul [i.e. from the internal, self-referential point of view (*nishchaya naya*)], is the characteristic of *moha*, while from the external, other-referential point of view (*vyavahara naya*), the absence of kindness is the characteristic of *moha* (PS 85 JS). In other words, Jayasena was saying that from *nishchaya naya* or *shuddha nishchaya naya*, compassion or kindness (*karunabhavo*) is the characteristic of infatuation (*moha*), while from *vyavahara naya*, the absence of compassion (*karunaya abhava*) is an attribute of infatuation.

In this way, he apparently felt that he was resolving the problem but he did not succeed in his attempt. He, in fact, complicated the issue thereby, in as much as it amounted to saying that one can justify anything, even wrong assertion or act by making use of one or the other viewpoint with or without the context and that *nishchaya naya* is opposed to *vyavahara naya*, which are only apparently contradictory, but are not opposite to each other. In their introductory remarks to *Pravachanasara* 189 both Amrtachandra and Jayasena state that there is non-opposition (*avirodha*) between *nishchaya naya* and *vyavahara naya*, which are complimentary to one another, and not antonyms.

The problem is further complicated by the fact that in case kindness is considered a characteristic of infatuation (*moha*), whether it should be regarded as characteristic of perception or view-deluding infatuation (*darshan-moha*) or of conduct-deluding (*charitra-moha*). Since feeling of kindness implies certain degree of commendable attachment (*prashasta raga*), in which external condition of disease, hunger, etc. of other being acts as an auxiliary factor (*nimitta*), it should properly belong to conduct-deluding type of infatuation. *Prashasta raga*, as already discussed, is part of good or auspicious disposition or righteousness (*dharma*), which has purifying effect and helps in the attainment of liberation and hence cannot be considered *adharma*.

Moreover, only from the perspective of *vyavahara naya*, but not from the transcendental perspective (*paramartha*) that the attributes of affective, cognitive and volition or conduct (*darshan*, *jnana* and *charitra*) can be predicated to consciousness, i.e. the conscious self, which is in reality the indivisible unity of these attributes (SS 7 and SS 7 AC), which cannot be separated from one another. Similarly, in spite of the distinction between the three roles of infatuation (*moha*), viz. *moha*, *raga* and *dvesh*, i.e. the two divisions of perception-deluding and conduct-deluding, they are, in fact an integrated whole and an indivisible unity; they are differentiated from or spoken of as distinct only from external, other-referential *vyavahara naya*, not from the transcendental perspective of *paramartha*.

Distorted Views of Kanjipanthi on Compassion

Proceeding from their perverted logic and one-sided thinking, similar to their views on *punya* and *shubha*, the Kanjipanthi, including Kanji Svami himself, have several misperceptions in regard to compassion:

1. That animals and people are miserable only due to their deluded view (*mithyatva*) regarding the nature of the self is wrong because people experience suffering due to the coming into operation, rise, or fruition of painful (*asata*) *vedaniya* (feeling producing) *karman*, i.e. sinful deeds. This can be rectified by the fruition of pleasure-causing (*sata*) category of *vedaniya karman* (TS 6.12), i.e. meritorious activities (*punya*) or good psychic dispositions (*shubha bhava*).

2. To argue that the cause of kindness (*karuna*) is always with reference to the other being is incorrect because the other person/ living being merely acts as an auxiliary factor (*nimitta*), not the direct cause [the feeling of compassion is the inherent nature of *jiva* (self)].

3. That kindness is *prashasta raga* (commendable attachment) which only causes karmic bondage and has no role or contribution in the attainment of liberation, has already been refuted in the above discussion on *shubha* or *punya*. *Karuna*, like *punya*, has a dual role: it results in a small stain, yet it is a means, even if indirect, leading gradually to liberation (PS 254 AC).

4. The argument that kindness is the result of either feeling of attachment or sense of mineness (*mamatva*) towards other living being or the thought of killing or protecting the other, imbued with a sense

of pride/superiority is flawed. It ignores the advice mentioned in *Pravachanasara* that we are enjoined to render aid to others disinterestedly without any *apeksha* (*nirpeksha*), i.e. interest, expectation or feeling of superiority, pride, etc. of any kind (PS 251). It is not in our hands to kill or save another. We can only be a *nimitta* (an auxiliary factor) in alleviating the suffering of others. Kanji Svami errenously does not assign any role for *nimitta*.

5. That the other substance or living being is only knowable (*jneya*), worth only observing and knowing and that one should desist from doing anything in regard to alleviating his suffering as any deed (*karma*) would only result in the karmic bondage. This perception is the result of the distorted concept of *akartratva* or *akarta* (non-doer) of the Kanjipanthi. In fact, this is quite contrary to Kundakunda's description of the self as being *karta* (doer) and *bhokta* (experiencer of one's deeds) (PKS 27).

The self is also said to be the architect of his own destiny (*prabhu*) and as such responsible for one's well-being (PKS 27). Kundakunda never denied the utility and significance of being a responsible person, taking charge of one's life, and being an agent of action (*karta*) concerned about one's own well-being (physical, mental, and spiritual) (*sva-kartratva*). He only said you are not responsible and cannot act for the other. In other words, he denied being an agent of action of the other person (*para-kartratva*). One cannot spend one's life being merely a spectator and let things drift or happen. . . and things do happen. People often speak of and cite Kundakunda's emphasis on being both knower (*jnata*) and observer (*drashta*). They also cite J. Krishnamurti's "choiceless awareness", or being a witness (*sakshi bhava*). They tend to forget that these statements or prescriptions are made in the context of avoiding indulgence in attachment, aversion and anger, etc. passions or evil psychic dispositions, and not in the sense of being an inactive and lazy person.

The Kanjipanthi acknowledge that intelligent persons (*jnani*) can also have feelings of compassion or kindness, that kindness can never be (*kadapi*) the characteristic of conduct-deluding and view-deluding *karma*, and that cruelty (absence of kindness or mercy) is the characteristic of view-deluding (*mithyatva*). However, they make contradictory statements and continue to persist in their distorted and one-sided thinking. They make selective and out of context use of some words/sentences in Jain texts or commentaries of Amrtachandra or Jayasena, thereby corrupting Kundakunda's noble concepts, and propagating views which go against all Jain scriptures.

Concept of *Svayambhu* (Self-Sufficient)

The concept of *Svayambhu* (PS 16) signifies that the self, possessed of conscious attentiveness, is capable of accomplishing virtually anything by itself (*svayameva*). This includes the destruction of *karmas* and even attaining the highest state of *paramatman* (supreme soul), independent of any other factor, i.e. without the help or assistance of any other object or substance (PS 192). That the self itself realizes itself by itself, through its own instrumentality and for itself is best described by Amrtachandra in the form of six components of action called six cases (*karakas*) (see PS 16 AC).[92] This concept is a sure prescription for self-reliance/self-restraint and self-discipline as described in *Niyamsara*. This finds expression in "*appa so paramappa*" (*Paramatma Prakash* 312) or "*appa divvena jaladi*" as Jains say. It is also reflected in the *Gita*, which speaks of *atmanam atmaneva uddhareta*, i.e. elevate yourself by your own self as well as the Buddhist teaching *appa divo bhava*, i.e. be your own light or guide.

Concept of Omniscience *(sarvajnata)*

Pravachanasara 16 states that the self, when purified in psychic-attention through the annihilation of four destructive *karmans* (*ghatia karman*) which results in the removal of obstacles, becomes omniscient (*sarvajna*) by itself and is called self-sufficient, or self-become (*svayambhu*), i.e. one who realizes his full potentiality by his own efforts. The reason why the soul is capable of knowing all the objects of the whole universe is explained in these words: "The soul is co-extensive with knowledge, knowledge is said to be co-extensive with the knowable [i.e. the objects of knowledge]; the knowable comprises the physical and non-physical universe, therefore, knowledge is omnipresent." (PS 23)

Moreover, it is stated: "The great *Jina* is omnipresent [see PS 23], and all the objects (*arthas*) in the world are within his grasp or belongs to him. The *Jina* is embodiment of knowledge; and the objects which are said to be within his grasp belong to him because they are objects-of-his-knowledge (*vishaya*)." (PS 26). Moreover, "The holy Omniscient

Lord or the absolute Knower does not seize (accept) or release and does not evolve into anything else; but without exception he sees and knows everything all around" (PS 32).

While the Kanjipanthi have misused the concept of omniscience in support of their mistaken concept of non-doing/non-doership principle and determinism of sequence bound modifications (*krama-baddha paryaya*), etc.,[93] Kundakunda categorically states: "From the external, other-referential (*vyavahara*) point of view, the omniscient Lord intuits and knows all [physical and non-physical objects, the self and other substances] (*sarvajna*); from the internal, self-referential (*nishchaya*) point of view, the omniscient necessarily intuits and knows his own self (*atmajna*)." (NS 159) This signifies that while the omniscient can have direct intuitive awareness, experience or knowledge of his own self, one cannot possibly have that direct experience or intuitive awareness in regard to other objects. His knowledge of all other objects in the universe is, therefore, considered by Kundakunda as a social or religious necessity from the *vyavahara* viewpoint.

"With Kundakunda," A.N. Upadhye remarks, "*sarvajnata* (omniscience) is a dogma, a religious heritage and an essential part of the doctrine he represents," in the circumstances when different schools of thought have been struggling hard "to prove and establish the omniscience of their respective prophets, for on that depended the very life and death of their systems: it was the omniscience that could give infallibility to their prophets and therefore automatically to their scriptures that constituted the utterances of these prophets." *Sarvajnata* (omniscience), Upadhye adds, thus, "came to be accepted and discussed only as a religious necessity."[94]

The Exposition of Knowledge

Speaking of the "unique contribution" of Jainism, particularly Kundakunda in the field of epistemology and its "outstanding solution of the relation between the soul and its knowledge," Hari Mohan Bhattacharya observes:

> *Jnana* or knowledge is to (Jaina) in relation of identity, the essence of the soul. Kundakundacharya, who is perhaps the oldest of the Jaina epistemologists and stands as a link between the canonical and later classical ways of thinking, remarks in his *Pravachanasara* (PS 35): *jo janadi so*

nanam; he whose knowledge is to be of real significance must be regarded as identical in essence with the soul, which in knowing only modifies itself into knowledge; there is no separation possible of any kind between the knower and its knowledge, the soul which is *parinami* cannot be regarded as something different from its *parinama. Knowledge* as *parinama is the soul knowing.*[95]

Relation between the Soul and Knowledge

The above statement refutes the view of both the *Naiyyayika* and the *Mimamsaka* who have taken the separatist view of the relation between the soul and its knowledge. To the *Naiyyayika*, the soul is a static reality to which knowledge comes and goes according to the presence or absence of the collection of the conditions (*karanasamagri*) of knowledge. The *Naiyyayika* goes to the extent of presuming that since knowledge is the source of *karma* and therefore of all sin, it should be eliminated to attain *moksha.* The *Mimansaka* fare no better in explaining the relation of knowledge to the soul since they describe it as an *avastha* or state that comes and goes just like the curved state (*kundalavastha*) or the straight state (*arjavavastha*) in the body of a snake in its intrinsic character.

Jains also feel that the Advaitist errs since the *Advaita* theory regards the soul as only the *antahkarana vrittis* [the psychosis of the internal organ as the determinant of the consciousness is knowledge] which do not have the intrinsic character of illumination of its object for the *antahkarana*, though an internal sense is no better than the outer sense which is *jada* or unilluminating in reality. The Advaitist tries to save himself from this difficulty by his supposition of the soul as *sakshi* or transcendental witness to all intellectual activities. Nevertheless, as a witness the soul cannot lend its illumining character to knowledge of objects.

Even the Advaitist concept of *anatmamatmopacarat*, by stressing the principle of *adhyasa* (viz. the empirical application of the transcendental power of *avidya* which rules the realm of empirical knowledge), does not resolve the problem of illumination. The argument that *anatamatva* of the *antahkarana* is transformed into anything of the *atman* by mere magic of *adhyasa* and as such the *antahkarana jada* by nature fails to account for the illumination or knowledge of objects.

We also notice the same inaccuracy in explaining knowledge owing to failure of the Advaitist to see that knowledge is always by the soul and occurs in the soul if it occurs anywhere as its own modification and knowledge shares in the illumining character of the soul of which it is a modification. Jains also criticize Buddhists in general for denying that mind as a reality ought to enter into the relation with knowledge.

The Jaina insists that both the soul and knowledge are closely interrelated, that knowledge is both self-revealing and also revealing its object as a *parinama* or evolution of the self-luminous soul. Thereby, the Jaina avoids the difficulties encountered by other Indian systems of thought. Thus, the Jaina insists that a proper relation is imperative between the soul and its knowledge.

Misplaced Criticisms of Kundakunda by I.C. Shastri

There are other critics like Indra Chandra Shastri, who is well-versed in Shvetambara Canons, but have only a superficial understanding of the select verses (PS 23-26 and PS 28-32) of Kundakunda's *Pravachanasara* (and Amrtachandra's commentary thereon). Shastri is hardly aware of his other works like *Samayasara, Niyamsara,* etc., and does not holistically comprehend his ethico-spiritual standpoints of *nishchaya, vyavahara* and transcendental aspects. Yet he finds fault with Kundakunda's views in the matter. Such criticism is quite misplaced and reflects his strong prejudice and bias against both the author of *Pravachanasara* and his commentator Amrtachandra.

Referring to Kundakunda's example of a sapphire-gem placed in milk (PS 30), Shastri states: "The knowledge operates on [is related to] objects, just as the sapphire (gem), thrown (placed) in the milk, pervades the whole of it with its lustre (splendour)." The same translation is quoted by Shastri himself [pp. 151-152 of his book], but he goes on to observe: "Kundakunda cites the example of sapphire placed in milk. The sapphire makes the milk appear green without pervading the entire area."[96] Thus, although Kundakunda specifically mentions "*indraneel ratna*" (sapphire-gem), which makes the milk appear "blue," not green as Shastri states. Moreover, Kundakunda uses the word "*abhibhuya*," which means dominating, overwhelming or all-pervasive. One wonders if the sapphire-gem does not pervade the whole of it, then how can it make the whole milk appear blue?

The main purpose of this example is to prove that consciousness (*samvedana*), which, because it is not separated from the self, constantly receives its inherent character in its function of agent or instrument. In other words, in its character of knowledge, consciousness pervades all the knowable appearances (as effects) of all the objects (as causes). Thus, when one metaphorically remarks that by reason of their relation of cause and effect, that "knowledge, dominating or pervading the objects, abides (in them)," there is no contradiction (PS 30 AC, see also PS 35 AC).

In the earlier two verses, Kundakunda states in clear terms:

> The Knower possesses knowledge as his innate nature; the objects, surely, possess the character of knowables with regard to the knower, like shapes or forms with reference to the eye. But they do not abide in each other (PS 28).
>
> The Knower, neither entering nor shunning to enter the knowables, verily, in consequence of his surpassing the sense-organs, knows and sees the whole world, as the eye knows and sees the shapes or forms, i.e. the objects of sight (PS 29).

Explaining these verses in detail, Amrtachandra observes:

> The Knower and the objects, owing to their separateness (*prthakatva*), which forms their individual-nature (*sva-lakshan*), do not possess occurrence within each other; but they merely possess a mutually related occurrence, effected by the relation between their innate natures as knowledge and knowable. For instance, as the eyes and the things having shapes or forms, which are their objects are respectively ready to receive and to occasion the appearances of the knowables, even without mutual penetration, so the self and the objects are ready to receive and to occasion the appearances of all knowables, without being identical with one another (PS 28 AC).
>
> Just as the eyes, not entering, i.e. not taking hold of shapes or forms of the substances with its own spacio-infinitesimal-constituents (*pradeshas*), nor shunning to enter them, i.e. really appropriating their distinguishable appearances, knows and sees, likewise the soul – of which, since it surpasses the sense-organs, we need not doubt at all that it acts independently of approach – not entering, i.e. not taking hold, with its own *pradeshas*, of all the things which function as knowables, nor shunning to enter them, i.e. as it were uprooting and then devouring all the knowable appearances which abide in the things, with the aid of the manifoldness of its efficacy,

> knows and sees. So that, as concerns the knower, who develops an activity (*yoga*) of manifold efficacy, his entrance into the things, attains just as much reality as his non-entrance (PS 29 AC).

Amrtachandra explains the apparently contrary statements regarding *Pravachanasara* verses 26 and 27 with the help of Jaina doctrine of *anekant* (multifacetedness or many-sided view of the reality of things). He states that from the internal, self-referential (*nishchaya*) perspective, the worthy Lord, "knows without moving himself towards all the appearances of the knowables, since he never leaves his own reality *svatattva.*" From an external, other-referential (*vyavahara*) aspect, the worthy Lord is said to have omniscient knowledge since all the objects in the world are within his grasp (PS 26-27 AC). In *Niyamsara*, Kundakunda categorically states: "From *vyavahara* point of view, the worthy Lord knows and intuits all (objects), i.e. he is omniscient; from *nishchaya* point of view, he necessarily knows and intuits his own self" (NS 159).

Unable to properly understand the Jaina doctrine of *anekant* and the ethico-spiritual viewpoints of Kundakunda, I.C. Shastri mistakenly accuses Kundakunda of causing "confusion". He blames Amrtachandra for taking "the position of Sautantrika, in holding that "knowledge takes the form of object" (pp. 177 and 175 of *Jaina Epistemology*), when he (Amrtachandra) unambiguously states that "all substances abide in their own characteristic nature" (PS 26 AC) and that "all the knowable appearances . . . abide in the things" and that the soul, "with the manifoldness of its efficacy, knows and sees" (PS 29 AC).

Knowledge, Amrtachandra adds,

> evolves onto all the distinguishable appearances which exist besides knowledge; and we may say that all the objects which are the causes of all the knowable appearances, which are (really) the effects of self-evolving knowledge, in a certain way reside in knowledge (PS 35 AC).

Shastri's contention that both Amrtachandra and Jayasena take "different courses to explain" (p. 175 of his book) Kundakunda's views pertaining to the exposition of knowledge also has no basis since both of them state that the knowable appearances may be compared to the reflection images (when located in the mirror of consciousness) (see PS 31 AC and PS 31 JS). Jayasena uses the word "*adarsha*", and Amrtachandra mentions "*mukura*", both terms meaning mirror. Shastri cites "*adarsha*" on p. 175 of his book.

Apparently Shastri is unable to comprehend the logic of Kundakunda's statement: "The soul is co-extensive with knowledge, knowledge is said to be co-extensive with the knowable [i.e. the objects of knowledge]; the knowable comprises the physical and non-physical universe, therefore, knowledge is omnipresent." (PS 23). As stated earlier, both Kundakunda and Amrtachandra categorically state (see PS 28 and 28 AC) that the knower inherently possesses knowledge as his innate nature whereas the objects possess the character of knowables. In other words, the two are quite separate from each other. However, Shastri erronously argues that Kundakunda's statement that "knowledge is coextensive with the objects of knowledge" is tantamount to "physical mixing." (p. 177 of his book) He is therefore unable to acknowledge the Jaina view of "the limitedness of the soul," which is "co-extensive with the body". This, Shastri contends, is reconciled by Kundakunda with the Vedanta view of all-pervasiveness which Kundakunda does "under the influence of the Vedanta" (p. 177 of his book). He is, thus, unable to see the logic of Kundakunda and unable to understand the validity of the *vyavahara* point of view.

I.C. Shastri is also unable to comprehend the rationale of the Jaina concept of the soul, in its embodied existence, which has the same dimensions as the large or small body, in which it resides. As a result, sensation (*samvedana*) is felt in all parts of the body. The Jaina concept of *jiva* or consciousness, which is equal in extent to its body, also ensures that the subjective experience of a person is his own personal experience and not of any third person.

Moreover, the Jaina view that the soul is co-extensive with the body apparently anticipates contemporary somatic philosophers like Moreleau-Ponty, Gabriel Marcel and Michael Polanyi. However, there is one difference. Unlike the Jaina view that the body can only have physical qualities, the somatic philosophers contend that the body consists of emotions, which is contrary to common experience. The position of the Sankhyas is also untenable because they maintain that "unconscious *prakrti* carries both psychological and physical qualities" whereas the *purusha* (self) remains "totally isolated," because its involvement in matter is illusory.

On the authority of Shvetambara scholar Yashovijaya, Shastri argues that the Jaina concept of *samudghata* alone can be considered to explicitly support the view that the soul is all-pervasive insofar as its power is concerned.[97] In the *Nyayakhanda Khadyatika, karika* 70 (pages 648-649), Yashovijaya confirms that the soul can pervade the entire universe and is therefore all-pervasive. However, as far as its activities are concerned it is confined to the body.

Digambara scholars have also dealt with the subject of the *samudghata*, which is altogether different from Kundakunda's description of all-pervasiveness or omnipresence of knowledge. *Samudghata* is "the emanation of the soul-particles or space points from the body, without discarding it wholly and for good". The whole soul does not leave the body. It is, in fact, only "a sort of overflow for some particular reason and the soul returns to the body to be re-absorbed by it" Seven kinds or varieties of *samudghata* are recognized in Jaina philosophy.

Again, Shastri cites the definition of *jiva* as given in Digambara text *Dravya Sangraha* (DS 2) by stating that it is characterized by *upayoga*, etc., without mentioning *chetana* (consciousness), which can equally be cited as the definition of *jiva*. He mistakenly observes: "Kundakunda also agrees with the same" (in this regard he refers to PKS 27) (p. 143 of his book), whereas Kundakunda specifically declares in that verse that the soul (*jiva*) is consciousness (*chetana*), having a particular characteristic of *upayoga*, viz. manifestation or function of consciousness in the two cognitive forms or modes of knowledge and perception. (PKS 27).

I.C. Shastri also does not seem to give importance to Kundakunda's deep insight distinguishing the soul (*jiva*), soul substance (*jiva dravya*) or the essential principle of *jiva* (*jiva tattva*), viz. consciousness-as-such from the embodied souls of different classes of living beings (*jiva nikaya*), possessing bio-energies (*pranas*) (PS 182) and consisting of two distinct substances, *jiva* and matter (*pudgal*), though having unity or oneness (*aikibhuta*) in consequence of mutual penetration yet distinct in their innate nature (*svabhava - bhedatparatvena*, PS 240 AC), or even when united as one (*aikya*) like milk and water in one body yet not one due to the distinctness in nature (*bhinna svabhavat*), PKS 34 AC) and thus having separateness from the body. As a result, the two substances have their own distinct characteristics (*jiva* or soul possessing its subjective attributes of cognition, feeling and volition, while material body, an inanimate entity possessing its own characteristic sense qualities of touch, taste, smell and colour).

Jaina Concept of the Soul and its Relation to Knowledge

Knowledge, according to Kundakunda, constitutes the inalienable attribute or quality of soul or consciousness (*chetana*). He states: "He who knows is knowledge (*jo janadi so nanam*); but the self does not by the help of its knowledge becomes something-that-is-knowing (*jnayaka*)"; knowledge evolves by itself, and all the objects reside in knowledge (PS 35). Knowledge is the evolution (*parinama*) of the soul knowing though the evolution cannot be separated from the evolving self. The forced supposition (*klesh kalpana*) of a separation of knower and knowledge is superfluous (PS 35 AC).

In this context, H.M. Bhattacharya observes:

> A conscious reality is never divorced from its own conscious modifications and qualities in which lies its very life. . . A *parinama* [state-of-evolution] or modification issuing from the *parinami* [the evolving being] or the modifying, and yet not in essential relation with the *parinami*, is as false an abstraction as the *aparinami* [unchanging] or immutable real without any *parinama* or modification.[98]

This conception of the self or soul as a dynamic or evolving eternal reality (*parinami nitya*) something persisting or enduring through its modes cannot be differentiated from knowledge. This view of the self and its relation to knowledge is quite different from the Samkhya "conception of the self as a static and unmodifying (*aparinami*) eternal principle which does not enter into the constitution of knowledge, but which merely looks on it from a distance as it arises, as a modification of an unconscious principle (*prakrti*). This virtual separation between the self and knowledge (*buddhi*) entails an actual stultification of each of them."[99] In this context, Nathmal Tatia remarks:

> Consciousness of the *jiva* manifests itself in cognitive acts, and is not like the unchanging principle of consciousness in the Samkhya-Yoga school which ascribes the cognitive acts of *buddhi* (intelligence) which is an evolute of the unconscious principle of *prakrti*. . . Consequently [Jainism] does not differentiate the metaphysical soul (*jiva*) from the epistemic subject (*jnata*) as is done in Samkhya-Yoga and monistic Vedanta.[100]

The Jaina concept of the soul and its relation to knowledge also differs from the *Mimansakas* and the *Vaisheshikas*, who maintain that *jnana* or knowing capacity is not the nature of the soul. They regard it as an accidental or adventitious quality generated in the soul on account of its contact with the body, mind, and sense organs. *Jnana* (knowledge) is, thus, considered to be a distinct entity from the soul. It is said to be brought in association with the soul or *jivatma* by combination (*samavaya*) whereby the soul becomes the knower. In other words, the quality of consciousness (*chetana*) and substance of the soul (*atmadravya*) are two different entities occasionally or accidentally brought together by extraneous circumstances.[101]

If after giving up sinful undertakings and practicing good and auspicious conduct, one does not get rid of infatuation (*moha*), both view-deluding as also conduct-deluding (viz. attachment and aversion), one does not find the "pure" self (PS 79). Abstention or rejection of every censurable activity of mind, speech and body and being satisfied in the practice of good psychic attention or auspicious conduct is not an end in itself, especially as the danger of submission to the army of infatuation exists or is near at hand. As a result, one obviously girds up one's loins for the victory over the army of infatuation (PS 79 AC). The means of overcoming *moha* is described in the next verse (PS 80).

He who knows the *arahanta* (one who has destroyed the internal enemies of infatuation, attachment, aversion, anger, etc. passions) with reference to substance, quality and modification knows the self; his infatuation (*moha*) indeed perishes (PS 80).

The sense or the purport (*abhipraya*) of the verse is that when one compares one's own self with the *arahanta*, he necessarily comes to know the difference. While *arahanta* has destroyed both view-deluding as well as conduct-deluding (viz. attachment and aversion) infatuation (*moha*), he is not free from those impurities of a deluded view, attachment and aversion, which are the direct cause of bondage (SS 188-189, SS 178, PKS 149; see also SS 164-165 JS). Accordingly, one feels inspired to get rid of them, just as after knowing the existence of dirt on the face by looking into a mirror, one necessarily tries to remove that dirt. Though attachment to *arahanta* is a factor in the bondage of auspicious (*shubha*) karmas, knowledge in regard to him is the cause of inhibition (*samvara*) and dissociation (*nirjara*) of *karmas*.

The Exposition of Joy

The practice of [prescribed] conduct by *shramanas*, saints and householders in whom excellent attachment (*prashasta raga*) is primary is said to lead to the highest happiness (*param sokkham* in Pk. and *param saukhyam* in Sk.) (PS 254). This is equated with *nirvana sukh* (happiness or bliss of liberation) (PS 254 AC). In *Samayasara*, Kundakunda states that the conscious self, who having [carefully] read the *Samaya Prabhratam* or *Samayasara* (the treatise on the nature and essence of the soul), and understood its real meaning and purport, firmly sticks to it, will attain excellent happiness (*uttam sukha*) (SS 415). This is said to be of the nature of *anakulata*, i.e. devoid of mental agitation, anxiety, eagerness, uneasiness or distress (SS 415 AC).

In *Ratnakaranda Shravakachara* (Verse 2), Samantabhadra defines *dharma* (righteousness or piety) as that which liberates living beings from the pain, misery or suffering of the worldly existence and installs in or begets them excellent happiness (*uttam sukha*).

In order to understand the nature of *uttam sukha*, one has to distinguish it from sensual pleasures, which is in fact misery in the guise of happiness. This is explained in *Pravachanasara* in the following words:

> That happiness which is dependent (i.e. rests on something else); connected with detriment or amenable to disturbances (for it is utterly confused, since it is attended by different longings, such as hunger, thirst etc.); interrupted or terminable (for oppositions are noticed in different longings); cause of *karmic* bondage (*karma* means crystallized effects of past activities of energies which brings in its train the army of the vices, passion, etc. trailing along the road of sensual enjoyments); unequal (for it is utterly unsteady since it evolves through increase and decrease and is not same for different persons); and acquired by means of the senses is indeed misery in disguise (PS 76 and PS 76 AC).

The lords of men, demons and gods, oppressed by their natural (*sahaja*) organs of senses, unable to withstand that misery, find pleasure in satisfying (*ramya*) objects (PS 63), which serve to soothe their disease (PS 63 AC). Misery is inherent or natural (*sabbhava* in Prakrit and *svabhava* in Sanskrit, PS 64 and PS 64 AC) in the lives of those who find satisfaction in sense-objects, i.e. in sensorial pleasure (PS 64). If this were not their natural urge, there would not be any attempt on their part for obtaining the objects of senses (PS 64). Those who seek pleasure in the satisfaction of sense-enjoyments remain discontented because that necessarily makes them thirst and hanker after the pleasures of senses for more and more sense-objects due to their craving (*tanha* or *trashna* in Sk.). As a result, they are afflicted by misery till death (PS 74-75 and PS 74-75 AC).

If happiness lies in the external objects of senses, then the pleasure we get in eating the first few pieces of a tasty sweet, say 2-3 *rasgullas*, then why we do not get similar pleasure in eating 5 or 10 such pieces.

Another Jain text, *Prashamratiprakaran* of Umasvami or Umasvati (Verse 234) observes:

> The happiness of heaven is indirect, it is beyond our experience. Thus, we may be disinterested in it. The happiness of salvation is still more indirect. Hence, we may have doubts about it. On the other hand, the peace and calm brought about by the subsidence or quelling down the excitement of passions and the happiness resulting therefrom can be directly experienced right here. This happiness is not dependent on other objects, things or beings. It is not perishable either.

The so-called pleasures of worldly life, viz. sensual pleasures, are always accompanied by pain. They are never full and unadulterated. They are preceded and followed by suffering. They are transient, passing and short-lived. What people in general consider happiness is mostly sensual pleasure which by its very nature is dependent on worldly objects pleasing to our senses. *Prashamsukha*, i.e. happiness derived from or resulting from calmness of mind and equanimity, is free from all these shortcomings.

The Exposition of Knowlable *(Jneya)*

The object of knowledge (*jneya*, i.e. knowable) is substance (*dravya*), which by its nature is an existent reality (*sat*) (PS 99, 105, PKS 10 and TS 5.29), and is subject to evolution (*parinama*) (PS 99). Substance is characterized by an indivisible unity of substance (*dravya*), attributes or qualities (*guna*) and modes or modifications (*paryaya*) (PS 93). While a substance does not forsake its innate nature, it is combined (*samavedan* in Pk., *samavetam* in Sk.) of stability or persistence (*dhruva*), origination, and destruction at one and the same moment (*ekkammi cheva samaye* in Pk., *ekasmin chaiva samaye* in Sk.) (PS 95, 99, 103).

In another of his works *Panchastikayasara* (PKS), Kundakunda states that the existent reality is the characteristic of substance (*dravya sat lakshanam*, PKS 10; also *sat dravya lakshanam*, TS 5.29). The existent reality, he adds, is that which is *nitya* (permanent) (PKS 6). Yet, at the same time, *parinami* or *traikalika bhava parinata* (PKS 6), i.e. one that undergoes modifications in all three times (past, present and future), thereby manifesting the characteristic of *dravya bhava* (PKS 6), *dravati* (PKS 9) or *dravyatva*, i.e. "that which by nature, flows towards its modes". The substance is permanent (TS 5.4) and permanence (*nityam*) is indestructibility of the essential nature (quality) of the substance (*tad bhavavyayam nityam*, TS 5.31).

The intrinsic nature of substance (*tadbhava*) is the existence of the past nature in the present. It is that existence, condition or mode, which is the cause of recognition or remembrance. In other words, a thing is seen as having the same nature with which it was seen formerly. So it is recognized in the form, "This is the same as that". "This is that only" is recognition.[102]

Thus, recognition of the object in future proves its permanence. It is noteworthy that while the intrinsic nature of a substance is permanent, it is also evolvent (*parinami*), i.e. undergoes modifications or changes in its modes. It is, therefore, called *parinami nitya*. Modification (*parinama*) of a substance means the continuity of the essential nature of substance and its qualities (*guna*) through changes (*tadbhavah parinamah*, TS 5.42).

In other words, a substance is the combination of the contradictory characteristics/points of view (*sa-pratipaksha*) of *dhrauvya* (indestructibility, constancy or continuity) while undergoing *utpad vyaya* (origination and destruction), i.e. change or modifications (*bhangotpad-dhrauvyatmika sa-pratipaksha* (PKS 8), (*utpad vyaya dhrauvya sambaddham*) (PS 95) or *utpad vyaya dhrauvya yuktam sat* (TS 5.30). Thus, a substance (i.e. existent reality) is neither absolutely changeless or permanent (*sarvatha nitya*) nor absolutely impermanent, transitory or changing (*sarvatha kshanik*) (PKS 8 AC). What appears and disappears are modes (*paryaya*); what persists is substance. Origination and cessation coexist with persistence/stability.

There is, Kundakunda elaborates, no coming-into-existence or origination without destruction. There is no destruction devoid of origination. Thereby, he declares that there is necessary concomitance (*avinabhava*) between one another. By stating that origination and destruction are possible only when there is an abiding something existing as constant or stable (*dhruva*) (PS 100), he seeks to resolve the argument among philosophers in regard to *satkaryavada* and *asatkaryavada* (PS 100)[103]

In this manner, when the necessary concomitance (*avinabhava*) is proved between the triple characteristics (origination, destruction and stability), then depending on the view of non-differentiation, Acharya Kundakunda points out that at the same moment (*samaya*) the same substance takes the forms, modes, names or states of origination, persistence and destruction, which certainly are inseparably rolled into one. All the three are, therefore, indeed the substance (PS 102).

Definition of Substance

Substance (*dravya*) is defined as that which, while it does not "forsake its innate nature [i.e. consciousness in the case of *jiva* (soul substance)] [TS 5.29], is characterized by origination, annihilation and stability [TS 5.30] and which possesses or is endowed with qualities and modifications [TS 5.38], is called a substance" (PS 95 and PKS 10) (also in TS 5.29, 30 and 38). And again: "Existence is the innate nature of a substance, which is accompanied by qualities and various modifications of its own, and by origination, annihilation and stability at all times" (PS 96). Substance, he adds, is neither created nor destroyed; the coming into existence or origination and ceasing to exist or destruction take place in the modes (PKS 11, 15).

Dravya (substance) is indivisible. There is an integral unity of its qualities (*guna*) and modifications (*prayaya*), which appear and disappear, originate and undergo annihilation. Kundakunda categorically affirms: "There is without substance no quality whatever and no modification" (PS 110). There is, he adds, neither mode and quality without substance nor substance without mode (*paryaya*) and quality (PKS 12-13).

As *dravya* (substance), the conscious entity of *jiva* is endowed or characterized with *dravyatva* (flow of consciousness in various ways), i.e. that which by nature flows towards or evolves into its modes or modifications (*paryaya*). These modifications are of two kinds. Firstly, there are modifications in qualities (*guna paryaya*), which are simultaneous (*sahabhavi* or *sahavarti*). Secondly, there are modifications, which take place in the conditions (*gati*) or modes, such as hellish, human, etc. states of living beings in their empirical, mundane existence, which are successive (*kramabhavi* or *kramavarti*) and extrinsic. These are called modes of substance (*dravya paryaya*).

The affective, cognitive and volitional qualities along with their modifications in being deluded (*mithya*) or enlightened (*samyak*) are simultaneous (*sahabhavi* or *sahavarti*) with and intrinsic to the substance or internal aspect or mode of consciousness (*sva samaya*, SS 2). This is the nature of that (substance), i.e. thatness or the inner principle (*antas tattva*) of self itself (*atman*) (PS 94 AC). The substance, undifferentiated from the existence-of-own nature, evolves by itself from one quality into another. It is, therefore, remarked that the quality-modifications (*guna paryaya*) are indeed the substance (PS 104).

Apart from consciousness, *jiva* is also said to be endowed with *upayoga* (function, manifestation or attentiveness of consciousness) (PS 127, PKS 16, 27), i.e. a functional self, i.e. an evolving reality. Affective, cognitive and volitional or conative attributes are the three aspects or functions of consciousness, viz. the internal self-referential aspects or modes of consciousness (*sva-samaya*) (first line of *Samayasara* 2). These three attributes (*guna*) or functions of consciousness (*upayoga*) are subject to modifications (*guna paryaya*) and these can be *gunantara* (PS 104). In other words, they can be transformed from one quality into another, including distorted or deluded (*mithya*) and enlightened (*samyak*). If these attributes are deluded, they are the cause of transmigratory existence (*samsara*) of *jiva*. If they are enlightened, they constitute the path of liberation (*moksha marg*) (TS 1.1).

The very term *dravya* (substance) signifies *dravyatva*, i.e. "that which flows or evolves towards its modes". Thus, the soul (*jiva*, consciousness) accepts the character of its state-of-evolution, good or evil, pure or impure, and possesses the nature [form, mode or state] of that through which it evolves during the time of the evolution (PS 8-9).

Inseparability of Substance, Quality and Modification

There is identity (*avyatiriktabhava* or *abheda*) of substance and qualities, i.e. there is neither quality without substance nor substance without quality (PKS 13). Similarly, there is the necessary concomitance (*avinabhava*) of origination, annihilation and stability or persistence, meaning thereby that there is necessary concomitance (*avinabhava*) between substance (*dravya*) and its modification (*paryaya*). In other words, there is no coming into existence or origination without destruction. There is no destruction devoid of origination.

Moreover, there is neither origination nor destruction without stability (PS 100).

The inseparability of these three constituents is categorically confirmed in the following words: "In the absence of substance, there can be neither quality nor modification" (PS 110). The quality modifications are modifications of one substance, hence quality modifications are indeed substance only (*eva*) (PS 104 AC). Kanji Svami himself admits at one place that in *Pravachanasara* "even *vikar* (agitated, altered or impure states of the mind) are said to be *dharma* (characteristics or traits) of *atma* (soul) because it is also the *paryaya* (mode or modification) of the soul."[104]

Moreover, a substance is the substratum of both attributes/qualities and modes (*dravyam guna paryayashrayam*, PKS 10, and TS 5.38). However, while qualities reside permanently in substance, modifications of substance (*dravya paryaya*) as well as qualities (quality modifications or *guna paryaya*) appear and disappear. As such, any particular modifications, including distortion or deviation (*vibhava*) of affective, cognitive, etc. (*darshanadi*) qualities of self, are transitory, impermanent or "occasional".[105]

In view of the clear-cut statements cited above, the modification (*paryaya*) is (*ananya*, PS 114), i.e. not separate or different from the substance/entity, which is the substratum (*ashrya*, PS 93 AC) of that modification. The modification(s) exist within the substance. There is a necessary concomitance (*avinabhava*) of origination, annihilation and persistence or stability. Indeed, they depend on modification, which are parts (*ansha*). These modifications, in turn, depend on, rest upon or are sustained by substance. Hence, all these are only substance which is the union, combination or aggregate (*samudaya*) of all these (PS 101 AC). The necessary concomitance (*avinabhava*) or inseparability of the three constituents of a substance is described in *Pravachanasara* 100-103.

The substance undergoes modifications by itself, including evolution from one quality into another (*gunantara*), i.e. quality-modification or modification of quality (*guna paryaya*). However, the essential nature/characteristic of a substance (e.g. consciousness-as-such or sentiency (*chetana*)) persists (*sat avasthitam*, PS 99 or *sat vishishtam* (PS 104). In other words, *jiva* (the self or soul) substance, invariably subsists or remains as the background or forms the substratum of all its changes or modifications. These include inauspicious, auspicious, or pure states of consciousness or the manifestations, or modes of cognition, feeling and volition, which are inalienable attributes of conscious entity.

And this is what constitutes the stability (*dhrauvya*) constituent of a substance, something stable, persisting or enduring through its modes or in the midst of its changes, modifications or evolutions and makes the existent reality (substance), including *jiva*, a dynamic, evolvent, permanent reality (*parinami nitya*), in Jainism, not an unchanging, unevolving, unmodifying entity as is the case in Samkhya system of philosophy and Advaita Vedanta.

The substance, quality and modification are said to be inseparable (*aprathak*). There is no differentiation of place or location. They occupy the same locale (*avibhakta pradesh*). Nevertheless, there is distinctnessor otherness (*anyatva*) because there is non-identity (*a-tad-bhava*) among them (PS 106).

Logical Distinction between Substance, Quality and Modification

To fully comprehend reality, it is evident that there is a logical and conceptual distinction between substance, quality and modification. However, they must necessarily be taken together as they are inseparably rolled into one. Any separation (*prthakatva*) between them would suggest a cleavage between the evolutes and the evolvent reality, which will reduce each one of them into non-existent entity.[106] The qualities and modifications are both distinct (*bhinna*) as well as not distinct (*abhinna*) from the substance. "Metaphysically, they are non-distinct or having identity/unity with the *dravya* (substance), but logically they are distinct from it." Without this logical distinction, there is no other way of apprehending the substance as substance, qualities as such, and *paryaya* (modification) *per se.*[107]

In other words, substance and attributes are inseparable. However, the substance is not the same as its attributes and the attributes are not similar to substance. The difference between the two is only a difference of reference, not one of existence, even though it is a fact that it is the substance that manifests its nature through its attributes. A substance without attributes and attributes dissociated from the underlying substance would all be meaningless abstractions. Attributes therefore can neither exist without the substance nor can the substance be divorced from the attributes. Hence, in the world of reality, there can be no separate existence either of substance or attributes from each other.[108] Likewise, there is "no substance that is devoid of modification, nor there is any modification without an abiding something, a substance" The trinity which comprise a substance are origin, decay and continuance.[109]

Misperceptions of Kanjipanthi concerning Substance and Mode

This section highlights several misperceptions of Kanjipanthi regarding substance and mode in the light of our previous discussion. Firstly, Kanji Svami's assertion that *paryaya* (modifications) and *dravya* (substance) are distint existent realities or two separate ontological entities. (*bhinna sattayen*)[110] is mistaken. It is, in fact, a gross deviation from Kundakunda's teachings and all other Jain texts, including the *Tattvartha Sutra.* In making such an argument, the motive of Kanji Svami is apparently two-fold. On the one hand, he seems to want to pave the way for the self being declared *aparinami* (without modification). Secondly, he aims to emphasize that psychic dispositions (*ragadi bhava*) like attachment are not *vibhava* (distorted, deluded psychic dispositions of self), but *para bhava*, i.e. psychic states pertaining to or concerning other substance or entity and as such it is not the responsibility of self to make efforts to purify the impurities of attachment, etc.

Accordingly, the self or soul is said to be *aparinami* (changeless). It is said to be "separate from its modification (*paryaya*)" from *nishchaya naya.* Kanji Svami, thus, declares that "the absence or negation of *paryaya* in the substance, in which there is no *paryaya.*"[111] Kanji Svami further declares: "I am changeless (*aparinami*) in all three times (*trikali*) even in the present time."[112]

The second misperception of Kanji Svami is that he asserts: "It is not that I have the capacity or the potentiality of becoming perfect supreme soul (*purna paramatma*), but that I am perfect supreme soul (*purna paramatma*) at present - think as that."[113] "My soul (*atma*)," he goes on to state "is eternally pure consciousness and bliss (*nitya shuddha chit-ananda*)." This implies that the self, which is said to be already *paramatma* or "pure consciousness", need not make efforts or adopt moral and spiritual means (*sadhan*) to purify the soul, thereby making it perfect.

Such deviations, innovations or misperceptions, harboured by Kanjipanthi (a group of Digambara Jains, which are followers of Kanji

Svami, a Shvetambara saint, who joined the Digambara sect) are gross distortions of Kundakunda's teachings and Jain scriptures (*agam*) as such. The Kanjipanthi opine that *dhruva* (constancy) signifies *aparinami chaitanya tattva*, i.e. changeless consciousness.[114] In reality, however, *dhruva* actually signifies that which exists, subsists or persists as a constant factor in all three times (*trikali*). This constant factor in *jiva* (self) is consciousness-as-such (*jivatva* or *parinamika bhava*, i.e. *atma* or soul), which is evolvent (*parinami*) and the substratum of its attributes of cognition, feeling and volition as also all psychic states, changes or modifications, pure or impure.

Substance (*dravya*), according to Kundakunda, is characterized by permanence or continuity and change. The *dhruva* (constant, eternal) element in substance comprises its "*svabhava*, i.e. own nature" (in the case of *jiva*, its *jivatva*, i.e. consciousness-as-such), which it never leaves (*aparityakta*). The evolving or change aspect is concerned with the modifications (*paryaya* or *parinama*) of substance and its qualities or attributes (PS 95-96).

The soul, which is *parinami*, H.M. Bhattacharya points out, cannot be regarded as something different from its *parinama* (evolution, change or modification).[115] Apart from the conscious self, the static self without its conscious modification and mere modifications are both equally meaningless abstractions.[116] The soul in its essence (*chaitanya*) is a conscious entity/substance, which undergoes modifications (*parinama*). The self, according to Jainism, is a "dynamic reality, something stable in the midst of its changes, a unity in diversity, a being in becoming."[117] Bhattacharya further observes:

> A conscious reality is never divorced from its own conscious modifications and qualities in which lies its very life. . . . A *parinama* or modification, issuing from the *parinami* or the modifying, and yet not in essential relation with the *parinami*, is as false an abstraction as the *aparinami* or immutable real without any *parinama* or modification.[118]

If there is no permanence, B.K. Matilal points out, there cannot be any change/fluctuation, for it is only the permanent that can change. It is only the persisting soul that can transmigrate[119] from animal into a human, etc. form, condition (*gati*) or mode (*paryaya*).

Jainism, including Kundakunda, upholds that substance, including soul (consciousness) substance, the essence of *jiva* (self), is an existent reality, which is eternal (*nitya*) in the sense of existing, in all three times (past, present and future) (*trikali dhruva*). At the same time, it is a dynamic evolvent (*parinami* or *parinamansheel*) reality. Contrary to this, the Kanjipanthi, believing in changeless consciousness (*aparinami chaitanya tattva*),[120] assert that "I am changeless or unchanging (*aparinami*) in all three times (*trikali*) even in the present time."[121] This contention is similar to that of the Samkhya and Vedanta.

Although the indivisible unity, inseparability and necessary concomitance of substance, quality and modification has been categorically declared by Kundakunda, Amrtachandra and others, Kanji Svami asserts that *paryaya* (modification) and *dravya* (substance) are two separate existent realities or two separate/different ontological entities (*bhinna sattayen*).[122] This is a gross deviation from Kundakunda's teachings and all other Jain texts.

The Mechanism of Bondage

Substances essentially consist of *jiva* (self or soul) and *pudgala* (matter). The essential characteristic of *jiva* (living being) is sentiency or consciousness (*chetana*). Its manifestation or function is called *upayoga* (PS 127 and PKS 16, 27). The self is indeed the agent or doer of its own states (*sagassa bhavassu* in Pk. *svakasya bhavasya* in Sk.) (PS 184). Matter, on the other hand, is a non-sentient, corporeal and inanimate entity possessing characteristic sense qualities/attributes of touch, taste, smell and colour. The two substances are the agents (*karta*) of their own conditions, states, or modes (modifications).

In his worldly, empirical existence, the living being is necessarily associated with *karmic* particles or the material *karman*. While experiencing the rise (*udaya*) or coming into operation of the *karmic* particles, a person who identifies oneself and evolves into a deluded view (*moha*), attachment and aversion, experiences *karmic* bondage (PS 43 and PS 43 AC). These three, viz. attachment, aversion and a deluded view, are the cause of *karmic* bondage (PS 42 and 43 JS).

Karmodaya *is not the Direct Cause of Karmic Bondage*

Karmic bondage does neither emanate from the conscious/the knowing nature of a living being nor from the coming into operation of the *karmas* devoid of attachment, etc. After becoming operational, the *karmic* particles (i.e. the genes, neurons or brain cells, the RNA, DNA, etc.) of different varieties (knowledge-obscuring, particular emotion producing, etc.), result in good or bad (*shubha* or *ashubha*) effects. They also disappear [i.e. the *karmas* fall off or the shedding of those particular *karmic* particles takes place] and do not cause [fresh] *karmic* bondage if the self does not evolve into the psychic states of attachment, etc. Deluded view, attachment, and aversion [are *jivasya svakasya bhavah*, i.e. the self's own conscious states]. In *Samayasara*, attachment, aversion and deluded view are declared to be the self's own inalienable states-of-evolution (SS 371). Together they constitute [*mohaniya karman*], which are the [real or direct] cause (*karana*) of the [fresh] karmic bondage, not *karmodaya* (the *karma-udaya*, the rise or the coming into operation of the karmas) (PS 43 JS and SS 164-165 JS).

In *Pravachanasara* 45, it is stated that the activities of the self, arising from the operation of the *karmas* are considered *audayiki* alone (*eva*), i.e. the coming into operation of the *karmas*. In the absence of being affected, infected or coloured (*uparanjaka*) by the deluded view, attachment and aversion, they do not cause distortions or perversions (*vikar*) in consciousness (*chaitanya*). They remain *audayiki*, i.e. always of an *audayiki* nature. Hence, they are considered to be destructive (*kshayiki*) of the *karmas*, in as much as the coming into operation of the *karmas* is not the cause of *karmic* bondage, i.e. having the effect of producing [fresh] bondage of *karman* (PS 45, PS 45 AC).

Jayasena also asserts that *karma-udaya* devoid of attachment, etc. is not the cause of *karmic* bondage. Being devoid of a deluded view, etc., it is unable to produce the sense of mineness (*mamakara* in other objects) and pride (*ahankara*). The *audayiki bhavas* (psychic effects or states resulting from the coming into operation of *karmas*) become the cause of *karmic* bondage only when they are accompanied by deluded view, attachment, etc. If *karma-udaya* alone is considered to be the cause of *karmic* bondage, then due to the *karma-udaya*, which is omnipresent in worldly persons, they will always continue to cause (fresh) bondage. Consequently, they will not be able to attain *moksha* (liberation) (PS 45 JS).

Owing to its inherent nature (*svabhava*), if the self does not evolve into an impure mode or state [on the auxiliary condition of the previously bound *karmas* coming into operation], there is no fresh bondage of *karmas*. As a result, there will be no transmigration of the cycle of births and deaths (i.e. *samsara*) for the living beings (PS 46).

In its unmixed, non-relational (*karma-nirpeksha*) *parinamika bhava* (i.e. in the sense of SS 6 AC) the self is not liable to lose its nature of consciousness and does not get transformed into a material, inanimate object. It also does not evolve into impure states. When all these conditions/causes of *karmic* bondage [the coming into operation of the previously bound *karmas* and the presence of attachment, aversion and deluded view], are absent, living beings, by their very nature, will become eternally liberated souls (*nitya-muktam*). At that stage, there will be absence of *samsara*.

The self evolves into auspicious (*shubha*) and inauspicious (*ashubha*) nature (*svabhava*) because of its own evolving nature and because *karmas* come into operation. This is similar to a crystal, which by its own nature, evolves or assumes the colours of red and black because of the condition or the association of red *japa* flower and black *tamal* flower (PS 46 AC). Thus, attachment, etc. are the cause of *karmic* bondage (PS 46 JS).

In *Pravachanasara* 173, the question is posed as to how the self (*atman*)– the conscious entity having quite opposite qualities to those possessed by corporeal (*murta*) material substance – bind material *karman*? The answer to this question is given in the subsequent verses.

Through its likes and dislikes and its perception and knowledge of the objects of senses (PS 174, 176), the self possesses an innate nature of psychic-attention (*upayoga*), which is conditioned, affected, tinged or stained (*uparakta*) (PS 175 AC) by deluded view, attachment or aversion. The physical *karma* or *material karman* (i.e. neuro-physiological processes), acts as the condition or auxiliary cause thereof (*nimitta*, PS 174 AC). It also affects, influences or conditions subjective psychic bondage (*bhava bandha*) (PS 174-175 AC), which is an evolution into attachment, etc. (Amrtachandra's introductory remark to PS 179).

In its external association/interaction with both desirable (*ishta*) and undesirable (*anishta*) sense objects irrespective of the psychic states, the soul perceives or knows them. However, the soul gets stained by attachment and aversion because of its own likes and dislikes. This inevitably leads to *karmic* bondage (PS 176 JS).

Kundakunda categorically states that [only] a attached person binds [fresh] *karman* (*ratto bandhadi kammam*). A person, he adds, who is devoid of attachment is liberated from *karmas*. This is a brief summary of the discussion about the bondage of souls (PS 179). Psychic bondage, in turn, acts as the supportive factor/the auxiliary cause that affects, influences or conditions binding of material *karman* (*bhava bandha pratyaya dravyabandha*) (PS 176 AC and PS 179 AC).

The two types of bondage (the psychic and physical or material bondage) are, thus, mutually related as cause and effect, each of the other, and interact with one another. Each one of them acts as indirect, extrinsic, supportive factor or auxiliary cause (*nimitta karana*) of the other (PS 177-179, AC). Though material *karman* is said to be the indirect, extrinsic, auxiliary cause of psychic dispositions or mental states, the self is indeed the [substantive] causal agent or doer of its own *bhavas* (conscious states) (PS 184). Although the soul exists at all times in the midst of matter, it does not accept, grasp or appropriate *karman*. It also does not abandon or release the material *karman*. Hence, it is not the substantive cause of the evolution or modification of material *karman* (PS 185 and PS 185 AC).

Nishchaya and *Vyavahara* Points of View

When tainted with deluded view, attachment and aversion, the self is also sullied by the dust of *karma*. In the Jaina scriptures, this is described as bondage (PS 188). This is briefly the genesis summary of the bondage of souls as preached by the worthy Lord (*Arahantas*) from an internal self-referential point of view (*nishchaya naya*). However, from an external other-referential standpoint (*vyavahara naya*), it is expressed differently (PS 189).

Commenting on *Pravachanasara* 189, Amrtachandra states that the self is the agent (*karta*) of its own evolution into psychic dispositions like attachment. According to internal, self-referential *nishchaya naya*, the self is also the appropriator as well as the renouncer thereof (PS 189 AC). Thus, the perspective of *nishchaya naya* is considered to be the most effective means of accomplishing (the task) (*sadhaktam*) of purity because the self not only acts as the agent of attachment, etc. but also as a renouncer thereof (i.e. the self also acts as the agent of transforming or purifying the impure mental states into pure mental states). *Nishchaya naya* is therefore regarded as the most effective means of attaining the objective of the purity of the self.

According to external, other-referential *vyavahara* point of view, the non-pure state of soul substance (PS 189 AC) regards the evolution of matter as "the self's *karman*". In other words, the *karmic* matter belongs to the soul because of acts performed by the soul. This view also regards the self as "the agent [*karta*] of the evolution of matter and appropriator and renouncer thereof".This description consists in describing the non-pure state of soul substance (PS 189 AC). In other words, from *vyavahara naya*, the self is viewed as the agent of material (*pudgala*) *karma* and their modifications.

Both these viewpoints, Amrtachandra adds, are correct since substance is conceived in both pure and impure forms (PS 189 AC). In this manner, Kundakunda exhibits the absence of opposition (*virodha*) between *nishchaya naya* (NN) and *vyavahara naya* (VN) (*atha nishchaya vyavahara avirodham darshayati*) (Introductory remark of both Amrtachandra and Jayasena to PS 189 and SS 58-60).

That *nishchaya naya* (NN) and *vyavahara naya* (VN) are the internal and external aspects of the same reality and therefore complementary and not contradictory or opposed to each other, is also emphasized in other places. Thus, "if one wants to follow the tenets and principles of Jainism, one should not give up VN or NN. Abandoning VN will amount to undermining the path of rules and guidelines (*tirtha*) laid down by the worthy Lord. The abandonment of NN undermines one's understanding of the *tattvas*, i.e. the reality of the things as they are or the nature of principles of life (SS 12 AC). The Jaina concept of *syadavada* (method of conditional predication) is destructive of the opposition between the two *nayas* (*ubhaya naya virodha dhvansini*) (SSK 4).

Padmaprabhadeva, the commentator of *Niyamsara*, also finds no contradiction between *nishchaya* and *vyavahara naya* (commentary on NS 187). He emphasizes that the teaching of relying only on one *naya* is not worth accepting; only the teaching which relies on both the standpoints is *grahya* (acceptable) (commentary on NS 19).

Though *nishchaya naya* and *vyavahara naya* are apparently contrary perspectives (*sapratipaksha*) (PKS 8) to one another or may seem to be irreconcilable aspects (*pratisiddha*, SS 272), the doctrine of *anekant* reconciles the apparently contradictory viewpoints because they coexist in the same object as inalienable parts thereof. They do not negate, deny or repudiate each other. (Repudiate implies a disowning or casting off as untrue, unauthorized, or unworthy of acceptance.)

To negate is to deny the existence, truth, or fact of something.

To contradict is to flatly deny the truth of an assertion and usually to imply the reverse is true. To deny is to reject as untrue or invalid or to refuse to concede the existence or claims of (something).

Contrary can imply extreme divergence (e.g. of opinions, motives, or intentions). It can in particular be used in formal logic or diametrical opposition. In logic, *contrary* propositions are those in the relation of affirmative and negative within the same degree of generality.

Vyavahara naya and *nishchaya naya* provide an alternative/optional course or choice in given circumstances. Alternative implies a necessity to choose, usually between two apparently contradictory things.

Option stresses a specifically given right or power to choose among two or more mutually exclusive items, e.g. took an *option* to buy a farm; the many *options* for careers open to present-day youth. Choice usually implies the right or privilege to choose freely from a number (e.g. of persons, things, or courses). It implies a set of things (called opportunities) that are available. It implies a criterion of selection. This, in turn, implies a wide range of choices and often the need of thought and discrimination in choosing, according to the purport (*abhipraya*) of the chooser/selector (*nayo jnatur abhiprayo*, Akalanka, *Laghiyastriya* 52).

Contradictory applies to two things that completely negate each other so that if one is true or valid the other must be false or invalid, e.g. the two suspects made contradictory statements to the police; the real trouble with love is that people want contradictory things out of it. Opposite is an inclusive term, which may replace any of the others but finds its typical application in the description of abstract things that stand in sharp contrast or complete antagonism, e.g. *opposite* views on a problem; attraction and repulsion are *opposite* forces; a person of the *opposite* sex; the boys went in *opposite* directions. Antithetical stresses clear and unequivocal diametric opposition.[123]

Thus, *nishchaya* and *vyavahara* aspects or perspectives are not contradictory but complementary to one another. The lack of opposition between them is best expressed in the Jaina doctrine of *anekant*, which regards them as coexisting simultaneously as inalienable parts of an object, or relative and complementary to one another (*paraspara sapeksha*). This phenomenon is also explained by the Jaina concept of *arpita anarpita* (TS 5.32) whereby a certain aspect/characteristic is said to occupy a position of prominence or considered primary (*mukhya*) because of some use, need, relevance or purpose, while the other aspect is considered secondary (*gauna*) (there being no contradiction between them). This is also evident from the Amrtachandra's example of a milkmaid engaged in churning butter-milk wherein one side of the string is brought in the foreground of attention/focus, while the other aspect/side recedes into the background (PSU 225).

The accomplishment of any task [including liberation], Samantabhadra observes, requires or depends on coordination of both internal and external causes [the internal cause is regarded as primary or substantive cause, while the external cause is considered as secondary, supportive, auxiliary cause or its co-adjunct] is said to be in the very nature of things (*dravyagatah svabhavah*), (Samantabhadra, *Svayambhu Stotra*, verses 59-60).

Material *Karman* and Psychic States

Panchastikayasara verse 134 explains how the empirical self (*jiva*) by its nature is in itself spiritual and incorporeal (*amurta*) appears corporeal (*murta*) because of material or physical *karman* coming into contact with the possibility of appropriate and mutual interpenetration in the transmigratory (*samsaric*) state. In the process, the self experiences fresh accretion of *karmas* and the consequent bondage (PKS 134). The beginningless material *karman* acts as the supportive or auxiliary factor (*nimitta*) in attachment, anger, etc. psychic states of *jiva*. These psychic states, in turn, function as the supportive or auxiliary factor (*nimitta*) of (knowledge-obscuring, etc.) material *karmas*. Thus, the two are mutually related as cause and effect, one to the other (PKS 134 AC).

Without the corresponding changes in the material *karmas*, the four psychic states of coming into operation or rise (*audayika*), subsidential, destructive, or partly destructive and partly subsidential, cannot happen in the consciousness of *jiva*. These psychic states or dispositions (*bhavas*) may, therefore, be said to be the effects of physical or material *karman* (*karmakrta*) (PKS 58). They should be considered and accepted as such (*anumantavyah*) (PKS 58 AC).

These four psychic states, Amrtachandra points out, are, in fact, the states or conditions (*avastha*) of *karma*, having reference to material *karman*. They are not consciousness-as-such (*parinamika bhava*), which is beginningless, without end, natural, having no relation or reference to karmic adjuncts or encumbrances (*nirupadhi*). The four altered states of consciousness are produced by the coming into operation of *karmas*, etc. or mutations of material *karman* acting as the supportive factor (*nimitta*) or auxiliary cause. In this situation, even the physical or material *karma* acquire the doership or the agency of action (*kartratva*) of the states of consciousness from the external, other-referential point of view (*vyavahara naya*) (PKS 58 AC). In reality, the self is the doer or agent of action (*karta*) of its own psychic states (PKS 59) from the internal, self-referential point of view (*nishchaya naya*) (PKS 59 AC).

The material *karmas* are the doer (*karta*) of the psychic states of *jiva* in the capacity of supportive or the auxiliary factor (*nimitta*). Similarly, the psychic states are the doer (*karta*) in the capacity of extrinsic, supportive or the auxiliary factor (*nimitta*) of material *karma* from external, other-referential point of view (*vyavahara naya*). However, from an internal, self-referential point of view, *jiva* is the doer or causal agent of its own psychic states and material *karman* is the doer or causal agent of its own mutations or modifications. Moreover, neither the modifications of the psychic states of *jiva* nor the modifications in material *karman* can occur without some doer (PKS 60 and PKS 60 AC). In this case, the author makes a distinction between the substantive causal agent (*upadana karta*) and the extrinsic, supportive or auxiliary causal agent (*nimitta karta*).

In the transmigratory embodied existence, the self does not renounce or abandon the consciousness-as-such *parinamika bhava*. However, it undergoes distorted impure modifications of its own psychic states, which lead to an adhesive quality of deluded view, attachment, aversion since it is conditioned and affected by the beginningless *karmic* bondage. Similarly, *karmic* particles mutate into *karma-bhava* [of knowledge-obscuring, etc. *karmas*, PKS 66 AC] [that have the power to condition and affect psychic states] merely by close proximity and mutual interpenetration of the distorted or perverted psychic states acting as the extrinsic, supportive or auxiliary factor (*nimitta*) in this regard (PKS 65 and PKS 65 AC). There is, however, no direct causal relation between *jiva* and matter or material *karma*

(PKS 66 AC). *Jiva* and matter are the causal agent of their own respective modes or mutations from the internal, self-referential point of view (*nishchaya naya*), yet from the extrinsic (or external), other-referential point of view (*vyavahara naya*) they are said to be mutually related as cause and effect each of the other.

Jivas and *karmic* matter are closely interlinked. However, when the time for their separation comes they become separate. The self (*jiva*) experiences both pleasure and pain, which are the result of the coming into operation or fruition of material *karma* (PKS 67) because *jiva* is of the nature of consciousness (PKS 68). The self, being the architect of his own destiny (*prabhu*), is an active agent (*karta*), responsible for his own actions, good and bad, physical and mental. It is also the enjoyer or experiencer (*bhokta*) of the fruits thereof, and covered by infatuation (*moha*) roams about endlessly in the transmigratory existence of births and deaths (PKS 69).

In *Tattvartha Rajvarttika* (TRV), Akalanka states that the contention that the incorporeal (*amurta*) self (*atma*) cannot be subject to or be subjugated by *karmic* matter, which is corporeal, is an incorrect conclusion since the self (*atma*), which possesses the inherent trait of consciousness (*chaitanya*), attains or develops special capabilities or energies owing to beginningless *karmic* bondage. As the beginningless evolvent (*parinamika*) consciousness-as-such, the self is an evolving conscious entity. Its particular modes, such as hellish, etc. conditions of the existence of the self and sensory states of knowledge, etc. also have the character of consciousness. Thus, the self, due to its beginningless association with the material (*karman*) body, is in some respect corporeal (*murtimana*). It is not absolutely or completely incorporeal (*amurtika*) (TRV on TS 2.7.24).

Since the self is bound by *karmas*, it is in some respect (*syat* or *kathanchit*) corporeal. However, since it does not leave or renounce its intrinsic characteristics like knowledge, it is also partially incorporeal (*amurta*). Just as after drinking alcohol, a person becomes deluded or confused and loses his memory, so also as a result of the coming into operation or rise (*udaya*) of material *karman*, the intrinsic qualities of knowledge, etc. of the self get affected or conditioned. Alcohol intoxicates, deludes or confuses only the conscious entity, but not the inanimate container of alcohol or the senses, which are devoid of consciousness (TRV on TS 2.7.25-27).

Although the self is bound by *karmas* since beginningless time, its independent existence is proven because of its own intrinsic characteristics like knowledge. It is said: "There is unity or union (*aiyattam* in Pk. and *ekatva* in Sk.) between the self and *karmas* from the point of view or with respect to *karmic* bondage still the two are distinct or different with respect to their own distinctive characteristics. Thus, the self cannot be said to be absolutely or merely one-sidedly (*ekantah*) incorporeal (*amurta eva*) (SAS commentary of Pujyapada on TS 2.7).

Depending on the condition of the supportive factor of the self (*jiva*), imbued with attachment, the material particles mutate or are transformed into material *karman* (*karmatvam*). The consciousness or psychic states of *jiva* also mutate or are transformed into distorted states like attachment depending upon the condition or the supportive factor of the material *karman* (*Yogasara-Prabrata* of Amitgati, Verse 2.31). Thus, the distorted psychic states and the material *karma* act as the supportive factor (*nimitta*) or the auxiliary cause (*nimitta karana*) of one another. They are not the substantive cause (*upadana karana*) of one another (Ibid., 9.50 and SS 80-81). Neither does *karma* destroys the intrinsic attributes of the soul nor does the *jiva* destroy the attributes of the material *karma.* There is no mutual relation of the destroyed and the destroyer between the *jiva* and *karma* (Ibid., 9.49).

How changes or modifications in the material objects affect the feelings (*bhava*) or the attitudes of persons because of their intense attachment to them is aptly described by Samantabhadra in the following words: "Persons desirous of a pot, a crown and gold become sad, happy and indifferent at the destruction (of the pot), origination (of the crown), and persistence (of gold) on account of their causes." (Samantabhadra, *Apta-Mimansa,* Verse 59) Though the psychological states of sadness, happiness, and indifference are generated in the self, their causes lie in the modifications that take place in the material object existing in the external world.

Thus, changes in the conscious mental states and changes in material particles or the neurophysiological states or processes are determined by and linked with their own antecedent or preceding states or events. Nevertheless, each one of them acts as the indirect, extrinsic, subsidiary or auxiliary cause (*nimitta karana*) of the corresponding changes in the other. The innate nature of things is the reason why only the intrinsic cause or internal factors can be regarded as the direct or substantive cause (*upadana karana*) of changes or modifications within their own respective entities. On the other hand, extrinsic causes or external factors can be *considered only as* indirect, subsidiary cause or the supportive factor (*nimitta*) of changes in the other.

The extrinsic, indirect and auxiliary kind of causal interaction does not in any way violate the principle of classic physics that "the physical realm is causally closed in the sense that nothing non-physical can enter into it and act as a cause"[124] and that "each physical event lay in an unbroken series of antecedent physical events". It also does not violate William James' principles of psychology that "psychological events never take place in a vacuum without some reference to the preceding events".[125]

Psycho-physical Parallelism

The Jaina contention that the two events – brain states and mental states – while interacting with one another, remain quite distinct processes and independent series or sequences (physical and psychic) seems to suggest a kind of psycho-physical parallelism. However, this parallelism is not merely "a temporal correspondence of the two series, but transcended and reconciled by the Jaina concept of *nimitta karana*"[126] (each one acting as an extrinsic, indirect, auxiliary, supportive or subsidiary factor or cause of the other). Jaina parallelism is, thus, quite distinct from other parallelist theories based on "divine intervention" (Malebranche) and mysterious "pre-established harmony" (Leibniz), which speak only of co-occurrences and never of interaction or causal relationship between the mental and physical realms.[127] The Jaina view differs not only from other systems of Indian philosophy but also from the disjunctive substance dualism of Descartes, property dualisms of David Chalmers and Thomas Nagel, John Searle's "causal reduction," and Max Velmans so-called "complementarity," which is based on deterministic physical laws or processes.[128]

In this way, the Jaina concepts of *jiva*, the evolving nature of reality, the dual (physical and psychic) aspects of mind, and *nimitta karana* (the conscious states and brain activities acting as extrinsic, indirect, auxiliary cause or supportive factor of each other) provides "the correct approach to the mind-body problem". This is the goal which Thomas Nagel has been seeking, viz. that it should preserve the mental-physical distinction, which must be "essentially biological, not functional or computational", and "necessarily both subjectively mental from the inside and objectively physical from the outside – just as we are".[129]

Internal and External Aspects

The strand of duality of internal and external, psychic and physical or subjective and objective aspects of the self runs throughout the Jaina system, including Jaina psychology and spiritualism. For instance, the *jiva* is both incorporeal and corporeal and has both internal and external *pranas*. Similarly, the senses, mind, *karma*, etc. have both physical as well as psychic aspects in the living organism. It is in the very nature of things (*dravyagatah svabhavah*) that the accomplishment of any task or deed requires or depends on coordination of both internal and external causes [the intrinsic cause is regarded as primary and substantive cause, while the extrinsic cause is considered as secondary, supportive factor or auxiliary cause].[130]

In *Pravachanasara*, it is stated that it is only when the self evolves into attachment (desire) is it bound by fresh (new) material *karma*. However, when it is free from attachment, the self is not bound since it is released (*muchyate*) by any fresh (new) material *karma* as well as by the old accumulated material *karma* (PS 179). Thus, psychic disposition of attachment is the most effective [cause] of material bondage. This is a decisive (*nishchayatah*) summary of the bondage of living beings, i.e. bondage from an internal, self-referential point of view (*nishchaya naya*) (*nishchayena bandha*) (PS 179 and PS 179 AC). Subsequently, it is stated that when the self is tainted by a deluded view, desire or attachment and aversion it is sullied by *karma* dust, which is described as bondage (PS 188).

In his introductory remark to the next verse (PS 189, and SS 58-60), Amrtachandra states that Kundakunda elaborates on the absence of opposition, conflict or contradiction between *nishchaya naya* and external other-referential point of view (*vyavahara naya*) (*atha nishchaya vyavahara avirodha darshayati*) as follows: "This is the summary account of the bondage of souls, preached by worthy Lord (*Arhats*) from *nishchaya naya*, from *vyavahara naya* it is expressed otherwise" (PS 189 AC). In other words, from the *nishchaya* point of view, the self (*jiva*) is the *karta* of a deluded view (*moha*), attachment, aversion and passions, etc. psychic bondage (*bhava bandha*). On the other hand, from the *vyavahara* point of view, the self is said to be the *karta* of *dravya* (material or *pudgala*) *karmic* bondage (PS 188-189).

In this context, Amrtachandra states that since the self is the causal agent (*karta*) of its own states-of-evolution of psychic dispositions like attachment, he is both the appropriator and the renouncer thereof from the perspective of *nishchaya naya* (PS AC 189). He, thus, emphasizes the internal aspects of the purity of the self. In other words, the self is the agent of impure mental states as well as the agent of transforming or purifying such impure mental states into pure psychic dispositions, because it is attachment that binds *karma* (PS 179 and SS 150).

In this way, *nishchaya naya* is said to describe or emphasize the internal self-referential purity aspect. However, *vyavahara naya* (PS 189 AC) stresses that "the evolution of matter is the self's *karman*". In other words, the *karmic* matter belongs to the soul or are deeds done by the soul, and that "the self is the agent [*karta*] of the evolution of matter and appropriator and renouncer thereof". The preceding sentences describe the impure state of the empirical self. In other words, from *vyavahara naya*, the self is viewed as the agent of material (*pudgala*) *karma* and their modifications. Amrtachandra further observes that "both these viewpoints are correct, since substance is conceived in both forms, as pure and as impure". However, in this case *nishchaya naya* is considered to be the most conclusive (*sadhaktam*) because by emphasizing the internal purity aspect of the thing, the internal self-referential viewpoint of *nishchaya naya* is regarded as the most effective way of achieving the objective of purifying the self (PS 189 AC).

In all his works, Kundakunda lays greater emphasis on or assigns higher priority or importance to internal aspects, though external aspects are not lost sight of. The intrinsic cause (*svanimitta*), Amrtachandra points out, is considered the primary factor in the transformation of a person, while the other external factors act as subsidiary or auxiliary cause (*para nimitta*), which must also be present.[131] In *Pravachanasara* also, Amrtachandra states that of the two kinds of negligence in self-restraint, viz. external and internal (PS 211-212 AC), the internal one is the more serious one (*baliyan*), and not the external (PS 217 AC). The importance accorded to the inner aspects or psychic dispositions is reflected in Kundakunda's views regarding the mechanism of bondage. It is also evident from the description of conduct of living beings, including the practice of non-violence, etc. which is the subject matter of Book III of *Pravachanasara.*

The internal aspects are obviously more important than the external aspects since it is the sole responsibility of the *jiva* (self), who alone, being the agent of its own psychic states of attachment, aversion, passions, etc., can get rid of them. Since these perverted, impure psychic states and passions are the cause of (*karmic*) bondage, the only way of annihilating physical or material *karman* (neuro-physiological processes) is to either abstain or get rid of them. They cannot be removed by any surgical procedure.

Moreover, it is generally recognized that the mind or mental states alone are the cause of both bondage as well as liberation (*mana eva manushyanam karanam bandha mokshayoh*) of men. W.J. Johnson's failure to comprehend this leads him to mistakenly criticize both Kundakunda and Amrtachandra for stressing the "internalized or dematerialized cause of *karmic* bondage", thereby making it [primarily] a matter of infatuation and passions, and also criticizing them for "internalization of *himsa*" (violence).[132]

The Concept of Non-violence *(ahimsa) in Pravachanasara*

There are a number of verses in *Pravachanasara* dealing with the concept of non-violence. Amongst these, the most important ones are verses 216-219. *Pravachanasara* 205 speaks of being devoid of violence, etc. But what constitutes *himsa*? Is it the "harm unto living beings," i.e. avoidance of external violence, such as destruction of the material vitalities of others? Or is violence primarily the result of internal negligence (*pramad*), i.e. passion-infected psychic disposition, or both. In the Shvetambara "canonical texts", particularly *Bhagavati, Thanang* and the *Uttarajjhayana,* Johnson states that the emphasis is on "the physical and material"[133] aspects of violence, i.e. "harm unto living beings". On the other hand, Kundakunda and Amrtachandra as well as *Tattvartha Sutra* of Umasvami or Umasvati, along with Pujyapada's commentary of *Sarvarthasiddhi* give greater importance to internal negligence or passions, i.e. injuring the psychic dispositions of his own self through passion-infected thoughts and emotions.

Thus, we have two translations of *Pravachanasara* 216. The translation by A.N. Upadhye states: "Careless activities of a monk [*shraman*] when sleeping, sitting, standing, and walking are always known as continuous harm unto living beings."[134] The words "unto living beings" do not exist in the original Prakrit verse. The other translation of *Pravachanasara* 216, based on Kundakunda's views in the matter and Amrtachandra's commentary thereon, is reflected in Faddegon's translation: "Heedless action in lying, sitting, standing, going, etc. is considered to be at all times continual hurt (*himsa*) to the *shramana*-state" (PS 216).

Negligence is an impure mode or manifestation of consciousness. As such, it is violative of the innate nature of *jiva* or the real identity of the self. This point is explained and clarified in verse 217 as follows: "A living being may die or live, on the part of the careless one the act of hurting is certain: by the mere fact of hurt he who is careful in his observances incurs no bondage." (PS 217). Commenting on this verse, Amrtachandra remarks:

> Impure psychic-attention is internal negligence; the taking of another's life is external. Whether the taking of another being's life occurs or does not occur, to the actual impure psychic-attention, proved by the careless conduct, which does not occur without it, the nature of hurting certainly belongs: and to the non-existence of impure psychic-attention, proved by the careful conduct, which occurs without it, the nature of hurting certainly does not belong, as is shown by the fact that the taking of another's life does not involve bondage: therefore internal negligence is the more serious, and not the external (PS 217 AC).

The additional verse (PS 217/3) in Jayasena's recension adds: "Even so, the external should be recognized, simply as being an occasion for the internal negligence." (PS 217/3)

Greater Emphasis on Psychic Dispositions

A *shraman* of careless conduct is deemed to be the cause of taking the life of beings [and consequently incurs bondage]. However, if one always behaves with care, then, like a lotus in water, one remains unassoiled or uncontaminated (PS 218). This means that if, in spite of the dispassionate activities of mind, body and speech, any living being is injured, it cannot be called *himsa* (violence), since the corrupting element of passion is missing (Amrtachandra in PSU 45).

In *Samayasara*, Kundakunda categorically states: "Whether one kills or not kills living beings, the bondage is caused by the psychic-disposition or thought/impulse (of killing or violence) (*adhyavasana*); this is the epitome of the bondage of souls from the internal, self-referential point of view" (*nishchaya naya*) (SS 262). In *Jai Dhavala* (41, page 93), it is stated: "Whatever action is performed by a person imbued with attachment, aversion or deluded-view leads to violence and hence he is considered a violent person. In other words, attachment etc. thought activities or psychic dispositions alone is the cause that instigates or promotes violence."

When the *jiva* causes harm to the *pranas* of the self and other living beings (*jivayoh*) owing to infatuation and hatred (aversion), it definitely leads to bondage of *karman*, such as knowledge-obscuring, etc. (PS 149). The material vitalities (*dravya pranas*) of "the other" (*para-jiva*) are sometimes hurt and sometimes not hurt. By being passionate, the soul always causes injury (*himsa*) to the subjective *pranas* or psychic vitalities of the self. It therefore binds itself with knowledge-obscuring, etc. material *karman*.

Thus, injury to the psychic vitalities, i.e. *bhava himsa*, of the self through passions becomes the cause of material *karman* (*paudagalik karman*) (PS 149 AC). The internal negligence or passions of anger, hatred, etc. (*pramad*), which cause violence to the self and later result in violence or injury to others, is undoubtedly more serious (PS 217 AC) and not the external, physical violence (*dravya himsa*). In any case, injury to other living beings should be avoided for purifying one's own thought activities (*parinama vishuddhi*) (PSU 49 AC).

Since the *jiva* (i.e. *prani*, one having or possessing *pranas*, i.e. bio-energies or material, physical vitalities) and the vitalities (*pranas*) are bound together in the organism and closely united (*aiyatta* in Pk., and *ekatva* in Sk.), they cannot be completely distinguished or considered distinct (*vibhakt*). Therefore, it is inevitable that the *jiva* will experience pain (*dukkha*) when these bio-energies separate. Thus, it is evident that the destruction of the bio-energies, or vitalities of living beings (*prani*) is the obvious cause of pain. Such violence (*himsa*) is certainly considered *adharma* (absence of righteousness or piety) (TSV commentary on TS 7.13, Vol. 6, p. 566).

In Jainism, *himsa* (violence) is of two kinds, viz. psychic violence and physical violence. The destruction of psychic vitalities (*pranas*) is inevitable in one's passionate activity or careless conduct (TSV on TS 7.13, Vol. 6, p 570).

Amrtachandra considers all sins like falsehood to be "external forms of violence" of the purity of psychic states of the soul (PSU 42). Moreover, since these sins are destructive of the inherent nature of the self (*atma-svabhava*), they are tantamount to violence. Generally speaking, non-violence is defined as the transformation of one's conduct characterized by self-restraint whereby no physical or mental harm is caused to others.

First of all, non-violence makes us conscious of the existence of other. It takes into account the convenience and inconvenience of all and declares the right of all to remain alive. It is reflected as non-violence in conduct, *syadavada* (method of conditional predication) in speech or expression, and *anekant* (multifacetedness of reality) in thought. This is the philosophy of life of Lord Mahavira.

The non-appearance of thoughts or feelings of attachment, passions, etc. is undoubtedly non-violence (*ahimsa*) whereas their appearance is *himsa* (violence). In brief, this is the essence of non-violence in Jain texts (PSU 44). Amrtachandra adds: "He, who, not knowing the true nature of things, relies solely or one-sidedly on the internal aspects of negligence alone (*eva*), is an ignorant person (*balah*); he is careless and lazy in external conduct and destroys all external, moral discipline related to others" (PSU 50). In other words, moral accountability is directly conditioned by subjectivity. The avoidance of external violence is considered desirable and advisable as a means for maintaining the purity of the thought activities or mind by an agent.

In comparison to psychic dispositions or thought activity undertaken knowingly or with the use of intellect (the discriminating faculty), sometimes those undertaken unknowingly, without the use of intellect, leads to bondage of greater sin. Therefore, ignorance or lack of discriminative insight or knowledge (*ajnana*) is considered a special (type) of fault or sin and counted as one of the [five] kinds of delusion (TSV commentary on TS 7.13, Vol. 6, p 570).

Tattvartha Sutra on Non-violence

The internal aspects of violence are discussed and emphasized by not only Kundakunda and his commentator Amrtachandra, but also by Umasvati in the *Tattvartha Sutra*, Pujyapada's *Sarvarthasiddhi* commentary thereon as well as in certain Shvetambara texts and scholars. In *Tattvartha Sutra* (TS 7.13), *himsa* is defined as *pramattayogat pranvyaparopanam himsa*, i.e. the destruction of bio-energies, life-principles, or vitalities (*prana*) due to negligence or passion is *himsa.* Muni Vidyananda defines violence as the passionate state together with the separation/ ending of bio-energies (*pranas*) of the self (*sva*) or other (*para*). In other words, violence occurs when a passionate activity of body, speech or mind causes harm, injury, or separation of one's own or someone else's psychic or physical *pranas* (TSV commentary on TS 7.13, Vol. 6, p. 564).

The contention that *himsa* does not merely hurts vitalities of living beings but that injury even results owing to the mental condition of passions and negligence is said to be a revision of the concept of violence as enumerated in Shvetambara canonical texts such as *Bhagavati*, and *Thanang*, which lay emphasis on merely physical aspects of violence.

The *Tattvartha Sutra*, Johnson opines, is the earliest extant Jaina work in Sanskrit written between 150 C.E. and 350 C.E. He affirms: "It is not only the one text that both Digambaras and Svetambaras recognize as authoritative," but the commentaries on it, whether by Digambara or Svetambara authors, "present almost identical explications of Jaina doctrine". In any case, the differences between the Svetambara and Digambara doctrine are not relevant for our discussion, which focuses on the problems which are fundamental to both traditions.

Johnson admits that he himself has used the *Sarvarthasiddhi* of Pujyapada (Devanandin) (c. fifth century C.E.) in conjunction with the *Tattvartha Sutra* "rather than the alleged auto commentary, the *Tattvarthadhigama Bhasya* (also known as the *Svopajna Bhasya*)" since there is considerable doubt whether Umasvati himself wrote the "auto commentary". Bronkhorst has presented a convincing case for attributing it to a Svetambara of the fourth century C.E. (at the earliest) whereas Zydenbos dates it to the fifth century A.D.

The *Sarvarthasiddhi*, Johnson adds, might be using a version of the *Tattvartha Sutra* which is "at times closer to the original than that used in the *Bhasya*". There is also some evidence that the *Tattvartha Sutra* itself was composed in "a Digambara milieu, while the *Bhasya* has marked Svetambara features [he cites Bronkhurst and R. Williams in that regard]. . . The *Sarvarthasiddhi* . . . often develops the logical implications of doctrines which are merely stated or formulated in the *Tattvartha Sutra*".[135]

In stating that merely a "passionate attitude even without the severance of vitalities constitutes violence,"[136] *Sarvarthasiddhi* stresses the internal-psychic disposition of the agent, i.e. the passion and its effect on the agent (*himsa* to oneself).[137] This is *sva-himsa*, which occurs first and the severance of vitalities of other beings happens thereafter. A passionate person first hurts one's own self by himself, the severance of other's vitalities happens afterwards or may not happen at all (TSV on TS 7.13, Vol 6, p 570). Pujyapada further observes:

> He who acts with negligence commits injury whether death is caused to organisms or not. And he who proceeds with proper care does not contract bondage of *karma* by mere injury. [this seems to be the reproduction of PS 217 as it is exactly similar to it]. . . He who has passions causes injury to himself by himself. Whether injury is then caused to other living beings or not, it is immaterial.[138]

In his *Sarvarthasiddhi* commentary on *Tattvartha Sutra* (TS 7.1 and TS 6.12), Pujyapada remarks that self-restraint (*samyam*) implies restraining oneself from evil, undesirable, inauspicious (*ashubha*) activities of injury, etc. It also signifies the observance of vows like non-violence, truthfulness, which is regarded as morality, virtuous activities (*punya*), righteousness and piety (*dharma*). One of the ways to inhibit (*samvara*) *karmic* inflow is through five of the ten moral virtues (*dharma*) (TS 9.6), which are only positive aspects of non-violence, etc. five moral rules (vows) of conduct (TS 9.2, 9.3).

Dual Role of Moral Virtues

Pravachanasara states that non-violence is the necessary concomitant of purification (*vishuddhi*) (PS 155 AC and 180 AC) partly because it signifies abstention from evil and vicious (*papa*) activities. The five moral virtues are said to have a paradoxical dual nature in that they are instrumental in the inhibition of the influx of *karma* when practiced with detachment and no vestige of passion; they also generate *karmic* influx of beneficial (pleasure producing) *karma* when practiced with attachment (*sarag samyam*) as being compassionate towards living beings in general in the worldly sense.

It is noteworthy that Shvetambara *Svopajnya Bhashya* commentary on *Tattvartha Sutra* and Kanjipanthi speak of the vow of self-restraint (TS 7.1) as the cause of (beneficial) karmic inflow only. As a result, it leaves unanswered the question "How can a vow both inhibit and generate *karmic* inflow?"[139] The answer to that paradox is given in the Digambara *Sarvarthasiddhi* commentary on *Tattvartha Sutra* and in Amrtachandra's commentary on *Pravachanasara* verses.

In his introductory remark and commentary on *Pravachanasara* 69, Amrtachandra states [that after transcending the state of evil or inauspicious (*ashubha*) psychic-attention PS 69 AC] good or auspicious (*shubha*) psychic-attention (*upayoga*) of the self, comprising of attachment to the veneration of the worthy Lord, ascetic and the teacher, to charity, to moral precepts or moral conduct of self-restraints (*su-shila*), to fasting and the like, (which is a self with good or auspicious (*shubha*) psychic-attention (*upayoga*), (PS 69), is a means (*sadhan*) to sensorial pleasure (PS 69 AC). In subsequent verses (PS 70-76), it is stated that while manifold sensorial pleasures may make one apparently happy, but this happiness is tantamount to misery because it is dependent, accompanied by distraction, and interruption. It is the cause of bondage, and unequal since it is acquired by means of the senses. (PS 76)].

In *Pravachanasara* verses 155, 180, 245-260 and the commentary thereon, both Kundakunda and Amrtachandra state that while evil/ inauspicious (*ashubha*) is inherently characterized by affliction, distress or morbidity (*sanklesh*) (PS 155, 156 and 180 AC), *shubha* or *punya* (righteousness or piety, i.e. *dharma*) has a dual role. When it is a mere means of sensorial pleasure (PS 69 AC) or a supportive factor (*nimitta*) of enjoyment of sense objects (*dhammam bhoga nimittam*, SS 273-275), it has the effect of karmic bondage and is unable to get rid of *karmas* (SS 273-275). However, when it is a commendable attachment (*prashasta raga*) oriented towards sanity, it has a purifying (*vishuddhi*) effect (PS 155 AC and PS 180 AC) that is capable of inhibiting and getting rid of *karmas*. This, in turn, *gradually* (*kramatah*) leads to the highest happiness of *nirvana* (liberation) (PS 254 and PS 254 AC), and, thus, not only leads to liberation (PS 259 and PS 259 AC) but also helps others to attain liberation (PS 260 and PS 260 AC).

Commenting on non-violence, Akalanka remarks: "The entire universe – the seas, the lands and the sky – is full of living beings.

He who practices self-restraint and is careful is not liable to any violence (though physical violence may be there)."[140]

Even when one kills a living being, Siddhsena remarks, one is not guilty of the sin of killing if he is *apramatta* (i.e. careful, not infected with passion and not negligent).[141] The same sentiment is found in *Oghaniryukti* (748, 749). In *Visheshavashyakabhashya* (a Shvetambara canon), Acharya Jinabhadra observes: "It is the intention that ultimately matters."[142] Muni Nyayavijaya too remarks: "Even in the absence of actual overt act of injuring the life forces of others, an evil act of violence is committed through mere entertaining ill-will or ill-thought."[143]

In view of all that is stated above, one is at a loss to understand why Johnson obstinately persists in his belief that A.N. Upadhye's definition of *himsa* would seem to be "the most natural rendering, i.e. *himsa* is harm to living beings as a result of careless physical actions on the part of the monk". Johnson feels that *prima facie himsa* is "a purely orthodox doctrine such as might be found in the *Dasavaikalika Sutra* [Shvetambara canon]".[144] *Sarvarthasiddhi*, he adds, thereby "shifts the whole emphasis of *himsa* on to the internal state of the agent, i.e. on to passion and its effect on the agent: *himsa*. . . to oneself".[145]

Like violence (*himsa*), *parigraha* (*upadhi*, PS 219)—the passionate mental state of attachment to or being infatuated (*murchha*) (PS 221) with external, physical objects – is considered more important than mere possession of worldly objects. *Upadhi*, i.e. *parigraha*, is primarily internal negligence, and is therefore worth abandoning (Amrtachandra's introductory remark to PS 219).

The feeling of attachment or sense of "mineness" (*mamatva*) invariably binds the soul and leads to possession of external things (external *parigraha*). This, in turn, acts as the indirect, auxiliary (*nimitta*) cause of internal *parigraha*, i.e. attachment to objects (PSU 113). One should, therefore, abandon all (*sarva*) *upadhi* (*parigraha*) (PS 219), both external and internal (*bahittham majjhattham* (PS 273). How can one (who is favourably disposed towards *parigraha* be free from infatuation (*murchha*) and worldly concerns (*arambha*) and practise self-restraint (*samyam*)? And how one who is attracted towards and engrossed in other things, can understand and realize the real identity of his self or the real nature of his soul (*atma*, i.e.

consciousness)? (PS 221).

Conduct in *Pravachanasara*

Book III of *Pravachanasara* deals with conduct and path of liberation. There are several misperceptions in that regard and Kundakunda has sought to rectify them. According to "purely orthodox doctrine," as found in *Dasavaikalika Sutra* and other Shvetambara "canonical texts", particularly *Bhagavati*, *Thanang* and *Uttarajjhayayana*, Johnson states, Jaina asceticism was usually and primarily viewed in physical and material terms,[146] i.e. painful penance and mortification of the body.[147] The glorious sufferings of Lord Mahavira, engaging himself in 12 years of "self-mortifications" and "wandering about leading a life of austerities and bearing hardships of all kinds", portrayed in *Acharanga Sutra*, seemed to serve as an illustration and "set a high example of the true ascetic life".[148]

Thus, Jainism along with Samkhya and Buddhist philosophy came to be considered as "essentially pessimistic in worldly outlook," and "temperamentally ascetic,"[149] with austerities (*tapasya*) "emanating from the darker and gloomier view of life".[150] "Self-mortification" by several kinds of austerities thereby seemed to assume utmost importance in the Jaina order, including the shedding of *karmas.*[151] Nakedness was supposed to be "the excellent type of Jaina aceticism".[152] The term "*achela*" signifies an unclothed state of nakedness, i.e. completely devoid of clothes on the body as well as scantily clothed.[153] Nakedness is symbolic of extreme non-attachment to worldly objects to the extent of not having clothes on the body and as such is prescribed in both Shvetambara[154] and Digambara texts.

Balance between Internal and External Aspects of Conduct

In these circumstances, in *Pravachanasara* Kundakunda sought to rectify the undue importance attached to the infliction of undue and painful physical hardships on oneself in the name of austerities in the belief that it led to the much desired balance and sanity between internal and external aspects. Internal aspects had "precedence" over the external ones. Kundakunda's concern for balance is reflected in the statement that a *shraman* does not desire/have any attachment to either food or fasting, either lodging (i.e. residence) or wandering (PS 215). Such a balanced approach is considered appropriate in regard to food and wandering (*yukta ahara vihara*) (PS 226).

While not neglecting austerities (*tapa*) (*tapa* is mentioned in PS 202, 214, 227, 263-264 and 268-269), Kundakunda lays stress on the internal aspects or mental attitude. The *shraman*, who is free from all desire or longing for food, he points out, is, in fact, observing the [internal] penance or austerity of fasting (the first of the external austerities (*bahya tapa*), as he is devoid of the desire (*eshana dosha*) [the fault against the observance of carefulness or self-regulation in eating, i.e. *eshana-samiti*]; for "the internal is more important [than the external]. Although taking food, those *shramanas* are really not taking food and are really abstainers from food" (PS 227 AC). Thus Kundakunda, Johnson remarks, is "consciously reacting to acting against the excessive formalization, the mechanistic pursuit of physical austerity".[155]

*28 Primary Qualities (*Mulagunas*) of* Samana

In this way, Kundakunda seems to remind the readers that the 28 primary or fundamental qualities (*mula-guna*) (PS 208-209) of *shramanas* prescribed by *Jinas* are not to be viewed merely in external, physical, material terms. In his introductory remarks to *Pravachanasara* 205-206 and *Pravachanasara* 207 and in his commentary on *Pravachanasara* 277, Amrtachandra specifically mentions both external and internal characteristics of *shraman.*

Of the 28 *mula-gunas* of *shraman*, except for seven (see PS 208), the remaining 21 characteristics have both internal and external dimensions. These include five vows (*vratas*) or moral rules of conduct (besides non-violence and *parigraha*, truthfulness, non-stealing and chastity), the five observances of carefulness or self-regulation (*samiti*) (besides carefulness in taking food, i.e. *eshana*, carefulness in walking, speaking, handling of things and disposing of excrements i.e. cleanliness), restraint of five senses (*indriya-rodha*) and six essential duties (*avashyaka*) (see PS 207 AC). [For the significance of the study of scriptures (*svadhyaya*, the 5th *avashyaka*) see PS 232-237].

The seven *mula-guna* includes *achailakya*, which signifies the unclothed state of nakedness as well as the scantily-clothed state. Kundakunda has also used *jadhajadaruva* (*yatha jata rupa* in Sk.) (PS 204, 205 and 225), which could mean the nature of self at birth, the child-like simplicity as also the state of nakedness of a newly-born child. A *shraman* is required to be earnest in regard to the observances of *mula-guna* (PS 214). In case of negligence, a *shraman* should seek to rectify it by self-reflection and acceptance (*alochana*) of his fault (PS 211-212).[156] The word "*samana*" (*shraman* in Sk. which means one who makes efforts), is used throughout *Pravachanasara* (except in PS 234 where *sahu, sadhu,* or a *sajjan purush*, i.e. a noble, simple, straightforward person is used), comes from the root *sama, samo,* meaning "to quiet," (*shama* in Sk.). It is also a state of equipoise (PS 241 AC).[157] Thus, *shama,* i.e. self-restraint (self-control or subsidence of passions), is considered the primary trait of *samana* (PS 236-237, 240). In fact, at several places (PS 201, 213, 214, 242, 246, 267 and 274), Kundakunda uses the word "*samanya*" (*shramanya* in Sk.), meaning the state of *samana.* The word "*samana*" is used for Lord Mahavira as well as religious and moral persons.[158]

Equanimity

Equanimity is referred to in *Pravachanasara* 7 (see *supra*) and explained in *Pravachanasara* 241. Apart from equanimity, the other attributes of a self-restrained (*sanjado* in Pk. and *sanyat* in Sk.) *shraman* are the practice of five self-regulations (*samiti*), the three restraints of mind, speech and body (*gupti*), control of five senses, the subsidence of passions, and being endowed with intuition and knowledge (PS 240). Self-restraint is both internal and external (PS 211-212 AC). A *shraman* is also not attached to food or fasting, lodging or wandering (*vihara*), possession of things, and other *shramanas.* He also has no interest in useless, idle talk or gossip (*vikatha*) (PS 215).

In *Niyamsara,* Kundakunda categorically declares: "What is good of residing in a forest, the mortification of the body, observance of various fasts, study of the scriptures and keeping silence, etc., if the *samana* is devoid of equanimity?" (NS 124)

The characteristic features of an equanimous person are said to be: freedom from all sinful, unwholesome actions (NS 103 and 125), observance of three-fold self-restraint of mind, speech and body (*gupti*) and control of senses (NS 125), equality with all living beings (NS 126), observance of self-restraint rules (*niyam*), austerities (NS 127), freedom from distorted psychic dispositions arising from attachment and aversion (NS 128), abstention from mournful and cruel concentrations (NS 129), renunciation of meritorious and demeritorious or sinful mental states (NS 130), of scornful laughter, indulgence in sense objects, sorrow and hatred (NS 131), disgust, fear, and sexual inclinations of all kinds (NS 132), and practice of righteous and pure concentrations (NS 133).[159]

Thus, self-restraint or subsidence of passions (*shama* or *prasham*) has necessary concomitance with equanimity. One without the other is not sustainable. Amrtachandra observes:

> Self-restraint (*samyam*) is conduct accompanied by enlightened (*samyak*) intuition and knowledge. Conduct is *dharma*; *dharma* is equanimity; equanimity is state-of-evolution of the self devoid of infatuation (*moha*) perturbation or mental agitation (*kshobha*) [resulting from attachment and aversion]. Therefore, equanimity is the characteristic of the self-restrained (PS 241 AC).

In *Uttarajjhayana* (25.32) a *samana* is defined as one who is endowed with equipoise (*samayaye samano hoi*). The same characteristic of a saint (*sadhu*) is found in Emperor Ashoka's inscriptions in Girnar (13, Girnar). In Buddhist literature as well, the word "*samana*" is frequently used and a *samana* is described as one who has controlled all his sins and subdued his passions and is tranquil (*Dhammapada* 19.10).

Importance of Self-restraint

Significantly, self-restraint (*sanjam* in Pk., *samyam* in Sk.) is considered synonymous with *samana*. How can one be a *samana* without self-restraint? (PS 236). A *samana* is considered to be self-restrained (*sanyat*) if he practices five-fold self-regulations (*samiti*), the three restraints (*gupti*) (of mind, speech and body), controls his five senses, has conquered his anger, pride, greed, etc. passions (*kashaya*) and is completely endowed with intuition and knowledge (PS 240, see also PS 263-264 and 268-269).

The three-fold restraint (*gupti*), which does not figure in the 28 *mula-guna*, is emphasized in *Pravachanasara* 238, which states: "That *karman* which one without knowledge destroys in hundreds of thousands of crores of existences (lives), a knower (*jnata*) possessing threefold restraint (*gupti*) [of mind, speech and body] destroys in a mere breath." In *Pravachanasara* 226, Kundakunda speaks of being free from passions. In *Pravachanasara* 268, he advocates the subduing (*shamit*) or subsidence of passions. In *Pravachanasara* 272, he speaks of the self being in a peaceful and calm state (*prashanta atma*). Since indulgence in sense objects and passions are described as a sin in

Jaina texts (PS 258), one should abstain from them.

According to 28 *mula-gunas* (PS 208-209) of *samana*, which have both external and internal aspects, apparently only a homeless ascetic can be a *samana*. However, this is not necessarily so. Kundakunda recognized that the immaculate performance of the 28 primary rules/ values/qualities, especially regarding pure psychic-attention, which is expected of an ideal or complete *shraman* state (*shramanya*) (PS 214), is not possible for all *samanas*, all the time. That is why he stressed the possibility that external negligence in bodily activities (*kaya cheshta*) (PS 211) and internal negligence in psychic-attention (*Pravachanasara* 211-212 AC) can occur. He therefore emphasized the need to reestablish them on the correct path, which finds mention in *Pravachanasara* 208-214. For instance, apart from the worthy Lord *Arhantas*, the supreme *shramanas*, who have themselves abandoned all *upadhi* (external possessions as well as internal *parigraha* of attachment, aversion and passions) (*Pravachanasara* 219 AC), it is impossible for a *samana* to remain in and forever maintain the state of pure psychic attention.

In the mundane existence of the embodied self, the psychic disposition is invariably unstable because one has to harmonize and strike a balance between not neglecting self-restraint and not neglecting the body. The former is of fundamental importance as a means towards realizing the principle of the pure self (*shuddha atma tattva*) whereas the latter is indispensable as a means to self-restraint (PS 230 AC). Kundakunda has therefore emphasized the need to strike a balance and not commit any excess in either food or fasting and lodging or wanderings, i.e. the need for proper food and wandering (*yukta ahara vihara*) (PS 213, 215, 226-231).

Amrtachandra stresses that one should avoid excess of everything (*ati sarvatra varjayeta*), keeping in view one's age, and capacity for suffering, etc. (PS 230 AC). One should also, he adds, practice austerities and renunciation according to one's capacity (*shakti tapas tyaga*). The body, he adds, is the means to *dharma* (righteousness) (*sharira madyam khalu dharma sadhanam*), which, in turn, is the means to peace and happiness and gradually leads to liberation (PS 254 AC). However, at the same time, he categorically states that even if one has the slightest infatuation or mental clinging (*murchha*) in regard to the body, etc., one does not attain liberation, even if one knows all the scriptures (PS 239).

Exposition of Good Psychic-attention *(Shubha Upayoga)*

The issue of *shubha* occupies an important place in the path of liberation. The subject was earlier described in 22 verses (PS 69-92) as also in another seven verses (PS 155-159 and PS 180-181) and is again discussed in 26 verses (PS 245-270). Taking a realistic view of things, Kundakunda categorically states that in the Jaina scriptures that *shramanas* can be endowed with either pure psychic-attention or with auspicious psychic attention (*shubha upayoga*). Amongst them, those with pure psychic-attention are free from karmic inflow (*asrava*); others are subject to karmic inflow (PS 245). Therefore, those with auspicious psychic-attention may not be equated or coordinated with those having pure psychic-attention, though they are also considered as *shraman* (PS 245 AC). Jayasena states that *shramanas* with pure psychic attention are primary, while those with auspicious psychic-attention are secondary (PS 245 JS). Therefore, Kundakunda and Amrtachandra did not deem it necessary to rule them out of the state of *shramanya* (*shraman*-hood).

Amrtachandra's commentary (PS 245 AC) advances several arguments why persons with good or auspicious psychic-attention should also be regarded as *samana*. These are:

1. They are in the proximity of pure psychic-attention, i.e. they are not deprived of having pure psychic-attention for some time.

2. Although they are not able to ascend to the stage of pure psychic-attention due to not being completely free from passions, they are subject to karmic inflow (SS 245). However, they have only mild passions or "small particles of passion" (PS 245 AC), which, unlike those endowed with inauspicious or evil psychic attention, does not prevent them from practicing rules or values of *shraman*-hood.

3. Since good or auspicious psychic-attention coinheres with righteousness (*dharma*) and since the "self evolves through righteousness" (PS 11), persons possessing it would be *shramanas.*

4. Such *shramanas* of good psychic-attention, whether householders or ascetics (PS 251), engage themselves in devotion to *arahantas* (PS 246). They show respect coupled with praise and homage to other *shramanas* (PS 247). They render disinterested assistance to others through compassion, which is to be practiced with no consideration

or expectation whatsoever (*nirpeksha*) of any kind or desire of fruit of one's acts of good or righteousness, even though it may result in a small stain (*alpa lepa*) (PS 249-254). They gradually attain the highest happiness of *nirvana* (*moksha*) (PS 254 and PS 254 AC).

5. Since a *shraman* is endowed with good psychic-attention and has refrained from sin, he has an attitude of equality towards all righteous persons. He is someone who is endowed with meritorious qualities, and is therefore on the right path (*sumagga* in Pk., *sumarga* in Sk.) (PS 259), i.e. on the path of liberation (PS 259 AC.

6. Such *shramanas*, who are devoid of evil or inauspicious psychic attention and endowed with either good or pure psychic-attention, through being themselves an abode of liberation, are able to help others to cross the (mundane existence), i.e. attain liberation (PS 260 and PS 260 AC).

However, *shramanas* with good psychic-attention cannot be equated with *shramanas* of pure psychic-attention (for definition of pure psychic attention, see PS 14) because they are not of the same level (PS 245 AC) and because they are not completely free from passions. The former are therefore subject to karmic inflow (PS 245 and PS 245 AC) whereas the latter are devoid of all passions and free from *karmic* inflow (PS 245 and PS 245 AC), which is the direct cause of liberation.

Ascetic *shramanas* having good psychic-attention and householders share a number of characteristics and activities. However, unlike the former, the latter cannot be totally free from worldly concerns and possessions (*upadhi* or *parigraha*) (PS 219). As a result, the activities of rendering assistance to others and service, etc. is more prominent in householders (PS 254).

Accordingly, Acharya Mahaprajna observes: "The vow of non-possession cannot be prescribed for a householder. For, an individual totally devoid of possessions cannot make material and economic development, nor can he solve the problem of hunger. . . [Hence] putting a limit on one's possessions, i.e. to put a limit on one's own accumulation of wealth and putting a limit to one's consumption, i.e. to put a voluntary limit to one's individual consumption" are considered foremost [or significant] vows of the code of conduct for the householder.[160]

Nevertheless, despite Kundakunda's emphasis on internal aspects, it was no longer possible to consider a Jaina householder to be "an anachronism,"[161] even if it was so when Jaina asceticism was viewed in "purely physical terms". Jain teachings, Johnson states, were from its beginnings so ascetic-oriented that "*prima facie*" lay Jainism "would seem to be a contradiction in terms".[162] We cannot, however, bifurcate the duties of *shramanas* and householders into watertight compartments.

In Kundakunda's works, particularly *Pravachanasara*, the householders (*sagara*, i.e. persons with homes) occupy a significant place and even considered *samana*. The words "*sagara*" and "*anagara*" (homeless) are frequently referred to in *Pravachanasara* (see PS 250, 251, 254 and 275).

Meaning of *Samana*

The word "*samana*" in Prakrit (*shraman* in Sk.) is used very frequently in *Pravachanasara* as well as other works of Kundakunda. It has several meanings: subsidence (*shaman*) of [negative] emotions i.e. anger, etc. passions, or restraint of one's senses; equanimity (*sama, samata, samana*), one having equanimous attitude as regards enemy or friend, pleasure or pain, praise or blame, life or death, etc; and one who is inclined towards making efforts or exerts himself (*shrama* or *shraman*) for his moral and spiritual uplift, i.e. a noble or enlightened person. The word "*samana*" can also be interpreted as *sa+manas*, i.e. one endowed with mind of his own or equanimous mind.

The word "*samana*" as described and explained in *Pravachanasara*, according to the present author of this introduction, does not necessarily mean an ascetic (the word *sahu* or *sadhu* in Sk. also signifies a noble person), even though it is generally used in the sense of an ascetic by many scholars. For that matter, It is also incorrect to conclude, as is often said, that Kundakunda's works are written and meant only for ascetics. The code of conduct for the householders, written by Samantabhadra categorically states: "The householder, who is devoid of delusion, has enlightened view [of the reality of things], and is established in the path of liberation, is superior to an ascetic who is deluded and is devoid of enlightened view" (RKS 33).

In *Pravachanasara* itself, the following characteristics are said to qualify or define *samana*:

(1) a person who has no desire or attachment to sense objects in

this world and has no expectation in regard to the other [i.e. next world], is self-controlled in food and wandering (*yukta-ahara-vihara*), and is free from passions (*kashaya*) is *samana* (PS 226);

(2) a person whose view (*ditthi* in Pk. and *drashti* in Sk.) or conviction is not in accordance with scriptures, cannot be self-restrained (*sanyat*) and one who does not practice self-restraints, how can he be considered *samana*? (PS 236), i.e. he is not *samana*; and

(3) a person who maintains equanimity among groups of enemies and friends as the same, treats pleasure and pain as the same, regards praise and blame as the same, clay and gold as the same, and, moreover, maintains an equanimous attitude in regard to life and death by considering them to be the same (PS 241).

It is noteworthy that in the three works of Kundakunda, viz. *Pravachanasara*, *Samayasara* and *Niyamsara*, no distinction is made in vows as major-scale vows (*mahavratas*) and minor-scale vows (*anuvratas*), meant for ascetics and householders respectively. Moreover, in *Niyamsara* the five rules of moral conduct like non-violence and five-fold self-regulation (*samiti*) as well as three restraints (*gupti*) (of mind, speech and body) (NS 56-70) (excluded from 28 *mula-gunas* of *samana*, PS 208-209) have been described as *vyavahara charitra*. They are also considered as a practice of austerities (NS 55), i.e. conduct of self-restraint from the external, other referential (*vyavahara*) point of view, relevant, desirable and applicable to householders as well as *samanas* alike.

Eighty-two verses of *Niyamsara* (verses 77 to 158) discuss in detail issues like conduct from the internal, self-referential point of view (*nishchaya charitra*) of psychological techniques of self-introspection, repentance (*pratikraman*), etc., aimed at purifying the mental states at the inner level.[163] They are briefly described as *pratikraman*, *alochana*, and *pratyakhyana* in *Pravachanasara* (see PS 207 AC). Interestingly, in *Pravachanasara*, the conduct which is endowed with equanimity is said to be free from infatuation (*moha*) and mental disturbance (*kshobha*) caused by attachment and aversion (PS 7).

Faulty Criticism of Johnson of Kundakunda's Views on Conduct

Kundakunda's emphasis on the internal aspects of conduct without denying the importance of physical, external, social aspects is criticized by W. J. Johnson as "internalization".[164] Apart from threatening "the ethical norm of lay community", Johnson argues, internal aspects of conduct also jeopardize the "ascetic practice, and thereby the entire structure of Jaina religious and social identity".[165] This allegation has no basis whatsoever because Kundakunda truly places the moral and spiritual conduct of both householders and ascetics on the solid foundations of a rational and balanced approach of external self-restraint and internal self-discipline or morality and spirituality.

One of the earliest codes of moral conduct for the householders (*Ratnakarnda Shravkachara,* RKS), written by Samantabhadra in the second century A.D., begins the chapter "Necessity for the Adoption of Enlightened Conduct," by stating that "*sadhu* [one can translate it as the noble or enlightened person or *samana* of PS] starts to practice the rules of moral conduct by getting rid of attachment and aversion" (RKS 47). "As a result of renunciation of attachment and aversion, one [necessarily] abstains from violence (*himsa*), etc. sins" (RKS 48). Renunciation is an attitude of mind that is manifested through word and deed; it is an ideal to be attained and it is possible only by cultivating detachment.

Johnson blames Kundakunda for his doctrine of *upayoga* (conscious attentiveness), his "internalization" of *karmic* bondage and his concept of *himsa* (violence), etc. However, Paul Dundas, the reviewer of his book *Harmless Souls,* maintains that Kundakunda's emphasis on inner aspects or "interiorisation of the various components of Jaina practice and the concomitant attempt to move the ascetic's ultimate concern away from his relationship with the external world toward his inner being" makes him a "reformer",[166] who is "consciously reacting against excessive formalization, the mechanistic pursuit of physical austerity".[167] Thus, "external, ascetic practice" which had become "meaningless" and "without spiritual significance", Dundas stresses, "had to be reinterpreted by Kundakunda". Kundakunda was well aware that although the "inner state has precedence and conditions the outer", external moral conduct of vows (*vrata*), self-regulation (*samiti*), etc. (*vyavahara charitra*) has its importance and value. The moral rules of conduct are the "objective correlative" of the subjective state or attitude.[168] Internal purification in the sense of subsidence of the passions is the necessary concomitant (*avinabhava*) (PS 216 AC) of external moral conduct of non-violence, etc.

The recognition of the necessity and importance of the value of external moral discipline ensures that Jainism does not become what Johnson calls a "private soteriology".[169] Kundakunda, Paul Dundas remarks, represents a "middle point between two main historic propensities within Jainism: excessive formalization and ritualisation of behavior which diminish the spiritual dimensions of the path and excessive interiorisation of values",[170] which denies the need for external moral conduct (*vyavahara charitra*) in relation to others.

Nishchaya and *Vyavahara* Charitra (Conduct)

This remark of Paul Dundas is very relevant in the discussion of conduct, especially *nishchaya* and *vyavahara charitra* (conduct). There are numerous persons who one-sidedly cling to only external, other-referential *vyavahara charitra.* As a result, they diminish the internal, spiritual dimension of the path of liberation. There are others, particularly Kanjipanthi, who exclusively depend on excessive interiorisation and deny the validity and relevance of *vyavahara charitra* altogether under the guise of internal, self-referential *nishchaya charitra* of their own thinking (which is not the same as *nishchaya charitra* of repentance (*pratikraman*), etc. described in *Niyamsara*).

Thus, H.C. Bharill adheres to the mistaken assertion of his preceptor (*guru,* whom Bharill describes with respect as *gurudeva,* i.e. preceptor-God), viz. Kanji Svami, that "conduct is only of one kind alone, and that is of the nature of non-attachment, i.e. completely devoid of attachment (*veetraga bhavarupa*); *charitra* with attachment is not conduct at all; he who respects it, accedes to it or believes in it is a deluded person (*mithyadrashti*)". Bharill adds: "*Nishchaya* (point of view) *charitra* is the term used only for the non-attached mental state; in reality *vyavahara charitra,* which has [some degree of] attachment, is not conduct at all, it is only the fault of conduct."[171]

In this regard, Bharill refers to the introductory remark of Amrtachandra to *Pravachanasara* verse 6, to the effect that conduct without attachment has desirable result (*ishta phala*) and therefore, is worth-acquiring (*upadeya*), while conduct with attachment has undesirable result (*anishta phala*) and hence to be avoided (*heya*). This remark in fact points out that as compared to the conduct with attachment or *vyavahara charitra,* the conduct free of attachment (*veetraga charitra*), which is the direct and immediate cause of liberation, is preferable and worth acquiring. Since *vyavahara charitra* has some degree of attachment, which is the cause of bondage, it does not have that privilege since it gradually (*kramtah*), not directly or immediately, brings about liberation (PS 254 AC).

Moreover, the above-mentioned remarks of Amrtachandra has to be seen in the context in which it has been made. Conduct without attachment, anchored or based on enlightened view and knowledge, is the [immediate and direct] cause of liberation. Hence, it is definitely preferable to conduct with attachment whereby one gets the troubles of the heavenly and kingly power, etc. (PS 6 AC). However, Amrtachandra also states that *vyavahara charitra*, i.e. conduct based on commendable attachment (*prashasta raga*), which is characterized by subsidence of passions, veneration of the worthy Lord (*Arhat*) and practice of moral conduct of self-restraint including non-violence, also has a purifying (*vishuddhi*) effect (Amrtachandra's commentary on PS 155, 156, 180). This gradually (*kramatah*) brings about the highest happiness of *nirvana* (liberation) (PS 254 and PS 254 AC), and not only leads to liberation of oneself (PS 259 and PS 259 AC), but also helps others to attain liberation (PS 260 and PS 260 AC).

In *Panchastikayasara* (PKS), Amrtachandra states that an external/other-referential inclination (*para-samaya pravrtti*) [i.e. *vyavahara charitra*] of the nature of veneration of the worthy Lord (*Arhant*) [etc.] is not the direct/immediate condition of liberation but traditionally (*paramparya*) has the disposition or tendency (*sadbhava*) of being the [indirect] condition (*hetu*) of liberation (Introductory remark of Amrtachandra to PKS 170), even with the troubles (*klesha*) of heaven, etc. (PKS 170 AC).

According to Jayasena, both *nishchaya* and *vyavahara* paths of liberation (*moksha marg*) are the cause of liberation (PKS 106 JS). Amrtachandra contends that the *vyavahara* path of liberation is the means (*sadhan*) of *nishchaya* path, which is the direct cause of liberation (PKS 160-161 AC). This apparently implies that without the practice of *vyavahara* path of liberation it is not possible to attain liberation. Thus, if someone argues that *vyavahara moksha marg* is the sole cause of transmigratory existence (*sansara*), and not of liberation, would, indeed, be considered to be filled with excessive stubbornness.

Summing up his exposition of the proper assessment of *nishchaya* and *vyavahara charitra* (conduct) or *nishchaya* and *vyavahara moksha-*

marg, Amrtachandra observes:

> One should first give up the tendency to indulge in *ashubha* (inauspicious or evil) activity (*nivarita ashubha karma pravrtti*), and adopt *vyavahara moksha-marg* of the *shubha* (good or auspicious) activities (*samupatta shubha karma pravrttyah*), consisting of subsidence of passions, enthusiasm for righteousness and piety, compassion, acceptance of reality of things, the study of scriptures, non-violence, etc. five rules (*vrata*) of conduct of self-restraint, the restraints (*gupti*) of activities of mind, speech and body (*yoga* in Jain terminology), the five carefulness or self-regulation (*samiti*), various kinds of austerities etc. All these rules of moral code of conduct, called *vyavahara moksha-marg* are, in fact, self-restraints (*samyam*) (PKS 172 AC).

Amrtachandra further points out:

> One should not cling one-sidedly (*ekantena*) to only *vyavahara moksha-marg* considering it to be diverse from or completely separate from the objective of *nishchaya moksha-marg* (*bhinna sadhya-sadhan bhava*); in that case he will suffer extreme grief or distress. He should certainly understand the two paths (*marg*) properly, along with the compatibility and the harmony between the two paths and thus realize the ideal of non-attachment (*veetragatva*) as the immediate and the direct cause of *moksha* (liberation). Only by the practice of *vyavahara* and *nishchaya* [paths] being complementary, not contradictory or opposed to each other (*avirodhena*), one can attain the objective of non-attachment, (*veetragata*), *not otherwise* (*na punar anyatha*) (PKS 172 AC).

Pandit Todarmal's *manglacharan* (opening verse in Hindi) to his translation of Amrtachandra's *Purusharthasiddhyupapa* is also quite relevant in regard to conduct from *vyavahara naya* and *nishchaya naya.* He states:

> There are those who from *nishchaya naya* mistakenly assume self (*atma*) to be pure like liberated souls (*siddha-samaan*) even in its empirical existence and hence become lazy and negligent about purification of self and make no effort in getting rid of attachment, aversion, passions, etc. internal impurities and thus become unrestrained in their behaviour, not recognizing or caring about purity of their own self, [i.e. renunciation of attachment, aversion, passions, etc. internal impurities]. And there are those who consider that mere auspicious thought-activities of charity, *sheel* (good conduct), and austerities from *vyavahara naya* alone (*hi*), even when devoid of internal purification, serves the true well-being of the self, and thereby they do not give up their foolishness. Moreover, there are others,

who recognize the path of *vyavahara naya* and that of *nishchaya naya* to be separate and different paths and thus become arrogant and insolent. It is only when one has proper understanding of the distinctive features and true nature of both the *nishchaya naya* and *vyavahara naya* and regards the former as the cause (*karana*) [i.e. the primary (*mukhya*)], or substantive cause (*upadana* cause) and the latter as supportive (*upachaar*) factor [or auxiliary cause, *nimitta karana*], then only one becomes truly enlightened or wise.

Apart from Amrtachandra's introductory remark (to PS 6), Bharill also states that a similar view is expressed by Jayasena in his commentary of the said verse. However, Bharill fails to mention Jayasena's observation that as a result of the special kind of karmic bondage of virtuous nature (*vishishta punya bandha*) that occurs due to conduct with attachment, one gets the kingly power, etc. and that *vishishta punya bandha* also customarily (*paramparya*) brings about liberation (*nirvana*) (PS 6 JS).

The Path of Liberation

Any discussion of conduct is incomplete without the description of liberation — the highest objective of human endeavour. The path of liberation is discussed in 13 verses (PS 232-244). The first four verses (PS 232-235) emphasize that the study of scriptures is important and necessary for ascertaining with certainty the reality of the principles of life or categories (*tattvas* or *padarthas*), particularly the knowledge of the self and the non-self, (*sva* and *para*, i.e. other). In other words, the self (*atman*) and 'other' than self (*paratman*) have the potential to become the supreme self (*param atman*). The self and not-self have the psycho-physical nexus and interaction as to how the mental state (*chitta vrtti*) get stained with the faults (*doshas*) of attachment and aversion due to being involved in duality by the division of things as favourable and unfavourable or desirable and undesirable (*ishta anishta*). The material or physical *karman* also affect, condition or influence (i.e. acting as *pratyaya*) psychic states, thereby staining mental states with delusion, etc. (*mohadi*). One devoid of above knowledge is unable to destroy the physical and psychic *karman* (*dravya-bhava karman*) (PS 232-233 and PS 232-233 AC).

Knowledge by itself is not sufficient to destroy *karmas*. *Pravachanasara* 236 states that persons who do not possess enlightened view of things because they really lack a discriminative insight between the self and other, and because they believe in identity of the self with the passions (*kashaya*). As a result, the body does not restrain his longing for sense-objects.Without self-restraint, there can be no *shramana*-state, otherwise known as the path of liberation. Hence the path of liberation can be nothing but a simultaneity of Scripture-knowledge, conviction in the principle and categories and self-restraint (PS 236 and PS 236 AC).

Pravachanasara Verse 237 states that one does not attain liberation by means of scriptural knowledge if one is devoid of enlightened world-view of the nature of reality of things. Similarly, someone having enlightened world-view of things does not attain liberation if he is devoid of self-restraint (*samyam*) (PS 237). Due to his indulgence in sense-objects and passions, the self continues to lack self-restraint (PS 237 JS). Moreover, a person, who has even the slightest attachment (e.g. to the body) does not attain perfection (*siddhi*) even if he knows all the scriptures (PS 239). Only a person who is free from desire or attachment and the sense of 'i-ness' and 'mine-ness' (PS 190 and SS 19-23) towards worldly objects is capable of enlightenment and salvation.

All the three (viz. scriptural knowledge, enlightened world-view and self-restraint) are necessary for attaining liberation. All three together are imperative for the attainment of liberation (PS 237 JS). In other words, one cannot attain liberation by sticking to a single path of liberation separately or independently of the other two, viz. devotion, enlightened world-view of the reality of things, knowledge alone, or action/inaction only. The example that one can reach the top of the mountain by following any one direction or path, does not apply in the case of the liberation of the self. The self can only be liberated by all three because it is an indivisible unity of its attributes or modes of intuition, knowledge and volition or conduct which are interactive, interdependent and mutually inter-penetrating.

The three-fold self-restraints of mind, speech and body (*gupti*) enables an enlightened person (*jnani*) to destroy the *karman* in a mere breath (PS 238), i.e. in no time. Unless the mind is controlled, it keeps wavering and drifting about without direction. Hence, restraint of mind is extremely important because it is the sole means to control the mind and to uproot disquietude and agitation (*kshobha*) caused by attachment and aversion, and thereby attain the state of equanimity (*samya*, PS 7).

Description of Self-restraint

Describing self-restraint (*sanjad* in Pk. and *samyat* or *samyam* in Sk.), Kundakunda states: "That *samana* (*shramana* in Sk.) who has five self-regulations (*samiti*), the three self-restraints (*gupti*) of mind, speech and body, control of five senses, has conquered his passions (*kashaya*) and is fully endowed with intuition and knowledge, is called self-restrained" (PS 240). Moreover, a *samana* is "he, who considers the groups of enemies and friends as the same, pleasure and pain as the same, praise and blame as the same, clay and gold as the same and maintains an equanimous attitude in regard to life and death" (PS 241).

Commenting on it, Amrtachandra observes:

> Self-restrained (*samyam*) is conduct accompanied by enlightened (*samyak*) world-view and knowledge. Conduct is *dharma*; *dharma* is equanimity; equanimity is a state-of-evolution of the self devoid of infatuation or deluded view (*moha*) and perturbation or mental agitation (*kshobha*) [caused by attachment and aversion]. Therefore, equanimity is the characteristic of the self restrained (PS 241 AC).

Thus, *sama* (equanimity), *sanyat* or *samyam* (conduct of self-restraint), [or *shaman*, i.e. subsidence of passions, etc. as also *samiti*, i.e. self-regulation] and *samana* (*shraman* in Sk.) [i.e. one who is oriented towards the path of liberation and makes efforts in the direction of sanity and purification], are considered to be closely inter-related terms. A *samana* is one who is self-restrained or who practices self-restraint. This is evident from the categorical statement that without self-restraint how can one be a *samana* (*shramana*)? (PS 236). The *shramana*-state is also equated with the path of liberation. Amrtachandra states: "And for one who has not attained self-restraint there can be no *shramana*-state, otherwise called the path of liberation, which is convincingly held to be in a state of mental concentration (*ekagra gatatva rupam*)" (PS 236 AC).

Enlightened World-view, Knowledge and Conduct constittue the Path of Liberation

In *Pravachanasara* 242, it is categorically stated that the *shramanya* (i.e. practice of moral and spiritual self-restraints and self-discipline) of a person who is endowed with enlightened world-view, knowledge and conduct [devoid of attachment and aversion], the three together (*yugapat*) with mental-concentration or one-pointed attention (*ekagratah*), is complete (PS 242). In other words, such a person is capable of attaining liberation Or that the three together constitute the path of liberation.

In *Samayasara* also, it is declared by the worthy Lord (*Jina*) that the enlightened world-view, knowledge and conduct jointly comprise the path of liberation (SS 410). In *Panchastikayasara* (PKS), enlightened conduct, devoid of attachment and aversion, together with enlightened world-view and knowledge is described as the path of liberation (PKS 106).

In his commentary on *Pravachanasara* 242, Amrtachandra states that just as in the case of *panak* (a drink mixture) there is an experiencing of one, though consisting of many, so also the path of liberation, otherwise called *shramana*-hood, is said to be characterised as mental concentrations (*ekagrata*) or repose in itself (*atma-nishthtva*), though comprising of the three modes (*paryaya*) [characterised by mutual-interpenetrations, i.e. mutually inter-dependent and inter-active] of the self or soul substance, viz. *darshan*, *jnana* and *charitra* (enlightened view, knowledge and conduct).

Amrtachandra further states that according to the external, other-referential point of view (*vyavahara-naya*), which, since it involves differentiations (*bheda*), considers chiefly the modes, the statement is that "enlightened view, knowledge, and conduct are the path of liberation." According to the internal, self-referential point of view (*nishchaya-naya*), which, since it consists in an identity (*abheda*), consider chiefly the substance, it is that "mental-concentration is the path of liberation." (PS 242 AC)

According to reliable evidence (*pramana*), everything consists in difference and identity (PS 242 AC).

Thus, that path of liberation, which, according to the attitude of the conceiver, becomes plural, though one, and thereby exhibits triple characteristics and again oneness, - that path, stable, with existence is dependent upon [the purport (*abhipraya*)] of seer and knower (*drashtr-jnatr*) (PS Kalash 16). *Naya* is defined, described and explained as the purport (*abhipraya*) of the knower (Akalanka, *Laghiyastraya* 49). *Samayasara* (verse 7) states that *darshan*, *jnana*, *charitra*, are said to be [three modes of consciousness] from *vyavahara naya*. However, from the [transcendental perspective] there is no such differentiation, just pure consciousness-as-such (*janago-suddho* in Pk. and *jnayak-shuddha* in Sk.).

If a *shraman*, who is ignorant about the nature of the reality of things, is infatuated because of addiction to the "other" substance, and feels either attachment or aversion, then he is bound with various *karmans* (PS 243). However, if a *shraman* is not infatuated with objects and does not have either attachment or aversion (*dvesha*), then he inevitably destroys the *karmans.* (PS 244). Freedom from infatuation or deluded view (*moha*), attachment (*raga*) and aversion (*dvesha*) play the most significant role in liberation (PS 243-244). A person devoid of self-restraint does not attain liberation even if he has knowledge of scriptures or is convinced of the nature of reality of things (see PS 237).

In the earlier verses as well, it is stated that without the renunciation of worldly concerns, devoid of all consideration or expectation, the purification of intentional mental states does not take place. When the mind is not pure, how can the annihilation of the *karman* take place (PS 220) or the liberation of the self take place? One must understand that renunciation is a state/an attitude of mind. It is a state of detachment, not necessarily asceticism (e.g. going to the forest). In *Niyamsara*, it is categorically stated: "What is the good of residing in a forest, mortification of the body, observance of various fasts, study of the scriptures and keeping silence, etc., if the *samana* is devoid of equanimity" (NS 124).

It is simply impossible for a person favourably disposed towards worldly objects (*upadhi, parigraha*) to be free from infatuation (sense of mineness), incidental sins inevitable in worldly activities (*arambha*) and lack of self-restraint (*asamyam*). A person, who is engrossed in other, external things, cannot understand or realize the real nature of or the true identity of his soul (PS 221 and PS 221 AC).

In *Pravachanasara* 14, a *shraman* is described as a person who has the following qualities. A person is a *shraman* if one is of pure psychic-attention, when one is well aware of the categories (*padarthas*), including the self and the non-self, and the *sutras* (the scriptures) [for the definition of *Sutra*, see PS 34] which explain them, when he possesses self-restraint (*samyam*) and practices austerities (*tapas*), gives up attachment and considers pleasure and pain the same (*sama*). Obviously, pure psychic-attention (*shuddha upayoga*) is the direct means of attaining pure self or pure consciousness, i.e. the liberated state.

Distortion of the Path of Liberation by Kanjipanthi

Liberation usually means getting rid of one's *karmas.* In this context, K. Ramakrishna Rao observes: "In Indian thought, one's actions good or bad deposit *karma.* Good actions produce meritorious *karma* and bad actions deposit black [bad] *karma.*" The accumulated *karma* lies dormant in the *chitta* (the mental stuff which contains instinctual tendencies inherited from previous lives and the effects of past actions) like a seed in the ground to sprout at an appropriate time. When *karma* leads to action in this manner, that action, in turn, again produces new *karma.* This cycle continues indefinitely unless broken by efforts towards self-realization, i.e. liberation (*moksha*) or *nirvana.*[172]

According to Patanjali's *Yoga Sutra, karma* is said to be "recorded in the unconscious by any action or thought a person has done". The *karmic* memory trace (*samskara*), it adds, remains in the unconscious as "a predisposition toward doing the same action or thought again in the future".[173] To this description, one may add that in Jainism *karma* is material in nature recorded in neuro-physiological processes (physical or *dravya karma* or physical mind). It has the power to affect, influence and condition the *adhyavasana bhavas* (SS 190), i.e. psychic states like *bhava karma* (e.g. passions like delusion (*mithyatva*), lack of self-restraints (*avirati*), anger, etc. passions, and vibratory activity of mind, speech and body (*yoga*).

The material or physical (*dravya*) *karma* and the psychic (*bhava*) *karma* act as the auxiliary cause (*nimitta karana*), and not the substantive cause (*upadana karana*), of one another (SS 80-81). Moreover, it is action, imbued with attachment or desire that is considered to bind the self with *karman* (PS 179), not each and every physical action, which is devoid of attachment, etc. psychical states (*bhava*). Accordingly, attachment, aversion and deluded view (*mithya darshan*) are said to be *asrava bhava* (SS 177-178), i.e. the direct cause of the influx of *karma* and the consequent bondage. In other words, psychological bondage is more significant than material bondage of physical *karma.*

Moreover, the coming into operation, rise (*udaya*) or fruition (*vipaka*) of material *karma* alone is not the cause of fresh karmic bondage. This does not produce *karma* again (thereby continuing the karmic cycle indefinitely as some systems of philosophy in Hinduism seems to imply). This occurs only when the self (*jiva*) itself evolves into psychic states of the nature of attachment, etc. (SS 132-136 and 164-165 JS). In other words, the only way to get rid of karmas and attain liberation (*moksha*) is by completely renouncing attachment, aversion and deluded view.

Faulty View of Bronkhorst regarding Liberation

Johannes Bronkhorst proceeds from the assumption that actions produce *karma* and the accumulated *karma*, on coming into operation or *karmic* seed sprouting at an appropriate time, produce fresh *karma* again. This results in the (*karmic*) cycle (*karma santati*, i.e. continued succession of *karma*) continuing indefinitely, He presents a strong, logical case in arguing that since actions produce *karma*, one can only escape the results of one's actions by inaction or somehow putting an end to all activity. He states:

> The early Jainas, and many other Indian ascetics with them, applied this principle literally, and suppressed all bodily and mental activity [restriction of the mind, of the sense organs or quite simply all bodily and mental activities, indicative of severe practice of external penances and austerities of the ascetics]. The pains and suffering which these kinds of practices provoke were looked upon as signs that old *karma* was being destroyed. Once all the old *karma* is destroyed [by asceticism], no new *karma* being added [due to non-performing of new actions], it was sufficient for the ascetic to [come across natural death or] fast to death, motionlessly, and no new births would await him.
>
> The other method shares the same essential concern. One can only be freed from the result of actions by not committing them. According to this second method, one has to discover that one is not identical with the active parts of the personality. All that is required is that one realizes this important insight. Once one stops identifying with the body and the mind, i.e. with all those aspects of the person that are active, one is no longer bound by the actions that have been committed by those parts. Usually this insight consists in the discovery of one's real self, one's soul, which is [thought to be] completely inactive by nature.

These two methods of liberation are or organically related to the doctrine of *karma*. They constitute, in a way, natural answers to the problem posed by this doctrine: Rebirth being occasioned by one's actions, only inaction can stop it.[174] [Escape from the cycle of rebirths was accepted as the highest religious aim.]

It is believed that the "insight into the true nature of the self is the necessary, or even [a] sufficient condition for the attainment of liberation from the cycle of rebirths. The self, it is believed, has to be permanent and unchangeable, precisely because it does not participate in any actions."[175] Accordingly, the knowledge of the inactive or non-active nature of the self, or concerning the need to practice mental and physical inaction, is considered sufficient in order to be liberated from the effects of one's actions.

In this context, Bronkhorst observes:

> Why did this knowledge of the self signify, for so many Indian [Samkhya and Kanjipanthi] liberation from the effects of one's actions? Precisely because it implied that one is not identical with the active parts of one's personality, i.e. the body and the mind.
>
> Well, this is exactly what the [liberating insight of the] knowledge of the not-self does for the Buddhists. It teaches that none of the constituents of the personality are the self. If we understand this to mean that one should not identify with these constituents, we come to the same kind of insight as that of the self for the non-Buddhists. A major difference is, of course, that an empty spot seems to remain there where the non-Buddhists believed to find a soul, but the effect of non-identification with one's action is exactly the same.[176]

This passage, Bronkhorst states, illustrates how "a doctrine that was explicitly rejected, found its way into the Buddhist texts through a back-door". "The reason," he adds, is "easy to guess: because in the case of such an insight it was clear why it could constitute a solution to the problem posed by the doctrine of *karma.* The effects of action can only be avoided through non-action. Knowing that one's active parts are not really one's self, implies not being affected by the results of those actions".[177]

The first method of Bronkhorst, viz. of undergoing pains and suffering by undertaking extreme practices of external penances and austerities and suppression of all bodily and mental activity, for the destruction of *karmas,* did not particularly appeal to Kundakunda because he has consistently laid greater emphasis on internal aspects of renouncing deluded view, attachment and aversion in order to get rid of the *karmas* and attain liberation. As for the second method of Bronkhorst, viz. of not identifying with body and mind, the active parts of the self and being completely inactive, Kundakunda specifically states that the self in the doer of *yoga* (the activities of mind, speech and body) and *upagoya (*function *of* conciousness) (SS 100) and the self in the doer (*karta*) and experiencer (*bhokta*) of his actions (PKS 27).

Mistaken Concept of Non-doership or Inactive Self of Kanjipanthi

As already stated, the objective of liberation can only be realized by enlightened world-view of the reality of things, knowledge and conduct, which necessarily involves will and effort. The very concept of psychic-attention (*upayoga*), which is the nature of the self and on which Kundakunda lays emphasis, signifies active consciousness and permanent and yet evolvent personality, not inactive, unchangeable (*aparinami*) self. Therefore, Kanjipanthi's advocacy of an inactive self and exclusive emphasis on knowing the permanent and unchangeable self is contrary to the teachings of Kundakunda.

In *Pravachanasara*, Amrtachandra asserts that a person who first has recourse to an active behaviour (*pravrtti*) based on good psychic attention (*shubha upayoga*), and gradually (*kramatah*) by proper self-restraint advances to complete abstinence (*nirvrtti*), experiences an absolutely everlasting state, consisting in knowledge and bliss (PS Kalash 17). In other words, it is only in "an absolutely everlasting state of . . . knowledge and bliss," i.e. the liberated state of soul, that one can be said to be *krta-krtya*, i.e. he has nothing more to do or accomplish anything. But till that stage of "complete abstinence (*nivrtti*)" is reached, one has to "take recourse to active behaviour (*pravrtti*)."

In his commentary on *Panchastikayasara* verse 59, Amrtachandra asserts that non-doership (*akartrtva*) of *jiva* (soul) is not desirable and acceptable (PKS 59 AC). Yet the Kanjipanthi persist in harping on the concept of the inactive self (*akarta* or *akartrtva*). Thus, Hem Chand Jain, a Kanjipanthi adherent/follower, mistakenly states: "Jain philosophy is basically that of non-doing/non-doership as this principle is established with omniscience and the sequence bound modifications (*krama baddha paryaya*)."[178] This means that whatever "particular modification will take place in a particular substance at a particular time is pre-determined". This so-called novel concept of *krama baddha paryaya*, which is propagated by Kanji Svami and his followers, is extremely detrimental and deterministic concept that robs the soul of its independence. It gives rise to inactivity and laziness. It denies the importance and significance of the effort, which is against Jain principles, and is not mentioned in any Jain scripture.[179]

According to Kundakunda, external, other-referential (*vyavahara*) moral conduct (*charitra*) consists of self-restraint, five vows (*vrata*) of non-violence, etc., five self-regulations or carefulness in action (*samiti*) and three restraints of mind, speech and body (*gupti*) (NS 56-70), which have characteristics of *dharma* (righteousness and piety), *samyam* (self-restraints) and *tapa* (austerity, NS 55). The internal, self-referential (*nishchaya*) conduct of repentance (*pratikraman*), etc. includes methods of spiritual self-discipline (NS 77-158). Along with enlightened view and knowledge of reality of things, *vyavahara* and *nishchaya* conduct are considered to be the authentic means (*sadhan*) of liberation.

The ascetic activities of *tapas*, according to the orthodox ideology, comprises performance of six external (*bahya*) practices and six internal (*abhyantar*) austerities or penances (*tapas*), including *prayashchitta* (*pratikraman*, etc.). These are also oriented towards external aspects. For instance, the performance of Shvetambara annual *samvatsari pratikraman* on the eighth day of *Paryushan* is primarily a congregational ritual action (*kriya*). In this tradition, recitation of a Prakrit liturgy is recited accompanied by various hand gestures and bodily postures. In this endeavour, each Jain publicly recognizes all possible wrong thoughts, statements, and deeds from the previous year, and strives to minimize their karmic effects through the statement of disavowal of intention behind them. One of the most public expressions of these themes of confession and community harmony comes at the conclusion of the performance of *Samvatsari Pratikraman*, when the members of the congregation say to each other individually, "*micchami dukkadam*" – a Prakrit phrase that literally means, "may my improper actions be without consequence."[180]

Kundakunda's self-disciplinary methods like *pratikraman* are described in detail in *Niyamsara*. Those are well-tried psychological techniques of self-transformation, which are directly related to the internal purification of the soul. Only when one indulges in self-introspection and self-analysis and acknowledges one's faults and weaknesses, can one remove those shortcomings and the accumulated evils of the past. There is simply no other way. However, this has to be a continuous process if one really wants to change onself. However, the Kanjipanthi maintain that knowledge of the inactive self is the easy way to liberation of the self from the cycle of births. They are averse to the adoption of means (*sadhan*) for the purification of the self through the efforts of *vyavahara* and *nishchaya charitra* (conduct), which are prescribed in *Niyamsara*, or the adoption of self-restraints (*samyam*) and austerities (*tapas*) described in *Pravachanasara* (PS 14).

In *Pravachanasara*, knowledge of the reality of things or categories (*padartha*), including the self and the non-self, *samyam* (self-restraints) and *tapa* (austerities), along with detachment and equanimity in pleasure and pain, are significant constituents of pure psychic attention (*shuddha upayoga*) (PS 14). Psychic activity is stated to be good (*shubha*) since it leads to accumulation of *punya* [karma]; if it is evil (*ashubha*), it leads to accretion of sinful (*papa*) [*karma*]. However, in the absence of both psychic attention, there is no accession [of *karmas*] (PS 156).

A person whose psychic-attention (*upayoga*) is purified (*vishuddha*) puts an end to all the pain and miseries relating to the body (PS 78). Such pure self or pure consciousness (*shuddha atma*) is, in fact, devoid of *karmas* (*karma-rahita*). It is considered the supreme soul (*paramatma*) or liberated soul, which can only be attained by efforts of moral self-restraints and spiritual self-discipline, which have been described in *Niyamsara* and *Pravachanasara*.

Though Kanjipanthi profess to hold Kundakunda in high esteem and consider themselves to be *mumukshu* (desirous of *moksha*), they do not concur or adhere to his prescription of *vyavahara* and *nishchaya charitra* (conduct) for attaining the highest objective of human endeavour, i.e. (*moksha*). They continue to emphasize and harp on the inactive self, whose knowledge, they feel, will liberate one from the cycle of births. In their mistaken one-sided conviction, they do not feel any need to make any efforts in that regard. The only duty/obligation of the soul (*atma*) is knowing. This alone, they maintain, is sufficient for the destruction of deluded view as well as conduct-deluding attachment and aversion.[181]

Undue Emphasis on Knowledge as the only Cause of Liberation

The only thing, Bharill asserts, that one has to do is to know the self and continue to know it. To know the self is knowledge, while to continue to know the self is meditation (*dhyan*), and that meditation [of self] is conduct (*charitra*). He maintains that one need not make any other effort or activity whatsoever to destroy *karmas.*[182] However, he mistakenly believes that one binds *punya* (*karma*) by the worship and meditation of the supreme soul (*paramatma*). The meditation of one's own soul, on the other hand, Bharill says, leads to both the destruction of *karmas* and delusion (*mithyatva*).

Kanjipanthi also erroneously maintain that whatever good activity (*shubha* or *punya*) a person undertakes will only beget him material for sense enjoyments (*bhog samagri*). This is the inherent nature of pain/misery and the cause of transmigratory existence (*sansara*).[183] Knowledge of the self is in itself considered to lead to the destruction of *karmic* bondage and liberation. This belief of the Kanjipanthi sect is similar to that of Shankara – the proponent of Advaita Vedanta – who consistently rejects the view that in addition to knowledge action is also necessary for achieving liberation (*jnana karma samuchchayavada*).

Delusion (*mithyatva*), i.e. ignorance about the nature of the self, Bharill argues, results from the mistake of regarding *punya* as desirable or worth acquiring (*punya mein upadeya buddhi*). This mistake pertains to the nature of reality of things, particularly the soul (*tattva sambandhi bhool*). According to him, this is a great heinous crime (*maha bhayankara papa*) which makes one continuously wander in the transmigratory existence (*sansara*) till he rectifies that mistake.[184] This statement is a gross distortion of Kundakunda's views.

Attachment, aversion and deluded-view (*mithya darshan*, not *mithyatva*), according to Kundakunda, are the cause of influx and bondage of *karmas* (SS 177-178) as well as of transmigratory existence (*sansara*). The various misperceptions and misconceptions entertained by Kanjipanthi regarding good (*shubha*) and righteousness (*punya*) have already been discussed earlier.

For the destruction of infatuation (*moha*) and for obtaining or acquiring or acquisition of enlightened world-view, knowledge and conduct, Bharill observes, one has to merely (*matra*) know the supreme soul (*paramatma*). Except knowing, he claims, one does not have to do anything else. *Paramatma*, he argues, is other (*para*) than self. Nevertheless, as "a consequence of knowing *paramatma* [*arihant*] one is able to know one's own soul or self (*atma*) and he who knows one's own self (*atma*), his infatuation (*moha*) perishes".[185]

Bharill adds:

> Soul's work is only to know [thereby denying or side-tracking all other activities, properties or attributes of soul, including *darshan* and *charitra*], to know self (*sva*) and other (*para*); therefore only know, know, know and know; know the other, know the self, know the self and other; know self different from other, know and continue to know. Continue to know your own self as own self, continue to know uninterrupted or constantly and nothing else is to be done. By this alone, enlightened world-view, knowledge and conduct all will be accomplished and not only view-deluding (*moha*) but conduct-deluding (*moha*) [i.e. attachment and aversion] will also be destroyed. You yourself will become (*Bhagawan*, God) in your present *paryaya* (condition, state or mode of existence). You are *Bhagawan* (God) by nature; if you want to be God in your present state (*paryaya*), then continue to know self in this way . . . you will be omniscient (*sarvajna*), completely devoid of all attachment (*veetragi*).

In this way, it is determined that for the destruction of infatuation (*moha*) the only means or way (*upaya*) is to know one's own *bhagawan atma* (divine soul), and if one wants to proceed further, one can include in this knowing the nature of God with respect to substance, attribute and mode (*dravya-guna-paryaya*).[186]

The above quotation highlights that Bharill not only presents a very perverted argument, which is not only contradictory to what Kundakunda has written but is also against all authentic Jain texts. Let us examine in detail the above statement of Bharill, which is made as a commentary on *Pravachanasara* verse 80. It may be pointed out that the word "*moha*" that is used in this verse only refers to view-deluding *moha* (*darshan moha*) and not conduct-deluding *moha*, comprising of attachment and aversion. This has also been pointed out by Jayasena (PS 80 JS). [Even Bharill is well aware of this as he has himself acknowledged it.][187]

The next verse makes this amply clear. It states that even after getting rid of deluding view (*moha*, *mithyadarshan*) and properly grasping the reality of the self, if one gives up attachment and aversion, then only one obtains the pure self (PS 81). One must therefore remain fully awake in order to get rid of attachment and aversion (PS 81 AC). It is only in this manner that all the enlightened souls have become emancipated (PS 82).

Earlier verses specifically state that he who understands the reality of things and gets rid of attachment and aversion (*raga dvesha*) purifies his *upayoga* (PS 78). Again, if after giving up sinful activities and even getting ready to undertake efforts of good conduct, one does not get rid of infatuation, etc. (*mohadi*) [i.e. both view-deluding and conduct-deluding, attachment and aversion, etc.], then he does not attain the pure self (PS 79). This is because deluded view, attachment and aversion are the cause of bondage of *karmas.* It is only by renouncing them that one can attain liberation. Since attachment and aversion are part of conduct-deluding *moha,* one can get rid of them only through undertaking action, conduct, efforts or adoption of means (*sadhan*) for the purification of the self.

Mithyatva *is the only Cause of* Karmic *Bondage?*

On the other hand, Bharill's mistakenly maintains that delusion (*mithyatva*) or *darshan-moha* (deluded-view or *mithya darshan*), is the cause of *karmic* bondage "in spiritualism" (*adhyatma*). "The agitation or disturbance (*gadabad*) concerning *charitra-moha* (conduct-deluding, i.e. attachment and aversion)", he argues, is only external or superficial (*upari*). This assertion of Bharill is totally mistaken in view of Kundakunda's categorical statement that "attachment and aversion and *moha* (deluded view) are the soul's own inalienable states, modes, or states-of evolution (*ananya parinama*)" (SS 371). Bharill also states that "any confusion or disturbance concerning *darshan-moha* is internal" [i.e. much more serious].[188]

In this regard, it is worth noting that in his commentary on *Pravachanasara* 189, Amrtachandra states that the self is an agent (*karta*) of its own evolution into psychic dispositions such as attachment, etc. It is therefore the appropriator as well as the renouncer thereof from internal, self-referential *nishchaya* point of view (PS 189 AC). As a result, it acts as the agent of transforming or purifying the impure mental states into pure mental states. In this sense, the adoption of *nishchaya naya* is considered the most effective means of achieving the objective of the purity of the self (PS 189 AC).

In this context, Jayasena raises the question as to how can *nishchaya naya,* that speaks of the self as the agent or doer (*karta*) and enjoyer or experiencer (*bhokta*) of attachment, etc. mental states, be considered worth acquiring (*upadeya*)? He answers the question himself by stating that only when the self knows that it is an agent of mental states like attachment, that these psychic states alone become the cause of bondage, it is only then that the self will contemplate/think of renouncing mental states like attachment. It is only then that the self will become pure (PS 189 JS). Since impure mental states like attachment are the self's own psychic dispositions (SS 371), the self alone has the capacity and the power to get rid of them.

Either Bharill apparently does not know or chooses to deliberately refrain from making the distinction between *mithyatva* and *mithya-darshan*. Unlike the former, *mithya-darshan* includes, besides *mithyatva*, the most intense/tenacious passions like anger (*anabtanubhandhi kashaya*), which are related to conduct and requires immense effort for its eradication. Since passions (*kashaya*) characterize evil (*ashubha*) (PS 158), it is only through subsidence of passions (*upasham* or *prasham*), i.e. in the condition or state of *shubha* (good) that one obtains enlightened view (*samyak-darshan*) and proceeds further in the direction of self-restraints (*samyam*) and austerities (*tapa*), etc. These are the characteristics of pure psychic-attention (*shuddha upayoga*) (PS 14), leading to pure self (*shuddhatma*), i.e. liberation.

Again, Veer Sagar Jain, a Kanjipanthi adherent/follower, echoing Bharill's above-mentioned mistaken view, states:

> *Mithyatva* (delusion) alone is the basic or fundamental cause of all the miseries and sufferings, not anything else . . . Anger, pride etc. passions (*kashaya bhava*) are not, in fact, the basic malady (*mool roga*, i.e. basic disease) as they are only the symptoms; the basic malady is delusion alone because it is only due to that *jiva* considers other objects as favourable or unfavourable, and which gives rise to anger, pride etc. [similar to Bharill's mistaken view that attachment, aversion are extrinsic (symptoms)] . . . Therefore, just as a skilled physician attends to and treats the real malady, not the (external) symptoms, which are automatically set right, so also with the destruction of delusion, anger, pride, etc. psychic states are automatically, on their own are destroyed. Moreover, the unfailing remedy or the means for the destruction of delusion is . . . experiencing of self (*atmanubhuti*) alone, none else . . . *Atmanubhuti* is the essence of all the scriptures (*sampurna dvadashanga*), because the path of liberation, begins only with that, undergoes development or growth thereby and also reaches its completion thereby, i.e. leads to liberation.[189] [In this easy path of liberation, there is no mention of adopting any means of self-restrains and austerities, etc.]

Samvara and *Nirjara* are Essential for Liberation

The path of liberation or the destruction of *karmas*, including deluding *karma*, consists of the prevention of the influx of new *karma* (*samvara*) and the shedding off previously accumulated *karma* (*nirjara*). The solution to the problem of *karma* is based on the strategies of *samvara* and *nirjara*. The two have been analyzed in terms of both the [external] physical processes (*dravya*) and the psychology of *bhava* (intention), which is considered primary and of much greater significance. That the accomplishment of any task or deed is contingent on the coordination of both internal and external causes [the intrinsic cause is regarded as primary and substantive cause, while the extrinsic cause is considered as secondary, supportive, or auxiliary cause] is said to be in the very nature of things (*dravyagatah svabhavah*)" (Samantabhadra, *Svayambhu Stotra*, verse 60).

Kundakunda's scheme of *vyavahara* self-restraints consist of *samiti*, *gupti*, etc. (*samyam*) and *nishchaya* self-disciplinary activities consist of *pratikraman*, etc., also called *tapas*. These have been described in *Niyamsara* and have been discussed above. They are real psychological practices concerning the prevention of the influx of new *karma* (*samvara*) and the shedding off of previously accumulated *karma* (*nirjara*), which is essential for attaining liberation (*moksha*). The *samyam*, *tapas*, and equanimity mentioned in *Pravachanasara* 14 are in fact, *samvara* and *nirjara*. They are considered to be important constituent parts of pure psychic-attention (*shuddha upayoga*), which alone is said to be the only refuge (*sharan*) for human beings (PS 78 AC).

The discussion of *samvara* focuses upon limiting and controlling one's behaviour in accordance with the goal of attaining a state of total [self-restraints or] equanimity (*samyam*) in order to reduce and ultimately stop the influx of new *karma*. This is to be done through observances such as the three restraints (*gupti*) and the five self-regulations (*samiti*). However, the discussion of *nirjara* focuses "upon conscious . . . activities (*tapas*) designed to scrub off *karma* that is already binding the soul".[190]

Bharill's contention that attaining godhood does not require anything beyond knowing one's own self and continuing to know that, goes against the age-old wisdom: "It is only by effort that any task or work is accomplished, not by mental wish or desire, just as the deers do not enter the mouth of the sleeping lion." The lion has to make efforts to catch the deer. "The only place," as Donald Kendall states, where success comes before work is in the dictionary.[191]

Empirically speaking, *moksha* is *krta-sadhya*, 'what is yet to be'; what is yet to be accomplished through man's knowledge, will, and effort. To bring the desired objective (*moksha* liberation is the highest objective to be attained) into existence or to realize it involves will or effort; value arises therefore by the conscious effort we make to realize it, and realizing it means overcoming the obstacles to its realization.[192]

In the introductory verse to *Tattvartha Sutra*, the worthy Lord is said to be "the destroyer of the mountains of *karmas*" (*bhettaram karma bhubhratam*), and the destruction of *karmas* is not an easy task; it requires great deal of effort.

In spite of what is stated above, Bharill still persists in his mistaken view that the one and only one (*eka matra*) means (*upaya*) of attaining liberation, of being happy, of getting rid of transmigratory existence (*samsara*), and of putting an end to the psychic states or modes of infatuation (*moha*), attachment and aversion, is the path comprising of the method, technique or the process (*prakriya*) of knowledge of the self (*atmajnana*) and meditation of the self (*atma-dhyana*) alone.[193] In support of this mistaken view, Bharill does not hesitate to distort the important concepts of pure psychic-attention (*shuddha upayoga*), meditation (*dhyana*), conduct (*charitra*), etc., given in Jain texts, including Kundakunda's works.

Although it may be said that he who knows *Arahant* (the worthy Lord) with reference to substance, qualities and modes, knows the self (*atma*). This can be considered as [one of the] the means for the destruction of deluding-view (PS 80). However, to argue that it is the sole method for the destruction of conduct-deluding attachment and aversion is totally incorrect. In fact, Amrtachandra states, that the verse emphasizes that after attaining enlightened view, one must eradicate attachment and aversion in order to realize the pure self lest the soul be robbed of the valuable enlightened world-view due to negligence (*pramad*). Therefore, one must be fully awake, in order to get rid of attachment and aversion (PS 81 AC), which is possible only through the conduct of self-restraints (*samyam*) and austerities (*tapas*) which are the characteristics of pure psychic-attention (*shuddha upayoga*) (PS 14), and the means of attaining the pure self (*shuddhatma*).

Kanji's Distortion of Pure Psychic-attention

Bharill, however, distorts the meanings of *shuddhatma* and conduct, etc. when he tries to prove that the method to get rid of attachment and aversion is "experiencing of pure self" (*shuddha atmanubhuti*) or/ and meditation of self (*atma dhyana*). Conduct, he adds, "completely devoid of attachment (*veetraga*) is of the nature of experiencing of the pure self". This is "restrictive or obstructive (*pratibandhak*) of attachment and aversion," thereby getting rid of them.[194] He seems to rely upon Kanji Svami's interpretation of *Pravachanasara* verse 14 that "pure psychic-attention (*shuddha upayoga*) is attention-oriented towards the nature of self, moving away from good and evil (*punya* and *papa*)", and that "stability or constancy (*sthirata*) in the nature of self is austerity (*tapa*)."[195] Kanji is deliberately distorting the meanings of pure psychic-attention and austerity (*tapa*).

The twelve kinds of external and internal austerities are referred by Jayasena (PS 14 JS) and are described in detail in Jain texts, including *Tattvartha Sutra*.[196] Kundakunda has also explained austerities (*tapa*) both from an external, other-referential (*vyavahara*) point of view and internal, self-referential (*nishchaya*) point of view in detail in *Niyamsara* (NS 56-70 and 77-158), which are also said to be *vyavahara* and *nishchaya* conduct.[197]

The concept of pure psychic-attention (*shuddha upayoga*) is described in clear terms in these words: "A *shramana* is called a man of pure psychic-attention, when he knows well the categories (*padarthas*), [including self and non-self, and their interaction], and the *sutras* (the scriptures) [for the definition of *Sutra*, see PS 34] which explain them, when he possesses self-restraint (*samyam*) and practices austerities (*tapas*), gives up attachment and considers pleasure and pain the same (*sama*)" (PS 14).

Bharill's description of meditation of the self (*atma dhyana*), which is said to be the method and path of getting rid of attachment and aversion and attaining liberation, viz. "knowing and continuing to know the self"[198] is also a distortion of what Kundakunda has written. Kundakunda states: "He, who observes rules of self-restraint, *niyam* and austerities, and meditates on his true self through virtuous concentration (*dharma-dhyana*) and pure concentration (*shukla dhyana*), (is said) to have supreme equanimity (*param samadhi*)" (NS 123). This cannot be divorced from *atma-dhyana*. Virtuous and pure concentrations or meditations (*dhyana*) are described in *Tattvartha Sutra* and other Jaina texts.[199]

Thus, Bharill seeks to present an easy way or soft option to people of knowing and inaction, which has no basis whatsoever in Jaina texts, including the works of Kundakunda by propagating certain myths. These include his presentation of *atma jnana* (knowledge of self), without the knowledge of the non-self and other derivative categories that are resultant categories due to the interaction of the self and non-self, without the firm conviction of the reality of the nature of the nine categories, including *punya* and *papa*. A second myth is his so-called *atma dhyana* (meditation of self) of the nature of continuing to know the self, and *atmanubhava*, *shuddhatmanubhuti*, *atmasakshatkara*, etc. A third myth is the concept of *shuddha upayoga* advocated by the Kanjipanthi. The three are mere myths which are *ingenious inventions* meant to confuse people, distract their attention from the true path of *sadhana* (adoption of proper means) of self-restraints (*samyam*), etc. for purification and liberation. Bharill's intention is to present an easy way or soft option of knowing and inaction, which has no basis whatsoever in Jaina texts, including the works of Kundakunda.

Bharill's *atma jnana* is not the *atma jnana* that *Pravachanasara* speaks of. *Atma jnana* (self-knowledge or knowledge of self), according to *Pravachanasara*, is only possible when it is simultaneously accompanied by knowledge of the Scriptures, faith or conviction in principles or categories of *jiva*, *ajiva*, etc. and self-restraint (*sanyat* or *samyam*) (as described in PS 240) (PS 240 AC). Similiarly, the pure psychic-attention (*shuddha upayoga*), which can lead to salvation, discussed by either Bharill or Kanji Swami is different from what has been described, defined and explained in *Pravachanasara* (verse 14).

Moreover, Bharill's so-called *atma dhyana* (self-meditation) is neither the virtuous meditation (*dharma dhyana*) nor the pure meditation (*shukla dhyana*) of Jain scriptures, including *Tattvartha Sutra*. It is also not similar to Kundakunda's supreme equanimity or mental concentration (*param samadhi*), which has been described in *Niyamsara* (verse 123).

To support his mistaken view regarding getting rid of attachment and aversion, Bharill also cites Jayasena's commentary of *Pravachanasara* verse 81. This verse describes conduct-deluding attachment and aversion as restrictive/obstructive of conduct which is completely devoid of attachment (*veetraga charitra*) having the characteristic of experiencing pure self (PS 81 JS). However, Bharill deliberately omits the most crucial qualifying conditional word "*if*" in Kundakunda's original text "(*jahadi jadi* in Pk. and *jahati yadi* in Sk.) and Jayasena's words "*yadi tyajati*". In other words, one acquires or obtains the pure self (*appanam lahadi suddham*, PS 81) and then and only then does he becomes liberated *if he gives up* attachment and aversion (PS 81 JS).

In this regard, Bharill also refers to Jayasena's observation that "*abheda ratnatrya parinata jiva*," i.e. the soul evolved as identity of enlightened view, knowledge and conduct obtains pure self and becomes liberated (PS 81 JS). He adds: [The soul] "does not attain liberation through'*bheda ratnatrya*,' i.e. the three – enlightened view, knowledge and conduct together."[200] This addition is conspicuous by its absence in Jayasena's commentary and is against statements of both Amrtachandra and Jayasena that they as well as identity of them, i.e. both *bheda* and *abheda*, i.e. three and one (identity/unity thereof) or *vyavahara* and *nishchaya* conduct constitute the path of liberation (PS 242 AC and PS 242 JS). The method of getting rid of attachment and aversion, is only through self-restraints and austerities as discussed in Kundakunda's works (NS 56-158, PS 14, 240's etc.) and other Jain texts.

As for Bharill's observation that except for knowing the self, nothing else is to be done and that by harping on the inactive self (*akarta*) one can attain godhood, it may be said that action is the insignia of life. As long as one lives one must act. "None can ever remain inactive even for a moment" (*Gita* 3.5); action is superior to inaction and even the maintenance of one's body would not be possible by inaction (*Gita* 3.8); and that one cannot attain perfection by mere renunciation of action (*Gita* 3.4).

If we remain ignorant of the real nature of the self, we will undoubtedly be inclined to perform activities (of mind, speech and body) in bondage to body consciousness (the self is body alone), and in accordance with our instinctive impulses of fear, sexual desire, mere satisfaction of sensual pleasures, passions like anger, pride, and greed,delusion and non-restraint. Therefore, ascertainment and knowledge of the reality of things or categories (*padarthas*), including the real nature of the self, is a necessary first step. However, that alone does not suffice for attaining godhood or liberation.

It is also essential to know the psycho-physical nexus and interaction, including the fact that the bondage of various *karmas* takes place because of infatuation (*moha*), attachment and aversion with reference to other objects (PS 243). By getting rid of these impurities, one invariably destroys various *karmas* (PS 244). To that end, one has to adopt means (*sadhan*) and undertake efforts for the purification (*vishuddhi*) of the self through self-restraints (*samyam*) and austerities (*tapas*) (PS 14), as well as five self-regulations (*samiti*), three self-restraints of mind, speech and body (*gupti*), control of senses and conquering passions like anger, pride, and greed (*kashaya*) (PS 240).

When the soul cannot remain without doing something, if it does not consciously undertake dispassionate action in the direction of self-restraint (*samyam*) and austerities (*tapas*), along with detachment and equanimity (*shuddha upayoga*) or sanity and purification (*vishuddhi*), i.e. *shubha upayoga* (PS 155, 156, 180 AC, PS 259, 260 and 259-260 AC), its activities will be based on instinctive impulses and sub-conscious motivations. As a result, the self slides into unrestrained behaviour of sense-gratification and anger, etc. passions (*vishaya kashaya*), i.e. the evil conscious action (*ashubha upayoga*) (PS 257, 258).

Active and Evolvent Aspect of the Self

The essential nature of the soul, according to Kundakunda, is consciousness (*chetana*). It is characterised by *upayoga* (PKS 16, 27, PS 127), which represents the active, functional and evolvent (*parinami*) aspect of the self. The self, he points out, possesses the nature of that through which it evolves during the time of the evolution (PS 8). In other words, it accepts the character of its state-of-evolution. When the soul evolves through the good or the evil, it becomes good or evil. And when it evolves through the pure, it becomes pure (PS 9).

If the soul is not considered to be evolvent (*parinami*, changeable) in nature, or if it is described as unchangeable, the soul, which is associated with *karma* since beginningless time, will not be able to get rid of the karmas and become pure self (*shuddhatma*) or pure consciousness, i.e. liberated soul. Only the liberated soul (*siddha* state of the soul) is said to be *krta krtya*, i.e. he has accomplished all that needs to be accomplished and no longer needs to do anything else.

While consciousness-as-such (*parinamika bhava*) is the fundamental reality of the being, pure consciousness of the soul or self (*shuddhatma* or *Paramatma*) is becoming, i.e. an effectual reality thereof. This being is not separate from the becoming but present in it. That being and becoming are not mutually incompatible but necessarily concomitant of one another is possible only when we accept the fundamental reality of the self as a dynamic or evolvent eternal reality (*parinami nitya*). It is something stable in the midst of its changes, a being in becoming, or persisting through its modes, i.e. one characterized by both continuity and change, as Jainism states. In this context, H.M. Bhattacharya observes:

> A conscious reality is never divorced from its own conscious modifications and qualities in which lies its very life… A *parinama* [state-of-evolution] or modification issuing from the *parinami* [the evolvent being] or the modifying, and yet not in essential relation with the *parinami*, is as false an abstraction as the *aparinami* [unchanging] or immutable real without any *parinama* or modification.[201]

The evolutionary characteristic or *atman* of the being (consciousness-as-such) forms the background or the substratum of changes of the states or modes of consciousness. It is devoid of any relational modes and relative aspects of *karmas* (*karma nirpeksha*), i.e. neither pure nor impure. This makes possible the evolution of the *jiva* or the empirical soul or the self, which is impure due to *karmic* bondage since beginningless time, becoming pure consciousness (*shuddhatma*). The Sankhya system of philosophy and Advaita Vedanta uphold the concept of the eternal self as an unevolving, unchanging or unmodifying (*aparinami*) and "pure". If one endorses this argument, the question arises that if the nature of the self (being) is held to be unchanging and "pure", how and when does it initially come into contact with the *karmas* and become impure and how the soul, associated with *karmas* since beginningless time, become pure?

There are people who mistakenly hold that Kundakunda's works, including *Pravachanasara* are meant only for ascetics. This is belied by what we have discussed above and by the frequent references to *sagara* (persons with homes) and *anagara* (those without homes) (see PS 250, 251, 254 and 275) and by the characteristics of *samanas* described in *Pravachanasara*. That *Pravachanasara* is written and meant as much for both householders and ascetics is clearly stated by Kundakunda in the concluding verse (PS 275), which observes: "He, who, practicing the conduct of householders or the homeless, [properly] understands this scripture [entitled *Pravachanasara*], acquires the essence (*sara*) of the Divine Discourse(s) (*pavayana* in Pk. *Pravachana* in Sk.)." He, thus, understands the real nature of the reality of things, including the self (never before experienced). The self persists throughout the endless stream of the three times (past, present and future) and is the foremost among all substances. It realizes the noble objective for living beings, viz. the supreme state of the self (*bhagwanta atma*), which is endowed with the nature of the self-intuiting divine knowledge and bliss (PS 275 AC).

NOTES

1 R.G. Bhandarkar, *Report on the Search for Sanskrit Manuscripts* (MSS), 1883-84, p. 91.

2 Peterson, *Report* for 1983-1984, p. 80.

3 This is the conclusion that A.N. Upadhye reaches after a long survey of the available material and detailed examination of the views of different scholars on the subject of Kundakunda's date. See A.N. Upadhye, *Sri Kundakundacharya's Pravachanasara* (Agas, Gujarat: Paramshruta Prabhavak Mandal, 1984), Introduction, pp. 10-23. *Pravachanasara* was first published before 1935.

4 Upadhye, n. 3, p. 49.

5 Ibid., p. 48.

6 See H.C. Bharill's article in *Darshan, Jnana Charitra* (Delhi), August 2008, p. 15.

7 Upadhye, n. 3, p. 49.

8 Ibid., pp. 49-50. Upadhye observes: "My tentative conjecture is that Amrtachandra was too spiritualistic to enter into sectarian polemics; and possibly he wanted to make his commentary along with it the sublime utterances of Kundakunda, acceptable to all the sects by eliminating the glaring and acute sectarian attacks." However, it seems that he has no objection to the phrase "*jatha-jada-ruva*" (*yatha jatarupa* in Sk.) or the natural form as of a child on birth (nudity) of a monk (PS 204-206 and 225). The phrase is also mentioned in the Shvetambara text *Uttradhyayan Sutra* 22 and 34. See Upadhye, n. 3, pp. 51, 52 and footnote 5 on p. 51.

9 The only comparable references to this topic, raised in these 11 additional verses of third group, which Upadhye could cite are from "*Ashta-prabhrata* or *Ashta-pahuda*," ("Eight Presents"). This is also generally attributed to Kundakunda, though W. Denecke doubts Kundakunda's authorship. Dialectically, he finds that six *pahudas* are earlier than

Samayasara, etc. The presence of *Apabhramsa* in these *pahuds* is cited as the reason. While other works of Kundakunda has thematic unity, this work (*Ashta-pahuda*) is of compilatory character. It is clear from the contents that each *pahuda* is meant to be an independent treatise. There are several other factors in regard to *Ashta-pahuda* to which A.N. Upadhye has also drawn our attention.

In some of them like *Charitra* (Conduct) *Pahuda* and *Bodha* (Enlightenment) *Pahuda,* the exposition of the subject matter is very systematic, while in others like *Sutta* (Scripture) and *Bhava* (Psychic State or Disposition) *Pahuda* appear to be merely compiled that is why perhaps the ascetic emblem prescribed for women is included in *Sutta-pahuda. Bhava-pahuda* contains legendary references and its contents are extensively varied (*Upadhye,* n. 3, pp. 34-35). The other four *pahudas* are *Darshan* (view, attitude or conviction), *Moksha* (Salvation), *Linga* (Insignia) and *Sheel* (Morality) *pahudas. Linga-pahuda* discusses the issue of *dravya-linga* (a monk having mere external appearance) and *bhava-linga* (having immaculate psychic dispositions), while *Sheel-pahuda* is particularly concerned with chastity aspect.

The first six of these *pahuds* (*shat-pahuda*), grouped together as an independent work, is commented upon in Sanskrit by Shrutasagar. His commentary is very dogmatic in nature containing severe criticism of other religions reflecting religious intolerance with the result that the editor of this work was compelled to remove such references. See Saubhagyamal Jain Ranvka, ed. *Shat-prabhratam* (*Shat-pahuda*) together with Sanskrit commentary by Shrutasagar, Hindi translation by Aryika Suparshvamati (Jaipur: Shanti-devi Badjatya, Gauhati, 1983), *Do Shabda* by editor, p. 19.

Upadhye opines that it is imaginable that "traditionally compiled texts might be attributed to Kundakunda because of his literary reputation". However, he is reluctant "to cancel the current tradition" that Kundakunda be accepted as the author of these *pahudas.* Upadhye, n. 3, p. 35.

Siddhasen Divakar, on the other hand, was frank enough to tell King Vikramaditya that he would not support the traditions which had been established by our ancestors and which had passed the test of time, unless they held true on examination. He observes: "I am not here to justify it for the sake of saving the traditional grace of the dead irrespective of the wrath I may have to face." Cited in Jagdish Prasad Jain, *Fundamentals of Jainism* (New Delhi: Radiant Publishers, 2005), pp. 297-298.

Since most of verses in *Ashta-pahuda* are significant and add to our understanding of various moral and other issues, we are not opposed to that work being considered to be a work of Kundakunda. However, one must be cautious about both unnecessary additions/interpolations as well as misinterpretations/distortions of Kundakunda's ideas in the commentaries of the works attributed to Kundakunda.

10 Ahimsa Mandir Prakashan, *Samayasara* (New Delhi: Ahimsa Mandir, 1959), Introduction by A.N.Upadhye, English Translation of text by Rajkrishna Jain, p. 1.

11 Ibid., p. 2.

12 Ibid., p.1.

13 Ibid., p.2.

14 See Jagdish Prasad Jain, *The Art and Science of Self-Realization: Purushartha Siddhhyupaya* of Amrtachandra Suri (New Delhi: Radiant Publishers, 2007), p. 26.

15 Upadhye, n. 3, p. 50.

16 Ibid., pp. 51-52.

17 Ibid., p. 48.

18 The concept of ***nirvana*** is discussed in detail by Kundakunda in his work *Niyamsara*. See Jagdish Prasad Jain, *Salvation through Self-discipline: Niyamsara* of Kundakunda (New Delhi: Radiant Publishers, 2005), verses 179-183.

19 See *Fundamentals of Jainism*, n. 9, pp. 201-202.

20 See Monier Williams, *Sanskrit English Dictionary* (Delhi: Motilal Banarasidass, 1999), pp. 1082 and 310.

21 *Jiva nikaya* consists of six kinds of *jivas* (the five classes of earth-bodied, etc. one-sensed (immobile) (*sthavara*) *jivas* and the mobile (*trasa*) *jivas* (living beings), having two to five senses, as also body, mind, etc., which includes animals and human beings. We also know that in Jain texts, both Digambara and Shvetambara there are no other *jiva(s)*, other than the six classes of *jiva*, except liberated souls and it is these *jiva-nikaya*, none else, that are embodied and transmigrate in the world or are liberated. The liberated souls are different from them, but they are not meant here. If it were so, Kundakunda himself would have mentioned it or the commentators would have referred to it.

22 See *Sanskrit-English Dictionary*, n. 20.

23 Upadhye, n. 3, p. 390.

24 W.J. Johnson, *Harmless Souls* (New Delhi: Motilal Banarsidass, 1995), pp. 97-100.

25 J.L. Jaini, ed. , *Tattvartha Sutra* by Umasvami (Delhi: Barrister Champat Rai Jain Trust, 1956), p. 39; *Sarvarthsiddhi* commentary on *Tattvartha Sutra* by Pujyapada, see S.A. Jain, *Reality* (Madras: Jvalamalini Trust,

1992), p. 55; and Tatia, Nathmal, *That Which Is*, translation of *Tattvartha Sutra* (San Francisco: Harper Collins, 1994), p. 39.

26 See A. Chakravartinayanar, *Panchastikayasara: The Building of the Cosmos* (New Delhi: Bharatiya Jnanapitha, 1975), pp. 12, 20 and xxviii.

27 See J.L. Jaini, *The Sacred Books of the Jainas*, Vol. VIII, *Samayasara* by Kundakunda Acharya (New Delhi: Today & Tomorrow Printers & Publishers, 1990); A. Chakravarti, *Samayasara of Kundakunda* (New Delhi: Bharatiya Jnanapitha, 1971); and J.S. Zaveri, *Samayasara* by Acharya Kundakunda (Ladnun: Jain Vishva Bharati University, 2009).

28 Indra Chandra Shastri, *Jaina Epistemology* (Varanasi: P.V. Research Institute, 1990), pp. 142-143.

29 See J.L. Jaini, tr., *The Sacred Books of the Jainas*; Vol V: *Gommatsara Jiva-Kanda* (The Soul) (GSJK), by Nemichandra Siddhanta Chakravarti (Lucknow: Central Jaina Publishing House, 1927), Introduction, pp. 38-39.

30 *Harmless Souls*, n. 24, pp. 97-98.

31 Ibid., pp. 98-99.

32 Ibid., pp. 99-100.

33 Ibid., p. 100.

34 Ibid, pp. 100-101.

35 See Jagdish P. Jain, "Jaina Psychology," in K. Ramakrishna Rao, et al, ed., *Handbook of Indian Psychology* (New Delhi: Cambridge University Press under the imprint of Foundation Books, 2008), pp. 57-74.

36 David Michie, "Test Cricket and Mindfulness," *Times of India*, 11 August 2011.

37 Hacker Andrew, *Political Theory: Philosophy, Ideology, Science* (Toronto: The Macmillan Company, 1969), pp. 6-7 and 20.

38 Kamal Chand Sogani, "Ethical Philosophy of Kundakunda," in Pandit Bechardas, *Doshi Smrti Granth*, edited by Madhusudan Dhaky and Sagar Mal Jain (Varanasi: Parsvanath Vidhyashram Shodha Sansthan, 1987), pp. 7-8.

39 See Kanaknandi, *Punya Papa Mimansa* (Baraut, Meerut: Dharma Darshan Vijnana Shodha Prakashan, 1992), pp. 5 and p. x.

40 Pujyapada's *Sarvarthasiddhi* (SAS) commentary on *Tattvartha Sutra* (TS) 6.3, translation mine.

41 See Akalankadeva, *Tattvartha-Vartika* (*Rajavartika* (also called *Tattvartha Rajvartika* (TRV), commentary on *Tattvartha Sutra* 6.3 (New Delhi: Bharatiya Jnanapitha, 1993), on TS 6.3, translation mine.

42 Cited in *Punya Papa Mimansa*, n. 39, p. 10.

43 *Tattvartha Rajvartika* , n. 41, pp. 507-508.

44 *Tattvartha Shloka Vartika* (TSV) commentary on TS 5.16, Commentator Manakchand Kaundeya, ed. and published by Pandit Vardhaman Parshvanath Shastri (Sholapur, 1969), Vol. 6, p. 439.
45 Ibid., p. 440.
46 Nagin Shah's commentary on Samantabhadra's *Apta-Mimansa* (AM): *Critique of an Authority*, translated by Nagin Shah (Ahmedabad: Jagruti Dilip Sheth, 1999), p. 83.
47 Samantbhadra, *Devavgam aparnama Apta-Mimansa*, translated by Jugal-Kishore Mukhtar (Delhi: Veer Sewa Mandir Trust, 1967), p. 98. Translation mine.
48 *Tattvartha Shloka Vartika* commentary on TS 6.3, See n. 44, p. 443.
49 Cited in *Economic Times*, 19 August 2009.
50 C.R. Jain, *Jaina Psychology* (Allahabad, 1929), p. 13.
51 Todarmal, *Mokshamark Prakashak* (MMP), edited by Parmananda Shastri (Delhi: Sasti Granthmala Karyalaya, Veer Sewa Mandir, 1950), pp. 301-302 (published 16 years before this work was first published by Kanjipanthi from Sonagarh in 1966).
52 Ibid., p. 301.
53 Ibid., pp. 332-333.
54 Ibid., p. 301.
55 Ibid.
56 Ibid., pp. 301-302.
57 Ibid., p. 302.
58 Ibid.
59 Ibid., p. 303 and 305.
60 Ibid., p. 302.
61 Ibid., pp. 302-303 and 305.
62 Ibid., pp. 313-314 and 305-306.
63 Ibid., pp. 305-306.
64 Hukum Chand Bharill, *Pravachanasara Anushilan*, Vol 1 (Jaipur: Pandit Todarmal Smarak Trust, 2005), p. 312.
65 Ibid., pp. 331 and 334.
66 Ibid., p. 343.
67 Ibid., p. 301.
68 *Moksha Marg Prakashak*, n. 51, pp. 301-302.
69 Bharill, n. 64, p. 328.
70 Bharill's talk on Zee Zagran TV, 11 July 2010.
71 Bharill, n. 64, p. 340.
72 Ibid., p. 299.
73 Kanji Svami, *Divyadvanisara*, p. 142, cited in ibid., p. 306.

74 Ibid., p. 317.
75 Kanji, n. 73, p. 159, cited in ibid., p. 321.
76 Ibid., p. 301.
77 Ibid.
78 Kanji, n. 73, p. 155, cited in ibid., p. 318.
79 Ibid., p. 301.
80 Kanji, n. 73, p. 158, cited in ibid., p. 321.
81 Ibid.
82 See also detailed discussion on compassion in this Introduction.
83 Bharill's talk on Zee Zagran TV, 15 July 2010.
84 Bharill, n. 64, p. 336.
85 Bharill, n. 83.
86 See K. Vijayaraghavan, "Twice blest and sublime virtues," *Economic Times*, 29 June 2009.
87 Ibid.
88 K. Vijayaraghavan, "Spare a thought for the less fortunate," *Economic Times*, 6 July 2009.
89 See Ibid., 29 June 2009.
90 See Samantabhadra, *Svayambhu Stotra*, translated by Jugal Kishore Mukhtar (Saharanpur, 1951), p. 81 footnote.
91 Samantabhadra, *Svayambhu Stotra*, Verse 119. See D.K. Goyal, *The Path to Enlightenment: Svyambhu Stotra of Samantabhadra* (New Delhi: Radiant Publishers, 2000), p. 182.
92 See also Jagdish Prasad Jain, ed., *The Enlightened Vision of the Self: Svarupa Sambodhana of Akalanka* (New Delhi: Radiant Publishers, 2005), Foreword, pp. 57-58.
93 See Br. Hem Chand Jain, "Omniscience," in International School for Jain Studies, *Study Notes*, V.2.0 (New Delhi, 2008), p. 312. For a critical appraisal of *krama-baddha paryaya*, see Jagdish Prasad Jain, ed., *Jain Dharma: Vyakti-svatantrya aur Svavalambana ka Dharma (Krambaddha-rupi Ekanta-niyativada)* (New Delhi: Jain Mission, 2005). See also Jagdish Prasad Jain, ed., *Jo jo Dekhi Veetraga ne, so so hosi Veera re athava hoi hai vahi jo Ram rachi rakha; Sarvajnata aur Niyativada* (New Delhi: Jain Mission, 2005).
94 Upadhye, n. 3, pp. 76-77 and footnote 1.
95 Hari Mohan Bhattacharya, "Essentials of Jaina Metaphysics and Epistemology," in Nalin K. Shastri, ed., *Namami* (Tijara/Alwar, Rajasthan: Shri 1008 Chandraprabha Digambara Atishaya Kshetra, Dehra, Tijara, 2005), pp. 316-317.
96 *Jaina Epistemology*, n. 28, p. 174.

97 Ibid., p. 150.
98 See *The Jaina Antiquary* (Arrah), June 1939, pp. 24-25. Cited in *The Enlightened Vision of the Self*, n. 92, p. 17.
99 *Prameya Kamal Martanda*, pp. 25-26 and *Pramana/Mimansa*, p. 49. Cited in Ibid., p. 15.
100 Nathmal Tatia, cited in ibid., p. 16
101 See ibid., p. 5.
102 See *Reality*, n. 25, pp. 156-157.
103 Malvania, Dalsukh, *Agam yug ka Jain Darshan* (AJD) (Jaipur: Prakrit Bharati Academy, 1990), p. 239.
104 Harilal Jain, *Atma Prasiddhi: Kanjiswami's Discourses on 47 Spiritual Qualities of Soul*, translated by Maganlal Jain (Agra: Shri Kundakunda Kahan Granthamala, 1994), p. 33.
105 See *Reality*, n. 25, p. 166.
106 See *The Enlightened Vision of the Self*, n. 92, Appendix 1, p. 93.
107 Kalipada Mitra, "The Jaina Theory of Existence and Reality," *Indian Culture* (Calcutta, 1939), pp. 322-323.
108 Chakravartinayanara, n. 26, p. 92.
109 Siddhasena, *Sanmatisutra*, ch. 1, Verse 12, cited in *The Enlightened Vision of the Self*, n. 92, Appendix 1, p. 91.
110 Nagardas B. Modi, et al, compiled, *Dravyadrashti Jineshwar: Kanjiswami's Discourses*, translated by Maganlal Jain (Bambai: Shardaben Shantilal Shah-pariwar, 1996), p. 48.
111 Ramesh Chandra Sogani, ed., *Dravya-drashti Prakash* (Bhavanagar: Veetrag Sat-sahitya Prasarak Trust, 2004), *Bole* 586, p. 200.
112 Ibid., p. 204.
113 *Dravya-drishti Jineshwar*, n. 110, p. 2 and quote of Kanji in the very beginning of the book
114 *Dravya-drishti Prakash*, n. 111, p. 202.
115 Cited in *The Enlightened Vision of the Self*, n. 92, p. 15.
116 See ibid., p. 16.
117 See ibid., p. 17.
118 Ibid.
119 Cited in ibid., p. 38.
120 *Dravya-drashti Prakash*, n. 111, p. 202.
121 Ibid., p. 204.
122 *Dravya-drashti Jineshwar*, n. 110, p. 48.
123 *The Merriams-Webster Pocket Dictionary of Synonyms* (New York: Pocket Books, 1972), pp. 270, 84, 51, 90, 352.
124 J.R. Searle, *Mind: A Brief Introduction* (New York: Oxford University

Press, 2004), p. 207.

125 Cited in W.E. Craighead and C.B. Numeroff, eds., *The Corsini Encyclopaedia of Psychology and Behavioural Science*, 3rd ed., vol. 1 (New York: John Wiley and Sons, 2001), p. 357. For a detailed discussion on mind-body interaction, see also *Fundamentals of Jainism*, n. 9, pp. 24-41.

126 See Chakravarti, n. 27, p. 54.

127 *Fundamentals of Jainism*, n. 9, pp. 40-41.

128 See Jain, n. 35.

129 See ibid.

130 *The Path of Enlightenment: Svambhu Stotra of Samantabhadra*, n. 91, Verse 60.

131 Amrtachandrasuri, *Laghu Tattva Sphota*, ed. by Padmanabha S. Jaini (Ahmedabad: L.D. Institute of Indology, 1978), Verse 391, p. 133.

132 *Harmless Souls*, n. 24, pp. 142, 146, 154 and 159.

133 Ibid., pp. 48-49.

134 Upadhye, n. 3, p. 404.

135 *Harmless Souls*, n. 24, pp. 46-47.

136 *Reality, n.* 26, p. 197.

137 *Harmless Souls*, n. 24, p. 197.

138 *Reality*, n. 25, p. 197.

139 Translation mine, based on Nathmal Tatia, *That Which Is:* tr. of *Tattvartha Sutra*, n. 25, pp. 169 and 156; *Reality*, n. 25 and original *Sarvartha siddhi*.

140 See Akalankadeva, TRV commentary on TS 6.3, n. 41, translation mine.

141 *Siddhasena, Dvatrinshika*, 3.16, cited in *Fundamentals of Jainism*, n. 9, p. 160.

142 Cited in ibid., p. 160.

143 *Nyayavijaya*, Muni, cited in ibid., pp. 160-161.

144 *Harmless Souls*, n. 24, p. 157.

145 Ibid., p. 52.

146 Ibid., p. 157 and 48-49.

147 Y.K. Mishra, *Asceticism in Ancient India* (Vaishali: Research Institute of Praktit, Jainology & Ahimsa, 1987), pp. 18, 30, 37, and 65.

148 Ibid., p. 34.

149 Upadhye, n. 3, preface.

150 Mishra, n. 147, pp. 18 and 15.

151 Ibid., p. 65.

152 Ibid., p. 35.

153 Ibid., p. 36.

154 *Acharang Sutra*, 1.9.1.

155 *Harmless Souls*, n. 24, p. 223.
156 For details, see *Salvation through Self-discipline*: *Niyamsara* of Kundakunda, n. 18.
157 See also Mishra, n. 147, p.6.
158 Ibid., p. 7.
159 For details, see *Salvation through Self-discipline*, n. 18.
160 Acharya Mahaprajna, "Spiritual Solution to economic problems," *Economic Times* (New Delhi), 20 April 2009.
161 *Harmless Souls*, n. 24, p. 27.
162 Ibid., introduction, p. 1.
163 For details, see *Salvation through Self-discipline*, n. 18.
164 *Harmless Souls*, n. 24, p. 165.
165 Ibid., p. 184.
166 Paul Dundas, "The Laicisation of the Bondless Doctrine: A New Study of the a Development of Early Jainism, A Review of W.J. Johnson *Harmless Souls*," *Journal of Indian Philosophy*, Vol. 25(5), October 1997, p. 502.
167 *Harmless Souls*, n. 24, p. 223.
168 Ibid.
169 Ibid., p. 223.
170 Dundas, n. 166, pp. 502-503.
171 Bharill, n. 64, pp. 41 and 39.
172 K. Ramakrishna Rao, *Consciousness Studies: Cross Cultural Perspectives* (North Carolina: McFarland & Co., 2005), p. 205 and 201:
173 Harold G. Coward, "Psychology and Karma," *Philosophy East and West*, 33:1(January 1983), p. 54.
174 Johannes Bronkhorst, "The Boddha and the Jainas Reconsidered," in N. K. Wagle and Olle Quarnstrom, eds., *Approaches to Jaina Studies: Philosophy, Logic, Ritual and Symbols* (Ontario: The Centre for South Asian Studies, University of Toronto, 1999), pp. 87-88.
175 Ibid., p. 89.
176 Ibid.
177 Ibid.
178 See Hem Chand Jain, n. 93.
179 See Jagdish Prasad Jain, n. 93.
180 John E. Cort, "Fistfights in the Monastery: Calendars, Conflict and Karma among the Jains," in *Approaches to Jaina Studies*, n. 174, p. 37.
181 Bharill, n. 64, pp. 373 and 364.
182 H.C. Bharill's TV Talk on Zee Zagran, 14 June 2010.
183 Ibid.

184 Bharill, n. 64, p. 336.
185 Ibid., p. 375.
186 Ibid.
187 Ibid., p. 380.
188 Bharill's TV Talk on Zee Zagran, 15 July 2010.
189 See Veer Sagar Jain, "*America mein hui adhyatma ki sukshma charcha*," in *Shruta Samvardhini* (Lucknow), December 2009, pp. 9-10.
190 Cort, n. 180, pp. 48-49.
191 *Span* (New Delhi), July-August 2010, p. 16.
192 N.A. Nikam, "Some Basic Concepts of Indian Culture," in Krishna Roy and Chhanda Gupta, *Essays in Social and Political Philosophy* (New Delhi: Indian Council for Philosophical Research, 1983), pp. 199 and 196.
193 H.C. Bharill, *Samayasara ka Sara*, p. 104, cited in Bharill, n. 64, p. 378.
194 Ibid., p. 381.
195 Cited in ibid., pp. 81-82.
196 For a detailed discussion in the matter, see *Fundamentals of Jainism*, n. 9.
197 For a detailed discussion on this subject, see *Salvation through Self-discipline*, n. 18.
198 Bharill's TV Talk, 14 June 2010.
199 For detailed discussion in the matter, see *Fundamentals of Jainism*, n. 9.
200 Bharill, n. 64, p. 381.
201 See *The Enlightened Vision of the Self*, n. 92, p. 39.

Translator's Preface

I owe great thanks to Professor [F.W.] Thomas for having helped me with the English idiom of the translation. When some years ago I acccepted Prof. Thomas's invitation to translate the *Pravachanasara* and *Tattvadipika* [commentary of Amrtachandra thereon] for the Jain Literature Society, I was not sufficiently aware of the difficulties which the commentary, with its intricate syntax, would give me.

I am deeply grateful to Prof Thomas for undertaking to write the introduction. . . at a time when an indisposition due to a constitutional nervous disease hindered me from doing it myself.

Despite such personal drawbacks during these last years I have realized the joy of a deeper and better understanding of the Jain religion.

Amsterdam 1934 **B. Faddegon**

Jaina texts (PS 258), one should abstain from them.

According to 28 *mula-gunas* (PS 208-209) of *samana*, which have both external and internal aspects, apparently only a homeless ascetic can be a *samana*. However, this is not necessarily so. Kundakunda recognized that the immaculate performance of the 28 primary rules/values/qualities, especially regarding pure psychic-attention, which is expected of an ideal or complete *shraman* state (*shramanya*) (PS 214), is not possible for all *samanas*, all the time. That is why he stressed the possibility that external negligence in bodily activities (*kaya cheshta*) (PS 211) and internal negligence in psychic-attention (*Pravachanasara* 211-212 AC) can occur. He therefore emphasized the need to reestablish them on the correct path, which finds mention in *Pravachanasara* 208-214. For instance, apart from the worthy Lord *Arhantas*, the supreme *shramanas*, who have themselves abandoned all *upadhi* (external possessions as well as internal *parigraha* of attachment, aversion and passions) (*Pravachanasara* 219 AC), it is impossible for a *samana* to remain in and forever maintain the state of pure psychic attention.

In the mundane existence of the embodied self, the psychic disposition is invariably unstable because one has to harmonize and strike a balance between not neglecting self-restraint and not neglecting the body. The former is of fundamental importance as a means towards realizing the principle of the pure self (*shuddha atma tattva*) whereas the latter is indispensable as a means to self-restraint (PS 230 AC). Kundakunda has therefore emphasized the need to strike a balance and not commit any excess in either food or fasting and lodging or wanderings, i.e. the need for proper food and wandering (*yukta ahara vihara*) (PS 213, 215, 226-231).

Amrtachandra stresses that one should avoid excess of everything (*ati sarvatra varjayeta*), keeping in view one's age, and capacity for suffering, etc. (PS 230 AC). One should also, he adds, practice austerities and renunciation according to one's capacity (*shakti tapas tyaga*). The body, he adds, is the means to *dharma* (righteousness) (*sharira madyam khalu dharma sadhanam*), which, in turn, is the means to peace and happiness and gradually leads to liberation (PS 254 AC). However, at the same time, he categorically states that even if one has the slightest infatuation or mental clinging (*murchha*) in regard to the body, etc., one does not attain liberation, even if one knows all

Introductory Remarks by F.W. Thomas

The *Pravachana-sara*, 'Essence of the Scripture' (or 'of the Doctrine,' since *pravachana* does not necessarily imply writing), is an early and authoritative Jaina text in Prakrit *Gatha* stanzas, embodying the teaching of the Digambara sect.. . .Of the two Sanskrit commentaries one, the *Tattva-dipika,* 'Lamp of Truth,' or *Tattva-pradipika,* 'Illuminator of Truth,' by Amrtachandra Suri, is a *tika* expounding the whole text; the other, the *Tatparya-vrtti,* 'Exposition of Purport,' by Jayasena Acharya, is of a more general, less literal, character. . . . The present English translation represents the Prakrit stanzas of Kundakunda together with the commentary of Amrtachandra but the *Tatparya-vrtti* by Jayasena and the Hindi exegesis in the Braj dialect by Hemaraja have been consulted.

Kundakunda was a *kavi,* writing in Prakrit verse for a wider public ...there is in it, especially in the *Prabhrtas,* a warmth more characteristic of a preacher than of a plain dogmatist, and poetry is by no means absent. The very fact that Kundakunda's work is in Prakrit is highly significant, seeing that every one of his famous successors in the Digambara school preferred Sanskrit exclusively ...

In the works attributed to Kundakunda there are no allusions to particular scriptures, and it would be a difficult task, and premature, to estimate his relation to the pre-existing texts. The expression *sara,* 'essence,' occurring in the titles of four of his works, the *Pravachana-sara* (also a sub-title of the *Panchasti-kaya-gatha*), *Niyama-sara, Rayana-sara, Samaya-sara,* does not imply a mere summary of the content of books; and in fact all his titles have reference to topics, not to treatises. Upon the perfection and all-sufficiency of the Scriptures he constantly dwells, as in *Moksha-prabhrta,* v. 90: ...

'Righteousness is faith in the *Nirgrantha* doctrine, a religion void of *himsa*, free from the eighteen faults, divine.'

But he is a preacher who lays stress upon the topic in hand : and so in the most affecting of his compositions, the *Bhava-prabhrta*, treating of *bhava*, 'realization' or 'sincerity,' we read (v. 164)...

'Why babble at length? Gain, religion, pleasure and final release, and other pursuits, all depend upon sincerity.'

And in the *Sila* [*Sheel*]*-prabhrta*, on morality (v. 19), he declares that...

'Mercy to living creatures, self-restraint, truth, honesty, chastity and contentment, right faith and knowledge, and austerity are [but] the entourage of morality.'

His manner of working, therefore, is that of a teacher at home in his subject and its several parts (and how should a Jaina dogmatist not be so?); and not of mere popularizer of pre-existing compositions. He would have disclaimed, as emphatically as does Ishvarakrshna, any departure from the strictest orthodoxy of his school; but his celebrity is that of a poet (*kavi*), sage (*muni*), ecclesiastic (*patta-dharin*), not of a commentator...

The *Pravachana-sara*, as arranged in the commentary, is in three chapters, containing respectively 92, 108 and 75 *Gatha* stanzas. In the commentary the chapters (*shruta-skandha*) are entitled —

I. *Jnana-tattva-prajnapana*, 'Exposition of the truth as to Knowledge';
II. *Jneya-tattva-prajnapana*, 'Exposition of the truth as to the Knowable';
III. *Charananusuchika-chulika*, 'Appendix, hints on Conduct.' The second commentary, by Jayasena, supplies and discusses a number of extra stanzas [*gatha*] and stanzas 24-34 of Chapter II seem out of place and have the air of an interpolation.

The first chapter treats of the soul and its evolution, knowledge and its relation to objects, the perfect knowledge of the saint, bondage and release, pleasure and pain, merit and demerit. The second chapter discusses objects, existence, substance, quality and state; the *syad-vada* and *naya* doctrine (*'quodammodo'* doctrine of 'aspects'); matter, origination and destruction; time, space, atoms, vital powers; souls and their evolution, the self, *karma* and bodies, soul-activity and contemplation. The third chapter deals with conduct, including the topics of renunciation, self-restraint, discipline, the recluse, food, residence, association, psychical attention (*upayoga*), faith and study of scripture...

There is nothing in Kundakunda's doctrine which did not pre-exist in the actual Jaina canon. As we know from the inscriptions published by Buehler (*Epigraphia Indica,* I, pp. 371 sqq., II, pp. 195 sqq.), the organization of the Jaina community was in the first century A. D. in full maturity, and the several orthodoxies will have been elaborately systematized. Kundakunda was posterior to this; and in regard to his works the only question concerns the emphasis which he lays upon particular doctrines. This also can be considered only in relation to the present text, the *Pravachana-sara,* since, as we have seen, the several writings are concerned with most departments of Jaina doctrine and religious life.

Of the more general logico-epistemological doctrines the *syad-vada,* or *anekanta* view, is everywhere affirmed, and in II.22-23, the *nayas* and the accompanying *sapta-bhang* are clearly expounded. Allied to this doctrine, which regards the truth of all true statements as relative to a context or an 'aspect,' is the conception of substance elaborated in the text (II.1, sqq.). A substance is an universal, identical with the existence of the thing, and embracing the thing and its qualities (*guna*), and its states or modifications (*paryaya*) and their qualities. The nature of a substance is its evolution as a single principle in states composed of the three 'moments' of origination (*utpada, sambhava*), persistence (*dhrauvya, sthiti*), and annihilation (*vyaya, nasha*). While these 'moments' are logically and epistemologically antithetic, their real status is an inseparable unity, the substance (II. 3-8). In this connection (II.1) appears the distinction between 'lengthwise' (*ayata, urdhva*) and 'crosswise' (*vistara, tiryak*) generality (*samanya*), the former being the identity of successive states of a thing, the 'concrete universal,' while the latter is community of property in separate things.

The substance to which this conception is most prominently applied is the self (*atman*), which is identified with knowledge (I.27 sqq). The self is a generality, embracing all its particular states, whereof it is also the creator (*kartr,* II. 92-94). In its perfect condition (*kevala*) it is omniscience and truth and identical with the Jaina faith (*samaya*) itself (I.8, 92). Essentially it never loses this condition, and no other action is performed by it (II. 92-93). All other states or acts attributed to it are due to matter (*karma* or *pudgala*) wherewith it is associated. From this association results the condition of *jiva,* or soul, which is self combined with vital powers (*prana*, II. 53-55); the various stages manifested in saints, divinities, human beings, animals, plants, denizens of hell, etc.; and the four not perfect kinds of knowledge known as *mati* (=*smrti*= sense knowledge), *shruti* (inference, etc.), *avadhi* and *manah-paryaya* (III. 34-35). Properly the self knows by direct intuition (*pratyaksha*) all substances, states, etc., in all times and places, without operation of senses. Sense-knowledge is indirect (*paroksha*), the senses being a material accretion. The stages (*avagraha*, *iha*, etc.) in a sense-perception which are known to the canonical works are clearly contemplated in the text (I.21, 59).

In Kundakunda's very frequent reference to *upayoga* there must be some special point. The word has very rarely been cited by European writers on Jainism; we can mention only Cowell, in Colebrooke's *Essays*, vol. I, p. 446, who renders it by 'the true employment of the soul's activities'; Jacobi (translation of Umasvati's *Tattvarthadhigama-sutra*, in the *Zeitschrift der Deutschen Morgenlandischen Gesellschaft*, vol. 60, p. 302), who gives 'geistige Funktion (Vorstellen),' 'mind-functioning (presentation)'; Dr. L. D. Barnett (*The Antagada-dasao and Anuttarovavaiyadasao translated from the Prakrit*, pp. 141-142), who prefers 'energy'; and Professor Von Glasenapp (*Der Jainismus*, p. 177), who renders by *Vorstellen*, 'presentation'. The Sanskrit dictionaries do not refer to the technical use of the word; but it is clearly expounded in Umasvati's own commentary upon his *Tattvarthadhigama-sutra* and in editions of Jaina texts published in India, e.g. in the *Dravya-samgraha* of Nemichandra (ed. S. C. Ghoshal, p. 9), as 'a sort of inclination which arises from consciousness,' in the *Gommata-sara, Jiva-kanda* (ed. J. L. Jaini, p. 326), as 'conscious attentiveness or attention'; while in the great Prakrit dictionary, *Abhidhana-rajendra*, the equivalent *uvaoga* is the subject of a long article. *Upayoga* is the fundamental property of a living soul, the power of attending; and, as it exists even in the lowest forms of life, it corresponds, in its range, to the modern expression 'response'. In creatures of superior intelligence it embraces, as *darshan* and *jnana* respectively, a general or formless awareness of things (*anakara-jnana*, Dr. Barnett's 'indefinite apprehension') and a determinate awareness (Dr. Barnett's 'definite apprehension'). When free from error, *darshan*, as a general 'outlook,' is identical with the Jaina faith. This conception of *upayoga* appears in Kundakunda's other works (e.g. *Panchastikaya-gatha*, v. 40, *Samaya-sara*, v. 107); its prominence in his writings and its rarity in Shvetambara books may indicate a superior importance in the Digambara teaching.

Attention may be drawn also to the discussion of time (II.48 sqq.), as an infinite of one dimension, passing through each infinitesimal (*pradesha*) of space. There are also some other special features in the Jaina doctrine of infinitesimal particles. The distinction of infinite (*ananta*) and incalculable (*asamkhyeya*) numbers is likewise of interest: see J. L. Jaini in *Gommata-sara, Jiva-kanda*, pp. 20 sqq. The *nigodas*, or *nikotas*, minute living creatures, are mentioned in *Sutra-prabhrta*, v. 18)

The commentator, Amrtachandra, composed commentaries also on the *Samaya-sara* (*Tatparya-vrtti*) [*Atma-khyati*] and the *Panchastikaya-gatha*. He is known, moreover, as author of independent works, *Purushartha-siddhy-upaya, Samaya-sara-kalasha-nataka*, and *Tattvartha-sara*. . . . His commentary on the *Pravachana-sara* is elaborate and of a severe, almost painful, precision, which leaves nothing to be supplied and by no means shrinks from reiteration. He is an excellent master of Jaina Sanskrit: he employs a fullness of phrase which not unfrequently gives an impression of an enjoyment of sonorous circumlocution and complicated sentences rather than of a simple striving for exactitude, and which renders the work of interpretation and translation extremely difficult; but no special charity is required for recognizing in the remorselessness of style the outcome of an inflexible religious faith. Like other Jaina writings, the commentary is entirely void of personal display; but there are some few passages where it adopts a strain of enthusiasm and even indulges in verse.

In the long travail of composing and verifying the translation, which may, it is hoped, convey a fairly correct impression of Digambara thought and style, Professor Faddegon and his editor have been much indebted to Brahmachari Shitalaprasada of Surat, who has perused the whole, for valuable suggestions and corrections and to Mr. Herbert Warren for much loyal and patient cooperation.

2

Summary of Significant Concepts

A N Upadhye

[Note: The figures in brackets indicate Verse no.]

1. The Doctrine of Three Upayogas

The soul is constituted of the manifestation of consciousness [*upayoga*] which is in the form of knowledge or cognition and which flows in one of the three channels: inauspicious, auspicious or pure (9, 155).

A being of inauspicious manifestation of consciousness (*ashubha upayoga*) is steeped in sensual pleasures and passions, is given to false scriptures, evil intentions and wicked works, is cruel, and goes astray (158). The inauspicious one is a cause of sinful *karmic* influx (156, 245). Under the influence of this *upayoga* the soul wanders for long as a low graded human being, a sub-human being and a hellish one subjected to thousands of miseries (12).

The auspicious manifestation of consciousness (*shubha upayoga*) is characterised by devotion of God, ascetic or preceptor and by the practice of philanthropy, virtues, fasts, etc. (69) and by compassion towards all the living beings (157). It incurs only the meritorious influx of *karmas* for the soul (157, 245). It leads the soul to heavenly pleasure; and even if one is born as a sub-human, human or divine being there are plenty of pleasures of senses (11, 70). A monk with *Shubhopayoga* shows a respectful behaviour towards elderly monks, offers instructions on faith and knowledge, maintains students, and helps co-monks without causing harm to any living beings (247-248).

Immunity from the contagion of the above two *upayogas* is the characteristic of pure manifestation of consciousness (*shuddha upayoga*) which is not open to *karmic* influx (156, 245) and leads to the annihilation of all the miseries (181). The soul with this *upayoga* develops religious experience (*dharma*), which is a spiritual state of transcendental, self-born, super-sensuous, unparalled, indestructible. . . happiness (13-14). In *Shuddhopayoga* the physical pains are no more, and one knowing the nature of reality is above attachment and aversion. . . he is equanimous (7, 78).

2. The Principle of Knowledge

Really speaking, the soul (*atman*) is the knower and essentially an embodiment of knowledge (127, 28 etc.). Knowledge is the self, and knowledge cannot subsist anywhere else than in the self; self and knowledge are co-extensive, neither less nor more (23); if the self is smaller, then knowledge being insentient cannot function; if larger, it cannot know in the absence of knowledge (24-5). In a sense, however, the self can be taken as wider than knowkedge (27), because it has other characteristics like *sukha* (happiness), *virya* (vigour), etc. In view of its being an embodiment of knowledge, the soul is capable of knowing itself, objects other than itself and the combinatory products of the two (36). But this essential knowing ability of the soul is crippled because of its long association with *karmic* matter (in the form of knowledge-obscuring *karman*, etc.); and it has come to possess the sense-organs (55, 145). The senses are material in nature (*paudgalika*) and hence foreign to the real nature of the soul. Whatever is apprehended through the senses is indirect (*paroksha*), because the soul is not directly apprehending the object of knowledge; that would be direct apprehension (*pacchakkham vinnanam*) when the soul apprehends all by itself without the aid of senses (56-58). The sense-perception is graded and mediate (*ajugavam* and *parokkham*), because it has four stages: outliner grasp (*avagraha*), discrimination (*iha*), judgement (*avaya*) and retention (*dharana*) (40).

After manifesting pure consciousness when the soul becomes free from knowledge-obscuring, conation-obscuring, obstructive and deluding *karmas*, it comes to be self-constituted and possessed of omniscience (15-16). This omniscience is supersensuous; therein the apprehension of the objectivity takes place directly by the soul without the aid of sense-organs; there are no sensational stages, but the apprehension is instantaneous and simultaneous; it is endowed with the potencies of all the senses together as it were; and there is nothing that is not visualised in omniscience. (20-22). The omniscient knows and sees the whole world, the variegated and unequal objectivity of the present or otherwise, neither entering into nor entered into by the objects of knowledge, just as the eye sees the objects of sight (27, 47).

Omniscience operates on the objects, just as a sapphire thrown in milk pervades the whole of it with its lustre; omniscience is ubiquitous in its functions, and therefore the omniscient is called omnipresent; and all the objects are within His knowledge (28-31, 35). The external objectivity does not affect Him, though He sees and knows everything completely (32). It is the supernatural characteristic of omniscience that therein are visualised all present and absent modifications of all those types of substances as if in the present (37-39). Omniscience being an extra-sensory form of knowledge (*atindriya-jnana*) knows any substance with or without space-points, with or without form and those modifications which have not come into existence and those that had come (41). It is also called *kshayika-jnana*, because this knowledge is the result of the destruction of *karmas* and does not involve fresh *karmas* (42, 52). Omniscience is the only knowledge worth the name, because its apprehension is simultaneous and sudden; a single substance has infinite modes, and infinite are the classes of substances: so to know one is to know all and to know all is to know one; it is impossible to exhaust them if they were to be known one after another; thus omniscience is the only knowledge that can really grasp the objectivity (48-51).

The development of omniscience is necessarily accompanied by . . . happiness (59, 19); there is no trace of misery, since the destructive *karmas* are all exhausted (60). As the sun has light and warmth, so the *Siddha*, the liberated soul, has . . .knowledge and happiness (68). This happiness is independent of everything, and hence eternal; it is not physical but spiritual (65). It should be completely distinguished from the pleasures of senses after which all the worldly beings are so much enamoured; the pleasures of senses are miseries in disguise, because they are dependent on something else, amenable to destruction, terminable, a cause of bondage and dangerous [unequal] (63-64, 76). . . .

3. The Principle of Knowable (Jneya): Substance, Quality and Modification

Substances (*dravya*), qualities (*guna*) and modification (*paryaya*) are called the object of knowledge (87). . . .The substance forms the substratum of qualities and modifications, and it is constantly endowed with origination, destruction and permanence without leaving its existential character (87, 95, 99, 105). It is the very nature of the substance to be amenable to these three states (99); origination and destruction are simultaneous and interdependent, and are not possible in the absence of the substance (100). This trio refers to modifications and qualities, and the substance, as it forms the essential basis of the three, comes to be predicated of them at that moment (101). The object of knowledge has always one or the other modification (18). One modification originates and the other passes away, while the substance is permanent (103). There is nothing as absolute production or destruction in this world: what is the production of one is the destruction of the other (119). That condition or state (*parinama*), which in fact forms the nature of the substance is quality, which is a distinguishing mark too (129-130). The transformation of one (form of the) object into the other is the modification with its varieties of figuration (152). The substance, quality and modification are existential (105); as to the relation between the three they are non-separate (*aprthaktva*) and non-identical (*anyatva*): they cannot be separate because they are the co-occupants of the same spatial extense, and they are non-identical because one is not the other (106-110). To illustrate: Soul is a substance; manifestation of consciousness is its quality; and its modifications are hellish, sub-human, human and ... [gods, i.e. denizens of heaven] embodiments which are caused by *Nama karman*, or even the state of a *Siddha*, behind all these modifications the soul is essentially the same and permanent (112,113,117-119). The substance is one in view of its substantial it, but it comes to be manifold because of the modifications pervading it for the time being (115). . . .

4. Nature of Spirit and Matter, or Jiva *and* Pudgala

The *jiva* is essentially constituted of sentiency (*chetana*) and manifestation of consciousness (*upayoga*) (127); but from beginningless time it is already tainted with *karman* (121). The development [or expression] of its sentiency is threefold: with regard to knowledge which consists in the comprehension of the objectivity, with regard to *karma* which consists in whatever is done (*samaraddham*) by the soul, and with regard to the fruit of *karma* which is either happiness or misery; and these three are predicated of the soul (123, 124, etc.). Likewise the manifestation of consciousness (*upayoga*) is towards *jnana* and *darshana* (155) and flows in three channels; inauspicious, auspicious and pure (9), which respectively indicate impiety, piety and purity (11, etc.). Auspicious and inauspicious channels are indicative of transmigratory condition; when the soul is free, it has the pure manifestation (46). The soul in its pure [natural] condition is without sense-qualities, is all the quality of sentiency, is beyond inferential mark and has no definable shape (172); but, here, being in the association of karmic matter, it has received a concrete embodiment (55. 117). The various grades of existence to which the soul is subjected in this round-of-rebirths are due to *karmas* (117-118). When passionate conditions are developed, the soul though non-concrete is bound by *karmas* which are concrete, just as the soul though devoid of colour, etc. is able to see colour, etc. (173,174). The soul really speaking is not the direct agent of *karmas* but only of its states of consciousness which being already tinged with passions etc. receive the *karmas* (183,184,190).

Matter (*pudgala*) is a permanent substance belonging to non-sentient class of substances (127). . . .Matter is concrete possessed of sensory qualities to its last unit (132). The world is full of material bodies (168), and the aggregatory process is going on because of their inherent qualities of cohesion and aridness (163, etc.). The matter molecules capable of becoming *karmas*, coming into contact with passional development of the soul, are transformed into *karmas* (169); further they inflow into the soul and remain there binding it (178). Thus the passionate states give rise to bondage (179-180). . .

Being already associated with *karman* which results in further *karmas*, the soul, in its embodied condition, comes to have many material adjuncts: the body, mind, speech are all material (161-162). Matter-bodies which are transformed into *karmas* go to form the bodies that serve as the transmigratory equipments of the spirit; there are five such bodies: the physical, transformatory, electric, translocational and *karmic* (170-171). The four life-essentials, namely, sense-organs, channels of activity [mind, speech and body], duration of life and respiration which characterise an embodied soul are all material being caused by the *karmas* (147-148, etc.). Thus the sense-organs too are made of matter, and the soul in *samsara* comes to have them, whether it is born in movable (*trasa*) or immovable (*sthavara*) bodies (57, 182).

5. Syadvada, or the Theory of Conditional Predication

. . . A substance is endowed with qualities (or attributes) and modifications; though the substance is the same, it expresses differently because of its passing through different modifications; so when something is to be stated about a substance, viewed through a flux of modifications, there would be seven modes of predication: according to some modification or the other it is stated that a substance is, is not, is indescribable, 'is and is not', 'is and is indescribable', 'is not and is indescribable', and is, is not and is indescribable (114-115)...

6. The Mechanism of Bondage and Liberation

The soul being tainted with *karman* develops states of consciousness which being auspicious or inauspicious receive *karmic* influx; and it is this *karman* that binds the soil and revolves it in *samsara.* Essential characteristics of the soul are all crippled by the *karmic* encrustation of eight kinds (187/1). The soul in this round-of-rebirths is subject to attachment, aversion and other psychic states tinged with passions which occasion further *karmas* (243). The way out of this *samsara* consists in Right [Enlightened] vision, Right [Enlightened] knowledge and Right [Enlightened] conduct (6). The first consists in believing in the nature of things or realities as they are. . . the second consists in comprehending the whole range of objectivity as preached by *Arahantas* or from the *Agamas* (81-2; 233 etc.); and the last consists in adopting . . .equanimity while practising the essential duties and penances . . . [of the householder and the ascetic] that go to stop the influx and exhaust the deposit of *karmas* [and thus the self gradually attains the stage of *siddha*, the liberated soul, by his own efforts].

When the soul is free from the four destructive or malignant types of *karmas*, namely *Jnanavaraniya, Darshanavaraniya, Mohaniya* and *Antaraya,* it . . . [comprehends all things knowable by itself (15); Having thus realised its real nature and become omniscient],. . . the soul is called self-sufficient (*Svayambhu*) (16). There the spirit develops excellent infinite strength, excessive lustre and super-sensuousness (19).

. . . Then he becomes *Siddha* [liberated soul] after the remaining four *aghati-karmas* are destroyed. Just as the sun is all lustre and warmth. He is all knowledge and happiness and a Divinity (68).

Book I
The Principle of Knowledge

Book I

The Principle of Knowledge

***Only the Original Verses are given in bold. The rest is Amrtchandra's commentary.* EDITOR**

TATTVA-DIPIKA "THE LAMP OF TRUTH"
(Commentary by AMRTACHANDRA SURI)

Benedictory Poetic Composition (Manglacharan) by AC

Homage to the Self, which in its innate nature is one principle of consciousness-as-such, that permeates all its attributes and modes, and which attains by its own efforts, the supreme state of soul consisting of knowledge and bliss. (PS *Kalash* 1)

This splendour, this truth, which consists of *anekant* (the doctrine of the multifaceted nature of reality), and illuminates the world, subdues the mass of darkness of great infatuation (*moha*) and easily removes it. (PS *Kalash* 2)

This commentary on the *Pravachana-sara* explains the nature of substances or things as they really are and is composed for the good of fortunate persons desirous of drinking the nectar-juice of Highest Bliss. (PS *Kalash* 3)

[Introductory Remarks by the Commentator in Prose]

Here now someone who possesses knowledge of the further and the nearer shores of mundane existence (*samsara*) — whose light of understanding has expanded abundantly; who, in consequence of attaining the divine many-sided knowledge (of the doctrine of *anekant*), has lost the conceit of knowledge proclaimed by all one-sided views; who has become ultimately impartial (*madhyastha*), because he has given up all bias or preference of particular views; and who, moreover, realizes that the imperishable bliss of liberation, containing the ultimate truth, available to us because of the five holy *parameshthins* and exclusively wholesome for the self, since it embraces all human aims, is an object worthy of acceptance adores the five blessed *parameshthins* (*Siddhas, Arhats, Acharayas, Upadhyayas* and *Sadhus*), preceded by the present *Tirtha-nayaka* (Spiritual Guide, i.e. Lord Mahavira) and the other *Tirthankaras*, with homage in the form of prostration (*pranamana*) and eulogy (*vandana*); and after this, embracing with all his power the way of liberation, he states his intention.

BENEDICTORY VERSES (VERSES 1-5)

Detailed Comments on Kundakunda's Verses

1. I now prostrate myself before *Vardhamana*, the *Tirtha* (landing place in the ocean of Transmigration, i.e. Spiritual Guide), promulgator of the law or path of *dharma*, praised by the best of gods, demons and men, free from the stains of destructive *karman*.

I now, the person perceived by means of self-consciousness, having for self the self of vision and knowledge in their generality, prostrate myself before the holy Vardhamana, the mention of whose name is auspicious and is worthy of being praised by the most excellent Masters (*Bhattarakas*), Great Gods, Tutelary Deities and Supreme Lords (*Parameshvaras*). I first bow before him, because he is our present Guide. He is the *guru* of the three worlds, because he is praised by the best of gods, demons and men; he possesses the rank of a Supreme Lord, which rank is one of unlimited efficacy and fitted for benevolence towards the world, because he is free from the stains of destructive *karman*; he is capable of saving us, because he is the *Tirtha* of the *yogins*; he is the institutor of a conduct of a wise nature, because he is propounder of the Law, i.e. the path of *dharma*.

2. (I pay obeisance) also to the other Tirthankaras (the promulgators of the order or the path of *dharma*) and all the *Siddhas* (liberated souls), and the *Shramanas* (saints) of pure nature who are engaged in the practice of knowledge, *darshan* (vision), conduct, austerities and energy (*virya*).

Then I bow before the other, former *Tirthankaras*, whose innate pure vision and knowledge may be compared to genuine gold, emerged from the fire, because they themselves are pure; and I bow before all the *Siddhas* and before the *Shramanas*, namely the *Acharyas*, the *Upadhyayas* and the *Sadhus*, who have reached the stage of the highest, pure psychic-attention (*upayoga*), because they are possessed of the practice of the exercises of knowledge, faith, conduct, penance and energy.

3. I pay homage to all of them conjointly and individually, and to the *Arhats* (perfect souls) existing at present in the region inhabited by man.

Thereafter, fixing my attention on the present time, I glorify all these five *Parameshthins* in their respective individualities, including the *Tirtha-nayakas* who now abide in the human region (*manushya-kshetra*) — for, though at present no *Tirthakaras* abide in this region of ours (*Bharat-kshetra*), they do exist in the great *Videha*-country — so then I venerate these *Parameshthins* collectively and separately with laudatory speech as it is taught by the *Krtikarma-shastra*, namely with the pronouncing of benedictions similar to those used at the time of their consecration in sainthood, which is the bridal day of the Glory of Deliverance.

4. Having thus paid homage to the *Arhats, Siddhas, Ganadharas* (direct disciples of *Tirthankaras*), the groups of *Adhyapakas* (Teachers) and all the *Sadhus* (saints).

After having thus paid homage to the *Arhats, Siddhas, Acharyas, Upadhyayas* and all the *Sadhus* - a homage which, although it proceeds in the two-fold form of prostration (*pranati)* and the pronouncing of eulogies (*vandana*), still is one, in as much as every distinction between ourselves and others fades away in consequences of an intensive mutual union, resulting from the relation of object worshipped and worshipper.

5. And having approached their holy station, devoted primarily to purifying vision and knowledge, I rely upon the equanimity (*samya)* leading to *nirvana*.

And by abundance of purified knowledge and vision having approached the holy station of these *Arhats, Siddhas, Acharyas, Upadhyayas* and all *Sadhus* - which station leads to right vision (*samyag-darshan*) and right knowledge (*samyag-jnana*), both characterized by the experience of belief in the reality of soul as having for its innate nature pure vision and knowledge, and so being in possession of right vision and knowledge, and having left far behind, although it takes place by degrees, the conduct influenced by attachment (*raga*) cause of the attainment of bondage through merits, since the soul is still blind through its passions (*kashaya*) - I now rely upon the tranquillity called the conduct free from attachment, cause of the attainment of *nirvana,* since the soul is freed from all the filth of the contest of passions.

Thus I have obtained the mental-concentration which consists in the oneness of right vision, right knowledge and right conduct; this is what I profess; thus I here am surely following the clear path of liberation.

The author now explains how conduct free from attachment and conduct based on attachment have desirable and undesirable results and therefore are to be sought and to be avoided:

SELF AND ITS STATES-OF-EVOLUTION (VERSES 6-12)

6. The *nirvana* of the soul, together with the powers or the splendour *(vibhava)* of kings (i.e. the best) of gods, demons and men, is reached by means of a conduct based on vision and knowledge.

Liberation is reached by a conduct which is based on enlightened world-view and knowledge and free from attachment (*raga*). For the same reason bondage, which troubles the kingly powers of gods, demons and men, results from conduct based on attachment. Hence, he who desires liberation should follow a conduct without attachment, as having a desired fruit, and conduct with attachment, as having undesired fruit, he should forgo.

Now he explains the characteristic nature of conduct:

7. Conduct is *dharma. Dharma* is defined as equanimity (*sama*); and equanimity is said to be a state-of-evolution (*parinama*) of the soul, in which it is free from infatuation (moha) and disturbance (*kshobha*).

Conduct is behaving according to one's own nature; activity obeying one's (innate) laws. And this being the nature of things is *dharma*; it means the manifestation of pure consciousness [pure in the sense that it is different from other substance(s) and not different from its own properties (PS 192, AC)]. And this is equanimity; for in it we possess the qualities of the self as they are. And equanimity is a state-of-evolution of the soul, a state which is completely exempt from blemish because there is no longer any infatuation and disturbance, which were caused by the arising (*udaya*)(the arising of *karman* out of its latent condition) of vision-infatuating (*darshan-mohaniya*) and conduct-infatuating (*charitra-mohaniya*) *karman.*

Now he investigates what is to be understood by the conduct of the self:

8. A substance possesses the nature of that through which it evolves during the time of the evolution. Therefore the soul, evolved through *dharma*, must be considered to be *dharma*.

Whatever substance evolves at a certain time through a certain form of existence takes at that time the nature of that existence, like a piece of iron evolved through heat. Therefore this soul, evolved through *dharma,* is *dharma*; thus is settled what we must understand by the conduct of the soul.

Now he investigates the good (*shubha*), evil (*ashubha*) and pure (*shuddha*) states of the soul:

9. The soul accepts the character of its state-of-evolution. When the soul evolves through the good or the evil, it becomes good or evil. When it evolves through the pure, it becomes pure.

When the soul evolves through a mental-state (*bhava*) of attachment (*raga*), either good or evil, it becomes good or evil, possessing the character of its state-of-evolution; like a crystal evolved through the colour (*raga*) of the China rose (*japa*) or the *Tamala* flower (*tapiccha*). But, when it evolves through a pure mental-state exempt from attachment, it becomes pure, possessing the character of its state-of-evolution; like a crystal evolved through the pure, colourless condition. Thus is settled what we must understand by the good, evil and pure condition of the soul.

Now he investigates evolution, as being the innate nature of things:

10. There is no object without a state of evolution; there is no state-of-evolution without an object (*arth*); the object, in the form of substance, attributes and modifications, has developed from existence (*astitva* or *satta*).

No thing (*vastu*) receives existence without evolution, because a thing evolves through substance, etc., because these are never seen apart, because anything without evolution would resemble a donkey's horn, and because it would be repugnant to the evolution which is seen, for instance, in cow's milk. Neither does evolution receive existence without a thing, because, if there were nothing for it to abide in, the unwished-for consequence would be that this evolution without an abode would be a void (*shunya*). But the thing, founded in the substance, which forms its general-aspect according to the vertical-direction (*urdhvata-samanya*, i.e the common features belonging to one thing in succession of time), in the attributes (*gunas*), which are the particular concomitants (*sahabhavi-vishesha*), in the modifications, which are the particular stages (*kramabhavi-vishesha*), has developed from, and still develops through, existence, which consists in origination (*utpada*), perishing (*vyaya*) and continuance (*dhrauvya*). So then evolution is its innate nature.

Now he considers the fruit (*phala*) of the pure and good states-of-evolution, which arise during the contact with the state-of-evolution called conduct (*charitra*), in order that one may accept or reject it:

11. When the soul, whose self evolves through *dharma* (i.e. righteousness and piety) is conjoined with pure psychic-attention (*upayoga*), then it attains the happiness of *nirvana;* or, when engaged in good psychic-attention, it attains the happiness of heaven.

When this soul, with its innate nature evolved through *dharma,* carries out the evolution of pure psychic-attention, then its efficacy (*shakti*) does not meet with resistance, and thus its conduct is capable of doing what is to be done, and the soul itself reaches manifest liberation. But, when the soul, although having its innate nature evolved through *dharma,* is in contact with the evolution-state of good psychic-attention, then its efficacy, meets with resistance, and thus it is unfit to do what is to be done; its conduct in bringing about what is to be done is to a certain extent checked; and the soul itself reaches bondage, in this case heavenly happiness, as a man sprinkled with *ghi* (oil) hot from the fire [incurs] the pain of burning. Therefore pure psychic-attention should be accepted, good psychic-attention avoided.

Now he considers the fruit of evil psychic-attention, which is utterly to be rejected; for here takes place no contact with a state-of-evolution called (lawful) conduct:

12. By the arising of the evil *(ashubha)* (psychic disposition) the self becomes a rogue, an animal or inhabitant of hell; And, always beset by thousands of pains, it strays incessantly.

When this self, not partaking at all of the evolution of *dharma,* gives itself up to the evolution of evil psychic-attention (*ashubha upayoga*), then it experiences the bondage of a thousand pains, whilst it wanders about as rogue, animal or inhabitant of hell. Therefore, because of the lack of even a grain of (lawful) conduct, this evil psychic-attention must be completely abandoned.

And the soul, thus throwing off all engagement (*vrtti*) in good and evil psychic-attention, and adopting the engagement in pure psychic-attention, gains a prerogative (*adhikara*) with reference to pure psychic-attention. And further, in order to rouse the self, he praises the fruit of pure pyschic-attention:

Pure, Psychic Attention

13. The happiness of those advanced in pure psychic-attention is transcendent, springing from the self, supersensuous, incomparable, endless and uninterrupted.

The nectar of joy in those who are perfect in pure psychic-attention is: (1) transcendent, (2) springing from the self, (3) surpassing objects, (4) incomparable, (5) endless and (6) uninterrupted; and therefore it should be sought in every way, (i) because it is an extreme, wonderful joy having no precedent all the *samsara* through, (ii) because it continues based only on the self, (iii) because it is independent of any other abode, (iv) because it is utterly different from anything else, (v) because it does not decrease in the longest succession-of-time (*ayati*), (vi) because it comes forth without pauses.

Now he describes the characteristic nature of self, when evolved through pure psychic-attention:

14. A *shraman* is called a man of pure psychic-attention, when he knows well the categories (*padarthas*) and the *sutras* (the scriptures) [For the definition of *Sutra*, see PS 34] which explain them, when he possesses self-restraint (*samyam*) and practises austerities (*tapas*), gives up attachment and considers pleasure and pain the same (*sama*).

He knows well the categories and the *sutras* which explain them, because he is capable of decisions (*vidhana*) and masters a complete knowledge of the distinction between his own (self's) substance and other substances by means of his understanding the contents of the *sutras.*

He possesses self-restraint and has practised austerities (*tapas*), (1) because he restrains the self in its pure characteristic nature by keeping it away from the different forms (*vikalpa*) of the longings of the five sense-organs and from the different forms of destroying the bodies of the six kinds of living beings (the five kinds of one-sensed *sthavara*-souls (immobile ones earth-borne, water-borne, air-borne, fire-borne and plant life) and the *trasa* (mobile) souls, i.e men and animals etc. possessing from two up to five sense organs), and (2) because he brings to brightness (*pratapati*) his intelligence, motionless and acquiescent in its characteristic nature.

He has given up attachment, because the unblemished characteristic nature of self has been revealed to him by a facility in realizing (*bhavana-saushthava*) the discrimination of the effects (*vipaka*) of all the infatuating *karmans.*

He considers pleasure and pain the same, because even under the most subtle examination he no longer experiences the manifold evolutions due to pleasure and pain which arise from the ripening of delightful (*sata*) and painful (*asata*) sensation-*karman* (*vedaniya-karman*). Thus the *Shraman* is called a man of pure psychic-attention.

Now he describes the attainment of the nature of the purified self, which is the acquisition of pure (*shuddha*) psychic-attention:

15. He who is pure in psychic-attention and has thrown off the filth of obscuring (*avaraniya*), obstructing (*antaraya*) and infatuating (*mohaniya*) *karmans* becomes himself the self and comprehends all things knowable.

He who has become and remains purified according to his power by means of psychic-attention, i.e. evolution of his intelligence, obtains an excellent efficacy of purity which springs up at every step, and an intelligence completely free from blemish, because the very strong knot (*granthi*) of infatuation, bound together all the *samsara* through, is untied; he obtains an efficacy of self expanding without obstacles, because he has thrown aside all *karmans* which obscure knowledge and intuition, and those *karmans* which obstruct; having himself become thus, he reaches the boundary of all things which can be known. Here then the innate nature of self is knowledge; and knowledge is nothing less than the things knowable; so then the self, owing to its pure attention, attains the self, which in its nature consists of knowledge, which knowledge, again, pervades everything that is knowable.

Now he explains how the acquisition of the innate nature of pure self, originating from pure psychic-attention, depends exclusively on the self, inasmuch as it is independent of any other factor:

16. Having thus realised (the full potential of) his nature and become omniscient, deserving of respect from the lords of all the worlds, being himself the self, he is called the self-being *(svayambhu).*

This self in its innate nature is intelligence provided with pure, unlimited efficacy; for all its destructive *karman* disappears through the dignity of the internal-state (*bhavana*) of pure psychic-attention;

it claims *kartrtva* (agency, or the function of the grammatical nominative), because of its independence; for it is in its innate nature a knower, possessing pure, unlimited efficacy;

it bears *karmatva* (the relation of the accusative towards the verb), because of its being arrived at; for it is in its innate nature an evolution-state of knowledge, possessing pure, unlimited efficacy;

it shows *karanatva* (the nature of an instrumental), because of its great effectiveness; for it is in its innate nature an evolution-state of knowledge, possessing pure, unlimited efficacy;

it manifests *sampradanatva* (the nature of a dative) because of its being the goal of an action; for it is in its innate nature an evolution-state of knowledge, possessing pure, unlimited efficacy;

it accepts *apadanatva* (the character of an ablative), because of its being based on immobility; for in its innate nature it is original (*sahaja*) knowledge, even when at the moment of an evolution-state of knowledge, possessing pure, unlimited efficacy imperfect knowledge in its innate nature, existing previously, withdraws;

it appropriates *adhikaranatva* (the character of a locative), because of its being the abode of the innate nature of an evolution-state of knowledge, possessing pure, unlimited efficacy;

thus by itself (*svayam*) arising in the form of the six *karakas* (the six cases of a noun which bear on a verb), it is called *svayambhu* (self-arising). Or[1] it is called thus because it comes itself (*svayam*) forth, throwing off in proportion to its rise the destructive *karmans,* divided into kinds according to their material nature (*dravya-bhava*).

Thus on strict examination (*nishchaya*) there is no relation of causality (condition of being a factor, *karakatva*) between the self and anything else (*para,* something else than the soul, i.e. *ajiva* or non-soul);[1a] for such beings as are intent on the search for means to the realization of the innate nature of their own pure selves are independent.

Now with regard to this self-existent being he considers the absolute impossibility of loss (*anapayitvam*) in the realization of the innate nature of the pure self, and its connection in a certain sense with origination, perishing and continuance:

17. There is in him origination without destruction, annihilation devoid of origination; and, on the other hand, also an inherence (*samavaya*) of persistence, origination or becoming and annihilation.

The origination which is found in the self according to its innate nature of *pure* self and which is due to pure psychic-attention is exempt from destruction; for in that respect there is no dissolution. And the annihilation which takes place because the *impure* exists no more is devoid of commencement; for there does not happen a new production. And, since this is ascertained, neither is there a loss. So then the inherence of persistence, becoming, and annihilation in him is not contradictory; for we find here the inherence of an origination exempt from decay, an annihilation devoid of commencement, and a substance [we should read *dhrauvyena* (permanence) instead of *dravyena* (substance)] which is the abode of both.

Now he explains how the triad of origination, etc., common to every substance, necessarily belongs to the pure self as well:

18. Origination and annihilation are found in every object whatever, and each existent object exists with reference to some mode or other.

Just as origination is seen in real gold by way of its modification as a bracelet, and annihilation with reference to a modification such as a previously existing finger-ring, and continuance, because this gold, in both regards, neither undergoes origination nor annihilation with reference to such modifications as yellowness, so we must acknowledge that in all substances there is origination with regard to one modification, annihilation with regard to a second, and continuance with regard to a third. Thus existence (*astitva*), characterized as substance and consisting of the triad origination, etc., is necessarily found in pure self as well.

Now he refutes the doubt how, through the power of pure psychic-attention, without sense-organs, knowledge and joy of this self, which is self-existent, can occur:

19/2. He whose destructive *karman* has perished, whose energy (*virya*) is sublime without limits, whose splendour is abundant, who

has risen above the realm of the senses—he himself evolves into knowledge and bliss.

This self, when its destructive *karman* has disappeared, because pure psychic-attention is capable of this; when it has risen above the realm of the senses, in consequences of being unblended with the knowledge and vision due to combined suppression (*upasham*) and annihilation (*kshaya*); when it possesses unlimited sublime energy, in consequence of the annihilation of all obstructive (*antaraya*) *karman*, when it abounds in splendour, called absolute (*kevala)* knowledge and vision (*darshan*), resulting from the complete perishing of all obscurations (*avarana*) of knowledge and vision (*darshan*)— this self, reaching the self, which in its innate nature is pure intelligence—absolutely unblemished, because of the absence of all infatuating (*mohaniya*) *karmans*, evolves itself by becoming knowledge, i.e. illumination of the self and the other (*svapara*, self and other; i.e self and non-self),[1b] and bliss, i.e. absence of confusedness. So then knowledge and bliss are the innate nature of the self. And, since innate nature does not depend on anything else, knowledge and bliss of the self arise even without sense-organs.

Now he explains how bodily pleasure and pain do not belong to the pure self, because it is without the senses:

20. Bodily pleasure or pain does not belong to him who possesses absolute knowledge or omniscience (*kevala-jnana*). Know that it is because he has transcended the realm of the senses.

Since the pure self does not possess the assemblage of sense-organs, just as little as the fire possesses the entire manifestation of matter which has met together in the iron ball, therefore bodily pleasure and pain, corresponding to the series of impacts of terrible hammer (*ghana*) blows, does not belong to it.

Now he gives the fuller explanation of the characteristic nature of knowledge and the fuller explanation of the characteristic-nature of happiness in two successive passages [see *gathas* 21-52 and 53-68]; and here he first explains how the perfect-sage (*kevalin*) has perception of all things, because he has evolved into supra-sensorial knowledge:

Exposition of Knowledge (Verses 21-52)

21. For him, who is evolving into knowledge, directly perceives all substances and their modifications; he does not know them by

means of stages such as apprehension of an object or sensation (*avagraha*), etc.

Since the perfect-sage does not obtain knowledge by the aid of the senses through the precedent series of *avagraha* (the taking up the object of knowledge by the senses), *iha* (the readiness to know more about the things perceived) and *avaya* (the finding out the determinate or ascertained cognition of a thing), and since he himself, at the moment of the annihilation of all obscurations (*avaranas*), having accepted in the function of a cause (*karana*) the innate nature of knowledge which has no beginning, no end, no cause (*hetu*) and has nothing in common with anything else, evolves, becoming the psychic-attention of arising absolute-knowledge, which immediately follows the annihilation of *avaranas*—therefore the modifications of all the substances are perceptible for him, since they conjointly become a basis for his consciousness inasmuch as all substances, times, places and forms-of-being (*bhava*) are appropriated by him simultaneously.

Now he commences the topic that nothing is hidden from the perception of the Holy One, because he has evolved into supra-sensorial knowledge:

22. Nothing is indirect to him, who himself has become one with knowledge, and who is rich in all qualities of the sense-organs, who always transcends the realm of the senses.

Nothing whatever is imperceptible to the Holy One at the very moment of the destruction of all obscurations; for he has surpassed the senses, each of which takes up its respective objects and causes the setting to work of the forces necessary for the arising of mundane distinctions (*parichchitti*); he is rich at all points (since they have for him the same savour) in all qualities of the senses in the form of the distinctions (*parichcheda*) in touch, taste, smell, colour and sound; he himself illuminates the self and the other by his completeness; he is become miraculous (*lokottara*) knowledge without restraint; so nothing is imperceptible to him, owing to his simultaneous grasping of all substances, places, times and forms-of-being.

Now he explains the equal extension of the knowledge and the self and the omnipresence of this knowledge:

23. The soul is co-extensive with knowledge; knowledge is said to be coextensive with the knowable [i.e. the objects of knowledge]; the knowable comprises the physical and non-physical universe;

therefore knowledge is omnipresent.

According to the saying "the substance has its qualities and modifications equivalent to itself," the self is the extension of the knowledge; for it evolves without becoming more or less than the knowledge; and knowledge is the extension of the knowable; for it abides therein, as fire in the fuel. The knowable is as much as everything; it is the totality of the six substances; it is annihilation, origination and continuance; divided into the division of universe and the beyond-the-universe; revealing itself in characteristic-natures (*svarupa*) which are covered by an endless series of modifications. Therefore knowledge is omnipresent; for at the very moment of the annihilation of all obscurations it has reached the (other) shore of all the appearances (*akara*) of objects, divided into the division of universe and beyond-the-universe, and remains in this way for ever unshaken.

He states two alternatives which arise when one does not accept the self as having the extension of knowledge, and refutes them:

24. He who does not accept the self as coextensive with knowledge, the self surely becomes smaller or larger than knowledge.

25. If the self is smaller, then knowledge (outside the self), being of unconscious nature, does not know; if the self is larger than knowledge, how does this self then without knowledge know?

If we allow that the self is smaller than knowledge, in that case knowledge–which may be compared to qualities such as shape (in material things)–going beyond the self, will be unconscious (*achetan*), because it no longer inheres in the conscious substance which was its abode, and so then does not know. If we admit the other alternative, that it is larger than knowledge, then necessarily the self–which in our comparison ranks together with (material things), such as pots and pieces of cloth–standing by itself and going beyond knowledge, does not know without this knowledge. Therefore this self must be taken as possessing the same extension as knowledge.

Now he declares that the omnipresence of self, like its knowledge, is proved by logic (*nyaya*):

26. The great *Jina* is omnipresent, and all the objects (*arthas*) in the world are within his grasp; the *Jina* is the embodiment of knowledge; and the objects are said to be within his grasp, because they are objects-of-his-knowledge (*vishaya*).

Knowledge, embracing the appearances (*akara*) of all knowables, arranged as the modifications of all substances in the three times, is called omnipresent. And also the Holy One, because he consists of such like knowledge, is omnipresent. And so all objects (*artha*), inasmuch as they are the objects (*vishaya*) of omnipresent knowledge, are called the objects (*vishaya*) of the Holy One, who is never deprived of omnipresent knowledge; and, since they are so called, they belong to him.

According to the [internal, self-referential] *nishchaya*-mode of statement, the Holy One, it is true, knows without moving himself towards all the appearances of the knowables, since he never leaves his own reality (*svatattva*), i.e. knowledge with the extension of the self, characterized by its being the abode of a consciousness (*samvedana*) of bliss demarked by serenity; however, according to the [extgernal, other-referential] *vyavahara*-mode the Holy One is said to be everywhere.

Similarly, the objects are said metaphorically to belong to him, whilst one considers the appearances of knowables which are auxiliary causes (*naimittika*) to be based on the self; but in the transcendental sense (*paramarthena*) of the word there is no mutual going towards each other, since all substances abide in their own characteristic-nature. The same argumentation must be understood with reference to knowledge.

Now he considers the identity and non-identity of self and knowledge:

27. The doctrine is that knowledge is the self. There is no knowledge without the self; therefore knowledge is the self. But the self is knowledge and something else [also].

Since knowledge cannot exist without the self—for knowledge arises, requiring, and using as basis, the self alone, which shows towards it a beginning-less and endless relation of inherence, ensuing from its innate nature, and which, with reference to all other, unconscious things (*vastu*), has no tendency towards such a relation of inherence—therefore we may say that knowledge is the self. But the self, inasmuch as it is the seat of innumerable properties (*dharma*), may be knowledge owing to its property of knowledge, while owing to some other property it may be something else. Moreover, the many-sided view (*anekant*) here prevails. By the one-sided view (*ekanta*), according to which the self is knowledge, the non-existence of knowledge would be the absence of consciousness (*chetanatva*); or (in other words) the non-existence of the self would follow from the absence of its characteristic qualities (*vishesha-guna*).

(For), were the self in every respect knowledge, then, in the case of absence of knowledge (i.e. when the self is in another state than cognition) there would arise for the self non-existence of its other modifications, as having no basis, and of itself also, since it is necessarily-concomitant (*avinabhavin*) with these.

Now he refutes a mutual approach of knowledge and knowable:

28. The knower possesses knowledge as his innate nature; the objects, surely, possess the character of knowables with regard to the knower, like shapes or forms with reference to the eye. But they do not abide in each other.

The knower and the objects, owing to their separateness (*prthakatva*), which forms their individual-nature (*sva-lakshan*), do not possess occurrence within each other; but they merely possess a mutually related occurrence, effected by the relation between their innate natures as knowledge-and knowable. For instance, as the eyes and the things having shapes or forms, which are their objects are respectively ready to receive and to occasion the appearances of the knowables, even without mutual penetration, so the self and the objects are ready to receive and to occasion the appearances of all knowables, without being identical with one another.[1c]

Now he explains the variety in efficacy which causes the activity (*vrtti*) of the knower towards the objects, although he is inactive (*a-vrtta*) with reference to them:

29. The knower, neither entering nor shunning to enter the knowables, verily, in consequence of his surpassing the sense-organs, knows and sees the whole world, as the eye knows and sees the shapes or forms, i.e. the objects of sight.

Just as the eye, not entering, i.e. not taking hold of the shapes or forms of the substances with its own spacial-infinitesimal-constituents (*pradeshas*), nor shunning to enter them, i.e. really appropriating their distinguishable appearances, knows and sees, likewise the soul— of which, since it surpasses the sense-organs, we need not doubt at all that it acts independently of approach[2] not entering, i.e. not taking hold, with its own *pradeshas*, of all the things which function as knowables, nor shunning to enter them. i.e. as it were uprooting and then devouring all the knowable appearances which abide in the things, with the aid of the manifoldness of its efficacy, knows and sees. So that, as concerns the knower, who develops an activity (*yoga*) of manifold efficacy, his entrance into the things attains just as much reality as his non-entrance.

Now he explains how knowledge is located in the things:

30. As the sapphire-gem, placed in milk, by its own splendour constantly dominates (the colour of) the milk or pervades the whole of it with its lustre, so is knowledge related to the objects.

Just as the sapphire-gem, located in milk, is observed to dominate or pervade it constantly with the mass of its splendour, so see we that consciousness (*samvedana*), which, because it is not separated from the self, receives the character of the self in its function of agent, constantly in its function of instrument, i.e. in its character of knowledge, pervades all the knowable appearances (as effects) of all the objects (as causes). So, when it is metaphorically said, by reason of their relation of cause and effect, that "knowledge, dominating or pervading the objects, abides (in them)," there is no contradiction.

Now he explains how the objects abide in knowledge:

31. If the objects do not exist in knowledge, then knowledge is not all-pervasive or omnipresent; alternatively, if knowledge is all-pervasive or omnipresent, how should the objects not exist or abide in knowledge?

If all the objects do not appear in knowledge, by penetrating into it and committing to it their own complete knowable appearances, then we must agree that knowledge is not omnipresent. But if you agree that it is omnipresent, then the immediate (*sakshat*) causes[3] of their own respective appearances, which are fit-objects-for-consciousness (*samvedya*) and may be compared to reflected-objects, coming down to the surface of the mirror of consciousness, are the indirect (*paramparaya*) causes of appearances-in-our-consciousness (*samvedya*), which appearances may be compared to the reflection-images (when located in the mirror of consciousness). So then it is ascertained (read *katham na*) that the objects abide in knowledge.

Now he explains the complete isolation (*viviktatva*) of (the Omniscient) who sees and determines everything; for, although there is a mutual activity (*anyonya-vrtti*) of knower and objects, yet neither does he take hold of them, nor let them loose, nor evolve into them:

32. The Holy Omniscient Lord or the Absolute Knower does not seize (accept) or release and does not evolve into anything else; but without exception he sees and knows everything all around.

This self, because according to its innate nature no seizing, no releasing, no evolution into anything else takes place, evolves owing to its characteristic nature of absolute (*kevala*) knowledge, which is its own principle (*tattva*), and thus, standing forth like a genuine jewel of motionless and radiant light, it possesses an everywhere glittering efficacy of vision and knowledge; so then it becomes by itself in itself aware of the self in its entirety without remainder. Or, to explain otherwise, by a simultaneous, intuitive-perception (*sakshat-karana*) of the multitude of all things wavering of notion is excluded, and there is cessation of all supposed acts such as grasping or releasing; in this way (the self as Omniscient Lord or the Absolute Knower), by firstly evolving into all distinguishable appearances and then again not evolving into any appearance, yet sees and knows everything without exception everywhere, whilst remaining in isolation (read *vivikta eva).*

Now he makes an end to the craving *(akanksha)* to know the difference between a *kevala-jnanin* (possessor of absolute-knowledge) and a *shruta-jnanin* (possessor of scriptural-knowledge), by showing that there is non-difference:

33. He who by means of scripture knows the self, which in innate nature is something-knowing (*jnayaka*), is called by the rshis (sages), the lights of this world, a *shruta-kevalin* (possessor of absolute knowledge, due to the knowledge of scripture).

In the same way as the Holy One is a *kevalin* (possessor of absolute-knowledge) by means of his realization (*samchetana*) — by the aid of his absolute-knowledge, amply provided with all the particular forms of consciousness (*chaitanya*) simultaneously evolved of the self in the self by the self, which self is absolute because it is one with its natural knowing capacity (*chetaka-svabhava*), and which is (the same as) the great general consciousness (*chaitanya*), realized by him (*sva-samchetyamana*) as beginningless and endless, uncaused and unparalleled, likewise is this man a *shruta-kevalin* by means of his realization—by the aid of his scripture-knowledge, amply provided with several particular forms of consciousness successively evolved of the self in the self by the self, which self is absolute because it is one with its natural knowing capacity (*chetaka-svabhava*), and which is (the same as) the great general consciousness, realized as beginningless and endless, uncaused and unparalleled.

Enough now of this craving to know the difference (between the *kevalin* and *shruta-kevalin*)! We stand firm in our characteristic-nature.

Now he refutes with reference to knowledge a distinction based on the *shruta* as an additional condition (*upadhi*):

34. The "sutra" is taught by the Jina with words consisting of material-substance.[4] The understanding of it is called both the understanding of the sutra and knowledge.

Now scripture is the *sutra*, and that is the sacred science as the word, materialized with the expression "*quodammodo*" (*syadvada*) as a characteristic, and first pronounced by the Holy Omniscient *Arhat*. Knowledge is the understanding of it. The expression "the word heard" (*shruta*) is metaphorically used for knowledge, inasmuch as it is the cause thereof. Consequently the understanding of the *sutra* means as much as "scripture-knowledge." If this "*sutra*" is disregarded, because it is an additional-condition (*upadhi*), then the understanding is left (as that which is essential). And this understanding by the *kevalin* and the *shruta-kevalin* is equal in regard to the realization of the self. Therefore there is no division of knowledge due to scripture as a condition.

Now he refutes the division which is made between self and knowledge, based upon their functions as agent and instrument:

35. He who knows is knowledge; but the self does not by the help of its knowledge become something-that-is-knowing (*jnayaka*); knowledge evolves by itself, and all the objects reside in knowledge.

He who knows by himself–because his self develops an activity (*yoga*) of the highest supremacy in efficacy, in which agency and instrumentality are united–is knowledge; in the same way as we call fire–in which there rests independently a most effective efficacy of heat–hot, because its action in burning is patent.

But the self does not become something-that-is-knowing as Devadatta becomes a cutter owing to a separately existing knife. If it were so (i.e. If the *self* only became knowing by a separately existing *knowledge*), then both (i.e. self and knowledge) would be unconscious, and on the conjunction of two unconscious entities no distinguishing could arise. And, even if we accept a process of distinguishing in two entities existing one outside (i.e. independently of each other) the other, then a distinguishing in the one in consequence of a process of distinguishing in the other, and an origination of distinction, bearing on objective-being (*bhuti*), etc., would be without any rule. Furthermore, knowledge evolves into all the distinguishable appearances which exist besides knowledge; and we may say that all the objects which are the causes of all the knowable appearances, which are (really) the effects of this self-evolving knowledge, in a certain way reside in knowledge. So then the forced supposition (*klesha kalpana*)[5] of a separation of knower and knowledge is superfluous.'

Now he explains what knowledge is and what the knowable:

36. Therefore the soul is knowledge; and substance, explained as threefold, is the knowable. This substance then is the self and "the other" evolutions.

Since the soul itself evolves in the form of distinguishing and distinguishes by itself independently, therefore the soul alone is knowledge; for other substances cannot evolve and distinguish in this way.

But the knowable is substance, which is without beginning and end; for it is connected with the three aspects of time, inasmuch as it shows a varying series of modifications in past, present and future. And this substance, possessing the property of being knowable, is twofold, i.e. it is divided into the self and "the other." For we must accept such a twoness in the object of an experienced, which is aware of a distinction of the self and the other.[6]

But (in this paragraph the author discusses self-consciousness) how (it is asked) can there be a distinguishing of the self, since it is contradictory that an act should take place upon one's *self*? Well, what is this act and what the contradiction means? The act which is (supposed to be) contradictory is either origination or understanding (*jnapti*). An act of (spontaneous) origination, however, is contradictory: since according to the words of scripture not one thing originates from *itself*. But no refutation occurs with reference to an act in the form of understanding; for the difficulty here is removed by conformity with the act of illuminating. For when a lamp, as illuminator, illuminates another thing as illumin and, then for its own illumination we need not search for a second illumination, since we observe an act of illuminating on its own part; similarly, when the self, as distinguisher, distinguishes something else as distinguend, then for its own distinction we need not search for a second distinguisher, since we observe an act of distinguishing on its own part.

Whence is it that the self has the form of knowledge of the substances; and the substances that of knowables for the self? Because they are connected with evolutions. Since self and substances are connected with their evolutions, therefore the evolution of self through knowledge, which finds its basis in the substances, and the evolution of the substances through knowable appearances, which base themselves on the knowledge, appear to be not contradictory.

Now he explains how past and future modifications of the substances may be separately contents of knowledge, just as well as those which take place in the present time:

37. All the modifications, existent and non-existent, of these kinds of substances appear, with their particularities, in knowledge, like those of the present.

All possible modifications, existent and non-existent, with the fullness of their characteristic natures appearing successively (which is due to the fact that the stages through which their self-realization passes are defined by the three times) all these modifications of all kinds of substances receive at one (The commentator explains the *gathas* as referring to perfect-knowledge) moment their place on the white-wall of attention (*avabodha*), with all their particular characteristics well marked notwithstanding the utmost blending, and they appear even as those of the present.

And this is not unfit. For, firstly, it is not contradicted by our daily-experience (*drshta*). Namely, when even a *chadmastha* (someone who has not reached absolute-knowledge) reflects on a past or future thing (*vastu*), its appearance (*akara*) founded on consciousness is perceived, as in the case of reflection on a present thing.

And, secondly, consciousness (*samvid*) may be compared to a picture. As delineable appearances of past, future, and present things are immediately visible in a picture at one moment, so happens on the wall of consciousness.

And lastly, all knowable appearances are not contradictory to present time. As delineable appearances of past and future events are present, so are the knowable appearances of past and future modifications present.

Now he explains how non-existent modifications are in a certain respect existent:

38. The modifications, which have not yet originated, and those which after origination have disappeared. Those non-existent modifications are yet directly perceptible (*pratyaksha*) to knowledge.

The modifications which do not yet partake of origination, and those which have gone to annihilation after having originated what they are, are although non-existent, well-defined with reference to mental-distinction and therefore liable to immediate-perception by means of knowledge; so then they are existent, since their characteristic nature has been planted firmly, like past and future gods hewn out in stone columns.

Now he confirms this fact that non-existent things can be perceived by knowledge:

39. If a not yet arisen and an annihilated modification were not directly perceptible to knowledge, who would call that knowledge divine (*divya*)?

If knowledge does not (insert *na* before *karoti*) cause the whole set of modifications, with their forms-of-being not yet experienced or previously experienced, to be bound to the self, whilst it in force invades (*akramya*) these modifications with its great power of splendour, opening out without impediment and unbroken, so that the entirety of their characteristic-natures is simultaneously (*akrama*) delivered up, how could there be any divinity in this knowledge? Therefore all this is possible for discernment, when it reaches the highest point.

Now he examines how sensorial knowledge[7] cannot know that which has passed or has not yet arisen:

40. Those who, by means of *iha* ("the readiness to know more"), etc., know the object present to the senses are not capable of knowing that which transcends the senses; thus it is taught.

Those who, accepting "contact" of objects and sense-organs, i.e. a coming together of the object-of-perception (*vishaya*) and the perceiver-of-the-object (*vishayi*), distinguish by means of *iha,* etc., which arise successively, cannot distinguish the concrete-existence (*svastitva*) which has passed, nor the time of the concrete-existence not yet arisen, owing to the impossibility (in this case) of the described relation of "thing-to-be-grasped" (*grahya*) and "grasper."

Now he states that everything that may be mentioned falls under the reach of supra-sensorial knowledge:

41. The knowledge which grasps things with or without space-points, corporeal (*murta*) and incorporeal things, modifications not yet arisen and modifications annihilated, is called supra-sensorial knowledge.

Sensorial knowledge takes place by the aid of indication (*upadesh*),[8] the internal organ, the sense-organs, etc., as heterogeneous (*virupa,* heterogeneous, i.e. non-intellectual) causes, and the becoming aware, the putting together (of ideas), etc., as internal and homogeneous (read *sarupa* instead of *svarupa*) causes.

And, when it takes place, it perceives-with-certainty only things which possess space-points (*pradeshas*), because it perceives what is gross (*sthula*); but it does not ascertain things which lack these space-points. It apprehends only corporeal things, because its existence depends upon such-like objects-of-the-senses; but it does not comprehend incorporeal things. It distinguishes merely that which is in present time, because only then can the object-to-be-perceived and the perceiver encounter each other; but it does not distinguish that which has happened and will happen.

But for knowledge (knowledge and self are here identical) free from obscurations (*avarana*) and loose from the senses—just as fuel, characterized by various nature, remains fuel for the lightened fire, because the property of being combustible is not outgone,—thus for the self (both the thing-with-space-points and) the thing-without-such-space-points, the corporeal as well as the incorporeal, the not yet arisen and the past set of modifications are distinguishable, because they do not outgo the property of being knowable.

Now he expresses his belief that the act, i.e. the evolution into the knowable object, does not spring forth from (superior) knowledge:

42. If the knower evolves into the knowable object (to evolve into the object = to identity oneself with the object, to feel attachment for it), then he does not possess *kshayika*-knowledge (knowledge which appears on the destruction of *karman*); thus the best of *Jinas* have declared him to be experiencing or enjoying the fruit of *karmans.*

If the distinguisher evolves into the thing to be distinguished, then there is not found in him an innate (*svabhavika*) cause (*nidana*) of distinction, engaged in destroying the whole capital of *karmans*; or, in other words, he does not possess knowledge. For the best of *Jinas* declare him whose mind is an instrument for the experience (*sambhavana*) of the water of the mirage, by reason of his evolution into the respective objects, to be experiencing (merely) the heavy burden of *karmans.*

Now he investigates whence the act, i.e. the evolution into the knowable thing, and its fruit originate:

43. It is said by the best of *Jinas* that as a result of *karman*-particles coming into operation or rise,[9] he who is filled with infatuation, attachment and aversion[10] necessarily incurs bondage.

The soul abiding in the cycle of existences of necessity possesses particles of material-*karman* in the origination-stage. And he who, being conscious of their existence, evolves into infatuation, attachment or aversion, joins himself with action, which consists in evolution into the knowable thing. Therefore he experiences bondage, which is the fruit of action. So then action and the fruit of action originate from the arising of infatuation, but not from knowledge.

Now he teaches that in the case of Absolute-Sages even the act does not produce the fruit of the action:

44. Standing, sitting down, moving about and teaching of moral rules, etc. activities, which are necessary activities for the *Arhats* at times, are similar to the [natural] activities of *maya* [*mata*, i.e. mother] in the case of women.

As women, without any effort, simply because their aptitudes are such, show a natural conduct enveloped in an envelopment of deceit, so the Absolute-Sages, without any effort, simply because their aptitudes are such, perform natural deeds such as standing, sitting, wandering and teaching the law. And this is not contradictory; for we have the example of the cloud. Just indeed as movement, rest, resounding and the throwing out of water are seen in the matter (*pudgala*) evolved into the form of a cloud, whilst no human effort takes place, thus occur standing, etc., in the Absolute-Sages, without attendant consciousness. Therefore this standing, etc., although kinds of action, are, since they are not preceded by the rising of infatuation, no causes of bondage, i.e. of the fruit of action, in the case of Absolute-Sages.

Now he makes it clear that consequently the ripening of merits (*punya*) has no effect for the *Tirthankaras*:

45. The *Arhats* owe their status to or enjoy the fruit of their merits; but their activities, though consequence of or originating from

rising-*karman* (*audayika-karman*), are exempt from infatuation, etc.; therefore it is considered to be annihilative (*kshayika*).

For the *Arhats* the fruits of the Wishing-tree of merits are generally and completely full-ripe. Whatever action takes place in them is originated-from-rising-*karman*, since the self's capacities (*sambhuti*) are realized (*sambhavita*) by the experience of this rise (of *karmans*). Thus even action as described, taking place when the residence of the anointed king Great-Infatuation is utterly destroyed, does not acquire a causality with reference to changes in the spiritual-principle (*chaitanya*), because the affecting or colouring (*uparanjaka*) factors, namely infatuation, attachment and aversion, do not exist. So then this act, although always of an originative (*audayika*) nature, is at the same time annihilative, inasmuch as it is not a cause of bondage (as effect), but is a cause of liberation (as effect). For surely, if this were not accepted, then the ripening of their *karmans* would tend to the deterioration of their innate nature.

Now he refutes the opinion that, just as in the case of Absolute-Sages, so with anybody no deterioration of innate being takes place:

46. If the self by itself, by innate nature, were devoid of auspicious or inauspicious (good or evil) psychic dispositions, then there would be no *samsara* (transmigratory existence) in the case of embodied *beings*.

If the self absolutely does not evolve through its innate nature of good and evil states, then it abides merely in the pure innate state without deterioration, at every time, under every circumstance. And so all the multitudes of beings would enjoy eternal emancipation, because of their being devoid of all causes of bondage; for their innate nature would be free of its restless unrest.[11] Now this is not admitted; the self, that is, having the property of its evolution, shows a good or evil nature in the same way as the crystal shows as innate nature the colour of the China rose or the *Tamala* flower.

Now again, in connection with the subject under discussion, he greets supra-sensorial knowledge as omniscience:

47. That knowledge which simultaneously (*yugapat*) knows presently existent things (and) the other objects, all in every direction, various and dissimilar as they may be, is called *kshayiki* (i.e. the result of the destruction of *karmans*).

Knowledge due-to-annihilation knows in one moment indeed both the object with an occurrence in the same time and the object with an occurrence in past or future time, and knows them in all directions completely, although they possess a variety (*vaichitrya*), showing itself in separateness, individual, accidental, and manifested in several forms, and a dissimilarity (*vaishamya*), accentuated by mutual opposition and called forth by their generic differences.

To this knowledge are simultaneously (*tulya-kalam*) revealed the multitude of objects coexistent and the multitude of objects belonging to another time, because of the total absence of knowledge-obscuring (*jnanavaraniya*) *karmic* matter in the destructional-subsidential state,[12] which is the cause of the coming forth in succession.

And (these multitudes of contemporary and not contemporary objects) are revealed (to the soul) in every direction, inasmuch as it is purified in every respect, whilst the purification in a limited respect is merged therein.

And all objects are revealed to it, because, as all obscuring *karmans* perish, the partially-obscuring destructional-subsidential condition (of *karmans*) no longer persists.

Objects, even various, are revealed, because, as the *karman* which obscures omniform knowledge perishes, the destructional-subsidential condition of *karman* which obscures non-omniform knowledge is dissolved.

Objects, even dissimilar, are revealed because, as the *karman* which obscures heterogenous knowledge perishes, the destructional-subsidential condition of *karman* which obscures homogeneous knowledge is on the decline.

But enough of over-elaboration: knowledge due-to-the-annihilation-of-*karman* (*kshayika*) necessarily knows everything everywhere at every time and in every respect; for it abounds in illumination whose coming forth is unchecked.

Now he certifies that one who does not know everything does not know even one thing:

48. He who does not know simultaneously the objects located in the three worlds (heavens, hells and earth) and three times is not capable of knowing even one substance with all its modifications.

There is one space-substance, one substance called the principle of motion, one substance called the principle of stationariness, innumerable time-substances (in every infinitesimal-particle of space there is one time), an unlimited number of soul-substances, and material substances in an unlimitedly more unlimited number. The modifications of these substances, considered one by one, are unlimited, whirling round in a series of existences without limitation, divided into the kinds past, future and present. The knowable, then, is all this collected; and confronting it there is only some single soul-substance as knower. Then, as a fire, burning all fuel, evolves into a self which has the appearance of one total fire that evolves through all the modifications of the appearances of the fuel, appearances due to all these fuels, so the knower, knowing all knowables, evolves into a self which has the appearance of one total knowledge that evolves through all the modifications of the appearances of the knowables, appearances due to all these knowables; into a self which is perceptible for self-experience (*svanubhava*), because it is a spiritual-being (*chetana*). Thus indeed is the innate nature of the substances.

But he who does not know every knowable is like a fire that does not burn every fuel and so does not evolve (read *atmanam aparinaman dahana iva*) into a self which has the appearance of one total fire that evolves through all the modifications of the appearances of fuel, appearances due to all these fuels; similarly (he who does not know everything) does not evolve into a self which has the appearance of one total knowledge that evolves through all the modifications of the appearances of the knowables, appearances due to all these knowables; and this holds true, although the self, as a spiritual being, remains perceptible for self-experience. Thus it appears that he who does not know everything does not know the self.

Now he certifies that one who does not know one thing does not know all things:

49. If one does not know one substance with its unlimited modifications, or the unlimited number of kinds of substances how should he know everything simultaneously?

The self is merely knowledge, since only as consisting of knowledge is it a knower. Knowledge, on the other hand, is a great generality (*chaitanya-samanya-mahiman*), consisting of illumination (*pratibhasa-maya*) and occurring in the individual souls. And this (great-generality) penetrates infinite species (*visheshas*) (species of consciousness=forms of knowledge=notions concerning objects) in phenomenal form; and these again find their basis in the modifications of all substances.

Suppose, now, that one cannot by his self-experience perceive the self in this form of a great generality which in phenomenal form penetrates infinite species, based on the modifications of all substances; how could this man embrace in his perception all the modifications of substances, which modifications are the basis of the infinite species in phenomenal form penetrated by a great-generality in phenomenal form? Thus it appears that he who does not know the self does not know all things. So then it is proved that from omniscience arises self-knowledge, from self-knowledge omniscience. Consequently, although knower and knowable really differ from the self, which, consisting only of knowledge, possesses consciousness in itself, yet the phenomenon and that which appears encounter each other in their common condition in such a way that it is totally impossible to separate them; so then everything is as it were implanted (*nikhata*) in the self. And, if this were not so, then, since the knowledge would not meet with complete consciousness in the self, neither could the knowledge be proved to belong to a single complete self.

Now he certifies that omnipresence of knowledge does not take place by a process going on successively:

50. If the knowledge of the knower arises by way of successive awareness of the objects, then it is not eternal, not the result of the-annihilation-of-*karman*, and not omnipresent.

Knowledge which arises by supporting itself successively now on this, then on that object is not eternal; for it arises whilst relating to one object, and perishes whilst it is directed towards another object. Neither is it due-to-*karman*-annihilation; for it receives one specialized-form (*vyakti*) and again another through the arising of *karmic* matter. Nor, lastly, is it omnipresent; for it is unable to dominate the infinite substances, places, time and forms-of-being (*dravya-kshetra-kala-bhava*).

Now it is settled that omnipresence of knowledge is secured simply by a process of simultaneity:

51. The (knowledge) of the *Jina* [(*jonham=jaina-jnanam* (*Tatparyavrtti*)=*jainam* (*Tattva-dipika*). Oh the grandeur of (that) knowledge, it knows simultaneously all things, which are constantly altered by the three times, in their entirety in all places and varieties.

Knowledge due to the annihilation of *karman* is a supreme greatness of knowledge, an abode of transcendence. When knowledge proceeds by basing itself simultaneously on all objects, then it assumes an eternal nature owing to its finding a place for the appearances of all knowable objects, steady as if carved by an axe (*tankotkirna*), and its *kshayika*-ness appears with its true nature, manifested by the fact that it reaches all individual-objects (*vyakti*).

Discerning, in its entirety, the great-multitude of all objects (*sarvartha-sambhutim* corresponds with *sarvatra sambhavam* in the *gatha*), constantly altered by the three times and possessing a manifoldness due to innumerable genera—this knowledge, displaying a wonderful grandeur, is omnipresent, inasmuch as it simultaneously arrives at the innumerable substances, places, times and forms-of-being.

Now, summarizing, he denies, in the case of an action of comprehension (*jnapti*) by a knower, bondage as fruit of the action:

52/1. The self does not evolve into the objects, does not grasp them, and does not arise in them [i.e. is not produced by them or become one of them], although it knows them; therefore it is said to be free from bondage.

In *sutra*, 43 the author has taught that, when the particles of material *karman* are at the rising stage, then in consequence thereof, the soul while being conscious of this, evolves itself into infatuation, attachment and aversion, and thus being united with action in the form of evolution into the knowable object, experiences bondage as fruit of that action; but this is not due to knowledge, since bondage was at the outset explained as the fruit of the action of evolution into the object.

And since in *sutra* 32 he has ascribed to the pure self a non-existence of actions such as evolution into objects, bondage, in the form of the fruit of action, does not happen to the self, though an action of awareness or understanding (*jnapti*) takes place, since it does not evolve into the objects, does not grasp them, or arise in them.

"When owing to the absence of infatuation the self, although knowing completely and simultaneously everything, present, future and past, does not evolve into 'the other (*para,* the other),' all its *karmic* matter being hewn off (annihilated), then it remains liberated, a manifestation of knowledge, illuminating separately and non-separately the threefold world, whilst the knowable appearances are swallowed (*pita,* i.e. drunk, enjoyed) by the expansion of its mightily unfolded understanding." (PS *Kalash* 4)

Here ends the section KNOWLEDGE

Now, detailing the characteristic nature of happiness, not divided from knowledge, he considers how both knowledge and happiness are sometimes to be abandoned and sometimes to be accepted:

EXPOSITION OF JOY (VERSES 53-68)

53. There is with reference to objects, material (*murta)* and immaterial, a supra-sensorial and a sensorial knowledge; and similar is the case of happiness; what then of these is the best, should be known.

Now knowledge and happiness which are material and born from the senses are one thing. And the immaterial and supra-sensorial are a second. Of these four the immaterial and supra-sensorial should be known as by reason of their superiority acceptable.

The former of these, arising—by means of material energies of psychic-attention for which combined-annihilation-and-precipitation-of-*karman* is characteristic—from such-like sense-organs, is accidental, owing to dependence on outside factors; it proceeds by succession, finds opposition, is subject to increase and decrease; for this reason this knowledge and happiness, as being destructive, should be abandoned.

The second pair, arising, by means of immaterial energies of self-evolution, which are obedient to intelligence and are unaccompanied, from the like supra-sensorial evolutions of natural thought-appearance, is eternal owing to its absolute dependence on the self; it proceeds simultaneously, does not find opposition, is devoid of increase and decrease; for this reason this knowledge and happiness, as being primary, should be accepted.

Now he praises supra-sensorial knowledge as acceptable, being a means to supra-sensorial happiness:

54. The knowledge of him who beholds the immaterial, the supra-sensorial in material objects (*murtani)*, and the hidden, complete, (embracing) the self and the other, is called *pratyaksha* (direct/ immediate):[13]

Now supra-sensorial knowledge beholds the immaterial, the supra-sensorial even in material objects, and the hidden complete (read *yat sakalam*), whether included in own or in other. Such knowledge surely is a seer, owing to its immediateness, with reference to— immaterial (*amurta*) substances, such as the principles of motion and stationariness, material, but supra-sensorial substances, such as the ultimate atom, that which is hidden in respect of substance, e.g. time; that which is hidden in respect of place, e.g. the *pradeshas* of space locates outside the world; that which is hidden in time, e.g. non-present modifications; that which is hidden in respect of forms-of-being, namely fine (*sukshma*) modifications latent within gross (*sthula*) modifications; thus with reference to all things, distinguished as own and other.

Immediate knowledge indeed, bound to a single self, called the *aksha* (*aksha*, from which *pratyaksha* is derived, is taken as a synonym of *atman*), and having the immediacy of its manifested infinite purity and beginningless connection with the generality of perfect intelligence (*siddha-chaitanya-samanya*), does not search for exterior means (read *itara-samagrim*), enjoys infinity, because of its possession of infinite energies. Knowledge enjoying such prestige, seeing that the knowable appearances no more outgo knowledge than combustible appearances the fire, what can resist such knowledge? Therefore it is acceptable (*upadeya*).

But now he rebukes sensorial knowledge, cause of sensorial pleasure, as deserving rejection:

55. The soul in itself immaterial or incorporeal,[14] becoming incorporeal in material form and then, apprehending with this material (form or body), the material (world), sometimes knows and sometimes does not know that-which-is-fit-for-knowledge *(yogya)*.

Sensorial knowledge requires a material instrument-of-perception (*upalambhaka*) and a material object-of-perception (*upalabhya*). The soul, in possession of this, although itself immaterial, occupying the material body, provided with the five sensories, apprehends with the material body, as instrument of perception, by way of the applications of its forces (*bala*)[15] to the production of notion (*jnapti*), the material thing, predominantly touch, etc., which, having acquired the property-of-being-perceptible (*upalabhyata*), is fit-for-knowledge: and by this apprehension the soul sometimes—repeatedly—if pureness recurs in regard to it, grasps the object, but sometimes, owing to the lack of pureness, does not grasp, by reason of indirectness (*parokshatva*).

Indirect knowledge—based on an extreme unsteadiness in the self, which, in consequence of being enveloped in a knot of very dense ignorance-darkness, has its eye closed and in spite of its beginningless connection with the generality of perfect intelligence is unable by itself to distinguish the object, and distracted in a search for the apparatus of exterior means, which it partially obtains and partially does not obtain; excessively enfeebled through the loss of its unlimited energy; and, though aiming at evolution into the other, at every step disappointed because the wrestler Great-Infatuation (*maha-moha*) is still alive—deserves according to deeper truth (*paramarthatah*) to be regarded as non-comprehension (*anupalambha*). Hence it should be abandoned.

Now he observes that, since the organs of sense are not capable of proceeding simultaneously towards the totality of their objects, sensorial knowledge must be abandoned:

56. Touch, taste, smell, colour and sound are the material objects (*pudgalas*) for the sense-organs; the sense-organs do not grasp them simultaneously.

The substrata of touch, taste, smell and colour, moreover sound (sound is a material substance according to Jainism), are material objects, fit for being grasped by the sense-organs. But even they are not grasped by the sense-organs simultaneously; for the requisite energy due to destructive subsidence is not present. In the case of the sense-organs the interior discerning efficacy, which is termed destructive-subsidence of [knowledge-obscuring]- *karman*, proceeds successively, like a crow's eyeball,[16] and is incapable of illuminating in many directions; hence, although the communications between sense-organs and objects are open, an awareness (*avabodha*) of the objects of all the senses will not take place simultaneously, because of the indirectness (of sensorial experience).

Now he ascertains that sensorial knowledge is not direct:

57. The sense-organs are called an exterior (*para*) substance, and not an innate nature of the self; how then could that which is grasped by them be direct or immediate perception for the self?

Absolute knowledge (*kevala-jnana*), belonging to the absolute (*kevala*) self, is immediate. But that which arises through observation by means of the sense-organs, which have not the slightest connection with the innate nature of the self and are allotted to the group of exterior substances, inasmuch as they are provided with a separate existence, cannot be immediate-perception for the self.

Now he gives in addition a sub-definition of indirect and immediate knowledge:

58. Knowledge of objects from another (agency, i.e. the senses) is called indirect; but, if knowledge is acquired by the soul alone (*kevala-jiva*), then it is indeed direct.

If discrimination of a thing which has become an object-of-knowledge to us is brought about by something other, which functions as a means, whether inner sensorium, a sense-organ, information by another person, a positive-probans (*upalabdhi*), latent-physical-impression (*samskara*), or light, etc., then this knowledge, arising from another, is indicated as indirect.

But discrimination which, disregarding every exterior substance, whether internal-organ, organ-of-sense, information by another person, positive-probans, latent-physical-impression, or light, and whatever else of that kind, and taking its own nature as sole cause, in its rise embraces simultaneously all the modifications of all substances,—this discrimination is indicated as direct knowledge, since it arises from the self alone. Here accordingly this, being means to natural (*sahaja*) pleasure, is approved as the Great-Direct-Knowledge.

Now he puts forward this immediate knowledge as supremely real happiness:

59. Knowledge, self-born, complete, extended over an infinite number of objects, stainless, devoid of stages such as avagraha (apprehension of an object or sensation), is called exclusive joy.

Since it is self-born, complete, extented over an infinite number of objects, without stain, devoid of stages such as *avagraha*, this immediate knowledge is ascertained to be exclusive joy. For the one definition of happiness is absence of perturbation.

Indirect knowledge, in fact, is excessively perturbed by dependence on something else; since it arises from something else; closure of the other doors of knowledge; since it is incomplete; wish to know other objects; since it is connected with [only] a certain number of objects; imperfect awareness (*a-samyag-avabodha*); since it is stained; fatigue of successively taking up the objects; since it is bound to stages such as *avagraha*.

Hence it is not ultimately real (*paramarthatah*) happiness.

But this knowledge is unperturbed by reason of–

self-dependence, since, being born from itself, it stands of itself extending with great expansion over the inner nature of the beginningless generality of knowledge;

opening of all doors, since, complete in the form of the psychic-attention of supreme, immediate knowledge, it stands pervading all the spacial units of the self (read: *samastatma-pradeshan*);

freedom from all desire to know things, since, extended over an infinite number of objects, it stands pervading a supreme multifariety wherein are exhausted the knowable appearances of all things;

perfect awareness, since, stainless, transcending all *karmans* which impede its complete energy, it stands pervading its own nature brilliant with clearest light;

freedom from the trouble of successively taking up the objects, since, devoid of stages such as *avagraha*, it stands pervading the world and that which is beyond the world, which simultaneously yield up their characteristic three-time nature.

Hence it is ultimate happiness.

Now he refutes the opinion that for the Absolute-Sage even exclusive happiness does not exist, since by the door of evolution trouble (*kheda)* is possible:

60. The knowledge, which is called Absolute or omniscience (*kevalajnana*) is happiness, and it is evolution; no trouble therefrom is mentioned; for the destructive *karmans* are gone[17] to annihilation, i.e. destroyed.

As to this: what trouble? what evolution? what difference between pure knowledge and joy, so that pure knowledge should not be joy?

The destructive *karmans* are abodes of trouble; but mere evolution simply is not such. For, since the destructive *karmans*, creating the great infatuation and instilling the notion of A in regard to non-A, as with one disordered in intellect, cause (read *parinamayanti*) the self to evolve in regard to an object to be discerned, therefore they become a source (*nidana*) of trouble (for the soul), which grows wearied in evolving again and again from object to object. But in pure knowledge, as these are absent, how can there be outbreaks of distress?

And, since Absolute Knowledge, evolving by itself, possessing an unlimited characteristic nature, resembling a picture-wall (*chitra-bhitti*), serving as locus for the manifestation of the manifoldness of the discernible appearances belonging to all objects (*padartha*) characterized by the three times—since this Absolute Knowledge is itself the evolution, how can there be any other evolution by which trouble can come to pass?

Add, since simply Absolute Knowledge—while, with its infinite energies in free play owing to absence of all impediments to its proper nature, it pervades the whole three-time appearance of world and non-world, yet stands in its aloofness absolutely immobile and having undistinguished from itself a freedom from perturbation which is the mark of happiness—is happiness, whence a difference between Absolute Knowledge and happiness?

Hence absolute knowledge should by all means be agreed to be exclusively joy.

Now again describing the identity of perfect knowledge with joy, he summarizes:

61. This knowledge reaches the limits of (all) objects; it is an intuition (*drshti*) expanded over the physical and super-physical universe; in it everything that is undesirable is destroyed, but everything desirable is attained.

Happiness indeed is caused by the absence of hindrances to one's innate nature. Intuition and intellect are the innate nature of the self. And there does not exist any hindrance to them, since they both open out at will, expanding over the world and the non-world and reaching the limits of objects. Hence happiness caused by this is, if we wish to express the non-difference (*abheda*), the characteristic nature of perfect knowledge. But, moreover, absolute knowledge is simply happiness, because in it all undesirables are given up and all desirables are obtained. For in the condition of absolute knowledge, since every ignorance which leads to pain, the opposite to the reaching of joy, perishes, and since complete knowledge, leading to joy, arises, therefore absolute knowledge is happiness—so enough of amplification!

Now he would have us believe that supremely-real (*paramarthika*) joy belongs only to Absolute-Sages:

62. The not-qualified (*abhavya*)[18] do not believe, when they hear that among joys the highest happiness is that of those whose destructive *karmans* have vanished; but the qualified admit it.

To those who have abundance of infatuating and other *karmans* there may be here a semblance of joy; but because of hindrances to their inner nature and because of perturbation it is an unreal (*aparamarthika*), popular use of the word "joy". But the holy Absolute-

Sages, whose destructive *karmans* are annihilated, being free from repugnance to their innate nature and from perturbation, have a joy supremely real, since the above described cause is present and the definition applies. Thus we must believe.

But those, not-qualified, who have not this belief, are far from the nectar-beverage of the joy of liberation, and only see the water-mass of a mirage. Those, again, who forthwith accept this world, worthy receptacles of auspicious bliss, are qualified-from near (*samasanna-bhavya*); but those who accept it for the future are qualified-from-far (*dura-bhavya*).

Now he examines the sensorial joy, not supremely real, of those who possess indirect knowledge (*paroksa-jnana*):

63. The lords of men, demons and gods, oppressed by their natural (*sahaja*) organs of sense, unable to withstand that misery, find pleasure in satisfying (*ramya*) objects.

Those creatures who through lack of immediate knowledge take refuge in indirect knowledge have a congenial affection for their organs of sense, which are the equipment therefor. So in these persons, having this affection for their sense-organs and, while devoured by the flaring *kala*-fire[19] of great infatuation, utterly longing and thirsty, like heated balls of iron (These cause an immediate evaporation of the water fallen on them), and unable to withstand the vehemence of this misery, there arises a satisfaction (*rati*) with these satisfying (*ramya*) objects, which serve to soothe their disease. Hence, since the sense-organs must be compared to a disease and the objects to means for soothing the disease, no really-true joy exists for those who have a limited knowledge (*chadmastha*).

Now he argues that misery is natural as long as there are sense-organs:

64. Know misery to be natural in those who find satisfaction in sense-objects; for, if this were not natural, there would not be any on their part for obtaining the objects of senses.

In those for whom these detestable sense-organs are alive (*jivad-avastha*) misery does not depend on accidental-conditions (*upadhi*), but is natural; for we see their satisfaction with the sense-objects.

We behold how, enslaved by the feelings of their incontrollable senses, they rush (*abhipata*) for objects, although on the point of perishing (*asanna-nipata*); like the elephant for the touch (*sparsha*) of the harlot she-elephant; the carp for the taste (*svada*) of the bait on the hook; the bee for the fragrance (*amoda*) of the *aravinda* on the point of closing; the moth for the visual-appearance (*rupa*) of the lamp-flame; the antelope for the sound (*svara*) of the hunter's song. But, if we could admit that their misery was not natural, then this activity of theirs towards sense-objects would not be seen any more than perspiration in one cured of cold fevers, use of *aranala*-gruel by a patient cured of inflammatory fever, salving with the *vata*-salve by one whose affection of the eye has passed, filling with calf's urine (read *vatsa-mutra*) by one who no longer suffers from ear-ache, application of a salve by one whose wound has closed. But it *is* seen. Hence the possessors of indirect knowledge, whose sense-organs are alive (read *jivadavasthendriyah*), are naturally subject to misery.

Now, in order to show the joy of the liberated self, he refutes the idea that the body is a means to joy:

65. The self, evolving naturally and obtaining the sense-objects desired and approachable to its touch, is itself pleasure; but the body is not.

To this self, even in the embodied condition, it is not the body that we perceive to be the means to the attainment of pleasure. For even then, while passing through an imperfect state due to the senses, which under the influence of pronounced delusion, as if they had quaffed maddening draughts, run after objects successively, deeming that "they are desired by us," the self, evolving by its own nature, which, though its main energy is obstructed, has knowledge, vision and power and is the cause of certain truth, of itself attains to happiness. But the body, since, because of its unconscious nature, it cannot be accepted as the cause of certitude of the evolution called happiness, surely does not function as happiness (In Jainism, the substance and its state are one and identical).

Now he confirms this:

66. The body indeed does not in any way cause pleasure to the transmigrating soul, even in heaven; but the self itself by virtue of the sense-objects becomes enjoyment or pain.

The tenet (*siddhanta*) here is that "the body, even when it is an angelic plastic body (*vaikriyika-sharira*), does not suffice for pleasure"; so that the self itself, by virtue of desirable or undesirable sense-objects, becomes pleasure or pain.

Now he illustrates how, inasmuch as the energy for evolving into pleasure belongs to the self itself, the objects are ineffectual:

67. When the eye of a person removes darkness, then there is no use for a lamp; similarly the self itself is pleasure, what use the sense-objects therefor?

Just as some night-walkers, inasmuch as their eyes possess energy for the removing of darkness, do not require for this purpose e.g. the radiance of a lamp, so for this self, in trans-migration as well as in liberation, evolving itself through the state of joy, what should avail the sense-objects, although uselessly sought by ignorant people under the idea that they are means for joy?

Now he confirms by an example [the view] that the innate nature of self is happiness:

68/1. As the sun is by itself a light, and is warm, and a god in the sky, so is the liberated soul (*siddha*) having knowledge, happiness and godhood in the world.

As the sun in the sky is by itself, without dependence on another cause, a light, since it abounds in the expanding brightness of its characteristic nature, radiant with a great quantity of light;

and as it is warm, because it enjoys a constant evolution into heat, as a piece of iron occasionally evolves into heat;

and as it is a god, since its innate nature is adapted to the continuous rise of the *nama-karman* of a god's condition;

similarly in our world the holy self itself, without dependence on another cause, is knowledge, since it is identical with an inborn consciousness, of unerring, unlimited energy capable of manifesting the self and "the other";

likewise it is happiness, since it is at ease owing to absence of perturbation and to complete delight originated from satisfaction with itself;

and likewise it is a god; for it possesses the characteristic nature of a divine soul, through its associations with majesty and laudation when it appears carved on the stone-columns of the minds of intelligent men, coloured by nearness to the realization of the essence of the self. Hence enough of sense-objects, which merely in appearance are means to the happiness of this self.

Here ends the explanation of JOY.

Next the chapter on GOOD EVOLUTION.

Now, entering upon the examination of the characteristic nature of sensorial joy, he propounds the characteristic nature of the means thereto:

GOOD (*SHUBHA*) PSYCHIC ATTENTION (VERSES 69-92)

69. The self which is attached to the veneration of the worthy Lord, ascetics and the teacher, to charity, to moral conduct (*su-shila*), to fasting and the like, is a self with good or auspicious (*shubha*) psychic-attention.[20]

When the self, transcending the stage of evil psychic-attention which shows itself as attachment to sense-objects and as hatred, the effect of which is misery, embraces the love of righteousness (*dharma*), a love which manifests itself as satisfaction with the veneration of the worthy Lord, the teacher and ascetics, with charity, moral precepts and fasting, then we may say that it has ascended the stage of good psychic-attention, which is a means to sensorial pleasure.

Now he describes sensorial pleasure as a result of good psychic-attention:

70. A self in possession of the good, whether it be an animal, man or god, receives in that period manifold sensorial pleasure.

By its fitness for good psychic-attention, which is a means to sensorial pleasure, this self, having reached one or other of the three stages of animal, man or god, which stages are the place therefor, obtains manifold sensorial pleasure, as long as it abides there.

Now, having thus extolled sensorial pleasure, he denounces it as misery:

71. Happiness born from innate nature is not in the Teaching [of *Jina*] assigned even to gods. Pained by the sensations of the body, they take pleasure in enjoyable sense-objects.

The inhabitants of heaven, surely, are the foremost of those who experience sensorial pleasure; yet even for them there is no innate happiness: on the contrary, innate misery is observed in them. For, besides themselves as they are with the torment of the demon (*pishacha*), their body, i.e. of the five sense-organs, they fly to delightful sense-objects, in place of falling from precipices.

After having by argumentation (*yukti*) premised that sensorial pleasure should be classified as misery, he now premises that good psychic-attention, which effects merit, cause of sensorial pleasure, is not different from the class of psychic-attention, the evil attention, which effects sin, cause of pain.

72. **If men, hell-inhabitants, animals and gods, have misery, born from the body, then how is there in these souls (distinction of) good and evil psychic-attention?**

If even gods, etc., in the plenitude of their merits, gained by good psychic-attention, and the hell-inhabitants, etc., involved in the ruin of sin, due to evil attention, both indistinguishably experience simply misery, conditioned by the body, i.e. by the five sense-organs; then, since both miss innate happiness of transcendental nature (*parmarthatah*) a relation of separateness (*prthaktva*) between good and evil psychic-attention does not hold.

Now, having admitted, for the purpose of refutation, a separate fruit-bearing merit, caused by good psychic-attention, he raises a point:

73. **Those who, bearing a thunderbolt as weapon (i.e. Indra) or ruling an empire, nourish the body, etc., by enjoyments, due to good psychic-attention, attached thereto, seem to be happy.**

Because *Shakras* and Emperors, thriving in body, etc., by enjoyments available at will, and extremely fond of these pleasures, as leeches of foul blood, give the impression of being happy, therefore fruit-bearing merits are seen to have arisen from good psychic-attention.

Now he suggests that the merits just admitted are causes of the germ of misery:

74. **Though there are manifold merits, resulting from (good psychic states of) evolution, they make the souls, including those of the gods, to thirst for sense-objects (*vishaya trasna*).**

If it is granted that there exists various merits, whose origin is due to the evolution through good psychic-attention, then these necessarily make a thirst for sense-objects to arise in all the transmigrating souls, including even those whose food is nectar. Assuredly, without thirst the activity of all transmigrating souls towards sense-objects, as of leeches towards bad blood, would not be seen; and it is seen. Let us therefore not deny that merits are a base (*ayatana*) for such craving or thirst for sense objects.

Now he proclaims the triumph of merit as germ of misery:

75. **These souls, then, their thirst roused and made unhappy by thirstings, wish for obtaining till death the pleasures of sense-objects,**

thereby being burnt by misery.

Then all these transmigrating souls, including the thirsty (gods), their thirst roused and made utterly unhappy by thirstings, even by those originated from merit, since this is a germ of misery, expect pleasures from sense-objects, like water from the mirage. And, not capable of withstanding the tremendous burning of this misery, they experience, like leeches, (the pleasures of the) sense-objects, until they die. For, as leeches, gradually overcome by the victorious sprout-of-misery (*duhkhankura*) having its root in thirst, covet the bad sweet blood and even while enjoying it are afflicted with annihilation, so these adherents of merit, like the adherents of sin, gradually dominated by the triumphant sprout of misery, of which the germ is thirst, covet the sense-objects and, enjoying them, are afflicted until the end. Therefore merits may be considered as causes of actual misery in the guise of happiness.

Now he explains in manifold ways how sensorial pleasure originated from merit is misery:

76. Therefore that happiness which is acquired by means of the senses, is dependent, accompanied by obstacles or distractions, interrupted or terminable, cause of bondage, and unequal is indeed misery.

Sensorial pleasure, although originated from merit, is actually misery; for it is dependent, accompanied by obstacles or distractions, interrupted, cause of bondage, unequal.

It is dependent; for it rests on something else, since it has in something else its condition.

It is accompanied by obstacles or distractions; for it is utterly confused, since it is attended by different longings, such as hunger, thirst, etc.

It is interrupted; for oppositions are noticed in it, since we realize it as proceeding by the rise of good emotional-*karman* (*sad-vedya=sata-vedaniya*) disturbed by the rise of bad emotional-*karman*.

It is a cause of bondage; for in its outcome it is hard to bear, since it is covered with a thick mass of dust of *karman*, collecting in the train of the army of the vices, passion, etc., trailing along the road of sensual enjoyments.

It is unequal; for it is utterly unsteady, since it evolves through increase and decrease. And it is, indeed, misery only. Thus even merit turns out to be, like sin, the means of misery.

Now, certifying that there is no difference between merit and demerit, he summarizes:

77. He who will not believe that there is nothing particular or special (*vishesha*) between merit (*punya*) and sin (*papa*) [i.e. there is no difference between the two or the two are similar in the way or sense stated above] moves about, covered with infatuation, in the terrible cycle of transmigratory existence (*samsara*).

Thus, in the way described, a duality of merit and sin, like a duality of good and evil psychic-attention or of pleasure and pain, does not, according to deeper transcendental reality (*paramarthatah*), exist; for on both sides equally we have not to do with a property really belonging to the soul.

But he who, conceiving an egotistical (*ahankarika*) difference between this pair—like two gold and iron fetters!—depending upon the desire or expectation for future sense-pleasures (*nidan*), thinking "I am the cause (*nidana*)[21] of my prosperity, for instance of my rank as *Indra* (Lord of Heaven)," still more leans on attachment (*anuraga*) to righteousness (*dharma*), experiences bodily misery as long as *samsara* lasts, his ability for pure psychic-attention being obscured, because the region or wall of his consciousness has become coloured (*uparakta*).

Having thus settled that there is no particular difference between good and evil psychic-attention, now, dismissing all duality of attachment and aversion, and resolved to destroy misery totally, he abides in pure psychic-attention:

78. He who understands the reality of things thus and no more entertains attachment or aversion towards objects, thereby purifying psychic-attention, puts an end to pain originating from the body.

He who has correctly distinguished the characteristic nature of things, by completely perceiving the identity of the good and evil psychical-states, and completely banishes attachment and aversion towards all objects with all their modifications, dependent as they are upon distinction of self and other, gives up every dependence on other substances, because he is utterly pure in his psychic-attention; and he puts an end to bodily pain; like fire, which, leaving a piece of iron and not adhering to the essence (*sara*) of the iron, no longer undergoes the series of violent blows by the hammer. Therefore, this pure psychic-attention is my only refuge.

"If now I, although bent upon conduct free from every censurable activity (of mind, body and speech) (*yoga*), do not eradicate infatuation, etc., in consequence of my adherence to good psychic-attention, then the attainment of the pure self is entirely impossible for me." So he stands up and gets ready in full might:

79/1. If any one, after giving up sinful undertakings and even applying himself to good conduct, does not get rid of infatuation, etc., then he does not attain the pure self.

Although one has taken up the strictest doctrinal [equanimous][22] conduct, characterized by the rejection of every censurable activity (*yoga*), if he, visited by the strolling lady, called Life-of-good-psychic-attention, dopes not make an end (read *vidheyatam vikirati*) to his submission to the army of infatuation, then it is impossible for him, whilst the danger of great misery is near to grasp the not-confused (*avipluta*) self. Therefore, I gird myself for the victory over the army of infatuation.

In answer to the question "how must I gain this victory over the army of infatuation?" he now examines the means:

80. He who knows the *Arahanta* [the worthy Lord] with reference to substance, quality and modification knows the self; his infatuation indeed perishes.

He who discriminately knows the *Arhanta* (the worthy Lord) with reference to substantiality, possession of qualities and modifications, surely knows the self, because from the internal, self-referential point of view (*nishchaya*) there is no difference between the two. The *Arhat*, moreover, possesses a purified form of self, like thoroughly molten gold; therefore on discriminately knowing him we discriminately know every self.

In this case the substance is the constant (*anvaya*); the quality is the qualifier (*visheshana*) of the constant; the modifications are the divergences (*vyatireka*) in the constant.

In the holy *Arhat*, pure in every respect, we may see a threefold similarity to our own mind:

That which is the constant, indicated as being "this conscious being," is the substance; the qualifier, which is based on the constant and indicated as "consciousness," is the quality; the divergences in the constant, which are separated from each other, inasmuch as their extension covers a time measured by one moment (*samaya*),[23] are the modifications or, what is the same thing, the nodes in the mental-changes (*cnid-vivartana*).

Now, if anyone considers the three times as one and sums up the mental-changes in consciousness only, as pearls in one long necklace; and if he then puts an end[24] to the transitory impression[25] of a separate qualifier and a thing-to-be-qualified, and allows the consciousness to be comprised (*antarhita*) in conscious being, as the whiteness in the necklace; and if he distinguishes merely the self in the manner of the mere necklace, then the differences between agent, object-of-deed and deed in successive moments will die away; and, whilst he thus becomes aware of an actionless state-of-being (*bhava*), which is only consciousness-as-such, he will resemble a jewel whose spotless light shines motionless, and the darkness of his infatuation will necessarily fade, since it has no longer a basis. If so, then I have acquired the means for vanquishing the army of infatuation.

Then he keeps awake with the thought "though I have obtained this talisman, there is the thief, 'heedlessness'. (*pramada*):[26]

81. If the soul, whose infatuation (deluded view) has gone and which has properly grasped the reality of the equanimous nature of the self, forsakes attachment and aversion, then it realises the pure self.

If, by the means thus described in their characteristic nature, one throws off infatuation and receives the perfect truth about the self, and if one then eradicates attachment and aversion, he realizes the pure self. But, should again and again these two (feelings) return to him, then, under the influence of heedlessness robbed of the talisman of the comprehension (*upalambha*) of the truth of the pure self, he is inwardly troubled. Therefore, I must remain fully awake, in order to expel attachment and aversion.

Now he expounds the view that "this is the one, supremely-real, path towards the Highest Good, shown by the Holy Ones after having experienced it themselves personally:"

82/1. All the *Arahantas*, after having in the manner described, have destroyed the particles of *karman* and teaching the same, became emancipated. Homage to them!

Since all the holy Spiritual Guides, who experienced their progressive career in the past and who, after their own experience of the destruction of all *karmic* particles in the one self same way, without becoming aware of any twofoldness (for no other way is possible!), then, having as highest authorities taught it thus to others desirous of liberation in present and future times, obtained supreme bliss, therefore that there is no other road to *nirvana* is ascertained. Enough now of loquacity! My thought is settled! Homage to the Holy Ones!

Now he explains the innate nature and the roles of infatuation, which way lays the attainment of the pure self:

83. An infatuated (*mudha*) state (*bhava*) of the soul with reference to substance, etc., is called *moha* (infatuation); covered (*avachchanna*) with this, the soul is agitated, having acquired attachment or aversion.

That infatuated state of the soul, as of one intoxicated with drink, a state characterized by not understanding the truth about substances, qualities and modifications, as described (in *gatha* 80), is called infatuation. The self which has its self form covered with this, conceiving the other "strange" substance[27] as if it were the substance of self, the quality of other substance as if a quality of self, the modifications of other substance as if states of self; taking hold (*upadana*) day after day of the other strange substance, since the psychical impression of this is full-grown and stronger; proceeding in duality (the opposed feelings of pleasure and pain), when there is really non-duality, in consequence of the preferences (*ruchi*) of the execrable organs of sense; embracing attachment and aversion with reference to agreeable (*ruchita*) and disagreeable things; splitting into two like a dam, beaten against by the rush of swollen water-masses—thus it becomes entirely subject to unrest (*kshobha*)·(in *gatha* 7). Therefore this infatuation possesses three roles (*bhumika*) of infatuation, attachment and aversion.

Now, designating infatuation a cause of undesirable consequences, he expounds its annihilation in all its three roles:

84. Manifold bondage takes place for the soul which is evolved through infatuation, attachment and aversion; therefore these must be destroyed.

For him (whose mental-eyes are) closed in non-apprehension of the truth and who evolves through infatuation (*a*) or attachment, (*b*) or aversion, (*c*) as for an elephant who either has got into a trap covered by a layer of leaves (*i*) or who has become attached, (*ii*) to the body of a harlot of a female elephant, or who is enraged and violent[28], (*iii*) at the sight of a hostile elephant–there is manifold bondage. Therefore, this infatuation, attachment and aversion, as causes of undesirable consequences, must be radically destroyed by him who wishes for liberation.

Now he discerns that these (three vices), discovered by their distinctive marks, must be destroyed as soon as they appear:

85. Wrong perception of things, i.e. other than as they really are, absence of a feeling of compassion[29] towards animals and men, and indulgence in sense-objects, these are the characteristics (*linga*) of infatuation.

Infatuation, which has three roles inasmuch as it admits of taking, according to its three characteristics, the nature of infatuation through acceptance of wrong perception and knowledge about objects, through a feeling of compassion towards animals and men, who are only worthy of observation, the thought of attachment through inclination towards desired objects, and the thought of aversion through dislike of undesired objects, should be killed at its very rise.

Now he considers another means to the destruction of infatuation:

86. By him[30] who understands the reality of things as they are from the scripture of the *Jina* with intuition and other direct means of valid knowledge, etc., the accumulation of infatuation is destroyed; therefore the scripture must be studied.

Whereas from a knowing of the *Arhat* in his inner nature as substance, qualities and modifications a similar knowledge of the self was accepted above (see comments on verse 80) as a means to the destruction of infatuation, that indeed requires another means, as follows:

The accumulation of infatuation, which causes the mental-habit (*samskara*) of attachment to that which is not the truth, is destroyed by him:

> who has reached the first stage (of the road towards liberation),
>
> and who, having mastered the Word as source of knowledge, trustworthy in every respect and guaranteed by the authority of the Omniscient, plays with it and has at his command a full energy of special assuredness (*samvedana*), emphasized by the mental-habit (of studying this Word),
>
> and who by perception or any other means of knowledge not contradictory thereto, which give an ebullition of bliss, and which impart a splendour of bliss to the mind of feeling and intelligent men, distinguishes (read

paricchindatah) the totality of things according to truth.

Therefore the utmost application to study-of-the-sacred-word, well applied with an evolution supported by the knowledge of the meaning (*bhava*), is another means to the destruction of infatuation.

Now he considers how in the sacred-word of the *Jinendra* the discrimination of objects is set out:

87. Substances, their qualities and modifications are understood by the term *artha* (object); among these the soul substance is the substratum of the qualities and modifications; thus runs the teaching.

Substances, qualities and modifications, although designated specially, may be united under a single term, *artha*. Here the substances are *arthas*, because they go (read *iyrati* instead of *prati*) to the qualities and modifications or because they "are gone to" (*aryante*) by the qualities and modifications; the qualities are *arthas*, because they go to the substances for an abode or because they "are gone to" by the substances which offer the abode; the modifications are *arthas*, because they go (read *krama-parinameneyrati* instead of *parinameneti*) to the substances in as far as (they form) a successive evolution or they "are gone to" by the substances in as far as (these are subject to) a successive evolution.

For just as gold, which we will take here as an example of a substance, going (read *iyrat* instead of *iyarti*) to such qualities as yellow, etc., to such modifications as a ring, etc., or "gone to" by them, is an *artha*; and just as the qualities yellow, etc., going to the gold for an abode or "gone to" by the gold which functions as abode (read *asrayabhuta* instead of *aryabhuta*), are *arthas*; and just as the modifications, ring, etc., going (read *kramaparinameneyratah*) to the gold in its successive evolutions or "gone to" by the gold in its successive evolutions, are *arthas*, so elsewhere.

And just as in the case of this gold, its qualities, such as yellowness and its modifications, such as a ring, the gold is "the self" of the qualities "yellowness," etc., and of the modifications "ring," etc., because they do not exist separately (*prthak*) from the gold, so in the case of substance, qualities and modifications in general the substance is "the self" of the qualities and the modifications, because they do not exist separately from the substance.

Now, since, even when we accept the teaching of Lord *Jina*, which is a means to the destruction of infatuation, it is manly effort that produces an effect, he sets manly effort to work:

88. Whosoever, having grasped the teaching of the *Jina*, destroys infatuation, attachment and aversion, attains within a short time emancipation from all miseries.

Whosoever on this very long path (of *samsara*), full of ever restless unrest (cf. *Tattva-dipika* on verse 46), has in some way or other obtained the teachings of the kingly *Jina*, and brings it down, like a sharp sword's edge, with force on his infatuation, attachment and hatred, quickly obtains liberation from all misery; and no other operation, as a gloved hand, is capable of that. Therefore with all my might I resort to manly effort for the destruction of infatuation.

The destruction of infatuation follows solely from discriminating (*viveka*) between the self (*sva*) and "the other" (*para*).

Therefore, he exerts himself to effect this partition of self and other:

89. If, one really knows the self as constituted of knowledge, and the other, both as connected with (their own) substantial nature, then he effects the annihilation of infatuation.

Whoso according to strict examination distinguishes the self, connected with its own, spiritual, substantiality, and "the other," connected with the appropriates "strange" substantiality, he, having thus completely attained discrimination between self and other, destroys infatuation completely. Therefore I exert myself for discrimination between self and other.

Now he summarizes the attainment of the discrimination between self and other must by all means be effected with the aid of the Scriptures:

90. Therefore in accordance with the teaching of the *Jina* one should understand the self and the other among substances by means of [or with regard to] their qualities, if his soul wishes for itself freedom from infatuation.

By means of some of the infinitely-many qualities mentioned in the Scriptures, namely by means of those which have in addition to generality a characterizing effect (*visheshana*), so as to exclude application to something else, let intelligent people whose minds are inclined to the giving up of infatuation take up, among the endless series of substances, the discrimination between self and other.

To wit, this intelligence which is mine, which belongs to me, which by its fullness of internal and external light is fit for discrimination of self and other, and which, being without another thing as condition, is self-caused (*svatah siddha*)—by means of this intelligence which, apart from any other substance, either homogeneous or heterogeneous, abides in my self, I know myself's self as a substance firm in the three times.

Likewise by means of characteristics which, excluding any other substance, possess separateness (*prthaktva*) and always abide in the same particular substance I examine strictly (read *nishchinomi*) space, *dharma* (the principle of motion), *adharma* (the principle of rest), time, matter and the strange soul, which are all substances firm in the three times. So then I am not space, not *dharma*, not *adharma*, not time, not matter, not another soul, because amid all this ordered multitude of things, resembling the mass of light of many lamps lit in one apartment, my intelligence not swearing from its characteristic nature, shows myself to be something apart. So then for this self, which has determined the discrimination of the self and the other, the sprout of infatuation which causes agitation (*vikara*) would not come forth.

Now he considers how attainment of Duty does not take place without belief in the doctrine taught by the *Jina*:

91. He who, in his state of *shramanya*, does not believe in these categories (*padarthas*), with their related generality of existence and various particularities, is not a *shramana*, therefore *dharma* does not accrue to him.

He who, while controlling himself by ascetism, does not accept with belief, or define, by means of the distinction between self and other, the substances, which obey a general nature, inasmuch as they enjoy a similar existence, and which are yet accompanied by particularities, inasmuch as they possess an existence of characteristic nature, is really no ascetic. Therefore the attainment of *dharma*, which consists in the attainment of the essence of the self, free from affections (*anuraga*), cannot take place, just as we cannot expect gold in the case of a person who, not distinguishing between particles of sand and gold, washes dust.

After having, with the words "I rely upon the tranquillity leading to *nirvana*," introduced (in verse 5) the subject-matter and having, with the words "the conduct is *dharma*; *dharma* is defined as equanimity, examined (in verse 7) the *dharma* of equanimity, he began (in verse 8) with the words "it is taught that substance possesses the nature of that through which it evolves," etc., to explain in what the *dharma* of the self consists. Then, in order to explain this, with the verse (11) "When the self whose self evolves through *dharma* is conjoined with pure psychic-attention, it reaches happiness undisturbed," he began to discuss pure psychic-attention as a means to the attainment of the happiness of *nirvana*; then good and evil psychic-attention, contraries, were rejected (cf. 46), and the nature of pure psychic-attention was described; finally, emphasizing the innate knowledge and happiness of the soul, which arise by grace of this (pure attention), he detailed the characteristic nature of consciousness (*samvedana* and *jnana* are equivalent here) and of pleasure.

Therefore, having with attention attained, by the grace of his pure psychic-attention, a total absence of longings for what is "strange" (to the soul), whilst he resorts to a behaviour, lordly and proud (or should we read *atma-trptam* instead of *atma-drptam*?) of the self, he now attains complete acquittance of his task, becomes entirely unperturbed, and, with the transitory-impression of preference-and-dislike (*bheda*) faded away, stands fast in the thought "I myself personally am *dharma*."

92/1. That noble-minded *shramana*, whose deluded view is destroyed, who is well conversant with the Scriptures, and who has established himself in conduct of detachment, is described as *dharma* itself.

It is certainly my wish that the self may become *dharma*: this is hindered only by an external perception-infatuation. And this infatuation is destroyed by conversancy with Scripture and knowledge of the self; then for me it will never come into re-existence. So this my self, with its earthly career guided by a conduct devoid of attachment, becomes itself Duty, and, since all its hindrances are thrown off, for ever remains steadfast. Enough of disquisition!

Hail to Holy Tradition (*shabda-brahman*), preached by the Lord *Jina* and sealed with the *syadvada* (the formula "*quodammodo*")! Hail to the acceptance of the truth of the self, which acceptance is based on that (tradition) and by grace whereof the knot of infatuation, tied since the beginning of *samsara*, is at once unfastened! Hail to pure psychic-attention, consisting in conduct utterly free from attachment, by grace whereof the self is become itself *dharma* !

"The self, becoming itself *dharma*, having attained pure psychic-attention, and, whilst it enjoys the flowing forth of an eternal bliss, engrossed into the principle (*tattva*) of knowledge, obtains the glory which without the slightest agitation shines motionlessly forth from the jewel-lamp spontaneously flashing with ebullient radiance (*sphurjaj-jyotih* is here the first member of a compound. A "jewel-lamp," a fabulous lamp in which a jewel is used for a light)". (PS *Kalash* 5)

"Having thus ascertained without doubt and as it is, the principle of knowledge whose substratum is the soul, and for this purpose desiring to know the principle of the knowable, with a view to its tranquillity, it considers all objects from the point of view of quality, substance and modification, in order that the sprout of infatuation may never again manifest itself." (PS *Kalash* 6)

Here ends, in the *Lamp of Truth,* a commentary on the *Essence of the Scripture,* composed by Amrtacandra-Suri, the first scriptural book, called the *Teaching of the Principle concerning Knowledge.*

Book II

The Principle of the Knowable

NOTE: II. 1, II. 2, etc. denotes *gatha* (verse) No. 1, 2, etc. of Book II in serial number, while *gatha* Nos. 93/2, 94, etc. at the end of translation denote consecutive numbering of *gathas* starting from Book 1, which tallies with the *gatha* numbering of the original *Prakrit* text given at the end of this edition and most editions of the work in Hindi.

SUBSTANCE IN GENERAL (VERSES 93-126)

Now begins the explanation of the principle (*tattva*) concerning the knowable. Here he explains the proper characteristic nature of the thing as substance, quality and modification:

II. 1 The object, indeed, consists of substance; the substances are said to have their essence in qualities. And through these [i.e. both substance and qualities] are the modifications. Those, who are deluded *(moodh)* in regard to the modifications, are *para-samaya*, i.e. those who hold the view of reality of things, including the self, "other" than what it is.[31] (93/2)

(1a) Whatever object (*padartha*) is distinguished by us consists of substance (*dravya*), inasmuch as it results from the substance, which is an aggregation (*samudaya*) of cross-wise-generality (*vistara-samanya*) and lenghtwise-generality (*ayata-samanya*).[32]

(1b) The substances again have their essence in [or chracterised by their] qualities, inasmuch as they result (from the qualities, i.e.) from cross-wise particularities (*vistara-vishesha*), which abide in one thing.

(1c) The modifications, again, have both the substance and the quality for essence; for being themselves lenght-wise particularities

Book II
The Principle of the Knowable

(*ayata-vishesha*), they result no less from the just now defined substances and qualities both.

(1d) The substantial-modification (*dravya-paryaya*) has for condition the apprehending of an unity which contains many substances. It is of two kinds, homogeneous and heterogeneous.

(1d-1) The homogeneous substantial-modification consists of several particles of matter (molecules), thus of two, three atoms, etc.

(1d-2) Heterogeneous substantial-modifications are e.g. a god, a man; they consist of soul and matter.

(1e) The qualitative-modification (*guna-paryaya*) has for condition the apprehending of lengthwise-manifoldness (*ayata-anaikya*) owing to qualities. It also is of two kinds, modifications of innate-nature (*svabhava*) and modifications of derivative-nature (*vibhava*).

(1e-1) The innate qualitative-modification belonging to all substances is their being subject to manifoldness of increase and decrease, which take place in the six *sthanas*[33] and arise in succession of time through their respective *a-guru-laghu*-qualities.[34]

(1e-2) The derivative qualitative-modification of colours, etc., and intellections [cognitive], etc., is the accession of a manifoldness of particular innate nature, which manifoldness is shown by a higher-or-lower-degree (*taratamya*) with reference to former and later states, and is conditioned by the thing itself or something else (*sva-para pratyaya*).

This now he confirms by an example:

(2a) Just as every piece of cloth results from a persisting collection of crosswise-generalities and a passing collection of lengthwise generalities, and consists of these,[35] so every object (*padartha*) results from a persisting collection of crosswise-generalities and a passing collection of lengthwise-generalities, which collections bear the name of substance; and it consists of substance.

(2b) And, just as in the piece of cloth the persisting collection of crosswise-generalities or the passing collection of lengthwise-generalities, as resulting from the qualities, has the qualities for self, since it is not perceived apart from the qualities, so in [all] objects the persisting collection of crosswise-generalities or the passing collection of lengthwise-generalities, which bears the name of substance, as resulting from the qualities, has the qualities for self, since it is not perceived apart from the qualities.

(2b-1) And, just as a homogeneous substantial-modification may consist of several pieces of cloth, for instance, two or three pieces, so a homogeneous substantial-modification may consist of several material-components, for instance, two or three atoms.

(2b-2) And, just a heterogeneous substantial-modification may consist of several—e.g. two or three—pieces of silk and cotton, so a heterogeneous substantial-modification may consist of several components, soul and matter; instances are a god or a man.

(2c) And, just as in a piece of cloth we see the innate qualitative-modification, i.e. the undergoing of manifoldness owing to an evolution which takes place in a manifold and successive form, by way of such *a-guru-laghu*-qualities as determine gross (*sthula*) nature, so in all substances we find an innate qualitative-modification, i.e. their being subject to the manifoldness of increase and decrease[36], which take place in the six *sthanas* and arise in succession of time by way of their respective *a-guru-laghu*-qualities.

(2c-1) And, just as in a piece of cloth we see the derivative qualitative-modification of colours, etc., in the accession of a manifoldness of particular innate natures, which manifoldness is shown by a higher-or-lower-degree with reference to former and later states, and is conditioned by (the piece) itself or something else (*sva-para pratyaya*), so in all substances we find a derivative qualitative-modification of colours, etc., or intellections, etc., in the accession of a manifoldness of particular innate natures, which manifoldness is shown by a higher-or-lower-degree with reference to former and later states, and is conditioned by the substance itself or something else (*sva-para pratyaya*).

For so, and not otherwise, is the preferable exposition of all objects, as it was preached by the Highest Lord, whereby is revealed the innate nature of substance, quality and modification; for many people, basing themselves merely on the modifications and becoming subject to delusion, which is characterized by not properly understanding the reality [the innate nature of self as it is] become *para-samaya*, i.e. accept only the conditioned modes of consciousness.

Having thus commenced incidentally (the topic of the) distinction of *sva-samaya* and *para-samaya* persons, he summarizes it as follows:

II.2 The souls, who are constantly engaged in, attached to or find satisfaction only in the modifications, are called *para-samayikas* but

those who rely on the innate nature of the self are known as *svaka-samayas [sva-samaya].* (94)

Those who, trusting in the heterogeneous substance-modifications, (*asaman jatiya dravya paryaya*) consisting in (the combination of) soul and matter–which modification is the one root of all forms of ignorance–become impotent to realize the innate-nature of soul as described, and incur an incapacity in respect of even that,

give free rein to an uncontrolled one-sided view, deceived by the notions *I* (*ahankara*) and *mine* (*mamakara*), and thinking "I here am a man," alone and "this human body is mine" only;

fallen away from the use of the word "self" (*atma-vyavahara*), which means being engrossed exclusively and unwaveringly in the innate nature of consciousness,

and taking refuge in the use of the word "man" (*manushya-vyavahara*), in which is ensconced the whole household of actions,

loving and hating [being engaged in attachment or aversion] become through attachment to the "other" substance, *karmic* matter, *para-samaya.*

But those who, relying on the sublime innate nature of soul substance which is well established in its qualities and modifications and which is the one root of all knowledge–become able to realize the innate nature of soul, as described, and, overcoming attachment merely to the modifications alone, maintain a firm stand on the innate conscious nature of soul,

destroy by their natural appearing many-sided view their acceptance of any one-sided view; they hold no more the notions *I* and *mine* with reference to human and other conditions of existence (*gatis*), or to the bodies belonging to them;

taking hold of the self as indivisible unity, which resembles a jewel lamp, carried round through many apartments, they keep thus true to the conception-of-self, which exclusively means the appearance of unwavering spirituality,

and, not taking refuge in the use of the word "man" (*manushya-vyavahara*) and all the activities relating thereto,

they find–whilst the manifestation of attachment and aversion ceases–rest in the highest indifference (*audasinya*); and, because every contact with "the other" substances is abandoned and the contact with the own substance is exclusively maintained, they become *sva-samaya.*

Hence, *sva-samaya* is the essence or inner principle (*antas tattva*) of the self (*atman*) itself.

Now he gives the definition of substance:

II.3 That which, whilst it does not forsake its innate nature, is characterized by origination, annihilation and stability and which possesses or is endowed with qualities and modifications, is called a substance. (95) [see also TS 5.29, 5.30 and 5.38]

A substance is that which, without commencing a differentiation (*bheda*) of its innate nature, is characterized by the twofold set of qualities and modifications and the triple set of origination, annihilation and continuation.

Here we understand by the innate nature (*svabhava*) of a substance its connection with existence-in-general (*astitva-samanya*). This existence will be explained as twofold: *svarupa-astitva* (existence-of-characteristic-nature) and *sadrshya-astitva* (existence-of-common-nature).

By origination we here understand coming forth, by annihilation decay, by stability continuance.

Qualities are crosswise-particularities; they are twofold, in as far as they may be general (*samanya-guna*) or particular (*vishesha-guna*).

Here the general qualities are existence, non-existence; oneness, otherness; to be a substance (*dravyatva*), to be a modification (*paryayatva*); omnipresence, non-omnipresence; possession of spacial units, non-possession of spacial units; materiality, immateriality; possession of action, non-possession of action; consciousness, unconsciousness; agency, non-agency; being-an-enjoyer, not-being-an-enjoyer; the set of *a-gurulaghutva*, etc. qualities.

Particular qualities are the being a cause of "penetrability" (*avagaha*), the being an occasion of moving, the being a factor of standing-still, the being the cause of modification of substances, the possessing of colour, etc., consciousness[37] and so forth.

Modifications are lengthwise-particularities. They have been previously described as fourfold.[38]

To (the notions mentioned), origination, etc., or qualities and modifications, substance is related as that which is to be defined to that which defines; but notwithstanding this differentiation there is no real difference, since the substance in its own nature is "suchlike" (*tathavidha*), as we may understand from the case of an upper-garment.

(1) As an upper-garment which has been subject to a state of filthiness, but, being washed, is originating with reference to a state of spotlessness, is then defined (*lakshyate*) by this origination and in connection with this does not undergo a differentiation in its own nature, but by its own nature adheres to being suchlike.

so any substance which has been subject to an original state, and, owing to the vicinity of the proper external causes, passes into a state qualitatively different or quantitatively greater, and, helped (read *anugrhitam*) by its innate nature—i.e. by its fitness as an own nature, agent and instrument—as an internal favourable condition, is originating with reference to the later state, is then defined by this origination; and in connection with this it does not undergo a differentiation in its own nature, but by its own nature adheres to being suchlike.

(2) And, as the same upper-garment, originating with reference to a state of spotlessness and being annihilated with reference to a state of filthiness, is defined by this annihilation, and, in connection with this, does not undergo a differentiation in its own nature, but by its own nature adheres to being suchlike.

so the same substance, originating with reference to the later state and becoming annihilated with reference to the original state, is defined by this annihilation, and, in connection with this, does not undergo a differentiation in its own nature, but by its own nature adheres to being suchlike.

(3) And, as the same upper-garment, simultaneously originating with reference to spotlessness, and becoming annihilated with reference to filthiness, and partaking of stability, with reference to its constant state of being a garment, is defined by this stability, and in connection with this, does not undergo a differentiation in its own nature, but by its own nature adheres to being suchlike.

so the same substance, simultaneously originating with reference to the later state, and becoming annihilated with reference to the original state, and partaking of stability with reference to its state of being a substance, is defined by this stability, and in connection with this, does not undergo a differentiation in its own nature, but by its own nature adheres to being suchlike.

(4) And, as the same upper-garment is defined by qualities—i.e. by crosswise-particularities–and, in connection with these, does not

undergo a differentiation in its own nature, but by its own nature adheres to being suchlike,

so the same substance is defined by qualities—i.e. by crosswise-particularities–and, in connection with these, does not undergo a differentiation in its own nature, but by its own nature adheres to being suchlike.

(5) And, as the same upper-garment is defined by threads which are in its modifications–i.e. its lengthwise-particularities–and in connection with these does not undergo a differentiation in its own nature, but by its own nature adheres to being suchlike,

so the same substance is defined by modifications–i.e. by lengthwise-particularities–and in connection with these, does not undergo a differentiation in its own nature, but by its own nature adheres to being suchlike.

Now in succession he mentions twofold existence, existence-of-own-nature and existence-of-common-nature (*sadrashya-astitva*), and of these he describes here *svarupa-astitva* (existence-of-own-nature):

II.4. Existence is the innate nature of a substance, which permeates its qualities and various modifications of its own, as also its origination, annihilation and stability at all times.[39] **(96)**

Existence, indeed, is the innate nature of a substance. For why should not this existence be the innate nature of a substance, partaking as it does of oneness with the substance?

For–

both are independent of any other means;

both always go on without beginning or end, and in a conditioning, uniform occurrence (*vrtti*);

both differ from that which makes up derivative-nature (*vibhava*);

although there exists a manifoldness in them, inasmuch as the one is the existence and the other the existent, they are not subject to a differentiation with reference to *pradeshas* (infinitesimal units of space).

The full completeness of this (existence) is not seen in a substance, quality or modification, when taken singly, as if they were different substances; for inasmuch as their reality (*siddhi*) is realized by mutual assistance, their existence (*astitva*) is one, as may be seen by the case of gold.

For,[40] as of gold, which is associated with a process proceeding in company with a manifestation of the qualities yellow etc. and the modifications ring etc., as its agent, instrument and seat, the existence by way of the qualities yellow etc. and the modifications ring etc.—which, not perceived in respect of substance, or place, or time, or being apart from the gold, are associated with an actualization actualized by the existence of the gold—is the own nature: so of substance, which is associated with a process proceeding in company with a manifestation of qualities and modifications, as its agents, instrument and seat, the existence by way of qualities and modifications—which, not perceived in respect of substance, or place, or time or being apart from the substance, are associated with an actualization actualized by the existence of substance, —is the own nature.

And, as of gold, which is not perceived in respect of substance or place or time or being apart from the qualities yellow, etc. and the modifications ring, etc., and which is associated with an actualization actualized by the qualities yellow, etc. and the modifications ring etc., associated with a process proceeding in company with a manifestation of gold, as their agent, instrument and seat, the existence actualized by these as the fundamental means is the self-nature: so of substance,which is not perceived in respect of substance or place or time or being apart from qualities and modifications, and which is associated with an actualization actualized by qualities and modifications, associated with a process proceeding in company with a manifestation of substance as their agent, instrument and seat—the existence actualized by them as fundamental means is the self-nature.

Furthermore, as of gold, which is associated with a process proceeding in company with a manifestation of origination, annihilation and stability of ring, bracelet, yellowness, etc., as its agent, instrument and seat, the existence by way of origination, annihilation, and stability of ring, bracelet, yellowness etc.—which, not perceived in respect of substance or place or time or being apart from the gold, are associated with an actualization actualized by the existence of the gold–is its own nature: so of substance, which is associated with a process proceeding in company with a manifestation of origination, annihilation and stability, as its agent, instrument and seat, the existence by way of origination, annihilation and stability—which not perceived in respect of substance or place or time or being apart from substance, are associated with an actualization actualized by the existence of substance–is the own nature.

And, as of gold, which is not perceived in respect of substance or place or time or being apart from origination, annihilation and stability of ring, bracelet, yellowness, etc., and which is associated with an actualization actualized by origination, annihilation and stability of ring, bracelet, yellowness, etc., associated with an actualization, actualized by origination, annihilation and stability of ring, bracelet, yellowness, etc. associated with a process proceeding in company with a manifestation of gold as their agent, instrument and seat—the existence realized by these as the fundamental means is the self-nature: so of substance, which is not perceived in respect of substance or space or time or being apart from origination, annihilation and stability—and which is associated with an actualization actualized by origination, annihilation and stability, associated with a process proceeding in company with a manifestation of substance, as their agent, instrument and seat—the existence actualized by these as the fundamental means is the self-nature.

Now he states the expression "it is" for existence-of-common-nature (*sadrashya-astitva*):

II.5. The *Jina* (the worthy Lord), when he preached the *dharma*, declared that one, common characteristic, "to be an existent," belongs here to all things with their manifold characterizations. (97)

Here in all substances, although (1) characterized by a proper existence of their own, (2) proceeding with a developed manifoldness exclusive of other substances and (3) serving as specific characteristic drawing the boundaries between substances, we must recognize an "existence" of common nature, one, (1) a common characteristic, omnipresent, termed "existence," (2) proceeding with sublation of the developed manifoldness and (3) breaking through the border-line drawn between substances.

So the expression "it is" and our discrimination expressed by "it is" concern all objects. If this were not so, then one thing should be called "existent," another thing "not-existent," again another thing "existent-and-not-existent," and again another thing "impossible to describe" (i.e. the *syad-vada* would with one only of its members prevail for each object). This now is contradicted and cannot be realized, as for instance in the case of trees.

As in the case of many manifold trees the manifoldness, founded upon their existence-of-characteristic-nature, which is a particular mark (*vishesha-lakshana*) and is individual in every case, is sublated by the oneness, constituted by the genus "trees," which is a general-mark (*samanya-lakshana*) and manifests itself in common so in the case of many manifold substances the manifoldness, founded upon their existence-of-characteristic-nature, which is a particular mark of theirs and is individual in every case, is sublated by the oneness, constituted by their "being," expressed in the words "it is existent," which is a general mark and manifests itself in common.

And, as in the case of these trees, although sublated by the oneness constituted by the genus "tree," as a general mark, and manifesting itself in common, the manifoldness founded upon their existence-of-characteristic-nature, as a particular mark and individual in each case, still shines forth: so in the case of all substances, although sublated by the oneness constituted by their "being," expressed in the words "it is existent," as a general mark and manifesting itself in common, the manifoldness founded upon their existence-of-characteristic-nature, as a particular mark and individual in each case, still shines forth.

Now he refutes the opinion that by substances there is originated another substance and that existence is an object different from substance:

II.6. The *Jinas* have correctly *(yatharthatah)* stated that substance is existent reality, and is proved *(siddha)* by its innate nature. Whosoever does not from Scripture accept it as so proved (*siddha*), is indeed *para-samaya.* (98)

Substances are not produced by other substances, because all substances are realized by their innate nature. And their being realized by their innate nature results from their having no beginning or end. For that which has no beginning or end does not depend on any other efficient factor or cause (*sadhan*), but is something existent, with its realization realized (*siddha-siddhimat*) by itself, being provided with its own main efficient cause (*mool sadhan*), the innate nature of its self, which is the self again of its qualities and modifications. On the other hand, that which is originated by substances is not a new substance, but, because of its accidentality, is a modification, as a double atom, etc., or a man, etc. A substance, on the other hand, being infinite and constant in the three times, cannot be such.

Let us observe in the same way that, as a substance is realized simply by its innate nature, so an existent (*sat*) is realized simply by its innate nature. For it has a form-of-being whose development is developed (*nishpanna-nishpattimat*) (parallel with *siddha-siddhimat* in the precedent paragraph) by its own innate nature, which has moreover (read *sattatmana*) existence for self. On the other hand, existence (*satta*) does not present itself as an object different from substance, so that the substance should be through inherence thereof something-existent (*sat*). And the existent (*sat*) and the existence (*satta*) are not different objects, (*a*) on the basis of *yuta-siddhatva*,[41] because we do not see in them this mutual separability (read *yuta-siddhatvasyadarshanat*), as in the case of a stick and the bearer of the stick. Nor (*b*) does (the thesis) hold by way of mutual-inseparability. And, if one should object that it arises from (read *upadyate*) the notion "this in that" (*ihedam*), then we ask on what is this notion "this in that" based?—It is founded on differentiation (*bheda*). What is this differentiation? Is it of local nature (*pradeshika*) or (logical) non-identity (*atadbhavika*)? It is not local, since we have already rejected *yuta-siddhatva.*—If it is non-identity, that is given already by the saying "that which is a substance is not a quality." But this differentiation, called non-identity, does not by itself suffice as the condition of the notion "this in that," since this notion emerges or is submerged independently. If a substance is caused-to-be-approached (*arpyate*, cf. *Tattva-dipika* on PS 87 and the explication there given of "*artha*") by a modification, then emerges the differentiation of non-identity, "this substance possesses a quality," "this is its quality," "this upper-garment is white," "this white quality," and so on (read *ityadivat prapashyatah*). But, when the substance is caused-to-be-approached by a substance, then every unfolding of an impression (*vasana*) of a quality is lost in us, and regarding only "the suchlike substance,"(cf PS 95) for instance a white upper-garment, the differentiation of non-identity is utterly submerged; and, since this differentiation is submerged, any notion based on it is submerged; and again, this being submerged any other object–an idea dependent on *a-yuta-siddhatva*–is submerged. Consequently the entire substance is left as an unity. On the other hand, when differentiation emerges, then, as it emerges, the notion conditioned by it emerges; and, when this notion emerges, the idea of a second object–due to inseparability (*a-yuta-siddhatva*)–emerges. But even then, emerging as a modification thereof, it is not separate from the object, as little as the water-wave from the water-mass.

This being so, the substance is itself an existent. And he who does not accept this must be considered to be *para-samaya.*

Now he explains that substance, although it consists in origination, annihilation and continuance, is an existent:

II.7. The substance is an existent reality, resting in its innate nature; for every evolution of a substance in the world-of-objects is its innate nature, combined of stability, origination and destruction. (99)

The substance, namely, here is an existent, inasmuch as it eternally rests in its innate nature; and the innate nature of a substance consists in its evolution or oneness of stability, origination and annihilation.

(*A*) For as the volume (*vastu*) of a substance, although in its integrity, one, contains infinitesimal-spacial-constituents (*pradeshas*), which are its fine portions and are engaged in effecting its ordered extension (*vishkambha*): so the occurrence (*vrtti*) of a substance, although in its integrity one, contains evolutions, which are its fine portions and are engaged in effecting its ordered process (*pravaha*).

(*B*) And, as the order of the extension is conditioned by the mutual exclusion (*vyatireka*) of the infinitesimal-spacial-constituents: so the succession in the process is conditioned by the mutual exclusion of the evolutions.

(*C*) And, as these infinitesimal-spacial-constituents uphold themselves, having origination, annihilation and stability for self, because in their own spot (*sthana*) they arise and perish by way of their precedent and subsequent forms, and are exempt from origination and decay, inasmuch as everywhere one and the same volume is effected by their being mutually strung together: so these evolutions uphold themselves, having origination, annihilation and stability for self, because at their own point-of-time (*avasara*) they arise and perish by way of their precedent and subsequent forms, and are exempt from origination and decay, inasmuch as everywhere one and the same process is effected by their being mutually strung together.

(*D*) And, as the limitation-of-volume (*vastu-simanta*), which consists in the destruction of the precedent infinitesimal-spacial-constituents, is the same as the volume-limitation which consists in the origination of the subsequent infinitesimal-spacial-constituents, and the same as the volume-limitation which consists in both together, inasmuch as the one volume is produced by their mutually being strung together: the limitation-of-process which consists in the destruction of the precedent evolution is the same as the limitation-of-process which consists in the origination of the subsequent evolution, and the same as the limitation-of-process which consists in both together, inasmuch as the one process is produced by their mutually being strung together.

In this manner we must admit that existence possesses a threefold character, because it–(i.e. this existence, or, what comes to the same thing, the described process (*pravaha*) or series of evolutions)–does not transgress its innate nature, luxuriating, as it does, in the threefold course of evolutions. To take the example of a necklace of pearls:

As in the case of a hanging necklace of pearls, of 'efinite length, the threefold is obvious, because, whilst all the pearls are visible each in its place,

each subsequent pearl arises (before our perception) in a subsequent place,

each precedent pearl does not arise in the subsequent place,

the whole necklace (*sutraka*), which-strings-them-together (*sutraka*) by means of a mutual stringing together, is present in all their places:

in the same manner in the case of a substance, developing with definite eternal activity (*vrtti*), the threefoldness is obvious, because, whilst all the evolutions are visible each in its own point-of-time,

each subsequent evolution arises in a subsequent point-of-time,

each precedent evolution does not arise in the subsequent point-of-time,

the whole process (*pravaha*), which strings-them-together by means of a mutual stringing together, is present in all their points-of-time.

Now he confirms the necessary concomitance (*avinabhava*) of origination, annihilation and stability:

II.8. There is no coming-into-existence or origination without destruction; there is no destruction devoid of origination; and there is no origination and destruction without stability or persistence. (100)

There is no creation without dissolution; no dissolution without creation; there is neither creation nor dissolution without permanence, nor permanence without creation and dissolution. Creation is dissolution, and dissolution is creation; and both creation and dissolution are the permanence, and the permanence is the creation and dissolution.

For instance, the creation of the jar is the dissolution of the clod, since being appears as an innate nature of not being another being. And the dissolution of the clod is the creation of the jar, since not-being appears as an innate nature of being another being. And both the creation and dissolution of jar and clod are the permanence of the clay, since the sameness (*anvaya*) only appears by means of the divergence (*vyatireka*)(For the terms *anvaya* and *vyatireka* of commentary on *gatha* 80). And the permanence of the clay is the creation and dissolution of jar and clod, since the divergences do not overpass, transgress or transcend the sameness.

And, if this is not accepted, it follows that the creation is something apart, the dissolution something apart, and the permanence again something else.

(I) In that case, since there is no cause for the origination of a pot when it asks only for creation, there would either be no coming into being *(bhavani)* whatever, or an origination of a non-existent.

(A) And thus, if the pot does not come into existence, there would be no arising of anything;

(*B*) in the case of the origination of a non-existent there would be origination of sky-flowers, etc.

(II) Likewise, since there is no cause for the destruction of the clod which is undergoing annihilation only, there would be either, no annihilation *(samharani)* whatever or the putting-an-end to a thing-really-existent (*sat*).

(*A*) And here, in the case of the clod's not being destroyed, there would be no annihilation of anything;

(*B*) in the case of the putting-an-end to an existent there would be an end to the conscious-being (*samvid,* i.e. the soul), and so on,

(III) Likewise, since in the clay, if admitting only continuance, there is no constancy, i.e. continuance, dominated by divergence, there would be no continuance *(asthani)*, or merely the eternality of the momentary.

(*A*) In the case of the non-continuance of the clay there would be non-continuance of all existence;

(*B*) in the case of the eternality of the momentary there would be eternality of the momentary-contents-of-consciousness (*chitta-kshana*).[42]

Consequently we must inevitably accept a substance characterized by a threefold-aspect coming forth without obstacle and inseparably connected (*avinabhuta*) with creation of a series of posterior divergences (*vyatireka*), destruction of a series of prior divergences, and stability of constancy.

Now he shows summarily that origination, etc., are not (read *dravyad anarthantaratvam*) objects (*arthas*) different from the substance:

II.9. Origination, continuance and destruction are in the modifications; the modifications, indeed, are in the substance; therefore necessarily all that is the substance or substance is the substratum of all of them. (101)

Origination, decay and stability are dependent (*alambante*) on the modifications; these modifications again are dependent on the substance. Therefore all that is one substance, and there is no other substance. On the substance the modifications rest; since that which consists of an aggregation (*samudaya*) has the aggregation for self, as e.g. a tree. As, namely, a tree which consists of an aggregation, has the aggregation of stem, root and boughs for self and appears only as that on which stem, root and boughs are dependent, similarly a substance which consists of an aggregation has the aggregation of the modifications for self and appears only as that on which the modifications are dependent.

And the modifications are that on which origination, dissolution and stability are dependent, since origination, dissolution and stability have the property of being portions, as we may see by the example of germ sprout and tree. As, namely, the three portions, termed the states of germ, sprout and full-grown tree, which belong to the tree as the whole, are envisaged together when the properties (*dharmas*) of each, i.e. destruction, appearance and stability rest upon them: so the three portions, characterized as passing off, coming forth and remaining, which belong to the substances as the whole are envisaged together when the properties of each, i.e. destruction, appearance and stability rest upon them.

But if destruction, origi..ation or stability were upheld merely in respect of substance, then everything would be confounded (*viplavate*).

(*I*) For in the case of mere destruction (*A*) *shunyata* of all substance would result, since all the substances, for which the *kshana-bhanga* (the momentary destruction) is eagerly watching, would be destroyed in one and the same moment (*kshana*); or (*B*) there would occur the destruction of the existent.[43]

(*II*) And in the case of mere production (*A*) there would be in each case an endless number of substances, stamped with an origination recurring every instant, or (*B*) there would occur the origination of a non-existent.

(*III*) And in the case of mere stability there would either be (*A*) the non-existence of any substance, since there would be no successively existing existences, or (*B*) *kshanikatva* (perpetual momentariness).

Hence origination, destruction and continuance must be dependent on the modifications, and the modifications on the substance, so that all this is merely one substance.

Now, rejecting a differentiation of origination, etc., with reference to moments-of-time (*kshana*), he explains that the very term *dravya* (substance) signifies *dravyatva*", i.e. "that which by nature flows towards its modes":

II.10. The substance at one and the same moment (*samaya*) takes the forms, modes, names or states of origination, persistence and destruction, which certainly are inseparably rolled into one. Therefore all the three are indeed the substance. (102)

(Opponent:) "The moment of birth of a thing (*vastu*), since it is pervaded (*vyapta*) merely by this birth, is neither a moment of continuance nor a moment of annihilation. The moment of continuance is neither a moment of origination nor a moment of annihilation, since it luxuriates (*durlalita*) in the interspace of both. The moment of annihilation, since it belongs to something which becomes annihilated after previous origination and continuance (read *utpadyavasthaya*), is neither a moment of birth nor a moment of stability. Thus reasoned out, the differentiation of origination, etc., with reference to moments-of-time no doubt obtains an entrance into the mind. And, if it so enters, then it is admitted that substances arises by itself (*atmana*), persists by itself and perishes by itself."

This is not proved. Originations, etc., belong merely to the evolutions; wherefore a differentiation with reference to the moments?

To wit, as, when the finishing of the pot, effected by the potter with stick, wheel and rag, is present, that moment of coming-into-existence of the produced object is the same as the moment of annihilation of the clod and the same as the moment of persistence of the clayness, which is found on both sides-of-the-process (*koti-dvaya*): in the same way, when the finishing (of any thing whatever), effected by internal and external causes, is present, then the moment of coming-into-existence of the posterior modification is the same as the moment of annihilation of the prior modification, and the same as the moment of the persistence of the substantiality found on both sides-of-the-process.

And, as origination, annihilation and continuance, which respectively inhere, one in the product, one in the clod and one in the clayness, are conjointly seen at one moment in the clay, which has contact with a threefold innate nature: similarly origination, annihilation and continuance, which respectively inhere, one in the posterior modification, one in the prior modification, and one in the substantiality, are conjointly seen at one moment in the substance, which has contact with a threefold innate nature.

And, as the origination, annihilation and stability, which abide in the product, the clod and the clayness, are the clay, and nothing else: in the same way the origination, annihilation and stability, which abide in the posterior modification, the prior modification and the substantiality, are the substance, and not another object.

Now he considers the origination, annihilation and continuance of a substance by means of the modifications of several substances:

II.11. One modification of a substance originates and another vanishes; the substance has not vanished and has not originated. (103)

For, as here one triple atom of homogeneous nature, a modification of several substances, vanishes and another, fourfold, atom arises, and, as these three or four matter-particles remain constant, not vanishing and not arising: in the same way all homogeneous modifications of substances vanish and arise, whilst the homogeneous substances remain constant, not vanishing and not arising.

And, as one, characterized as man and possessing a heterogeneous nature, vanishes, and another, god (heavenly being), arises, but the two, soul and the matter, remain constant, not vanishing and not arising: in the same manner all heterogeneous modifications of substances vanish and arise, whilst the heterogeneous substances remain constant, not vanishing and not arising.

Thus the substances, in themselves constant, but becoming origination and annihilation through the substance-modifications, are origination, annihilation and permanence.

Now he considers the origination, annihilation and continuance of a substance through the modifications of one substance:

II.12. The substance, undifferentiated from the existent, evolves by itself from one quality into another; therefore it is said that the quality-modifications (*guna paryaya*) are indeed the substance. (104)

The quality-modifications are modifications of one substance, since the quality-modifications are one substance. For their being one substance may be explained by a *sahakara* (mango) fruit.

As the *sahakara*-fruit, which, evolving by itself from the green state into the yellowish [white, Faddegon] state, has its own existence affected by the successive states of green and yellowish [white, Faddegon] colour, is with these states of green and yellowish [white, Faddegon] colour one object and not a different object, inasmuch as its existence is undifferentiated from them:

in the same manner the substance which, evolving by itself from the quality of the precedent condition into the quality of the subsequent condition, has its own existence affected by the qualities of these successive conditions, is with these qualities of successive conditions one substance and not a different substance, inasmuch as its existence is undifferentiated from them.

And, as the *sahakara*-fruit, originating with reference to the yellowish [white, Faddegon] colour, decaying with reference to the green colour, permanent in its being a *sahakara*-fruit, is origination, annihilation and stability in consequence of these being modifications of one thing (*vastu*):

in the same manner the substance, originating with reference to the quality of the subsequent state, decaying with reference to the quality of the precedent state, permanent in the quality of being a substance (*dravyatva-guna*), is origination, annihilation and stability in consequence of these being modifications of one substance.

Now he supplies a proof that existence and substance are not different objects:

II.13. If the substance is not an existent reality, then necessarily it is a non-existent; so how is it a substance: Or is it perhaps something else? Therefore the substance is itself existence. (105)

If the substance be not by characteristic nature an existent, then there is a double possibility: it is a non-existent, or it exists apart from existence.

If it were a non-existent, then, since there would be no stability, it would not maintain itself, and thus the substance would come to its end.

If it were without existence, then, maintaining itself apart from existence, it would do away with existence, which has merely that purpose.

If, on the other hand, in itself existent, then maintaining itself, because of admitting stability, substance will come about, and maintaining itself without being separate from existence, it will allow existence, which has merely that purpose, to come about.

Therefore, the substance, in itself, must be admitted to be existence, since existence and the existent, being not separated, are not different.

Now he discloses the definition of separateness and "otherness":

II.14. Separateness *(prthaktva)* is occupying of different place; thus runs the teaching of the Vira *(Mahavira)*; other-ness *(anyatva)* is non-identity *(a-tad-bhava)* [i.e. it is not the same] [a relation between two objects A and B may be formulated as "A is non-B" - Faddegon]; how could what is not "that" be one with it? (106)

Now occupying of different places is the definition of separateness. This is not attributed to existence and substance; since the quality and that which possesses the quality do not occupy different places, as in the case of a white upper-garment. As, namely, the places of the white quality are also the places of the upper-garment which possesses the quality, so that there is between them no differentiation of place, in the same way the places of existence as a quality are also the place of the substance which possesses the quality, so that there is between them no differentiation of place.

Even so there is otherness between them; for the definition of that notion is applicable here. Non-identity (*a-tad-bhava*) is, in fact, the definition of "otherness"; and this is found in existence and substance, since there is no identity (*tad-bhava*) between the quality and that which possesses the quality, as in the case of the white upper-garment.

For, as the white colour, which becomes an object of only one sense-organ, namely the eye, but transcends the reach of the set of all other sense-organs, is not the garment, which falls under the reach of the complete set of sense-organs, and as the garment, which falls under the reach of the complete set of sense-organs, is not the white colour, which becomes an object of only one sense-organ, namely the eye, but transcends the reach of the set of all other sense-organs, so that the two are not identical, in the same manner existence, which: (1) occurs as inhering, (2) lacks qualities, (3) is composed of one quality, (4) is a characteristic (*visheshana*), (5) a predicate (*vidhayika*) and (6) has occurrence (*vrtti*) for characteristic nature, is not substance, which (i) occurs as non-inherent, (ii) possesses qualities,(iii) is composed of several qualities, (iv) is a thing for characterization (*visheshya*), (v) a subject of predicates, and (vi) is by nature that wherein occurrence takes place; and substance, which does occur as non-inherent, possesses qualities, is composed of several qualities, is a thing for characterization, a subject of predicates, and is by nature that wherein occurrence takes place, is not existence, which occurs as inherent, lacks qualities, is composed of one quality, is a characterizer, a predicate and has occurrence for characteristic nature. Therefore there is not identity of these, existence and substance. For this reason, although in a certain respect they are not different objects (*arthas*), yet we must not suppose their complete oneness; for "being that" (*tad-bhava*) is the definition of oneness. And that which cannot be thought of as "being that" (i.e. being the same, *tad-bhavat*), how could it be one? Nay, in their function of quality and that which possesses the quality they are simply not one. This is what is meant.

And now, making non-identity (*a-tad-bhava*) his topic, he expounds:

II.15. The substance is an existent, the quality is an existent, and the modification is an existent; in this way is its extension (*vistara*).[44] Not being that (*tad-abhava*), which is the "non-existence of that," (*tasya-abhava*) is *a-tad-bhava* (the non-identity). [That *tad-abhava* ("the not being A") which is the "non-existence of A" (*tasya abhava*) is *a-tad-bhava* ("the being non-A," the non-identity). – Faddegon] (107)

As one pearl-necklace extends itself (*vistiryate*) over a triplicity, namely, the necklace, the string and the pearl, so the one substance extends itself over a triplicity, namely, the substance, the quality and the modification.

And, as the white quality of the one pearl-necklace extends itself over a triplicity, namely, the white necklace, the white string and the white pearl, in the same way the existence quality of the one substance extends itself over a triplicity, namely, the existent substance, the existent quality and the existent modification.

And, as in the one pearl-necklace the white quality is not the necklace, or the string, or the pearl, and as the necklace, the string and the pearl are not the white quality, so that they have mutual "not being that," and this *a-tad-bhava* (the fact of being non-*A*), defined as "not being that," is based on the fact that one is different (*anya*) from the other,

in the same way in the substance the existence-quality is not the substance, or another quality (of the substance), or a modification, nor are the substance, the other quality and the modification the existence-quality; so that they have mutual "not being that," and this *a-tad-bhava,* defined as "not being that," is based on the fact that one is different (*anya*) from the other.

Now he rejects *a-tad-bhava* ("esse non-*A*) as a definition of non-existence in general:

II.16. The substance is not the quality, and the quality is not the *tattva* (substance), indeed; for, according to the teaching [of *Jina*], this *a-tad-bhava* is not non-existence simply. (108)

In one substance that which is the substance is not the quality, and that which is the quality is not the substance; thus the non-existence of the substance under the aspect of quality, or of the quality under the aspect of substance, a non-existence under-a-certain-aspect (*tena*), is *a-tad-bhava.*

And, since this suffices to justify the notion-of-otherness (*anyatva*), we may not define *a-tad-bhava* as non-existence simply, so that, for instance, substance should be non-existence of quality and quality non-existence of substance. For, were this true, then the result would be either plurality of the substance, or "nothingness" (*shunyata*) of both substance and quality, or their form as negation (*apoha*).[45]

For (I) as the non-existence of thinking substance is unthinking substance and the non-existence of unthinking substance is thinking substance, so that there is a plurality in them, in the same way the non-existence of substance would be quality, and the non-existence of quality would be substance, so that there would be plurality in substance, although it is one.

(II) Or, as in the case of non-existence of gold there is non-existence of gold-in-general (*suvarnatva*), and in the case of non-existence of "being gold" there is non-existence of gold, and thus absolute-nihility (*shunyatva*) of both, in the same way in the case of non-existence of substance there would be non-existence of quality, and in the case of non-existence of quality there would be non-existence of substance, consequently absolute-nihility of both.

And, as the pot would be merely the non-existence of the piece of cloth, and the piece of cloth merely the non-existence of the pot, so that both would have the form of *apoha* (negation), in the same way quality would be merely the non-existence of substance, and substance the non-existence of quality, so that both would have the form of *apoha.*

Therefore he who wishes oneness, non-nihility (*a-shunyatva*) and the non-negationness (*an-apoha*) of substance and quality, must accept *a-tad-bhava* (non-identity) as described.

Now he establishes between existence and substance a relation of quality and that-which-possesses-the quality:

II.17. The evolution, having the substance as innate nature, is the quality, not distinguished from the existent (*sad-avishishta*, "the same as," "identical with the existent," "called existence" cf. *Tattva-dipika* on 105 and 106); the substance, reposing in its innate nature, is the existent; this is the teaching of the *Jina.* (109)

Substance has previously (PS 99) been proved to be the existent reality, since it is always reposing in its innate nature. The innate nature of substance has been called the evolution. That evolution which is the innate nature of the substance is likewise quality, not separated from the existent; this will now be proved.

The same *astitva* (the actuality-of-existence)–which is an occurrence of the characteristic nature of a substance and is termed "existent" (*sat*), because it reveals what is most essential in the substance–is the evolution, which, being a quality not separated from that existent, is the innate nature of the substance.

In the first place, the evolution forms the innate nature of the substance, because the occurrence (*vrtti*) of the substance, whilst reaching the threefold-aspect (*tri-koti*) of time (*samaya*), is evolving every moment through this innate nature.

And, further, (this evolution) is a quality, which, undistinguished from the existent, is a predicator (cf commentory on 106) of the substance, because it consists in the occurrence of the substance, i.e. in the actuality-of-its-existence (*astitva*).

Thus is established between existence and substance the relation of quality and that which possesses the quality.

Now he refutes the idea of diversity of the quality and that which has the quality:

II.18. There is without substance no quality whatever, and no modification; to be a substance (*dravyatva*) means to be (*bhava*); therefore substance is in itself existence. (110)

There can not be any quality or any modification, separately (*prthak*) from substance, as e.g., separately from the gold, its yellow colour or its ring shape. Then in the substance its being a substance, which consists in the occurrence of its characteristic nature and is called the actuality-of-its-existence, does this, whilst it is also a quality, called its being that, occur separately from the substance? Indeed, it does not. Therefore let the substance be the existence, its very self.

Now he shows, with reference to substance, that there is no contradiction between its origination from an existent (*sat-utpada*) and its origination from a non-existent (*a-sat-utpada*):

II.19. Substance, which in innate nature is suchlike always, attains a manifestation which, under the substance-aspect and the modification-aspect, is bound to an existent and a non-existent nature. (111)

Substance, whose marks are, in the manner described, in their totality undefiled, and which is in nature without beginning or termination, attains manifestation; and this manifestation of substance, when considered under the denotation of substance, is bound to an existent nature, but, when considered under the denotation of modification, bound to a non-existent nature. For

(*A*) When it is called substance and not modifications, then the substance, while–by means of the energies (*shakti*) of sameness of nature (*anvaya*, general nature), which (1) are exempt from commencement and termination, (2) proceed simultaneously, and (3) develop the substance–assuming now these, then those particular (*vyakti*) divergences (*vyatireka*), which (1) are characterized by commencement and termination, (2) proceed in succession, and (3) develop modifications, has a manifestation bound to an existent nature (*sad-bhava*); as in the case of gold.

For, when it is called gold and not modifications, for instance a bracelet, then the gold, while–by means of the energies of its general-nature (*anvaya*), which (1) exists as long as the gold exists, (2) proceeds simultaneously, and (3) develops the gold–assuming now these, then those particular divergences, which (1) exists as long as the modifications, such as a bracelet, exist, (2) proceeds in succession, and (3) develops the modifications such as a bracelet, has a manifestation bound to an existent-nature.

(*B*) But, when called modifications, and not substance, then the substance, while–by means of now of these, then of those, particular divergences, which (1) are characterized by commencement and termination, (2) proceed in succession, and (3) develop modifications–assuming the energies of sameness of nature, which (1) are exempt from commencement and termination, (2) proceed simultaneously, and (3) develop the substance, has a manifestation bound to a non-existent nature, as in the case of gold.

For, when it is called modifications, such as a bracelet, and not gold, then the gold, while–by means now of these, then of those particular divergences, which (1) exist as long as the modifications, such as the bracelet, exist, (2) proceed in succession, and (3) develop the modifications, such as the bracelet, –assuming the energies of its sameness of nature, which (1) exist as long as the gold exists, (2) proceed simultaneously, and (3) develop the gold, has a manifestation bound to a non-existent nature.

(*C*) But even in the case of denotation by the term "modifications," when thus origination from a non-existent takes place, the respective particular divergences, which develop the modifications, will, as attaining a simultaneous procedure, share in the nature of the energies of the sameness of nature (*anvaya*, "general nature"), and make the modifications into a substance.

So, through the particular divergences, which develop the modifications, such as a bracelet, and which, as attaining a simultaneous procedure, share in the nature of the energies of the sameness of nature, the modifications (read *angadadi-paryaya api*), such as a bracelet, will become gold.

(*D*) And likewise in the case of denotation by the term "substance," when thus origination from an existent takes place, the energies of the sameness of nature, which develop the substance, will, as attaining a successive procedure, share in the nature of the particular divergences, and make the substance into modifications.

Thus, through the energies of the sameness of nature, which develop the gold and which in a successive procedure share in the nature of the particular divergences (read *tad-tad-vyatireka-vyaktitvam apannabhir*), the gold will become the very modifications, bracelet, etc.

Therefore the thesis "origination from the existent takes place in accordance with the denotation under a substance-aspect, and origination from the non-existent in accordance with the denotation under a modification-aspect" is without fault.

Now he ascertains origination from the existent to be *un-anyatva* (not being another):

II.20. The soul which is will be a man or god (celestial being), becoming each time another. Does it then lose its substantiality (*dravyatva*) [the state-of-evolution]? Not losing this, how does it become another? (112)

In the first place, the substance is an existent reality, never forsaking its energy of sameness of nature, which makes up its substantiality [see *Tattva-dipika* on PS 111(A)].

And further, even in the manifestation (*pradur-bhava*) of a particular divergence, which is a modification of the substance, the energy of sameness of nature (*anvaya*) is not lost; and so the substance is not-another (*un-anya*). Therefore in virtue of negation-of-otherness, origination from an existent (*sad-utpada*) is proved for the substance.

Thus, the soul, being a substance, will necessarily, since the occurrence (*vrtti*) of a substance craves for a modification, exists in accordance with one of the modifications, hell-inhabitant, animal (*tiryag*), man, god or liberated soul. Does it, in becoming that, thereby forsake its energy of sameness of nature, which consists in the substance? It does not. If it does not, how could it be "another"; consequently it must be the same with its existence (*satta*) exhibiting a three-sided aspect (*tri-koti*) [i.e. its existence in all three times] (The same expression occurs in commentary on PS 109).

Now he ascertains origination from the non-existent to be *anyatva* (being another):

II.21. A man is not a god, nor is a god a man or a liberated soul; being thus "not," how does (the soul) admit of identity (*un-anya-bhava*)? (113)

The modifications [This and the following paragraph correspond to commentary on PS 111(B) and (C)], since they exist exclusively during the time of their own particular divergence (*vyatireka*), which is the modification, are therefore at other times not existent.

And, as regards the manifestation of the modifications, which takes place in the time given, according to succession, and threaded through them with its energy-of-sameness, which has a substance-character, in regard thereto the modifications of nature, since they do not exist before their own several divergences, which constitute the respective modifications, are "others".

Therefore, through this relation of otherness between the modifications it is ascertained that in substance–which is not separated from its modifications, inasmuch as it is the characteristic nature, the agent, the instrument and the abode[46] of the modifications–origination from a non-existent takes place.

Thus, a man is not a god or liberated soul; neither is a god a man or liberated soul; being "not" (read *asan* instead of *asat*) in this way, "other," and so that a soul-substance whose modification as man, for instance, is being effected–like a piece of gold, whose secondary state of armlet, for example, is coming into existence–should not be at each stage (*pratipadam*) "other"?

Now he repudiates a contradiction between the *anyatva* and *un-anyatva* in the one substance:

II.22. The soul substance when viewed from the point-of-view-of-substance *(dravyarthikena)*, is the same (not other) in all its altered modifications, but when viewed from the point-of-view-of-modification (*paryayarthikena),* it is other and not other from the modifications because during a certain time it possesses the nature of that through which it evolves during the time of the evolution. (cf PS 8). (114)

With reference to any thing whatever, since it has generality (*samanya*) and particularity (*vishesha*) for self, those who consider its characteristic nature possess two (mental)-eyes, which successively distinguish the generality and the particularity, namely one eye for the substance-aspect and another for the modification-aspect.

When one looks with only the eye of the substance-aspect open, whilst the eye of the modification-aspect is decidedly closed, then to those who observe only the one generality of soul, placed in the differentiations consisting in being hell-inhabitant, animal, man, god and liberated soul, and do not observe the differentiations, all that manifests itself as soul-substance.

When one looks with only the eye of the modification-aspect open, whilst the eye of the substance-aspect is decidedly closed (Insert *vidhaya* in the text), then to those who observe only the several differentiations disposed in the soul-substance, such as the modifications hell-inhabitant, animal, man, god and liberated soul, and do not observe the generality, it manifests itself as something else, and again something else. For the substance is, during the times of its several particularities, not other than the particularity of each time, because it has the nature of it; as in the case of fire, which has the nature of the collected (material, *gana*), of grass, or leaves, or wood.

But when with both eyes, the one for the substance-aspect and that for the modification-aspect simultaneously open, one looks in the two directions, then the soul-generality disposed in the modifications such as hell-inhabitant, animal, man, god and liberated soul, and the soul-particularities, consisting in these modifications, hell-inhabitant, animal, man, god and liberated soul, and abiding in the soul-generality, are simultaneously observed.

Here the one-eye-view is a partial view, and the two-eye-view is the complete view. In this complete view the *anyatva* and *un-anyatva* of substance are not contradictory.

Now he introduces the *sapta-bhangi*,[47] which prohibits all contradictory-assertions (*vipratishedha*):

II.23. With regard to some modification or other, it is stated that a substance is (1), is not (2), is indescribable (3), is both ()[48] or something else.[49] (115)

(1) *Quodammodo* (*syat*), it is,

(2) *Quodammodo*, it is not,

(3) *Quodammodo*, it is indescribable,

(4) *Quodammodo*, it is and is not (= 1 + 2),

(5) *Quodammodo*, it is and is indescribable (= 1 + 3),

(6) *Quodammodo*, it is not and is indescribable (= 2 + 3),

(7) *Quodammodo*, it is, is not, and is indescribable (= 1 + 2 + 3),

B. (1) With reference to (*rupena*) itself.

(2) With reference to another.

(3) With regard to simultaneously of reference to itself and reference to another,

(4) With regard to the succession of reference to itself and reference to another (= 1 + 2),

(5) With regard to reference to itself, and simultaneity of reference to itself and reference to another (= 1 + 3),

(6) With regard to reference to another, and simultaneity of itself and reference to another (= 2 + 3),

(7) With regard to reference to itself, reference to another, and simultaneity of reference to itself and reference to another (= 1 + 2 + 3),

If in this sevenfold way the substance is described:

(1) As being, with reference to itself,

(2) As not being, with reference to another,

(3) As indescribable simultaneously, with reference to itself and another,

(4) As successively being and not being, with reference to itself and another,

(5) As being and indescribable, with regard to reference to itself, and simultaneity of reference to itself and reference to another,

(6) As not being and indescribable, with regard to reference to another, and simultaneity of reference to itself and reference to another,

(7) As being, not being, and being indescribable, with regard to reference to itself, reference to another, and simultaneity of reference to itself and another,

thus with reference to each single property of substance, with its unlimited number of properties, this sevenfold-formula-of-restriction, interposing, with its partly meant and partly not meant affirmation (*vidhi*) and negation (*pratishedha*), the infallible magic charm of the invariably enunciated word *Quodammodo* dispels the entire infatuation of contrariety (*vipratishedha*), unexhausted by the word *eva* (exclusively).

Now, in regard to the soul, which is taken for example as being the object of inquiry, he explains the "otherness" of its modifications, such as man, etc., as being the fruit of actions:

II.24. There is no modification [such as man, etc.] which can be called "this one" is eternal; no deed, originated from (any one's) innate nature, is non-existent [i.e. there is no activity which is not the outcome of its nature]; for there is no deed without fruit, although (the fulfilment of) the highest *dharma* is without fruit. (116)

For here, in the case of a soul which is subject to *samsara* and with transformations (*vivartana*) every moment conditioned by the vicinity of a beginningless *karmic* matter as accessory-condition (*upadhi*), every deed is originated (read *nirvrttasti*) from (the soul's) innate nature. Therefore among the modifications such as man, etc., to which the soul is subject, there is no one, carved out (*tankotkirna*), whom we could call "the real one," since each later one is disqualified, as being the fruit of actions directed to the destruction of the respectively precedent, or they may be regarded as fruit of action, due to the soul being still encumbered with infatuation. The action, namely, of a thinking being (*chetana*) is an evolution of his thinking, characterized by a previous and subsequent state. And this evolution bears fruit for the soul imbued with infatuation, since it causes effects such as human life, etc., in the same way as the evolution of an atom, which is connected with another atom, causes an effect such as a double-atom (diatomic molecule).

But, when, at the disappearance of the conjunction with infatuation, it does not produce any effect such as the state of man, etc.,—as the evolution of the atom, which has ended its connection with another atom has no longer the double atom as effect—the action is without fruit and is called the highest *dharma*, since it is the own nature of highest substance.[50]

Now he explains how for the soul the modifications man etc., are the results of actions:

II.25. ***Karmic*** **matter called [physique or body-making] "name** ***karma*** **(*****nama-karman*****)"[51] dominating by its own nature or class or** ***karma*****, the nature of the soul, makes it (the self) man, animal, hell-inhabitant or god (celestial being). (117)**

The action is indeed self's *karma*, because it is "the thing to be attained" (*prapta*)[52] by the self; and matter, whose evolution is attained (*prapta*) by that occasion [i.e. the action of the self which acts as the auxiliary cause (*nimitta*) thereof], is likewise *karman*; moreover, the modifications, such as man, which are its (It, i.e. of the *karman* in the precedent meanings) effects, may be called the fruit of deed, because they arise from the soul's deed, which is the principal-cause (*mula-karana*). For, when there is no deed, matter is not *karman*, because the modifications, which are its effects, do not arise.

How now do these (modifications of the self) attain the nature of the effects of *karman*? It is because the action takes place with domination of the own-nature of the soul by the own-nature of the *karman*; as in the case of the lamp-light.

As, namely, the lamp-light is the effect of the light-substance (*jyotis*) because it is effected by the own nature of the light-substance, dominating the own nature of the oil, so the modifications, such as man, etc., are the effect of *karman*, because they are effected by the own nature of *karman*, dominating the own nature of the soul.

Now he answers the question how in the modifications, man, etc., the own nature of soul yields to this domination:

II.26. The *jivas* (living beings), viz. men, hell-inhabitants, animals or gods (celestial beings) are originated from *nama-karman;* for, while evolving through their *karman* (deeds, or conjunctions with matter, or consequences of deeds), these souls do not realize their own nature. (118)

In the first place, these modifications, such as man, are originated from the *karmic* matter called *nama-karman*. But it is not simply by this that the own nature of soul becomes subdued, just as little as does the ruby in bracelets with rubies set in gold. But that which hinders the soul from maintaining even then its own nature is its evolution into its *karma*; as in the case of water. As, namely, water does not maintain its own nature of (independent) substantiality and sweetness, whilst evolving, with its infinitesimal-spacial-constituents and its taste, into trees such as the *picumanda* or the sandal-tree, so neither does the soul maintain its own nature, that is to say, its immateriality, and its possession of unstained pureness, whilst evolving, with its infinitesimal-spacial-constituents and its mental-state (*bhava*), into *karman*.

Now he explains how the soul, although permanent in its substantiality, is non-permanent in regard to its modifications:

II.27. In the midst of the universe-of-souls, subject every moment to annihilation and origination, no one is born, or dies. For origination of one modification is destruction of another. Yet the origination and destruction are different. (119)

Here indeed no one is born or dies. Yet, on the other hand, the world of souls, men, gods, animals and hell-inhabitants, annihilation and origination carries with it every moment annihilation and origination, because they evolve with the moment. And this is not contradictory, because origination and annihilation are one as well as different. When decay and origination are one, then we have the "thesis" (*purva-paksha*); but, when they are many, then the "antitheses" (*uttara-paksha*).[53]

For, as in the affirmation "the pot is the pitcher," since oneness of the characteristic-natures of pot and pitcher is not possible, the clay which is the base (*adhara*) of them both shows itself, so in the affirmation "origination is annihilation," since oneness of the characteristic natures of originations and annihilation is not possible, the permanence which is the base of them both shows itself. Consequently, when the modification god, e.g., arises and the modification man, e.g., vanishes, then, with the understanding that the origination is here the annihilation, the soul-substance, which possesses permanence and is the base of the two states mentioned, is conceived. So at all times, whoso lives, is, in respect of substantiality, carved out [clearly].

But further: as in the affirmation "the pot is something else, and the pitcher is something else," since "otherness" of the clay, the common base of both, is not possible, the characteristic natures of pot and pitcher show themselves, so in the affirmation "origination is something else, and annihilation is something else," since "otherness" of permanence, which is the common base of them both, is not possible, the characteristic natures of origination and annihilation show themselves. Consequently, when the modification (*paryaye*) god, e.g., arises and (read *chanyah* instead of *vanyah*) the modification [*paryaye*] man, e.g., vanishes, then, upon the understanding that the origination is something and the annihilation is something else, the two modifications, e.g. god and man, which represent origination and annihilation, are conceived. So every moment the soul in respect of the modifications is non-permanent.

Now he expounds the cause of this non-permanence of the soul:

II.28. Therefore during the transmigratory existence (*samsara*) no one ever remains stable in its same nature; and this transmigration [in mundane existence] is action of the transmigrating substance. (120)

Since the soul, although permanent in regard to substantiality (*dravyatva*), is non-permanent with respect to modifications, we understand how no one in transmigration is at rest in his own nature. And of this non-permanence *samsara* is the cause, since it is suchlike by its characteristic nature; for it has modifications such as man, etc., for self.

And the evolution, called action, which belongs to the evolving substance and consists in giving up a former state and accepting a following state, is the characteristic nature of this transmigration.

But whence arises adhesion (*slesha*) of matter to soul during *samsara* (which in essence is evolution), so that it receives the nature of modifications such as man? This question he here settles:

II.29. The soul, stained with *karmic* matter, undergoes evolution, connected with *karman*; thus the *karman* adheres; therefore *karman* may be called the evolution. (121)

This self-evolution, called *samsara*, being such as we have described, is the cause of the adherence of material-*karman*.[54] But what again is the cause of such an evolution? The material-*karman* is the cause of it. For the self undergoes this adherence, as being conjoined with material-*karman*.

But, if so, have we not the fallacy of mutual dependence (*itaretarashraya*)? No; since the self, which is bound by material-*karman*, existent without beginning, adopts the previous material-*karman* as cause.

So, since new and old material-*karman* functions as effect and cause, this suchlike evolution of the self is (speaking metaphorically, figuratively or as formal usage, *upachara*)) the material-*karman*; and the self, as agent of its own evolution, is, metonymously, the agent[55] of the material-*karman*.

Now he explains how in the transcendental sense of consciousness-as-such (*paramartha*) the self is not the agent of material-*karman*:

II.30. The self itself is the evolution; and this evolution is considered to be action, which consists of soul; and action is taken as *karma;* so (the self) is not the agent of the [material] *karman*. (122)

The self itself is the evolution of the self; for that which evolves is nothing else than the evolution, since it is the agent of the characteristic form of the evolution.

And its suchlike evolution is action (*kriya*), consisting of soul; for in the case of all substances action (*kriya*), characterized as evolution, is acknowledged to be the self (of these substances).

And action again is a *karma*; for it is attained (*prapyate*) by the self independently.

Therefore, according to the higher transcendental sense, the self is the agent of that subjective-*karma* (*bhava-karman*, or conscious deed), which is essentially an evolution of the self; but it is not the agent of material-*karma* (*dravya-karman*), which is essentially an evolution of matter.

Then who is the agent of the material-*karman*?–Matter itself is the evolution of matter; for that which evolves is nothing else than the evolution, since it is the agent of the characteristic nature of the evolution and its suchlike evolution is the action (*kriya*), as far as it consists of matter; for in the case of all substances action (*kriya*), characterized as evolution, is acknowledged to be the self (of these substances). And this activity again is a *karman*; for it is attained (*prapyate*) by matter, independently.

Therefore, in the higher sense, the self of matter is the agent of the material-*karman (dravya-karman)*, which is essentially an evolution of the self (of matter); but it is not the agent of the subjective-*karma*, which is essentially an evolution of the self.

So then the self evolves with its characteristic form of self, but not with the characteristic form of matter.

Now he gives an answer to the question "What is the characteristic form with which the self evolves?":

II.31. The self evolves as consciousness (*chetana*); the consciousness is considered to be threefold, i.e. with regard to knowledge, *karma* (deed or action) and fruit of action *(karma-phala)*. (123)

Since, namely, the self's being consciousness means its pervasion of its own quality, therefore consciousness-as-such is the characteristic form of self, and therewith the self evolves. No single evolution of the self departs from consciousness–that is the intent.

Consciousness, again, is threefold; for it may be knowledge, deed and the fruit of deed.[56] Here the knowledge-consciousness is evolution through Knowledge; the deed-consciousness is evolution through the deed; and the consciousness of the deed-fruit is evolution through this fruit of the deed.

Now he describes the characteristic form of knowledge, deed and fruit of deed:

II.32. Knowledge is comprehension *(vikalpa)* of objects; deed is

that which is undertaken by the soul; it is said to be manifold; its fruit is either pleasure or pain. (124)

Knowledge is comprehension of objects. What do we mean here by object? Everything which stands out with distinction (*vibhaga*) between self and other. Clear-distinction (*vikalpa*) [between self and other] is the presentation of the object's appearance (*akara*). So we call knowledge the clear-distinction of an object with reference to its own appearance and appearances strange to it, both showing themselves simultaneously as in the interior expanse of a looking-glass.

The deed is the thing done by the self: that positive-existence (*sadbhava*) which is every moment effected by the self, assuming now this and then that mental-state (*bhava*), is called a deed (*karman*); for it is attained (*prapyate*) by the self. And, though uniform, it is manifold (successful or futile); according as the vicinity of material-*karman* as a condition (required for the purpose) occurs or does not occur.

The pleasure or pain to be brought about by the deed is the fruit of the deed. The fruit of a deed, when due (insert *yad*) to the negation of the vicinity of material-*karman* as an accessory-condition, is characterized by serenity (*anakulatva*) and is normal (*prakrti-bhuta*); it is happiness. But the fruit of a deed, when due to the occurrence of the vicinity of material-*karman* as an accessory-condition, is abnormal (*vikrti-bhuta*), since the characteristic of happiness is absent; it is misery.

Thus we have ascertained the characteristic form of knowledge, deed, and the fruit of deed.

Now he ascertains that knowledge, deed, and the fruit of deed are the self:

II.33. The self is evolvement by nature; this evolution is with reference to knowledge, deed or fruit of the deed; therefore knowledge, deed, and fruit of the deed must be considered to be the self. (125)

Now the self has evolution for self, because we have ourselves stated that "the self is itself evolution." The evolution, since it has here consciousness for self, is fit to be knowledge, deed, or fruit of the deed, since consciousness consists of these. Therefore, knowledge, deed, and fruit of the deed are the self.

Since with this definition of pure substance no connection with strange substances is possible, and since the modifications are dissolved in the substance, therefore the self consists in pure substance.

Accordingly, since from the certitude that the self, when evolved into or reduced to the state of being knowable (*jneyatam apanna*) (cf. *Pravachanasara*, 32 and 42) is not pure, a realization of the principle (*tattva*) of pure self entity results from establishment of the principle (*tattva*) of knowledge,

welcoming now this (realization of the principle of pure self), he concludes the exposition of substance in general:

II.34. If the *shramana* is sure in his conviction that the soul itself is agent, instrument, act and fruit, and does not evolve into something else, then he conceives the [real nature of the] pure self. (126)

He who, after having thus ascertained that the self is agent, instrument, act and fruit of the act, no more evolves into the strange [other] substance, attains the pure self, which has exhausted its commingling with strange substances and whose modifications are dissolved in its substance; but none else succeeds in this.

Thus, in the days when the manifestations (*vrtti*) of my self were coloured by passion (*uparaga*), which rushed forth owing to the vicinity of accessory conditions, namely the bondage by material-*karman*, familiar from all time, –like a crystal gem, whose manifestations are coloured by a hue (*uparaga*) which rushes forth owing to the vicinity of the China rose–and when I was a transmigrating soul with a secondary-nature (*vikara*), superinduced by "the other," even then no one belonged to me;

even then I, alone, was agent, independent as I was by my thought-nature, although impassioned;

even then I, alone, was instrument, nearest-cause (*sadhakatama*) as I was by my thought-nature, although impassioned;

even then I, alone, was deed, attained by the self as I was, through the innate nature of the evolutions of my thought, although impassioned;

even then I, alone, was the fruit of the deed, happiness, or, with reversed qualities, misery, effected by the innate nature of the evolutions of my thought, although impassioned.

And at present, when the manifestations of the self, completely pure and original, flash forth in consequence of the dissolution of the presence of an accessory-condition, namely bondage by material-*karman*, familiar from the beginning,–like a crystal gem, when the manifestations of its self, completely pure and original, flash forth through the disappearance of the vicinity of the China rose–when I am exclusively desirous of liberation and have exhausted the secondary-nature, superinduced by "the other," now also no one belongs to me;

now also I, alone, am agent, independent through my completely pure thought-nature;

now also I, alone, am instrument, nearest cause as I am through my completely pure thought-nature;

now also I, alone, am deed, attained by myself as I am, through the innate nature of the evolutions of my completely pure thought;

now also I, alone, am the fruit of the deed, called happiness and characterized as serenity, effected by my completely pure thought-nature.

Thus to one realizing that the self is one only in the path of bondage as well as of liberation—like an ultimate atom, with its oneness realized–no longer does an evolution into other substance take place. And, like that atom, realizing his oneness, he is no more connected with "the other"; then through non-connection with other substance he becomes completely pure. Realizing that the agent, the instrument, the deed and the fruit of the deed are all himself, he no more becomes commingled with the modifications; and owing to not being commingled with modifications he becomes completely pure.

"Dissevering the self from intercourse with other substance and cleansing by generality the complete set of particularities; thus the pure mode-of-considering-things (*naya*) plunders the grandeur of Infatuation, and distinguishes the reality [of the nature of self] through deep discriminative insight." (PS *Kalash* 7)

"When the evolution into 'the other' has stopped and the delusion of difference between agent, act, etc., has disappeared, this consciousness, having at last realised the principle of pure self, and concentrated in the pure splendour, consisting of consciousness alone, will stand for ever liberated, whilst its innate grandeur shines forth." (PS *Kalash* 8)

"Having thus levelled the mind in the knowledge of substance in general, (the author) now erects the precipitous heights of the knowledge of its species (*vishesha*)." (PS Kalash 9)

Thus the exposition of SUBSTANCE IN GENERAL.

Here begins the exposition of the particularities (*vishesha*)of substance: wherein he first ascertains the particularization (*vishesha*) of substance as soul and non-soul:

SUBSTANCE IN PARTICULAR (VERSES 127-144)

II.35. Substance is soul and non-soul. Soul, again, is constituted of consciousness (*chetna*) and psychic-attention (*upayoga*); non-soul is devoid of consciousness, primarily material-substance. (127)

Substance, even while not forsaking the generality (*samanya*) of substance, which is the condition (*nibandhana*) of oneness, yet, since there exist differential characteristics, "mounted" upon this (generality), admits the particularization of soul and non-soul, in consequence of their mutual exclusion (*vyavaccheda*).

Of these two, the soul has only one specialized-form *(vyakti)*, the self-substance. But of non-soul there are five specialized-forms, (1) material substance, (2) substance *dharma* (principle of motion), (3) the substance *adharma* (principle of rest), (4) the substance time, (5) the substance space.

The differential (i.e. only belonging to one class of substances, and therefore used in the definition) characteristic (*vishesha-lakshana*) of soul is the fact that it consists of consciousness with its manifestation or psychic-attention; of non-soul, again, it is being without consciousness.

The soul is that (substance) in which we see installed a manifestation of consciousness, august, in the form of conscious awareness (*samvitti*), never absent, and since it penetrates its own properties, shining with characteristic nature,

and of psychic-attention, characterized as an evolution thereof and having the form of a functioning of the substance.

Where, on the other hand, we see installed an insentient-nature (*achetana*), inwardly and outwardly, due to absence of consciousness, accompanied by psychic-attention and with characteristics as described, that is non-soul

Now he defines the differentiation between the universe and the beyond (*a-loka*):

II.36. That which is located in space, provided with time and *asti-kayas* (those having extension in space), *dharma* and *adharma* [the principles of motion and rest], and conjoined with soul and matter, is at all times the universe [loka]. (128)

Of substance (read *dravyam*) there is what is differentiated by differentiation as universe and the beyond, because th ese have each its own characteristics.

The universe, namely, is characterized by the fact that it consists in inherence of the six substances; but the beyond (or non-universe) is characterized by consisting merely of space.

Wherein and with what extension of extremely large space, pervading all substances, soul and matter, which have movement and rest for properties, enact movement and rest; and *dharma* and *adharma*, which are the conditions (*nibandhana*) of their movement and rest, are present enveloping them; and time, the cause (*nimitta*) of the revolving (*vartana*) of all substance, for ever luxuriates (*durlalita*): that which has for definition the consisting of the assemblage of that so extended space and of all other substances without exception is universe.

On the other hand, in what extension of space the movement and rest of soul and matter do not take place, and *dharma* and *adharma* do not abide, and time does not luxuriate, that is the beyond.

Now he ascertains the differentiation of existence-as-action (as motion, *kriya-bhava*) and qualitative-existence (*tad-bhava*):[57]

II.37. Origination, permanence and annihilation of the universe, comprising of souls and matter, take place by evolution, combination and separation.[58] (129)

There is a differentiation of substance according to its possession of action and its possession of mere (qualitative-) being. Matter and soul are both in the possession of (qualitative-) being and of action, because they arise, are permanent and vanish by evolution, separation and combination. But the other substances possess mere states-of-evolution of their own being, because they arise, are permanent and vanish exclusively by evolution. This is certain.

Here being is characterized as only its own state-of-evolution; action as movement [or vibration, *parispandan*].

All the substances are in possession of being; for, being through evolution endowed with constancy (*anvaya*) and divergence (*vyatireka*), and being permanent, arising and vanishing (by evolution), they have evolution as their proper nature.

But material substances possess action as well; for, being separated by movement and combined by combination, and being, on the other hand, permanent, arising and vanishing through separation, they have movement as their proper nature.

In the same way, souls possess action also; for, being by movement separated from material-substances functioning at that time as *karman* or *no-karman*, and being combined with them by combination, and, moreover, arising, being permanent, and vanishing through separation, they have movement as their proper nature.

Now he teaches that differentiation of the substances results from differentiation of the qualities:

II.38. As marks *(linga)* by which the substance is distinctly-known as soul or as non-soul we must consider the qualities differentiated by non-identity[59] (with the substances) and by being of an incorporeal or corporeal nature (*murta-amurta*). (130)

Qualities are marks, because by them, as belonging to substance and not to anything else, substance is marked, gone to (*lingyate* = *gamyate*). And, being differentiated from substance by non-identity (*a-tad-bhava*), according to the saying "the substance is not the qualities, and the qualities are not the substance (cf. *Pravachana-sara*, 108)," they function as marks thereof, when the mark and the possessor-of-the-mark are known.

And these qualities cause in the substances such differentiations as "this is a soul," and "this is a non-soul"; for they themselves are endowed with differentiation through the fact that (the substances) are differentiated by their distinctive-being (*tad-bhava*). And, because the differentiation of the (qualities) arises from the fact that a substance is differentiated by this, or that proper nature, therefore, as the corporeal and incorporeal substances are differentiated by their respective-distinctive-being, i.e. by either corporeality or incorporeality, we have certain differentiation of the qualities, "these qualities are corporeal, and those are incorporeal."

Now he expounds the definition and relation of corporeal and incorporeal qualities:

II.39. Corporeal *(murta)* qualities, which can be perceived by the sense-organs, characterise the material substances (*pudgala-dravya)* and are manifold. The qualities of incorporeal substances should be considered incorporeal (*amurta*). (131)

Perceptibility by the sense-organs is the definition of corporeal qualities; and the very opposite holds true of the incorporeal qualities. And these corporeal qualities belong to material-substance, since this alone is corporeal. The incorporeal qualities belong to the other substances, since all substances, other than matter, are incorporeal.

Now he teaches the qualities of the corporeal matter-substance:

II.40. Colour, taste, smell, and touch are found in matter, beginning with fine substance[60] and ending with earth. But sound is a manifold (*chitra*) material-substance. (132)

Touch, taste, smell, and colour are perceptible to the sense-organs, since they form objects for them. And these, perceived or not perceived, according as the sensorial-perceptibility has a manifest-(*vyakti*) or latent-form (*shakti*), belong, in the character of special qualities, to every kind of matter without exception, beginning with the ultimate atom, the fine modification consisting of one substance, and ending with the earth-aggregate, the gross modification, consisting of several substances; and, since owing to their corporeality, they do not inhere in other substances, they prove the existence of matter.

That sound also, as perceived by a sense-organ, is a quality should not be suggested; for, inasmuch as it exhibits a manifoldness due to variety-of-nature (*vaichitrya*), it is taken to be a modification of matter, consisting of many substances.

For, if a quality, then, in the first place, sound is not a quality of an incorporeal substance, since the incorporeal substance also would be an object of the auditory sense-organ, inasmuch as quality and that-which-possesses-the-quality, as not possessing separate infinitesimal-spacial-constituents (*pradesha*), are realized in the same realization of intuitive awareness.

Nor is it a quality of corporeal substance, since the characteristic of a quality is here eradicated by the characteristic of a modification. The characteristic of a modification is, in fact, incidentality; and the characteristic of a quality is constancy (*nityatva*). So sound, in which durability is eradicated by incidentality, is not a quality. As for the durability found in it, that, we should notice, belongs to the components of the several (objects) and to their qualities, such as touch, etc., and is not found in the modification called sound.

But, if sound is a modification of matter, then it is not necessary that it should be, like the aggregate earth, an object for the tactile organ, etc.; for (1) water is not an object of the olfactory organ, (2) light not of the olfactory and gustatory organs, (3) wind not of the olfactory, gustatory and visual organs. And yet water, light and wind (Read *evam ab-jyotir-marutah*) do not accordingly (1) lack smell, (2) lack smell and taste, (3) lack smell, taste and colour, since it is believed that all the kinds of matter possess the fourfold set of qualities, touch, etc. For we see that the same material-components which give rise to (*a*) the moon-stone, (*b*) the fire-stick and (*c*) the barley-corn, which possess the fourfold set of qualities, touch, etc., in manifest-form (*vyakta*), likewise originate (*a*) water (read *ab-jyotir* or *ap-pradyotir* instead of *apradyotir*) with unmanifest smell, (*b*) light with unmanifest smell and taste, and (*c*) the wind in the stomach with unmanifest smell, taste and colour.

And the fact that some quality in some circumstances possesses sometimes a manifest as well as a not-manifest-form, dependent upon a manifoldness of incidental evolutions, is not opposed to the innate nature of an eternal substance.

Let it be then that sound is a modification of matter.

Now he mentions the qualities of the other incorporeal substances:

II.41. The function of space is giving room; the *dharma*-substance is cause of motion; the substance opposite to *dharma* has for quality the effecting of rest; (133)

II.42. The quality of time is the rolling-on (of events) (*vartana*); the manifestation of consciousness or psychic-attention is said to be the quality of self. Thus, in short, you should know the qualities of the substances devoid of corporeality. (134)

The typical-quality of space is to be the cause of giving universally and simultaneously room to all substances.

That of *dharma* to be at once a cause of movement to all souls and material-components possessing movement as evolution.

That of *adharma* to be at once a cause of rest to all souls and material-components possessing rest as evolution.

That of time to be a cause of the fact that all other substances without exception occur according to their modification in a certain moment (*samaya*).

That of soul to be an evolution of consciousness.

Thus in this concise enumeration of typical-qualities there is proof-of-existence (*linga*) of the incorporeal-substances.

The fact of providing a common room (*avagaha*) for all substances at the same time, since by reason of non-omnipresent it does not belong to any other substance, suffices to prove space.

The fact of causing at one moment, as far as the universe reaches, the movements of all souls and material-components which are evolving through movement,–which property does not belong to time (cf commentary on 48) and the material components, (i.e. ultimate atoms), since these do not possess (several) infinitesimal-spacial-units; or to soul, since this possesses, except in the case of *samudghata,*[61] only an "innumerable" (*asamkheya*) (the soul contains "innumerable *pradeshas*", cf. next *gatha*) portion of the universe; or to space, since there is no fluctuation of the limit of the universe and the beyond; nor to *adharma,* since this is cause of an opposite effect–proves *dharma.*

Similarly, the fact of causing at one moment, as far as the universe reaches, the rest of all souls and material-components, which are evolving through rest–which property does not belong to time and the material-components, since these do not possess (several infinitesimal-spacial-units; or to soul, since this possesses, except in the case of *samudghata,* only an "innumerable" portion of the universe; or to space, since this is independent of the limit between the universe and the beyond; or to *dharma,* since this is cause of an opposite effect–proves *adharma.*

Similarly, the fact of causing all other substances without exception to occur in moments according to their modifications–which property does not belong by nature to these (other substances), since the occurrence characterized by moments must be effected by another cause–proves time.

Similarly, the evolution through consciousness–which evolution does not belong to any of the other substances, since they are insentient–proves soul.

Thus the differentiation of substances may be known by the differentiation of the qualities (cf. Amrtachandra's introductory remark to PS 130).

Now he teaches the differentiation of the substances with reference to their possessing or not possessing (several) infinitesimal-spacial-units:

II.43. ***Jivas,*** **material-aggregates,** ***dharma, adharma*** **and space possess innumerable space-points or infinitesimal-spacial-units; but time has no space-points. (135/1)**

Souls, matter, *dharma, adharma* and space are possessed of infinitesimal-spacial-units (*pradeshas*); for they contain several *pradeshas.* The time-atom (*kalanu*), however, is devoid of *pradeshas*; for it is only a (single) *pradesha.*

The possession of (several) infinitesimal-spacial-units holds true of soul, because in both its contraction (*samvarta*) and expansion (*vistara*) it never leaves the (region of) the innumerable infinitesimal-spacial-units which are coextensive with the space of the universe[62];

of matter, because although it is *a-pradesha*, particle-less, when considered as a substance (i.e. atom), owing to its extending over only one *pradesha*–yet it possesses a fluctuating number of infinitesimal-spacial-units, through its modifications having a numerable number, two, etc., an innumerable and an infinite number;

of *dharma*, because it has the nature of extending over innumerable infinitesimal-spacial-units which pervade the whole universe;

of *adharma*, because it has the nature of extending over innumerable infinitesimal-spacial-units which pervade the whole universe;

of space, because it has the nature of extending over an infinite number of infinitesimal-spacial-units which pervade everything.

But the time-atom (*kalanu*) is devoid of infinitesimal-spacial-units (*a-pradesha*), because, considered as a substance, it covers only one infinitesimal-spacial-units, and, considered in its modifications, it has no intermingling.

Therefore the time-substance is without spacial-units, and all other substances have spacial-units.

Now he teaches where situated are these substances with and without infinitesimal-spacial-units:

II.44. Space or sky is in the universe (*loka*) and that which is beyond the universe (*aloka*); *dharma, adharma* [the principles of motion and rest][63] are stretched over the universe; so is time, with the remaining [two] substances, souls (*jivas*) and material-components. (136)

Space is in and outside the universe, since it occurs without any difference as to containing or not containing the six substances.[64]

Dharma and *adharma* are in the whole universe, because it is not possible that souls and matter, which move and rest through their causation, move or rest outside the universe or only in one region thereof.

Time, too, is in the universe; for its modifications, such as moments (*samaya*) etc., are found in the evolutions of souls and matter; but it covers one infinitesimal-spacial-unit of the world, since it does not possess *pradeshas*.[65]

Souls and matter are in the universe, for good reason, because the world has the inherence of the six substances for self. But, since soul has the property of expansion and contraction over (more or fewer) infinitesimal-spacial-unit, and since matter has the property of smooth (or viscid, *snigdha*) and rough (*ruksha*) qualities, which are the cause of its cohesion (*bandha*)[66], there is no restriction of time[67], souls and matter between (the limits of) one infinitesimal-spacial-unit (*desha*, here=*pradesha*) and the whole universe; thus with reference to their single substantiality[68] their limit is one spacial-unit, but with reference to several substances it is the whole universe, on the principle (*nyaya*) of the box full of perfumed powder.[69]

Now he explains generally the manner in which possession or non-possession of several infinitesimal-spacial-units takes place:

II.45. As are the infinitesimal-spacial-units of space, so are the infinitesimal-spacial-units of the other substances: the ultimate atom is without (plurality of) spacial-units or space-points. By this is explained how the [possession of] infinitesimal-spacial-units[70] originates. (137)

[The author] will himself in *sutra* 48 give the definition of an infinitesimal-unit of space, as that which is pervaded by an ultimate atom. Here it is taught that there is oneness in the way of defining the infinitesimal-spacial-unit, seeing that, as are the infinitesimal-units of space, so are those of the other substances. Therefore, as space, which is measured (read *ganyamanasya*) by a portion (*amsha*) pervaded by one ultimate atom, contains an unlimited number of infinitesimal-units, since it possesses an unlimited number of such portions, so *dharma, adharma* and the single soul, each measured by a portion which covers one ultimate atom, contain an innumerable number of infinitesimal-spacial-units, since they possess an innumerable number of such portions.

And, as the number of infinitesimal-spacial-units contained by *dharma* and *adharma*, which have a definite extension, is innumerable, so the number of infinitesimal-spacial-units contained by soul is innumerable, although it possesses an indefinite extension, varying with expansion and contraction—as leather varies in size with dryness and wetness, since its own portions are neither few nor many. The proof of its incorporeal contraction and expansion can be given by mere self-consciousness, since it pervades the body, stout or lean, the infant and the boy.

As concerns matter, although we have seen that, considered as a substance, it is devoid of infinitesimal-spacial-units, since it only covers one infinitesimal-spacial-unit, yet it has origination of infinitesimal-spacial-units owing to its innate nature of being capable of an evolution into viscid (*snigdha*) and rough (*ruksha*) qualities of such a kind that they are the cause of the origination of two infinitesimal-spacial-units, etc. So then, in the case of matter, we must infer a possession-of-infinitesimal-spacial-units numerable, namely two, etc., innumerable and infinite, because through modification it can have a plurality of infinitesimal-spacial-units.

Now he ascertains the absence of infinitesimal-spacial-units in the time-atom (*kalanu*):

II.46. The moment (*samaya*) lacks infinitesimal-spacial-units; it occurs (*vartate*), while a material-substance (*dravya-jata*, i.e. atom; cf. note 68) which covers only one infinitesimal-spacial-unit or space-point traverses an infinitesimal-unit of the space-substance. (138)

The time-moment lacks infinitesimal-spacial-units, because it covers, as a substance, only one infinitesimal-spacial-unit. And it does not, as is the case with matter, through modification have several infinitesimal-spacial-units; for though it is innumerable substance of infinitesimal-spacial-units stretched in a continuous expanse, yet, since these do not commingle, it remains with the extent of only a spacial-unit, occupying the space-units one by one, and its only occurring is while an ultimate (material-) atom traverses, with slow movement, the one space-particle in which this (particular time-stream) inheres.[71]

Now he makes known the substance and modification of the time-object (*kala-padartha*):

II.47. A moment (*samaya*) is what is equal to the movement of (an ultimate material-atom) traversing a spatial particle. The object (*artha*) which is before and after that (moment) is time. The moment is subject to origination (*utpanna*) and annihilation. (139)

When an ultimate (material-) atom with slow motion passes through the spacial particle which is pervaded by a time-object measuring one particle in extension, then that moment (*samaya*), a minute occurrence of that time-object, and equal to the duration (*parimana*) of that passing through that one particle, is a modification of the time-object. Therefore that object (*artha*) (*artha* = *padartha* = everything that exists objectively) which possesses an eternity manifested (read *vyanjita-nityatvo*) by its existence in an occurrence anterior and posterior to the so-described modification is a substance. So substantial-time (*dravya-samaya*)[72] is not-originated and exempt from annihilation; but modificational-time (*prayaya-samaya*) is both originated and subject to annihilation.

And this *samaya* (moment) is without portions (*amsha*):[73] otherwise the thesis that the spacial-particle is without portions would not hold good. But not even if one ultimate-atom could move to the end of the world in one moment, would the *samaya*, for that reason, possess portions, since it would be a particular (*vishishta*) evolution of movement, like a particular evolution of spacial-containment (*avagaha*). As, that is, an aggregate of an endless number of ultimate-atoms, which aggregate owing to a particular evolution of spacial-containment (cf. n. 62) has the extension of one ultimate-atom, does not prove for the atom the possession of an endless number of portions (for it does not even possess portions), in the same way the innumerable number of time-atoms,[74] –whilst an ultimate (material) atom, owing to a particular evolution of movement, moves from one end of the world to another within one moment (*samaya*), which is delimited by the evolution of passing through one space-particle pervaded by one time-atom–does not prove that the time-moment possesses an innumerable number of portions (for it does not even possess portions).

Now he gives a definition of the infinitesimal-particle of space:

II.48. Space, as occupied (*nivishta*) by a material-atom, is termed *pradesha* (infinitesimal-spatial unit or space-point); it[75] is capable of affording room to all material-atoms. (140)

A part (*amsa*) of space which can be pervaded by one atom is a spacial infinitesimal-particle. And, this, although one, is capable of affording room to the infinitesimal-particles of the other five substances and, moreover, to aggregates of an endless number of ultimate atoms, if these are evolved through an ultimate fineness.

And space, although one undivided substance, may be supposed to consist of parts; for otherwise it would not be capable of affording room to all material-atoms.[76]

I. But,[77] if one should think that space does not possess parts, then let him lift up two fingers in space and inquire, "Is this one spot (*kshetra*) or more? And, if one, is it one as a continuous substance whose parts are not distinguished-from-one-another (*bhinna*) or as a continuous substance whose parts are distinguishable?"

(*IA*) In case it is one continuous (*a-vibhaga*) substance whose parts are not distinguished, then, since the occupied by one finger is, as a part of space, not distinguishable from that of the other finger, one of the two parts does not exist; and therefore, since there are not two or more parts, space would contain merely one infinitesimal-particle, as a material-atom does.

(*IB*) And, in case it is one continuous substance whose parts are distinguishable, this involves the supposition of one continuous substance having (many) parts.

(*II*) If (the interlocutor thinks that the spots of the two fingers are) more than one, is it as several non-continuous substances or as one continuous substance?

(*II A*) If as several non-continuous substances, then space, as one substance, would be an endless number of substances.

(*IIB*) If as one continuous substance, then this involves the supposition of one continuous substance with (many) parts.

Now he announces the two conglomerations, in transverse and vertical direction (*triyag-urdhva-prachayau*):[78]

II.49. The infinitesimal-space points contained by substances are either one, two, many, or transcending number, or endless (in number). But time has only one space-point, viz. *samaya* or moment. (141)

The conglomeration of infinitesimal-particles is a conglomeration in a transverse direction. And the conglomeration whose occurrence is characterized by moments (*samaya*) is a vertical conglomeration of them.

A conglomeration in a transverse direction exists:

for space, because it possesses a fixed, endless number of *pradeshas*;

for *dharma* and *adharma*, because they possess a fixed innumerable number of *pradeshas*;

for the soul, because it possesses an unfixed, innumerable number (cf *Tattva-dipika* on 136) of *pradeshas*;

for matter, because, considered as a substance, it possess one *pradesha* with the capability (*shakti*) of forming several *pradeshas*, and, considered as modification, it possesses two and many *pradeshas*.

But it does not exist for time, because, whether in potential-form (*shakti*) or in manifest-form (*vyakti*), it possesses only one *pradesha.*

The vertical conglomeration is not excluded from any substance, since the occurrence of all substances, in its connection with the three aspects (*koti*) (of time), possesses parts. But there is this difference: the vertical conglomeration of the substances other (than time) is a conglomeration whose occurrence is characterized by the time-moments; but the vertical conglomeration of time is a conglomeration of the time-moments themselves. For the occurrence of the other substances, being something else than the moment (*samaya*), has qualification by the moment; but the occurrence of time, being identical with the moment, has not that.

Now he refutes the opinion that the vertical conglomeration of the time-substance would lack identity (*anvaya*)[79]:

II.50. If origination and annihilation within one moment are found in any *samaya*, then that *samaya* (time-moment) is established in its own nature. (142)

The moment, indeed, is the occurrence-part of the time-object (*samaya-padartha*); in this moment we necessarily find the origination and annihilation of something, because, as arising through the traversing (*vyatipata*), of a material-atom, it is preceded by a cause.

Should these two belong to the occurrence-part, does this then happen simultaneously or successively? If simultaneously, there is no simultaneity, because two contradictory qualities of one thing cannot occur together. And, if successively, there is no succession, since there is no division (*vibhaga*) in the occurrence-part, owing to its fineness (*sukshmatva*).

Therefore we must necessarily search for something that has the occurrence (*vrttimat*); and this is the time-object. For of that, even in its single occurrence-part there is origination and annihilation; thus:

that same which,
in regard to something which has occurrence
is, in its occurrence-part,
as qualified by that occurrence-part, origination
is for the same object which has occurrence,
in its occurrence-part
as particularized by the precedent occurrence-part, annihilation.

If thus origination and annihilation occur in the one occurrence-part, how is there absence of identity in the time-object? For, even though, as qualified by the precedent and subsequent occurrence-parts, it simultaneously acquires annihilation and origination, why should it not possess permanence owing to its not being annihilated or produced in innate nature? So we have proved that origination, annihilation and permanence belong to the time-object in one occurrence-part.

Now he proves that origination, annihilation and permanence belong to the time-object in all its occurrence-parts:

II.51. In one moment exist the things (*arthas)* which are called origination, permanence and disappearance of time (*samaya*); at all times, therefore, this forms the existence (*sad-bhava*) of the time-atom (*Kalanu,* time-stream in one spacial *pradesha*). (143)

In all its occurrence-parts origination, annihilation and permanence of the time-object are present, since we see this in one occurrence-part. And this proves right, because the existence of the particular could not be justified without the existence of the generality. The existence of the time-object follows thus: if both the existence of the particular and the existence of the generality are proved, then in no way whatever can they exist without existence (*astitva*) itself.

Now he proves that time possesses only one *pradesha*, since otherwise time could not exist:[80]

II.52. That object in which no (plurality of) *pradeshas*[81] exists, and which is not known[82] to contain in fact[83] even one *pradesha*, must be admitted to be a *shunya* (void); for it is [then] an object different from existence. (144)

(*A*) Existence (*astitva*),[84] in fact, is an occurrence, consisting of an union of origination, annihilation and permanence. And this occurrence, if propounded without (even one) *pradesha*, does not belong to time; for in the absence of *pradeshas* there is absence of that which occurs. But this (absence) is a void, since the term existence is a synonym for occurrence.

(*B*) Moreover, time cannot be mere occurrence, because occurrence, without something that occurs, is unaccountable. Or, if you would still accept such, how could it have for self an union of origination, annihilation and permanence?

(*C*) If (you then should maintain this as true), because each of the precedent parts is annihilated, each of the subsequent parts effected, and the one own self permanent, inasmuch as this one own self depends on many beginningless, endless and uniterrupted parts,

Then no! Whence, indeed, could this oneness be, since there can be no simultaneity of that part, where the annihilation, and of the part, where the origination proceeds? And whence could there be stability, which abides in this oneness of annihilation and origination; since the annihilated part has totally disappeared, and the originating part is just attaining its self, which is brought into existence? This being so, the threefold set of characteristics comes to nought; *kshana-bhanga* (universal-momentariness) is triumphant; eternal substance has its sunset; momentarily annihilated existence-forms (*bhavas*) raise their heads. Therefore, for fear lest all truth should become confused, we must necessarily search for something that has the occurrence, and that is its abode. Now this is the *pradesha* (infinitesimal-particle), because a correspondence (*anu-vidhayitva*) to presence and absence cannot belong to what is not *pradesha* (*a-pradesha*).

(*D*) If time thus has *pradesha*, why not agree that it contains an innumerable number of *pradeshas*, equal to the space of the universe, as the condition of its being one substance?

The reason is non-admission of modificational–time. It is the modification of an ultimate atom passing through the substantial-time, which covers only one *pradesha*, that we admit as the moment. If the substantial-time consisted of an innumerable number of *pradeshas* equal to the space of the universe, whence could that be established?

If it is urged that, even if this, as one total substance, possesses innumerable *pradeshas*, equal to the space of the universe, the moment might result from the ultimate atom passing through one *pradesha* of the substantial-time.

Not so, because an occurrence of a part cannot consistently be an occurrence of the whole. The moment is the minute occurrence-part of the whole-time object, not of such and such a single part. Moreover, it would follow that conglomeration in transverse directions conglomeration in vertical direction (cf. the introduction which *Tattva-dipika* gives to 141). Thus, (the moving ultimate atom) first abides with one *pradesha* (of the supposed innumerable time-*pradeshas*), then with another, then again with another, so that conglomeration in transverse direction, becoming conglomeration in vertical direction, proves the substance to contain only one *pradesha*.

(*E*) Therefore, whoever does not wish to assert that a

conglomeration in transverse direction is the same as a conglomeration in vertical direction must from the very first conclude that the time-substance contains only one *pradesha*.

Now, after having thus stated the Principle concerning the Knowables, he examines the self by aid of a distinction between knowledge and knowable; and, in order to have the self (*atma*) completely distinguished, he reveals the reason for the embodied being of the external, other-referential [i.e. from the manifest physical, objective, external characteristic of bio-energies aspect] (*vyavahara*) soul-condition (*jivatva*):

DISTINCTIVE FEATURES OF JIVA SUBSTANCES (VERSES 145-200)

II.53. The world is eternal, complete and consummate with objects having infinitesimal-space-points; what knows that world is the *jiva*, connected with the fourfold set of *pranas* (vitalities or bio-energies). (145)

Of this world, complete and consummate with all the objects, whose possession of infinitesimal-particles has been examined by us, beginning with space and ending with time, the knower is the soul only, and no other, because of the inconceivable fullness of energy (*shakti*) which the soul, although placed in the midst thereof, possesses for discrimination between self and "other."

Thus the remaining substances are knowable only; the soul substance is both knowable and knowledge. Such is the division between knowledge and knowable.

And, although this soul possesses, as cause of an innately-manifested and endless knowledge-energy, and characterized by persistence in the three times, and never absent, inasmuch as it is really its (the soul's) characteristic being,–its true soul-nature (*nishchaya-jivatva*) [the conscious vital force or consciousness-as-such], yet in the state of *samsara*, inasmuch as its self is vitiated by adhesion of matter, proceeding in a beginningless stream, we must distinguish a reason for its external, other-referential (*vyavahara*) soul-condition (*jivatva*), viz. its being connected with the fourfold set of *pranas*.

Now he states what the *pranas* are:

II.54. The *prana* of the senses, the *prana* of force *(bala)*, the *prana* of duration of life, the *prana* of respiration,[85] –these are the *pranas* of the *jivas*. (146/1)

The *pranas* of the senses are the fivefold set of touch, taste, smell, eye sight and ear hearing; the *pranas* of force (*bala*) are the body, the voice and the mind; the *prana* of duration of life (*ayu*), which is the supportive factor (*nimitta*) of that, aims at the maintenance of transmigratory existence (*bhav dharan*); the *prana* of inhaling and exhaling is respiration, characterized by upward and downward movement.

Now by means of an explanation of the *pranas* he teaches how they are a reason for the condition of soul (*jivatva*), and, moreover, how they are material:

II.55. That which by means of the four *pranas* (vitalities) lives, will live, and has previously lived, is called a *jiva* (a "liver," or soul). But the *pranas* have arisen from material substances. (147)

The soul (the "liver") lives, will live and has previously lived by means of the material vitalities (called *prana*) in general. Since, as these vitalities are coming together (of soul and matter) in a beginningless series, and located (in one place) in the three times, is the (external) condition (*hetu*) of the soul principle (*jivatva*). Nevertheless, it is not the innate nature of soul, since it has arisen from material substances.

Now he proves the materiality of the *pranas*:

II.56. The soul, endowed with the *pranas*, bound with *karman* of infatuation, etc., enjoying the fruit of *karman* (*karmaphala),* binds itself with fresh *karman.* (148)

Because the soul, through being bound with the material *karmans* of infatuation, etc., is connected with the *pranas*, and because, by enjoying the fruit of material *karman* (action) through being bound by *pranas*, it binds itself again with fresh material *karman,* therefore the *pranas*, by reason of being effects of material *karmans* and causes of material *karmans,* are proved to be material.

Now he reveals how the *pranas* are causes of material *karmans*:

II.57. When the soul causes, by its infatuation or aversion,[86] injury to the *pranas* of self and other living beings, then this means bondage in consequence of such *karman* as knowledge-obscuration, etc. (149)

By its *pranas* the soul enjoys the fruit of *karman*; enjoying this, it takes up infatuation and aversion; by these it causes injury (*badha*) to the *pranas* of the own soul and another soul. Then, sometimes causing, and sometimes not causing, injury to the material-*pranas* (*dravya-prana*)[87] of "the other," but (always), through being impassioned, causing injury to the subjective-*pranas* (*bhava-prana*) of itself, the soul binds (itself with) *karmans*, of knowledge-obscuring kind, etc. Thus the *pranas* become causes of material-*karman* (*paudgalika-karman*).[88]

Now he teaches the interior cause of the serial recurrence of material-*pranas* (*pudgala-prana*):

II.58. The self, stained with *karman*, acquires again other and other *pranas*, so long as it does not give up the notion of "mine" with reference to sense-objects, primarily its body. (150)

Of this (read *yeyam atmanah*) serial recurrence of material-*pranas* the root is beginningless material-*karman*, enveloping the self; attachment (*uparaktatva*), showing itself as the idea of "mine" with reference to the body, etc., is the interior cause.

Now he teaches the interior cause of the cessation of this series of material-*pranas*:

II.59. He who conquers the senses, etc., and meditates on the self *(atmakam = Prakrit appagam = atmanam)* endowed with psychic-attention is not affected by *karmans*. How then could the *pranas* follow him? (151)

Non-existence of attachment, which is the root of material-*karman*, is the interior cause of the cessation of this series of material-*karman*. And this absence accrues to him who has conquered all other substances such as the senses, like a crystal-gem withdrawn from the influence (*anuvrtti*) of any support, and who abides in the only (*kevala*) and stable self, completely pure and consisting merely of psychic-attention.

Here the purport is as follows: to effect the final distinctness of the self (from that which is other to it) the material *pranas*, as the cause of the (external, other-referential *vyavahara* condition of soul's state (*jivatva*) as such, must be annihilated.

Now again, in order to effect the complete distinctness of the self, he describes minutely the characteristic-nature of the modifications, which are the cause of the *vyavahara* condition of soul's state as such, characterized by *gati* (kind-of-existence):

II.60. A modification is a thing (*artha*) [e.g. a man, a god, etc.], belonging to a thing (*artha*) [e.g. the soul] which is certified as existent, and originating by coming into contact with another [i.e.material] thing (*artha*) (e.g. the conditions or modifications), with

varieties such as configuration (*samsthana*) (the shape of body in which the soul temporarily lives), etc. (152)

When of one thing certified as existent in its characteristic nature, which is its definite individuality, there is in another thing, likewise certified in its characteristic nature, which is its definite individuality, a self-attainment achieved under a specialized form, that [other] thing, consisting of more than one substance, is a modification. Such a modification of soul in matter, as of matter in other matter, arising through qualification by configuration and so forth, is actually experienced. And such a modification is logical. For the modification of a single substance, differentiated from the pure (*kevala*) soul simply as consisting in a connection with more than one substance, is discerned unimpaired within (the composite thing).

Now he instances particular modifications:

II.61. Men, beings in hell *(naraka)*, animals, and *devas*, are modifications of souls, metamorphosed by configurations and so forth, through the arising (*udaya*) of name-*karman* (*nama-karma*) (For the term *udaya*, see note 9 and note 12; for *nama-karman*, see note 51). (153)

Beings in hells, lower animals, men, *devas*–these in fact are modifications of souls. These, assuredly, as consisting of conjunctions with more than one substance–since this is the cause of the ripening of name-*karman* matter –have been metamorphosed by configurations and so forth; like the modifications of fire, chaff-fire, coal-fire and so forth through configurations such as agitation, vibration (for *khilva* read *khela*), and so on.

Now, as the reason for the distinction of own and others, he emphasizes the self's possession of existence, which, despite its mixture with other substances, makes it known as a thing:

II.62. Whoso knows the own nature of substance, dependent upon existence (*sad-bhava*), stated as triple [stability, origination, annihilation] and having varieties (*vikalpa*), will not be infatuated with other substance. (154)

The own nature of a substance is that possession of existence in a form of its own, which is the individuality and is called that which makes it known as a thing; since the own nature of a substance is dependent upon existence. Inasmuch as the own nature of a substance, when recognized as assuming, in the form of substance, quality and modification and in the form of stability, origination and annihilation, a triple variety, dispels infatuation for other substance and so is reason for the distinction of own and other, therefore, in order to effect the distinction of own and other, we must at every point take note of possession of existence in ones own form. Thus: That which has for own nature possession of existence, triple as being (1) substance characterized by unfailing presence of 'being conscious,' (2) quality, characterized by non-difference from the consciousness, and (3) modification characterized by divergence from the 'being conscious' and also triple as (1) stability by way of 'being conscious,' which extends to the prior and posterior divergences, and (2) origination and (3) evanescence, as diverging from prior and posterior, that, myself here, is one thing. That which has for own nature possession of existence, triple as being (1) substance, characterized by unfailing presence of not-being conscious, (2) quality, characterized by non-difference from the non-conscious, (3) modification, characterized by divergence from the not-being conscious, and also triple as (1) stability by way of not-being conscious, which extends to the prior and posterior divergences, and (2) origination and (3) evanescence, as diverging from prior and posterior, that, matter, is another. I have no infatuation: I have distinction of own and other.

Now, with a view to an absolute distinctness of the self, he considers the characteristics of the cause of its conjunction with other substance:

II.63. The self (*appa* in Pk., *atma* in Sk.) is of the nature of psychic-attention (*upayoga*): psychic attention is stated as knowledge and intuition [vision]. And this psychic-attention of the self is auspicious (*shubha*) or inauspicious (*ashubha*) good or evil]. (155)

Now the cause of the self's conjunction with other substance is a species of psychic-attention. Psychic-attention, indeed, is the own nature of the self, since it evolves in obedience to its (the self's) character as consciousness. And that *upayoga* is knowledge and intuition, since consciousness, according as it is definite or indefinite, has both forms. Now this psychic-attention is specialized in two ways, according to purity and impurity. Of these the pure is without attachment; the impure is with attachment, which again is twofold, good (*shubha*) and evil (*asubha*), because of the twofold character of the attachment, as being in the form of sanity or morbidity.

Now he informs us what psychic-attention is cause of conjunction with other substances:

II.64. If the psychic-attention is auspicious or good, it leads to accumulation or increase of the soul's virtue or merit (*punya*); if inauspicious or evil, its sinfulness (*papa*) likewise is accumulated or increases. In the absence of both there is no accession or accumulation [of *karmas*]. (156)

Psychic-attention, when impure, is cause of the soul's conjunction with other substance. As effected by attachment in the form of sanity (i.e. purifying effect, *vishuddhi*) or morbidity (affliction, distress, *sanklesh*), it receives a double aspect, as good or evil, and is active as cause of conjunction with other substance, which receives a double aspect, as merit and sin. But, when non-existence of this impure in both forms is effected, then only pure psychic-attention remains: and this, on the other hand, is no cause of conjunction with other substance.

Now he delineates the characteristic form of good psychic-attention:

II.65. Whoso knows the great *Jina*, respects the Liberated Souls and also the Homeless Ones [saints][89] and is compassionate to the living beings, his psychic-attention is good. (157)

Good psychic-attention, which,–as it consists in a recurrence of vision-infatuating and conduct-infatuating matter reposing in the special condition of destruction and subsidence[90]–embraces an attachment of a good kind, is engaged in entertaining faith in the *Arhats*, those Supreme Lords, Super-*Devas* of Great *Devas*, Supreme Gods, and the *Siddhas* and *sadhus*, and in practising compassion towards the totality of living beings.

Now he delineates the characteristic form of evil psychic-attention:

II.66. He whose psychic-attention is sunk in passion for sense-objects, addicted to hearing words that defile and pollute the mind, bad thoughts, bad companionship, [and] is violent and inclined to perverse ways, is evil. (158)

Evil psychic-attention,—since, as it consists in a recurrence of vision-infatuating and conduct-infatuating matter reposing in the specialized condition called *udaya* [arising of *karman*], it embraces an attachment of an improper kind,—is engaged in entertaining faith in perverse ways, other than the *Arhats*, those Supreme Lords, Super-

Devas of Great *Devas*, Supreme Gods, and the *Siddhas* and *Sadhus*, and in practising sense-gratification, passionate thought, bad hearing, bad intention, bad companionship, and violence.

Now he essays the destruction of the cause of conjunction with other substance:

II.67. Being free from evil psychic-attention and, not uniting with good conscious attentiveness in regard to other substance, I, becoming established in the real nature of self (*majjhatth* in Pk.) [*madhyastha* in Sk., i.e. being neutral or indifferent], meditate upon the self, which is of the nature of some-thing knowing. (159)

This impure psychic-attention, set forth as cause of conjunction with other substance, proceeds simply from dependence upon recurrence of other substances, reposing in a state of slow or vehement *udaya*, and not from anything else. Therefore I here become neutral to all other substance. Becoming so, I, released, through non-dependence upon recurrence of other substance, from impure psychic-attention, good or evil, and having, through embracing a recurrence of the absolute (*kevala*) self-substance, an evident pure psychic-attention, stand with my self of psychic-attention, ever immovably intent (read *upayunjams tishthami*) upon the self alone. This is my essay to destroy conjunction with other substance.

Now he proclaims neutrality in regard to other substance, such as body and so on:

II.68. I am not body, not mind, nor again voice, nor cause of these: neither the doer of action, nor getting it done by others, nor consenting or approving the same. (160)

Body and voice and mind I apprehend as other substance: hence I have no partiality for them. In regard to them all I am absolutely neutral. Thus: I am not unconscious, material substance, acting as basis of the characteristic forms of body, voice and mind: these, in fact, maintain their own characteristic forms even without me as an object (read *artham antarena*) to be basis of their characteristic forms. Hence, having shaken off partiality to body, voice and mind, I am absolutely neutral. Nor am I unconscious substance which is cause of body, voice and mind: these, in fact, are cause even without me as cause. Hence, having shaken off partiality to being their cause, I am absolutely neutral. Nor I am [worker of] unconscious substance which is independent cause of body, voice and mind: these, in fact, are worked even without me as a worker. Hence, having shaken off partiality to their being things worked by me, I am absolutely neutral. Nor I am instigator of unconscious substance which is independent worker of body, voice and mind: these, in fact, are worked even without me as instigator of that which works them. Hence, having shaken off partiality to being instigator of what works them, I am absolutely neutral. Nor am I approver of unconscious substance which is independent worker of body, voice and mind: they, in fact, are worked even without me as approver. Hence, having shaken off partiality to being approver of that which works them, I am here absolutely neutral.

Now he ascertains body, voice and mind to be other substance:

II.69. Body, mind and voice are declared to consist of material substance: material substance, again, is a mass of subtlemost particles of material substances (*paramanu dravyanam pindhah*). (161)

Body, voice and mind, all three, are other substance, because they consist of material substance. And they are material substance, because they are ascertained to have an existence of characteristic form which is the individual mark of material substance. Now such material substance is an evolution, in the modification of a single mass, of more than one sub-atomic (*paramanu*) substance: because, despite the plurality of the existences of characteristic form which are the individual marks of the plural sub-atomic (*paramanu*) substances, in a way they appear as an unity.

Now he establishes that the self is not other substance and not what acts upon other substance:

II.70. I am not composed of matter, nor is material substance made by me into a mass. Therefore I am neither the body, nor the maker or active agent (*karta*) of that body. (162)

As to this other substance, called body, comprising the pair, voice and mind, which in this section has been made out as consisting of matter, I am not it, because there is incompatibility in me, not composed of matter, being body, which consists of matter. Nor am I what works the body, whether by way of cause, or by way of agent, or by way of instigation of the agent, or by way of approver of the agent, because it is in every way incompatible that I, not agent of the evolution of plural material substance in its modification as a single mass, should be agent of the body, which consists in an evolution of plural material substance in a modification as a single mass.

Now he averts the doubt how there is evolution of plural substance in a modification as a mass:

II.71. The ultimate atom, itself not possessing spacial units or space-points, having the extent of one spacial unit only, and soundless, experiences, as smooth or rough, the condition of extension over two spacial units and so on. (163)

The ultimate atom, since it has not two or more spacial units, is without spacial units; since it has one spacial unit, it is of the extent of one spacial unit only; since it has not itself the particular modification, sound, which consists in plural substance of ultimate atoms, it is soundless. Because, existing without opposition to the four[91] touches, the five tastes, the two smells, and the five colours, it may be either smooth or rough, thence comes its experience, in the form of evolution into the modification "mass,"[92] of the condition of extension over two spacial units and so on. Thus, accordingly, smoothness and roughness bring about the condition "mass."

Now he states what-like are that smoothness and roughness of the ultimate atom:

II.72. Beginning with [extension over] one, the smoothness or roughness of the atom is said to increase, through its evolution, by units, until it experiences the condition of infinite number. (164)

The ultimate-atom has evolution, since that, as the innate nature of things, is unescapable. Subject to variation[93] from time to time in consequence of that evolution,—since the atom is adapted to diverse qualities,—smoothness or roughness results, including distinctions in an unbroken series, which, beginning with one, through addition of unit ends in infinity.

Next he here states from what kind of smoothness or roughness the condition of mass arises:

II.73. The smooth or rough evolutions of atoms are either even or odd: when exceeding the even by two, they are combined, except at the beginning.[94] (165)

The general rule is "combination resulting from smoothness or roughness in excess of the even by two degrees"; because a difference of two in degree of smoothness or roughness is, as cause of evolution, efficient of combination (allowed). The exception is "no combination resulting from smoothness or roughness in the first degree"; because smoothness or roughness in the first degree is, as not a cause of evolution in the thing to be evolved, not efficient of combination (forbidden).

Now he discerns the above-stated causality in the case of the "mass" condition of ultimate atoms:

II.74. The second degree in respect of smoothness undergoes combination with the smooth of the fourth degree, or with the rough:[95] the atom, in the third degree, is combined when associated with the fifth degree. (166)

The "mass" condition of ultimate atoms must be recognized as having the above-stated cause; for combination of two atoms of the second and fourth, and of the third and fifth degrees is admitted (Read *bandhasya prasiddheh*), if they are both smooth, or both rough, or one smooth and the other rough. And it is said:

"material-particles are combined smooth with smooth and rough with rough;

material-particles are combined, smooth and rough, similar and dissimilar in degree.[96]

There[97] is combination of the smooth with the smooth two degrees higher, of the rough with the rough two degrees higher:

there is combination of smooth with rough, in case of odd or even, excepting of the lowest degree."[98]

Now he discerns that the self is not agent of a material mass:

II.75. Aggregates extending over two or more spacial units–fine or gross; having configurations; earth, water, fire and wind–are originated by their own several evolutions. (167)

These thus originated aggregates,–extending over two or more spacial units; undergoing varieties of smoothness or roughness in consequence of varying potentialities of occupying space [see n. 33, and in general the *Tattva-dipika* on PS 93-2 (in the translation the portions numbered H and h]; assuming diverse configurations in consequence of varying potentialities of bearing shapes; subject each to its several potentiality of manifesting or veiling the fourfold set of touch and so on (touch, colour, smell, taste)—come into being merely by their own several evolutions, earth, water, fire, wind. Hence it is discerned that the soul is not agent of the mass [state] of material-particles, beginning with the double atom and ending with the infinite (read *dvyanukadi-anantanta-pudgalanam*).

Now he discerns that the self is not conveyor of a material mass:

II.76. The universe is in all directions densely packed, as room-filled, with material bodies, fine and gross, unadaptable and adaptable. (168)

Since the universe is of itself in all directions densely packed with material bodies — evolved in fineness and evolved in grossness; in case of not excessive fineness and grossness, possessed of potentiality for evolving as *karmic*-matter; in case of excessive fineness and grossness, lacking the same; by reason of being qualified by a power of room-filling not impeding one another—therefore it is discerned that the soul is not conveyor of a material mass.

Now he discerns that the self is not agent of the *karma*-condition of material masses:

II.77. Aggregates adaptable to *karma*-condition, when they meet with a soul's evolution, attain the state of *karman*; but they are not made to evolve by the soul. (169)

Since, in dependence upon an exterior means, namely the mere evolution of a soul, located in the same spot, material aggregates, being themselves equipped with a potentiality of evolving in the *karma*-condition[99] even without a soul to evolve them, evolve of themselves in the *karma*-state, therefore it is discerned that the soul is not agent of the *karma*-condition of material masses.

Now he discerns that the self is not maker of the body consisting of material substance evolved in the *karma*-condition:

II.78. Such and such material aggregates, having attained a *karma*-condition, give rise, further, to the soul's bodies, in its transitions to other bodies. (170)

Whatever material aggregates, merely on the occasion of a soul's evolution, evolve of themselves in *karma*-condition, the same, in dependence upon the soul's transition to another body in the course of its beginningless, continuous, activity, themselves give rise to bodies. Hence it is discerned that the soul is not the maker of the body, which consists of material substance evolved in *karma*-condition.

Now he discerns that the self is not body:

II.79. The physical, the plastic, the magnetic (electric), the emanatory and the *karmana* bodies all consist of material substance. (171)

Since the physical (*audarika*), the plastic (*vaikriyika*), the emanatory (*aharaka*), the magnetic (*taijas*) and the *karmana* bodies all consist of material substance, therefore it is discerned that the soul is not body.

Now he states what then is the soul's special, unshared, characteristic which effects its discrimination from all other substance, body and so on:

II.80. Know the soul to be tasteless, colourless, odourless, without the manifest touch quality (*avyakta* here = *asparsha*), with its quality of sentiency or consciousness, soundless, without apprehension by a mark, without any defined configuration. (172)

Since it is the self's proper nature to be without the qualities of taste, colour and odour, to be without manifestation of the touch quality, to be without modification as sound, and in consequence of this to be unapprehensible by a mark, also to be without any configuration, it has for the effecting of its discrimination from material substance tastelessness, colourlessness, odourlessness, unmanifestedness, soundlessness, inapprehensibility by a mark, non-configuration. Also its having consciousness for quality effects its discrimination from all non-soul substance, whether material or non-material. And this of itself, since, as inhering only in its own substance, soul, it carries with it its character as having a particular nature, effects the discrimination from the remaining other substances.

Whereas the expression without apprehension by a mark is used where "not apprehendible by a mark" might have been used, that is for the purpose of conceiving more meanings. Thus: (1) understanding "that whose apprehension is not when it is apprehensive by marks, i.e. by sense-organs," we conceive its consisting of supra-sensual knowledge; (2) understanding "that whereof there is not apprehension, as apprehendible by marks, i.e. sense-organs," we conceive its not being object of sense-perception; (3) understanding "that whereof there is not apprehension through a mark within reach of the senses, as of fire through smoke," we conceive its not being subject of inference implying sense perception; (4) understanding "that whereof there is not apprehension by others merely through a mark," we conceive its not being merely a thing inferred; (5) understanding "that whose apprehension (insert *grahanam*) of others is not merely through a mark," we conceive its not being merely an inferer (i.e. the soul is not an agent of inference only, but also of perception); (6)

understanding "that whose apprehension is by its own nature not through a mark," we conceive its being a direct knower (i.e. it has *paramarthika-pratyaksha, Outl.* p. 113): (7) understanding "that where of the apprehension, i.e. its basis as a knowable object, is not through a mark, i.e. its characteristic termed psychic-attention," we conceive its not being knowledge with external things for basis (the self is really of only the nature of knowing); (8) understanding "that whose apprehension, i.e. self-appropriation,[100] is not of a mark, i.e. the characteristic termed psychic-attention," we conceive its being non-extrinsic knowledge; (9) understanding "that whereof the apprehension, i.e. the appropriation by another, is not of a mark, i.e. of the characteristic termed psychic-attention," we conceive its being knowledge which cannot be taken away (read *yasyeti aharyajnanatvasya*); (10) understanding "that in the mark whereof, i.e. in the characteristic termed psychic-attention, there is not interference, like eclipse in the sun," we conceive its innate nature as pure psychic-attention; (11) understanding "that which has not apprehension, i.e. appropriation of material *karman*, through its mark, i.e. its characteristic termed psychic-attention," we conceive its freedom from coalescence of substantial *karman*; (12) understanding "that which has not apprehension, i.e. enjoyment of objects (read *upabhogo*), through its mark, i.e. sense-organs," we conceive its not being enjoyer of objects;[101] (13) understanding "that, the soul, of which there is not apprehension from the 'mark' self, defined (read *lakshanasya*) as sense-organs, etc. (*adi* refers to the sexual organs)," we conceive its not being governed by semen and menstruation; (14) understanding "that which has not taking of a mark, i.e. a delusive appearance (read *mohana* for *mehana*)," we conceive its not being merely a worldly expedient; (15) understanding "that which has no apprehension, i.e. winning of people (*Loka-vyapti*), by a mark, i.e. delusive appearance," we conceive its not winning people by appearances, which are the familiar expedients of cheats (*kuhuka=kuhaka*); (16) understanding "that which does not assume marks, i.e. the sensations of female, male and neuter," we conceive its not being female, male or neuter substance; (17) understanding "that which does not assume marks, i.e religious badges," we conceive its not being the external marks of ascetics; (18) understanding "that whose apprehension, i.e. awareness of things, is not a mark, a quality (read *lingam guno*)," we conceive its being pure substance, untouched by particular quality; (19) understanding "that whose apprehension, i.e. particular awareness of things, is not a mark, a quality modification," we conceive its being pure substance, untouched by particular modification; (20) understanding "that whose apprehension, i.e. general awareness of things, is not a mark, i.e. a cause of recognition,"[102] we conceive its being pure modification, untouched by substance.

Now, in view of the question "How can there be bondage of the self, since, being incorporeal, it is without smoothness or roughness?," he propounds the *prima facie* opinion:

II.81. The corporeal, having qualities of colour and so on, is bound by mutual forms of touch [viz. smoothness and roughness]: how can the self, the opposite thereof, bind material *karman*? (173)

On the part of two corporeal material substances, indeed, since they are associated with qualities, colour and so on, mutual bondage, due to a particular touch, smoothness or roughness as described, is in fact recognized: but on the part of self and *karma*-matter how is it recognized? Though the *karma*-matter, as associated with qualities, colour and so on, can have a particular touch, smoothness or roughness as described, yet, since the incorporeal self, as not being associated with qualities, colour and so on, cannot be credited with a particular touch, smoothness or roughness as described, we have inadequacy on the one side.

Now he states the approved view that there is bondage of the self, though incorporeal:

II.82. Just as, though devoid of colour and so on, it [the self] sees and knows substances having colour, etc. qualities; in this way, understand, it is bound with them. (174)

In the same way as, though deprived of colour and so on [the self], it sees and knows coloured substances and their qualities, similarly of course, though deprived of colour and so on, it is bound by *karma*-material, having colour, etc. For otherwise it is impossible to evade the further interrogation "How does it, being incorporeal, see and know the corporeal?" Nor is this made the subject of an example by reason of the difficulty of giving a solution: rather is it by means of an example made plain even down to the boy and the cowherd. Thus: as on the part of a boy or a cowherd, who sees and knows a clay bull or a bull, standing apart from them, there is not union with the bull, but the common understanding of an union with the bull is justified by an union with a seeing or knowing which has the form of a bull and which is erected upon a psychic-attention occasioned (*nimitta*) by a bull standing in the condition of an object, so the self, since, being colourless, it is void of touch, has indeed no union with *karma*-material, but the common understanding of bondage by *karma*-material is justified by an union with states of passion, dislike and so on, erected upon a psychic-attention occasioned (*nimitta*) by *karma*-material existing in the condition of taking up the same space [as the parts of the soul].

Now he makes known the characteristic nature of subjective bondage (*bhava-bandha*):[103]

II.83. The soul, which is constituted of psychic-attention or function of consciousness, becomes infatuated, or attached, or averse on encountering the various sense objects; so it is bound up with them.[104] **(175)**

This self, indeed, is in its entirety, since it consists of discursive (*sa-vikalpaka*) and intuitive (*nir-vikalpaka*) mental-distinguishing, composed of psychic-attention. Whatever of it, on meeting with the various distinguishable things, falls into either infatuation or attachment, or aversion, that, since it has its innate nature affected (*uparakta*) by infatuation, attachment or aversion conditioned by "the other"—like a crystal gem which has its innate nature coloured (*uparakta*) by blueness, yellowness, or redness, conditioned by a blue, yellow, or red accessory—becomes itself bondage, since it is accompanied by their natures.

Now he makes known the proof of subjective bondage and the characteristic nature of substantial bondage (*dravya-bandha*):

II.84. With whatever [mental] state a soul sees and knows the objects [of senses] (read *vishayam or vishayan*) which has come within its ken, thereby it is affected: *karman* is thereby bound – this is the teaching. (176)

With whatever state, in the form of infatuation, of attachment, or of aversion, this self sees and knows the things which, since it consists of mental-distinguishing, definite (*sakara*) and indefinite (*nirakara*)[105], fail to be distinguished [by it], by that same it is affected, This affection it is that is subjective bondage, corresponding to smoothness and roughness. Then again there through material *karman* is bound: so we have here substantial bondage conditioned by subjective bondage.

Now he makes known the characteristic nature of bondage of matter, soul, and the two together:

II.85. Bondage of material things is through their touches, of soul through attachment and so on: mutual interpenetration is said to be [bondage] of matter and soul [together]. (177)

The evolution of *karmans* into union through particular touches, smoothness or roughness, is bondage of matter only. The evolution of the soul into union with conditioned modifications, infatuation, attachment, aversion, is bondage of soul only. The mutual penetration, on the other hand, of soul and *karma*-matter, which is better described as merely occasion of their mutual evolutions, is the bondage between the two.

Now he revives the fact that substantial (material) bondage is caused by subjective bondage:

II.86. The self has spacial units (space-points): into those spacial units enter material aggregates according to their suitability (cf. gathas, PS 168-169): they stay and go; or they are bound. (178)

This self, as having innumerable spacial units as many as the world space, has spacial units (cf. *Tattva-dipika* on PS 136). So, according as in those spacial units is its vibration, dependent upon the atom-groups (*vargana*) of body, voice and mind, aggregates of *karma*-material having of themselves similar vibration enter and stay in them. If the soul is in a subjective state in the form of infatuation, attachment, or aversion, it is also bound. Hence it is discerned that subjective bondage is cause of substantial (material) bondage of *karman* (*dravya bandh*).

Now he proves that subjective bondage, which is simply an evolution into attachment, is, as being cause of substantial material bondage of *karman* (*dravya bandh*), the veritable [*nishchaya*] bondage:

II.87. Attached, the self binds *karman;* when it is devoid of attachment, it is liberated from *karmans.* This, be assured, in verity sums up the bondage of souls. (179)

Since only when evolved into attachment is [the self] bound by the fresh *karman*, and not when evolved into detachment; since from the fresh *karman* it is not released when evolved into attachment, but only when evolved into detachment; since, when evolved into attachment, it is bound by [any] new material *karman* which even comes into contact with it and is not released by the old, long familiar; whereas when evolved into detachment, it is released by any fresh material *karman* which comes into contact with it and also by the old, long familiar and is not bound; therefore it is discerned that, as being the thing most really effective of substantial bondage, evolution into attachment is the veritable bondage.

Now he reveals the fact that evolution is qualified by attachment, which is the thing most really effective of substantial (material) bondage; also the qualification:

II.88. From evolution comes bondage; evolution is attended by attachment, aversion and infatuation. Infatuation and aversion are evil (inauspicious): attachment is good (auspicious) or evil. (180)

Substantial bondage comes from evolution qualified: and the being qualified is by way of being composed of attachment, aversion and infatuation. It admits of duality according to the goodness or evilness therein: through being composed of infatuation or aversion it is evil; through being composed of attachment it is both good and evil, because attachment has a double character according as it includes sanity (*visuddhi*) or morbidity (*sanklesha*).

Now, metonymically substituting effect for cause, he illustrates the qualification of the qualified evolution and the non-qualified evolution:

II.89. Good evolution in regard to other things is termed merit, bad is termed sin: evolution not entering into other things is in [due] time cause of evanescence (destruction) of misery. (181)

Evolution, indeed, is of two kinds, proceeding in other substance or concerned with own substance. Of these, that proceeding in other substance is, as being affected by the other, qualified evolution; that proceeding in own substance is, as not affected by the other, non-qualified evolution. Among these, qualified evolution is said to have two qualifications, good evolution and evil evolution. Of these, good evolution, as being cause of binding of meritorious matter, is merit; evil evolution, as being cause of binding of sinful matter, is sin. Of pure evolution, on the other hand, since, as being pure, it is one, there are no special forms. Being, in course of time,[106] cause of evanescence of *karma*-material, which is cause of *samsara* misery, it is liberation, consisting in evanescence of *karma*-material, which is cause of *samsara* misery.

Now, with a view to the soul's activity and abstention in regard to own and other substance [respectively], he exhibits the distinction of own and other:

II.90. The classes of souls *(jivas)*, earth-bodied, etc. and the mobile, are said to be other immobile like (*anya)* than the [essential nature of] soul, and the soul is also [essentially] other (*anya)* than they. (182)

The six classes of souls, earthen and so on, admitted with distinction of mobile and immobile, are, due to being (combined with) as being (only) unconsciousness, other than the soul, and the soul also, as being conscious, is other than they. Here, the six classes of souls are substance other than the self (*atmanah*): the self (*atma*) alone is own substance (*sva-dravyam*).

Now he discerns knowledge and non-knowledge of the distinction of own and other as occasioning the soul's activity in regard to own and other substance:

II.91. Whoso does not in this manner know the other (*para*) and the self, according to their characteristic natures, makes for himself through infatuation the conviction [of other being self and belonging to self, such as] "I am this," and "this is mine." (183)

Whoso does not in this manner, through the respectively invariable characteristic natures as conscious and unconscious, see the distinction of soul and matter as own and other, he only, and no other, has through infatuation the conviction of other substance being self and belonging to self, "I, am this" and "this is mine." Therefore what occasions the soul's activity in regard to other substance is merely the absence of clear distinction of its own and the other; and consequently (*samarthyat*) what occasions activity in regard to own substance is the negation thereof.

Now he describes what is the self's *karman* (act):

II.92. Working out its own inner nature, the self is indeed the agent of its own state; but of all states composed of material substance it is not the agent. (184)

The self is indeed agent of its own state; for that is its own property, since that must necessarily be effected by the self, as it possesses potentiality of so becoming. And, independently effecting this, it must necessarily be the agent thereof; and, being effected by the self, its own state, being that which it has to attain, must be result (*karman,* its accusative). Thus the *karman* of the self is its [the self's] own evolution: the self does not bring about states of matter; for these are properties of the other, since they are not effectible by the self, as it has no potentiality of so becoming. Not effecting them, it cannot be agent of them; and, not being effected by self, they cannot be its *karman*. Thus evolution of matter is not act (*karman*) of the self.

Now he rebuts a doubt as to how evolution of matter can fail to be *karman* of the self:

II.93. Although existing at all times in the midst of matter, the soul, in fact, does not grasp, does not release, and is not the agent of material *karman*. (185)

Assuredly evolution of matter is not *karman* (effect) of the self, since this is exempt from appropriation or surrender of other substance. For whatever is perceived to be cause of evolution in another thing is not (insert *na*) perceived to be exempt from appropriation and surrender thereof : as in the case of fire in regard to a mass of iron. But the self, although existing in identical space, is in fact exempt from appropriation and surrender of other substance: hence it cannot be cause of the evolution of material components into the state of *karman*.

Now he describes how, accordingly, there is appropriation or surrender of the self by material *karmans*:

II.94. He, being at present [in this transmigratory condition] the agent of his own evolution, constituted of its own substance, is at times appropriated [i.e. bound up with] and released by *karman*-dusts. (186)

This self, though exempt from appropiration and release of other substance, now, in the transmigrant state, exercising agency only in regard to his own substantive evolution,—for which the evolutions of other substance serve only as occasioning causes [i.e. the supportive or auxiliary factor (*nimitta*)—is, so long only, appropriated, by way of a particular kind of interpenetration, by the dusts of matter, which, merely using the occasion (*nimitta*) of his own self-evolution, assumes evolution into *karman*; and sometimes he is released [by them].

Now he describes how produced is the variety of material *karmans*:

II.95. When the self, associated with attachment and aversion, evolves into good and evil, *karma*-dust, in the state or form of 'knowledge-obscuring' and so on, enters into it. (187/1)

Assuredly, at the time of the self's evolving into good and evil, there exists independently a variegated evolution of *karma*-matter; just as at the time of evolution of a new cloud's water into conjunction with the earth there exists a variegated evolution of other matter. Thus: just as, when the water of a new cloud evolves into conjunction with the earth, then other material components independently evolve in variegated states as green-swards, mushrooms, cochineal insects, so, when this self, under the sway of attachment or aversion, evolves into a good or evil state, then other *karmic*-material-components, entering it through its vibratory activity, evolve independently in variegated states, "knowledge-obscuring" and so on. Hence the variety of *karmans* is produced by their innate nature, and not produced by the self.

Now he states that the self alone is bondage:

II.96. The self, which has spacial units (space-points), when stained with deluded view, attachment and aversion, is, at that time embraced by *karma*-dust, described as bondage in the scripture. (188)

Just as in the world a single garment, having spacial units, is, through being stained with *lodhra* and so on, observed to be dyed with colour of madder and so on, so the self also, having spacial units, is, at time, through being stained with infatuation, attachment and aversion, to be regarded as a single bondage, embraced by *karma*-dusts: for the thing contemplated by strict verity [internal self-referential viewpoint] (*nishchaya naya*) is the pure substance.

Now he exhibits the absence of contradiction between internal self-referential viewpoint [strict verity, Faddegon] (*nishchaya naya*) and external other-referential standpoint [common acceptance, Faddegon] (*vyavahara naya*):

II.97. This [in brief] is the summary account of the bondage of souls, described by *Arahantas* to the *yatis* as strict verity (*nishchaya naya*) [i.e. from the internal self-referential point of view]; common acceptance (*vyavahara-naya*) [i.e. from the external, other-referential standpoint] it is expressed differently. (189)

Only evolution into attachment is *karman* of the self: It is a duality of merit and sin. That the self is agent only of evolution into attachment and so on and appropriator and renouncer of that only is the view of *nishchaya naya*, which consists in describing the pure substance. But that which says that "the evolution of matter is the self's *karman*[107], and that is a duality of merit and sin: the self is agent of the evolution of matter and appropriator and renouncer thereof" is the view of *vyavahara naya,* which consists in describing non-pure substance. Both these two are correct, since substance is conceived in both forms, as pure and as not pure. However, in this place the view of *nishchaya naya* is adopted, as being the most effective: for, as emphasizing the purity of the thing in view, viz. substance in its purity, the view of *nishchaya naya* is the most effective means of accomplishing the task (*sadhaktam*), not the view of *vyavahara naya,* which emphasizes the impure.

Now he states that from the point of view of the impure we get only an impure self:

II.98. But whoso does not abandon the notion of mineness, such as "I am this", "this is mine," in regard to body and wealth forsakes the state of *sramana* and takes a wrong path. (190)

The self, in fact, which, regardless of and being non-relative (*nirpeksha*) the view of *nishchaya* [pure] *naya,* consisting in description of [undefined, transcendental] pure substance, and infatuated with the view of *vyavahara naya,* consisting in the description of impure substance, does not abandon the notion of mineness in regard to body, wealth and so on, which are other substance, thinking them to belong to the self, "I am this," "this is mine," leaves afar the path of *sramana*-hood, which has the form of evolution into the pure self, and takes actually a wrong path, in the form of evolution into impure self. Hence it is discerned that through the point of view of the impure we get only an impure self.

Now he discerns that from the point of view of the pure we get simply the pure self:

II.99. Whoso contemplates thus, "I do not belong to other: others do not belong to me: I am only something of the knowing nature alone," that self in its contemplation is a contemplator of the [real] self.[108] (191)

Whoso, in fact, being neutral in the sense of having no opposition[109] in regard to the view of *vyavahara naya,*–which consists in discerning impure substance and is active only upon its own objects, and having cast away infatuation by means of the view of *nishchaya* [pure] *naya,* which consists in discerning pure substance,—has dissipated any connection of mutual ownness and ownership between self and other, thinking, "I do not belong to others: others do not belong to me," and, conceiving that "I am one [alone],[110] pure knowledge," lets go the non-self and, taking on the self as self, turns away from other substance and confines his thought to the single point, the self, such an one assuredly, confining his thought one-pointedly, will in that moment of confining his thought one-pointedly be pure self. Hence it is discerned that only from the point of view of the pure do we get the pure self.

Now he teaches that on ground of being eternal (*dhruvatva*) only the pure self should be resorted to:

II.100. Thus I deem the self as pure because it is knowledge and intuition, a great thing, supra-sensual, supreme reality (*mahartha*), eternal (*dhruva*), stable [immobile, Faddegon] (*achala*), without prop or support. (192)

The self, in fact, is pure and only the pure self is eternal (*dhruva*) existent (*sat*) and without a cause, it is without beginning or end and since it is self-established; nothing else is so. And purity belongs to the self, since through discrimination from other substance and through non-discrimination from its own properties it is an unity (*ekatva*). And this [unity] is because of consisting of knowledge and intuition, because of supra-sensual, supreme reality, because of being stable, and because of being without prop. As to these, it has unity because, bearing in itself knowledge and being of itself intuition, it is absolutely discriminated from other substance and undiscriminated from its own properties; likewise it has unity because, transcending the several senses, which grasp each its restricted quality, touch, taste, smell, colour, and also the mode of sound, and being itself one supreme reality apprehending all the qualities, touch, taste, smell, colour and also the mode of sound, it is discriminated from other substance, consisting in the sense-organs, and not discriminated from its own property, consisting in apprehension of touch, etc.: likewise it has unity because, being stable through taking and leaving the discernible modifications in their process of instantaneous evanescence, it is discriminated from substance consisting in the discernible modifications, and not discriminated from its own property, consisting in discerning the presentations thereof; likewise it has unity, because, being without prop, as not being propped upon discernible substance in its perpetual process, it is discriminated from discernible "other" substance and not discriminated from its own property, consisting in discerning the presentations thereof. Thus the self is pure, because the view of the pure, which is simply consciousness, discerns only what is no more than that, and it alone, because of its being eternal (*dhruvatva*), is to be taken to: what of other unstable things, which correspond to the numerous shadows of way-side trees coming in contact with the limbs of the traveller?

Now he teaches that on ground of unsteadfastness nothing other than the self is to be resorted to:

II.101. Neither bodies nor possessions, neither pleasure nor pain, neither enemies nor friends are steadfast or eternal *(dhruva)* for the soul; the self, which is constituted of psychic-attention, is steadfast or eternal. (193)

Nothing else whatever is steadfast or eternal (*dhruva*) for the soul, because it has beginning and end, inasmuch as something impermanent (*asat*) has produced it and because it is brought into being by another thing; for everything [with the exception of self] results in impurity, since it is not distinct from "the other" substance and is distinct from the self's own properties, which are infected by the "other". The self alone, which has psychic-attention for self, is steadfast and pure. Therefore I do not resort to the unsteadfast, impermanent body, etc., although they are resorted to; but I resort to the pure self, which is eternal (*dhruva*).

Now as regards the question "what results from this resorting (*upalambha*) to the pure self?" he explains:

II.102. He who, having thus discerned the pure self, contemplates on the supreme reality of that self, whether he is a householder or an ascetic,[111] destroys the evil knot of infatuation. (194)

He who in the manner described approaches the pure steadfast (*dhruva*) self attains, through his activity in regard to it, pureness of self. Being then the supreme reality of self and nothing else than consciousness with unlimited energy (*shakti*), he attains contemplation, which is characterized as deep, attentive thoughtfulness. Then, since in one activley occupied with formed thought (*sa-sakara*) there is an arising of an attentive thoughtfulness without deviation, he attains the unfastening of the coil-knot (*granthi*) of infatuation, bound very tightly throughout his transmigration. Thus a breaking of the knot of infatuation is the fruit of restoring to the pure self.

Now as regards the question "what happens from the breaking (*bheda*) of the knot of infatuation?" he explains:

II.103. He who, having destroyed the knot of infatuation and having made an end to attachement and aversion, abides in the state of a shraman, counting pleasure and pain as the same, acquires imperishable happiness. (195)

From the destruction of the knot of infatuation ensues the destruction of attachment and aversion, whereof that is the root. Thence follows an abiding in the state of a *shraman*, characterized as the perfect equanimity (*madhyastha*) of one who counts pleasure and pain as the same. Thence follows attainment of imperishable happinss, characterized as absence of perturbation. Thus imperishable happiness is the fruit of the breaking of the knot of infatuation.

Now he certifies that contemplation (*dhyana*) characterized as deep, attentive thoughtfulness, does not lead to impurity of self:

II.104. Whoso, having destroyed the stains of infatuation and being detached from sense objects, restrains his mind and abides in his innate nature, becomes a contemplator of the self. (196)

To the self whose stains of infatuation are destroyed belongs detachment from sense-objects, because it abstains from activity towards the "other" (substance), whereof that (infatuation) is the root. Then comes restraint (*nirodha*) of the internal-sense, which has nothing else for refuge because there is no other substance which could be its resting-place (*adhikarana*); like a flying bird for which there is only one bark in mid-ocean. Thereupon, through the disappearance of flightiness, whereof that (not restrained internal-sense) is the root, comes steadfastness in his innate nature, which is unlimited innate consciousness. And that, because of being an unperturbed, deeply attentive, thoughtfulness, proceeding (*pravrtta*) in its own nature, is entitled "contemplation." Hence contemplation, as being an abiding in one's inborn nature, is the self, since it is not anything other than the self.

Now he propounds the question what the possessor of complete knowledge (*sakala-jnani*), who has attained the pure self, contemplates:

II.105. What does the *shraman*, who has annihilated the dense destructive *karman* and directly knows the reality of all existences and has reached the limit of the knowable, contemplate, free from doubt? (197)

The ordinary man is seen to contemplate an object of which,— because he is full of longings (*trshna*), while there exist in him infatuation and hindrance of the energy of knowledge, and because he has no immediate knowledge and no well-defined object,—he is desirous, curious and in doubt. But the revered Omniscient does not feel desire, curiosity or doubt, because he has eradicated all longings, while there exists for him no infatuation, or hindrances to the energy of knowledge, inasmuch as he has destroyed the dense destructive *karman,* and because the truth of all existences is immediately perceptible to him and the limit of the knowbale attained. How then can there be to him an object (*artha*) of desire, curiosity or doubt? In these circumstances what does he contemplate?

Now he propunds the answer: the possessor of complete knowledge, who has attained (read *upalabdha-shuddhatma*) the pure self, contemplates this:

II.106. Set free from all afflictions and hindrances, rich with complete happiness and knowledge in all his faculties, elevated above the sense-organs, he without sense-activities (*aksha*) contemplates supreme happiness. (198)

This self, as soon as–in consequence of the absence of sense-activities, which are abodes of hindrance to innate happiness and knowledge and abodes of such happiness and knowledge as do not extend in all directions and do not comprise the whole soul–it is itself, without sense-organs, immediately, being elevated above others and the sense-organs, it becomes free from all afflictions, because it has untroubled innate happiness and knowledge, and rich with complete happiness and knowledge in all its faculties, because it is full of such happiness and knowledge as extend in all directions and comprise the whole soul. And in this state, though every desire, wish for knowledge and doubt are absent, it contemplates the highest happiness, unprecedented and characterized as absence of perturbation: that is to say, it abides as simply a deeply attentive consciousness, accompanied by absence of perturbation. And such a state is, in fact, attainment of perfection, whose essence is innate knowledge and bliss.

Now he determines that this itself is the path of liberation, characterized as attainment of the pure self:

II.107. Thus, my homage to those, who following the path [of liberation] have attained the state of the *Jinas,*[112] the best of *Jinas,*[113] the *shramanas,* and liberated souls *(siddhas).* And homage to that path of *nirvana.* (199)

Since all those, the spiritual guides (*tirtha-kara*), who are for the last time embodied, and the aspirants to liberation, not for the last time embodied, have beem sanctified by following a path towards liberation proceeding in just the manner described and characterized as a striving for the truth of the pure self, and since there has been no other way, therefore it is determined that there is only this one road to liberation and no second. And enough of elaboration! To those who strive towards the truth of the pure self, and to that Path of Liberation which consists in the striving towards the truth of pure self, while the difference between the object of adoration and the adorer has not yet been superseded, be Homage then in non-essentials (*noagama*) and in heart. The path of liberation has been determined; the due action is (to be) carried out.

Now, carrying out the former pledge contained in the words "I depend on the tranquillity" etc. (PS 5), he sets forth this striving towards the pure self, which striving is the path of liberation:

II.108. Therefore, having in this way conceived the self as essentially of knowing nature *(jnayak)*, I relinquish the notion of "mineness," adopting the idea of non-attachment or negation of "mineness." (200/1)

This I, qualified (*adhikarin*) for liberation,–by surrender of the idea of "mine" and adoption of the idea of negation of "mineness," preceded by acquaintance with the truth of the self as essentially something-that-knows,–strives with all its might towards the pure self, since it has no other task. Thus: I now am essentially of knowing nature (*jnayaka*), and, as only *jnayaka*, I have with everything a connection characterized as that of naturally knowable and knower, not any other connection, such as that of possession and possessor. For me, therefore, there is in respect of nothing as being "mine," in respect of everything a negation of "mineness." The pure self, then– which, since the knowing capacity has the nature of realizing all knowables, in one moment intuits,–as it were carved in relief, engraven, implanted, pinned down, hobbled down, actually present, mirrored, – the whole mass of things, deep, of unfathomable, nature, a mountain of variegated modifications, successive, infinite, past, present and future –and which, while assuming uniformity, because of impossibility of discrimination due to the inevitability of the relation of knowable and knower, yet never abandons uniformity in virtue of its essence as a knower of infinite natural potency and in that same permanence persists everlastingly, though through infatuation otherwise regarded,–to that pure self, as it really is, I having eradicated infatuation, adhere without the least wavering. Towards this self, which, in consequence of in disinclination to weaknesses, –by reason of being actively occupied in perfect knowledge having its root in purity of conviction, –is, although a practising saint (*sadhu*), yet already perfected (*siddha*), and also towards similar supreme selves, may there spontaneously arise a perpetual mental adoration, characterized as a sole intentness[114] upon them.

"Thus, having rightly penetrated the Jaina doctrine, the expositor of the truth of knowable, the bounteous Absolute in the form of speech, we abide perpetually rapt in the one-pointed attitude (*vritti*) which is nothing but the pure self-substance."[115] (PS *Kalash* 10)

"Making truly everything to the utmost limit a knowable, making the knowable, with its differences superseded, a knowledge and making that knowledge, though seemingly different from self, into self, the self shines forth, having straightway attained the Absolute." (PS *Kalash* 11)

"The conduct follows the substance; the substance follows the conduct; the two are surely *sapeksha*, i.e. mutually complementary to one-another or interdependent. Let him, therefore, who is desirous of liberation climb the path of liberation, whether having envisaged the substance or having envisaged the conduct." (PS *Kalash* 12)

Here ends *The Lamp of Truth*, a commentary on *Pravachanasara*, composed by Amrtachandra Suri, the second sciptural book, entitled *The Teaching of the Truth of the Knowable.*

Book III
The Conduct

Book III
The Conduct

NOTE: III.1, III.2, etc. denote *Gatha* (verse) No. 1, 2, etc. of Book III, while *Gatha* Nos. 201, 202, etc. at the end of translation denote consecutive numbering of *gathas* starting from Book 1, which tallies with the *gatha* numbering of the original *Prakrit* text given at the end of this edition and most editions of the work in Hindi.

Now begins the Supplement expository of the Conduct, containing an examination of conduct for others.

"With attainment of the substance comes attainment of the conduct; with attainment of the conduct, attainment of the substance"–made aware of this, let others, who have not yet desisted from [sinful] action (*karman*), follow a conduct not repugnant to the substance. (PS Kalash 13)

In this way he stimulates others to observe the conduct, i.e. as described in *gathas* 201-203:

CONDUCT INCLUDING NEGLIENCE (VERSE 201-231)

III.1. Thus having bowed before the *Siddhas,* the great *Jinas,* and the *shramanas,* one should take refuge in the state of *shramana,* if one wishes liberation from misery. (201)

Just as my own self, desirous of liberation from misery, in *gathas* 4 and 5 paid veneration, in the form of prostration and salutation, to the *Arhats, Siddhas, Acharyas, Upadhyayas* and *Sadhus,* and after this has for itself adopted the state of a *shramana,* which, consisting mainly in purifying intuition and knowledge, bears the name of equanimity (*samya*) and includes the state of well-being conceived in the two intervening (the first two books), books of our treatise,—so the selves of others also, if desirous of liberation from misery, should likewise adopt the same. Of the path of its adoption, as experienced, we here stand forth as guides.

Now he teaches what anyone desirous of becoming a *shramana* does first:

III.2. Having said farewell to his kindred; being released by his family, wife and sons; having applied himself to the practice of knowledge, intuition, conduct, austerity and energy (*virya*).[116] (202)

Now he who wishes to become a *shramana* begins by saying farewell to his kindred, effects his release from parents, wife and sons, and applies himself to the practice of knowledge, intuition, conduct, austerity and energy. Thus he bids farewell to his relatives in these terms:

"O selves who abide in the kindred of this person's body, this person's self belongs in no way to you; of this be assured. He has said farewell to you. This self, wherein the light of knowledge has burst forth, seeks the self, the self's primordial kinsman.

"O self of the father of this man's body, O self of the mother of this man's body, the self of this man has not been procreated by you; of this be you assured. Therefore do you release this self. This self, wherein the light of knowledge has burst forth, seeks the self, the self's primordial parent.

"O self of the wife (*ramani*) of this man's body, you do not impassion (*ramayasi*) the self of this man: of this be you assured. Therefore release this self. This self, wherein the light of knowledge has burst forth, seeks its own experience (*anubhuti*), the self's primordial (impassioner) wife.

"O self of the son of this man's body, you were not procreated by this man's self: of this be you assured. Therefore release this self. This self, wherein the light of knowledge has burst forth, now seeks the self, the self's primordial son."

In this way, he effects his release from parents, wife and son.

"Likewise exercise in knowledge, characterized by — (1) consideration of time (*kala*); (2) modesty (*vinaya*); (3) affection for knowledge (*upadhana*); (4) respect (*bahu-mana*); (5) non-concealment (*anihnava*); (6) the meaning (*artha*); (7) the words (*vyanjana*); (8) that which combines the last two mentioned (*tad-ubhaya-sampanna*); you do not belong to the purified self; of this I am assured. Yet I apply myself to you, until by your grace it[117] attains the purified self.

"O exercise in intuition, characterized by (1) absence of doubt (*nishankitatva*); (2) absence of desires for anything but self-realization (*nihkankshatatva*); (3) absence of hatred (of the poor and diseased (*nirvichikitsatva*); (4)freedom from foolish superstitions (*nirmudhadrshtitva*); (5) edification (*sthitikarana*); (6) causation of progress (*upavrmhana*); (7) tenderness (*vatsalya*); (8) promulgation of doctrine (*prabhavana*); you do not belong to the purified self: of this I am assured. Yet I apply my self to you, until by your grace it attains the purified self.

"O exercise in conduct, characterized by (1) - (5) the five great vows (*mahavrata*), causes of striving on the road of liberation; (6) - (8) the three restraints (*gupti*) of body, mind and speech; (9) - (13) religious observances (*samiti*), walking carefully so as not to hurt any living being, speaking relevantly, taking only pure food, carefully handling the few things which belong to a *shramana*, great care as to where to answer the calls of nature; you do not belong to the purified self: of this I am assured. Yet I apply my self to you, until by your grace it attains the purified self.

"O exercise in austerity, characterized by (1) fasting; (2) eating less than what one may desire; (3) accepting alms only if a particular thing is fulfilled; (4) renunciation and suppression of taste and tasteful things; (5) sitting and sleeping alone; (6) mortification of the body through refusing it many comforts; (7) penance in expiation of any fault; (8) eager zeal and humility; (9) service and attendance on old, infirm and sick *sadhus*; (10) reading the scripture; (11) contemplation; and (12) non-attachment to the body; you do not belong to the purified self: of this I am assured. Yet I apply my self to you, until by your grace it attains to the purified self.

"O exercise in energy, characterized by not hiding your potency promotive of all the other exercises; you do not belong to the purified self: of this I am assured. Yet I apply my self to you, until by your grace it attains to the purified self."

Thus he applies himself to the practice of knowledge, intuition, conduct, austerity and energy.

Now he teaches what like he thereby becomes:

III.3. Then before a *shramana*, a class leader, rich in merits, distinguished by family (*kula*), form and mature age, and highly

approved by (other) *shramanas,* he makes his bow and, after saying, "accept me," he receives favour. (203)

Then the person desirous of the state of a *shramana* bows reverentially and receives favour. Thus:

Approaching one who, through *shramana*-hood, which consists in a self which has practised and caused (others) to practise all the renunciations and activities both, is a *shramana*: who, through skill in practising and causing (others) to practise such *shramana*-hood, is rich in merits; who, through being fit to be honoured without hesitation by all people of the world and through being free from inherited defects such as usury,[118] etc. is of distinguished family: who, because an exterior clear colour (*shuddha-rupa*) is indicative of interior of pure colour, is of distinguished colour; who through freedom from all infirmity of mind due to infancy or old age, and through having a mind dissociated from perversion by the extravagancies of youth, is distinguished by mature age; through being by preference sought by all who long for liberation, since he has annihilated all human weaknesses in the sphere of practising and causing to be practised the above-defined *shramana*-hood, is highly approved by *shramanas*; who is a *ganin* (i.e. a class-leader), a teacher who succeeds in effecting the comprehension of the truth of the pure self—approaching such a teacher with the words "Favour me by promoting my understanding of the truth of the pure self," he bows before him. Being by him furnished with the objects of his request in the words "Yes, here is for you understanding of the truth of pure self," he receives favour.

Now he teaches what like he further becomes:

III.4. "I do not belong to others, and others do not belong to me; nothing whatever belongs to me"—firm in this conviction, conqueror of his senses, he *[shramana]* adopts *jadha jada-ruva* in Pk. *yathajatarupa* in Sanskrit), i.e. natural *rupa* (character) of a new born child. (204)

Further the person desirous of the state of *shramana* adopts his natural form. Thus: "In no respect do I belong to others nor are others anything to me, because in reality all substances are devoid of all connections with other substances; therefore in this world, which consists of the six substances, nothing else than myself belongs to me." Thus convinced in his mind and conqueror of his senses, through conquest of his senses and quasi-senses (*noindriya*), which are relations of possessor and possession between themselves and other substances, he indeed adopts his natural *rupa* (character), inasmuch as he adopts the pure *rupa* (nature) of the self-substance as it originally is.

Now of this adopting the natural *rupa,* which condition had until then been absolutely unattained, because of never having been practised during the whole precedent *samsara,* he mentions a number of characteristics, external and internal, which make evident the success which is being attained by the skill of his new practice:

III.5. The (external) characteristic of a *shramana* is (1) the possession of *rupa* (form) as it is by birth, (2) the extraction of hair and beard, (3) purity (of not being attached to things), (4) the absence of *himsa* (the injuring of living beings, etc.), (5) and devoid of decoration of body. *(apratikarma,* or *aparikarma,* see also PS 224 and 228). (205)

III.6. A (further) characteristic (of *shraman*), as described by *Jina* (the conquerors of internal enemies), is (1) absence of infatuation and sins pertaining to incidental activities, (2) being endowed with purity of psychic-attention (*upayoga*) and of the threefold activity (of body, speech and mind, *yoga*), (3) and independent of "the other," which puts a stop to further births.[119] (206)

In the self which has begun by itself, in the way described by us, to adopt a form as it is by original nature, there is an absence of states such as infatuation, attachment and aversion, causes of the possession of *rupa* different from that of original nature; in consequence of this non-existence, then, there belong to him who abides in such a state: (1) possession of a *rupa* as it was by original nature; (2) extraction of hair and beard; (3) purity; (4) absence of deeds such as the injuring of living beings;[120] (5) not decorating the body due respectively to negation of (1) wearing garments and adornment, (2) keeping hair and moustache, (3) possessing anything (*sakimchanatva*), (4) being engaged in blamable activity (*yoga*), (5) paying attention (*samskara*) to the body. This is the external mark.

Likewise, in consequence of the non-existence of states such as infatuation, attachment and aversion, causes of the possession of a *rupa* different from that of original nature,–which *rupa* is now expelled by the *rupa* of original nature,–there belong to him who abides in such a condition: (1) freedom from infatuation and sins pertaining to incidental activities; (2) possession of purity of psychic-attention and (threefold) activity; (3) independence of "the other" due (respectively) to the negation of (1) the evolution of the consequences of the notion "mine"; (2) the possession of impurity of psychic-attention infected by good (*shubha*) and evil (*ashubha*) and the like (threefold) activity following thereupon; (3) dependence on other substances. This is the internal mark.

Next, in the words, "by taking these two marks (Verses 205 and 206) and doing so and so he becomes a *shramana*", indicating the identity of subject of the verb "becomes"[121] and all the other actions (previously mentioned) of taking leave of kindred, etc., he teaches that so much suffices (*iyata*) for attainment of the state of *shramanas*:

III.7. Having adopted this sign or mark at the hands of his superior teacher, after reverencing him, heard what he should do, together with the vows, applying himself thereto, he becomes a *shramana*. (207)

Next, wishing to become a *shramana*, he (1) adopts the two characteristics, (2) reverences the teacher, (3) hears the vows and tasks, (4) applies himself, and by so doing becomes a *shramana*, possessed of all requirements of the *shramana*-state.

Thus, (1) Having by the act of acceptance honoured this external and internal characteristics, which lead to the adopting the form of original nature, and which are a gift,–as being customarily given, originally by the *guru*, the supreme Lord, the *Arhat*, but at the moment by the initiation-teacher, as demonstrating the procedure of acceptance, – he identifies himself therewith.

(2) Next, having by prostration honoured the original, the following and the subsequent *gurus*, who, by the forgetting all distinction between self and other, not distinguishing between the adorable, adorer and adoration, successively involving each other, have given their all, he identifies himself with adoration, praise (*stuti*), and homage (*vandana*) 2nd and 3rd essential daily duties (*avashyaka*).

(3) Then, knowing by study of the scriptures (*svadhyaya*, the fifth *avashyaka*), i.e. by hearing the one great vow defined as renunciation (*pratyakhyana*) (in the list of the *avashyakas*) of every blamable activity relating to mind, speech and body (*yoga*)–that the self evolves into the equanimous state of *samaya* (*jiva* or self), on knowing the essential nature of soul, ascends to the *samayika* (first *avashyaka*).

(4) Then, knowing the nature of soul as different from *karmas* in all three times (past, present and future) on hearing about repentance

of past misdeeds (*pratikraman*), confession of one's faults in the present (*alochana*) and resolve not to repeat the blamable activity in future (*pratyakhyana*) through the scriptures ascends the state of consciousness different from the activities related to body, speech and mind (4th *avashyava*).

(5) Then, continually basing himself without distraction on the one characteristic of own nature (*svarupa*), which possesses the *rupa* (form, character) of original nature, and having given up attachment to the body (*kayotsarga*; 6th *avashyaka*), as abode of every blamable activity, he applies himself. And, having applied himself in this way and adopting in all cases equal vision or view of equanamity (*samadrashtitva*) by regarding all things alike, he becomes really a *shramana*.

Now he teaches that even a *shramana* habituated to uninterrupted equanimity (*samayika*) requires sometimes correction of negligences (*chedopasthapana*):

III.8. (Five) vows (*vrata*), (five-fold) religious observances or self-regulations (*samiti*), restraint of five senses (*indriya-rodha),* pulling out the hair (*loch*), the daily duties (*avashyaka*) (six in number), unclothed state of nakedness or scantily clothed *(achailakya)*, not bathing (*asnana*), sleeping on the ground (*kshiti-shayana*), not brushing the teeth (a-*danta-dhavana*), taking food in a standing position (*sthiti-bhojana*), one meal a day (*eka-bhakta*). (208)

III.9. These (twenty-eight) are the primary or fundamental qualities[122] *(mula-guna)* of *shramanas,* prescribed by the best of *Jinas.* A *shramana* remiss in one of these becomes a corrector of negligence (*chedopasthapaka*). (209)

As being specialized forms of the one great vow defined as renunciation (*pratyakhyana*) of every blamable activity (*yoga*), abstinence from hurting (any living being), from falsity (in speech, thought and deed), from theft, from unchastity, from worldly concerns, this five-fold vow, and in attendance thereupon the five-fold religious observances or self-regulations,

the five-fold restraints of the senses, pulling out of the hair with one's own hands, the six daily duties, *achailakya*, not bathing, sleeping on the ground, not brushing the teeth, taking food in a standing position, one meal a day–are the fundamental qualities of a *shramana*, since they are branches of the indispensable *samayika*

(*Tattvarthadhigama Sutra*, IX. 18, *samayika-samyama* as first kind of *samyama*) self-restraint.

When in respect to these the *shramana* is remiss because, while established in the indispensable *samayika* self-restraint, he has not practised the branches, then, reflecting that "for one who desires simply gold sometimes an earring, a bracelet, a ring and so forth are good: he cannot on all occasions have (merely) gold," he corrects himself by one of the branches and so is a corrector of negligences.

Now by giving information concerning the different kinds (*vikalpa*) of teachers (*acharya*), he shows that, like the giver of ordination, the corrector of negligences is another person (*para*):

III.10. In the adoption of the marks the giver of ordination is called *guru*; the other *shramana* who give advice as to correction *(upasthapaka)* of the faults are *niryapakas*. (210)

Since that teacher who, at the time of the adoption of the marks, effects ordination by teaching indispensable self-restraints is the *guru*; and, since, on the other hand, the teacher who later by expounding the self-restraint of correction of negligences (*chedopasthapana*)[123] in regard to the branches (*vikalpa*) corrects in respect of negligences, and also the teacher who, when a negligence exists, corrects by teaching the way of repairing (*pratisamdhana*) the omission, is a *niryapaka*, therefore the corrector of negligences is another.

Now he teaches the way of repairing (*pratisamdhana*) a neglected self-restraint:

III.11. When a *shramana* commits a negligence in a bodily activity earnestly undertaken, then an action, combined with self-reflection and confession of fault (*alochana*) is prescribed for him. (211)

III.12. When a *shramana* practised negligence [of mental intent], then he must approach a *shramana* expert in the doctrine of the *Jina*, and after self-reflection confess *(alochana)* his fault before him and do what is advised. (212)

There are two kinds of negligences in self-restraint, external and internal. That which relates only to bodily action is external; that which relates to psychic-attention is internal. If in the course of an earnestly undertaken bodily activity of a *shramana* properly intent there somehow occurs an external negligence, then, since it is altogether clear of internal negligence, the reparation is by an action, accompanied by reflection. But, when the same person, inasmuch as the negligence relates to intent, has been intent upon a patent negligence, then reparation is made by resorting to a *shramana*[124] expert in the rules of conduct as prescribed by the *Jina*, and further by reflection and by the procedure advised by him.

Now he teaches that inclinations towards other substances, as occasioning negligences in the state of a *shramana*, should be rejected:

III.13. In the teacher's abode *(adhivasa)* or in solitude *(vivashe)*,[125] let the *shramana* who has become free from negligences in regard to the *shramana*-state live (*viharatu)*, ever avoiding (*pariharamana*)[126] attachments. (213)

All inclinations towards other substances are, as infecting the psychic-attention, occasions of negligences in the *shramana*-state, which is psychic-attention free from infection; simply from absence thereof (of those inclinations) comes *shramana*-hood void of negligences. Hence in an abode constantly appropriated (*adhikrtya*) in his own mind to himself, or in a dwelling distinguished (*vishishta*) for its *gurus*, let this *shramana* who has become free from negligences in regard to the *shramana*-state abide, always rejecting inclinations to other substances.

Now he teaches that inclination towards one's own substance is to be cultivated, as occasioning completeness of the *shramana*-state:

III.14. The *shramana* who moves about ever attached to knowledge, with faith in the forefront, and is earnest in regard to the fundamental qualities (*mula-guna*)[127] has complete *shramana*-hood. (214)

For inclination towards one's own substance, being purificatory of the psychic-attention, of itself occasions completeness of the *shramana*-state, which is purified psychic-attention. Therefore, earnest in regard to the fundamental qualities, he must live ever attached to knowledge, intuition, etc.: that is to say, he must be simply pure existence, attached to the pure self-substance, which has for essence knowledge and intuition.

Now he teaches that even a slight (*sukshma*)[128] inclination towards other things, even such as is natural in ascetics, must be rejected, as occasioning negligence in the *shramana*-state:

III.15. A *shramana* does not enterain any desire or attachment to food or fasting, lodging or wandering *(vihara)*, anything of worldly concern *(upadhi)*,[129] for another *shramana* or useless and idle gossip (*vikatha)*.[130] (215)

For food merely taken as a means of sustaining the body, which is an auxiliary cause of the modification called the *shramana*-state; for fasting, which, without contravening such a sustaining of the body, takes place conformably to the *sutra* ordinance of a passionless and still repose of the pure self-substance; for a lodging, such as a cave in a high mountain, frequented in order to secure a passionless and calm internal substance; for the business of wandering, undertaken in order to find means for sustaining the body as above mentioned; for any *upadhi* (anything that complies with one's needs), which is limited to the body merely and, as being an auxiliary means to the modification called the *shramana*-state, is not prohibited; for a *shramana*, familiar to him in one way or another, merely in the mutual relation of one who gives and one who receives enlightenment; for talk (*vikathayam*), in which a portion of the wall-of-consciousness (*bhitti*) is stained by contact with sparkle of word particles, and which is opposed to the pure self-substance,–even for these things an inclination must be rejected, so that the wall of consciousness is no more painted with these fancies (*vikalpa*).

Now he informs us, what is a negligence (*chheda*):

III.16. Heedless[131] action in lying, sitting, standing, going, etc., is considered to be at all times continual hurt *(himsa)*[132] to the *shramana*-state. (216)

A negligence is an impure (*ashuddha*) psychic-attention; for it "breaks," "destroys," the *shramana*-state, which consists of pure psychic-attention. Negligence is thus itself hurt (*himsa*). Therefore heedless action on the part of the *shramana* in lying, sitting, standing, going, etc., which is necessarily accompanied by impure psychic-attention, is for him a hurt, at all times in continuous progress and in no way different from negligence.

Now he teaches two kinds of negligence, as being internal or external:

III.17. Let the creature die or live, on the part of the careless one the act of hurting is certain: by the mere fact of hurt he who is careful in his observances incurs no bondage. (217/1)

Impure psychic-attention is internal negligence; the taking of another's life is external. Whether the taking of another being's life occurs or does not occur, to the actual impure psychic-attention, proved by the careless conduct, which does not occur without it, the nature of hurting certainly belongs: and to the non-existence of impure psychic-attention (read *asadbhavasya*), proved by the careful conduct, which occurs without it, the nature of hurting certainly does not belong, as is shown by the fact that the taking of another's life does not involve bondage : therefore internal negligence is the more serious, and not the external.

Even so, the external should be recognized, simply as being an occasion for the internal negligence.

Now he teaches that internal negligence must in any case be rejected:

III.18. A *shramana* of careless conduct in regard to the six bodies[133] is esteemed to be hurting them; but, if he always behaves carefully, then, like a lotus in water, he is un-assoiled. (218)

Since the existence of impure psychic-attention, proved by careless behaviour, which does not occur without it, is hurtful, inasmuch as bondage is known to result from the cause of taking the life of the six classes of bodies; and since non-existence of impure psychic-attention, proved by careful behaviour, which occurs without it, is non-hurtful,–for, inasmuch as it has not the slightest bondage resulting from the "other," it is known to be like a lotus luxuriating (*durlalita*) in the water, without assoil–for these reasons internal negligence, which has the form of impure psychic-attention, must be rejected in all cases where external negligence, in the form of taking another being's life, which is merely occasion of internal negligence, is entirely rejected.

Now he teaches that similarly appropriation (*upadhi*), since it is exclusively an internal negligence, should be rejected:

III.19. Bondage may arise or not arise when, in case of a bodily action, a living being is killed: but from appropriation or possessiveness (the *Tatparya-vrtti* paraphrases *upadhi* by *parigraha)* bondage certainly results; therefore *shramanas* have abandoned it entirely. (219)

Whereas in the taking of another being's life through a bodily action the negligence-quality is held to be variable,–because its character as bondage is variable according to the presence or absence of impure psychic-attention,–with appropriation the case is different. Its negligence-quality is invariable, because its character as bondage is invariable owing to the invariable presence of impure psychic-attention, which is proved by its non-occurrence without the same. Therefore the holy *Arhats*, the supreme *shramanas*, have themselves abandoned all *upadhi* [external possessions as well as internal *parigraha* of attachment, aversion and passions]. Accordingly others also should from the first reject it, like internal negligence, because it does not occur without the same.

"Hereby, if a man reflects upon it, is said all that needs to be said. For the unreflecting, surely, the net of delusion is hard to escape even with the greatest expenditure of words." (PS *Kalash* 14)

Now he teaches that rejection of appropriation is in fact rejection of internal negligence:

III.20. Without the absolute renunciation *(tyaga)*[134] of worldly concerns, devoid of all consideration, regard or expection of any sort (*nirvekkho* in Pk., *nirpeksha* in Sk.), there does not take place purification (*visuddhi*) of mental states (*aasaya* in Pk., *aashaya* in Sk.) and when the mind is not purified, how can there be annihilation of *karman*? (220/1)

Given the existence of connection with an external (negligence), and given rejection of internal (negligence) having the form of impure psychic-attention, as of impurity of rice-grains when husks are present, we do not find only the fundamental pure psychic-attention. Therefore rejection of appropriation, ordained in view of a purpose, namely rejection of an internal negligence, namely impure psychic-attention, is in fact rejection of internal negligence.

Now, enlarging upon appropriation, he teaches that it is invariably internal negligence:

III.21. How can he (who is favourably disposed towards *parigraha)* be free from infatuation, incidental sins inevitable in worldly activities (*arambha)*[135] and lack of self-restraint *(samyama)*? And how one, who is attached to or engrossed in other substance, can realize the real nature of self? (221)

Since, given appropriation, there unavoidably results infatuation, characterized as an evolution of the idea of mine, worldly undertakings, characterized as an evolution through a series of acts having that for object, and lack of self-restraint, characterized as an evolution destructive of the character of pure self,

and since one associated with appropriation, being fond of other "substance," does not attain the pure self, we determine that appropriation is invariably internal negligence. The purport hereof is thıt, having determined the nature of appropriation to be such, we should entirely forgo it.

Now he teaches an exception, to the effect that for some person in some circumstances at some time in some way some appropriation is in fact not to be rejected:

III.22. That wherethrough negligence does not attach to the user either in taking or in leaving it [things], the *shramana* who has considered time and place may use it. (222)

That every appropriation must be rejected, since the self-substance is without any second, material, substance, is the main rule.

But here we have an exception, that by virtue of particular time and place some [appropriations] are not rejected. For, when a *shramana* who has undertaken a rejection of all appropriations cannot, although desirous of attaining the highest self-restraint in indifference, succeed in this, because his energies have failed owing to particular time and place, then, taking to a diminished self-restraint, he has recourse to appropriations, merely as external means. And the appropriation so resorted to is not only not a negligence through being an appropriation; on the contrary, it is a rejection of a negligence. A negligence is that which does not occur without impure psychic-attention; but this, accepted in order to avoid a negligence in the matter of taking and leaving, e.g. of taking food and voiding of excrements (*nirhara*), which are means for the life of the body,–itself required as an auxiliary means for the modification called the *shramana*-state,–is in every respect a rejection of negligence, since it does not occur without pure psychic-attention.

Now he teaches the characteristic nature of an appropriation which is (rightly) not rejected:

III.23. An appropriation which is (really) not objectionable and is not desired by people who lack self-restraint, and which does not beget infatuation, etc., a *shramana* should accept, but sparingly. (223)

That appropriation which is altogether unobjectionable, because it does not lead to bondage; which is not desired by people without self-restraint, because it is unusual except in the case of self-restraint; which does not beget infatuation, etc., because it takes place without an evolution such as attachment, is not rejected.

Therefore an appropriation of a nature as described may be accepted, but no other, however small, having a nature different from that described.

Now he teaches that the real duty (*dharma*) is the main rule, and not the exception:

III.24. "Why anything[136] at all?" one should reason that when the slightest thought "even to his body?",[137] on the part of him who dsires no rebirth, is considered attachment–thus have the best of *Jinas* extolled inattention (towards the body) (*nih-pratikarma*). (224/1)

Even in regard to the body,–so absolutely adopted and not an object of rejection, inasmuch as it is an auxiliary cause of the modification called the *shramana*-state,–the holy divine *Arhats* have extolled inattention, "Being other substance, this acquisition,[138] far from deserving favour, is an object of indifference." Then in connection therewith why should one who has a taste for the realization of the perception of the truth of pure self admit the other, residual, miserable, not agreed, acquisitions?

This is the evident intention (read *akutam* or *akutih*) of those (*Arhats*). Therefore it is determined that the "main rule" is the real Duty, and not the exception. The meaning here is that we must cling to the extreme *nirgrantha* condition; for it is the real Duty (*vastu-dharma*).

Now he teaches which are the different exceptions:

III.25. As instrumental on the path of the *Jinas* is mentioned the mark, i.e. the form as it is by birth; so also are prescribed the word of the *guru*, propriety of conduct (*vinaya*) and the study of the *sutras*. (225)

Whatever not-rejected appropriation is here excepted is in all cases such as is instrumental, as rendering service by being an auxiliary cause of the modification called the *shramana*-state; but no other object. Different kinds thereof are:

the material components of the body, which make up the external mark, inasmuch as they possess the native colour which corresponds with the natural colour, free form anything adventitious;

the mental word-components of the saint's teaching in illuminating the truth concerning the self, when heard as pronounced by the *gurus* who are giving instruction at the time;

the material *sutra*-components, being sounds which are means to scripture-knowledge, which, when studied, is perpetually instructive and able to illuminate the beginningless and endless truth of the pure self;

the material-components of the mind (*chitta*), which affect the modification in intuition and so on, revealing the truth of the pure self, and, in the so-modified person, the will for a disciplined condition.

The purport here is that, like the body, even speech and mind are not the essence of reality (*vastu-dharma*).

Now he teaches the procedure of maintaining the not-rejected appropriation which is confined to the body:

III.26. A *shramana* is indifferent to this world [i.e has no desires in this world] and has no expectations in regard to the other [i.e. next world], is self-controlled in food and wandering (*yukta-ahara-vihara*)[139] free from passions (*kashaya*). (226/1)

Being free from passions, since his innate nature is completely separate from the ripening of all *karmic* matter, because evolved through the truth of uniform pure self without beginning or end; being indifferent to this world, since, although at the time still belonging to mankind, he stands far aloof from all human business; being without inclination for the other world, since he is empty of longing (*trshna*) to experience future states, such as that of an immortal, etc.,

the *shramana* must be self-controlled in food and wandering, since he feeds and moves his body as a means for grasping the truth of the pure self, like a lamp filled and carried round as a means for perceiving an object to be examined.

The purport here is that, since he is free from passions, therefore he does not, through attachment to his present body or attachment to a heavenly body, live without self-control in respect of food and wandering, and he is self-controlled in food and wandering merely for the purpose of maintaining the modification, called the *shramana*-state, which leads to the comprehension of the truth of the pure self.

Now he teaches that one who controls himself in food and wandering is (as good as) actually without food and wandering:

III.27. He whose self is not-desirous of food,[140] is indeed austerity; and the *shramanas* who go and accept food, which is not the object of desire, are also considered abstainers from food. (227/1)

Since in essence he is abstinent from food (*anashana*) and since the alms are devoid of the fault of desire (*eshana-dosha*),[141] the self-controlled in food is in verity actually foodless.

Thus, if a man is at all times conscious only of the self, which is exempt from the taking of any material sustenance, his innate nature is in itself foodless, inasmuch as it is void of all longing for food. This, namely, is his abstinence from food (*anashana*), his austerity; for the internal is of more importance (than the external). Those who with this in view realize a nature in itself without food and, in order to preclude that (food), live by such, other, alms as are free from fault of desire (*eshana*), are, although taking food, really not taking food and are really abstainers from food, since, by reason of their self-control in food, every inclination based on their innate nature or the nature of other substance is absent. Likewise, it is to be understood, although not stated, that he who is self-controlled in wandering, is really without wandering, since his innate nature is in itself without wandering and since his wandering is purified by religious observances (*samiti*).

Now, in view of the question "how is self-control in food secured?," he teaches:

III.28. The *shramana*, possessing only a body and not attending[142] to that body, which he deems not his (i.e. has no sense of mineness in that), controls it by austerity, manifesting the energy (*shakti*) of his self. (228)

Since a *shramana*, although possessing only a body,—for he does not forcibly reject the appropriation consisting of his mere body, an auxiliary means for the evolution called the *shramana*-state,—yet omits every care (*samskara*) for it having taken to heart the meaning of the Highest Lord explained in a former *sutra*, "Why anything?" and so forth (224-1), and, thinking that "this (body) is not mine; so it deserves not favour, but indifference," pays no attention to it, for this reason, since he takes no improper food which would presuppose the notion of mine, control in diet may be duly his.

And, since, manifesting the full energies of his self, he with every effort keeps that body controlled by asceticism, characterized by an innate mature free from food (*anasana*), as described in the last preceding *sutra*, for this reason, his diet being that of one actually engaged in *yoga*, as he is without the loss of *yoga*, which consists in the proceeding of taking the food [to himself], control in diet may be duly his.

Now he teaches fully the characteristic nature of controlled or proper diet (*yukta-ahara*):

III.29. (The proper food consists of) a meal once a day; not filling the stomach; taken as given; collected by begging; in the day-time; without respect to taste; neither honey nor meat.[143] (229/1)

Food taken once a day is controlled (*yukta*) food, since so much suffices to sustain the body, which is an auxiliary means to the modification called the *shramana*-state. But food taken more than once is not controlled, since, being a habit due to attachment to the body, it is made into flagrant occasion for hurt; nor is it that of a self-controlled person, since it is habit due to attachment to the body.

Only food which does not fill the stomach is controlled food, since only by this is self-control (*yoga*)[144] not violated. But food which satisfies the stomach is not controlled, since, as violating self-control, it is to a certain extent an occasion of hurt; nor is it that of a self-controlled person, since it violates self-control.

Only food taken as given is controlled food, since only such food is free from attachment, characterized as a particular liking. But food not taken as given is not controlled, since, being a habit due to attachment, defined as a particular liking, it is made a flagrant occasion for hurt: nor is it that of a self-controlled person, since it is a habit due to attachment, characterized as a particular liking.

Only food collected by begging is controlled food, since that only is independent of effort. But food not collected by begging is not controlled, since it is clearly an occasion of hurt, as presupposing an effort: nor is it that of a self-controlled person, since internal impurity is manifested by such a food habit.

Only food eaten in the day-time is controlled food, since only then can it be properly inspected. But food which is taken not in the day-time is not controlled, since, not being properly inspected, it is an occasion of unavoidable hurt: nor is it that of a self-controlled person, since internal impurity is manifested by such a food habit.

Only food without respect to taste is controlled food, since only this is graced with internal purity. But food which has respect to taste is not controlled, since in consequence of internal impurity it is made a flagrant occasion of hurt: nor is it that of a self-controlled person, since it is a habit of internal impurity.

Only food not containing honey or meat is controlled food, since such food is no occasion of hurt. But food containing honey or meat is not controlled, since it is an occasion of hurt: nor is it that of a self-controlled person, since internal impurity is manifested by such a food habit. Here containing of honey and meat implies also (*upalakshana*) any [other] occasion of hurt: hence only food which is free from all occasion of hurt is controlled food.

Now he teaches the proper adjustment of conduct, in which main rule (*utsarga*) and exception (*apavada*) harmonize:

III.30. Boy or old man or tired or sick, let him follow a conduct appropriate to him in such a way that no fundamental negligence (*mula-cheda*) takes place. (230)

The main rule is that even by a boy, an old man, one tired or sick a conduct very rigorous and appropriate to one who practises self-restraint must be maintained in such a way that (read *na yatha syat*) there is no neglect of self-restraint (*samyama*), which is fundamental importance as a means towards the reality of pure self.

The exception is that by a boy, an old man, one tired or sick, a conduct mild and appropriate to a boy or an old man, one tired or sick, must be maintained in such a way that there is no neglect of the body, which is of fundamental importance as a means to the reality (*tattva*) of the pure self.

The main rule as affected by the exception is that a boy, an old man, one tired or sick, while maintaining a conduct very rigorous and appropriate to one who practises self-restraint, in such a way that there is no neglect of self-restraint, which is of fundamental importance, as a means towards the reality of the pure self, should maintain a conduct mild and appropriate to a boy, an old man, one tired or sick, in such a way that there is no neglect of the body, which is of fundamental importance as a means towards the self-restraint which is a means to the reality of the pure self.

The exception, as affected by the main rule, is that a boy, an old man, one tired or sick, while maintaining a conduct mild and appropriate to a boy, an old man, one tired or sick, in such a way that there is no neglect of the body, which is of fundamental importance as a means to self-restraint, which is a means towards the reality of the pure self, should maintain a conduct very rigorous and appropriate to one practising self-restraint, in such a way that there is no neglect of self-restraint, which is of fundamental importance as a means to the reality of the pure self.

Thus, in any case, by harmonizing main rule and abrogative rule a proper adjustment of conduct must be effected.

Now he teaches a misadjustment of conduct through conflict (*virodha*) between main rule and exception:

III.31. If a *shramana* with awareness of time and place, his tiredness [i.e. capacity for physical labour] forbearance and of *upadhi* [i.e. bodily condition], acts in regard to food and wandering, then he incurs a minor shortcoming (*lepa*).[145] (231)

Here the cause of exhaustion and sickness is fasting (*upavasa*); the *upadhi* is the body, the abode of youth and old age. Therefore the boy, the old man, the tired and sick are here brought in.

One who, though aware of place and time, proceeds in regard to food and wandering in accordance with his state of boyhood, old age, fatigue or sickness, does by acting on the line of mild conduct commit a minor shortcoming; therefore the main rule is preferable.

He who, though aware of place and time, proceeds in regard to food and wandering in accordance with his state of boyhood, old age, fatigue or sickness, commits by acting on the line of full-grown (*vrddha*) conduct only a minor shortcoming; therefore the exception is preferable.

He who, though aware of place and time, through fear of minor shortcoming does not proceed in regard to food and wandering in accordance with his state of boyhood, old age, fatigue or sickness and, by his adherence to very hard (*atikarkasha*) conduct, causes his body out of due course to fail (read *patayatah*), and then reaches heaven with his whole accumulation of the nectar of self-restraint lost, because his auserity has no opportunity, incurs an irreparable major shortcoming. For this reason the main rule, applied without regard to the exception, is far from superior.

He who, though aware of place and time, in disregard of a minor short-coming proceeds arbitrarily in food and wandering out of regard for his state of boyhood, old age, fatigue or sickness, and by his adherence to mild conduct destroys his self-restraint, and becomes on a level with persons lacking self-restraint, because at the moment his austerity has no opportunity, incurs an irreparable major shortcoming. For this reason the exception, applied without regard to the main rule, is far from superior.

Therefore in every way a misadjustment in conduct through clashing of the main rule and the exception must be rejected, and for that purpose the *syad-vada*,[146] in its developed form with main rule and exception in mutual harmony, should be adhered to in every case.

"Thus let the self-restrained person (*yati*), practising in accordance with the main rule and exception a conduct found beneficial by men of old times, who were full of special care, and gradually, after having proceeded through several distinct roles or stages, attaining a repose without compare, take his stand entirely upon his own substance, showing itself as a special and general form consciousness." (PS *Kalash* 15).

Here ends the discussion of CONDUCT

Now begins the discussion of the path of liberation, otherwise called the state of the *shramanas* and characterized as mental-concentration (*eikagrya*). Here he first sets to work upon the Scripture (*agama*), which is the chief means thereto:

THE PATH OF LIBERATION (VERSES 232-244)

III.32. He, who has reached mental concentration is *shramana;* mental concentration belongs to him who has certainty about objects: certainty arises from the Scriptures; therefore to be busy (*chesta*) with [the study of] the Scriptures is of primary importance. (232)

Now the *shramana* can only be one who has mental-concentration: mental-concentration belongs to him only who has certainty about objects: and this certainty about objects comes only from the Scripture. Therefore occupation with the Scripture is the main thing, and there is no other way. For neither can objects be ascertained without the Scripture, since only this possesses an internal depth, well-founded on a correct ascertainment of the whole multitude of objects, appearing with three characteristics[147] in threefold time: nor could mental-concentration be attained without certainty concerning objects, since in one who had no certainty about objects there would be constant distraction, sometimes through excessive eagerness, when, confused in mind by the wish to ascertain, he wavers in all directions; sometimes through unrest, exploding every moment, when, enslaved by the desire to do something and seeking to create everything himself, he evolves through all kinds of occupations: sometimes through extreme capriciousness, when, filled with desire to enjoy and assuming everything to be for his enjoyment, he is in a mental-state stained with the faults (*doshas*) of attachment and aversion, and, involved in duality by the division of things desirable and undesirable, changes his condition with every fresh object, so that, unable to arrive at certainty, he does not see the holy self without action or enjoyment, which, although exhausting everything simultaneously, is, as not being everything, one.

Nor could the *shramana*-state be attained without mental-concentration, since the *shramana*-state, which consists in applying oneself to the reality of pure self, cannot exist in one who, without mental-concentration, beholds that "surely a many is here," under the influence of such a presentation judges that "surely a many is here," and, filled with this experience and always acting with a mind distracted by such mental distractions (*vikalpa*) about each thing that "surely a many is here," in such a pitiable condition lacks mental-concentration upon the reality of pure self, in the form of vision, knowledge and activity proceeding through evolution into enlightened (*samyak*) view, knowledge and conduct, which have for characteristic natures the presentation, the realization and the activity of the one self.

Therefore, for the attainment of the *shramana*-state, otherwise called the path of liberation, one desirous of liberation must, in any case, be deeply versed in the Holy Word, explored by the venerable omniscient *Arhat*, with its distinctive banner of many-sidedness (allusion to the *anekanta-vada* = *syad-vada*).

Now he proves that destruction of *karmic* matter, called liberation, is not possible for anyone lacking the understanding of the Scripture:

III.33. A *shramana* who lacks the understanding of Scriptures knows not the self (or)[148] the "other." Not knowing the reality of things, how can he living on alms destroy the *karmas*? (233)

Now without the Scripture there could not be knowledge of the "other" self (*paratman*) or knowledge of the highest self (*paramatman*). Neither could one devoid of the knowledge of the other self, or devoid of the knowledge of the highest self, destroy the objective or physical and subjective or psychic *karma* (*dravya-bhava-karma*) of infatuation, etc., or the *karman* which consists in the perversion of knowledge.

To explain: One without Scripture,–who, in regard to this world, defiled with the pollution of great infatuation moving with the flow of the river of beginning and endless existences, has his discrimination inundated, as if he were drunk or insane, and who, though observing with a not discriminative (*avivikta*) light of knowledge, has not in regard to substances such as the body, ascertained as the place of each particular self, or in regard to psychical states such as infatuation, attachment and aversion, commingled with his psychic-attention, his own experience (*anubhava*) of the self, based on the instruction of the Scripture, which gives certainty about the self and the other (*sva* and *para* at the beginning of the commentary),—could not attain the knowledge "this is the other, this is the self."

Likewise also, one straining himself through having taken as object of knowledge the universe with its unfathomably deep nature—a mass of diverse modifications, manifested in the series of three times—could not, without his own experience of the self, based on the instruction of the Scripture, which gives certainty about this highest self, attain the knowledge of the one highest self, which has knowledge for nature.

Likewise again, one lacking the knowledge of the other self, and of the highest self, who imagines an oneness with body, etc., originated by objective *karman*, and with the psychical states such as infatuation, attachment and aversion, based on the body, etc., is, through failure to discriminate between that which destroys and that which should be destroyed, unable to attain to destruction of objective and subjective *karman* of infatuation, etc.

Likewise also–since without a basis in the highest self his worldly-experience, whilst, revolving with uncontrollable revolution since ever there was *samsara*, evolves through ups and downs with every single thing, because it is based on the knowable,—he could not attain the destruction of the *karmans* which consist in the perversions of knowledge.

Therefore those who are desirous of destroying *karman* must in any case study the Scripture.

Now he teaches that the Scripture, alone is the eye of those who are on the path to liberation:

III.34. The saint (*sadhu*) has the Scripture for eye; all creatures have their sense-organs for eyes; the *Devas* have eyes which see the remote (*avadhi*); but the liberated-souls (*siddhas*) have eyes which see in every respect. (234)

Now only the venerable liberated souls, because they consist of pure knowledge, have eyes which see everywhere. All other beings, because their perception is bound to corporeal (*murta*) substances, have sense-organs for eyes. The *Devas,* because they apprehend corporeal substances characterized by fineness (*sukshamatva*), have eyes which see the remote; and so they too, because, seeing only coloured substance, they are not distinguished from beings with sense-organs as eyes, have sense-organs for eyes. So then for all these beings moving in *samsara* and being themselves on the knowable, because they are maimed by infatuation, there could be no possession of eyes seeing everywhere, which is obtainable by realization of the reality of pure self, whereupon depends the basing one's self on knowledge.

So, in order to obtain this, the venerable *shramans* take the Scripture for eye; and, although, by reason of the mutual blending of the knowable and the knowledge, discrimination between them is impossible, yet, having effected a separation of the self and the other, they break through the great infatuation, and, having reached the highest self, they stand based on knowledge. Therefore those desirous of liberation should see everything with the eye of the Scripture.

Now he explains how with the eye of the Scripture everything is seen:

III.35. All objects together with their various qualities and modifications are established [known] by the Scripture; seeing [i.e. comprehending] by Scripture, the *shramanas* know them all. (235)

Now through the Scripture all substances are trustworthily known (*pramiyante*); for all the substances are free from contradiction by any argumentation.

And they are known as characterized (*vishishta*) by their various qualities and modifications; for the Scripture, as it consists of the many-sided-view (*anekanta*), which penetrates the several properties simultaneously or successively arising, can possess the character of a trustworthy means of knowledge.

Therefore, all objects are established by the Scripture. And, evolving by way of becoming the psychic-attention of study-knowledge (*shruta-jnana*), which consists in the many-sided-view (*anekanta*), pervading all substance, characterized by their various qualities and modifications, they become of themselves knowable to the *shramanas.* Therefore to those who have the eye of Scripture nothing can be imperceptible.

Now he shows that the road to liberation is nothing but the simultaneity of Scripture-knowledge, the consequent conviction (*shraddhan*) in the principles or reality of things (*tattva*) and categories (*artha*) and the self-restraint resulting from both of them:

III.36. He, who does not view reality of things, preceded by knowledge of Scripture, has not self-restraint; thus says the *sutra*. Without self-restraint how can one be a *shramana?* (236)

To one who is destitute of conviction, preceded by Scripture-(knowledge), which has the *quodammodo*-theory (*syad-vada*) for emblem, and characterized as conviction in the principles and categories; who, because he does not possess discrimination between self and other, is assured of identity with the passions (*kashaya*) and the body; who in consequence of not restraining his longing for sense-objects is a destroyer of the six kinds of soul-bodies; who, because he is without quietism (*nivrtti*) in any direction, is active (*pravrtti*) in every direction; also because he does not possess the knowledge of the highest-self nor is engaged in mental-concentration on the truth of self, which has the form of knowledge, whereas his worldly-opining (*jnapti*) invades without barrier (*nir-argala*) the circle of the knowable—to such a one even self-restraint is unattainable.

And for one who has not attained self-restraint there can be no *shramana*-state, otherwise called the path of liberation, whereof the nature is a convinced mental-concentration. Hence the path of liberation can be nothing but a simultaneity of Scripture-knowledge, conviction in the principles and categories and self-restraint.

Now he dispels (the idea) that non-simultaneity of Scripture-knowledge, of conviction in the principles and categories and of self-restraint could be the path of liberation:

III.37. One does not attain liberation by means of Scripture-knowledge, if he is not convinced of the nature of reality of things *(arthas)*; and one convinced of the nature of reality of things also does not attain liberation (*nirvana)* if he is lacking self-restraint. (237)

One does not attain perfection through knowledge produced by Scriptures, but destitute of faith [i.e. conviction with regard to the nature of reality of things]; or through faith combined with that knowledge, but devoid of self-restraint.

To explain: If a man, although clearly, with the help of the Scripture, reasoning out all the categories, yet does not understand (*pratyeti*) the self, which is one clear appearance-form (*akara*) of knowledge, combined with the appearance-form of the knowable in all the categories, then, not experiencing (*un-anubhavan*) the self as described, because he is devoid of faith in the self as described, how can he immersed as he is in the knowable and infatuated as to knowledge, become a knower? and for one who does not know what can the Scripture, though illumining the knowable, effect? Therefore through Scripture-knowledge, void of faith, there is no attainment.

Moreover, if a man, although believing in the self and experiencing it as one clear appearance-form combined with the appearance-form of the knowable in all the categories, does not live with it restrained within itself, then, because in his very self there abides a state of consciousness which capriciously moves to and fro between the substances owing to beginningless latent impressions (*vasana*) of infatuation, attachment and aversion, and because there does not exist in him a state of consciousness which is consolidated in this one truth (principle, *tattva*), free from latent impressions and agitation, how can he be self-restrained? And for one without self-restraint what can belief, which consists in apprehension (*pratiti*) of the truth (reality) of the self as described, or knowledge, which consists in experiencing (*anubhuti*) of the reality of the self as described, have any effect? Therefore from belief or knowledge, devoid of self-restraint, there is no attainment of liberation; hence [the idea] that non-simultaneity of Scripture-knowledge, conviction in the principles and categories, and self-restraint could be the path of liberation is refuted.

Now he makes clear that, even with simultaneity of Scripture-knowledge, conviction in the principles and categories, and self-restraints, the most effective means towards the path of liberation is knowledge of the self:

III.38. That *karman* which one without knowledge destroys in hundreds of thousands of crores of existences (lives), a knower (*jnani*) possessing threefold restraint (*gupti*) [of mind, speech and body] destroys in a mere breath. (238)

That *karman* which, as it ripens in a series of stages, beginning with the manifoldness of childish pains, the man without knowledge,—evolving through the transitory psychical states of pleasure, pain, etc., in consequence of his acceptance of attachment and aversion,—with difficulty escapes in hundreds of thousands of crores of existences, because it again repairs its continuity, that *karman*, brought to ripeness by a vigorous effort–because, possessing the quality of a knower, characterized by experience of the self's pure knowledge nature, obtained by the exceeding benefit of a simultaneity of (1) Scripture-knowledge, having for emblem the *quodammodo*-theory (*syadvada*), (2) conviction in the principles and categories (*tattvartha shraddham*), and (3) self-restraint, he possesses the three restraints, which function in refraining from (*uparama*) bodily, vocal and mental *karman*,—he who by repelling attachment and aversion has cast far away all weakness such as pleasure, pain and so forth, easily in the space of a mere breath brings to nought without renewal of its continuity. Therefore we must agree that knowledge of the self, given a simultaneity of Scripture-knowledge, faith in the principles and categories, and self-restraint (read *samyatatvanam*), is the most effective means to the path of liberation.

Now he teaches that for one who lacks knowledge of the self simultaneity of the knowledge of the complete Scriptures, faith in the principles and categories, and self-restraint is ineffective:

III.39. But, if anyone has delusion (*murcha*) [i.e. attachment or mental clinging] in regard to the body, etc., even to the extent of an ultimate atom, he does not attain perfection (*siddhi*), though knowing the Scriptures completely. (239/1)

If anyone, because the whole substance of the Scripture is to him a myrobalan in the hand, knows the self, which knows the whole mass of substances, characterized by their appropriate modifications and in their past, present and future existences, has faith and practises self-restraint, yet at some time, despite a simultaneity of Scripture-knowledge, faith in the principles and categories and self-restraint,—in consequence of being slightly defiled with infatuation,—does not make his self evolve in an uninfected psychic-attention (because infected by delusion of body and so on) and so experience the self as having knowledge for self, he does not reach perfection (*sidhyati*), since he is not released from *karmic* matter, which is pinned down, as it were, by a pin, by even that spot of impurity of infatuation. Therefore even a simultaneity of Scripture-knowledge, faith in the principles and categories and self-restraint, when destitute of knowledge of the self, is ineffective.

Now he establishes a simultaneity of self-knowledge with simultaneity of Scripture-knowledge, faith in principles and categories, and self-restraint:

III.40. That *shramana* who practises the five self-regulations *(samiti)* and the three restraints (*gupti)*, controls his five senses, has conquered the passions (*kashaya*) and is fully endowed with intuition and knowledge, is called self-restrained. (240)

He who through Scripture-knowledge, which has the many-sided-view as emblem, believes in the self and experiences the self as having its one clear appearance–form (*akara*) of knowledge combined with appearance-forms of the knowable in all the categories; who wishes to abide always in the self alone; who has made the vessel of the body a means of self-restraint carried out by a positive-behaviour (*pravrtti*) controlled by the fivefold set of *samitis*; who has gradually allayed (*samuparata*)(referring to the *guptis*) the activity (*vyapara*) of body, voice and mind by keeping the five senses controlled and checked; who has ascertained that the cause which makes the activity (*vrtti*) of consciousness hover over strange substances is—although become entirely one with the self, in consequence of mutual penetration, different from it by distinction in innate nature; and who, by himself, like a skilful wrestler, tightly squeezing and squeezing the group of the passions, makes them give up life, that man, being also void of all "other" substances, is patently self-restrained, because the activity (*vrtti*) of his consciousness is eternally unaffected owing to the ascertainment of the reality (*tattva*) of self, which in innate nature is simply pure conviction (*drshi*) [*drashti*] and knowledge (*jnapti*).

In him alone is attained a simultaneity of self-knowledge with a simultaneity of Scripture-knowledge, faith in the principles and categories, and self-restraint:

Now he teaches what is the characteristic of one who has become self-controlled through a simultaneity of self-knowledge with a simultaneity of Scripture-knowledge, conviction in the principles and categories and self-restraint:

III.41. Considering the groups of enemies and friends as the same, pleasure and pain as the same, praise and blame as the same, clay and gold as the same, the *shramana,*[149] moreover, considers life and death as the same. (241)

Self-restraint (*samyama*) is conduct accompanied by enlightened (*samyak*) intuition and knowledge. Conduct is *dharma*; *dharma* is equanimity; equanimity is a state-of-evolution of the self devoid of infatuation (*moha*) and perturbation or mental agitation (*kshobha*).

Therefore equanimity is a characteristic of the self-restrained.

So in regard to the two groups, enemies and friends, pleasure and pain, praise and blame, clay and gold, life and death, he is the same (*samah*).

Whoso,–being free from the infatuation, "this one is strange to me, this one belongs to me; this is a joy, this is a torment; this is an elevation to me, this is a humiliation; this man is useless to me and this thing is helpful; this means a maintaining of myself, and that is a complete destruction"– has not in regard to anything the duality of attachment and aversion; who continually experiences the self as having for nature pure faith and knowledge; who, having comprehended enemies and friends, pleasure and pain, praise and blame, clay and gold, life and death indistinguishably, merely as knowables, constantly abides in the self, which has knowledge for self, truly possesses equanimity in every regard.

That equanimity must be designated as a characteristic of him who is self-restrained, who has brought to perfection a simultaneity of self-knowledge with a simultaneity of Scripture-knowledge, conviction in the principles and categories and self-restraint.

Now he shows this self-restraint having a simultaneity of self-knowledge with a simultaneity of Scripture-knowledge, conviction in the principles and categories, and self-restraint to be identical with the path of liberation, otherwise called the *shramana*-state, characterized as mental-concentration:

III.42. He who is intent on the triad, world-view, knowledge and conduct together, is held to be in a state of mental-concentration; his *shramana*-hood is complete. (242)

When (1) through the modification of enlightened vision (*samyag-darshan*), characterized as comprehension (*pratiti*) of the principles (*tattva*) of knowable and knower as it is (read *jneya-jnatr-tattva-tatha-pratiti-lakshanena*), (2) through the modification of knowledge, characterized as experience (*anubhuti*) of the principles of knowable and knower as it is, (3) through the modification of conduct, characterized as abiding in the truth of seer and knower, which is effected by abstinence from any other action on the part of the knowable and the knower,–through these three modifications simultaneously the self,–by reason of intense mutual-interpenetration, manifested in a relation of thing enjoyed (*bhavya*) and enjoyer (*bhavaka*)–evolves through a part and whole relation and possesses a state of self-restraint together with a repose in itself; then, although there is an experiencing of a one consisting of a many,–as in the case of *panak* (a drink mixture),–we must, by reason of the rejection of all other substances, recognize the path of liberation, otherwise called *shramana*-hood, characterized as mental-concentration.

According to the external, other-referential [practical, Faddegon] point of view (*vyavahara-naya*), which, since it involves differentiation (*bheda*), considers chiefly the modes, the statement is that "enlightened view, knowledge, and conduct are the path of liberation."

According to the internal, self-referential [theoretical, Faddegon] point of view (*nishchaya-naya*), which, since it consists in an identity (*abheda*), considers chiefly the substance, it is that "mental-concentration is the path of liberation."

According to trustworthy proof (*pramana*) it is that "both are so," since everything consists in difference and identity.

"Thus that path of liberation, which, according to the attitude of the conceiver, becomes plural, though one, and so exhibits triple characterization and again oneness,–that path, stable, with existence dependent upon the purport of seer and knower (*drashtr-jnatr*), let men take by storm, in order that they may shortly storm an incomparable splendour of flashing thought." (PS *Kalash* 16)

Now he refutes this idea that non-mental-concentration is the path of liberation:

III.43. If a *shramana*, being ignorant about the nature of reality of things, is infatuated through addiction to the "other" substance, and feels attachment or aversion, then he is bound with various *karmas*. (243)

Whoso does not with simple concentration (*ekam agram*) realize the self, which has knowledge for self, necessarily addicts himself to the "other" substance, that is, the knowable. And, being addicted thereto and fallen away from the knowledge of the self, which has knowledge for self, he is himself without knowledge and either becomes infatuate or feels attachment or aversion; and, being so, he becomes bound and not released. Therefore, non-mental-concentration could not be the path of liberation.

Now determining that mental-concentration is the path of liberation, he summarizes:

III.44. If a *shramana* is not infatuated with reference to objects, and does not feel attachment, nor is subject to aversion (*dvesham*), then inevitably he destroys the various *karmas.* (244)

Whoso with single concentration realizes the self, which has knowledge for self, does not addict himself to the "other" substance, that is, the knowable. Not being addicted thereto, not fallen away from the knowledge of the self, which has knowledge for self, he stands fast himself as knowledge, and neither is infatuated, nor feels attachment or aversion; and, being so, he becomes released and not bound. Therefore it may be proved that only mental-concentration is the path of liberation.

Thus ends the exposition of the THE PATH OF LIBERATION.

Now begins the exposition of good pyshcic attention. Here it is stated that those who possess good psychic attention are also *shramanas*:

GOOD (*SHUBHA*) PSYCHIC ATTENTION (VERSES 245-270)

III.45. In the Jain scriptures (*samaye), shramanas* are those endowed with pure psychic-attention and with good psychic attention. Amongst them, those with pure psychic-attention are free from *karmic* inflow (*asrava*); the others are subject to *karmic* inflow. (245)

Those who, though pledged to *shramana*-hood, are, through survival of a small portion of the passions, unable to ascend to the stage of pure psychic-attention,—consisting in an actualization (*vrtti*) of the principle of the self, which has for nature quite pure convictions (*drshi*) and understanding (*jnapti*), both active (*pravrtta*) in renunciation (*nivrtti*) of all "other" substance—would they, being in the proximity or neighbourhood (*upakantha*) thereof, with their energies blunted (*kunthikrta*) by the passions and with their internal organ excessively full of longings (*utkanthula*), be *shramanas* or not? As to this a statement is given.

In the first place, good psychic-attention may coinhere with righteousness (*dharma*), since we have had (PS 11) the description "self evolved through righteousness."

Therefore, those who possess good psychic-attention would, by reason of the existence of righteousness in them, be *shramanas.* But they are not on a level (*sama-kastha*) with those who possess pure psychic-attention, since those who possess pure psychic-attention, having thrown off all passions, are without *karmic* inflow. The others on the contrary, having a particle of passion undispersed, are subject to inflow. For this very reason they may not be coordinated with the possessors of pure psychic-attention, but are also considered as *shraman*.

Now he sets forth the definition of a *shramana* with good psychic-attention:

III.46. If in the conduct of a *shramana* there is found devotion to *Arhats*, etc. and disinterested affection (*vatsalya*) for all who have applied themselves to the sacred writings (*pravachana*), then that conduct is said to be of good psychic-attention. (246)

He who, given the state of *shramana*, which consists in abandonment (*sanyasa*) of every attachment, is himself, through the influence of a particle of passion, unable to abide exclusively in the actualization of the pure self, yet is inspired by devotion and love for others, *Arhats*, etc. abiding exclusively in the actualization of the pure self, who, having applied themselves to the sacred writings, expound the exclusive abiding in the actualization of the pure self, would,–inasmuch as his actualization of the pure self is only so far commingled with activity towards the "other" substance, stimulated by a slight attachment,–exhibit a conduct of good psychic-attention. Therefore the characteristic of *shramana* of good psychic-attention is a conduct conjoined with affection (*anuraga*) for the pure self.

Now he exhibits the action of *shramanas* having good psychic-attention:

III.47. Respectful behaviour to *shramanas*, by rising in welcome and attendance upon them (when they go), combined with reverence (*vandana*) and homage (*namaskara*) and the removal of their fatigue, are not censurable in a conduct of affection. (247)

On the part of the persons of good psychic-attention, their conduct being conjoined with affection for the pure self, the proceeding of respectful behaviour, i.e. praise, homage, rising in welcome and attendance upon departure, towards *shramanas*, who have reached the actualization of the pure self, and the proceeding of removing their fatigue, with the aim of conserving the actualization of the pure self, would not be a fault.

Now he demonstrates that actions of this kind are proper only for those persons who apply themselves to good psychic-attention:

III.48. Instruction in vision and knowledge, receiving pupils and rearing of them and instruction in the worship of the best of *Jinas* are the conduct of those who have attachment [i.e. those with good psychic-attention]. (248)

The proceeding of instructing in intuition and knowledge, which proceeding implies a wish to show kindness, the proceeding of receiving pupils and the proceeding of rearing them and the proceeding of instructing them in the worship of the best of *Jinas* are only for those who have good psychic-attention, and not for those who have pure psychic-attention.

Now he determines that all [such] proceedings belong only to those who have good psychic-attention:

III.49. Whoso constantly renders help to the fourfold[150] community (*sangha*) of *shramanas* without doing hurt to (living) bodies is eminent among those who possess affection [of good psychic-attention]. (249)

Any proceeding in assistance of the fourfold community of *shramanas*, with the purpose of conserving their actualization of the pure self, and unaccompanied by doing hurt to the six (kinds of living) bodies,—seeing that there is a pledge of self-restraint (*samyama*),—is merely for those who have good psychic-attention, since it is mainly inspired by attachment, and never for those who have pure psychic-attention.

Now he forbids interference of active-behaviour with self-restraint:

III.50. If in an effort to render service and help with humility and respect (to *sadhus, vaiyavrtya)* he does hurt to [living] bodies, then he is not a *shramana*, but a householder (*agarin*): that should be the duty (*dharma*) of lay-followers (*shravaka).* (250)

Whoso, by his activity in administering with a view to conserving the actualization of the pure self, injures his own self-restraint, falls away from the *shramana*-state, inasmuch as he enters upon the duty of the householder (*grahstha*). Therefore every activity whatever must in any case be performed without detriment to self-restraint, since even in case of active behaviour the object is self-restraint.

Now he exhibits a distinction in active behaviour according to its object (*vishaya*):

III.51. Even though there should result a small stain, yet a layman or an ascetic, who are the followers of *Jina*, should through

compassion render disinterested aid *(nirvekkham* in Pk. or *nirpeksha* in Sk.) [i.e. without any consideration or expectation of any kind) to all. (251)

An activity characterized as rendering aid to others and due to compassion–in the case of the followers of *Jina* whose minds are purified by unalloyed kindness and who, inasmuch as their activity is directed toward pure knowledge and conviction, follow a stricter or freer line of life–is, even if bringing a small stain, unforbidden, inasmuch as it has regard to nothing but the attainment of the pure self. But activity is not forbidden under every circumstance and in every respect, on the ground of bringing [only] a small stain; for then there is nothing to prove that through such activity there is a conserving of another's and one's own actualization of the pure self.

Now he exhibits a distinction in active behaviour according to time:

III.52. Having seen a *shramana* overcome by disease, hunger, thirst or exhaustion, a *sadhu* (noble person) should render service and help with all his power. (252)

When to a *shramana* who has reached the actualization of the pure self there befalls some trouble which might cause the loss thereof, that is the time for the person of good psychic-attention to endeavour (*pravratti*) to counteract with all his power. But any other time is merely one for desisting (*nivratti*) from such activity with a view to his own attainment of the actualization of the pure self.

Now he exhibits a distinction, with its occasion, in the active behaviour of discourse with people of the world (read *pravrtteh sa-nimitta*):

III.53. Neither may one, in the case of (persons who apply themselves to) good psychic-attention, blame discourse with worldly people, if with a view to render service and help *(vaiyavrtya)* to infirm, venerable (*guru*), young or old *shramanas.* (253)

Discourse with people devoid of the actualization of the pure self is approved, if it is exclusively with the purpose of ministering to infirm, venerable, young or old *shramanas* who have reached the actualization of the pure-self; but not with another purpose.

Now he exhibits a distinction in good psychic-attention, as secondary (*gauna*) and primary (*mukhya*):

III.54. This conduct or activity of excellent attachment (*prashasta raga)* is observed by *shramanas,* while it is said to be primary for

lay-followers (*grahstha*); by this highest happiness is *[gradually]* attained [by lay followers]. (254)

Thus has been described good psychic-attention, having the form of excellent conduct on the part of persons possessing inclination (*anuraga*) towards the pure self.

Taking place by reason of the existence of a small amount of passion in those who have chosen complete abstention (*virati*) which reveals the pure self, this on the part of *shramanas* is secondary, because it is accompanied by attachment, which is repugnant to the actualization of the pure self.

But on the part of lay-followers, although it takes place in consequence of the existence of attachment,–inasmuch as, through lack of complete abstinence, they are without revelation of the pure self (read *shuddhatmano'nubhavat*, in agreement with the simile *arkatejasa iva*),–it is primary, since, like fuel experiencing the sun's heat through the intermediacy of the crystal, they experience the pure self in conjunction with attachment; and it gradually (*kramtah*) brings about the highest happiness of *nirvana.*

Now he proves that according to variant occasions (*karanavaiparitya*) good psychic-attention has variant effects (*phalavaiparitya*):

III.55. Excellent attachment brings variant fruits according to the particularity of its objects (*vastu*); as, at the time of harvest, do germs [seeds] fallen in different kinds of soil. (255)

Just as from similar germs [seeds] there is variance of produce due to variance of soil, so from similar psychic-attention, characterized as excellent attachment, there is variance of fruit, due to variance of receptacle (*patra*),[151] since different occasions lead to different effects.

Now he exemplifies the variance (*vaiparitya*) in occasions and variance in results:

III.56. One who finds satisfaction *(rati)* in vows (*vrata*), observances (*niyama*), study (*adhyayana*), contemplation (*dhyana*) and liberality or charity (*dana*) with reference to objects (objective deeds, *vastu)* ordained for those who have not yet reached enlightened wisdom (*chadmastha*) does not obtain liberation from rebirth; he obtains a state characterized by pleasure (*sata*). (256)

The results of good psychic-attention, applied to objects set forth by the Enlightened Lord, is attainment of liberation from rebirth, preceded by accumulation of merit.

There is, however, a difference in the result, due to variance of occasion. Here the variance of occasion is the objects set forth by those who have not yet reached enlightened wisdom. As regards these, the variant result of good psychic-attention applied to satisfaction with vows, observances, study, contemplation and liberality is the attainment of mere "outcast" (*apasada*) merit, without liberation from rebirth; it is the state of a high *Deva* or man.

He explains in full the variance of occasion and the variance of result:

III.57. Service, kindness or charity, bestowed on persons who do not know the transcendental (*paramartha*) nature of reality and in whom indulgence in sense objects and passions predominate, result (in a rebirth) among low levels of gods (*devas*) or men. (257)

The objects set forth by persons who have not yet reached enlightened knowledge being the variance of occasion, and the persons being those who do not know the highest aim and exceed in passion for sense objects,–inasmuch as they are devoid of clear discrimination of the pure self and have not attained actualization of the pure self,– the attainment of mere "outcast" merit by service, help or gift to these, inspired by good psychic-attention, is the variance of fruit; it is rebirth among low *Devas* and men.

Now he enforces the belief that from a variance (*vaiparitya*) of occasion a non-variant fruit does not arise:

III.58. Since indulgence in sense objects and passions are said in the sacred texts to be sin, how should men addicted thereto become saviours [i.e. be able to liberate themselves and help others to liberate themselves from the mundane existence, i.e. *samsara*]? (258)

Now passions for sense objects are sin; the men also who have them are sinful; those also who are fond of such men become sinful, inasmuch as they have affection for sinners.

Therefore, having passions for sense objects and depending upon the merits of those who are attached to them, how can they be fit to save others from *samsara*? Therefore from them a non-variant fruit could not arise.

Now he proves that an occasion which gives rise to a non-variant result is non-variant:

III.59. A man in whom there is cessation from sin, who possesses equanimity towards all righteous *(dharmika)* persons and strives for

the totality of meritorious qualities has entitlement for following the right path (for *guna-samididovasevi* probably one should read *guna-samidadovasevi*). (259)

The *shramana* who, through cessation from sin, neutrality (*madhyastha*) towards all righteous persons, and striving for the totality of meritorious qualities, has for portion the right path, consisting in mental-concentration, which results from evolution through a simultaneity of enlightened view, knowledge and conduct, must, since he is an abode of liberation and merit, be regraded as a non-variant occasion bringing about a non-variant result (read *aviparita-phala-karanam*).

Now he expounds a non-variant occasion which gives rise to a non-variant result:

III.60. Those who are devoid of evil psychic-attention and have pure psychic-attention or good psychic-attention are saviours of men: he who is devoted to them, receives what is excellent (merit). (260)

Shramanas, characterized as above, who through annihilation of infatuation, aversion and disapproved (*aprashasta*) attachment, are free from evil psychic-attention–being sometimes, through stoppage of every arising of passions (*kashaya*), possessed of pure psychic-attention and, sometimes, through ripening of excellent attachment, possessed of good psychic-attention,–are, through being themselves abodes of liberation, saviours of men; and others who manifest excellent feelings of devotion to them become partakers of merits.

Now in a pair of *sutras,* he indicates that the practice of reverence towards the non-variant occasion, which occasions a non-variant fruit, should be carried out in general and particular:

III.61. Having perceived a fit object (*vastu*) as described [say venerable saints], one should proceed with acts such as rising in welcome: then according to qualities distinction should be made–this is the teaching. (261)

With reference to a fit-object (*vastu*), such as we have described as a cause of purification of the self, it is not forbidden to *shramanas* to introduce an intensification of quality into their activity in action agreeable thereto.

III.62. Rising in welcome, hospitable reception, reverence, nourishing, respectful attention, folding of hands and prostration are said to be due in this life to superiors in meritorious qualities. (262)

Such forms of behaviour as rising in welcome, hospitable reception, reverence, nourishing, respectful attention, folding of hands and prostration, when shown to *shramanas* who in meritorious qualities are superior to oneself, are not prohibited.

Now he probihits all forms of (such) behaviour towards pseudo-*shramanas* (*shramanabhasa*):

III.63. (Only) *shramanas* skilled in the interpretation of the sutras and rich in self-control, austerities and knowledge, should be honoured by (other) *shramanas* with rising in welcome, reverence and prostration. (263)

Only in the case of *shramanas* possessing self-control, austerities, and knowledge of their own essence, inspired by familiarity with the *sutras* and their meaning, are proceedings such as rising in welcome unforbidden. In the case of others, pseudo-*shramanas,* they are forbidden.

Now he teaches what sort of person is a pseudo-*shramana*:

II.64. Although endowed with self-control, austerities and knowledge of the sutras, if one is not convinced of the (nine) categories (*arthas*) taught by the *Jina,* primarily the self, he is considered to be no *shramana.* (264)

Though knowing the sacred tradition, self-controlled and persistent in austerities, one who does not believe in the teaching of the *Jina,* which is full of categories not other (than he proclaimed), is entire, and,–inasmuch as by one's own self as knowable (everything) is exhausted–contains the self as its most important constituent, is a pseudo-*shramana.*

Now he shows that want of respect towards an equal (*sama*)[152] in *shramana*-hood leads to utter ruin:

III.65. He who on seeing a *shramana* abiding by the injunctions of the scripture reviles him from hatred and does not show respect to him in actions is a man of ruined conduct. (265)

The conduct of a man who from hatred reviles a *shramana* faithful to the doctrine and in actions does not show respect to him is ruined, in consequence of being infected with the passion of hatred.

Now he shows how utter ruin befalls the man who treats his superior in *shramana*-hood as an inferior:

III.66. If one inferior in merits expects reverence from another who is superior in merits, thinking "I am also a *shramana,*" he

wanders for ever in *samsara.* (266)

If one who himself possesses lower qualities, thinking from pride "I also am a *shramana*," expects reverence from others who are superior in merit, then, may be, owing to pride in his *shramana*-hood he wanders for ever in *samsara.*

Now he shows that utter ruin befalls the man superior in *shramana*-hood who treats his inferior as an equal:

III.67 If the superior in merits as regards *shramana*-hood show in their actions (respect) to those inferior in merits, they are imbued with delusion and debased conduct. (267)

Those who, themselves superior in merits, show in their actions (respect) to others inferior in merits, fall from (right) conduct, are perverted through infatuation.

Now he shows that association with those who are not good (*asat*) is forbidden:

III.68. If a man who possesses sure knowledge of the words and meanings of the *sutras*, whose passions are subsided (read *shamita* in the Sanskrit paraphrase) and who excels in austerities does not give up company with worldly people, then he is not self-controlled (*samyata*). (268/1)

Seeing that even one exceedingly self-controlled through possessing (1) a sure (*nishchita*) knowledge of the words and meanings of the *sutras*–through the method of internal, self-referential point of view [strict-examination, Faddegon] (*nishchaya-naya*) applied to (a) the complete Holy Word, having the existent for characteristic and expounding the world-totality (*vishva*), and (b) its complete import, having the existent for characteristic, and (c) the whole knowing reality, having the existent for characteristic and simultaneously pervading as the basis the knowable forms of both,–and (2) the quelling of his passions through his psychic-attention being free from inclination and (3) superiority in austerities because of motionless psychic-attention repeatedly practised, would through attachment to worldly people lose self-control, like water in contact with the god-of-seven-rays (fire),–some change is unavoidable,–therefore attachment to such people is in any case to be prohibited.

Now he adds a definition of worldly people:

III.69. If one who has left the world for the state-without-bonds *(nirgrantha)* still engages in mundane concerns, he is called a worldly

man, though equipped with self-control and austerities. (269)

Even one who through professed entrance into the sublime state-without-bonds (*nairgranthya*) has borne a great weight of self-control and austerities, if through gross infatuation he becomes slack in the business of pure thought and, tossed to and fro by human affairs, does not abstain from mundane acts, is called a worldly man.

Now he shows that association with good (*sat*) people should be practised:

III.70. Therefore, [in this state-without-bonds[153]] a *shramana* should always dwell with a *shramana* who is either equal in merit or superior in merits, if he wishes liberation from misery. (270)

Since, as it is the nature of the self to evolve, even a self-controlled man does lose his self-control by associating with worldly people,—some changes being unavoidable, as in the case of water in contact with fire,–therefore a *shramana* who seeks liberation from misery should always dwell with another *shramana* equal or superior in merits. Thus by association with one of equal merits he preserves his merit, like cold water placed in the corner of a cold room, and by association with one superior in merits (read *gunadhika-samgat* instead of *guna-samgat*) he increases his merit, like cold water mixed with still colder snow and hail.

"Thus let the monk (*yati*) who first has recourse to an active behaviour (*pravrtti*) based on good psychic-attention, and gradually (*kramatah*) by his facility in proper self-control advances to complete abstinence (*nivrtti*), experience an absolutely everlasting state, consisting in knowledge and bliss and bringing the delight of having easily mastered the (reality of the) whole outspread mass of things." (PS *Kalash* 17)

Here ends the exposition of GOOD PSYCHIC-ATTENTION.

Now (the five *gathas* called) the Five Jewels (*pancharatna*):

"Crest-ornament of this book, illuminating briefly in every part the doctrine of the Holy *Arhat* in its unique way, expounding (read *vyakurvaj*) the states of *samsara* and liberation, with their divergent paths, may the flawless Five Jewels be now triumphant with these [last] five *sutras* (gathas)." (PS *Kalash* 18)

Now he reveals the Reality of Transmigration-Principle (*Samsara-tattva*):

THE FIVE JEWELS (VERSES 271-275)

III.71. Those who in (comprehending) the scripture grasp the reality of things not as they are, being convinced (in their mistaken way) that "so and so are reality," wander through all later time (in the transmigratory existence), which brings them an endless fullness of *karmic* fruit. (271)

Those who, from their own lack of discrimination, conceive objects wrongly and, forming for themselves the conviction "thus is the truth," are for ever ignorant,–inasmuch as their minds are soiled with the continually accumulating dirt of great infatuation–these, although adhering to the doctrine, are only pseudo-*shramana*, because they have not attained to *shramana*-hood in the real sense; and with mental-moods (*vrtti*) unsettled by their gyrations through other births during an infinite time, terrible through its huge mountain of enjoyment of endless *karmic* fruit, they are to be understood as the transmigration-Truth (*tattva*).

Now he reveals the Reality of Liberation-Principle (*Moksha-tattva*):

III.72. He who is free from improper (a-*yatha*) conduct, who has convictions concerning nature of the reality of things (*padartha*) as they are (*yatha*), whose self is in repose (*nishchitah prashantatma*), and whose *shramana*-hood is consummated, does not live long in this unfruitful (a-*phale*) here [in this transmigratory existence]. (272)

He whose self, through habituation to the light of the lamp of spotless discrimination, which is, as it were, the crest jewel of the three worlds, is in constant repose (*upashanta*) and in its own being unmoved by longing,–which is at rest by his ascertained-knowledge of the categories as they are–and who, always acting with reference to his one characteristic-nature, is free from improper conduct and always a knower, is indeed a *shramana* of consummate *shramana*-hood; no more essaying the pitiable condition of an animate creature,–inasmuch as the fruit of all previous *karman* has been easily brushed aside and no fresh fruit of *karman* is brought to development,–and with his mental-mood, through absence of any transition to a second state, established in its pure innate nature, is to be understood as the Liberation-Truth.

Now he reveals the Principle/Reality of the Means of the Liberation [*moksha-tattva-sadhana-tattva*]:

III.73. Those who properly understand the reality of things or

the categories, who have given up external and internal appropriation (*upadhi*), and who are not attached to sense-objects, are designated pure (*suddha*). (273)

Those venerable men who are passionately fond of learning in regard to the true characteristic nature of the complete principles (*tattva*) of knower and knowable, considered according to the many-sided doctrine (*anekanta-kalita*); whose self-principle (*atma-tattva*) possesses a characteristic nature distinguished by a thoughtfulness of unlimited energy welling up within, and purified of adherence to any external or internal attachment;–and who,–inasmuch as the mood of their internal-principle (*antas-tattva*) is safeguarded (*gupta*), as if in deep sleep, by its characteristic nature,–experience no attachment whatever to objects,–these venerable men, possessing all forms of greatness (*anubhava*) and being pure, manifesting heroism by the bold determination wherewith they break open the huge portals of *karman,* closed throughout the [beginningless] *samsara,* should be understood as the reality of the means of the Liberation-Truth.

Now he extols the Principle/Reality of the Means of the Liberation-Truth as the centre of all desires (*sarva-manoratha-sthana*):

III.74. To the pure, it is said, belongs *shramana*-hood; to the pure belong intuition and knowledge; the pure attains liberation (*nirvana*); He alone is a perfect soul (*siddha*). Homage to him! (274)

Shramana-hood, which is the manifest road to liberation and is characterized as mental-concentration occupied with a simultaneity of enlightened view (*samyag-darshan*), knowledge and conduct, belongs to the pure alone.

Conviction and knowledge, which consist in the perceiving and conceiving of all generalities (*samanya*) and particularities (*vishesha*), i.e. the infinite constancies of things commingled with all their past, present and future divergencies, belong to the pure alone.

Nirvana, whose divine innate nature is stamped with inborn knowledge and bliss, revealing themselves without hindrance (read *nihpratigha-vijrmbhita,* with insertion of the syllable *gha*), belongs to the pure alone.

The venerable perfect one, deep through acquisition of the nature of the self, which self abides peacefully as if chiselled in its condition of the highest bliss, is alone pure.

Enough of expatiation! To the pure Truth of the means to the

Liberation-Truth, to that centre of all desires, be paid sincere homage, wherefrom all separation of self and other has disappeared, because the relation between worshipper and worshipped has developed as mutual relation of part and whole.

Now, furnishing the disciple with the fruit of the treatise, he completes the work:

III.75. He who, practising the conduct of a householder or the homeless [properly], understands this scripture acquires in a short time the essence (sara) of the [Divine Discourse(s) or] the Scripture (*Pavayana* in Pk., *Pravachana* in Sk.). (275)

Disciples who–inasmuch as they are intent in a mental-mood settled in its characteristic-form of well purified knowledge and intuition–are equipped with the stricter or freer form of conduct, and who, themselves realizing the true nature of the self by means of a realization preceded by psychic-attention upon Scripture-knowledge–condensing the extensive mass of all topics of the text-books,–understand this doctrine (read *shasanam etad budhyate*), take

hold of the never before realized self, which is the essence of (Divine) discourses or scriptures and which is persisting throughout the endless stream of the three times, and being the best among all the substances, realizes the existent reality (*bhutartha*) (which exists in all living beings in all stages of life's journey), the intuitive divine knowledge and bliss, i.e. the supreme reality of self (*bhagwant atma*).

Here ends in *The Lamp of Truth* (*Tattva-dipika*), a commentary on *The Essence of the Divine Discourse/Scripture,* composed by Amrtachandra Suri, the third scriptural book, entitled *Supplement Expository of the Conduct.*

Gathas given only in *Tatparya-vriti* of Jayasena

19/1. Souls who believe in the best [pure self] among all things and who is respected by the foremost of *Devas* (gods) and *Asuras* (demons), have their miseries brought to nought.

52/2. To him the world, combining (*sambandha*) the kings of *Devas*, *Asuras* and men, pays devoted homage always: and so do I.

68/2. He who has splendour, vision, knowledge, supernatural powers (*riddhi*), bliss, likewise "sovereignty" [affluence] (*aishvarya*), and majesty (*mahatmya*), of the lordship of the three worlds, is *Arhat.*

68/3. To that perfect [liberated] soul (*Siddha*), exceeding in good-qualities, who has transcended the dignity of kings of *Devas* and men and is not tied to rebirth, I again make prostration.

79/2. The purified (self), perfected in austerities and self-restraint, showing the way to heaven and liberation, and extolled by the kings of *Devas* and *Asuras*, stands at the summit of the world.

79/3. Men who adore the *Deva* of *Devas*, the *guru* of the three worlds, the foremost among the best of saints, attain never-waning happiness.

82/2. Men pure in conviction, pre-eminent in knowledge and standing firm in (right) conduct complete, deserve respectful adoration (*puja*), hospitality (*sat-kara*) and offering (*dana*); homage to them!

92/2. Whoso at the sight of such a person is pleased and, having risen in welcome, shows Him honour by praise, homage, etc., derives merit therefrom.

92/3. Men or animals, having thereby obtained the *Deva* or human state (*gati*), have their wishes always fulfilled in respect of powers (*vibhava*)[*Vibhava*= *vibhuti* (superhuman power)] and sovereignty [affluence] (*aishvarya*).

93/1. Therefore, having paid homage to Him (the worthy Lord) and continually fixing my mind on Him, I will concisely state the way to full certitude of the supreme reality.

135/2. Five of these substances–time being excluded–are called existence-aggregates (*asti-kaya*): aggregates, again, are accumulations of infinitesimal particles or space-points (*pradesha*).

146/2. The vitalities (*prana*) are ten: five sense-organs: three vital force (*bala*) of mind, speech and body; further, there is the vitality of inspiration and expiration [i.e. respiration]; together with the vitality of life duration (*ayuh*).

187/2. Through pureness [*Visohi* (instrumental), explained in the *Tatparya-vrtti.* as "a purification consisting in a strong attachment to righteousness"] [good thought-activity] comes a vehement or intense fruition (*anubhaga*) of good kinds of *karman*; in the case of affliction or morbidity (*samklesha*) (*Tatparya-vrtti, samklesha*, here= *tivra-samklesha*), [intense fruition] of evil kinds of *karman*; but in the (contrary or) opposite case fruition of all kinds of *karman* is milder.

200/2. To the liberated soul (*Siddha*) and saintly, purified in conviction, having the psychic-attention of enlightened (*samyag*) knowledge, and enjoying happiness without hindrance or afflictions, my homage and again homage!

217/2. When the foot of (a saint or monk) who observes the *irya-samiti* (the religious observance in walking with the eyes carefully directed $3^1/_2$ yards ahead) has been raised for movement, although, coming in contact therewith, a small living being is hurt or killed,

217/3. Yet not the slightest bondage from this cause is taught in Scripture, just as clinging to objects (*parigraha*) is regarded according (as it is due) to the attachment, etc. mental state of the nature of infatuation (*murchha*), not in physical acquisition of external objects.

220/2. If he accepts a piece of cloth or has a bowl—thus it is said in the *sutra* here—how has he given up dependence (*alamba*) on exterior things? or how is he free from worldly undertakings?

220/3. Indeed, should he take a piece of cloth, or a pot, or alms bowl, or anything else, there is injury (*arambha*) to life (*prana,* i.e. lives of others or his own spiritual life) and a distraction in his mind.

220/4. He takes, shakes, washes and dries his bowl, or piece of cloth, carefully depositing them in the sun, and feels fear or guards them from others [thereby giving up contemplation on his pure self].

224/2. The law preached by the Lord of *shramanas* has no regard to this world or the following. How then could there be in this law a separate *linga* [According to the *Tatparya-vrtti.* this *gatha* contains a *purva-paksha* (opponent's view). *Linga* is explained as *savarana-chihnam*, or concealed token consisting of clothing] for women?

224/3. Decidedly no attainment of [liberation] (*siddhi*) by women in their present existence is agreed. Therefore for women there is a separate *linga* [The second *gatha* contains the *parihara* (refutation). *Linga* is explained as *pravarana-sahitam chihnam*, a token provided with an upper garment.] suitable to their case.

224/4. The mental-mood (*vrtti*) of women consists by nature in heedlessness (*pramaad*); and so they are called "women" (*pramada*): therefore these *pramadis* are described as full of heedlessness.

224/5. Infatuation, aversion, fear, disgust and various kinds of deceit (*maya*) are unavoidable in the minds of women: for them, therefore, there is no *nirvana* [liberation in that very birth].

224/6. In the world of living beings no woman is free from even one of those (faults or shortcomings); nor is their body well covered: therefore they wear a covering.

224/7. There is necessarily found in them melting of [sexual urge in] the mind, unsteadiness, the menstrual loss of blood and sudden origination of tiny men [subtle human organisms]. [These "tiny men," says the *Tatparya-vrtti* are not seen even by subtle perception (*sukshma-labdhi-aparyapta*).]

224/8. In the womb, between the breasts, in the navel and loins or armpit this subtle origination [of human organisims] is said to take place. How could they be fit for self-control?

224/9. Although she is pure in conviction and even occupied with the study of the *sutras* [*Suttajjhayanena*, paraphrased in the *Tatparya-vrtti* by *ekadashanga-sutradhyayanena*, "the reading of the eleven *Angas* and the *Sutras*": *Outline of Jainism* by J.L. Jaini p. 135, etc.] or practises a severe course of conduct, for a woman no falling-away or shedding of (complete) *karmic*-matter (*nirjara*) is preached (prescribed).

224/10. Therefore a corresponding external-token [consisting of clothing] is prescribed for them by the *Jinas*. The nuns (*shramani*), distinguished by family (*kula*), appearance (*rupa*) and time of life, i.e. age (*vayas*), follow such and such a rule of conduct (*samachara*).

224/11. Any one of the three castes (*Brahmana, Kshatriya, Vaishya*) who has a sound body, is of an age capable of austerities, has a good countenance and is free from blame, is fit to receive the token-of-an-ascetic (*linga*) [a capable *shudra*, etc. also].

224/12. The loss of the three *jewels* is what the best of *Jinas* designate a deficiency (*bhanga*): by deficiencies in other respects one is disqualified for [voluntary] fasting unto death (*sallekhana*) [a practise indulged in case of incurable disease and impending unavoidable death].

226/2. Through the four (passions) [anger, pride, deceit and greed], [four kinds of] idle talk [about women, food, thieves and politics], the [five] objects of the senses, and when pre-occupied with affection and sleep [drowsiness], a *shramana* becomes guilty of [the fifteen kinds of] heedlessness (*pramada*).

229/2. In pieces of meat, cooked, raw and being cooked, there takes place a continuous origination of very smallest living beings (*nigoda*) of the same kind.

229/3. He who eats or touches a cooked or raw piece of meat kills a mass of many *kotis* (ten millions) of souls [beings].

229/4. A morsel (of food) which, although not forbidden (*apratikrushta*), has been in one's hand, should not be given to another; if given, it is not fit for eating, or the eater becomes liable to repentance (*pratikrushta*).

239/2. Renunciation, abstinence from worldly undertaking (leading to sin), indifference to sense-objects and annihilation of the passions are called self-restraint; especially in the state of a religious mendicant (*pravrajya*).

268/2. He who, seeing one thirsty, hungry or pained [miserable], is pained in mind and through pity assists him is "compassion."

Appendix
Concerning 47 Points of View regarding the Self

What is this self? and how is it approached? As to this question, what has been stated is here restated.

In the first place, the self is one substance having endless properties, pervaded by the generality of "consciousness"; because it is trustworthy known by self-experience (*svanu-bhava*), preceded by the valid-knowledge characterized as the scripture-knowledge pervaded by the infinitely-many points of view (*naya*), which in their turn pervade the infinitely numerous properties (*dharma*).

1. According to "the method of substance", (*dravya-naya*) it is only consciousness, like a simple piece of cloth.

2. According to "the method of modification" (*paryaya-naya*) it is simply intuition, knowledge, etc., like the threads (constituting the cloth).

3. According to "the method of considering (things) as existent (*astitva-naya*)"[154] it is, as having its own (a) substance, (b) place, (c) time and (d) character, something possessing existence (*astitvavat*): like an arrow (a) consisting of iron, (b) placed in the interspace of string and bow, (c) in the condition of insertion and (d) directed at the mark. [Similarly, the self consists of consciousness-as-such with respect to its own substances; it is placed in the physical universe with respect to its own place; it is having the form or mode existing in the present time with repect to its own time; and it is something of the nature of knowing things with respect to its own character].

4. According to "the method of non-existence" (*nastitva-naya*) it is, with reference to (a) another substance, (b) its place, (c) its time, and (d) its character, something that possesses non-existence; like the

arrow of a previous time, (a) not consisting of iron[155], (b) not placed in the interspace of string and bow, (c) not in the condition of insertion and (d) not directed at the mark.

5. According to "the method of combining existence and non-existence" (*astitva-nastitva-naya*) it is successively, with reference to its own and the other (a) substance, (b) place, (c) time, and (d) character, something that possesses and does not possess existence; like the arrow [and that] of a previous time, which (a) consisted of iron and thereafter no more consists of iron, (b) is placed in the interspace of string and bow and thereafter is not placed in the interspace of string and bow, (c) is in the condition of insertion and then not in the condition of insertion, and (d) is directed at the mark and then is not directed at the mark.

6. According to "the method of inexpressible" (*avaktavya-naya*) it is, with simultaneous reference (a) to its own and other substance, (b) its (own and the strange) place, (c) time, and (d) character, something which cannot be described; like the arrow [and that] of a previous time, which (a) consists and does not consist of iron, (b) is placed and is not placed in the interspace of string and bow, (c) is and is not in the condition of insertion, and (d) is directed and is not directed at the mark.

7. According to *astitva-avaktavya-naya* it is, with reference to (a) its own substance, (b) place, (c) time, and (d) character with simultaneous reference, (a) to its own and the other substance, (b) (its own and the strange) place, (c) time, and (d) character, something which possesses existence, but cannot be expressed; like the arrow [and that] of a previous time, which (a) consists of iron, (b) is placed in the interspace of string and bow, (c) is in the condition of insertion, and (d) is directed at the mark, and which, moreover, (a) consists and does not consist of iron, (b) is placed and is not placed in the interspace of string and bow, (c) is and is not in the condition of insertion, and (d) is directed and is not directed at the mark.

8. According to *nastitva-avaktavya-naya* it is, with reference to (a) another substance, (b) a strange place, (c) time, and (d) character and with simultaneous reference to (a) its own and the other substance, (b) (its own and the strange) place, (c) time, and (d) character, something which does not possess existence and cannot be described; like the arrow [and that] of a previous time, which (a) does not consist

of iron, (b) is not placed in the interspace of string and bow, (c) is not in the condition of insertion, and (d) is not directed at the mark, and which, moreover, (a) consists and does not consist of iron, (b) is placed and is not placed in the interspace of string and bow, (c) is and is not in the condition of insertion, and (d) is directed and is not directed at the mark.

9. According to *astitva-nastitva-avaktavya-naya* it is, with reference to (a) its own substance, (b) place, (c) time, and (d) character with reference to (a) the other substance, (b) strange place, (c) time, and (d) character, and with simultaneous reference to (a) its own and the other substance, (b) (its own and the strange) place, (c) time, and (d) character, something which possesses existence, does not possess existence and cannot be described; like the arrow [and that] of a previous time, which (a) consists of iron, (b) is placed in the interspace of string and bow, (c) is in the condition of insertion, and (d) is directed at the mark, and which, moreover, (a) does not consist of iron, (b) is not placed in the interspace of string and bow, (c) is not in the condition of insertion, and (d) is not directed at the mark, and which, finally, (a) consists and does not consist of iron, (b) is placed and is not placed in the interspace of string and bow, (c) is and is not in the condition of insertion, and (d) is directed and is not directed at the mark.

10. According to "the method of alternation" [or alternate thought constructions] (*vikalpa-naya*) it is something with alternative forms; like the single person who is child, youth and old man.

11. According to "the method of non-alternation" (*a-vikalpa-naya*) it is something without alternative forms; like the single person simply.

12. According to the "method of name"[156] (*nama-naya*) it is something which is connected with the sacred word (*sabda-brahman*); like a thing itself.

13. According to "the method of representation of one thing by another" (*sthapana-naya*) it is something which rests on all its material-substances; like corporeality.

14. According to "the method of substance" (*dravya-naya*) it is something which exhibits itself in past and future modifications; like a *shramana* as a king and a boy as a merchant.

15. According to "the method of present state or condition" (*bhava-naya*) it is something which shows itself in the modification of a certain

moment; like a woman who is acting as a man.

16. According to "the method of generality" (*samanya-naya*) it is something which pervades (*vyapin*); like the string which binds together the necklace.

17. According to "the method of particularisation" (*vishesha-naya*) it is something which does not pervade; like one pearl of that necklace.

18. According to "the method of the permanence" (*nitya-naya*) it is something which persists (in something else); like a [continually] dancing youth (read *natad-yuvavad*).

19. According to "the method of the non-permanence" (*a-nitya-naya*) it is something which does not persist (in something else); like (the two roles) Rama and Ravana.

20. According to "the method of the omnipresence" (*sarvagata-naya*) it is something which is everywhere; like an eye with eyelids open.

21. According to "the method of the non-omnipresence" (*a-sarvagata-naya*) it is something which abides in itself; like an eye with eyelids closed.

22. According to "the method of the vacuous" (*shunya-naya*) it is something which appears as its self alone; like an empty house.

23. According to "the method of the non-vacuous" (*a-shunya-naya*) it is something which appears as non-vacuous (with a content); like a ship loaded with passengers.

24. According to "the method of the unity [or non-duality] of knowledge and knowable" (*jnana-jneya-advaita-naya*) it is one thing; like fire, when evolved through a great mass of fuel.

25. According to "the method of the duality of knowledge and knowable" (*jnana-jneya-dvaita-naya*) it is several things; like a looking glass in combination with the images of other things.

26. According to "the method of the determinism" (or necessary, *niyati-naya*) it is something which appears as having a determined nature; like fire, which possesses heat as a determination.

27. According to "the method of the contingent" (*aniyati-naya*) it is something which appears as having a contingent nature; like water, which possesses heat not determined by necessity.

28. According to "the method of nature" (*svabhava-naya*) it is something for which manipulation is superfluous; like a thorn, which is sharp [by nature] without being sharpened.

29. According to "the method of non-nature" (*a-svabhava-naya*) it is something for which manipulation is necessary; like an arrow, which is sharp after having been whetted by the ironsmith.

30. According to "the method of (proper) time" (*kala-naya*) it has its effectuation dependent on the (proper) moment; like the mango fruit, which ripens in accord with summer days.

31. According to "the method of not (proper) time" (*a-kala-naya*) it has its effectuation not dependent on a (proper) moment; like the mango fruit, brought to ripeness by artificial heat.

32. According to "the method of human effort" (*purushkara-naya*) it has its effectuation brought about by effort; like those who maintain human effort in the case of the *madhu-kukkuti* (fruit of the citron-tree) obtained by human effort.

33. According to "the method of fortuitousness" (*daiva-naya*) it has its effectuation not brought about by effort; like those who maintain the fortuitousness of the ruby found in the citron-tree without "human effort."

34. According to "the method of Providence" (*ishvara-naya*) it is something which enjoys in dependence on something else; like a traveller's child forcibly suckled by a nurse.

35. According to "the method of denying Providence" (*un-ishvara-naya*) it is something which enjoys independently; like a lion tearing antelopes at will.

36. According to "the method of the thing with quality" (*guni-naya*) it is something that receives a quality; like a boy educated by a teacher.

37. According to "the method of the thing without quality" (*a-guni-naya*) it is something that is merely a witness; like the spectator of the boy educated by the teacher.

38. According to "the method of the agent" (*kartr-naya*) it is something which is the agent of such evolutions as dye-stain by the dyer.

39. According to "the method of the non-agent" (*a-kartr-naya*) it is something which is merely a witness; like a spectator of the dyer engaged upon his work.

40. According to "the method of the experiencer" (*bhoktr-naya*) it is something which experiences pleasure, pain, etc.; like a sick person who enjoys agreeable and disagreeable food.

41. According to "the method of the non-experiencer" (*a-bhoktr-*

naya) it is something which is mere witness; like the physician's servant who is a spectator of the illness of the experiencer of agreeable and disagreeable food.

42. According to "the method of action" (*kriya-naya*) it has its effectuation brought about principally by setting to work; like the blind man who obtained a treasure (read *-nidhanandhavad*) by means of an eye which started seeing as a result of getting rid of blood defect in his head when broken against a pillar.

43. According to "the method of knowledge" (*jnana-naya*) it has its effectuation brought about principally by discrimination; like the house-corner merchant who for a handful of peas bought a magic jewel.

44. According to "the external other-referential point of view" [the method of common sense, Faddegon] (*vyavahara-naya*) it is that which undergoes the duality of bondage and liberation; like an atom connected with another ultimate atom, which either binds it or lets it loose [i.e. the self undergoes bondage with the material *karman* and liberates it therefrom].

45. According to "the internal, self-referential point of view" [the method of verification, Faddegon] (*nishchaya-naya*) it is that which does not undergo the duality of bondage and liberation; like an atom which evolves through the qualities of smoothness (or adhesiveness, *snigdhatva*) and roughness (*rukshatva*), qualities which are suitable for bondage or liberation of whatever is simply bound or liberated [i.e. the self itself undergoes bondage and liberates it through its own attachment, etc. psychic dispositions or absence thereof].

46. According to "the method of the impure" (*a-shuddha-naya*) it is something having a nature provided with qualifications (*upadhi*); like earth specialized as pot or dish.

47. According to "the method of the pure" (*shuddha-naya*) it is something having a nature free from *upadhi*; like earth in itself (*kevala*).

With reference to this it has been said:

> "There are as many points of view, standpoints or expositions of methods (*naya*) as there are modes of speech or statements of speakers, and there are as many *para-samayas* (other modes of speech or expositions of methods) as there are standpoins."

These *para-samayas* (other modes of speech, expositions of methods or standpoints) are definitely wrong, incorrect, false and faulty (*michhham* in Prakrit, *mithya* in Sanskrit), when they make absolute assertion that their own particular exposition, or description of a thing, which is partially correct, is in every way, in every respect, entirely, completely (*savvaha* in Prakrit or *sarvatha* in Sanskrit) true or perfect. However, the statements, or expositions of methods that are qualified by the word "from a particular point of view," or "in a certain context" (*kahanchi* in Prakrit or *kathanchit* in Sanskrit) are spoken from a relative point of view [i.e. do not refute the possibility of other alternative aspects or viewpoints being correct from their own particular perspective], as in Jainism [in accordance with the *syadavada* method of conditional predication, which is complementary to *nayavada*, the Doctrine of standpoints], "are faultless or right (*samyak*) in their own respective spheres."[1]

Thus, described by way of innumerable views severally, each embracing innumerable attributes, the self-substance has a single-view essence, as set forth, because, like the ocean, wherein are commingled the white and blue masses of Ganges and Yamuna water, it is a single subject, pervading a single attribute of a non-variegated (*a-mechaka*) nature, since it is impossible in it to discriminate the innumerable attributes, as merely contradicting each other.

But, described by way of final truth [valid knowledge, *praman*], characterized as the single Scripture-knowledge, pervaded simultaneously by innumerable "views," each embracing innumerable attributes, it has a "many-view" essence, as set forth, because, like the single ocean consisting of a gathering of the water-floods of all rivers, it is a single subject, pervaded by innumerable attributes of variegated nature, since it is impossible to discriminate the innumerable attributes as distinct realities.

"If with the multitude of *nayas* dominated by the lotus [lustre] of the word "*quodammodo*" [*syatkara*] men behold, then also with final truth [valid knowledge, *praman*] they behold within them the substance of their own self, with its endless series of properties manifest, as nothing but pure consciousness." (PS *Kalash* 19)

Thus is expounded THE SOUL-SUBSTANCE.

Now the detail of its attainment is expounded:

Now this self, perpetually disturbed in its very self, like the ocean, through the moods of its very self, agitated by experiencing states of infatuation, occasioned by beginningless material *karman*;

revolving through particular cognitions in endless successions;

making friendships with particular external things, made knowable by being occasions of cognitions;

exclusively turned outwards through weakening of the discriminative insight of the self;

and following after the duality of attachment and aversion, leading to further accumulation of material *karman*,

is very far indeed from the attainment of itself.

But when this same, its whole knowledge-side provoked to action by the aggressive *karman*-side, accomplishes in regard to the beginningless material *karman*, first, a knowledge of the distinction of the destroyed and the destroyer, and then a distinction (of itself), and, with its mental-moods calmed in the majesty of its exclusive self-experience, abides absolutely undisturbed, like the ocean, in itself, and, pervading simultaneously all particular cognitions, no more changes, since for that there is no room, then it continues no more its friendship with particular external things, made knowable by being occasions of particular cognitions.

Then, exclusively directed inwards through well-established discriminative insight of the self;

and far from following after the duality of attachment and aversion, leading to accumulation of material matter;

it attains its holy self, never before realized and having for nature unparalleled knowledge and bliss!

May the world too reach the supreme self, having for self knowledge and bliss!

On this subject there is the verse:

"The Truth, deep sunk in the river of the Absolute State [omniscience state] moves along with its great flood of the ambrosia of bliss and having for its glorious face the great consciousness capable of beholding the universe, may the peoples, thanks to the doctrine of the *Jina*, which has for emblem the word '*Quodammodo*' (*syatkara*), attain, brilliant, their own, illuminated by the rays of the choice, genuine Jewels, and that what is worth realizing." (PS *Kalash* 20)

"Let the folk (men) not leap in the delusion that all universe is expoundable, and therewith the self, and that Amrtachandra Suri is the expositor in his garland of flower words to expound them. Let them leap now unperturbed, with a measure of purified enlightenment, having obtained, by the power of knowledge of the '*Quodammodo*' doctrine (*syadvada*), this its own true nature eternal in every Self." (PS *Kalash* 21)

"All that truth, high and low, which has here in no low tones been proclaimed, was once in [has been consummated in] consciousness (*chit*), like the oblation in the [sacrificial] fire (read *bhutkalpam*). May consciousness experience it to the full, since here is only consciousness and nothing else; the one supreme reality is consciousness." (PS *Kalash* 22)

Here ends the commentary, *The Lamp of Truth.*

Note

1. The translation of the two quotations in the Prakrit language, as given by Barend Faddegon (given below) is not at all proper and is, in fact, very damaging to Jainism. It appears to be based on his ignorance of Prakrit and failure on his part to understand the correct meanings of words "*para-samaya*", "*savvaha*" and "*kahanchit*" and their significance in properly understanding the Jaina Doctrines, particularly *Syadvada.* Faddegon's translation of the two quotations (cited from *Gommatsara Karmakanda*, verses 894-895) is given below:

   "So many speakers, so many expositions of methods (*naya*): so many expositions of methods, so many heterodox systems."

   "The word of the heterodox systems is, in whatever way stated, false; but the word of the Jainas is, however stated [from any point of view], perfect (*samyak*)."

Notes

1 The idea of the genitive case is not considered as *karaka.* The second interpretation of *svayambhu* does not seem to refer to grammatical notions.

1a The word *karaka* (relation expressed by a grammatical case; 2.factor) is ambiguous according to the two interpretations given of the word *svayambhu.*

1b Four means and four results are mentioned in this passage. Means: (1) lack of knowledge and vision due to combined supression and annihilation of obscuring *karman,* (2) annihilation of *antaraya karman,* (3) of *avarniya karman,* and (4) of *mohaniya karman.* Results: (1) independence with regard to sense organs, (2) sublime energy, (3) absolute knowledge and intuition, and (4) the distinction between the self and the other; the realization of bliss.

1c If the reading is not corrupt, *anyonya-vrtti* must have two different meanings at the end of the two sentences. Or should we for the second *anyonya-vrtti* read *mitho-vrtti?*

2 The author denies *prapya-karita,* "activity subsequent to approach."

3 In a wider sense of the word "cause" the substance is the cause of its qualities; the object the cause of its appearance. Read in the first occurrence *pratibimbi* in place of *pratibimba.*

4 The sounds consist, according to the Jainas, of a sound-matter.

5 A similar condemnation of too complicated supposition is found in the scholastic writings of Brahmanism.

6 i.e. the immediate impression which makes us believe in a duality of soul and objective world is not merely illusionary, but indeed trustworthy.

7 Sensorial-knowledge is (according to older Jainism) indirect-knowledge *a-pratyaksha.*

8 *Upadesha,* "the pointing out," here= *shabda?* Or should we read *upashlesha,* "contact?

9 Actions of the soul cause the assimilation or "binding" (*bandha*) of fresh *karmic* matter in the *karmic* body which envelops the soul. This *karman,* thus bound, is for a longer or shorter time in a latent condition (*satta*); every moment when the soul is in action some of this collected *karman* is used and is then said to be in a "rising condition" (*udaya*); but simultaneously and in consequence fresh *karman* is bound (H.V. Glasenapp, *Der Jainismus eine indische Erlosungsreligion nach der Quellen dargestellt von Helmuth v. Glasenapp* (Berlin 1925), p. 42), [if the soul evolves into attachment, aversion, etc. psychic states (SS 132-136 JS).]

10 "*Dushta.*"– Infatuation (*moha*), attachment (*raga*), and "shortcoming" (*dosha*), i.e. aversion (*dvesha*), form together *mohaniya-karman.* With this triple division compare the more intricate classification of *mohaniya-karman* in J.L. Jaini, *Outline of Jainism,* Indore: J.L. Jaini Trust, (1979), p. 32.

11 *ajavamjavabhava-svabhavatah.* The expression *ajavamjava* (= that which is quick up to quickness itself = *javaj javatara* = that which is quicker than quick), used as paraphrase for *samsara,* recurs in the commentary on PS 88.

12 *kshayopashamavastha.* The "mechanics" of *karmic* matter is treated in several dogmas of Jainism.

(a) In the theory of the seven *padarthas (Outline of Jainism,* n.10, p. 37) it is taught that the soul by its wrong belief, etc., attracts *karman,* which flows into the soul (*asrava*), and thus *karman* and the soul bind each other (*bandha*). Thus, when the soul acts, fresh *karman* is bound and *karman* previously collected is enjoyed and used (*vipaka-nirjara*). When, however, the soul raises itself and finds the truth preached by the *Jina,* it will succeed in checking (*samvara*) the inflow of fresh *karman,* and even in destroying latent *karman* (*a-vipaka-nirjara*).

In the first case a deed is accompanied by enjoyment and destruction of old *karman,* [or] by the binding of fresh *karman;* in the second case a deed will tend not only to the destruction of the *karman* used at that moment, but also to the annihilation of still resting *karman.*

(b) In the theory of *bandha, udaya* and *satta* (H.V. Glasenapp, n. 9, p. 42) *bandha* denotes the bondage of *karman* which penetrates into the soul in its present (*vartamana*) state in consequence of its passionate actions or even of actions in general. *Satta* means the latent state of previously collected (*samchita*) *karman. Udaya* demotes the "realization" (*prarambha*) of this latent *karman* and the formation, due to this, of external circumstances and internal properties which determine the soul's experience and character during its life; a part of this *karman* which is thus realized wears off naturally (*vipaka-nirjara*).

(c) In the theory of the five *bhavas* (psychical states, H.V. Glasenapp, p. 52; cf. J.L. Jaini, *Outline of Jainism,* n.10, p. 50) we meet with the terms *upashama* (i.e. the subsidence of *karman*), *kshaya* (i.e. the annihilation of *karman*) and *kshayopashamika-bhava* (i.e. the partial annihilation and the partial subsidence of obscuring matter.

13 Cf. *Outline of Jainism,* n.10 p. 113, *paramarthika-pratyaksha.*

14 The immateriality of the soul does not exclude its extension in space; but its infinitesimal particles are exclusively called *pradeshas,* never *anus* (atoms).

15 The three forces (*bala*) or powers (*virya*) are body, mind and speech. Their use is called *yoga. Outline of Jainism,* n. 10, p. 82, no. 4; Glasenapp, n. 9, p. 57.

16 *Kakakshitara,* the crow's eye-pupil, here metaphorically used for the eyeball. Crows are popularly supposed to have only one eye, which, as occasion requires, moves from the cavity on one side into that on the other. Jacobi, *Handful of Popular Maxims,* I, p. 18.

17 *Pravachana-sara: ghadi khayam jada,* i.e. *ghatikarmani kshayam jatani.* The expression, grammatically incorrect and due to contamination, is rightly paraphrased in the *Tatparya-vrtti* as *kshayam gatani.*

18 *Bhavya* and *abhavya,* qualified and not qualified refer to those who have the capacity for liberation from *samsara* and those who do not have that capacity; V. Glasenapp, n. 9, p. 79.

19 "Fire at the end of time," i.e. the fire which consumes the world.

20 The general duties mentioned in this *gatha* are cognate with the voluntary vows of the layman; *Outline of Jainism, n.* 10, p. 69. Compare *puja* (veneration) with *samayika* (first *shiksha-vrata,* or third *pratima*), *dana* (charity) with *atithi-samvibhaga* (third *shiksha-vrata*), *upavasa* (fasting) with *posadha* (second *shiksha-vrata* or fourth *pratima*).

21 The substance–here, the soul–is considered to be the cause of its properties.

22 *Samayika,* referring to the doctrine [equanimous] (*samaya*), devotional; cf. *samayika* (as a noun), worship; *Outline of Jainism,* n.10, p. 69.

23 Cf. the theory of the Vaisheshikas. holding that elementary states of conscience last one moment (*kshana*).

24 *antardhana* and *antarhita,* in the text, do not correspond in meaning.

25 *Vasana*: cf. the meaning of this term in Buddhistic philosophy.

26 According to the Jaina system of ethics, the stages towards perfection are, 1. the absence of wrong belief (*mithyatva*), 2. the absence of incontinence (*avirati*), 3. the absence of heedlessness (*pramada*), 4. the

absence of the passions (*kashayas*), 5. the cessation of all activity (*yoga*) of mind, body and speech. Cf. *Outline of Jainism,* n. 10, p. 94; Glasenapp, n. 9, p. 81.

27 The strange substance, or other substance, is all that which is not the soul; strange qualities are qualities belonging to the strange substances.

28 There is reference to the secondary meaning, "butting," of *parinata.*

29 One interpretation as per Amrtachandra's comments of *karunabhavo* is *karunya bhava*, the feeling of compassion. The *Tatparya-vrtti* adds a second interpretation, according to which *karunabhava* would mean *karunaya abhavah*, i.e. absence of compassion. [For a detailed discussion on this, see my Introduction].

30 The genitive *budhyamanasya* is not to be constructed with *niyamat*, but with *kshiyate* as a dative-like genitive: "the accumulation of infatuation comes to an end for him," etc. Compare the genitives in the commentary, where, however the noun *niyamat* is lacking.

31 There is much ambiguity in regard to the word "*para-samaya*", which is often explained as "*mithyadrashti*", i.e. one having deluded view in regard to the reality of things or as "heretic".

32 The commentary on *gatha* 93/2, offers many difficulties. It consists of two parts. The second of them is supposed to be an explanation of the first, but is really a little altered repetition. As to the subdivisions of the first portion I wish to observe:

Ad 1a. The term *padartha* is identical with *artha*, occurring in PS 87 and there defined as including substances, qualities and modifications. The crosswise-generality (*vistara-samanya*) and lengthwise-generality (*ayata-samanya*) are called in the *Tatparya-vrtti,* respectively transverse-generality (*tiryak-samanya*) and vertical-generality (*urdhvata-samanya*); the last-mentioned term occurs in the *Tattva-dipika* on PS 10. According to the *Tatparya-vrtti* the *urdhvata-samanya* refers to the features remaining the same in a substance during its successive evolutions; thus a man remains in a certain sense the same man during his youth, manhood and old age; the *tiryak-samanya* refers to the features common to the specimens of one genus.

Thus the first sentence of the passage means our "notions of substances, qualities and modifications," or, shortly, the objects (*padarthas*) find their basis in the substance; for the substance is not only identical with itself, but is also "the self" of qualities and modifications, according to *gatha* PS 87. Our notions of substances, again, are due to the fact that there is a similarity in one substance between the successive states, and a similarity between substances mutually.

Ad 1b. Compared with the substances as their abode, the qualities and modifications are particularities. The qualities represent coexistent relations; modifications represent successive relations.

Ad 1c. The *svabhava-guna-paryayas* relate to the density of all substances: thus even of such substances as soul and space. The *vibhava-guna-paryayas* are partly changes of physical or sensorial qualities, such as changes of colour, and partly physical qualities in their successive states, such as cognitions.

33 The six *sthanas* or aggregation-states are enumerated in *Outline of Jainism,* n.10, p. 21, not the two *sthanas* mentioned ibid., p. 33. Or are the six dimensions meant?

34 *Outline of Jainism,* n.10, p. 86, no. 16, "set of central attributes which sustain the others". [*Agurulaghutva* is that quality or property of substances which maintains them as they are and prevents them from being converted into other things].

35 Or should we translate, "of the latter," and "which latter collection bears,"? cf. *Tattva-dipika* on PS 10.

36 For an illustration how the degree of *sthulatva* or *sukshmatva* varies with the number of *pradeshas,* see Glasenapp, n. 9, p. 39.

37 By these particular or typical qualities are defined respectively space, *dharma, adharma,* time, matter, soul. Consciousness is enumerated under the general qualities as well.

38 We may summarize the Jaina doctrine of categories in the following tabular form:

Objects (*padarthas*) contain

1. substances; these are collections of lengthwise and crosswise generalities:

    they possess existence, divided into two kinds;
    they possess qualities and modifications.

2. qualities, divided into–

    a. general qualities : existence, oneness, etc.;
    b. special qualities, characterizing the six *dravyas.*

3. modifications, divided into–

    a. substantial modifications, *a.* homogeneous, *b.* heterogenous; *b.* qualitative modifications, *a.* connected with the fineness and grossness of substances, *b.* the rest

39 Whilst here existence is said to be the innate nature of the substance, it is taught in PS 97 that existence is *sarva-gata,* omnipresent, or belonging to everything [i.e. belongs to all things], and is a *lakshanam vividha-lakshananam,* common characteristic of that which for the rest shows

the greatest variety of characterization.

This variation in expression has led the commentator to think that the author distinguished existence-in-reference-to-the-substance or existence-of-characteristic-nature from existence-in-general. (see the beginning of the comments on PS 95).

In the same way the Vaisheshika system distinguishes existence in the *arthas* (substance, quality and action) from existence as positive being and opposed to negation.

40 In trying to find my way in this syntactical labyrinth I have taken *pitadigunaih kundaladi-paryayais cha* as an instrumentalis causae; and have construed *anupalabhyamanaih* with these nouns, in spite of the strange word-order.

41 The passage is directed against the Vaisheshika system, whose *darshan* is even quoted. Now we find in one of the oldest texts of this philosophy, Prashastapada's *Bhashya*, the notion *yuta-siddhi* or *ayuta-siddhi* mentioned in three passages (Dvivedin's edition, pp. 14, 141 and 152). The theory of this notion given there is not so clear as one would desire, since *samavaya* is defined by the notion *a-yuta-siddhi*, and *yuta-siddhi* with the help of *samavaya. Yuta-siddhi,* namely, is 1. the independent possession of movement of two, or one of two eternal things ; thus a moving atom is *yuta-siddha* in comparision with another atom of physical space; and 2. the relation of *samavaya*, in the case of transient substances; thus a stick and (the body of) the bearer of the stick are *yuta-siddha*, since they are both transient and inhere in separate groups of atoms. On the other hand, *samavaya* exists between objects which are not *yuta-siddha* and one of which is the recipients (*adhara*), whilst the other is the recipiendum (*adheya*:); thus there is *samavaya* between the aggregate and its portions, the quality and the substance, the genus called substance (*dravyatva*) and the particular substance, existence and the thing-existent.

42 The formulation of this alternative reminds us of the Buddhist *kshana-bhanga-vada* in the form in which it was accepted by the *Yogachara.*

43 The reader will be interested and surprised, when comparing the premises and conclusions given here and in the comments on PS 100. But, besides the inconsistency or capriciousness of argumentation, we must notice that the present passage attacks the Madhyamikas, according to which sect *sunyata* ("emptiness," "precipice") means the extreme confusion and logical anarchy to which all phenomena, physical and psychical, are subject ; and *kshanikatva* or *kshana-bhanga* the momentary duration and therefore unsteadiness of everything. Cf. Madhava-Acharya's chapter on Buddhism in his *Sarva-darshan-sangraha.*

44 *Tatparya-vrtti* : the "extension" of the quality "existence" over substance, quality and modification (*satta-gunasya dravya-guna-paryayeshu vistarah).*

45 The reasoning given in the following passage may be described as an *argumentatio ad absurdum,* or rather *ad absurdissimum* ; for the premise is shown to lead to two dogmas upheld by the abhorred Madhyamikas, the *sunyata-vada* and the *apoha-vada.*

The sunyata-vada taught the "nothingness," "absence," shallowness, contradictoriness of everything; the *apoha-vada* upheld the impossibility even of defining. For *genera* do not exist in nature, or even in our mind. If you will define a cow, you may say that it is not a horse, not an elephant, in short not a non-cow; but really you do not get further by that.

Brahmanic philosophers exerted themselves to show the contradictoriness of this theory of "definition by means of negation"; but certainly the Madhyamikas themselves must have been quite conscious of this nature of their *apoha-vada.* They intended to show the impossibility of defining; for their mysticism consisted just in their deep feeling of the helplessness of the human intellect before the enigma of existence.

46 *Svarupa-kartr-karanadhikarana*: cf. *Tattva-dipika*, PS 96, where a *dvanda,* formed of the three last members, occurs.

47 *Bhanga,* in the term *saptabhangi*, does not mean "paralogism," which rendering was given by Cowell, but "turn," or varied form (of idea or expression). The word *syat* [Faddegon's translation "may be" is not correct; *syat* means "in a certain context," in a certain sense, in some respect or from a particular point of view], in each *bhanga*, may be paraphrased "the proposition holds true, provided you take it in the right sense, in the correct proportion, namely, with other notions."

48 According to the context this must mean two of these three possibilities combined, 1 with 2, 1 with 3, 2 with 3.

49 i.e. the three possibilities combined.

50 *Parama-dravya=paramatman=* its quality, namely *–parama-dharma.*

51 *Outline of Jainism,* n. 10, p. 32. In the significance of *nama-karman* in early Indian philosophy we have to recognize a remote influence of "primitive thought," according to which the name is a quality of the thing. So in Jainism the *nama-karman* of a thing has become its central quality, around which the other qualities are grouped as specifications or effects.

52 The explanation of the first and second meaning of *karman* "responsible deed," and "*karmic* matter" bases itself on the use of the word *karman* for "direct grammatical object", cf. *Tattva-dipika,* on PS 16.

53 In Brahmanic philosophy *purva-paksha* = the view of the opponent; and *uttara* = the orthodox view.

54 In the compound *dravya-karman, dravya* means "material substance." Cf. the three meanings of *karman,* distinguished by the *Tattva-dipika,* on PS 117.

55 *Kartr,* agent, is the grammatical subject of a verb; *karman,* matter, or deed, the grammatical object; cf. *Tattva-dipika,* on PS 16.

56 With reference to these three sides of psychical life, intellect, will and emotion, pleasure and pain, we may notice (cf. here note 10) that *avarana-* and *darshan-mohaniya-karman* belong to the province of intellect, *antaraya-* and *charitra-mohaniya-karman* to the sphere of will and emotion, whilst *vedaniya-karman* represents the feelings of pleasure (*sata*) and pain (*asata*), and the rest of *aghatiya-karman* the objective conditions of these. *Hasya* (frivolity), *shoka* (sorrow) and the other *akashaya-[no-kashaya] karmans* presuppose a voluntary indulgence in the sentiments and are in this respect distinguished from *sata-* and *asata-karman.*

57 *Kriya,* in *kriya-bhava,* means "movement"; cf. the term *karman* in the Vaisheshika system.

58 *Parinama* in the Prakrit text seems to be an ablative and is explained as such in the commentary. Thus the Sanskritization of the *gathas* should run, *parinamaj jayante.* The *Tatparya-vrtti* reads the text as *uppada-tthidi-bhanga...parinamado jayadi,* which gives a correct meter, but offends against grammar.

Parinama, in general = "evolution," "evolution-stage," "change," i.e. "existence with its threefold aspect during a moment's duration (*Pravachana-sara,* 99), is used here in the specialized signification of "qualitative change."

59 The term *tad-bhava* has two significations in our text, (1) the "being-that" = "identity" (*Pravachana-sara,* 106-108*),* opposite to a-*tad-bhava* = *anyatva;* (2) "qualitative" or "distinctive being" (*Tattva-dipika,* on 149), opposite to *kriya-bhava.* The second line of the *gatha* begins thus, *te tad-bhava, visittha;* this is interpreted in the commentary first as *te 'tad-bhava-vishishtah* (cf. R. Pischel, *Grammatik der Prakrit-Sprachen,* 1900, p.175) and then as *te tad-bhava,* whilst *a-tad-bhava* is taken as *anyatva* and *tad-bhava* as "distinctive being"!

60 *Puggalassa suhumado* (i.e. *sukshmat; Tattva-dipika,* less correctly, *sukshmatvat; Tatparya-vrtti, paramanu-lakshana-sukshma-svarupadeh.* While the Jainas thus hold that sound is a substance and that matter in general possesses in its fine form the four qualities, colour, taste, smell,

and touch, all Brahmanic systems agree in taking sound for a quality; further the Vaisheshika-system teaches the accumulation-theory: the elements possess successively one quality more than the precedent one; and the Samkhya-*darshan* accepts the *tan-matra*-theory, holding that every element in its fine form only possesses one quality.

61 Jaini, *Outline of Jainism*, n. 10, p. 90, no. 30, "the conditions when some particles (*pradeshas*) of the soul expand and go out of the body and then come back to it, as in the case of the *aharaka*-body."

62 This seems to be in conflict with the fact that the material-atoms can be not only *asamkhyeya*, but also *ananta*. But we must remember that the Jaina system does not teach the impenetrability of matter; thus one infinitesimal-particle of space (*akasha-pradesha*) can hold an innumerable (*asamkhyeya*) or even endless (*ananta*) number of material-atoms (*pudgala-paramanus*). Cf. *Tattva-dipika* on PS 139, second paragraph.

63 The Sanskrit text of the *gatha* offers here a very strange anacolouthon, *dharma-dharmabhyam atato lokah sheshau pratitya kalo*; it is explained in the commentary, as if there *kalena cha* were read. By a simple emendation we can avoid this irregularity in the Prakrit text, namely by changing *dhammadhammehi adado logo...kalo* into *dhammadhamme hi adade* (nom. pl.) *loge* (locat, sing.)...*kalo*. The asyndeton here is hard, but not inconsistent with the style of the *gathas*.

64 One would have expected "the remaining five substances".

65 In other words, there are innumerable time-streams in the world, which are situated in the infinitesimal-spacial-units of the souls and the material atoms. These time-streams exist without any adhesion (*bandha*) or commingling (*samparka*) with one another. They all have the same properties: their modifications are *samayas* (moments), *nimishas* (time required for raising the eyelids), etc. One such time-stream covers one *pradesha* and is therefore called a time-atom (*kalanu*). Thus a *samaya* is the shortest time-duration; a *kalanu* is one time-stream, considered in its spacial extension.

66 For the theory of cohesion cf. *Tattvarthadhigama Sutra*, V. 32-36.

67 Since there is no cohesion between the *kalanus*, it is rather surprising to find time mentioned in this context.

68 Substance, i.e. one soul-particle or one material-atom. Cf above, note 4.

69 Which powder, that is on the box being opened, perfumes the whole room.

70 *Pradeshodbhava* is an inadequate expression of the author's intended thought, viz. *pradeshatvodbhava*. Cf. the last sentence of the commentary on the *gatha*.

71 In the text *tasthushah pradeshamatrasya* must not be constructed with the immediately following genitive *paramanos*, but with *tasya* (= *samayasya*) at the beginning of the clause (after *yatas*).

72 Here *samaya* means time; *dravya-samaya* thus = beginningless and endless time. In the immediately following sentence, however, *samaya* again means "moment."

73 Perhaps the drift of the argumentation comes to this: a moment is the duration in which an ultimate atom penetrates a space-particle, but the atom does not reach first one and then another portion of the space-particle, from which a division of the time-moment would ensue; but the space-particle is indivisible.

74 These time-atoms exist locally next to one another, and consequently with every such atom lying in its line of movement the atom would come in contact.

75 Thus one infinitesimal-particle of space can hold an endless number of material-atoms.

76 In other words, the *syad-vada* or *anekanta-vada* holds true in the case of space too; it is one and many according to our point of view. In the following the commentator attacks a one-sided view.

77 In the following argumentation we must take notice that the word "spot" (*kshetra*) has a vague meaning ; it depends on us what extent and limits we shall give to such a *kshetra*. "The two fingers are in one spot," "they are in two spots," both answers are possible. For the rest the author thinks that the problem gives rise to the following division:

I. The fingers are in one spot.
   A. This spot is one continuous substance with identical parts.
   B. It is one continuous substance with distinguishable parts.

II. The fingers are in more than one spot.
   A. These spots form several not-continuous substances.
   B. These spots form one continuous substance.

The alternatives I B and II B are accepted, as being the same as the Jaina doctrine on this point.

78 Cf. the similar expressions *urdhvata-samanya*, and *ayata-samanya*, *Tattva-dipika*, PS 10, 93/2 (see also note 32).

79 Cf. *Tattva-dipika* on PS 80, where the substance is called the identity; and the modifications the divergences (*vyatireka*) in the identity.

80 According to the commentaries on PS 142 and 143, time (*kala* or *samaya*) is a substance (*dravya*), because the moment (*samaya*) as its modification possesses existence, or occurrence (*vrtti*), i.e. the three aspects (*kotis*), origination, annihilation, and permanence, or the synthesis of

origination and annihilation.

Time is a substance, but not an *asti-kaya,* i.e. "something extensively-existent," or "something that, itself permanent like the atom, builds up by aggregation the transitory objects." Time is a substance, because it is that which is common to the successive moments, which is their identity (*anvaya*); and since in the moments changing substances possess origination, annihilation and permanence, the moments themselves, and indirectly time, may be said to possess existence and its three aspects.

81 In the commentary the singular *pradesha* is often given in the meaning of *pradeshatva,* i.e. "possession of one or more *pradeshas*".

82 In the *Tatparya-vrtti nadum* is explained as *jnatum sakyate,* and *padesha-mettam* is taken as beginning the main clause.

83 *tattvatah, Tatparya-vrtti: padarthatah,* considered as an object.

84 We can distinguish in the commentary the following parts:

A. Thesis. Existence or occurrence without *pradesha* cannot belong to time, and still less can time be occurrence itself.

[Note: in Jainism a substance is in a certain sense identical with its qualities; existence is considered as a quality of things; thus in general a substance is identical with (its) existence.]

B. First part of the argumentation. Time cannot be the occurrence itself, for the occurrence must rest on something which possesses the occurrence. And if we suppose that time were identical with the occurrence, then oneness of origination, annihilation, and permanence would be impossible.

C. Argument for the conclusion, drawn at the end of B. If the unity of originations and annihilation, with reference to a substance, were to consist in an uninterrupted series of origination and annihilation, without something in its modifications subject to these aspects, then the Buddhistic theory of momentariness, *kshana-bhanga*–horrible dictu!–would hold true. Time, therefore, consists of (one or more) *pradeshas.*

D. Second part of the argumentation. Should time consist of many *pradeshas,* then (as we must read between the lines) the only supposition, allowed, would be that it consists of an innumerable number of *pradeshas,* equal to the space of the universe. But this is excluded, because the moment could not come into existence.

E. Final conclusion (or the return to thesis). Time consists of one *pradesha* and, as such, according to the *gatha* it possesses existence. Had it not possessed even one *pradesha,* it would not have existed.

85 Read *ana-prana-prano* in agreement with the Prakrit text. The *pranas* are given in the *karman*-classification of Jainism as *bala* or *virya* (the fifth

antaraya-karman), *indriyani* (belonging to the group of *nama-karman*, sub-division *pinda-prakrtis*), *ayuh-karman*, and *ucchvasa-karman* (one of the *apinda-prakrtis* of *nama-karman*). Cf. the table of *karmans* in *Outline of Jainism* n.10, after p. 36.

86 In general Indian philosophy (cf. note 10) ignorance, attachment and aversion are the roots of the misery of existence. Ignorance forms the intellectual, attachment and aversion the emotional, side of this evil.

87 *Dravya-prana* may be compared with "*dravya-karman*". For *bhava-karman*, see *Tattva-dipika* on PS 122. *Para* = the other = all that is not oneself; thus all corporeal substances, but also other souls. However, as we may interpret our author, by our hatred we may, or may not, cause injury to the other souls, in any case we injure ourselves.

88 *Pudgala*-or *paudgalika-karman* is synonymous with *dravya-karman*.

89 The *Tatparya-vrtti* understands *acharyas, upadhyayas,* and *sadhus*.

90 On *darshan-mohaniya* and *charitra-mohaniya*, see *Outline of Jainism*, n.10, p. 32; on *kshayopashama* state and *udaya* state, see supra note 12 "the mechanics of *karman*."

91 As a rule we find in Jain works *eight* kinds of touch, viz. (1) light (*laghu*), (2) heavy (*guru*), (3) soft (*mrdu*), (4) hard (*khara*), (5) smooth, or sticky like oil (*snigdha*), (6) rough, or dry like ashes (*ruksha*), (7) cold (*shita*), (8) hot (*ushna*). Perhaps the four kinds mentioned in the text are the four pairs of opposites *laghu-guru, mrdu-khara,* etc. Or perhaps we may suppose an older doctrine; cf. the Vaisheshika system, which maintains three kinds of touch.

92 According to the text the ultimate atoms can evolve (*parinato-bhavati*—*Tatparya-vrtti*) through different qualities, losing some and gaining others. Thus, acquiring either *sneha* or *rukshatva,* they are capable of forming aggregates. In the Vaisheshika system, as expounded by Prashastapada, the ultimate atoms may likewise change in quality; but their aggregation as double, triple, etc. atoms is due either to the *apeksha-buddhi* of God or to the *adrshta* of souls: cf. the translator's work. *The Vaisheshika System,* p. 147 and pp. 165-8.

93 Thus according to the number of atoms in the aggregate the degree of smoothness or roughness in each atom seems to change.

94 This theory of the cohesion and adhesion of material substances is not very clear. We may make the following observations: The word *sama* has in the two lines of the *gatha* different meanings. In the first line it means "even." This interpretation is supported by the *Tatparya-vrtti*, "even" is the term for [atom] evolved into the second degree (*dvi-shakti*), fourth degree, sixth degree, etc.; 'odd' is the term for [atom] evolved into the

third degree, fifth degree, seventh degree, etc." This explanation is in accordance with the Prakrit *trishtubh* quoted in the *Tattva-dipika* on PS 166.

Further, we must observe that the Prakrit lacks a Dual; according to the sense the clause *samado duradhiga jadi bajjhante* should have been Sanskritized as *samato dvyadhikau yadi badhyete*, "when two [atoms] differ [in degree] by two from equal[ity], then they are bound." A more logical expression would have been "when of two atoms one is two degrees higher than the other, etc." The two atoms, differing by two in degree are called "the level" (*sama*) and "the higher" (*adhika*). Cf. *Tattvarthadhigama-sutra*, v. 36.

The expression *adi-parihina* is satisfactorily explained by the *Tattva-dipika* in the following *gatha*.

In general it is clear that the *pudgala-bandha* theory of the Jainas is only partly based on observation, and more on fancy. A similar remark holds good of the *try-anuka* theory of the Vaisheshikas; see the translator's work, *The Vaisheshikas System*, p. 368.

Comparing with European notions, we may say that the *bandha* between *ruksha* and *ruksha* is the cohesion and adhesion between solid substances (e.g. between the particles of a stone, between chalk and blackboard); the *bandha* between *snigdha* and *snigdha* the cohesion in a fluid; the *bandha* between *snigdha* and *ruksha* the adhesion between a solid and a fluid substance, e.g. the cohesion in a solution.

The theory of the degrees seems to have originated in speculation: its main thesis is that only when the exponents of the degrees of roughness or smoothness differ by two can two atoms "attract" each other and thus cause evolution (*parinamika*, *Tattvarthadhigama-sutra*, v. 36) in one another.

Finally, it deserves to be noticed that this theory of material cohesion or adhesion is given principally as an introduction to the exposition of "bondage" between soul and matter (*gathas*, 172-189).

95 i.e. the rough of the fourth degree. Similarly, the rough of the second degree combines with the fourth degree of either kind.

96 As a technical term, *rupin* is explained in the *Gommata-sara Jiva-kanda*, v. 614:"From the point of view of an atom with two degrees of smoothness an atom with two degrees of roughness is similar (*rupi*); and an atom with one, three and other degrees is dissimilar (*a-rupi*). The same applies to rough also."

97 The Prakrit of this *tristubh* verse differs from that of the *gathas*, e.g. it has the form *durahia* in place of the *duradhiga* of the *Pravachana-sara*.

98 *Jahanna-vajje. Vajje* developed out of Sanskrit *varjam* ("with exception of"), perhaps under influence of *krte* ("for the sake of").

99 Glasenapp, n.9, p. 39, "die Menge der *pradeshas* des *karman.*" *Shakti-yogin* corresponds to *yogya* in the *gatha.*

100 *Aharati* has here the same meaning as in *aharaka-jnana (Outline of Jainism,* n. 10, p. 44); the idea is that the self always possesses potentially pure psychic-attention.

101 Para. 13-15 are far from clear and seem to have suffered several corruptions. So I have been reduced to making a series of conjectures.

102 According to (PS 110) and (PS 111) the soul is a substance untouched by qualities and modifications; according to (PS 112) a modification untouched by substance. Here again we have an example of the Jaina *syadvada, anekanta-vada.* [In these paras, the "pure" substance is to be understood in the sense of *karma-nirpeksha parinamika bhava,* see J.P. Jain, "Introduction" on the nature of the self ir this volume.]

103 Cf. the terms *bhava-karman* and *dravya-karman,* n. 87.

104 *Tatparya-vrtti, taih sambaddho bhavati,* "is combined with them."

105 These two terms are equivalent to *sa-vikalpaka* and *nir-vikalpaka* [or the scripture].

106 *Samaye* is alternately rendered "in the doctrine or in the scripture".

107 Ambiguous: *karmic* matter belonging to the soul, or deed done by the soul. In the opinion of Barend Faddegon, to say "the evolution of matter is the self's *karman*" (PS 189 AC) is "ambiguous" because he thinks that how can "karmic matter be said to belong to the soul or deed done by the soul". This frank expression of doubt on his part is due to the fact that he does not seem to understand the Jaina concept of the *nimitta karana* and the role played by it in the doctrine of *karma* and mind-body interaction as also the intracacies of external, other-referential *vyavayara naya* and internal, self-referential standpoint (*nishchaya-naya*). In Jainism, the self's psychic states of attachment, etc. act as the supportive factor or auxiliary cause (*nimitta karana*) in the evolution of matter into material *karman*; that there is a difference between matter and material *karman. Karmic* matter is matter that has the capacity to evolve into material *karman,* but it cannot evolve into material *karman* unless psychic states act as *nimitta karana* thereof. It is for this reason that the evolution of matter is said to be the "self's *karman*" from external, other-referential *vyavahara* point of view (*naya*). For a detailed discussion in this regard, see Jagdish Prasad Jain, *Samaysara of Kundakunda* (New Delhi, forthcoming), chapter on *Karta-Karma.*

108 According to the Prakrit text *appanam havadi jhada,* a reading warranted

by the metre. But the *Tattva-dipika* translates *atma bhavati dhyata,* "he becomes the self, a contemplator.

109 Cf. the introduction to PS 189, *nishchaya-vyavaharavirodham darshayati.*

110 *ekam.* The *gatha* has *jnanam aham ekko.*

111 The Sanskrit paraphrase of the *gatha* in some books gives *sakaranakarah* (with form or formless); the original Prakrit *gatha* of Kundakunda, as also *Tatparya-vrtti* of Javasena mentions a second interpretation, namely as *sagaranagarah* ("while having home-life, or has given this up").

112 *Tatparya-vrtti: anagara-kevalinah,* the homeless possessors of perfect knowledge.

113 *Tatparya-vrtti: na kevalam jina jinendras cha tirthakara-parama-devah,* "not merely *Jinas,* but Kings of *Jinas,* highest Gods who are Spiritual Guides."

114 Read *parayanatva* in place of *parayanatattva.*

115 This and the following paragraph have in the original the form of *Shalini* verses ; the third verse is a *Vasanta-tilaka.*

116 Cf. *Outline of Jainism,* n. 10, p. 133, where the five *acharas* are called, "qualities of the *acharyas.*"

117 It–the purified soul just mentioned=the speaker himself.

118 *Krorya,* 'cruelty'?

119 In the original of the *gathas* neuter adjectives are used for abstract nouns. As concerns the interpretation, I have followed the *Tattva-dipika*; in the *Tatparya-vrtti* the second characteristic is divided into five kinds, (1-3), as in the *Tattva Dipika,* (4) the cause of liberation, (5) the obedience to the Jaina doctrine.

120 i.e. deeds prohibited by the *maha-vratas.*

121 Read *kriyayah* in agreement with *kriyanam,* which follows.

122 Cf. *Outline of Jainism n.*10, p. 133, subheading. V, the moral qualities of the *sadhu* (saints): the two lists coincide completely.

123 *Tattvarthadhigama Sutra,* III. 18, *chedopasthapya,* as the second kind of self-restraint.

124 Read *shramanashrayalochana.*

125 In the *Tarparya-vrtti* we meet with two interpretations of *adhivasa,* "living in the house of the teacher who is placed over (*adhi-krta*) one" and "staying in the pure self." *Vivasa* is explained there as "a dwelling left (*vi-rahita*) by one's *gurus.*" According to the *Tattva-dipika* one should render *adhivasa* by "abiding in the self," and *vivasa* by "a dwelling characterized (*vishishta*) by the presence of *gurus.*"

126 *Tattvarthadhigama Sutra,* IX. 18, *parihara-vishuddhi,* as the third kind of self-restraint.

127 Enumerated in PS 208.

128 *Tattvarthadhigama Sutra,* IX. 18, *sukshma-samparaya* as the fourth kind of *samyama.*

129 *Tyaga* is renunciation of all worldly concerns (*parigraha*), i.e. of possessions; *vyutsarga* is abandonment of all that may become seductive (*upadhi*), specially that which is required for the welfare of the body. Thus, *tyaga* and *vyutsarga, parigraha* and *upadhi* are nearly identical. On *parigraha-tyaga,* cf. *Outline of Jainism,* n.10, p. 133, 5th *mahavrata; Outline of Jainism,* n.10, p. 132, the 8th of the ten *dharmas; Outline of Jainism* n.10, pp. 69-70, the 5th, 6th, 8th-11th of the *pratimas.* On *vyutsarga, utsarga* or *kayotsarga* cf. *Outline of Jainism,* n.10, p. 97, the 5th of the *samitis; Outline of Jainism,* n. 10,p. 132, the 11th of *tapamsi; Outline of Jainism,* n.10, p. 133, the 6th of the *avashyakas.*

130 Cf. *Outline of Jainism,* n.10, p. 94, the four first forms of *pramada.*

131 Prakrit text, *apayatta; Tattva-dipika, aprayata; Tatparya-vrtti. aprayatna* (correct).

132 The usual and primary meaning of *himsa* is the destroying of any kind of life. Here the word receives a wider signification: and thus the *ahimsa-vrata* refers more to the intention (*bhava-himsa*) and obtains at the same time a formal strictness.

133 i.e. the bodies of the six kinds of souls; the five *sthavaras* and the *trasa* kind, *Outline of Jainism,* n.10, p. 8.

134 On *tyaga* and *upadhi* cf. note 129, and on the "mechanics" of *karman-*matter, note 12.

135 *Outline of Jainism,* n.10, p. 70 the 8th of *pratimas.*

136 Both commentaries, with the same mistake, read *kim kimchanam iti.*

137 *Dehe vi samgatti, Tattva-dipika, atha dehepi samga iti; Tatparya-vrtti, aho dehopi samga iti* ("Ah ! the body too is an attachment").

138 Cf. above, note 129.

139 *Vihara,* "wandering undertaken in order to find the means for sustaining the body," *Tattva-dipika,* on PS 215. The ascetic ethics of the *Jinas* attaches importance to the limitation of our bodily movements; cf. the *dig-virati-guna-vrata* and the *deshavakashika-sikshavrata,* both optional duties of the lay-follower (Bhandarkar, 2nd Report, pp. 114 and 115).

140 Prakrit, *jassa anesanam appa,* "whose self is non-desire." *Tattva-dipika, yasyaneshana atma,* "whose self is without desire."

141 Or "fault against the *eshana-samiti,*" *Outline of Jainism,* n.10, p. 134.

142 *Deha rahita-parikarma,* e.g. he does not bathe, or brush his teeth, *Pravachanasara,* 208.

143 *Ekabhakta*: see list of *mula-gunas, Pravachanasara,* 208; *aprati-*

purnodara=anavapta, 2nd *tapas, Outline of Jainism n.* 10, p. 131 ; *diva, na madhumansah, Outline of Jainism,* n.10, , p. 68, *dharmas* of the *pakshika-shravaka; rasa-parityaga*, 4th *tapas, Outline of Jainism*, n.10, p. 131, etc. The noun *bhakta* is made masculine in the Sanskrit paraphrase and commentary.

144 *Yoga* has a meaning cognate with that of the participle *yukta*, and cannot be translated in this passage by "activity of mind, body, or speech."

145 The *gatha* is a conclusion to the passage beginning with PS 222. For time and place, cf. PS 222; for *upadhi*, PS 223 etc., for *shrama* and *kshama*, PS 230.

146 The theory of holding that a statement is possibly, i.e. under restrictions, true; cf. above, note 47.

147 *Outline of Jainism*, n.10, p. 111.

148 The text of the *gatha, appanam param*, is explained in the *Tatparya-vrtti* as an asyndeton: the *Tattva-dipika* accepts two interpretations.

149 The Prakrit form *samana* presents a favourite similarity in sound to *sama*.

150 I am inclined to interpret "the fourfold multitude of *shramans*" as referring to the *Arhats, Siddhas, Ganadharas* and *Sadhus* mentioned in *Pravachana-sara*, 4. The benefiting, then, must be understood as practical assistance, partly as adoration. The *Tarparya-vrtti*, however, cites the four following classes: (1) *Rshis*, who possess miraculous power (*rddhi*) or absolute knowledge; (2) *munis*, who possess *avadhi, manah-paryaya-* or *kevala-* knowledge (*Outline of Jainism*, n.10, p. 59); (3) *yatis*, who mount the ascending stages (*shreni*) of the *upashamaka* and *kshapaka* state (Glasenapp), n.9, p. 85); (4) *sadhus* in general. Bhandarkar, second report, p. 100, takes *chaturvarnasya shramana-samghasya* as asyndeton of two nouns, the first of which he explains by the four classes of *shravakas, shravikas, yatis* ("ascetics") and *aryas [aryikas]*.

151 The value of deeds depends on the choice of "authority," i.e. adviser, and on the choice of the "person to be benefited" by the deed. *Patra* seems to be ambiguous. [*Patra* is one who receives benefit.]

152 The word "*sama*" is the antithesis to *adhika* and *adhara* in the following *gatha* (PS 266).

153 *Tanhi* refers to the noun *niggantham=nirgrantha=nairgranthya* in the preceding *gatha*. Jayasena explains *tanhi* as locative (*adhikarana*), governed by *adhivasadu*, and the accusative (*karma*) *samanam* as a grammatical attribute (*lakshana*) to this *tanhi*. In other words, the verb allows two constructions, which are here contaminated.

154 The sections 3-9 give an exposition of the *sapta-bhangi-naya*.

155 The example is not quite clear. Must we think of an arrow in general, or

of two arrows, one of iron and the other of another material, whilst the second replaces the first? Or of one arrow made from two materials?

156 For the sections 12-15, see *Outline of Jainism,* n.10, p. 47.

श्री कुन्दकुन्दाइरियकदो

पवयणसारो

ज्ञानतत्त्व--प्रज्ञापन

एस सुरासुरमणुसिदवंहिदं धोदघाइकम्ममलं ।
पणमामि वड्ढमाणं तित्थं धम्मस्स कत्तारं ।।१।।

सेसे पुण तित्थयरे ससव्वसिद्धे विसुद्धसब्भावे ।
समणे य णाणदंसणचरित्ततववीरियायारे ।।२।।

ते ते सव्वे समगं समगं पत्तेगमेव पत्तेगं ।
वंदामि य वट्टंते अरहंते माणुसे खेत्ते ।।३।।

किच्चा अरहंताणं सिद्धाणं तह णमो गणहराणं ।
अज्झावयवग्गाणं साहूणं चेव सव्वेसिं ।।४।।

तेसिं विसुद्धदंसणणाणपहाणासमं समासेज्ज ।
उपसंपयामि सम्मं जत्तो णिव्वाणसंपत्ती ।।५।।

संपज्जादि णिव्वाणं देवासुरमणुयरायविहवेहिं ।
जीवस्स चरित्तादो दंसणणाणप्पहाणादो ।।६।।

चारित्तं खलु धम्मो धम्मो जो सो समो त्ति णिद्दिट्ठो ।
मोहक्खोहविहीणो परिणामो अप्पणो हु समो ।।७।।

परिमदि जेण दव्वं तक्कालं तम्मयं त्ति पण्णत्तं ।
तम्हा धम्मपरिणदो आदा धम्मो मुणेयव्वो ।।८।।

जीवो परिणमदि जदा सुहेण असुहेण वा सुहो असुहो ।
सुद्धेण तदा सुद्धो हवदि हि परिणामसब्भावो ।।९।।

णत्थि विणा परिणामं अत्थो अत्थं विणेह परिणामो ।
दव्वगुणपज्जयत्थो अत्थो अत्थित्तणिव्वत्तो ।।१०।।

धम्मेण परिणदप्पा अप्पा जदि सुद्धसंपयोगजुदो ।
पावदि णिव्वाणसुहं सुहोवजुत्तो व सग्गसुहं ॥११॥

असुहोदयेण आदा कुणरो तिरियो भवीय णेरइयो ।
दुक्खसहस्सेहिं सदा अभिद्दुदो भमदि अच्चंतं ॥१२॥

अइसयमादसमुत्थं विसयातीदं अणोवममणंतं ।
अव्वुच्छिण्णं च सुहं सुद्धुवओगप्पसिद्धाणं ॥१३॥

सुविदिदपयत्थसुत्तो संजमतवसंजुदो विगदरागो ।
समणो समसुहदुक्खो भणिदो सुद्धोवओगो त्ति ॥१४॥

उवओगविसुद्धो जो विगदावरणंतरायमोहरओ ।
भूदो सयमेवादा जादि परं णेयभूदाणं ॥१५॥

तह सो लद्धसहावो सव्वण्हू सव्वलोगपदिमहिदो ।
भूदो सयमेवादा हवदि सयंभु त्ति णिद्दिट्ठो ॥१६॥

भंगविहूणो य भवो संभवपरिवज्जिदो विणासो हि ।
विज्जदि तस्सेव पुणो ठिदिसंभवणाससमवायो ॥१७॥

उप्पादो य विणासो विज्जदि सव्वस्स अट्ठजादस्स ।
पज्जाएण दु केणवि अट्ठो खलु होदि सब्भूदो ॥१८॥

तं सव्वट्ठवरिट्ठं इट्ठं अमरासुरप्पहाणेहिं ।
जे सद्दहंति जीवा तेसिं दुक्खाणि खीयंति ॥१९-१॥

पक्खीणघादिकम्मो अणंतवरवीरिओ अहियतेजो ।
जादो अणिंदिओ सो णाणं सोक्खं च परिणमदि ॥१९-२॥

सोक्खं वा पुण दुक्खं केवलणाणिस्स णत्थि देहगदं ।
जम्हा अदिंदियत्तं जादं तम्हा दु तं णेयं ॥२०॥

परिणमदो खलु णाणं पच्चक्खा सव्वदव्वपज्जाया ।
सो णेव ते विजाणदि उग्गहपुव्वाहिं किरियाहिं ॥२१॥

णत्थि परोक्खं किंचि वि समंत सव्वक्खगुणसमिद्धस्स ।
अक्खातीदस्स सदा सयमेव हि णाणजादस्स ॥२२॥

आदा णाणपमाणं णाणं णेयप्पमाणमुद्दिट्ठं ।
णेयं लोयालोयं तम्हा णाणं तु सव्वगयं ॥२३॥

णाणप्पमाणमादा ण हवदि जस्सेह तस्स सो आदा ।
हीणो वा अहिओ वा णाणादो हवदि धुवमेव ॥२४॥

हीणो जदि सो आदा तण्णाणमचेदणं ण जाणादि ।
अहिओ वा णाणादो णाणेण विणा कहं णादि ॥२५॥ जुगलं

सव्वगदो जिणवसहो सव्वेवि य तग्गया जगदि अट्ठा ।
णाणमयादो य जिणो विसयादो तस्स ते भणिदा ॥२६॥

णाणं अप्प त्ति मदं वट्टदि णाणं विणा ण अप्पाणं ।
तम्हा णाणं अप्पा अप्पा णाणं व अण्णं वा ॥२७॥

णाणी णाणसहावो अट्ठा णेयप्पगा हि णाणिस्स ।
रूवाणि व चक्खूणं णेरण्णोण्णेसु वट्टंति ॥२८॥

ण पविट्ठो णाविट्ठो णाणी णेयेसु रूवमिव चक्खू ।
जाणदि वस्सदि णियदं अक्खातीदो जगमसेसं ॥२९॥

रयणमिह इंदणीलं दुद्धज्झसियं जहा सभासाए ।
अभिभूय तं पि दुद्धं वट्टदि तह णाणमट्ठेसु ॥३०॥

जदि ते ण संति अट्ठा णाणे णाणं ण होदि सव्वगयं ।
सव्वगयं वा णाणं कहं ण णाणट्ठिया अट्ठा ॥३१॥

गेण्हदि णेव ण मुंचदि ण परं परिणमदि केवली भगवं ।
पेच्छदि समंतदो सो जाणदि सव्वं णिरवसेसं ॥३२॥

जो हि सुदेण विजाणदि अप्पाणं जाणणं सहावेण ।
तं सुयकेवलिमिसिणो भणंति लोगप्पदीवयरा ॥३३॥

सुत्तं जिणोवदिट्ठं पोग्गलदव्वप्पगेहिं वयणेहिं ।
तं जाणणा हि णाणं सुत्तस्स य जाणणा भणिया ॥३४॥

जो जाणदि सो णाणं ण हवदि णाणेण जाणगो आदा ।
णाणं परिणमदि सयं अट्ठा णाणट्ठिया सव्वे ॥३५॥

तम्हा णाणं जीवो णेयं दव्वं तिहा समक्खादं ।
दव्वं ति पुणो आदा परं च परिणामसंबद्धं ॥३६॥

तक्कालिगेव सव्वे सदसब्भूदा हि पज्जया तासिं ।
वट्टंते ते णाणे विसेसदो दव्वजादीणं ॥३७॥

जे णेव हि संजाया जे खलु णट्ठा भवीय पज्जाया ।
ते होंति असब्भूदा पज्जाया णाणपच्चक्खा ॥३८॥

जदि पच्चक्खमजादं पज्जायं पलयिदं च णाणस्स ।
ण हवदि वा तं णाणं दिव्वं ति हि के परुवेंति ॥३९॥

अत्थं अक्खणिवदिदं ईहापुव्वेहिं जे विजाणंति ।
तेसिं परोक्खभूदं णादुमसक्कं ति पण्णत्तं ॥४०॥

अपदेसं सपदेसं मुत्तममुत्तं च पज्जयमजादं ।
पलयं गदं च जाणदि तं णाणमदिंदियं भणियं ॥४१॥

परिणमदि णेयमट्ठं णादा जदि णेव खाइगं तस्स ।
णाणं ति तं जिणिंदा खवयंतं कम्ममेवुत्ता ॥४२॥

उदयगदा कम्मंसा जिणवरवसहेहिं णियदिणा भणिया ।
तेसु विमूढो रत्तो दुट्ठो वाबंधमणुभवदि ॥४३॥

ठाणणिसेज्जविहारा धम्मुवदेसो य णियदयो तेसिं ।
अरहंताणं काले मायाचारो व्व इत्थीणं ॥४४॥

पुण्णफला अरहंता तेसिं किरिया पुणो हि ओदइया ।
मोहदीहिं विरहिदा तम्हा सा खाइग त्ति मदा ॥४५॥

जदि सो सुहो व असुहो ण हवदि आदा सयं सहावेण ।
संसारो वि ण विज्जदि सव्वेसिं जीवकायाणं ॥४६॥

जं तक्कालियमिदरं जाणदि जुगवं समंतदो सव्वं ।
अत्थं विचित्तविसमं तं णाणं खाइयं भणियं ॥४७॥

जो ण विजाणदि जुगवं अत्थे तिक्कालिगे तिहुवणत्थे ।
णादुं तस्स ण सक्कं सपज्जयं दव्वमेगं वा ॥४८॥

दव्वं अणंतपज्जयमेगमणंताणि दव्वजादाणि ।
ण विजाणदि जदि जुगवं किध सो सव्वाणि जाणादि ॥४९॥

उप्पज्जदि जदि णाणं कमसो अट्ठे पडुच्च णाणिस्स ।
तं णेव हवदि णिच्चं ण खाइगं णेव सव्वगदं ॥५०॥

तिक्कालणिच्चविसमं सयलं सव्वत्थसंभवं चित्तं ।
जुगवं जाणदि जोण्हं अहो हि णाणस्स माहप्पं ॥५१॥

ण वि परिणमदि ण गेण्हदि उप्पज्जदि णेव तेसु अट्ठेसु ।
जाणण्णवि ते आदा अबंधगो तेण पण्णत्तो ॥५२-१॥

तस्स णमाइं लोगो देवासुरमणुअरायसंबंधो ।
भत्तो करोदि णिच्चं उवजुत्तो तं तहा वि अहं ॥५२-२॥

अत्थि अमुत्तं मुत्तं अदिंदियं इंदियं च अत्थेसु ।
णाणं च तहा सोक्खं जं तेसु परं च तं णेयं ॥५३॥

जं पेच्छदो अमुत्तं मुत्तेसु अदिंदियं च पच्छण्णं ।
सयलं सगं च इदरं तं णाणं हवदि पच्चक्खं ॥५४॥

जीवो सयं अमुत्तो मुत्तिगदो तेण मुत्तिणा मुत्तं ।
ओगेण्हित्ता जोग्गं जाणदि वा तेण जाणादि ॥५५॥

फासो रसो य गंधो वण्णो सद्दो य पुग्गला होंति ।
अक्खाणं ते अक्खा जुगवं ते णेव गेण्हंति ॥५६॥

परदव्वं ते अक्खा णेव सहावो त्ति अप्पणो भणिदा ।
उवलद्धं तेहि कधं पच्चक्खं अप्पणो होदि ॥५७॥
जं परदो विण्णाणं तं तु परोक्खं ति भणिदमट्ठेसु ।
जदि केवलेण णादं हवदि हि जीवेण पच्चक्खं ॥५८॥
जादं सयं समत्तं णाणमणंतत्थवित्थडं विमलं ।
रहिदं तु ओग्गहादिहिं सुहं ति एगंतियं भणिदं ॥५९॥
जं केवलं ति णाणं तं सोक्खं परिणमं च सो चेव ।
खेदो तस्स ण भणिदो जम्हा घादी खयं जादा ॥६०॥
णाणं अत्थंतगयं लोयालोएसु वित्थडा दिट्ठी ।
णट्ठमणिदं सव्वं इट्ठं पुण जं तु तं लद्धं ॥६१॥
णो सद्दहंति सोक्खं सुहेसु परमं ति विगदघादीणं ।
सुणिदूण ते अभव्वा भव्वा वा तं पडिच्छंति ॥६२॥
मणुआसुरामरिंदा अहिद्दुदा इंदियेहिं सहजेहिं ।
असहंता तं दुक्खं रमंति विसएसु रम्मेसु ॥६३॥
जेसिं विसयेसु रदी तेसिं दुक्खं वियाण सब्भावं ।
जइ तं ण हि सब्भावं वावारो णत्थि विसयत्थं ॥६४॥
पप्पा इट्ठे विसये फासेहिं समस्सिदे सहावेण ।
परिणममाणो अप्पा सयमेव सुहं ण हवदि देहो ॥६५॥
एगंतेण हि देहो सुहं ण देहिस्स कुणदि सग्गे वा ।
विसयवसेण दु सोक्खं दुक्खं वा हवदि सयमादा ॥६६॥
तिमिरहरा जइ दिट्ठी जणस्स दीवेण णत्थि कायव्वं ।
तह सोक्खं सयमादा विसया किं तत्थ कुव्वंति ॥६७॥
सयमेव जहादिच्चो तेजो उण्हो य देवदा णभसि ।
सिद्धो वि तहा णाणं सुहं च लोगे तहा देवो ॥६८–१॥

तेजो दिट्ठी णाणं इड्ढी सोक्खं तहेव ईसरियं ।
तिहुवणपहाणदइयं माहप्पं जस्स सो अरिहो ॥६८–२॥

तं गुणदो अधिगदरं अविच्छिदं मणुवदेवपदिभावं ।
अपुणब्भावणिबद्धं पणमामि पुणो पुणो सिद्धं ॥६८–३॥

देवदजदिगुरुपूजासु चेव दाणम्मि वा सुसीलेसु ।
उववासादिसु रत्तो सुहोवओगप्पगो अप्पा ॥६९॥

जुत्तो सुहेण आदा तिरियो वा माणुसो व देवो वा ।
भूदो तावदि कालं लहदि सुहं इंदियं विविहं ॥७०॥

सोक्खं सहावसिद्धं णत्थि सुराणं पि सिद्धमुवदेसे ।
ते देहवेदणट्टा रमंति विसएसु रम्मेसु ॥७१॥

णरणारयतिरियसुरा भजंति जदि देहसंभवं दुक्खं ।
किह सो सुहो व असुहो उवओगो हवदि जीवाणं ॥७२॥

कुलिसाउहचक्कधरा सुहोवओगप्पगेहिं भोगेहिं ।
देहादीणं विद्धिं करेंति सुहिदा इवाभिरदा ॥७३॥

जदि संति हि पुण्णाणि य परिणामसमुब्भवाणि विविहाणि ।
जणयंति विसयतण्हं जीवाणं देवदंताणं ॥७४॥

ते पुण उदिण्णतण्हा दुहिदा तण्हाहिं विसयसोक्खाणि ।
इच्छंति अणुभवंति य आमरणं दुक्खसंतत्ता ॥७५॥

सपरं बाधासहिदं विच्छिण्णं बंधकारणं विसमं ।
जं इंदियेहि लद्धं तं सोक्खं दुक्खमेव तहा ॥७६॥

ण हि मण्णदि जो एवं णत्थि विसेसो त्ति पुण्णपावाणं ।
हिंडदि घोरमपारं संसारं मोहसंछण्णो ॥७७॥

एवं विदिदत्थो जो दव्वेसु ण रागमेदि दोसं वा ।
उवओगविसुद्धो सो खवेदि देहुब्भवं दुक्खं ॥७८॥

चत्ता पावारंभं समुट्ठिदो वा सुहम्मि चरियम्हि ।
ण जहदि जदि मोहादी ण लहदि सो अप्पगं सुद्धं ॥७६/१॥
तव संजमप्पसिद्धो सुद्धो सग्गापवग्ग मग्ग करो ।
अमरासुरिंदमहिदो देवो सो लोयसिहरत्थो ॥७६/२॥
तं देवदेवदेवं जदिवरवसहं गुरुं तिलोयस्स ।
पणमंति जे मणुस्सा ते सोक्खं अक्खं अक्खयं जंति ॥७६/३॥
जो जाणदि अरहंतं दव्वत्तगुणत्तपज्जयत्तेहिं ।
सो जाणदि अप्पाणं मोहो खलु जादि तस्स लयं ॥८०॥
जीवो ववगदमोहो उवलद्धो तच्चमप्पणो सम्मं ।
जहदि जदि रागदोसे सो अप्पाणं लहदि सुद्धं ॥८१॥
सव्वे वि य अरहंता तेण विधाणेण खविदकम्मंसा ।
किच्चा तधोवदेसं णिव्वादा ते णमो तेसिं ॥८२/१॥
दंसणसुद्धा पुरिसा णाणपहाणा सम्मग्चरियत्था ।
पूजासक्काररिहा दाणस्य य हि ते णमो तेसिं ॥८२/२॥
दव्वादिएसु मूढो भावो जीवस्य हवदि मोहो त्ति ।
खुब्भदि तेणुच्छण्णो पप्पा रागं व दोसं बा ॥८३॥
मोहेण व रागेण व दोसेण व परिणदस्स जीवस्य ।
जायदि विविहो बंधो तम्हा ते संखवइदव्वा ॥८४॥
अट्ठे अजधागहणं करुणाभावो य तिरिएमणुएसु ।
बिसएसु य प्पसंगो मोहस्सेदाणि लिंगाणि ॥८५॥
जिण सत्थादो अट्ठे पच्चक्खादीहिं बुज्झदो णियमा ।
खीयदि मोहोवचयो तम्हा सत्थं समधिदव्वं ॥८६॥
दव्वाणि गुणा तेसिं पज्जाया अट्ठसण्णया भणिया ।
तेसु गुणपज्जयाणं अप्पा दव्व त्ति उवदेशो ॥८७॥

जो मोहरागदोसे णिहणदि उवलब्भ जोण्हमुवदेसं ।
सो सव्वदुक्खमोक्खं पावदि अचिरेण कालेण ॥८८॥
णाणप्पगमप्पाणं परं च दव्वत्तणाहिसंबद्धं ।
जाणदि जदि णिच्छयदो जो सो मोहक्खयं कुणदि ॥८९॥
तम्हा जिणमग्गादो गुणेहिं आदं परं च दव्वेसु ।
अभिगच्छदु णिम्मोहं इच्छदि जदि अप्पणो अप्पा ॥९०॥
सत्तासंबद्धेदे सविसेस जो हि णेव सामण्णे ।
सद्दहदि ण सो समणो तत्तो धम्मो ण संभवदि ॥९१॥
जो णिहदमोहदिट्ठी आगमकुसलो विरागचरियम्हि ।
अब्भुट्ठिदो महप्पा धम्मो त्ति विसेसिदो समणो ॥९२/१॥
जो तं दिट्ठा तुट्ठो अब्भुट्ठित्ता करेदि सक्कारं ।
वंदणणमंसणादिहिं तत्तो धम्ममादियदि ॥९२/२॥
तेण णरा व तिरिच्छा देविं वा माणुसि गदि पप्पा ।
विहविस्सरियेहिं सदा संपुण्णमणोरहा होंति ॥९२/३॥

ज्ञेयतत्त्व-प्रज्ञापन

तम्हा तस्स णमाइं किच्चा णिच्चं पि तम्मणो होज्ज ।
वोच्छामि संगहादो परमट्ठविणिच्छयाधिगमं ॥९३/१॥
अत्थो खलु दव्वमओ दव्वाणि गुणप्पगाणि भणिदाणि ।
तेहिं पुणो पज्जाया पज्जयमूढा हि परसमया ॥९३/२॥
जो पज्जयेसु णिरदा जीवा परसमइग त्ति णिद्दिट्ठा ।
आदसहावम्मि ठिदा ते सगसमया मुणेदव्वा ॥९४॥
अपरिच्चत्तसहावेणुप्पादव्वयधुवत्तसंबद्धं ।
गुणवं च सपज्जायं जं तं दव्वं ति वुच्चंति ॥९५॥

सब्भावो हि सहावो गुणेहिं सह पज्जएहिं चित्तेहिं ।
दव्वस्स सव्वकालं उप्पादव्वयधुवत्तेहिं ॥९६॥

इह विविहलक्खणाणं लक्खणमेगं सदित्ति सव्वगयं ।
उवदिसदा खलु धम्मं जिणवरवसहेण पण्णत्तं ॥९७॥

दव्वं सहावसिद्धं सदिति जिणा तच्चदो समक्खादा ।
सिद्धं तध आगमदो णेच्छदि जो सो हि परसमओ ॥९८॥

सदवट्ठिदं सहावे दव्वं दव्वस्स जो हि परिणामो ।
अत्थेसु सो सहावो ठिदिसंभवणाससंबद्धो ॥९९॥

ण भवो भंगविहीणो भंगो वा णत्थि संभवविहीणो ।
उप्पादोवि य भंगो ण विणा धोव्वेण अत्थेण ॥१००॥

उप्पादट्ठिदिभंगा विज्जंते पज्जएसु पज्जाया ।
दव्वं हि संति णियदं तम्हा दव्वं हवदि सव्वं ॥१०१॥

समवेदं खलु दव्वं संभवठिदिणाससण्णिदट्ठेहिं ।
एक्कम्मि चेव समये तम्हा दव्वं खु तत्तिदयं ॥१०२॥

पाडुब्भवदि य अण्णो पज्जाओ पज्जओ वयदि अण्णो ।
दव्वस्स तं पि दव्वं णेव पणट्ठं ण उप्पण्णं ॥१०३॥

परिणमदि सयं दव्वं गुणदो य गुणंतरं सदविसिट्ठं ।
तम्हा गुणपज्जाया भणिया पुण दव्वमेव त्ति ॥१०४॥

ण हवदि जदि सद्दव्वं असद्धुवं हवदि तं कहं दव्वं ।
हवदि पुणो अण्णं वा तम्हा दव्वं सयं सत्ता ॥१०५॥

पविभत्तपदेसत्तं पुधत्तमिदि सासणं हि वीरस्स ।
अण्णत्तमतब्भावो ण तब्भवं होदि कधमेगं ॥१०६॥

सद्दव्वं सच्च गुणो सच्चेव य पज्जओ त्ति वित्थारो ।
जो खलु तस्स अभावो सो तदभावो अतब्भावो ॥१०७॥

जं दव्वं तं ण गुणो जोवि गुणो सो ण तच्चमत्थादो ।
एसो हि अतब्भावो णेव अभावो त्ति णिद्दिट्ठो ॥१०८॥

जो खलु दव्वसहावो परिणामो सो गुणो सदविसिट्ठो ।
सदवट्ठिदं सहावे दव्वं त्ति जिणोवदेसोयं ॥१०९॥

णत्थि गुणो त्ति व कोई पज्जाओ त्तीह वा विणा दव्वं ।
दव्वत्तं पुण भावो तम्हा दव्वं सयं सत्ता ॥११०॥

एवंविहं सहावे दव्वं दव्वत्थपज्जयत्थेहिं ।
सदसब्भावणिबद्धं पादुब्भावं सदा लभदि ॥१११॥

जीवो भवं भविस्सदि णरोऽमरो वा परो भवीय पुणो ।
किं दव्वत्तं पजहदि ण जहं अण्णो कहं हवदि ॥११२॥

मणुवो ण हवदि देवो देवो वा माणुसो व सिद्धो वा ।
एवं अहोज्जमाणो अणण्णभावं कधं लहदि ॥११३॥

दव्वट्ठिएण सव्वं दव्वं तं पज्जयट्ठिएण पुणो ।
हवदि य अण्णमणण्णं तक्काले तम्मयत्तादो ॥११४॥

अत्थि त्ति य णत्थि त्ति य हवदि अवत्तव्वमिदि पुणो दव्वं ।
पज्जायेण दु केण वि तदुभयमदिट्ठमण्णं वा ॥११५॥

एसो त्ति णत्थि कोई ण णत्थि किरिया सहावणिव्वत्ता ।
किरिया हि णत्थि अफला धम्मो जदि णिप्फलो परमो ॥११६॥

कम्मं णामसमक्खं सभावमध अप्पणो सहावेण ।
अभिभूय णरं तिरियं णेरइयं वा सुरं कुणदि ॥११७॥

णरणारयतिरियसुरा जीवा खलु णामकम्मणिव्वत्ता ।
ण हि ते लद्धसहावा परिणममाणा सकम्माणि ॥११८॥

जायदि णेव ण णस्सदि खणभंगसमुब्भवे जणे कोई ।
जो हि भवो सो विलओ संभवविलय त्ति ते णाणा ॥११९॥

तम्हा दु णत्थि कोई सहावसमवट्ठिदो त्ति संसारे ।
संसारो पुण किरिया संसरमाणस्स दव्वस्स ॥१२०॥

आदा कम्ममलिमसो परिणामं लहदि कम्मसंजुत्तं ।
तत्तो सिलिसदि कम्मं तम्हा कम्मं तु परिणामो ॥१२१॥

परिणामो सयमादा सा पुण किरिय त्ति होदि जीवमया ।
किरिया कम्म त्ति मदा तम्हा कम्मस्स ण दु कत्ता ॥१२२॥

परिणमदि चेदणाए आदा पुण चेदणा तिधाभिमदा ।
सा पुण णाणे कम्मे फलम्मि वा कम्मणो भणिदा ॥१२३॥

णाणं अट्ठवियप्पो कम्मं जीवेण जं समारद्धं ।
तमणेगविधं भणिदं फलं त्ति सोक्खं व दुक्खं वा ॥१२४॥

अप्पा परिणामप्पा परिणामो णाणकम्मफलभावी ।
तम्हा णाणं कम्मं फलं च आदा मुणेदव्वो ॥१२५॥

कत्ता करणं कम्मं फलं च अप्प त्ति णिच्छिदो समणो ।
परिणमदि णेव अण्णं जदि अप्पाणं लहदि सुद्धं ॥१२६॥

दव्वं जीवमजीवं जीवो पुण चेदणोवओगमओ ।
पोग्गलदव्वप्पमुहं अचेदणं हवदि य अजीवं ॥१२७॥

पोग्गलजीवणिबद्धो धम्माधम्मत्थिकायकालड्ढो ।
वट्टदि आगासे जो लोगो सो सव्वकाले दु ॥१२८॥

उप्पादट्ठिदिभंगा पोग्गलजीवप्पगस्स लोगस्स ।
परिणामा जायंते संघादादो व भेदादो ॥१२९॥

लिंगेहिं जेहिं दव्वं जीवमजीवं च हवदि विण्णादं ।
तेऽतब्भावविसिट्ठा मुत्तामुत्ता गुणा णेया ॥१३०॥

मुत्ता इंदियगेज्झा पोग्गलदव्वप्पगा अणेगविधा ।
दव्वाणममुत्ताणं गुणा अमुत्ता मुणेदव्वा ॥१३१॥

वण्णरसगंधफासा विज्जंते पुग्गलस्स सुहुमादो ।
पुढवीपरियंतस्स य सद्दो सो पोग्गलो चित्तो ॥१३२॥
आगासस्सवगाहो धम्मद्दव्वस्स गमणहेदुत्तं ।
धम्मेदरदव्वस्स दु गुणो पुणो ठाणकारणदा ॥१३३॥
कालस्स वट्टणा से गुणोवओगो त्ति अप्पणो भणिदो ।
णेया संखेवादो गुणा हि मुत्तिप्पहीणाणं ॥१३४॥जुगलं॥
जीवा पोग्गलकाया धम्माधम्मा पुणो य आगासं ।
सपदेसेहिं असंखा णत्थि पदेस त्ति कालस्स ॥१३५ १॥
एदाणि पंचदव्वाणि उज्झियकालं तु अत्थिकाय त्ति ।
भण्णंते काया पुण बहुप्पदेसाण पचयत्तं ॥१३५/२॥
लोगालोगेसु णभो धम्माधम्मेहिं आददो लोगो ।
ऐसे पडुच्च कालो जीवा पुण पोग्गला सेसा ॥१३६॥
जध ते णभप्पदेसा तधप्पदेसा हवंति सेसाणं ।
अपदेसो परमाणु तेण पदेसुब्भवो भणिदो ॥१३७॥
समओ दु अप्पदेसो पदेसमेत्तस्स दव्वजादस्स ।
वदिवददो सो वट्टदि पदेसमागासदव्वस्स ॥१३८॥
वदिवददो तं देसं तस्सम समओ तदो परो पुव्वो ।
जो सो कालो समओ उप्पण्णपद्धंसी ॥१३९॥
आगासमणुणिविट्ठं आगासपदेससण्णया भणिदं ।
सव्वेसिं च अणूणं सक्कदि तं देदुमवगासं ॥१४०॥
एक्को व दुगे बहुगा संखातीदा तदो अणंता य ।
दव्वाणं च पदेसा संति हि समय त्ति कालस्स ॥१४१॥
उप्पादो पद्धंसो विज्जदि जदि जस्स एगसमयम्हि ।
समयस्स सो वि समओ सभावसमवट्ठिदो हवदि ॥१४२॥
एगम्हि संति समये संभवठिदिणाससण्णिदा अट्ठा ।
समयस्स सव्वकालं एस हि कालणुसब्भावो ॥१४३॥

जस्स ण संति पदेसा पदेसमेत्तं व तच्चदो णादुं ।
सुण्णं जाण तमत्थं अत्थंतरभूदमत्थीदो ॥१४४॥
सपदेसेहिं समग्गो लोगो अट्ठेहिं णिट्ठिदो णिच्चो ।
जो तं जाणदि जीवो पाणचदुक्केण संबद्धो ॥१४५॥
इंदियपाणो य तधा बलपाणो तह य आउपाणो य ।
आणप्पाणप्पाणो जीवाणं होंति पाणा ते ॥१४६/१॥
पंच वि इंदियपाणा मणवचिकाया य तिण्णि बलपाणा ।
आणप्पाणप्पाणो आउगपाणेण होंति दसपाणा ॥१४६/२॥
पाणेहिं चदुहिं जीवदि जीवस्सदि जो हि जीविदो पुव्वं ।
सो जीवो पाणा पुण पोग्गलदव्वेहिं णिव्वत्ता ॥१४७॥
जीवो पाणणिबद्धो बद्धो मोहादिएहिं कम्मेहिं ।
उवभुंज कम्मफलं बज्झदि अण्णेहिं कम्मेहिं ॥१४८॥
पाणाबाधं जीवो मोहपदेसेहिं कुणवि जीवाणं ।
जदि सो हवदि हि बंधो णाणावरणादिकम्मेहिं ॥१४९॥
आदा कम्ममलिमसो धरेदि पाणे पुणो पुणो अण्णे ।
ण चयदि जाव ममत्तिं देहपधाणेसु विसयेसु ॥१५०॥
जो इंदियादिविजई भवीय उवओगमप्पगं झादि ।
कम्मेहिं सो ण रंजदि किह तं पाणा अणुचरंति ॥१५१॥
अत्थित्तणिच्छिदस्स हि अत्थस्सत्थंतरम्हि संभूदो ।
अत्थो पज्जाओ सो संठाणादिप्पभेदेहिं ॥१५२॥
णरणारयतिरियसुरा संठाणादीहिं अण्णहा जादा ।
पज्जाया जीवाणं उदयादिहिं णामकम्मस्स ॥१५३॥
तं सब्भावणिबद्धं दव्वसहावं तिहा समक्खादं ।
जाणदि जो सवियप्पं ण मुहदि सो अण्णदवियम्हि ॥१५४॥
अप्पा उवओगप्पा उवओगो णाणदंसणं भणिदो ।
सो वि सुहो असुहो वा उवओगो अप्पणो हवदि ॥१५५॥

उवओगो जदि हि सुहो पुण्णं जीवस्स संचयं जादि ।
असुहो व तध पावं तेसिमभावे ण चयमत्थि ।।१५६।।

जो जाणादि जिणिंदे पेच्छदि सिद्धे तहेव अणगारे ।
जीवेसु साणुकंपो उवओगो सो सुहो तस्स ।।१५७।।

विसयकसायओगाढो दुस्सुदिदुच्चित्तदुट्ठगोट्ठि जुदो ।
उग्गो उमग्गपरो उवओगो जस्स सो असुहो ।।१५८।।

असुहोवओगरहिदो सुहोवजुत्तो ण अण्णदवियम्हि ।
होज्जं मज्झत्थोऽहं णाणप्पगमप्पगं झाए ।।१५९।।

णाहं देहो ण मणो ण चेव वाणी ण कारणं तेसिं ।
कत्ता ण ण कारयिदा अणुमंता चेव कत्तीणं ।।१६०।।

देहो य मणो वाणी पोग्गलदव्वप्पग त्ति णिद्दिट्ठा ।
पोग्गलदव्वं हि पुणो पिंडो परमाणुदव्वाणं ।।१६१।।

णाहं पोग्गलमइओ ण ते मया पोग्गला कया पिंडं ।
तम्हा हि ण देहोऽहं कत्ता वा तस्स देहस्स ।।१६२।।

अपदेशो परमाणु पदेसमेत्तो द सयमसद्दो जो ।
णिद्धो वा लुक्खो वा दुपदेसादित्तमणुभवदि ।।१६३।।

एगुत्तरमेगादी अणुस्स णिद्धत्तणं च लुक्खत्तं ।
परिणामादो भणिदं जाव अणंतत्तमणुभवदि ।।१६४।।

णिद्धा वा लुक्खा वा अणुपरिणामा समा व विसमा वा ।
समदो दुराधिगा जदि बज्झन्ति हि आदिपरिहीणा ।।१६५।।

णिद्धत्तणेण दुगुणो चदुगुणणिद्धेण बंधमणुभवदि ।
लुक्खेण वा तिगुणिदो अणु बज्झदि पंचगुणजुत्तो ।।१६६।।

दुपदेसादी खंधा सुहुमा वा बादरा ससंठाणा ।
पुढविजलतेउवाऊ सगपरिणामेहिं जायन्ते ।।१६७।।

ओगाढगाढणिचिदो पुग्गलकायेहिं सव्वदो लोगो ।
सुहुमेहिं बादरेहिं य अप्पाओग्गेहिं जोग्गेहिं ॥१६८॥

कम्मत्तणपाओग्गा खंधा जीवस्स परिणइं पप्पा ।
गच्छंति कम्मभावं ण हि ते जीवेण परिणमिदा ॥१६९॥

ते ते कम्मत्तगदा पोग्गलकाया पुणो वि जीवस्स ।
संजायंते देहा देहंतरसंकमं पप्पा ॥१७०॥

ओरालिओ य देहो वेउव्विओ य तेजसिओ ।
आहारय कम्मइओ पोग्गलदव्वप्पगासव्वे ॥१७१॥

अरसमरूवमगंधं अव्वत्तं चेदणागुणमसद्दं ।
जाण अलिंगग्गहणं जीवमणिद्दिट्ठसंठाणं ॥१७२॥

मुत्तो रूवादिगुणो बज्झदि फासेहिं अण्णमण्णेहिं ।
तव्विवरीदो अप्पा बज्झदि किध पोग्गलं कम्मं ॥१७३॥

रूवादिएहिं रहिदो पेच्छदि जाणादि रूवमादीणि ।
दव्वाणि गुणे य जधा तह बंधो तेण जाणीहि ॥१७४॥

उवओगमओ जीवो मुज्झदि रज्जेदि वा पदुस्सेदि ।
पप्पा विविधे विसये जो हि पुणो तेहिं सो बन्धो ॥१७५॥

भावेण जेण जीवो पेच्छदि जाणादि आगदं विसये ।
रज्जदि तेणेव पुणो बज्झदि कम्म त्ति उपदेशो ॥१७६॥

फासेहिं पोग्गलाणं बंधो जीवस्य रागमादीहिं ।
अण्णोण्णमवगाहो पुग्गलजीवप्पगो भणिदो ॥१७७॥

सपदेशो सो अप्पा तेसु पदेसेसु पोग्गला काया ।
पविसंति जहाजोग्गं चिट्ठंति हि जंति बज्झंति ॥१७८॥

रत्तो बंधदि कम्मं मुच्चदि कम्मेहिं रागरहिदप्पा ।
एसो बंधसमासो जीवाणं जाण णिच्छयदो ॥१७९॥

परिणामादो बंधो परिणामो रागदोसमोहजुदो ।
असुहो मोहपदोसो सुहो व असुहो हवदि रागो ॥१८०॥

सुहपरिणामो पुण्णं असुहो पावं त्ति भणिदमण्णेसु ।
परिणामो णण्णगदो दुक्खक्खयकारणं समये ॥१८१॥

भणिदा पुढविप्पमुहा जीवणिकायाध थावरा य तसा ।
अण्णा ते जीवादो जीवो वि य तेहिंदो अण्णो ॥१८२॥

जो णवि जाणदि एवं परमप्पाणं सहावमासेज्ज ।
कीरदि अज्झवसाणं अहं ममेदं ति मोहादो ॥१८३॥

कुव्वं सभावमादा हवदि हि कत्ता सगस्स भावस्स ।
पोग्गलदव्वमयाणं ण दु कत्ता सव्वभावाणं ॥१८४॥

गेण्हदि णेव ण मुंचदि करेदि ण हि पोग्गलाणि कम्माणि ।
जीवो पोग्गलमज्झे वट्टण्णवि सव्वकालेसु ॥१८५॥

स इदाणि कत्ता सं सगपरिणामस्स दव्वजादस्स ।
आदीयदे कदाइं विमुच्चदे कम्मधूलीहिं ॥१८६॥

परिणमदि जदा अप्पा सुहम्हि असुहम्हि रागदोसजुदो ।
तं पविसदि कम्मरयं णाणावरणादिभावेहिं ॥१८७/१॥

सुहपयडीण विसोही तिव्वो असुहाण संकिलेसम्मि ।
विवरीदो दु जहण्णो अणुभागो सव्वपडीणं ॥१८७/२॥

सपदेसो सो अप्पा कसायिदो मोहरागदोसेहिं ।
कम्मरएहिं सिलिट्ठो बंधो त्ति परूविदो समये ॥१८८॥

एसो बंधसमासो जीवाणं णिच्छयेण णिद्दिट्ठो ।
अरहंतेहिं जदीणं ववहारो अण्णहा भणिदो ॥१८९॥

ण चयदि जो दु ममत्तिं अहं ममेदं ति देहदविणेसु ।
सो सामण्णं चत्ता पडिवण्णो होदि उम्मग्गं ॥१९०॥

णाहं होमि परेसिं ण मे परे संति णाणमहमेक्को ।
इदि झायदि झाणे सो अप्पाणं हवदि झादा ॥१९१॥

एवं णाणप्पाणं दंसणभूदं अदिंदियमहत्थं ।
धुवमचलमणालंबं मण्णेऽहं अप्पगं सुद्धं ॥१९२॥

देहा वा दविणा वा सुहदुक्खा वाध सत्तुमित्तजणा ।
जीवस्स ण संति धुवा धुवोवओगप्पगो अप्पा ॥१९३॥

जो एवं जाणित्ता झादि परं अप्पगं विसुद्धप्पा ।
सागारोऽणगारो खवेदि सो मोहदुग्गंठिं ॥१९४॥

जो णिहदमोहगंठी रागपदोसे खवीय सामण्णे ।
होज्जं समसुहदुक्खो सो सोक्खं अक्खयं लहदि ॥१९५॥

जो खविदमोहकलुसो विसयविरत्तो मणो णिरुंभित्ता ।
समवट्ठिदो सहावे सो अप्पाणं हवदि झादा ॥१९६॥

णिहदघणघादिकम्मो पच्चक्खं सव्वभावतच्चण्हू ।
णेयंतगदो समणो झादि कमट्ठं असंदेहो ॥१९७॥

सव्वाबाधविजुत्तो समंतसव्वक्खसोक्खणाणड्ढो ।
भूदो अक्खातीदो झादि अणक्खो परं सोक्खं ॥१९८॥

एवं जिणा जिणिंदा सिद्धा मग्गं समुट्ठिदा समणा ।
जादा णमोत्थु तेसिं तस्स य णिव्वाणमग्गस्स ॥१९९॥

तम्हा तह जाणित्ता अप्पाणं जाणगं सभावेण ।
परिवज्जामि ममत्तिं उवट्ठिदो णिम्ममत्तम्हि ॥२००/१॥

दंसणसंसुद्धाणं सम्मण्णाणोवजोगजुत्ताणं ।
अव्वाबाधरदाणं णमो णमो सिद्धसाहूणं ॥२००/२॥

चरणानुयोगसूचक चूलिका

एवं पणमिय सिद्धे जिणवरवसहे पुणो पुणो समणे ।
पडिवज्जदु सामण्णं जदि इच्छदि दुक्खपरिमोक्खं ॥२०१॥

आपिच्छ बंधुवग्गं विमोचिदो गुरुकलत्तपुत्तेहिं ।
आसिज्ज णाणदंसणचरित्ततववीरियायारं ॥२०२॥

समणं गणिं गुणड्ढं कुलरूववयोविसिट्ठमिट्ठदरं ।
समणेहि तं पि पणदो पडिच्छ मं चेदि अणुगहिदो ॥२०३॥

णाहं होमि परेसिं ण मे परे णत्थि मज्झमिह किंचि ।
इदि णिच्छिदो जिदिंदो जादो जधजादरूवधरो ॥२०४॥

जधजादरूवजादं उप्पाडिदकेसमंसुगं सुद्धं ।
रहिदं हिंसादीदो अप्पडिकम्मं हवदि लिंगं ॥२०५॥

मुच्छारंभविजुत्तं जुत्तं उवजोगजोगसुद्धीहिं ।
लिंगं ण परावेक्खं अपुणब्भवकारणं जेण्हं ॥२०६॥

आदाय तं पि लिंगं गुरुणा परमेण तं णमंसित्ता ।
सोच्चा सवदं किरियं उवट्ठिदो होदि सो समणो ॥२०७॥

वदसमिदिंदियरोधो लोचावस्सयमचेलमण्हाणं ।
खिदिसयणमदंतवणं ठिदिभोयणमेगभत्तं च ॥२०८॥

एदे खलु मूलगुणा समणाणं जिणवरेहिं पण्णत्ता ।
तेसु पमत्तो समणो छेदोवट्ठावगो होदि ॥२०९॥

लिंगग्गहणे तेसिं गुरु त्ति पव्वज्जदायगो होदि ।
छेदेसूवट्ठवगा सेसा णिज्जावगा समणा ॥२१०॥

पयदम्हि समारद्धे छेदो समणस्स कायचेट्ठम्हि ।
जायदि जदि तस्स पुणो आलोयणपुव्विया किरिया ॥२११॥

छेदुवजुत्तो समणो समणं ववहारिणं जिणमदम्हि ।
आसेज्जालोचित्ता उवदिट्ठं तेण कायव्वं ।।२१२।।

अधिवासे व विवासे छेदविहूणो भवीय सामण्णे ।
समणो विहरदु णिच्चं परिहरमाणो णिबंधाणि ।।२१३।।

चरदि णिबद्धो णिच्चं समणो णाणम्हि दंसणमुहम्हि ।
पयदो मूलगुणेसु य जो सो पडिपुण्णसामण्णो ।।२१४।।

भत्ते वा खमणे वा आवसधे वा पुणो विहारे वा ।
उवधिम्हि वा णिबद्धं णेच्छदि समणम्हि विकधम्हि ।।२१५।।

अपयत्ता वा चरिया सयणासणठाणचंकमादीसु ।
समणस्स सव्वकाले हिंसा सा संतयि त्ति मदा ।।२१६।।

मरदु व जियदु व जीवो अयदाचारस्स णिच्छिदा हिंसा ।
पयदस्स णत्थि बंधो हिंसामेत्तेण समिदस्स ।।२१७/१।।

उच्चालियम्हि पाय इरियासमिदस्स णिग्गमत्थाए ।
आबाधेज्ज कुलिंगं मरिज्ज तं जोगमासेज्ज ।।२१७/२।।

ण हि तस्स तण्णिमित्तो बंधो सुहुमो य देसिदो समये ।
मुच्छा परिग्गहो च्चिय अज्झप्पपमाणदो दिट्ठो ।।२१७/३।।

अयदाचारो समणो छस्सु वि कायेसु वधकरो त्ति मदो ।
चरदि जदं जदि णिच्चं कमलं व जले णिरुवलेवो ।।२१८।।

हवदि व ण हवदि बंधो मदम्हि जीवेऽध कायचेट्ठम्हि ।
बंधो धुवमुवधीदो इदि समणा छड्डिया सव्वं ।।२१९।।

ण हि णिरवेक्खो चागो ण हवदि भिक्खुस्स आसयविसुद्धी ।
अविसुद्धस्स य चित्ते कहं णु कम्मक्खओ विहिदो ।।२२०/१।।

गेण्हदि व चेलखंडं भायणमत्थि त्ति भणिदमिह सुत्ते ।
जदि सो चत्तालंबो हवदि कहं वा अणारंभो ।।२२०/२।।

वत्थक्खंडं दुद्दियभायणमण्णं च गेण्हदि णियदं ।
विज्जदि पाणारंभो विक्खेवो तस्स चित्तम्मि ॥२२०/३॥
गेण्हइ विधुणइ धोवइ सोसेइ जदं तु आदवे खित्ता ।
पत्तं व चेलखंडं बिभेदि परदो य पालयदि ॥२२०/४॥
किध तम्हि णत्थि मुच्छा आरंभो वा असंजमो तस्स ।
तध परदव्वम्मि रदो कधमप्पाणं पसाधयदि ॥२२१॥
छेदो जेण ण विज्जदि गहणविसग्गेसु सेवमाणस्स ।
समणो तेणिह वट्टदु कालं खेत्तं वियाणित्ता ॥॥२२२॥
अप्पडिकुट्ठं उवधिं अपत्थणिज्जं असंजदजणेहिं ।
मुच्छादिजणणरहिदं गेण्हदु समणो जदि वि अप्पं ॥२२३॥
किं किंचण त्ति तक्कं अपुणब्भवकामिणोध देहे वि ।
संग त्ति जिणवरिंदा अप्पडिकम्मत्तमुद्दिट्ठा ॥२२४/१॥
पेच्छदि ण हि इह लोगं परं च समणिंददेसिदो धम्मो ।
धम्मम्हि तम्हि कम्हा वियप्पियं लिंगमित्थीणं ॥२२४/२॥
णिच्छयदो इत्थीणं सिद्धि ण हि तेण जम्मणा दिट्ठा ।
तम्हा तप्पडिरूवं वियप्पियं लिंगमित्थीणं ॥२२४/३॥
पइडीपमादमइया एदासिं वित्ति भासिया पमदा ।
तम्हा ताओ पमदा पमादबहुला त्ति णिद्दिट्ठा ॥२२४/४॥
संति धुवं पमदाणं मोहपदोसा भयं दुगुंछा य ।
चित्ते चित्ता माया तम्हा तासिं ण णिव्वाणं ॥२२४/५॥
ण विणा वट्टदि णारी एक्कं वा तेसु जीवलोयम्हि ।
ण हि संउडं च गत्तं तम्हा तासिं च संवरणं ॥२२४/६॥
चित्तस्सावो तासिं सित्थिल्लं अत्तवं च पक्खलणं ।
विज्जदि सहसा तासु अ उप्पादो सुहममणुआणं ॥२२४/७॥
लिंगम्हि य इत्थीणं थणंतरे णाहिकक्खपदेसेसु ।
भणिदो सुहमुप्पादो तासिं कह संजमो होदि ॥२२४/८॥

जदि दंसणेण सुद्धा सुत्तज्झयणेण चावि संजुत्ता ।
घोरं चरदि व चरियं इत्थिस्स ण णिज्जरा भणिदा ।।२२४/९।।
तम्हा तं पडिरूवं लिंगं तासिं जिणेहिं णिद्दिट्ठं ।
कुलरूववओजुत्ता समणीओ तस्समाचारा ।।२२४/१०।।
वण्णेसु तीसु एक्को कल्लाणंगो तवोसहो वयसा ।
सुमुहो कुच्छारहिदो लिंगग्गहणे हवदि जोग्गो ।।२२४/११।।
जो रयणत्तयणासो सो भंगो जिणवरेहिं णिद्दिट्ठो ।
सेसं भंगेण पुणो णो होदि सल्लेहणाअरिहो ।।२२४/१२।।
उवयरणं जिण मग्गे लिंगं जह जादरूवमिदि भणिदं ।
गुरुवयणं पि य विणओ सुत्तज्झयणं य णिद्दिट्ठं ।।२२५।।
इह लोग णिरावेक्खो अप्पडिबद्धो परम्मि लोयम्हि ।
जुत्ताहारविहारो रहिदकसाओ हवे समणो ।।२२६/१।।
जस्स अणेसणमप्पा तं पि तवो तप्पडिच्छगा समणा ।
अण्णं भिक्खमणेसणमध ते समणा अणाहारा ।।२२७/१।।
कोहादिएहिं चउहिं वि विकहाहिं तहिंदियाणमत्थेहिं ।
समणो हवदि पमत्तो उवजुत्तो णेहणिद्दाहिं ।।२२७/२।।
केवलदेहो समणो देहे ण ममत्ति रहिदपरिकम्मो ।
आजुत्तो तं तवसा अणिगूहिय अप्पणो सत्तिं ।।२२८।।
एक्कं खलु तं भत्तं अप्पडिपुण्णोदरं जहालद्धं ।
चरणं भिक्खेण दिवा ण रसावेक्खं ण मधुमंसं ।।२२९/१।।
पक्केसु अ आमेसु अ विपच्चमाणासु मंसपेसीसु ।
संतत्तियमुववादो तज्जादीणं णिगोदाणं ।।२२९/२।।
जो पक्कमपक्कं वा पेसी मंसस्स खादि फासदि वा ।
सो किल णिहणदि पिंडं जीवाणमणेगकोडीणं ।।२२९/३।।
अप्पडिकुट्ठं पिंडं पाणिगयं णेव देयमण्णस्स ।
दत्ता भोत्तुमजोग्गं भुत्तो वा होदि पडिकुट्ठो ।।२२९/४।।

बालो वा वुड्ढो वा समभिहदो वा पुणो गिलाणो वा ।
चरियं चरदु सजोग्गं मूलच्छेदो जधा ण हवदि ॥२३०॥
आहारे व विहारे देसं कालं समं खमं उवधिं ।
जाणित्ता ते समणो वट्टदि जदि अप्पलेवी सो ॥२३१॥
एयग्गगदो समणो एयग्गं णिच्छिदस्स अत्थेसु ।
णिच्छित्ती आगमदो आगमचेट्ठा तदो जेट्ठा ॥२३२॥
आगमहीणो समणो णेवप्पाणं परं वियाणादि ।
अविजाणंतो अत्थे खवेदि कम्माणि किध भिक्खू ॥२३३॥
आगमचक्खू साहू इंदियचक्खूणि सव्वभूदाणि ।
देवा य ओहिचक्खू सिद्धा पुण सव्वदो चक्खू ॥२३४॥
सव्वे आगमसिद्धा अत्था गुणपज्जएहिं चित्तेहिं ।
जाणंति आगमेण हि पेच्छित्ता ते वि ते समणा ॥२३५॥
आगमपुव्वा दिट्ठी ण भवदि जस्सेह संजमो तस्स ।
णत्थीदि भणदि सुत्तं असंजदो होदि किध समणो ॥२३६॥
ण हि आगमेण सिज्झदि सद्दहणं जदि वि णत्थि अत्थेसु।
सद्दहमाणो अत्थे असंजदो वा ण णिव्वादि ॥२३७॥
जं अण्णाणी कम्मं खवेदि भवसयसहस्सकोडीहिं ।
तं णाणी तिहिं गुत्तो खवेदि उस्सासमेत्तेण ॥२३८॥
परमाणुपमाणं वा मुच्छा देहादिएसु जस्स पुणो ।
विज्जदि जदि सो सिद्धिं ण लहदि सव्वागमधरो वि ॥२३९/१॥
चागो य अणारंभो विसयविरागो खओ कसायाणं ।
सो संजमो त्ति भणिदो पव्वज्जाए विसेसेण ॥२३९/२॥
पंचसमिदो तिगुत्तो पंचेंदियसंवुडो जिदकसाओ ।
दंसणणाणसमग्गो समणो सो संजदो भणिदो ॥२४०॥
समसत्तुबंधुवग्गो समसुहदुक्खो पसंसणिंदसमो ।
समलोट्ठुकंचणो पुण जीविदमरणे समो समणो ॥२४१॥

दंसणणाणचरित्तेसु तीसु जुगवं समुट्ठिदो जो दु ।
एयग्गगदो त्ति मदो सामण्णं तस्स पडिपुण्णं ।।२४२।।
मुज्झदि वा रज्जदि वा दुस्सदि वा दव्वमण्णमासेज्ज ।
जदि समणो अण्णाणी बज्झदि कम्मेहिं विविहेहिं ।।२४३।।
अट्ठेसु जो ण मुज्झदि ण हि रज्जदि णेव दोसमुवयादि ।
समणो जदि सो णियदं खवेदि कम्माणि विविहाणि ।।२४४।।
समणा सुद्धुवजुत्ता सुहोवजुत्ता य होंति समयम्हि ।
तेसु वि सुद्धुवजुत्ता अणासवा सासवा सेसा ।।२४५।।
अरहंतादिसु भत्ती वच्छलदा पवयणाभिजुत्तेसु ।
विज्जदि जदि सामण्णे सा सुहजुत्ता भवे चरिया ।।२४६।।
वंदणणमंसणेहिं अब्भुट्ठाणाणुगमणपडिवत्ती ।
समणेसु समावणओ ण णिंदिदा रागचरियम्हि ।।२४७।।
दंसणणाणुवदेसो सिस्सग्गहणं च पोसणं तेसिं ।
चरिया हि सरागाणं जिणिंदपूजोवदेसो य ।।२४८।।
उवकुणदि जो वि णिच्चं चादुव्वण्णस्स समणसंघस्स ।
कायविराधणरहिदं सो वि सरागप्पधाणो से ।।२४९।।
जदि कुणदि कायखेदं वेज्जावच्चत्थमुज्जदो समणो ।
ण हवदि हवदि अगारी धम्मो सो सावयाणं से ।।२५०।।
जोण्हाणं णिरवेक्खं सागारणगारचरियजुत्ताणं ।
अणुकंपयोवयारं कुव्वदु लेवो जदि वि अप्पो ।।२५१।।
रोगेण वा छुधाए तण्हाए वा समेण वा रूढं ।
दिट्ठा समणं साहू पडिवज्जदु आदसत्तीए ।।२५२।।
वेज्जावच्चणिमित्तं गिलाणगुरुबालवुड्ढसमणाणं ।
लोगिगजणसंभासा ण णिंदिदा वा सुहोवजुदा ।।२५३।।
एसा पसत्थभूदा समणाणं वा पुणो घरत्थाणं ।
चरिया परेत्ति भणिदा ताएव परं लहदि सोक्खं ।।२५४।।

रागो पसत्थभूदो वत्थुविसेसेण फलदि विवरीदं ।
णाणाभूमिगदाणिह बीजाणिव सस्सकालम्हि ॥२५५॥

छदुमत्थविहिदवत्थुसु वदणियमज्झयणझाणदाणरदो ।
ण लहदि अपुणब्भावं भावं सादप्पगं लहदि ॥२५६॥

अविदिदपरमत्थेसु य विसयकसायाधिगेसु पुरिसेसु ।
जुट्ठं कदं व दत्तं फलदि कुदेवेसु मणुवेसु ॥२५७॥

जदि ते विसयकसाया पाव त्ति परूविदा व सत्थेसु ।
किह ते तप्पडिबद्धा पुरिसा णित्थारगा होंति ॥२५८॥

उवरदपावो पुरिसो समभावो धम्मिगेसु सव्वेसु ।
गुणसमिदिदोवसेवी हवदि स भागी सुमग्गस्स ॥२५९॥

असुभोवयोगरहिदा सद्धुवजुत्ता सुहोवजुत्ता वा ।
णित्थारयंति लोगं तेसु पसत्थं लहदि भत्तो ॥२६०॥

दिट्ठा पगदं वत्थुं अब्भुट्ठाणप्पधाणकिरियाहिं ।
वट्टदु तदो गुणादो विसेसिदव्वो त्ति उवदेसो ॥२६१॥

अब्भुट्ठाणं गहणं उवासणं पोसणं च सक्कारं ।
अंजलिकरणं पणमं भणिदमिह गुणाधिगाणं हि ॥२६२॥

अब्भुट्ठेया समणा सुत्तत्थविसारदा उवासेया ।
संजमतवणाणड्ढा पणिवदणीया हि समणेहिं ॥२६३॥

ण हवदि समणो त्ति मदो संजमतवसुत्तसंपजुत्तो वि ।
जदि सद्दहदि ण अत्थे आदपधाणे जिणक्खादे ॥२६४॥

अववददि सासणत्थं समणं दिट्ठा पदोसदो जो हि ।
किरियासु णाणुमण्णदि हवदि हि सो णट्ठचारित्तो ॥२६५॥

गुणदोधिगस्स विणयं पडिच्छगो जो वि होमि समणो त्ति ।
होज्जं गुणाधरो जदि सो होदि अणंतसंसारी ॥२६६॥

अधिगगुणा सामण्णे वट्टंति गुणाधरेहिं किरियासु ।
जदि ते मिच्छुवजुत्ता हवंति पब्भट्ठचारित्ता ।।२६७।।

णिच्छिदसुत्तत्थपदो समिदकसाओ तवोधिगो चावि ।
लोगिगजणसंसग्गं ण चयदि जदि संजदो ण हवदि ।।२६८/१।।

तिसिदं बुभुक्खिदं वा दुहिदं दट्ठूण जो हि दुहिदमणो ।
पडिवज्जदि तं किवया तस्सेसा होदि अणुकंपा ।।२६८/२।।

णिग्गंथो पव्वइदो वट्टदि जदि एहिगेहिं कम्मेहिं ।
सो लोगिगो त्ति भणिदो संजमतवसंपजुत्तो वि ।।२६९।।

तम्हा समं गुणादो समणो समणं गुणेहिं वा अहियं ।
अधिवसदु तम्हि णिच्चं इच्छदि जदि दुक्खपरिमोक्खं ।।२७०।।

जे अजधागहिदत्था एदे तच्च त्ति णिच्छिदा समये ।
अच्चंतफलसमिद्धं भमंति ते तो परं कालं ।।२७१।।

अजधाचारविजुत्तो जधत्थपदणिच्छिदो पसंतप्पा ।
अफले चिरं ण जीवदि इह सो संपुण्णसामण्णो ।।२७२।।

सम्मं विदिदपदत्था चत्ता उवहिं बहित्थमज्झत्थं ।
विसयेसु णावसत्ता जे ते सुद्धा त्ति णिद्दिट्ठा ।।२७३।।

सुद्धस्स य सामण्णं भणियं सुद्धस्स दंसणं णाणं ।
सुद्धस्स य णिव्वाणं सो च्चिय सिद्धो णमो तस्स ।।२७४।।

बुज्झदि सासणमेयं सागारणगारचरियया जुत्तो ।
जो सो पवयणसारं लहुणा कालेण पप्पोदि ।।२७५।।

इति प्रवचनसार [पवयणसारो]

Glossary of Jaina Technical Terms

The English equivalent of words used in this work, given below in Sanskrit, may not always necessarily and exclusively have the same meaning in all contexts or indicate the same Jaina term. The references are to consecutive numbering of verses (*gathas*). The additional (extra) verses in the text, given only in Jayasena's commentary, are marked with an asterisk (*). Sk. stands for Sanskrit and Pk. stands for Prakrit.

Ajiva — Non-life or the insentient principle; nature of 127.

Adharma — The principle of stationariness or the fulcrum of rest; property of 133.

Anagara — An ascetic, or homeless 194.

Anyatva — Non-identity; defined 106.

Appadikammam — Non-attention towards the body 205, 224/1, also 228.

Appadikutha — Non forbidden by the sacred text 223, *229/4.

Abhavya — A non-liberable being; nature of 62.

Amurta — Incorporeal, Non-concrete; defined 131; see *guna.*

Arahanta — One who is worthy of worship, *Tirthankara*; nature of the (Sk. *Arhat*) activities of 44-45; glories of *68/2.

Artha — An existential entity; some characteristics of 10; defined 87; 93/2, *agama* as the proof of 235.

Avagraha — Apprenhension of an object, outlinear grasp 21, 59.

Avadhi — Clairvoyance; 234

Ashubhopayoga — Inauspicious psychic-attention or manifestation of consciousness; fruit of 12; demerit caused by 156; characteristics of 158; *karmic* influx in 245.

Astikaya	Existence-aggregate or magnitude, a technical name given to five substances, time being excepted; five kinds of and defined *135/2.
Akasha	Space, also sky; the property of 133; space-points of 135/1; two kinds of 136.
Agam	The Jaina scripture; importance of the study of 232; *karman* destroyed by the study of 233; monks see through 234; self-control obtained from 236.
Atman	The self; coextensive with knowledge, neither less nor more 23-24, 36; identity with knowledge 27; the happiness itself 67; contact and relation of *karma* with 121-122; the relation of three kinds of *chetana* with 125; agency, etc. in 126; property of 134; nature of 155; independence of 160; body not identical with 162; real nature of 192; external things and relations different from 193; see also *jiva* and *chetana*.
Arambha	Preliminary sin; all those activities which involve some slight harm to living beings *220/3.
Alochana	Report of defaults 211-212.
Avashyaka	Essential duty 208.
Asrava	The influx of *karmas*; causes of 245.
Ahara	Food, etc.; nature of monk's 229/1, *229/4; reasons for abstaining from non-vegetarian *229/2-3.
Aharaka (- *sharira*)	The emanatory or translocational body 171.
Indriya	The sense organ or the sense; simultaneous comprehension impossible for 56; not a part of the soul's nature 57; sense-perception not *pratyaksha* 57; nature of the happiness from 76.
Iha	Specific enquiry, discrimination 40.
Utpada-vyaya-	Origination, destruction or annihilation and permanence *dhrauvya* or stability; refer to modifications leaving *arthatva* 18, 101; interaction of 100; simultaneous presence of (in a substance) 102; relation of origination and destruction 119.
Upadhi	The same as *parigraha*, encumbrances 223.
Upayoga	Psychic-attention, manifestation or function of consciousness. It is a very mobile term, whose shade of meaning slightly changes according to the context. It

is a condition of the soul which is an embodiment of consciousness; three kinds of 9; two channels of 155.

Audarika (*-sharira*) The physical body 171.

Karman Karma, a subtle type of matter which inflows into the soul, when the latter is disturbed by passional vibrations etc.; *ghati-k.* destroyed by Mahavira 1; *ghati-k.* destroyed in *shuddhopayoga* 15; nature of and soul's contact and relation with 121-122; soul bound by 148; harm to vitalities as the cause of *jnanavaraniya-k.* etc. 149; vitalities are further incurred due to 150; a way of escaping from 151; transformation of material aggregates into 169; body of 171; illustration of the bondage of 174; possibility of the destruction of 220, 233, 244; causes of 243; *nama-k.* the states of existence fashioned by 117, 118. 153.

Kaya Body, an embodied being; six kinds of 218.

Karmana (*-sharira*) The karmic body 171.

Kala Time; property of 134; infinitesimal-spacial-units or space-points denied in the case of 135/1.

Kalanu The ultimate unit of time 143.

Kevala-jnana Omniscience; equated with happiness 19, 60; its direct comprehension without sensorial stages 21; the manner of its vision 29; as a reflector of present and absent modifications 37; scope of the comprehension of 41,48; its ability to know all substances with all their modifications 49; simultaneous comprehension of 50; glory of 51; *pratyakshatva* of 54.

Kevalin The omniscient; his exemption from physical feeling 20; no indirect perception in his case 22; the mode of his vision and comprehension 29; his immunity from disturbances when seeing and knowing 32; his immunity from bondage 52.

Kshayika-jnana Knowledge which originates after the destruction of armas; defined 42, 47.

Ganadhara An apostle, the direct disciple of *Tirthankara*, but sometimes equated with *acharya*, who is at the head of an ascetic group 4.

Guna Quality; modifications associated with 93/2; substance is the substratum of 110; *murta* and *amurta* distinction

	of 130.
Charitra	Conduct, equated with *dharma* and *sama* 7.
Chetana	Sentiency or consciousness; definition of and three kinds cf 123-124; see also *atman* and *jiva*.
Chadmastha	One who has not attained omniscience; fruit of following 256.
Cheda	Default (in the practice of primary virtues); and *Chedopasthapaka* is that monk who stands in need of re-establishment in the correct behaviour after he has committed a default 209; antidotal procedure against 211-212; guarding against 213, 222.
Jiva	Soul or the sentient principle; non-concrete or incorporeal nature of 55; as one that develops happiness 65-66; its difference and non-difference in different births explained 112-113; nature of 127; space-points of 135/1; as a knower endowed with four life-essentials or vitalities 145; incurrance of karmas by 148; modifications of 153; descriptions of 172; illustration of the karmic bondage of 174, 176; bondage resulting from the passional vibrations of 175-176; embodiment distinct from 182; conditions of material substances not caused by 184; discussion about the reception of karmas by 115; see also *atman* and *chetana*.
Jnana	Knowledge coextensive with the self and the objects of knowledge 23; all-pervasiveness of 23; the self identical with 27; its relation with *jneya* indicated with an illustration 28; its enlightenment of objects illustrated 30; equated with the understanding of the sacred text 34; equated with the knower 35; equated with the soul 36; two kinds of 53; its being *pratyaksha* 54; *pratyaksha*-, and *paroksha*-distinguished and defined 58; karmas instantaneously destroyed through 238.
Jneya	The object(s) of knowledge; coextensive with knowledge 23; scope of 23; reflected in and grasped completely by *Jina* 29; its relation with *jnana* illustrated 28.
Tapas	Penance, austerity; in the form of fast 227.
Taijasika (*-sharira*)	The magnetic (electric) body 171.

Trasa (-kaya)	Movable body (or being) that possesses more than one sense 182.
Deva	A god, a resident of heavens; nature of his happiness 71, 73-75.
Dravya	Substance; defined 49, 95; infinite number of and infinite modifications of 49; as made up of qualities 93/2; nature of 96; differentia of 97-98; origination etc., associated with the condition of 99; origination etc. intimately and simultaneously united with 102; existential character of and immunity from modificational disturbance 103; its relation with qualities and modifications 104; *satta* as the characteristic of 105, 109, 110; positive and negative aspects of 111; two kinds of 127; concrete and non-concrete qualities of 130; space-points of 141; three-fold nature of 154.
Dravyarthika(-naya)	substantial viewpoint; non-difference established by 114.
Dvesha	Aversion (Pk. form *dosa*) 81, 83. 84, 180: see *raga* (or attachment) with which it is generally coupled.
Dharma	equated with *charitra* and *sama* 7; the soul considered as 8; a designation of *shraman* 92.
Dharma	The principle or fulcrum of motion; property of 133; space-points of 135/1.
Dhyata	A meditator; qualifications of 196.
Niryapaka	An ascetic who establishes a defaulter-monk in the correct behaviour; defined 210.
Nirvana	*Nirvana* or liberation; a way of attaining 6: salutation to the path of 199; in the same birth women cannot attain *224/3-10, infatuation as a hindrance to 239; attainment of 259-260.
Pancha-parameshthin	The five dignitaries; enumerated and saluted 4.
Paramanu	A primary or subtle-most atom; a measure of space-point 137; nature of and the aggregates formed by 163; process, with illustration, of aggregates formed by 164-166.
Para-samaya	Those who do not understand the reality of the self and are affected or conditioned by "the other"; defined 93/2, 94, 98.

Murccha	Infatuation, excessive attachment 239; see also *parigraha.*
Murta	Concrete or corporeal; defined 131; see also *guna.*
Mulaguna	Primary virtue; twentyeight enumerated 208-209.
Moksha	Liberation, see *Nirvana.*
Moha	Delusion or Infatuation; destruction of 80, 86, 88-89, 194; defined 83; as a cause of bondage 84; characteristics of 85.
Raga	Attachment; as a hindrance to the realisation of spiritual purity 81; as a source of infatuation 83; as a cause of bondage 84, 179; two kinds of 180; illustration of the fruit of 255; see also *dvesha* with which it is generally coupled.
Linga	Emblem (*viz.* the ascetic emblem); description and two kinds of 205-206; that prescribed for women *224/2, etc.
Loka	Physical world 128; =*akasha* physical space; origination etc., in 129; constituents of 135/1.
Vardhamana	Vardhamana alias Mahavira, the last *Tirthankara* of the Jainas; he attained liberation in 527 B.C.; saluted along with previous and contemporary *Tirthankaras* 1-3.
Vikatha	Unhealthy gossip; four kinds of 215.
Vishaya	The objects of pleasure; as the source of misery 64.
Vaikriyika	(Pk. *Veuvviya*) (*-sharira*); The plastic or transformatory body 171.
Vrata	Vow 208.
Shabda	Sound; the material nature of 132.
Sama	Equanimity; defined and equated with *dharma* and *charitra* 7.
Sharira	Body; five kinds of 171.
Shuddha	The pure and the perfect one; defined 273; attainment of 274.
Shuddhopayoga	Pure manifestation of consciousness; fruit of 11; nature of happiness in 13; nature of a *shraman* endowed with 14; omniscience in 15; as a cause of destroying misery 78; absence of karmic influx in 245.
Shunya	Void; defined 144.
Shubhopayoga	Auspicious manifestation of consciousness; fruit of 11,

70; characteristics of 69, 157, 246; merit caused by 156; karmic influx in 245; activities sanctioned for a monk with 247-248.

Shraddhan — Conviction, faith; importance of 237; as a necessary qualification of a *shraman* 264.

Shraman — A saint, an ascetic; his qualifications 91-92, 226; *dharma* as a designation of 92; procedure, etc. to be observed at the time of the initiation of 202, 207; reflection and appearance of 204; his caution against *cheda* 213; commission of *himsa* by 216; careful activities prescribed for 218; responsibility of *himsa* on *217/2-3; foodlessness of 227; how least karma is incurred by 231; definition of a self-controlled monk 240-242; destruction of karmas by244; activities allowed for a *shraman* of *shubhopayoga* 247-249; mutual help among 252; the occasion when contact with commoners not forbidden for 253; formalities to be observed by 261-263; faith to be possessed by 264; malice and vanity leading to the fall of 265-266; his mistake in cooperating with a lower *shraman* 267; selection of a colleague by 220; attainments of perfect *shraman* 272.

Shramani — A nun *224/10.

Shramanya — *Shraman*-hood; misery destroyed by the adoption of 201; preliminary rites at the time of adopting 202; the preceptor, etc. from whom to adopt 203; description of the emblem of 205-206; definition of the perfect type of 214; the fruit of the perfect type of 272.

Shravaka — A householder or a layman 250.

Shruta-kevalin — A scriptural omniscient; defined 33.

Sanga — Attachment or association; defined 224.

Sat — Existence; scope of 107, *satta-* 110.

Saptabhangi — The doctrine of seven-fold predication, *quodammodo*, stated 115.

Samaya — Moment or instant, an unit of time which is coordinated with an atom of matter and a point of space; defined 138; origination, etc. in 139; initial nature of 142.

Samaya — Scripture; *para-* and *svaka*-defined 94, 98.

Samiti	Carefulness 208.
Sallekhana	Voluntary fasting unto death *224/12.
Samyam	Self-control or discipline; defined *239/2.
Samsara	Transmigratory existence, defined 120.
Sagara	A householder 194; duty of 250; the highest duty of 254; see also *shravaka.*
Siddha	A liberated soul; an embodiment of absolute happiness and omniscience, and also a Divinity 68/1; salutation to *68/3.
Siddhi	see *Nirvana.*
Sukha	Happiness; in *shubhopayoga* 11; in *shuddhopayoga* 13; equated with omniscience 19; of an omniscient 20; two kinds of 53; absolute happiness defined and equated with omniscience 59; happiness of senses is misery 76; absolute happiness as an object of meditation 198.
Sutra	The sacred text; its constitution and equation with knowledge 34.
Skandha	An aggregate; formation of 166-167.
Stri (-moksha)	Liberation of women; discussed *224/3-10.
Sthavara (-kaya)	Immovable being, i.e. those that possess only the sense of touch; they are five: earth, water, fire, air-bodied and vegetation or plants. 182.
Syadvada	see *saptabhangi.*
Svayambhu	The self-existent; definition of 16; as a collocation of origination, destruction and permanence 17.
Himsa	Harm unto beings; *shraman's* commission of 216; bondage due to 217.

Name Index

Title Index

Word Index

Subject Index